The American People

BRIEF SECOND EDITION

The American People

Creating a Nation and a Society

VOLUME I: TO 1877

GARY B. NASH
University of California, Los Angeles

JULIE ROY JEFFREY
Goucher College

JOHN R. HOWE
University of Minnesota

PETER J. FREDERICK
Wabash College

ALLEN F. DAVIS
Temple University

ALLAN M. WINKLER
Miami University

HarperCollinsCollegePublishers

Executive Editor: Bruce Borland
Developmental Editor: John Matthews
Project Editor: Robert Ginsberg
Text and Cover Designer: Nancy Sabato
Cover Illustration: Christine Francis
Art Studio: Vantage Art, Inc.
Photo Researcher: Leslie Coopersmith
Electronic Production Manager: Valerie A. Sawyer
Desktop Administrator: LaToya Wigfall
Manufacturing Manager: Helene G. Landers
Electronic Page Makeup: Americomp
Printer and Binder: RR Donnelley & Sons Company
Cover Printer: The Lehigh Press, Inc.

For permission to use copyrighted material, grateful acknowledgment is made to the copyright holders on p. 711, which is hereby made part of this copyright page.

The American People: Creating a Nation and a Society, Volume I: To 1877, Brief Second Edition

ISBN 0-673-99526-7 (single volume)
ISBN 0-673-99527-5 (volume 1)
ISBN 0-673-99528-3 (volume 2)

98 9 8 7 6 5

Contents in Brief

Detailed Contents

Maps and Charts

known American. Chapter 1, for example, starts with the tragic account of Opechancanough, a Powhatan tribesman whose entire life of nearly ninety years was consumed by a struggle against the land, hunger, and alien values brought by Spanish and English newcomers. This brief anecdote serves several purposes. First, it introduces the overarching themes and major concepts of the chapter, in this case the meeting in the North American wilderness of three societies—Native American, European, and African—each with different cultural values, life styles, and aspirations. Second, the personal story launches the chapter in a way that facilitates learning—by engaging the student with a human account. Last, the personal story suggests that history was shaped by ordinary as well as extraordinary people. At the end of the personal story a *brief overview* links the biographical sketch to the text by elaborating the major themes of the chapter.

We aim to facilitate the learning process for students in other ways as well. Every chapter ends with pedagogical features to reinforce and expand the presentation. A *conclusion* briefly summarizes the main concepts and developments elaborated in the chapter and serves as a bridge to the following chapter. A list of *recommended reading* provides supplementary sources for further study or research; novels contemporary to the period are often included. Finally, a *time line* reviews the major events and developments covered in the chapter. Each graph, map, and illustration has been chosen to relate clearly to the narrative.

THE BRIEF EDITION

This text is a Brief Edition of the very successful third edition of *The American People*. This shorter volume—approximately half the length of the complete version—will be particularly useful in one-semester courses and those courses that assign wide readings in primary sources, monographs, or articles in addition to the main text.

The foremost goal of the abridgement was to preserve the distinctive character of the complete text. The balance of political, social, economic, and cultural history remains the same, revolving around the same central, organizing themes previously described. The structure and organization of the text—parts, chapters, sections, and subsections—are largely unchanged. Deletions have been made on a careful line-by-line basis. All important topics are in place, as are the interpretive connections among the many factors molding our society. We have eliminated only detail, extra examples, and illustrative material within sections. While it might have been easier to delete more of the "humanness" of history, leaving room for facts and more facts, we have been careful to retain our focus on history as it is revealed through the lives of ordinary Americans, and the interplay of social and political factors.

We have also tried to provide the support materials necessary to make teaching and learning enjoyable and rewarding. The reader will be the judge of our success. The authors and HarperCollins welcome your comments.

ACKNOWLEDGMENTS

Over the years, as successive editions of this text were being developed, many of our colleagues read and criticized the various drafts of the manuscript. For their thoughtful evaluations and constructive suggestions, the authors wish to express their gratitude to the following reviewers:

Richard H. Abbott, Eastern Michigan University
Kenneth G. Alfers, Mountain View College
Gregg Andrews, Southwest Texas State University
Robert Asher, University of Connecticut, Storrs
Harry Baker, University of Arkansas at Little Rock
Michael Batinski, Southern Illinois University
Gary Bell, Sam Houston State University
Virginia Bellows, Tulsa Junior College

Spencer Bennett, Siena Heights College
James Bradford, Texas A&M University
Neal A. Brooks, Essex Community College
Jeffrey P. Brown, New Mexico State University
Sheri Bartlett Browne, Portland State University
David Brundage, University of California at
    Santa Cruz
Colin Calloway, University of Wyoming
D'Ann Campbell, Indiana University
James S. Chase, University of Arkansas
Vincent A. Clark, Johnson County Community
    College
Neil Clough, North Seattle Community College
Matthew Ware Coulter, Collin County
    Community College
David Culbert, Louisiana State University
John H. De Berry, Somerset Community College
Bruce Dierenfield, Canisius College
John Dittmer, DePauw University
Gordon Dodds, Portland State University
Richard Donley, Eastern Washington University
Robert Downtain, Tarrant County Community
    College
Mark Dyreson, Weber State University
Lori Clune Emerzian, California State University,
    Fresno
Rex L. Field, Palo Alto College
John L. Finnegan, Spokane Community College
Bernard Friedman, Indiana University–Purdue
    University at Indianapolis
Bruce Glasrud, California State University,
    Hayward
Richard Griswold del Castillo, San Diego State
    University
Colonel Williams L. Harris, The Citadel Military
    College
Robert Haws, University of Mississippi
Jerrold Hirsch, Northeast Missouri State
    University
Frederick Hoxie, McNickle Center for Study of
    American Indians
John S. Hughes, University of Texas
Donald M. Jacobs, Northeastern University
Delores Janiewski, University of Idaho, Mt.
    Holyoke

David Johnson, Portland State University
Richard Kern, University of Findlay
Monte Lewis, Cisco Junior College
William Link, University of North Carolina,
    Greensboro
Ronald Lora, University of Toledo
George M. Lubick, Northern Arizona
    University
John C. Massman, St. Cloud State University
Vern Mattson, University of Nevada at Las
    Vegas
Michael McCarthy, Community College of
    Denver
John McCormick, Delaware County
    Community College
Sylvia McGrath, Stephen F. Austin University
James E. McMillan, Denison University
Walter Miszczenko, Boise State University
Norma Mitchell, Troy State University
Gerald F. Moran, University of Michigan,
    Dearborn
William Morris, Midland College
Marian Morton, John Carroll University
Roger Nichols, University of Arizona
Paul Palmer, Texas A&I University
Al Parker, Riverside City College
Judith Parsons, Sul Ross State University
Neva Peters, Tarrant County Junior College
James Prickett, Santa Monica College
Noel Pugash, University of New Mexico
Juan Gomez-Quinones, University of California,
    Los Angeles
George Rable, Anderson College
Joseph P. Reidy, Howard University
Leonard Riforgiato, Pennsylvania State
    University
Randy Roberts, Purdue University
Mary Robertson, Armstrong State University
David Robson, John Carroll University
Sylvia Sebesta, San Antonio College
Herbert Shapiro, University of Cincinnati
David R. Shibley, Santa Monica College
Ellen Shockro, Pasadena City College
Sheila Skemp, University of Mississippi
Kathryn Sklar, Stanford University

Howard Smead, University of Maryland
Gary Scott Smith, Grove City College
James Smith, Virginia State University
John Snetsinger, California Polytechnic State
   University
Tommy Stringer, Navarro College
Joan E. Supplee, Baylor University
Tom Tefft, Citrus College
John A. Trickel, Richland College
Donna Van Raaphorst, Cuyahoga Community
   College
Morris Vogel, Temple University
Michael Wade, Appalachian State University
Jackie Walker, James Madison University

SUPPLEMENTS

For Instructors

- *Teaching the American People.* Authors Julie Roy Jeffrey and Peter J. Frederick have written this guide on the basis of ideas generated in the frequent "active learning" workshops held by the authors and have tied it closely to the text. In addition to suggestions on how to generate lively class discussion and involve students in active learning, this supplement also offers a file of exam questions and lists of resources, including films, slides, photo collections, records, and audiocassettes.

- *America Through the Eyes of Its People: A Collection of Primary Sources.* Prepared by Carol Brown of Houston Community College, this one-volume collection of primary documents portraying the rich and varied tapestry of American life contains documents concerning women, Native Americans, African-Americans, Hispanics, and others who helped to shape the course of U.S. history. Designed to be duplicated by instructors for student use, the documents have accompanying student exercises.

- *Discovering American History Through Maps and Views.* Created by Gerald Danzer of the University of Illinois at Chicago—the recipient of the AHA's 1990 James Harvey Robinson Prize for his work in the development of map transparencies—this set of 140 four-color acetates is a unique instructional tool. It contains an introduction on teaching history through maps and a detailed commentary on each transparency. The collection includes cartographic and pictorial maps, views and photos, urban plans, building diagrams, and works of art.

- *Primary Sources in Gender in American History.* Prepared by Ellen Skinner of Pace University, this collection includes both classic and unique documents from diverse perspectives covering the history of women and gender in American history. The book includes critical thinking questions, bibliography, and contextual headnotes and is available shrinkwrapped with *The American People* at a low cost.

- *Primary Sources in African American History.* Prepared by Roy Finkenbine of Hampton University, this compelling collection includes both social and political documents and covers the history of African-Americans in America. The book includes critical thinking questions, bibliography, and contextual headnotes and is available shrinkwrapped with *The American People* at a low cost.

- *American Impressions: A CD-ROM for U.S. History.* This unique and ground-breaking CD-ROM for the U.S. History course is organized in a topical and thematic framework which allows in-depth coverage with a media-centered focus. Hundreds of photos, maps, works of art, graphics, and historical film clips are organized into narrated vignettes and interactive activities to create a tool for both professors and students. The first volume includes: "The Encounter Period," "Revolution to Republic," "A Century of Labor and Reform," and "The Struggle for Equality." A Guide for Instructors provides teaching tips and suggestions for using advanced media in the classroom. The CD-ROM is available in both Macintosh and Windows formats.

- *Visual Archives of American History, 2nd ed.* This two-sided video laserdisc explores history from the meeting of three cultures to the present. It is an encyclopedic chronology of U.S. history offering hundreds of photographs and illustrations, a variety of source and reference maps—several of which are animated—plus 50 minutes of video. For ease in planning lectures, a manual listing barcodes for scanning and frame numbers for all the material is available.

- *A Guide to Teaching American History Through Film.* Written by Randy Roberts of Purdue University, this guide provides instructors with a creative and practical tool for stimulating classroom discussion. The sections include "American Films: A Historian's Perspective," a list of films, practical suggestions, and bibliography. The film listing is presented in narrative form, developing connections between each film and the topics being studied.

- *Video Lecture Launchers.* Prepared by Mark Newman, University of Illinois at Chicago, these video lecture launchers (each 2 to 5 minutes in duration) cover key issues in American history from 1877 to the present. The launchers are accompanied by an instructor's manual.

- *"This Is America" Immigration Videos.* Produced by the American Museum of Immigration, these two 20-minute videos tell the story of American immigrants, relating their personal stories and accomplishments. By showing how the richness of our culture is due to the contributions of millions of immigrant Americans, the videos make the point that America's strength lies in the ethnically and culturally diverse backgrounds of its citizens.

- *Visual Archives of American History.* This video laserdisc provides over 500 photos and 29 minutes of film clips of major events in American history. Each photo or film clip may be instantly accessed, making this collection ideal for classroom use.

- *Transparencies.* A set of more than 40 map transparencies drawn from the text.

- *Test Bank.* This test bank, prepared by Charles Cook, Houston Community College, and J. B. Smallwood, North Texas State University, contains more than 3,500 objective, conceptual, and essay questions. All questions are keyed to specific pages in the text.

- *TestMaster Computerized Testing System.* This flexible, easy-to-master computer test bank includes all the test items in the printed test bank. The TestMaster software allows you to edit existing questions and add your own items. Tests can be printed in several different formats and can include figures such as graphs and tables. Available for IBM and Macintosh computers.

- *QuizMaster.* This new program enables you to design TestMaster-generated tests that your students can take on a computer rather than in printed form. QuizMaster is available separately from TestMaster and can be obtained free through your sales representative.

- *Grades.* A grade-keeping and classroom management software program that maintains data for up to 200 students.

For Students

- *Study Guide and Practice Tests.* This two-volume study guide, created by Julie Roy Jeffrey and Peter J. Frederick, includes chapter outlines, significant themes and highlights, a glossary, learning enrichment ideas, sample test questions, exercises for identification and interpretation, and geography exercises based on maps in the text.

- *Learning to Think Critically: Films and Myths About American History.* Randy Roberts and Robert May of Purdue University use well-known films such as *Gone with the Wind* and *Casablanca* to explore some common myths about America and its past. Many widely held assumptions about our country's past come from or are perpetuated by popular films. Which are true? Which are patently not true? And how does a student of history approach documents, sources, and textbooks with a critical and discerning eye? This short handbook subjects some popular beliefs to historical scrutiny in order to help students develop a method of inquiry for approaching the subject of history in general.

- *Mapping America: A Guide to Historical Geography.* This workbook by Ken L. Weatherbie, Del Mar College, contains 35 sequenced exercises corresponding to the map program in the text, each culminating in a series of interpretive questions about the role of geographical factors in American history.

- *Mapping American History: Student Activities.* Written by Gerald Danzer of the University of Illinois at Chicago, this free map workbook for students features exercises designed to teach students to interpret and analyze cartographic materials as historical documents. The instructor is entitled to a free copy of the workbook for each copy of the text purchased from HarperCollins.

- *Concepts in American History.* This slim volume, written by Robert Asher of the University of Connecticut, contains brief essays on 13 key concepts in American history, including such topics as Republicanism, nativism, feminism, and capitalism.

- *SuperShell II Computerized Tutorial.* Prepared by Ken L. Weatherbie, Del Mar College, this interactive program for IBM computers helps students learn major facts and concepts through drill and practice exercises and diagnostic feedback. SuperShell II provides immediate correct answers, the text page number on which the material is discussed, and a running score of the student's performance maintained on the screen throughout the session. This free supplement is available to instructors through their sales representative.

- *TimeLink Computer Atlas of American History.* This atlas, compiled by William Hamblin of Brigham Young University, is an introductory software tutorial and textbook companion. This Macintosh program presents the historical geography of the continental United States from colonial times to the settling of the West and the admission of the last continental state in 1912. The program covers territories in different time periods, provides quizzes, and includes a special Civil War module.

GARY B. NASH
JULIE ROY JEFFREY
JOHN R. HOWE
PETER J. FREDERICK
ALLEN F. DAVIS
ALLAN M. WINKLER

About the Authors

Gary B. Nash received his Ph.D. from Princeton University in 1964. He is currently Director of the National Center for History in the Schools at the University of California, Los Angeles, where he teaches colonial and revolutionary American history. Among the books Nash has written are *Quakers and Politics: Pennsylvania, 1681–1726* (1968); *Red, White, and Black: The Peoples of Early America* (1974, 1982); *The Urban Crucible: Social Change, Political Consciousness, and the Origins of the American Revolution* (1979); and *Forging Freedom: The Black Urban Experience in Philadelphia, 1720–1840* (1988). His scholarship is especially concerned with the role of common people in the making of history. He wrote Part I and served as a general editor of this book.

Julie Roy Jeffrey earned her Ph.D. in history from Rice University in 1972. Since then she has taught at Goucher College. Honored as an outstanding teacher, Jeffrey has been involved in faculty development activities and curriculum evaluation. Jeffrey's major publications include *Education for Children of the Poor* (1978); *Frontier Women: The Trans-Mississippi West, 1840–1880* (1979); and *Converting the West: A Biography of Narcissa Whitman* (1991). She is the author of many articles on the lives and perceptions of nineteenth-century women. She wrote Parts III and IV in collaboration with Peter Frederick and acted as a general editor of this book.

John R. Howe received his Ph.D. from Yale University in 1962. At the University of Minnesota his teaching interests include early American politics and relations between Native Americans and whites. His major publications include *The Changing Political Thought of John Adams* (1966) and *From the Revolution Through the Age of Jackson* (1973). His major research currently involves a manuscript entitled "The Transformation of Public Life in Revolutionary America." Howe wrote Part II of this book.

Peter J. Frederick received his Ph.D. in history from the University of California, Berkeley, in 1966. Innovative student-centered teaching of American history has been the focus of his career at California State University, Hayward, and since 1970 at Wabash College (1992–1994 at Carleton College). Recognized nationally as a distinguished teacher and for his many articles and workshops for faculty on teaching and learning, Frederick has also written several articles on life-writing and a book, *Knights of the Golden Rule: The Intellectual as Christian Social Reformer in the 1890s*. He co-ordinated and edited all the "Recovering the Past" sections and co-wrote Parts III and IV of this book.

Allen F. Davis earned his Ph.D. from the University of Wisconsin in 1959. A former president of the American Studies Association, he is a professor of history at Temple University and Director of the Center for Public History. He is the author of *Spearheads for Reform: The Social Settlements and the Progressive Movement* (1967) and *American Heroine: The Life and Legend of Jane Addams* (1973). He is co-author of *Still Philadelphia* (1983), *Philadelphia Stories* (1987), and *One Hundred Years at Hull-House* (1990). He is currently working on a book on masculine culture in America. Davis wrote Part V of this book.

Allan M. Winkler received his Ph.D. from Yale University in 1974. He is presently teaching at Miami University, where he chairs the History Department. His books include *The Politics of Propaganda: The Office of War Information, 1942–1945* (1978); *Modern America: The United States from the Second World War to the Present* (1985); *Home Front U.S.A.: America During World War II* (1986); and *Life Under a Cloud: American Anxiety About the Atom* (1993). His research centers on the connections between public policy and popular mood in modern American history. Winkler wrote Part VI of this book.

The American People

part 1

A Colonizing People

America has always been a nation of immigrants, an elaborate cultural mosaic created out of the unending streams of people who for four centuries have flocked to its shores from every corner of the world. This intermingling began with the convergence of people from the three continents of North America, Europe, and Africa. We examine the mingling of their values, institutions, and lifeways during the fifteenth and sixteenth centuries in Chapter 1, "Three Worlds Meet." Chapter 2, "Colonizing a Continent," explores five regions of settlement along the Atlantic seaboard.

Chapter 3, "Mastering the New World," explores how colonists struggled against Native Americans to expand their land base and turned to slave labor in the southern colonies. The colonists also had to deal with social and political tensions among themselves at the end of the seventeenth century. At the same time, French territorial ambitions in North America threatened another kind of conflict.

Chapter 4, "The Maturing of Colonial Society," traces the development of the colonies of England, Spain, and France in the first half of the eighteenth century. It shows how economic growth, religious revival, and political maturation prepared the English colonists by 1750 for the epic events that would follow. Chapter 5, "Bursting the Colonial Bonds," describes the coming of the American Revolution.

chapter 1

....

Three Worlds Meet

In the late 1550s, a few years after Catholic King Philip II and Protestant Queen Elizabeth assumed the throne in Spain and England, respectively, Opechancanough was born in Tsenacommacah. In the Algonquian language, the word Tsenacommacah meant "densely inhabited land." Later English colonizers would rename this place Virginia after their monarch, the virgin Queen Elizabeth. Before he died in the 1640s in the ninth decade of his life, Opechancanough had seen light-skinned, swarthy, and black-skinned newcomers from a half dozen European nations and African kingdoms swarm into his land.

Opechancanough was only an infant when Europeans first reached the Chesapeake Bay region. A small party of Spanish had explored the area in 1561, but they found neither gold nor silver nor anything else of value. Upon departing, they left behind something of unparalleled importance in the history of contact between the peoples of Europe and the Americas: a bacterial infection that spread like wildfire through a population that had no immunity against it. Many members of Opechancanough's tribe died.

In 1570, when Opechancanough was young, the Spanish returned and established a Jesuit mission near the York River. Violence occurred, and before the Spanish abandoned the Chesapeake in 1572, they put to death a number of captured Indians, including a chief who was Opechancanough's relative.

Opechancanough was in his forties when three ships of fair-skinned settlers disembarked in 1607 to begin the first permanent English settlement in the New World. As relations with the whites worsened, his half brother Powhatan, high chief of several dozen loosely confederated tribes in the region, sent him to capture the English leader John Smith and escort him to the Indians' main village. Smith was put through a mock execution but then released. He later got the best of Opechancanough, threatening him with a pistol, humiliating him in front of his warriors, and assaulting one of his sons.

Opechancanough saw English settlements slowly spread in the Chesapeake region. Then, in 1617, he assumed leadership of the Powhatan Confederacy. Five years later, Opechancanough led a determined assault on the English plantations that lay along the rivers and streams emptying into the bay. The Indians killed nearly one-third of the intruders. But they paid dearly in the retaliatory raids that the colonists mounted in succeeding years.

As he watched the land-hungry settlers swarm in during the next two decades, Opechancanough's patience failed him. Finally, in 1644, now in his eighties, he galvanized a new generation of warriors and led a final desperate assault on the English. It was a suicidal attempt, but the "great general" of the Powhatan Confederacy, faithful to the tradition of his people, counseled death over enslavement and humiliation. Though the warriors inflicted heavy casualties, they could not overwhelm the colonizers, who vastly outnumbered them. For two years, Opechancanough was kept prisoner by the Virginians. Nearly blind and "so decrepit that he was not able to walk alone," he was fatally shot in the back by an English guard in 1646.

Over a long lifetime, Opechancanough painfully experienced the meeting of people from three continents. The nature of this violent intermingling of Europeans, Africans, and Native Americans on Chesapeake Bay is an essential part of early American history. But to understand how the destinies of red, white, and black people became intertwined in Opechancanough's land, we must look at the precontact history and cultural foundations of life in the homelands of each of them.

THE PEOPLE OF AMERICA BEFORE COLUMBUS

The history of humankind in North America began thousands of years ago, as nomadic hunters from Siberia migrated across a land bridge connecting northeastern Asia with Alaska. Paleoanthropologists remain divided on the exact timing, but the main migration apparently occurred either about 12,000 to 14,000 or 25,000 to 28,000 years ago.

Hunters and Farmers

For thousands of years, these early hunters trekked southward and eastward, following vegetation and game. In time, they reached the tip of South America and the eastern edge of North America.

Archaeological evidence suggests that as centuries passed and population increased, the earliest inhabitants evolved into separate cultures, adjusting to a variety of environments in distinct ways. By the 1500s, as Europeans began to explore the New World, the "Indians" of the Americas were enormously diverse in the size and complexity of their societies, the languages they spoke, and their forms of social organization.

The first phase of "Native American" history, the long Beringian epoch, ended about 12,000 B.C. A rich archaeological record from that time indicates that the hunters had developed a new technology. Big-game hunters now flaked hard stones into spear points and chose "kill sites" where they slew whole herds of Pleistocene mammals. This more reliable food source allowed population growth, and nomadism began to give way to settled habitations or local migration within limited territories.

In the Archaic era, from about 8000 B.C. to 500 B.C., human populations adapted to a warmer climate as the glaciers retreated. The Pleistocene mammals could not survive, but the people learned to exploit new sources of food, especially plant life. In time a second technological breakthrough, the "agricultural revolution," occurred.

When Native Americans learned to "domesticate" plant life, they began the long process of transforming their relationship to the physical world. To learn how to harvest, plant, and nurture a seed was to gain partial control over natural forces that before had been ungovernable. Over the millennia, humans progressed from doorside planting of a few wild seeds to systematic clearing and planting of bean and maize fields. Sedentary village life began to replace a nomadic hunting and gathering existence. The increase in food supply brought about by agriculture triggered the growth of larger populations and greater social and political complexity. Many societies empowered religious figures, who organized the common followers, directed their work, exacted tribute, and undertook to protect the community from hostile forces.

Regional trading networks carried commodities such as salt, obsidian rock for projectile points, and copper for jewelry. Technology, religious ideas, and agricultural practices were also transmitted. By the end of the Archaic period (about 500 B.C.), hundreds of independent, kin-based groups, like people in other parts of the world, had learned to exploit the resources of their particular area and to trade with other groups in their region.

Native Americans in 1600

The last epoch of pre-Columbian development, the post-Archaic phase, occurred during the 2,000 years before contact with Europeans. It involved a complex process of growth and environmental adaptation among many distinct societies—and crisis in some of them. In the American Southwest, the ancestors of the present-day Hopi and Zuni developed carefully planned villages composed of large terraced buildings, each with many rooms. By the time the Spanish reached the American Southwest in the 1540s, the indigenous Pueblo people were using irrigation canals, check dams, and hillside terracing to bring water to their arid maize fields.

Far to the east were the mound-building societies of the Mississippi and Ohio valleys. These societies declined about 1,000 years before Europeans reached the continent, perhaps because of attacks from other tribes or severe climatic changes that undermined agriculture. Several centuries later, another culture, based on intensive cultivation of beans, maize, and squash, began to flourish in the Mississippi valley. Its center, a city of perhaps 40,000, called Cahokia, stood near present-day St. Louis and included a temple that rose in four terraces to a height of 100 feet. This was the urban center of a far-flung "Mississippi" culture that encompassed thousands of villages from Wisconsin to Louisiana and from Oklahoma to Tennessee.

The influence of the Mound Builders passed eastward to transform the woodlands societies along the Atlantic coastal plain. The numerous small tribes that settled from Nova Scotia to Florida had added limited agriculture to their skill in exploiting natural plants for food, medicine, dyes, and flavoring and had developed food-procurement strategies that used all the resources around them—cleared land, forests, streams, shore, and ocean.

Most of the eastern woodlands tribes lived in waterside villages. Locating their fields of maize near fishing grounds, they often migrated seasonally between inland and coastal village sites or situated themselves astride two ecological zones.

As European exploration of the Americas drew near, the continent north of the Rio Grande contained perhaps four million people, of whom perhaps 500,000 lived along the eastern coastal plain and in the piedmont region accessible to the early European settlers. The colonizers were not coming to a "virgin wilderness,"

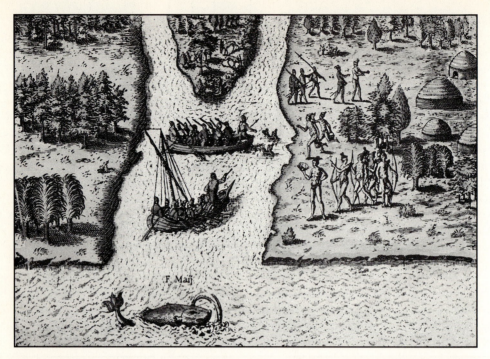

An engraving showing the French discovery of the River of May in Florida on May 1, 1654. As the illustration shows, many initial encounters between Native Americans and Europeans were friendly. Here, a party of the locally indigenous people swims out to meet the French with gifts, and another Native American leads a small group of French inland to a village.

as they often described it, but to a land inhabited for thousands of years by people whose village existence in many ways resembled that of the arriving Europeans.

In some important ways, however, Indian culture also differed from that of Europeans. Horses, for example, were not available to the native peoples of the New World as they developed their methods of farming, transportation, and warfare. Without draft animals such as the horse or ox, they had not developed wheeled vehicles or, for that matter, the potter's wheel, which also uses the wheel-and-axle principle. Many inventions—such as the technology for the smelting of iron, which had diffused widely in the Old World—had not crossed the ocean barrier to reach the New World. The opposite was also true: Valuable New World crops, such as corn and potatoes, which had been developed by Indian agriculturalists, were unknown in the Old World before Columbus.

Contrasting World Views

Colonizing Europeans called themselves "civilized" and typically described the people they met in the Americas as "savage," "heathen," or "barbarian." The gulf separating people in Europe and North America was defined not only by their material cultures but also by how they viewed their relationship to the environment and how they defined social relations in their communities. Having evolved in complete isolation from each other, European and Indian cultures exhibited a wide difference in values.

In the view of Europeans, the natural world was a resource designed for use by humans. Native Americans, in contrast, were "contented with Nature as they find her," as one colonist phrased it. In their ethos, every part of the natural environment was sacred. Rocks, trees, and animals all possessed spiritual power, and all were linked to form a sacred whole. To injure the environment, by overfishing or abusing it in any way, was to offend the spiritual power present throughout nature and hence to risk spiritual retaliation.

Regarding the soil as a resource to be exploited for humans' benefit, Europeans believed that land should be privately possessed. Their social structure directly mirrored patterns of land ownership, with a land-wealthy elite at the apex of the social pyramid and a mass of propertyless individuals forming the broad base.

Native Americans also had concepts of property, and tribes recognized territorial boundaries. But they believed that land was invested with sacred qualities and should be held in common. Observing the Iroquois of the eastern woodlands in 1657, a French Jesuit noted with surprise that they had no almshouses because "their kindness, humanity and courtesy not only makes them liberal with what they have, but causes them to possess hardly anything except in common. A whole village must be without corn, before any individual can be obliged to endure privation." Not all Europeans were acquisitive, competitive individuals. The majority were peasants scratching a subsistence living from the soil, living in kin-centered villages with little contact with the outside world, and exchanging goods and labor through barter. But in Europe's urban centers a wealth-conscious, striving individual who celebrated wider choices and greater opportunities to enhance personal status was coming to the fore. In contrast, Native American traditions stressed the group rather than the individual. Holding land and other resources in common, Indian societies were usually more egalitarian and their members more concerned with personal valor than personal wealth.

The European newcomers to North America encountered a people whose cultural values differed strikingly from theirs. They also found disturbing the matrilineal organization of many tribal societies. Family membership among the Iroquois, for example, was determined through the female line. A typical family consisted of an old woman, her daughters with their husbands and children, and her unmarried granddaughters and grandsons. When a son or grandson married, he moved from this female-headed household to one headed by the matriarch of his wife's family. Divorce was also the woman's prerogative. If she desired it, she merely set her husband's possessions outside their dwelling door. Clans were composed of several matrilineal kin groups related by a blood connection on the mother's side.

European women, with rare exceptions, were entirely excluded from political affairs. By contrast, in Native American villages, again to take the Iroquois example, designated men sat in a circle to deliberate and make decisions, but the senior women of the village stood behind them, lobbying and instructing. The village chiefs were male, but they were named to their positions by the elder women of their clans. If they moved too far from the will of the women who appointed them, these chiefs were removed—or "dehorned."

In the tribal economy, men were responsible for hunting, fishing, and clearing land, but women controlled the cultivation, harvest, and distribution of food. When the men were away on hunting expeditions, women directed village life. Europeans perceived such a degree of sexual equality as another mark of the uncivilized nature of tribal society.

In the religious beliefs of Native Americans, the English saw a final cultural defect. Europeans built their religious life around the belief in a single god, written scriptures, an organized

Micmac
MAINE
Malecite
Abnaki
NEW HAMPSHIRE
VERMONT
Passamaquoddy
Penobscot
MASSACHUSETTS
CONNECTICUT
RHODE ISLAND
Pennacook
Pocomtuc
Pennacook
Nipmuc
Massachuset
Nauset
Wampanoag
Narraganset
Pequot
Montauk
NEW JERSEY
DELAWARE
MARYLAND
Mahican
Mohawk
Oneida
Onondaga
Cayuga
Seneca
NEW YORK
PENNSYLVANIA
Susquehanna
Wenrohronon
Munsee
Delaware
Wappinger
Nanticoke
Powhatan
VIRGINIA
WEST VIRGINIA
Monacan
Nottoway
Weanoc
Tutelo
Pamlico
Secotan
NORTH CAROLINA
Weapemeoc
Coree
Cape Fear
Catawba
Tuscarora
Yuchi
Sewee
Stono
Edisto
SOUTH CAROLINA
Cusabo
Guale
Timucua
Guacata
Jedga
Tekesta
FLORIDA
Cree
Erie
OHIO
NORTHEAST
KENTUCKY
Shawnee
TENNESSEE
Cherokee
Upper Creek
GEORGIA
Lower Creek
Apola
Apalachee
Santa Rosa
Chatot
Pensacola
Mobile
ALABAMA
SOUTHEAST
Choctaw
Chickasaw
MISSISSIPPI
Tunica
Biloxi
Houma
Natchez
Washa
Chitimacha
Chawasha
Atakapa
LOUISIANA
Lake Superior
Lake Huron
Lake Michigan
Lake Ontario
Lake Erie
MICHIGAN
Potawatomi
WISCONSIN
Menomini
Winnebago
INDIANA
Miami
Weo
ILLINOIS
Kaskaskia
Peoria
Piankashaw
Cahokia
Kickapoo
Sauk
Fox
IOWA
MINNESOTA
Ojibwa
Santee Dakota
FARMERS
Missouri
MISSOURI
Quapaw
Osage
ARKANSAS
Caddo
Kichai
Tawakoni
Tonkawa
Karankawa
Coahuiltec
Yankton Dakota
WESTERN
Arikara
NORTH DAKOTA
Assiniboin
Mandan
Hidatsa
SOUTH DAKOTA
Hunkpapa
Sans Arc
Teton
Oglala Dakota
Brule
Ponca
Omaha
Oto
NEBRASKA
Pawnee
Kansa
KANSAS
Wichita
OKLAHOMA
Waco
Comanche
TEXAS
Lipan Apache
Llanero
Cheyenne
HIGH
PLAIN
Arapaho
Cheyenne
COLORADO
Jicarilla Apache
Faraon
NEW MEXICO
Eastern Apache
Mescalero
Blackfoot
Atsina
Piegon
MONTANA
Crow
WYOMING
Wind River Shoshone
Ute
Navajo
Zuni
Hopi
ARIZONA
SOUTHWEST
Tonto
Western Apache
Arivaipa Apache
Gileno
Mimbreno
Chiricahua
Opata
Blood
Pend D'Oreille
Kalispel
Coeur D'Alene
Flathead
Nez Perce
Lemhi
Bannock
IDAHO
Shoshone
GREAT BASIN
Gosiute
NEVADA
Western Shoshone
Southern Paiute
Northern Paiute
Mono
Panamint
Havasupai
Walapai
Yavapai
Maricopa
Pima
Papago
Yuma
Dieguefio
Cocopah
Yaqui
Squamish
WASHINGTON
Nisqually
Spokane
Palus
Walla Walla
Umatilla
OREGON
Klamath
Modoc
Washo
Miwok
Costanoan
Yokuts
CALIFORNIA
Salinon
Chumash
Serrano
Gabrielino
Luiseno
Cahuilla
Mojave
Chemehuevi
Makah
Quinault
Chehalis
Cowlitz
Klikitat
Chinook
Tenino
Tillamook
Siletz
Alsea
Yaquina
Siuslaw
Kalapuya
Tututni
Karok
Kusa
Shasta
Wintun
Patwin
Maidu
Yuki
Pomo
Yurok
Hupa

clergy, and churches. Most Native American societies believed in a spirit power dwelling throughout nature (polytheism).

AFRICA ON THE EVE OF CONTACT

Half a century before Columbus reached the Americas, a Portuguese sea captain, Antam Gonçalves, made the first European landing on the west coast of sub-Saharan Africa. If he had been able to travel the length and breadth of the immense continent, he would have encountered a rich variety of African peoples and cultures. The notion of African "backwardness" and cultural impoverishment was a myth perpetuated after the slave trade had begun transporting millions of Africans to the New World. During the period of early contact with Europeans, Africa, like pre-Columbian America, was recognized as a diverse continent with a long history of cultural evolution.

The Kingdoms of Africa

The peoples of Africa, estimated at about 50 million in the fifteenth century, when Europeans began making extensive contact with them, lived in vast deserts, grasslands, and tropical forests. As in Europe and the Americas at that time, most people tilled the soil. Part of their skill in farming derived from the development of iron production, which may have begun in West Africa while Europe was still in the Stone Age. More efficient iron implements increased agricultural productivity, which in turn spurred population growth.

By the time Europeans reached the west coast of Africa, a number of large empires had risen there. The first was the kingdom of Ghana, embracing an immense territory between the Sahara and the Gulf of Guinea and from the Atlantic Ocean to the Niger River. The development of large towns, skillfully designed buildings, elaborate sculpture and metalwork depicting humans and animals, long-distance commerce, and a complex political structure marked the Ghanaian kingdom from the sixth to eleventh centuries.

An invasion of North African Muslim people beginning in the eleventh century introduced a period of religious strife that eventually destroyed the kingdom of Ghana. But in the same region arose the Islamic kingdom of Mali, which flourished until the fifteenth century. Its city of Timbuktu contained a distinguished faculty of scholars with whom North Africans and even southern Europeans came to study. Lesser kingdoms such as Kongo, Songhay, and Benin had also been growing for centuries before Europeans reached Africa by water.

The African Ethos

The peoples of Africa had a rich diversity of cultures, but most of them shared certain ways of life that differentiated them from Europeans. As in Europe, the family was the basic unit of social organization. In many African societies, as in many Native American ones, the family was matrilineal. Property rights and political inheritance descended through the mother rather than the father. It was not the son of a chief who inherited his father's position but the son of the chief's sister. When a man married, he left his family to join that of his bride.

West Africans believed in a supreme creator of the cosmos, an assortment of lesser deities associated with natural forces such as rain, fertility, and animal life, and spirits that dwelt in trees, rocks, and rivers. Ancestors were also worshiped, for they mediated between the Creator and the living of the earth.

Social organization in much of West Africa by the time Europeans arrived was as elaborate as in fifteenth-century Europe. At the top of society stood the nobility and the priests, usually men of advanced age. Beneath them were the great masses of people. Most of them were farmers, but some worked as craftsmen, traders, teachers, and artists. At the bottom of society

The art of sixteenth-century West Africa, much of it ceremonial, shows a high degree of aesthetic development. On the left is Gou, god of war, a metal sculpture from the Fon culture in Dahomey; on the right is a pair of antelope headdresses (worn by running a cord through holes in the base and tying them atop the head) carved of wood by the Bambara tribe of Senegambia.

West African Cultures and Slaving Forts

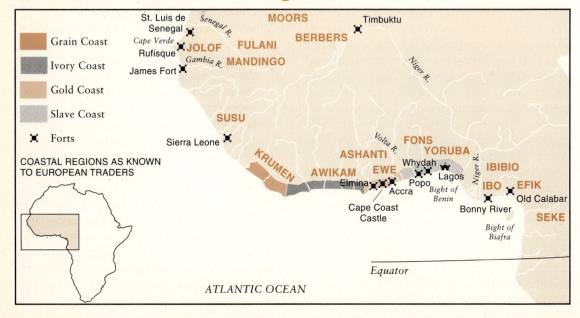

resided slaves. As in ancient Greece and Rome, they were "outsiders"—war captives, criminals, or sometimes persons who sold themselves into servitude to satisfy a debt. Slaves were entitled to protection under the law and allowed the privileges of education, marriage, and parenthood. Their servile condition was not permanent, nor was it automatically fastened onto their children, as would be the fate of Africans enslaved in the Americas.

EUROPE IN THE AGE OF EXPLORATION

In the ninth century, about the time that the Mound Builders of the Mississippi valley were constructing their urban center at Cahokia and the kingdom of Ghana was rising in West Africa, western Europe was an economic and cultural backwater. It was overshadowed by Christian Byzantium, which controlled Asia Minor, the Balkans, and parts of Italy, and by the Muslim culture of the Middle East, which had spilled across North Africa and penetrated Spain and West Africa south of the Sahara. Over the next six centuries, an epic revitalization of western Europe occurred, creating the conditions that enabled its leading maritime nations vastly to extend their oceanic frontiers. Thence began a 400-year epoch of the militant expansion of European peoples and European culture into other continents.

The Rise of Europe

The rebirth of western Europe, which began around A.D. 1000, owed much to a revival of long-distance trading from Italian ports on the Mediterranean. Venice, Genoa, Pisa, and other Italian ports grew wealthy and gradually evolved into merchant-dominated city-states that freed themselves from the rule of feudal lords in control of the surrounding countryside.

While merchants led the emerging city-states, western Europe's feudal system was gradually weakening. In the thirteenth and fourteenth centuries, kings began to reassert their political authority and to undertake efforts to unify their realms.

Early developments in England led to a distinctive political system. In 1215, the English aristocracy curbed the powers of the king when they forced him to accept the Magna Charta. On the basis of this charter, a parliament composed of elective and hereditary members eventually gained the right to meet regularly to pass money bills. Parliament was thus in a position to act as a check on the Crown, an arrangement unknown on the Continent. During the sixteenth century, the Crown and Parliament worked together toward a more unified state, with the English kings wielding less political power than their European counterparts.

Economic changes of great significance also occurred in England during the sixteenth century. Members of the landed class began to combine their estates in order to practice more intensive and profitable agriculture. In this process, they threw peasant farmers off their plots, turning many of them into wage laborers. The formation of this working class was the crucial first step toward industrial development.

Continental Europe lagged behind England in two respects. First, it was far less affected by the move to consolidate, or "enclose," land. Part of the explanation lies in the values of continental aristocrats, who regarded the maximization of profit as unworthy of gentlemen. French nobles could lose their titles for commercial activities. Second, continental rulers were less successful in engaging the interests of their nobilities, and these nobles never shared governance with their king, as did English aristocrats through their participation in Parliament. In Spain, for example, the bloody expulsion of the Muslims and the Jews in 1492 strengthened the monarchy's hold, but regional cultures and leaders remained strong. The continental monarchs would thus warmly embrace doctrines of royal absolutism developed in the sixteenth century.

The New Monarchies and the Expansionist Impulse

In the second half of the fifteenth century, ambitious monarchs coming to power in France, England, and Spain sought social order and political stability in their kingdoms. Louis XI in France, Henry VII in England, Isabella of Castile, and Ferdinand of Aragon all created strong armies and bureaucratic state machinery. In these countries, and in Portugal as well, economic revival and Renaissance culture, with its secular emphasis on human abilities, nourished the impulse to expand beyond known frontiers. The exploratory urge had two initial objectives: to circumvent Muslim traders by finding an eastward oceanic route to Asia and to tap at its source the African gold trade.

Portugal launched Europe's age of exploration at the end of the fifteenth century. Led by Prince Henry the Navigator, for whom trade was secondary to the conquest of the Muslim world, Portugal breached the geographical unknown. In the 1420s, Henry began dispatching Portuguese mariners to probe the unknown Atlantic "sea of darkness." His intrepid sailors were aided by important improvements in navigation, mapmaking, and ship design, all promoted by the prince.

By the 1430s, Prince Henry's captains had reached Madeira, the Canaries, and the Azores, lying off the coasts of Portugal and northwestern Africa. These were soon developed as the first European agricultural plantations located on the Continent's periphery. From there, the Portuguese sea captains pushed farther south.

By the time of Prince Henry's death in 1460, Portuguese mariners had reached the west coast of Africa, where they began a profitable trade in ivory, slaves, and especially gold. By 1500, they had captured control of the African gold trade monopolized for centuries by North African Muslims. In 1497, Vasco da Gama became the first European to sail around the Cape of Africa, allowing the Portuguese to colonize the Indian Ocean and to establish trade concessions as far east as the Spice Islands and Canton by 1513.

Reaching the Americas

The marriage of Ferdinand and Isabella in 1469 united the independent states of Aragon and Castile and launched the Spanish nation into its golden age. Leading the way for Spain was an Italian sailor, Christopher Columbus. The son of a poor Genoese weaver, Columbus had married into a prominent family of Lisbon merchants and thus made important contacts at court.

Like many sailors, Columbus had listened to sea tales about lands to the west. He may have heard stories about the voyages of the Viking explorer Leif Eriksson, who around A.D. 1000 set sail from Greenland and landed at "Vinland," which may have been located somewhere between New England and Virginia. Columbus may also have heard accounts of the Viking settlement in Newfoundland. At any rate, he believed that ships could reach the Indies by sailing west across the Atlantic, but for nearly ten years he failed to secure financial backing and royal sanction in Portugal for exploratory voyages. Finally, in 1492, Queen Isabella of Spain commissioned him, and he sailed west with three tiny ships manned by about 90 men.

Strong winds, lasting ten days, blew the ships far into the Atlantic. There they were becalmed. In the fifth week at sea—longer than any European sailors had been out of the sight of land—mutinous rumblings swept through the crews. But Columbus pressed on. On the seventieth day, long after Columbus had calculated he would reach Japan, a lookout sighted land. On October 12, 1492, the sailors clambered ashore on a tiny island in the Bahamas, which Columbus named San Salvador (Holy Savior). Grateful sailors "rendered thanks to Our Lord, kneeling on the ground, embracing it with tears of joy."

Oceanic Exploration in the Fifteenth and Sixteenth Centuries

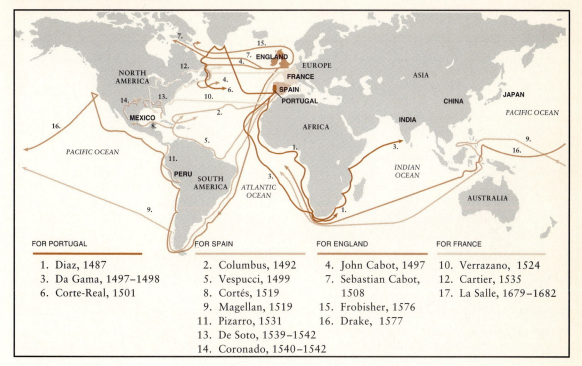

FOR PORTUGAL	FOR SPAIN	FOR ENGLAND	FOR FRANCE
1. Diaz, 1487	2. Columbus, 1492	4. John Cabot, 1497	10. Verrazano, 1524
3. Da Gama, 1497–1498	5. Vespucci, 1499	7. Sebastian Cabot,	12. Cartier, 1535
6. Corte-Real, 1501	8. Cortés, 1519	1508	17. La Salle, 1679–1682
	9. Magellan, 1519	15. Frobisher, 1576	
	11. Pizarro, 1531	16. Drake, 1577	
	13. De Soto, 1539–1542		
	14. Coronado, 1540–1542		

Believing he had reached Asia, Columbus explored the island-speckled Caribbean for ten weeks, landing on heavily populated islands that he named Hispaniola (shared today by Haiti and the Dominican Republic) and Cuba (which he thought was the Asian mainland). While homeward bound, he penned a report of his discoveries, still convinced that he had reached Asia.

Quickly printed and distributed throughout Europe, Columbus's report of his discoveries brought him financing for three much larger expeditions to explore the newfound lands. Though he led Spain to the threshold of a mighty empire, he reaped few rewards, dying unnoticed and penniless in 1506. To the end he believed that he had found the water route to Asia.

In time the real import of Columbus's discovery became clear, and he has long been celebrated as the bold explorer who initiated permanent contact between Europe and the Americas. He is attacked by some today as the ruthless exploiter of Indian peoples and lands, but Columbus is best understood in the context of his own times—an age of great brutality and violence, in which no race or nation had a monopoly on cruelty.

The expansion of Spain and Portugal into new areas of the world profoundly affected patterns of economic activity in Europe. Its commercial center now shifted away from the ports of the Mediterranean to the Atlantic ports facing the New World.

The New World also beckoned as a field of religious conquest. The heavily populated Americas offered millions of potential Christian converts. But the Catholic-Protestant division within Christianity complicated Christian dreams of converting a "heathen" continent. The people of western Europe, at precisely the time they were unlocking the secrets of the new worlds to the east and west in the sixteenth century, were being torn by religious schisms that magnified the era's national rivalries.

Religious Conflict During the Reformation

At the heart of Europe's religious strife was a continental movement to cleanse the Christian church of corrupt practices and return it to the purer ways of "primitive" Christianity, as practiced by the early Christians. While criticism of the worldliness of the Catholic church mounted during the Renaissance, a German monk, Martin Luther, became the first to break successfully with Rome and initiate a Protestant reformation of theology and practice. As Protestant sects multiplied, a Catholic Reformation grew up within the church, and the two groups began a long battle for the souls of Europeans.

Luther, an Augustinian monk, lost faith in the power of the age-old rituals of the church—prayer, the Mass, confession, pilgrimages to holy places, even crusades against Muslim infidels. He reasoned that salvation came through an inward faith, or "grace," that God conferred on those he chose. Good works, Luther believed, did not earn grace but were only the external evidence of grace won through faith. Luther had taken the revolutionary step of rejecting the church's elaborate hierarchy of officials, who presided over the rituals intended to guide individuals along the path toward salvation. The spread of printing, invented less than 70 years before, allowed the rapid circulation of his ideas.

Luther urged people to seek faith individually by reading the Bible, which he translated into German and made widely available for the first time in printed form. He also called on the German princes to assume control over religion in their states, directly challenging the authority of Rome.

The basic issue dividing Catholics and Protestants thus centered on the source of religious authority. To Catholics, religious authority resided in the organized Church, headed by the pope. To Protestants, the Bible was the sole authority, and access to God's word or God's grace did not require the mediation of the Church.

Building on Luther's redefinition of Christianity, John Calvin, a Frenchman, brought new intensity and meaning to the Protestant Reformation. In 1536, at age 26, he published a ringing appeal to every Christian to form a direct, personal relationship with God. By Calvin's doctrine, God had saved a few souls at random before Creation and damned the rest. Human beings were too depraved to know or alter this predestination, but good Christians must struggle to believe in their hearts that they were saved. Without mediation of ritual or priest but by "straight-walking," one was to behave as one of God's elect, the "saints." This radical theology spread among elements in all classes throughout Europe.

Calvin proposed reformed Christian communities structured around the elect few. Communities of "saints" must control the state, rather than the other way around. Elected bodies of ministers and dedicated laymen, called presbyteries, were to govern the church, directing the affairs of society down to the last detail so that all, whether saved or damned, would work for God's ends.

Calvin's radical program converted large numbers of people to Protestantism throughout Europe. Sixteenth-century monarchs regarded attacks on the Catholic church with horror. But many local princes adopted some version of the reformed faith. The most important monarch to break with Roman Catholicism was Henry VIII of England. Although Henry did not consider himself a Protestant, when Pope Clement VII refused him permission to divorce and remarry, he broke relations with Rome and established the Church of England, with himself as head.

The countries most affected by the Reformation—England, Holland, and France—were slow in trying to colonize the New World, so Protestantism did not gain an early foothold in the Americas. Catholicism in Spain and Portugal remained almost immune from the Protestant Reformation. So even while under attack, it swept across the Atlantic almost unchallenged during the century after Columbus's voyages.

THE IBERIAN CONQUEST OF AMERICA

From 1492 to 1518, Spanish and Portuguese explorers opened up vast parts of Asia and the Americas to European knowledge. At first, only modest attempts at settlement were made, mostly by the Spanish on Caribbean islands. The three decades after 1518, however, became an age of conquest. In some of the bloodiest chapters in recorded history, the Spanish nearly exterminated the native peoples of the Caribbean islands, toppled and plundered the great inland empires of the Aztecs and Incas in Mexico and Peru, discovered fabulous silver mines, and built a westward oceanic trade of enormous importance to all of Europe. The consequences of this short era of conquest proved to be immense for the entire world.

Portugal, meanwhile, restricted by one of the most significant lines ever drawn on a map, concentrated mostly on building an eastward oceanic trade to southeastern Asia. In 1493, to settle a dispute, the pope had demarcated Spanish and Portuguese spheres of exploration in the Atlantic. Drawing a north-south line 100 leagues (about 300 miles) west of the Azores, the pope confined Portugal to the European side of the line. One year later, in the Treaty of Tordesillas, Portugal obtained Spanish agreement to move the line 270 leagues farther west. Nobody knew at the time that a large part of South America, as yet undiscovered by Europeans, bulged east of the new demarcation line and therefore fell within the Portuguese sphere. In time, Portugal would develop this region, called Brazil, into one of the most profitable areas of the New World.

The Spanish Onslaught

Within a single generation of Columbus's death in 1506, Spanish conquistadores explored, claimed, and conquered most of South America (except Brazil), Central America, and the southern parts of North America from Florida to California. They were motivated by religion, growing pride of nation, and dreams of personal enrichment. "We came here," explained one Spanish footsoldier in Cortés's legion, "to serve God and the king, and also to get rich."

In two bold and bloody strokes, the Spanish overwhelmed the ancient civilizations of the Aztecs and Incas. In 1519, Hernando Cortés set out with 600 soldiers from coastal Veracruz and marched over rugged mountains to attack Tenochtitlán (modern-day Mexico City), the capital of Montezuma's Aztec empire. In 1521, following two years of tense relations between the Spanish and Aztecs, it fell before Cortés's assault. From the Valley of Mexico, the Spanish extended their dominion over the Mayan people of the Yucatán and Guatemala in the next few decades.

In the second conquest, the intrepid Francisco Pizarro, marching from Panama through the jungles of Ecuador and into the towering mountains of Peru with a mere 168 men, most of them not even soldiers, toppled the Inca empire. Like the Aztecs, the populous Incas lived in a highly organized social system. But also like the Aztecs, violent internal divisions had weakened them. Pizarro captured their capital at Cuzco in 1533. From there, Spanish soldiers marched farther afield, plundering other gold- and silver-rich Inca cities. Further expeditions into Chile, New Granada (Colombia), Argentina, and Bolivia in

Before the arrival of Cortés in 1519, Tenochtitlán was the capital and showplace of Montezuma's Aztec empire. The Spanish were astounded to see such a magnificent city, larger than any in Spain at the time. This modern rendering is based on archaeological evidence.

the 1530s and 1540s brought under Spanish control an empire larger than any in the Western world since the fall of Rome.

By 1550, Spain had overwhelmed the major centers of native population throughout the Caribbean, Mexico, Central America, and the west coast of South America. Spanish ships carried gold, silver, dyewoods, and sugar east across the Atlantic and transported African slaves, colonizers, and finished goods west. In a brief half century, Spain had brought into harsh but profitable contact with one another the people of three continents and established the triracial character of the Americas.

For nearly a century after Columbus's voyages, Spain enjoyed almost unchallenged dominion over the fabulous hemisphere newly revealed to Europeans. Only Portugal, which staked out important claims in Brazil in the 1520s, challenged Spanish domination of the New World.

The Great Dying

Spanish contacts with the natives of the Caribbean basin, central Mexico, and Peru in the early sixteenth century triggered the most dramatic and disastrous population decline ever recorded. The population of the Americas on the eve of European arrival had grown to an estimated 50 million or more. Europeans were members of a population that for centuries had been exposed to nearly every lethal microbe that infects humans on an epidemic scale in the temperate zone. Over the centuries, Europeans had built up immunities to these diseases. Such biological defenses did not eliminate smallpox, measles, diphtheria, and other afflictions, but they limited their deadly power. In contrast, the people of the Americas had been geographically isolated from these diseases and had no immunity whatsoever.

The results were catastrophic. On Hispaniola, a population of about one million that had existed when Columbus arrived had only a few thousand survivors by 1530. Of some 25 million inhabitants of the Aztec empire prior to Cortés's arrival, about 90 percent were felled by disease within a half century. Demographic disaster also struck the populous Inca peoples of the Peruvian Andes. Smallpox "spread over the people as great destruction," an old Indian told a Spanish priest in the 1520s. "There was great havoc. Very many died of it. They could not stir, they could not change position, nor lie on one side, nor face down, nor on their backs. And if they stirred, much did they cry out. . . . And very many starved; there was death from hunger, [for] none could take care of [the sick]." In most areas where Europeans intruded in the hemisphere for the next three centuries, the catastrophe repeated itself. In Spanish territories, the enslavement and brutal treatment of the native people intensified the lethal effects of European diseases. After their spectacular conquests of the Incas and Aztecs, the Spanish enslaved thousands of native people and assigned them work regimens that severely weakened their resistance to disease.

Silver, Sugar, and Their Consequences

Though Europeans looked for gold in the New World, more than three centuries would pass before they found it in windfall quantities on the North American Pacific slope and in the Yukon. Silver, however, proved abundant. Bonanza strikes were made in Bolivia in 1545 and in northern Mexico in the next decade, and much of Spain's New World enterprise focused on its extraction. The Spanish empire in America, for most of the sixteenth century, was a vast mining community.

Native people, along with some African slaves, provided the labor supply for the mines. At

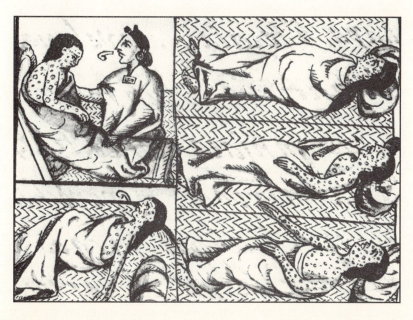

The devastating effects of smallpox on the Native American population were illustrated in this woodcut for a sixteenth-century book about Nueva España.

Potosí, in Bolivia, 58,000 workers labored at elevations of up to 13,000 feet to extract the precious metal from a fabulous sugarloaf "mountain of silver." The town's population reached 120,000 by 1570, making it larger than any in Spain at the time. Thousands of other workers toiled in the mines of Zacatecas, Taxco, and Guanajuato.

The massive flow of bullion from the Americas to Europe triggered profound changes. It financed further conquests and settlement in Spain's American empire, spurred long-distance trading in luxury items such as silks and spices from the Far East, and capitalized agricultural development in the New World of sugar, coffee, cacao, and indigo.

The enormous increase of silver in circulation in Europe after the mid–sixteenth century also caused a "price revolution." Between 1550 and 1600, prices doubled in many parts of Europe and then rose another 50 percent in the next half century. Landowning farmers got more for their produce, and merchants thrived on the increased circulation of goods. But artisans, laborers, and landless agricultural workers (the vast majority of the population) suffered because their wages did not keep pace with rising prices. The price revolution increased the number of people in western Europe living at the margins of society and thus built up the pressure to emigrate to the Americas.

While the Spaniards concentrated on the extraction of silver from the highlands of Mexico and Peru, the Portuguese staked their future on sugar production in the lowlands of Brazil. Adapting techniques of cultivation worked out earlier on their Atlantic islands, the Portuguese produced sugar for the export market. Whereas the Spanish mining operations used primarily Indian labor, the lowland Portuguese sugar planters scattered the indigenous people and replaced them with platoons of African slaves. By the 1630s this regimented work force was producing 32 million pounds of sugar annually. High in calories but low in protein, the sweet "drug food" revolutionized the tastes of millions of Europeans and caused the oceanic transport of millions of African slaves to the coast of Brazil and later to Colombia, Ecuador, and Peru.

From Brazil, sugar production jumped to the island-specked Caribbean. Here, in the early seventeenth century, England, Holland, and France challenged Spain for the riches of the New World. Once they secured a foothold in the West Indies, Spain's enemies stood at the gates of the Hispanic New World empire. In the seventeenth century they gradually sapped the strength of the first European empire outside of Europe.

Spain's Northern Frontier

The crown jewels of Spain's New World empire were silver-rich Mexico and Peru, with the islands and coastal fringes of the Caribbean representing lesser, yet valuable, gemstones. Distinctly third in importance were the northern borderlands of New Spain—the present-day Sun Belt of the United States. The early Spanish influence in Florida, the Gulf region, Texas, New Mexico, Arizona, and California indelibly marked the history of the United States.

Spanish explorers began charting the southeastern region of North America in the early sixteenth century, beginning with Juan Ponce de León's expeditions to Florida in 1515 and 1521. For the next half century, Spaniards planted small settlements there, and Franciscan priests attempted to gather the local tribes into mission villages and convert them to Catholicism.

The Spanish made several attempts to bring the entire Gulf of Mexico region under their control. From 1539 to 1542, Hernando de Soto, a veteran of Pizarro's conquest of the Incas, led an expedition deep into the homelands of the Creeks and explored westward across the Mississippi to Arkansas. In 1559, Spaniards marched northward from Mexico in an attempt to establish their authority in the lower Gulf region. Everywhere they went, they enslaved Indians and used them as provision carriers. In 1565, they built a fort at St. Augustine in Florida. They held Florida for more than two centuries.

The Southwest became the second region of Spanish activity in North America. Francisco Vásquez de Coronado explored the region from 1540 to 1542, never finding the legendary Seven Cities of Cíbola but opening much of Arizona, New Mexico, and Colorado to eventual Spanish control.

The Southwest, like Florida, proved empty of the fabled golden cities. Hence, in the seventeenth century, the region chiefly interested Jesuit and Franciscan missionaries. The Catholic mission became the primary institution of the Spanish borderlands. The Spanish missions operated differently, depending on the Indian cultures encountered. In Florida and California, where the native people lived in small, often seminomadic tribes, the Spanish used persuasion mixed with force to gather them within the sound of the mission bell. Setting the Indians to agricultural labor, the Spanish attempted slowly to convert them to European ways of life.

In New Mexico, however, the natives had lived in settled villages and practiced agriculture for centuries, so here the Spanish aimed to graft Catholicism onto Pueblo culture by building churches on the edges of ancient native villages. When they attempted to do more than overlay Indian culture with a veneer of Catholicism, they encountered fierce resistance. Such was the case in Popé's revolt in 1680. For five years, the Spanish padres had tried to root out traditional Pueblo religious practices. In response, a Pueblo leader named Popé led an Indian uprising that destroyed most of the churches in New Mexico and for more than a decade drove the Spanish from the region. Spaniards and Indians declared a kind of cultural truce: The Spaniards agreed to allow certain Pueblo rituals in return for nominal acceptance of Christianity.

ENGLAND LOOKS WEST

By the time England awoke to the promise of the New World, the two Iberian powers were firmly entrenched there. England was the most backward of the European nations facing the Atlantic in exploring and colonizing the New World. Only the voyages of John Cabot (the Genoa-born Giovanni Caboto) gave England any claim in the New World sweepstakes. But Cabot's voyages to Newfoundland and Nova Scotia a few years after Columbus's first voyage—the first northern crossing of the Atlantic since the Vikings—were never followed up.

At first, England's interest centered primarily on the rich fishing grounds of the Newfoundland Banks. Exploratory voyages along the eastern coast of North America hardly interested them. It was for the French that explorers Cartier and Verrazano sailed between 1524 and 1535. Looking for straits westward to India, through the northern landmass, which was still thought to be a large island, they made contact with many Indian tribes and charted the coastline from the St. Lawrence River to the Carolinas.

Changes occurred in the late sixteenth century that propelled the English overseas. The rising production of woolen cloth, a mainstay of the English economy, had sent merchants scurrying for new markets after 1550. Their success in establishing trading companies in Russia, Scandinavia, the Middle East, and India vastly widened England's commercial orbit and raised hopes that still other spheres could be developed. At the same time, population growth and rising prices depressed the existence of ordinary people and made them look to the transoceanic frontier for new opportunities.

England Challenges Spain

Queen Elizabeth, who ruled from 1558 to 1603, followed a cautious policy that did not include the promotion of overseas colonies. Ambitious and talented, she had to contend with Philip II, king of Spain and her fervently Catholic brother-in-law, whose long reign nearly coincided with hers. Regarding Elizabeth as a

Protestant heretic, Philip plotted incessantly against her.

The smoldering conflict between Catholic Spain and Protestant England broke into open flames. Elizabeth had been providing covert aid to the Protestant Dutch revolt against Catholic rule. Philip vowed to crush the rebellion and decided as well to launch an attack on England in order to wipe out this growing center of Protestant power. In 1585 Elizabeth sent 6,000 English troops to aid the Dutch Protestants. Three years later, Philip dispatched a Spanish armada of 130 ships, sails blazing with crusader's crosses, to conquer Elizabeth's England. For two weeks in the summer of 1588, a sea battle raged off the English coast. A motley collection of smaller English ships, with the colorful sea dog Francis Drake in the lead, defeated the Armada, sinking many of the lumbering Spanish galleons and then retiring as the legendary "Protestant wind" blew the crippled Armada into the North Sea. With Spanish naval power checked, both the English and the Dutch found the seas more open to their rising maritime and commercial interests.

The Westward Fever

In the last decades of the sixteenth century, the idea of overseas expansion captured the imagination of important elements of English society. Urging them on were two Richard Hakluyts, uncle and nephew. In the 1580s and 1590s, they devoted themselves to advertising the advantages of colonizing on the far side of the Atlantic. The New World offered land, opportunities for commerce, and heathen people in need of salvation. The Hakluyts publicized the idea that the time was ripe for England to break the Iberian monopoly on the riches of the New World.

England mounted its first attempts at colonizing, however, in Ireland. In the 1560s and 1570s, the English gradually extended their control over the country through brutal military conquest. Many of the leaders first involved in New World colonizing had served in Ireland, and many of their ideas of how to deal with a "savage" and "barbaric" people stemmed from their Irish experience.

The first English attempts at overseas settlement in the 1580s and early 1600s were small, feeble, and ill fated. Beginning in 1583, they mounted several unsuccessful attempts to settle Newfoundland, but perhaps their most dramatic failure was the "Lost Colony" of Roanoke.

Sir Walter Raleigh, a veteran of the campaign in Ireland and a favorite courtier of Queen Elizabeth, organized two attempts to establish a colony at Roanoke Island, off the North Carolina coast. The first group of settlers landed in August 1585 but, failing to receive needed supplies from England, left the island the following spring, taking passage on ships of Sir Francis Drake, who paid them an unexpected but welcome visit. A second expedition of 117 colonists was sent to Roanoke in 1587 under the command of John White, whose pregnant daughter was among the settlers. White's granddaughter, Virginia Dare, was born in Roanoke soon after the colonists landed and became the first child of English parentage to be born in America. White soon sailed back to England to obtain more supplies and settlers for Roanoke, but England's war with Spain prevented his immediate return to the colony. When he finally revisited Roanoke in 1590, he found that the colonists had vanished. Their fate to this day remains unknown, but they probably perished in attacks by a local tribe after killing a tribal leader and displaying his head on a pike.

Small groups of men sent out to establish a tiny colony in Guiana, off the South American coast, failed in 1604 and 1609, and another group that set down in Maine in 1607 lasted only a year. Even the colonies founded in Virginia in 1607 and Bermuda in 1612, although they would flourish in time, floundered badly for several decades.

English merchants, sometimes supported by gentry investors, undertook these first tentative efforts. They risked their capital and had little backing from the government, in subsidies, ships, or naval protection, though they had the blessing of their queen. The Spanish and Portuguese colonizing efforts, by contrast, were national enterprises, sanctioned, capitalized, and coordinated by the Crown.

Not until these first merchant adventures solicited the wealth and support of the prospering middle class of English society could colonization succeed. This support grew steadily in the first half of the seventeenth century, but even then, investors were drawn far more to the quick profits promised in West Indian tobacco production than to the uncertainties of mixed farming, lumbering, and fishing on the North American mainland. In the 1620s and 1630s, most of the English capital invested overseas went into establishing tobacco colonies in the flyspeck Caribbean islands of St. Christopher (1624), Barbados (1627), Nevis (1628), Montserrat (1632), and Antigua (1632).

Apart from the considerable financing required, the vital element in launching a colony was a suitable body of colonists. About 80,000 streamed out of England between 1600 and 1640, as economic, political, and religious developments pushed them from their homeland at the same time that dreams of opportunity and adventure pulled them westward. In the next 20 years, another 80,000 departed.

Economic difficulties in England prompted many to try their luck in the New World. Probably half the households in England lived on the edge of poverty in the early seventeenth century. "This land grows weary of her inhabitants," wrote John Winthrop of East Anglia, "so as a man, which is the most precious of all creatures, is near more vile among us than a horse or a sheep."

Religious persecution and political considerations intensified the pressure to emigrate from England in the early seventeenth century. The largest number of emigrants went to the West Indies. The North American mainland colonies attracted perhaps half as many, and the Irish plantations in Ulster and Munster still fewer.

Anticipating North America

The early English settlers in North America were far from uninformed about the indigenous people of the New World. Beginning with Columbus's first description of the New World, published in several European cities in 1493 and 1494, reports and promotional accounts circulated among the participants in early voyages of discovery, trade, and settlement.

Colonists who read or listened to these accounts probably held a split image of the native people. On the one hand, the Indians were depicted by Columbus and Verrazano as a gentle people who eagerly received Europeans. The natives, "graceful of limb and tawny-colored," Verrazano related in 1524, "came toward us joyfully uttering loud cries of wonderment, and showing us the safest place to beach the boat."

This positive image of the Native Americans reflected both the friendly reception that Europeans often actually enjoyed and the European vision of the New World as an earthly paradise where war-torn, impoverished, or persecuted people could build a new life. The strong desire to trade with the native people also encouraged a favorable view because only a friendly Indian could become a suitable partner in commercial exchange.

A counterimage, of a savage, hostile Indian, however, also entered the minds of settlers coming to North America. As early as 1502, Sebastian Cabot had paraded in England three Eskimos he had kidnapped on an Arctic voyage. They were described as flesh-eating savages and "brute beasts" who "spake such speech that no man could understand them." Many other accounts portrayed the New World natives as crafty, brutal, loathsome half-men, who lived, as the Italian navigator and explorer Amerigo Vespucci put it, without "law, religion, rulers, immortality of the soul, and private property."

The English were also aware of the Spanish experience in the Caribbean, Mexico, and Peru—and the story was not pretty. Many books described in gory detail the wholesale violence that occurred when Spaniard met Mayan, Aztec, or Inca. Immigrants embarking for North America wondered if similar violent confrontations did not await them.

Another factor nourishing negative images of the Indian stemmed from the Indians' possession of the land necessary for settlement. For Englishmen, rooted in a tradition of the private ownership of property, this presented moral and legal, as well as practical, problems. As early as the 1580s, George Peckham, an early promoter

of colonization, had admitted that the English doubted their right to take the land of others. But many argued that in return for land, the settlers would offer the natives the advantages of a more advanced culture and, most important, the Christian religion.

A more ominous argument arose to justify English rights to native soil. By denying the humanity of the Indians, the English, like other Europeans, claimed that the native possessors of the land were disqualified from rightful ownership of it. Defining the Native Americans as "savage" and "brutish" gave the settlers moral justification for taking their land. For their part, people like Opechancanough probably perceived the arriving Europeans as impractical, irreligious, aggressive, and strangely intent on accumulating material wealth.

CONCLUSION

CONVERGING WORLDS

The English migrants who began arriving on the eastern edge of North America in the late sixteenth century came late to a New World that other Europeans had been colonizing for more than a century. The English immigrants to Virginia were but a small advance wave of the large,

varied, and determined fragment of English society that would flock to the western Atlantic frontier during the next few generations. We turn now to the diversity of founding experiences of the English colonizers of the seventeenth century.

Recommended Reading

The rich pre-Columbian history of the Americas is surveyed in Dean Snow, *The Archaeology of North America: American Indians and Their Origins* (1980). Another fascinating analysis is Marshall Sahlins, *Stone Age Economics* (1972).

Excellent introductions to early African history in-

clude Basil Davidson, *The African Genius* (1969), and J. D. Fage, *A History of West Africa*, 4th ed. (1969).

Europe in the Age of Exploration can be studied in Ralph Davis, *The Rise of the Atlantic Economies* (1973); and Eric Wolf, *The People Without History* (1983).

A fine corrective to the much romanticized and often distorted story of the Spanish and Portuguese conquest of the Americas is James Lockhart and Stuart B. Schwartz, *Early Latin America* (1983). Also valuable is C. R. Boxer, *The Portuguese Seaborne Empire, 1415–1825* (1972).

The shape of English society as overseas colonization began is detailed in Carl Bridenbaugh, *Vexed and Troubled Englishmen, 1500–1642* (1968), and Peter Laslett, *The World We Have Lost* (1971). England's belated intervention in the Americas is followed in Nicholas P. Canny, *The Elizabethan Conquest of Ireland* (1976); David B. Quinn, *England and the Discovery of America, 1481–1620* (1974); and David B. Quinn, *North America from Earliest Discovery to First Settlements* (1977).

Time Line

	Pre-Columbian epochs	1513	Portuguese explorers reach China
12,000 B.C.	Beringian epoch ends	1515–1565	Spanish explore Florida and southern part of North America
6,000 B.C.	Paleo-Indian phase ends	1520s	Luther attacks Catholicism
500 B.C.	Archaic era ends	1521	Cortés conquers the Aztecs
500 B.C.–A.D.	Post-Archaic era in North America	1530s	Calvin calls for religious reform
		1533	Pizarro conquers the Incas
1420s	Portuguese sailors explore west coast of Africa	1540–1542	Coronado explores the Southwest
1492	Christopher Columbus lands on Caribbean islands	1558	Elizabeth I crowned queen of England
	Spanish expel Moors (Muslims)	1585	Roanoke Island settlement
1494	Treaty of Tordesillas	1588	English defeat the Spanish armada
1497–1585	French and English explore northern part of the Americas	1603	James I succeeds Elizabeth I
1498	Vasco da Gama reaches India after sailing around Africa	1607	English begin settlement at Jamestown, Virginia
1500	Kingdoms of Ghana, Mali, Songhay in Africa	1680	Popé's revolt in New Mexico

chapter 2

Colonizing a Continent

John Mason had emigrated from southeastern England as part of the flock of John Warham, a Puritan minister from the village of Dorchester. In Massachusetts, the group commemorated their origins by giving the name Dorchester to the area assigned to them.

Four years later, in the fall of 1636, Mason followed many of his Dorchester friends out of Massachusetts to the Connecticut River, 100 miles to the west. At their journey's end, they founded the town of Windsor, on the west bank of the Connecticut.

Six months later, when his new village was no more than a collection of crude lean-tos, militia captain John Mason marched south against the Pequots. He commanded several hundred men whom the fledgling Connecticut River towns had dispatched to drive the Pequots from the area. In the years before the English arrival, the powerful Pequots had formed a network of tributary tribes. Finding it impossible to placate the English as they swarmed into the Connecticut River valley, the Pequots chose resistance.

At dawn on May 26, 1637, Captain Mason and his troops approached a Pequot village on the Mystic River. Supported by Narragansett allies, the English slipped into the town and torched the Pequot wigwams. Then they rushed from the fortified village. As flames engulfed the huts, the Pequots fled the inferno, only to be cut down with musket and sword by the English soldiers, who had ringed the community. Most of the terrified victims were noncombatants—old men, women, and children—for the Pequot warriors were preparing for war at another village about five miles away. Before the sun rose, a major portion of the Pequot tribe had been exterminated. Mason wrote that God had "laughed at his enemies and the enemies of his people, . . . making them as a fiery oven."

Captain John Mason's actions at the Mystic River testify that the European colonization of America involved a violent confrontation of two cultures. We often speak of the "discovery" and "settlement" of North America by English and other European colonists. But the penetration of the eastern edge of what today is the United States might more accurately be called "the invasion of America."

Yet mixed with violence was utopian idealism. The New World was a place to rescue humankind from the ruins of the Old World. This chapter reconstructs the manner of settlement and the character of immigrant life in five areas of early colonization: the Chesapeake Bay, southern New England, the St. Lawrence to the Hudson rivers, the Carolinas, and Pennsylvania.

THE CHESAPEAKE TOBACCO COAST

As we saw in the previous chapter, England gained a foothold in North America when Walter Raleigh tried to establish a colony on Roanoke Island off the Carolina coast in the 1580s. The colony was too small and poorly financed to succeed. It served only as a token of England's rising challenge to Spain in the western hemisphere and as a source of valuable information for colonists later settling the area.

The Roanoke colony also failed resoundingly as the first sustained contact between English and Native American peoples. Although one member of the first expedition reported that "we found the people most gentle, loving, and faithful, void of all guile and treason," relations with the local tribes quickly soured and then turned violent. In 1591, when a relief expedition reached Roanoke, none of the settlers could be found. It is likely that in spite of their Iron Age weaponry, these "lost colonists" of Roanoke succumbed to Indian attacks. It was an ominous beginning for England's overseas ambitions.

Jamestown

In 1607, a generation after the first Roanoke expedition, a group of merchants established the first permanent colony in North America at Jamestown, Virginia. Under a charter from James I, they operated as a joint-stock company, an early form of a modern corporation that allowed them to sell shares of stock in their company and use the pooled investment capital to outfit and supply overseas expeditions. Although the king's charter to the Virginia Company of London began with a concern for bringing Christian religion to native people, most of the settlers probably agreed with Captain John Smith, who described the company as "making religion their colour, when all their aim was profit."

Profits in the early years proved elusive, however. Most of the early Virginia colonists died miserably of dysentery, malaria, and malnutrition. More than 900 settlers, mostly men, arrived in the colony between 1607 and 1609; only 60 survived. Moreover, one-third of the first three groups of immigrants were gold-seeking adventurers with unroughened hands. Others were unskilled servants, some with criminal backgrounds, who "never did knowe what a days work was," observed John Smith. Both types adapted poorly to wilderness conditions, leaving Smith begging for "but thirty carpenters, husbandmen, gardeners, fishermen, and blacksmiths" rather than "a thousand such gallants as were sent to me, . . . "

The Jamestown colony was also hampered by the common assumption that Englishmen could exploit the Indians of the region as the Spanish had done in Mexico and Peru. But in the Chesapeake the English found that the indige-

As seen in this sixteenth-century watercolor by John White, a member of the expedition to Roanoke Island, the natives who inhabited the village of Secotan lived much like English or Irish peasants.

nous peoples were not densely settled and could not easily be subjugated. Relations with some 40 small tribes, grouped into a confederacy led by the able Powhatan, turned bitter almost from the beginning. Powhatan brought supplies of corn to the sick and starving Jamestown colony during the first autumn. However, John Smith, whose military experience in eastern Europe had schooled him in dealing with people he regarded as "barbarians," raided Indian corn supplies and tried to cow the local tribes by shows of force. In

response, Powhatan withdrew from trade with the English and sniped at their flanks. Many settlers died in the "starving times" of the first years.

Despite these early failures, merchants of the Virginia Company of London poured more money and settlers into the venture. Understanding the need for ordinary farmers who could raise the food necessary to sustain the colony, they reorganized the company in 1609, promising free land to settlers at the end of seven years' labor for the company. In 1618, they sweetened the terms by offering 50 acres of land outright to anyone journeying to Virginia. More than 9,000 voyaged to Virginia between 1610 and 1622, but only 2,000 remained alive at the end of that period. "Instead of a plantation," wrote one English critic, "Virginia will shortly get the name of a slaughter house."

Sot Weed and Indentured Servants

The promise of free land lured a steady stream of settlers to Virginia, even though the colony proved a burial ground for most immigrants within a few years of arrival. Also crucial to the continued growth of the colony was the discovery that tobacco grew splendidly in Chesapeake soil. Tobacco proved to be Virginia's salvation. The planters shipped the first crop in 1617. By 1624, Virginia was exporting 200,000 pounds of the "stinking weed"; by 1638, though the price had plummeted, the crop exceeded three million pounds. Tobacco became to Virginia in the 1620s what sugar was to the West Indies and silver to Mexico and Peru. In London, men gibed that Virginia was built on smoke.

The cultivation of tobacco obliged Virginia's planters to find a reliable supply of cheap labor. The "sot weed" required intensive care through the various stages of planting, weeding, thinning, suckering, worming, cutting, curing, and packing. To fill their need, planters recruited immigrants in England and Ireland and a scattering from Sweden, Portugal, Spain, Germany, and even Turkey and Poland. Such people, called indentured servants, willingly sold a portion of their working lives in exchange for free passage across the Atlantic. About four of every five seventeenth-century immigrants to Virginia—and later Maryland—came in this status. Nearly three-quarters of them were male, and most of them were between 15 and 24 years old.

Few servants survived long enough to achieve their freedom. If malarial fevers or dysentery did not quickly kill them, they often succumbed to the brutal work routine harsh masters imposed. Masters bought and sold their servants as property, gambled for them at cards, and worked them to death since there was little motive for keeping them alive beyond their term of labor. When servants neared the end of their contract, masters found ways to add time and were backed by courts controlled by the planter class.

Contrary to English custom, masters often put women servants to work at the hoe. Sexual abuse by masters was common. Servant women paid dearly for illegitimate pregnancies. The courts fined them heavily and ordered them to serve an extra year or two to repay the time lost during pregnancy and childbirth. They also deprived mothers of their illegitimate children, indenturing them out at an early age. For many servant women, marriage was the best release from this hard life. Many willingly accepted the purchase of their indenture by any man who suggested marriage.

Expansion and Indian War

As Virginia's population increased, violence mounted between white colonizers and the Powhatan tribes. In 1614, the sporadic hostility ended temporarily with the arranged marriage of Powhatan's daughter, the fabled Pocahontas, to planter John Rolfe. However, the profitable cultivation of tobacco created an intense demand for land, and more and more settlers pushed up the rivers that flowed into Chesapeake Bay.

In 1617, when Powhatan retired, the leadership of the Chesapeake tribes fell to Opechancanough, who began building military strength for an all-out attack on his English enemies. The English murder of Nemattanew, a Powhatan war captain and religious prophet, triggered a fierce Indian assault on Good Friday in 1622 that dealt Virginia a staggering blow. More than one-quarter of the white population fell before the marauding tribesmen; the casualties in cattle, crops, and buildings were equally severe.

The devastating attack led to the bankruptcy of the Virginia Company. As a result, the king annulled its charter in 1624 and established a royal government, which allowed the elected legislative body established in 1619, the House of Burgesses, to continue lawmaking in concert with the royal governor and his council. The Virginia House of Burgesses is significant as the first elected legislative body in colonial America.

The Indian assault of 1622 fortified the determination of the surviving planters to pursue a ruthless new Indian policy of "perpetual enmity." The Virginians sent annual military expeditions against the native villages west and north of the settled areas. Population growth after 1630 and the recurrent need for fresh acreage by settlers who planted soil-exhausting tobacco intensified the pressure on Indian land. The tough, ambitious planters soon encroached on Indian territories, provoking war in 1644 and again in 1675, reducing the native population of Virginia to less than 1,000 by 1680. The Chesapeake tribes, Virginians came to believe, had little to contribute to the goals of English colonization; they were merely obstacles to be removed from the path of English settlement.

Proprietary Maryland

By the time Virginia had achieved commercial success in the 1630s, another colony on the Chesapeake took root. Rather than hoping for profit, George Calvert sought to establish in

Early Chesapeake Settlement

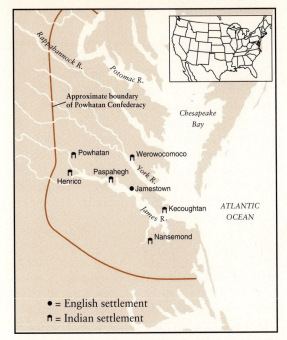

Approximate boundary of Powhatan Confederacy

Rappahannock R.

Potomac R.

Chesapeake Bay

Powhatan

Werowocomoco

Paspahegh

York R.

Henrico

Jamestown

Kecoughtan

ATLANTIC OCEAN

James R.

Nansemond

● = English settlement

⌂ = Indian settlement

Maryland a religious refuge for Catholics and a New World version of the English manorial countryside.

Catholics were an oppressed minority in England, and Calvert, Lord Baltimore, planned his colony as a place where they could start anew without fear of harassment. But knowing that he needed more than a small band of Catholic settlers, the proprietor planned to invite others as well. Catholics would never form a majority in his colony. They were quickly numerically overwhelmed by Protestants who jumped at the offer of free land with only a modest yearly fee to the proprietary family (a "quitrent") of two shillings per 100 acres.

Calvert died in 1632, leaving his 26-year-old son, Cecilius, to carry out his plans. The charter guaranteed the proprietor control over all branches of government and designated large estates for Calvert's relatives. Neither of these arrangements proved workable. Arriving in 1634, immigrants blithely ignored his plans, took up free land, imported as many indentured servants as they could afford, maintained generally peaceful relations with local Indian tribes, began to grow tobacco on scattered riverfront plantations like their Virginia neighbors, and governed themselves locally as much as possible. Although Maryland grew slowly at first, by 1700 its population of 33,000 was half that of Virginia's.

Daily Life on the Chesapeake

Though immigrants to the Chesapeake Bay region dreamed of bettering the life they had known in England, existence for most of them was dismally difficult. Only a minority could expect to marry and raise a family because marriage had to be deferred until after the indenture was completed, and there were three times more men than women. Once made, marriages were fragile. Either husband or wife was likely to succumb to disease within about seven years. The vulnerability of pregnant women to malaria frequently terminated marriages in the first few years, and death claimed half the children born before they reached adulthood. Few children could expect to have both parents alive while growing up. Grandparents were almost unknown. In a society so numerically dominated by men, widowed women were prized and remarried quickly. Such conditions produced complex families, full of stepchildren and stepparents, half sisters and half brothers.

The household of Robert Beverley of Middlesex County illustrates the tangled family relationships in this death-filled society. Between 1666 and 1687, Beverley had married in succession two widows who bore him nine children and had been stepfather to the eight children his two wives had produced with previous husbands. Not one of these 17 children, from an interlocking set of four marriages, reached adulthood with both a living mother and father.

Plagued by such mortality, the Chesapeake remained, for most of the seventeenth century, a land of immigrants rather than a land of settled families. Social institutions such as churches and schools took root very slowly amid such fluidity. The large number of indentured servants further increased the instability of community life.

The fragility of life showed clearly in the region's architecture. As in most New World colonies, the settlers at first erected only primitive huts and shanties, hardly more than windbreaks. After establishing crops, planters improved their habitats but still built ramshackle, one-room dwellings. "Their houses," it was observed in 1623, "stand scattered one from another, and are only made of wood ... so as a firebrand is sufficient to consume them all." Even as Virginia and Maryland matured, cheaply built and cramped houses, usually no larger than 16 by 24 feet, remained the norm. Life was too uncertain, the tobacco economy too volatile, and the desire to invest every available shilling in field labor too great for men to build grandly.

The crudity of life also showed in the household possessions of the Chesapeake colonists. Struggling farmers and tenants were likely to own only a straw mattress, a simple storage chest, and the tools necessary for food preparation and eating—a mortar and pestle to grind corn, knives for butchering, a pot or two for cooking stews and porridges, wooden trenchers and spoons for eating. Most ordinary settlers owned no chairs, no dressers, no plates or silverware. Among middling planters the standard of living was raised only by possession of a flock mattress, coarse earthenware for milk and butter, a few pewter plates and porringers, a frying pan or two, and a few rough tables and chairs. Even one of Virginia's wealthiest planters, the prominent Robert Beverley, had "nothing in and about his house but what was necessary ... good beds ... but no curtains, and instead of cane chairs, he hath stools made of wood."

MASSACHUSETTS AND ITS OFFSPRING

While some English settlers in the reign of James I (1603–1625) scrambled for wealth on the Chesapeake, others in England were seized by the spirit of religion. They looked to the wilds of North America as a place to build a tabernacle to God, a society dedicated to reforming the corrupt world. American Puritanism nurtured a belief in America's special mission in the world. But it also sought to banish diversity on a continent where the arrival of streams of immigrants from around the globe was destined to become a primary phenomenon.

Puritanism in England

England had been officially Protestant since 1558. Many English in the late sixteenth century, however, thought the Church of England was still ridden with Catholic elements. Because they wished to purify the Church of England, they were dubbed Puritans.

The Puritan movement attracted men and women who hoped to find in religion an antidote to the changes sweeping over English society. Many feared for the future as they witnessed the growth of turbulent cities, the increase of wandering poor, rising prices, and accelerating commercial activity. In general, they disapproved of the growing freedom from the restraints of gentry-dominated medieval institutions such as the church, guilds, and local government. The concept of the individual operating as freely as possible, maximizing both opportunities and personal potential, is at the core of our modern system of beliefs and behavior. But many in England cringed at the crumbling of traditional restraints of individual action. They worried that individualistic behavior would undermine the notion of community—the belief that people were bound together by reciprocal rights, obligations, and responsibilities. Especially they decried the "degeneracy of the times," which they saw in the defiling of the Sabbath by maypole dancing, card playing, fiddling, and bowling. Puritans vowed not only to purify the Church of England but to reform society as well.

One part of their plan was a social ethic stressing work as a primary way of serving God. The "work ethic" would banish idleness and impart discipline throughout the community. Second, Puritans organized themselves into religious congregations where each member hoped for personal salvation but also supported all others in their quest. Third, Puritans assumed responsibility for the "unconverted" people around them, who might have to be controlled. Religious reform and social vision were in this way interlocked.

When King James VI of Scotland succeeded the childless Elizabeth as James I of England in 1603, he spoke stridently for the divine right of the monarch and his own role as head of the church. He deplored the rising power of the Puritans, who had occupied the pulpits in hundreds of churches, gained control of several colleges at Oxford and Cambridge, and obtained many seats in Parliament. James promised to "harry them out of the land, or else do worse."

Among those he succeeded in harrying out of the land were a congregation of Puritan Separatists, who from 1608 on escaped in small numbers and over a period of years to Leyden in Holland. Unlike other Puritans, the Separatists did not seek to reform the Church of England; they wanted only to be left alone to realize their vision of a pure life. They were allowed to practice their faith freely in Holland, but eventually a number of them turned to America for a permanent home.

When King Charles I ascended the English throne in 1625, the situation worsened for Puritans. Determined to strengthen the monarchy and stifle dissent, the king adjourned Parliament in 1629. He then appointed William Laud, the bishop of London, to high office and turned him loose on the Puritans, whom Laud called "wasps" and "the most dangerous enemies of the state."

By 1629, many Puritans were turning their eyes outward to Northern Ireland, Holland, the Caribbean islands, and especially North America. The depression in the cloth trades, most severe in Puritan strongholds, was an added motivation to emigrate. To some distant shore, many Puritans decided, they would transport a fragment of English society and carry out the completion of the Protestant Reformation. As they understood history, God had assigned them a special task in his plan for the redemption of humankind.

Puritan Predecessors in New England

Puritans were not the first Europeans to reach the shores of New England, but no permanent settlement took root until the Pilgrims arrived in Plymouth in 1620. The *Mayflower* left England in September 1620 carrying 35 Puritan Separatists and 67 other colonists. The "Pilgrims," as they called themselves, suffered greatly during their first winter in the new land, half of them dying of sickness, cold, and malnutrition. With the help of friendly Indians, however, the survivors learned to grow corn and exploit the waters for seafood.

For two generations, the Pilgrims tilled the soil and fished while trying to keep intact their religious vision. But with the much larger Puritan migration that began in 1630, the Pilgrim villages nestled on the shores of Cape Cod Bay became a backwater of the thriving, populous Massachusetts Bay colony, which absorbed them in 1691.

Errand into the Wilderness

In 11 ships, 1,000 Puritans set out from England in 1630 for the Promised Land. They were the

John Winthrop was one of the lesser gentry who joined the Puritan movement and in the 1620s looked westward for a new life. Always searching himself as well as others for signs of weakness, Winthrop was one of the Massachusetts Bay Colony's main leaders for many years.

vanguard of a movement that by 1642 had brought about 18,000 colonizers to New England's shores. Led by John Winthrop, they operated under a charter from the king to the Puritan-controlled Massachusetts Bay Company. The Puritans set about building their utopia with the characteristic fervor of people convinced they are carrying out a divine task.

Their intention was to establish communities of pure Christians who collectively swore a covenant with God to work for his ends. To accomplish this, the Puritan leaders agreed to employ severe means. Their historic mission was too important, they believed, to allow the luxury of diversity of opinion in religious matters. Likewise, participation in government would be

limited to church members. Civil and religious transgressors would be rooted out and severely punished.

To realize their utopian goals, the Puritans willingly gave up freedoms that their compatriots sought. An ideology of rebellion in England, Puritanism in America became an ideology of control. Much was at stake, for as Winthrop reminded the first settlers, "We shall be as a city upon a hill [and] the eyes of all people are upon us." That visionary sense of mission would help to shape a distinctive American self-image in future generations.

As in Plymouth and Virginia, the first winter tested the strongest souls. More than 200 of the first 700 settlers perished, but Puritans kept coming. They "hived out" along the Back Bay of Boston, along the rivers that emptied into the bay, south into what became Connecticut and Rhode Island a few years later, and north along the rocky Massachusetts coast.

Motivated by their militant work ethic and sense of mission, led by men experienced in local government, law, and the uses of exhortation, the Puritans thrived almost from the beginning. Most of the ordinary settlers came as freemen in families. Trained artisans and farmers, they established tightknit communities in which, from the outset, the brutal exploitation of labor rampant in the Chesapeake had no place.

An Elusive Utopia

The Puritans built a sound economy based on agriculture, fishing, timbering, and trading for beaver furs with local Indians. Even before leaving England, the directors of the Massachusetts Bay Company transformed their commercial charter into a rudimentary government and transferred the charter to New England. Once there, they laid the foundations of self-government. Free male church members annually elected a governor and deputies from each town who formed one house of a colonial legislature. The

Early New England

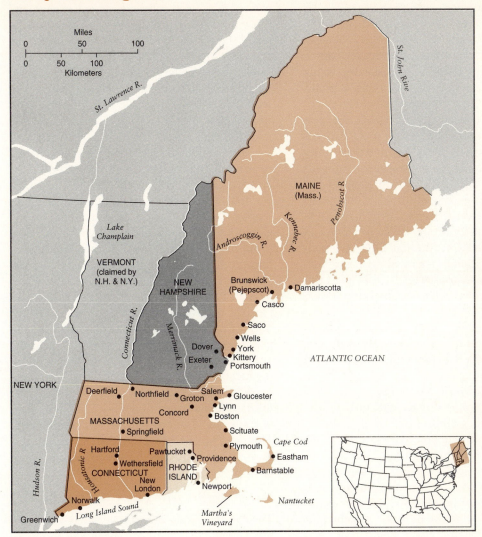

other house was composed of the governor's assistants, later to be called councillors. Consent of both houses was required to pass laws.

The Puritans established the first printing press in the English colonies and planted the seed of a university, Harvard College, which opened its doors in 1636 for the training of prospective clergymen. They also organized elementary and secondary schools, open to all.

In spite of these accomplishments, the Puritan colony experienced internal tensions and proved unable to reach a peaceful accommodation with the Native Americans, whose lands some colonists coveted. Others agitated for broader political rights and even briefly ousted Winthrop as governor in 1635.

Winthrop's troubles multiplied in 1633 when Salem's Puritan minister, Roger Williams, began to voice disturbing opinions on church and government policies. The visionary young man argued that the Massachusetts Puritans were not truly pure because they would not completely separate themselves from the polluted Church of England (which most Puritans still hoped to reform). He denounced mandatory worship and argued that government officials should not interfere with religious matters but confine themselves to civil affairs. Later to be celebrated as the earliest spokesman for the separation of church and state, Williams seemed in 1633 to strike at the heart of the Bible commonwealth, whose leaders regarded civil and religious affairs as inseparable. Williams also charged the Puritans with illegally intruding on Indian land.

In 1635, under threat of deportation to England, Williams fled southward through winter snow with a small band of followers to found Providence, a settlement on Narragansett Bay in what would become Rhode Island.

Even as they were driving Williams out, the Puritan authorities confronted another threat. Anne Hutchinson, who had arrived in 1634 with her husband and seven children, gained great respect among Boston's women as a practiced midwife, healer, and spiritual counselor. She soon began to discuss religion, suggesting that the "holy spirit" was absent in the preaching of some ministers. Before long Hutchinson was leading a movement labeled antinomianism, an interpretation of Puritan doctrine that stressed the mystical nature of God's free gift of grace while discounting the efforts the individual could make to gain salvation. She declared that God had communicated directly with her and that other true believers could also receive his message of grace and salvation directly. The importance of the clergy was thus diminished.

By 1636, Boston was dividing into two camps, those who followed the male clergy and those who cleaved to the theological views of a gifted though untrained woman with no official standing. Hutchinson doubly offended the male leaders of the colony because she boldly stepped outside the subordinate position expected of women. "The weaker sex" set her up as "a priest" and "thronged" after her, wrote one male leader.

In 1636 Hutchinson was tried and convicted of sedition and contempt and banished from the colony. Six months later, the Boston church excommunicated her for preaching 82 erroneous theological opinions. In the last month of her eighth pregnancy, Hutchinson, with a band of supporters, followed the route of Roger Williams to Rhode Island, the catch basin for Massachusetts Bay's dissidents.

But ideas proved harder to banish than people. The magistrates could never enforce uniformity of belief. Neither could they curb the appetite for land. Growth, geographic expansion, and commerce with the outside world all eroded the ideal of integrated, self-contained communities filled with religious piety. By 1636, groups of Puritans had swarmed not only to Rhode Island but also to Hartford and New Haven, where Thomas Hooker and John Davenport led new Puritan settlements in what became Connecticut.

New Englanders and Indians

The charter of the Massachusetts Bay Company proclaimed the goal of converting the natives to the Christian faith. But the instructions that Governor John Winthrop carried from England reveal other Puritan thoughts about the native inhabitants. According to Winthrop's orders, all men were to receive training in the use of firearms, Indians were prohibited from entering Puritan towns, and any colonist selling arms to an Indian or instructing one in their use was to be deported.

Only sporadic conflict with local tribes occurred at first because disease had catastrophically struck the Native American population of southern New England, which may have numbered as many as 125,000 in 1600, and left much of their land vacant. The settler pressure for new land, however, soon reached into areas untouched by disease. When land hunger mingled with the Puritan sense of mission, it proved an explosive mix. To a people charged with messianic zeal, the heathen Indians represented a mocking challenge to the building of a religious commonwealth that would "shine as a beacon" back to decadent England.

Making the "savages" of New England strictly accountable to the ordinances that governed white behavior was part of this quest for fulfilling their mission. In this the Puritans succeeded with the smaller, disease-ravaged tribes of eastern Massachusetts. But their attempts to control the stronger Pequots led to the bloody war in 1637 in which John Mason was a leader. The Puritan victory in that war removed the last obstacle to expansion into the Connecticut River valley. Missionary work, led by John Eliot, began among the remnant tribes in the 1640s. After a decade of effort, about 1,000 Indians had been settled in four "praying villages," learning to live according to the white man's ways.

The Web of Village Life

The village was the vital center of Puritan life. Unlike the Chesapeake tobacco planters, who dispersed along the streams and rivers of their area, the Puritans established small, tightly settled villages, and most pursued "open field" agriculture. Under this system, fields were divided into narrow strips of land that radiated out from the town, and a family might be allotted several disconnected strips. Each year a third or more of the village land was set aside to lie fallow so that it could regain its fertility. Farmers

trudged out from the village each day to work on their fields. They grazed their cattle on common meadow and cut firewood on common woodland. Such a system re-created agricultural life in many parts of England.

In other towns, Puritans employed the "closed field" system of self-contained farms that they had known at home. But in either system, families lived close together in compact towns built around a common, where the meetinghouse and tavern were located. These small, communal villages kept families in close touch and perfectly served the need for moral surveillance, or "holy watching" among neighbors. Puritans also prohibited single men and women from living by themselves, for this would put individuals beyond patriarchal authority and group observation.

At the center of every Puritan village stood the meetinghouse. These plain wooden structures, sometimes called "Lord's barns," gathered within them every soul in the village twice a week—on the Lord's day and during mid-week as well. The minister was the spiritual leader in these small, family-based, community-oriented settlements, which viewed life as a Christian pilgrimage.

The unique Puritan mixture of strict authority and incipient democracy, of hierarchy and equality, can be seen in the way the Massachusetts town distributed land and devised local government. Each town was founded by a grant of the colony's General Court, sitting in Boston. Only groups of Puritans who had signed a compact signifying their unity of purpose received settlement grants.

After receiving a grant, townsmen met to parcel out land. They awarded individual grants according to the size of a man's household, his wealth, and his usefulness to the church and town. Such a system perpetuated existing differences in wealth and status. But Puritans also believed that every family should have enough land to sustain it, and prospering men were expected to use their wealth for the community's benefit, not for conspicuous consumption. Repairing the meetinghouse, building a school, aiding a widowed neighbor—such were the proper uses of wealth.

Having felt the sting of centralized power in church and state, Puritans emphasized local exercise of authority. Until 1684, only male church members could vote, and as the proportion of males who were church members declined, so did the proportion of men who could vote. These voters elected selectmen, who allocated land, passed local taxes, and settled disputes. Once a year, all townsmen gathered for the town meeting, at which they selected town officers for the next year and decided matters large and small: Should the playing of football in the streets be prohibited? Might Widow Thomas be allowed £10 for a kidney stone operation for her son? What salary should the schoolteacher be paid?

The predominance of families also lent cohesiveness to Puritan village life. Strengthening this family orientation was the remarkably healthy environment of the Puritans' "New Israel." While the germs carried by English colonizers devastated neighboring Indian societies, the effect on the newcomers of entering the new environment was the opposite because the low density of settlement prevented infectious diseases from spreading.

The result was a spectacular natural increase in the population and a life span unknown in Europe. The difference was not a higher birthrate. The crucial factor was that chances for survival after birth were far greater than in England because of the healthier climate and better diet. In New England, nearly 90 percent of the infants born in the seventeenth century survived to marriageable age, and life expectancy exceeded 60 years—longer than for the American population as a whole at any time until the early twentieth century. About 25,000 people immigrated to New England in the seventeenth century, but by 1700 they had produced a population of 100,000. By contrast, some 75,000 immigrants to the Chesapeake colonies had yielded a population of about 70,000 by the end of the century.

Women played a vital role in this family-centered society. In the household economies of the Puritan villages, the woman was not only wife, mother, and housekeeper but also custodian of the vegetable garden; processor of salted and smoked meats, diary products, and preserved vegetables; and spinner, weaver, and clothesmaker.

The presence of women and a stable family life strongly affected New England's regional architecture. Well-constructed one-room houses with sleeping lofts quickly replaced the early "wigwams, huts, and hovels." Families then added parlors and lean-to kitchens as soon as they could. Within a half century, New England immigrants accomplished a general rebuilding of their living structures, while the Chesapeake lagged far behind.

A final binding element in Puritan communities was the stress on literacy and education, eventually to become a hallmark of American society. Placing religion at the center of their lives, Puritans emphasized the ability to read catechisms, psalmbooks, and especially the Bible.

An event in England in 1642 affected the future development of the New England colonies. King Charles I pushed his people into revolution by violating the country's customary constitution and trying to continue the reformation in the Anglican church. The ensuing civil war climaxed with the trial and beheading of the king in 1649. Thereafter, during the so-called Commonwealth period (1649–1660), Puritans had the opportunity to complete the reform of English religion and society. Migration to New England abruptly ceased.

The 20,000 English immigrants who had come to New England by 1649 were scattered from Maine to Long Island. To combat disper-

Reconstructed Chesapeake planter's house, typical of such simply built and unpainted structures in the seventeenth century.

sion, Puritan leaders established a broad intercolony political structure in 1643 called the Confederation of New England. This first American attempt at federalism functioned fitfully for a generation, though Massachusetts, the strongest and largest member, often refused to abide by group decisions when they ran counter to its objectives.

Although the Puritans fashioned stable communities and effective government, their leaders, as early as the 1640s, complained that the founding vision of Massachusetts Bay was faltering. Material concerns seemed to transcend religious commitment; the individual prevailed over the community. A generation later Puritans rarely mentioned the work of salvaging western Protestantism by example. Instead, they concentrated on keeping their children on the straight and narrow road.

Frequent complaints about moral laxness notwithstanding, New England had achieved economic success and political stability by the end of the seventeenth century. If social diversity increased and the religious zeal of the founding generation waned, that was only to be expected. One second-generation Bay colonist put the matter bluntly. His minister had noticed his absence in church and found him late that day at the docks, unloading a boatload of cod. "Why were you not in church this morning?" asked the clergyman. Back came the reply: "My father came here for religion, but I came for fish."

FROM THE ST. LAWRENCE TO THE HUDSON

The New Englanders were not the only European settlers in the northern region, for both France and Holland created colonies there. At the same time that Jamestown was founded, the French repeated their attempt to settle Canada, more successfully than in the 1540s. French explorer Samuel de Champlain established a small settlement in Port Royal, Acadia (later Nova Scotia), in 1604, and another at what would become the capital of New France, Quebec, in 1608. The primary interest of the French was the fur trade. The holders of the fur monopoly in France did not encourage emigration to the colony because settlement would reduce the forests from which the furs were harvested. New France therefore remained so lightly populated that English marauders easily seized and held Quebec from 1629 to 1632.

In 1609, Champlain allied with the Algonquian Indians of the St. Lawrence region in attacking their enemies the Iroquois to the south, earning their eternal enmity. The Iroquois traded furs to the Dutch on the Hudson River for European goods, and when they exhausted the furs of their own territory, they turned north, determined to destroy the French-allied Hurons of the Great Lakes region and seize their rich forests. In the 1640s and 1650s, the Iroquois smashed the Hurons and the French Jesuit missions among them. That ended all commerce in New France for a time and menaced Quebec and Montreal. The bitterness bred in these years colored future colonial warfare, driving the Iroquois to ally with the English against the French. But for the time being, in the mid–seventeenth century, the English remained free of pressure from the beleaguered French colonists, who numbered only about 400.

By the mid–seventeenth century, the Chesapeake and New England regions each contained about 50,000 settlers. Between them lay the mid-Atlantic area controlled by the Dutch, who had planted a small colony named New Netherland at the mouth of the Hudson River in 1624 and in the next four decades had extended their control to the Connecticut and Delaware river valleys. To the south of the Chesapeake lay a vast territory where only the Spanish, on their mission frontier in Florida, challenged the power of Native American tribes.

These two areas, north and south of the Chesapeake, became strategic zones of English colonizing activity after the end of England's civil war in 1660 brought the reinstallation of the English monarchy.

England Challenges the Mighty Dutch

Although for generations they had been the Protestant bulwarks in a mostly Catholic Europe, England and Holland became bitter commercial rivals in the mid–seventeenth century. By the time the Puritans arrived in New England, the Dutch had become the mightiest carriers of seaborne commerce in western Europe. By one contemporary estimate, Holland owned 16,000 of Europe's 20,000 merchant ships. By 1650, the Dutch had temporarily overwhelmed the Portuguese in Brazil, and soon their vast trading empire reached the East Indies, Ceylon, India, and Formosa.

In North America, the Dutch West India Company's New Netherland colony was small but profitable. Agents fanned out from Fort Orange (Albany) and New Amsterdam (New York City) into the Hudson, Connecticut, and Delaware river valleys. There they established a lucrative fur trade with local tribes by hooking into the sophisticated trading network of the Iroquois Confederacy, which stretched to the Great Lakes. At Albany, the center of the Dutch-Iroquois trade, relations remained peaceful and profitable for several generations because both peoples admirably served each other's needs.

By 1650, England was ready to challenge Dutch maritime supremacy. Three times between 1652 and 1675, war broke out between the two Protestant competitors for control of the emerging worldwide capitalist economy. In the second and third wars, the Dutch colony on the Hudson River became an easy target for the English. They captured it in 1664, lost it to the Dutch in 1673, and recaptured it almost immediately. By 1675, the Dutch had been permanently dislodged from the North American mainland. But they remained mighty commercial competitors of the English in Europe, Africa, the Far East, and the Caribbean.

New Netherland, where from the beginning Dutch, French Huguenots, Walloons from present-day Belgium, Swedes, Portuguese, Finns, English, refugee Portuguese Jews from Brazil, and Africans had commingled in a babel of languages and religions, now became New York, named for James, duke of York, brother of the king and heir to the English throne.

Under English rule, gradual intermarriage between the Dutch, the Huguenots, and the English—the three main groups—diluted ethnic loyalties. But New York retained its polyglot, religiously tolerant character.

PROPRIETARY CAROLINA: A RESTORATION REWARD

In 1663, three years after he was restored to the throne taken from his father, Charles II granted a vast territory named Carolina to a group of men who had supported him when he was in exile. Its boundaries extended from ocean to ocean and from Virginia to central Florida. Within this miniature empire, eight proprietors, including several involved in Barbados sugar plantations, gained large powers of government and semifeudal rights to the land. To lure settlers, they promised religious freedom and offered land free for the asking. Onto this generous land offer they grafted plans for a semimedieval government that provided themselves, their deputies, and a small number of noblemen with a monopoly of political power. A hereditary aristocracy of wealthy manor lords, they thought, would bring social and political stability to the southern wilds of North America and would check boisterous small landholders.

However, the reality of settlement in Carolina bore faint resemblance to what the planners envisaged. The rugged sugar and tobacco planters who streamed in from Barbados and Virginia ignored proprietary regulations about settling in compact rectangular patterns and reserving two-fifths of every county for an appointed nobility. Meeting in assembly for the first time in 1670, they refused to accept the proprietors' Fundamental Constitutions of 1667 and ignored the orders of the governor appointed in London. In shaping local government, the planters were guided mostly by their experience in the slave society of Barbados, whence most of them had come.

The Indian Debacle

Carolina was the most elaborately planned colony in English history but the least successful in achieving amicable relations with the natives. The proprietors in London had anticipated a well-regulated Indian trade limited to their appointed Carolina agents. But the aggressive settlers from the West Indies and the Chesapeake openly flouted proprietary policy. Those from Barbados, accustomed to exploiting African slave labor, saw that if the major tribes of the Southeast—the Cherokees, Creeks, and Choctaws—could be drawn into trade, the planters might reap vast wealth.

It was not the beaver that beckoned in the Indian trade, as in the North, but the deerskin, much desired in Europe for making warm and durable clothing. But what began as a trade for the skins of deer soon became a trade for the skins of Indians. To the consternation of the London proprietors, capturing Indians for sale in New England and the West Indies became the cornerstone of commerce in Carolina in the early years.

The Indian slave trade plunged Carolina into a series of wars. Local planters and merchants selected a tribe, armed it, and rewarded it handsomely for bringing in captives from another tribe. Even strong tribes that allied for trade with the Carolinians found that after they had used English guns to enslave their weaker neighbors, they themselves were sometimes scheduled for elimination. By the early eighteenth century, the two main tribes of the coastal plain, the Westos and the Savannahs, were nearly extinct.

Early Carolina Society

Carolina's fertile land and warm climate convinced many that it was "a second Paradize." Into the country came Barbadians, Swiss, Scots, Irish, French Huguenots, English, and even

Restoration Colonies: New York, the Jerseys, Pennsylvania, and the Carolinas

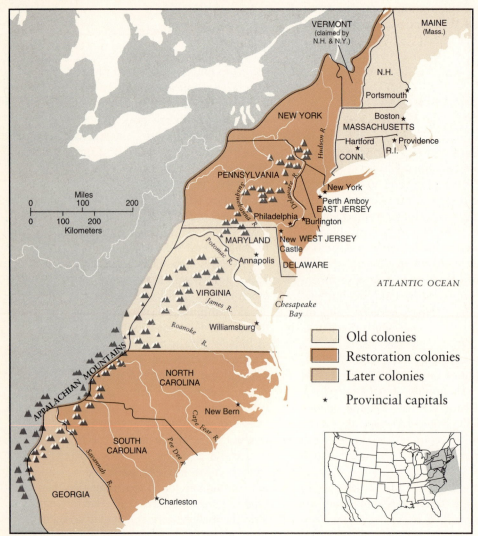

migrants from New England and New York. But far from creating paradise, this ethnically and religiously diverse people clashed abrasively in an atmosphere of fierce competition, brutal race relations, and stunted social institutions.

Settlements spread as the Indian population of the coastal region fell sharply. Planters experi-

mented with a variety of exotic crops, including sugar, indigo, tropical fruits, tobacco, and rice. It was this last that proved to be the staple crop upon which a flourishing economy could be built.

The cultivation of rice required backbreaking labor to drain the swampy lowlands, build

This painting of Mulberry Plantation in South Carolina shows the mansion house, built in 1708, and rows of slave huts constructed in an African style.

dams and levees, and hoe, weed, cut, thresh, and husk the crop. Since many of the early settlers had experience with African slaves in Barbados, their early reliance on slave labor came naturally to them. By 1720, when the colony's population had grown to 18,000, blacks outnumbered whites two to one.

As in Virginia and Maryland, the low-lying areas of coastal Carolina were so disease-ridden with malaria and yellow fever that population grew only slowly in the early years. "In the spring a paradise, in the summer a hell, and in the autumn a hospital," remarked one traveler. Malaria and yellow fever, especially dangerous to pregnant women, were the twin killers that retarded population growth, while the scarcity of women further limited natural increase."

In the healthier northern part of Carolina, mostly pine barrens along a sandy coast, a family-oriented society emerged. Populated largely by small tobacco farmers from Virginia seeking free land, the Albemarle region developed a mixed economy of livestock grazing, tobacco and food production, and the mining of the pine forests for naval stores—turpentine, resin, pitch, tar, and lumber. In 1701, North and South Carolina became separate colonies, but their distinctiveness had emerged before that. Slavery took root only slowly in North Carolina, which was still 85 percent white in 1720.

But in both North and South Carolina, several factors inhibited the growth of a strong corporate identity: the pattern of settlement, the ethnic and religious diversity, and the lack of shared assumptions about social and religious goals.

THE QUAKERS' PEACEABLE KINGDOM

Of all the utopian dreams imposed on the North American landscape in the seventeenth century, the most remarkable was that of the Quakers. During the English civil war, the Society of Friends, as the Quaker called themselves, had sprung forth as one of the many radical sects searching for a more just society and a purer religion. Their visionary ideas and their defiance of civil authority cost them dearly in fines, brutal punishment, and imprisonment. After Charles II and Parliament stifled radical dissent in the 1660s, they too sent many converts across the Atlantic. The society they founded in Pennsylvania foreshadowed more than any other colony the future religious and ethnic pluralism of the United States.

The Early Friends

Like their Puritan cousins, the Quakers regarded the English Protestant church (called the Church of England) as corrupt and renounced its formalities and rituals, which smacked of Catholicism. They also foreswore all church officials and institutions, persuaded that every believer could find grace through his or her own "inward light." By discarding the ideas of original sin and eternal predestination, the Quakers offered a radically liberating alternative to the reigning Calvinist doctrine. And their egalitarian doctrine of the light within elevated all lay persons to the position of the clergy and denied the primary place accorded the Scriptures.

Garbing themselves in plain black cloth and practicing civil disobedience, the Quakers presented a threat to social hierarchy and order. They refused to observe the customary marks of deference, such as doffing one's hat to a superior, believing that in God's sight no social distinctions existed. They used the familiar *thee* and *thou* instead of the formal and deferential *you*, they resisted taxes supporting the Church of England, and they refused to sign witnesses'

oaths on the Bible, regarding this as profane. They also renounced the use of force in human affairs and refused to perform militia service.

Quakers also affronted traditional views when they insisted on the spiritual equality of the sexes and the right of women to participate in church matters on an equal, if usually separate, footing with men. Quaker leaders urged women to preach and to establish separate women's meetings. Among Quakers who fanned out from England to preach the doctrine of the "inward light," 26 of the first 59 to cross the Atlantic were women. All but four of them were unmarried or without their husbands and therefore living, traveling, and ministering outside the bounds of male authority.

Intensely committed to converting the rest of the world to their beliefs, the Quakers ranged westward to North America and the Caribbean in the 1650s and 1660s. Nearly everywhere they were reviled, mutilated, imprisoned, and deported. Puritan Massachusetts warned them that their liberty in that colony consisted of "free liberty to keep away from us and such as will come to be gone as fast as they can, the sooner the better." The Bay Colony magistrates hanged several Quakers to show they meant business.

Early Quaker Designs

By the 1670s, the English Quakers were looking for a place in the New World to carry out their millennial dreams. Emerging as their leader in this dark period was William Penn, the son of Admiral Sir William Penn, who had captured Jamaica from the Spanish in 1654. Young William had been groomed for life in the English aristocracy, but he rebelled against his parents' designs for him. At age 23, he was converted by a spellbinding speech about the power of the Quaker inward light. After joining the Society of Friends in 1666, Penn devoted himself to their cause.

In 1674, Penn joined other Friends in establishing their own colony on former Dutch territory between the Hudson and Delaware rivers. They purchased the rights to the land, known as West Jersey, from Lord John Berkeley. Penn now helped fashion an extraordinarily liberal constitution for the budding Quaker colony. Legislative power and the authority to constitute courts were vested in an assembly chosen annually by virtually all free males in the colony. Election of justices of the peace and local officeholders was also mandated. Settlers were guaranteed freedom of religion and trial by jury. As Penn and the other trustees of the colony explained, "We lay a foundation for [later] ages to understand their liberty as men and Christians, that they may not be brought in bondage, but by their own consent; for we put the power in the people." Nowhere in the English world did ordinary citizens, especially those who owned no land, enjoy such extensive privileges.

Despite these idealistic plans, West Jersey sputtered at first. Only 1,500 immigrants arrived in the first five years. The focus of Quaker hopes lay across the Delaware River, where in 1681 Charles II granted William Penn a vast territory, almost as large as England itself, in payment of a large royal debt to Penn's father. To the Quakers' great fortune, the territory granted to Penn, the last unassigned segment of the eastern coast of North America, was also one of the most fertile.

Pacifism in a Militant World: Quakers and Indians

On the day Penn received his royal charter for Pennsylvania, he wrote a friend, "My God that has given it to me will, I believe, bless and make it the seed of a nation." The nation that Penn envisioned was unique among colonizing schemes. Penn intended to make his colony an asylum for the persecuted, a refuge from arbitrary state power. Puritans strove to nurture social homogeneity and religious uniformity, excluding all not of like mind. In the Chesapeake and Carolina colonies, aggressive, unidealistic men sought to exploit the region's resources. But

Penn dreamed of inviting to his sylvan colony people of all religions and national backgrounds and blending them together in peaceful coexistence. His state would claim no authority over the consciences of its citizens nor demand military service of them.

The Quakers who began streaming into Pennsylvania in 1682 quickly absorbed earlier Dutch, Finnish, and Swedish settlers. Primarily farmers, they fanned out from the capital city of Philadelphia, purchasing land from Penn at reasonable rates.

Even before arriving, Penn laid the foundation for peaceful relations with the Delaware tribe inhabiting his colony. He wrote to the Delaware chiefs: "The king of the Country where I live, hath given me a great Province; but I desire to enjoy it with your Love and Consent, that we may always live together as Neighbors and friends." Recognizing the Indians as the rightful owners of the land included in his grant, Penn pledged not to sell one acre until he had first purchased it from local chiefs. He also promised strict regulation of the Indian trade and a ban on the sale of alcohol.

A comparison between Pennsylvania and South Carolina shows the power of pacifism. A quarter century after initial settlement, Pennsylvania had a population of about 20,000 whites. Penn's peaceful policy had so impressed Native American tribes that Indian refugees began migrating into Pennsylvania from all sides. During the same 25 years, South Carolina had grown to only about 4,000 whites, but the area had become a cauldron of violence. Carolinians spread arms through the region to facilitate slave dealing, shipped some 10,000 members of local tribes off to New England and the West Indies as slaves, and laid waste to the Spanish mission frontier in Florida.

As long as the Quaker philosophy of pacifism and friendly relations with the Delawares and Susquehannocks held sway, interracial relations in the Delaware River valley contrasted sharply with those in other parts of North

Edward's Hick's Penn's Treaty with the Indians *was painted in the nineteenth century and in a romanticized version of the* Treaty of Shackamaxon *by which the Lenape Indians ceded the site of Philadelphia to Penn. The treaty was actually made in 1682, but Hicks was correct in implying that the Lenape held Penn in high regard for his fair treatment of them.*

America. But the Quaker policy of toleration, liberal government, and exemption from military service attracted to the colony, especially in the eighteenth century, thousands of immigrants whose land hunger and disdain for Indians undermined Quaker trust and friendship. Germans and Scots-Irish flooded in, swelling the population to 31,000 by 1720. Seeking farm land, neither of these groups shared Quaker idealism about racial harmony. They encroached on the lands of the local tribes, sometimes encouraged by the land agents of Penn's heirs. By the mid–eighteenth century, a confrontation of red and white inhabitants was occurring in Pennsylvania.

Building the Peaceable Kingdom

Although Penn's dream of a society that banished violence, religious intolerance, and arbitrary authority never completely materialized, the plain Quaker farmers prospered and retained a sense of common endeavor. They maintained their distinctive identity, allowing marriage only within their society, carefully providing land for their offspring, and guarding against too great a population increase (which would cause too rapid a division of farms) by limiting the size of their families.

Pennsylvania's countryside blossomed, and its port capital of Philadelphia also grew rapidly. By 1700, it had overtaken New York City in population, and a half century later it was the largest city in the colonies, bustling with a wide range of artisans, merchants, and professionals.

The Limits of Perfectionism

In spite of commercial success and peace with Native Americans, not all was harmonious in early Pennsylvania. Political affairs were often turbulent, in part because of Pennsylvania's weak leadership. Penn was a much-loved proprietor, but he did not tarry long in his colony to guide its course.

In England, Quakers had been bound to one another by decades of persecution. In Pennsylvania, the absence of persecution eliminated a crucial binding element, and factionalism developed. Meanwhile, Quaker industriousness and frugality led to such material success that after a generation, social radicalism and religious evangelicalism began to fade. As in other colonies, settlers discovered the door to prosperity wide open and surged across the threshold.

Where Pennsylvania differed from New England and the South was in its relations with Native Americans, at least for the first few generations. It also departed from the Puritan colonies in its immigration policy. Pennsylvania, it is said, was the first community since the Roman Empire to allow people of different national origins and religious persuasions to live together under the same government on terms of near equality. English, Highland Scots, French, Germans, Irish, Welsh, Swedes, Finns, and Swiss all settled in Pennsylvania. This ethnic mosaic was further complicated by a medley of religious groups, including Mennonites, Lutherans, Dutch Reformed, Quakers, Baptists, Anglicans, Presbyterians, Catholics, Jews, and a sprinkling of mystics. Their relations may not always have been friendly, but few attempts were made to discriminate against dissenting groups. Pennsylvanians thereby laid the foundations for the pluralism that was to become the hallmark of American society.

CONCLUSION

The Achievement of New Societies

Nearly 200,000 immigrants reached the coast of North America in the seventeenth century. Coming from a variety of social backgrounds, they represented the rootstock of distinctive societies that would mature in the North American colonies of England, France, Holland, and Spain. For three generations, North America served as a social laboratory for religious and social visionaries, political theorists, fortune seekers, social outcasts, and, most of all, ordinary men and women seeking a better life than they had known in their European homelands.

Nearly three-quarters of them came to the

Chesapeake and Carolina colonies. Most of them found this a region of disease and death rather than an arena of opportunity. In the northern colonies, to which the fewest immigrants came, life was more secure. Organized around family and community, favored by a healthier climate, and motivated by religion and social vision, the Puritan and Quaker societies thrived, even though utopian expectations were never completely fulfilled.

Recommended Reading

The early settlement of the Chesapeake is the subject of much exciting recent research. Newer works include Edmund S. Morgan, *American Slavery, American Freedom: The Ordeal of Colonial Virginia* (1975); Gloria L. Main, *Tobacco Colony: Life in Early Maryland* (1982); and Darrett B. Rutman and Anita H. Rutman, *A Place in Time: Middlesex County, Virginia, 1650–1750* (1984).

A good introduction to English Puritanism is Christopher Hill, *Society and Puritanism in Pre-Revolutionary England*, 2d ed. (1967). For information on the Puritans in their early New England communities, consult David G. Allen, *In English Ways* (1981); Philip Greven, Jr., *Four Generations* (1970); and Stephen Innes, *Labor in a New Land* (1983). Illuminating biographies of early Puritan leaders are Edmund S. Morgan, *The Puritan Dilemma: The Story of John Winthrop* (1958); and Robert Middlekauff,

The Mathers (1971). For rich analyses of Puritan-Indian relations, see Neal Salisbury, *Manitou and Providence* (1982); William Cronon, *Changes in the Land: Indians, Colonists, and the Ecology of New England* (1983); and James Axtell, *The Invasion Within* (1985).

Proprietary New York and Carolina are treated in Robert C. Ritchie, *The Duke's Province* (1977); Michael Kammen, *Colonial New York* (1975); M. Eugene Sirmans, *Colonial South Carolina* (1966); and Robert M. Weir, *Colonial South Carolina* (1983).

Quaker Pennsylvania is the subject of Gary B. Nash, *Quakers and Politics* (1968).

On indentured servitude, see David Galenson, *White Servitude in Colonial America* (1981), and Sharon V. Salinger, *"To Serve Well and Faithfully": Labor and Indentured Servitude in Pennsylvania* (1987).

Time Line

1590	Roanoke Island colony fails
1607	Jamestown settled
1616–1621	Native American population in New England decimated by European diseases
1617	First tobacco crop shipped from Virginia
1619	First Africans arrive in Jamestown
1620	Pilgrims land at Plymouth
1622	Powhatan tribes attack Virginia settlements
1624	Dutch colonize mouth of Hudson River
1630	Puritan migration to Massachusetts Bay
1632	Maryland grant to Lord Baltimore (George Calvert)
1633–1634	Native Americans in New England again struck by European diseases
1635	Roger Williams banished to Rhode Island
1636	Anne Hutchinson exiled to Rhode Island
1637	New England wages war against the Pequot tribe
1642–1649	English Civil War ends great migration to New England
1643	Confederation of New England
1659	Two Quaker men hanged on Boston Common
1660	Restoration of King Charles II in England
1663	Carolina charter granted to eight proprietors
1664	English capture New Netherland and rename it New York
	Royal grant of the Jersey lands to proprietors
1681	William Penn receives Pennsylvania grant

chapter 3

....

Mastering the
New World

Anthony Johnson, an African, arrived in Virginia in 1621 with only the name "Antonio." Caught as a young man in the Portuguese slave-trading net, he was purchased by Richard Bennett and sent to work at Bennett's tobacco plantation situated on the James River. On March 22, 1622, the Powhatan tribes of tidewater Virginia fell upon the white colonizers in a determined attempt to drive them from the land. Of the 57 persons on the Bennett plantation, only black Antonio and four others survived.

Antonio—anglicized to Anthony—labored on the Bennett plantation for some 20 years, slave in fact if not in law, for legally defined bondage was still in the formative stage. During this time he married Mary, another African, and fathered four children. In the 1640s, Anthony and Mary Johnson gained their freedom and at some point adopted their surname. Already past middle age, the Johnsons settled on Virginia's eastern shore. By 1650, they owned 250 acres, a small herd of cattle, and two black servants. By the late 1650s, however, as the lines of racial slavery tightened, the customs of the country began closing in on Virginia's free blacks.

In 1664, convinced that ill winds were blowing away the chances for their children and grandchildren in Virginia, the Johnsons began selling their land to white neighbors. The following spring, most of the clan moved north to Maryland, where they rented land and again took up farming and cattle raising. Five years later, Anthony Johnson died, leaving four children and his wife. A jury of white men in Virginia declared that because Johnson "was a Negroe and by consequence an alien," the 50 acres he had deeded to his son Richard before moving to Maryland should be awarded to a local white planter.

Johnson's children and grandchildren, born in America, could not duplicate the modest success of the African-born patriarch. By the late seventeenth century, people of color faced much greater difficulties. Anthony's sons never rose higher than tenant farmer or small freeholder. John Johnson moved farther north into Delaware in the 1680s. Members of his family married local Indians and became part of a triracial community that has survived to the present day. Richard Johnson stayed behind in Virginia. His four sons became tenant farmers and hired servants. By now, in the early eighteenth century, slave ships were pouring Africans into Virginia and Maryland to

replace white indentured servants, the backbone of the labor force for four generations. To be black had at first been a handicap. Now it became a fatal disability, an in-
delible mark of degradation and bondage.

Anthony and Mary Johnson and their children lived in a time of unrest and growing
inequality. This chapter surveys the fluid, conflict-filled era from 1675 to 1715, a time
when five overlapping struggles for mastery occurred. First, in determining to build a
slave labor force, the colonists struggled to establish their mastery over resistant
African captives. Second, the settlers sought mastery over Native American tribes.
Third, the colonists resisted the attempts of English imperial administrators to bring
them into a more dependent relationship. Fourth, within colonial societies, emerging
elites struggled to establish their claims to political and social authority. Finally, the
colonizers, aided by England, strove for mastery over French, Dutch, and Spanish con-
tenders in North America.

BLACK BONDAGE

For almost four centuries after Columbus's
voyages to the New World, European colonizers forcibly transported Africans out of their
homelands and used their labor to produce
wealth in their colonies. Estimates vary widely,
but the number of Africans brought to the New
World was probably not less than 12 million.
Of all the people who populated the New
World between the fifteenth and eighteenth
centuries, the Africans were by far the most numerous, probably outnumbering Europeans
two to one.

Slave traders took most Africans to the West
Indies, Brazil, and Spanish America. Yet those
who came to the American colonies, about
10,000 in the seventeenth century and 350,000
in the eighteenth, profoundly affected the destiny of American society. In a prolonged period
of labor scarcity, their labor and skills were indispensable to colonial economic development.
Their African culture mixed continuously with

that of their European masters. And the race relations that grew out of slavery so deeply
marked society that the problem of race has continued ever since to be the "American dilemma."

The Slave Trade

The African slave trade began as an attempt to
fill a labor shortage in the Mediterranean world
in the eighth century. Seven centuries later, Portuguese merchants reached the west coast of
Africa by water and began buying slaves captured by other Africans and transporting them
home by ship. These slaves were mostly criminals consigned to bondage in their own society or
unfortunate individuals captured in tribal wars.

More than anything else, sugar transformed
the African slave trade. By the seventeenth century, with Europeans developing a taste for
sugar almost as insatiable as their craving for tobacco, they vied fiercely for possession of the
tiny islands dotting the Caribbean and for control of the trading forts on the West African

coast. African kingdoms, eager for European trade goods, warred against one another in order to supply the "black gold" demanded by white ship captains.

The economy of the former West African kingdom of Dahomey, for example, relied heavily for several centuries on commerce in slaves. Some black slave traders also joined in the carrying trade. One former slave, Francisco Felix de Sousa, came to own a fleet of slave ships. But the carrying trade was mainly in the hands of Europeans.

Many European nations competed for trading rights on the West African coast. In the seventeenth century, when about one million Africans were brought to the New World, the Dutch replaced the Portuguese as the major supplier. But by the 1790s, the English were the foremost slave-trading nation in Europe. All in all, in the eighteenth century, European traders carried at least six million Africans to the Americas, probably the greatest forced migration in history.

Even the most vivid accounts of the slave trade cannot convey the pain and demoralization that accompanied the capture and subsequent treatment of slaves. Olaudah Equiano, an eighteenth-century Ibo from what is now Nigeria, described how raiders from another tribe kidnapped him and his younger sister when he was only 11 years old. He passed from one trader to another while being marched to the coast. Many slaves attempted suicide or died from exhaustion or hunger on these forced marches. But Equiano survived. Reaching the coast, he and others were confined in barracoons, fortified enclosures on the beach, where a surgeon from an English slave ship inspected him. Equiano was terrified by the light skins, language, and long hair of the English and was convinced that he "had got into a world of bad spirits and that they were going to kill me."

More cruelties followed. Some slaves were branded with a hot iron. Then the slaves were ferried in large canoes to the ships anchored in the harbor. An English captain recounted the desperation of the captives: "The Negroes are so loath to leave their own country, that they have often leaped out of the canoes, boat and ship, into the sea, and kept under the water till they were drowned."

Conditions aboard the slave ships were miserable. Equiano recounted the scene below decks, where manacled slaves crowded together like corpses in coffins. "With the loathsomeness of the stench, and crying together, I became so sick and low that I was not able to eat, nor had I the least desire to taste anything." The refusal to take food was so common that ship captains devised special techniques to force feed resistant Africans.

The Atlantic passage usually took four to eight weeks. It was so physically depleting and psychologically wrenching that one of every seven captives died en route. Many others arrived in the Americas deranged or near death. In all, the relocation of any African may have averaged about six months from the time of capture to the time of arrival at the plantation of a colonial buyer. During this protracted personal crisis, the slave was completely cut off from the moorings of a previous life—language, family and friends, tribal religion, familiar geography, and status in a local community.

The Southern Transition to Black Labor

English colonists on the mainland of North America turned only slowly to Africa to solve their labor problem. Indentured white labor proved the best way to meet the demand for labor during most of the seventeenth century. Beginning in 1619, a small number of Africans were brought to Virginia and Maryland to labor in the tobacco fields alongside white servants. But as late as 1671, when some 30,000 slaves toiled in English Barbados, fewer than 3,000 served in Virginia. They were still outnumbered there at least three to one by white indentured servants.

The transformation of the southern labor force from mostly white to mostly black began in the last quarter of the seventeenth century.

Origins and Destinations of African Slaves, 1526–1810

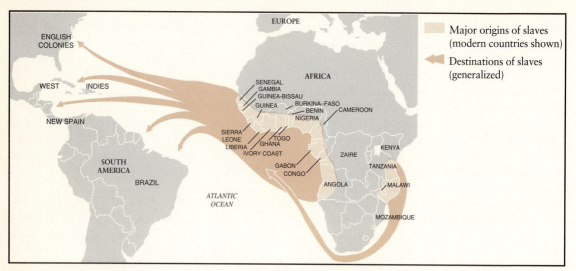

Three reasons explain this shift. First, the rising commercial power of England, at the expense of the Spanish and Dutch, swelled English participation in the African slave trade. Beginning in the 1680s, southern planters could purchase slaves more readily and cheaply than before. Second, the supply of white servants from England began drying up. Those who did arrive fanned out among a growing number of colonies. Finally, white servant unrest and a growing population of ex-servants who were landless, discontented, and potential challengers to established white planters led the southern elite to welcome a more pliable labor force. Consequently, by the 1730s, the number of white indentured servants had dwindled to insignificance.

Slavery in the Northern Colonies

Slavery never became the foundation of the northern colonial work force, for labor-intensive crops such as sugar and rice would not grow in colder climates. On the smaller family farms, household labor and occasional hired hands sufficed. Only in the cities, where slaves worked as artisans and domestic servants, and in a few scattered rural areas did slavery take substantial root.

Although the northern colonists employed few slaves, their economies were becoming enmeshed in the commercial network of the Atlantic basin, which depended on slavery and the slave trade. New England's merchant ships pursued profits in the slave trade as early as the 1640s. In New York and Philadelphia, building and outfitting slave vessels proved profitable. New England's seaports became centers for the distilling of rum, which was made from West Indian sugar and traded for slaves on the African coast. As the number of slaves in the Caribbean multiplied, the West Indies became a favorite market for codfish from New England, wheat from the middle colonies, and barrel staves and hoops from North Carolina. Thus, every North American colony participated in the racial exploitation in some way.

The System of Bondage

The first Africans brought to the American colonies came as bound servants. They served for a number of years; then, like Anthony and Mary Johnson, many of them eventually gained their freedom. Gradually during the seventeenth century, Chesapeake planters began to draw tighter lines around the activities of black servants. By the 1640s, Virginia forbade blacks, free or bound, to carry firearms. In the 1660s, marriages between white women and black servants were called "shameful matches" and "the disgrace of our Nation." Bit by bit, white settlers strengthened the association between black skin and slave status.

By the mid–seventeenth century, most white colonists were determined to fasten perpetual bondage on their black servants. In this dehumanization of Africans, which the English largely copied from their colonial rivals, the key step was instituting hereditary lifetime service. Once servitude became perpetual, relieved only by death, the elimination of all other privileges followed quickly. When the slave condition of the mother legally fell upon the black infant (not the case in other forms of slavery, such as in Africa), slavery became self-perpetuating, passing automatically from one generation to the next.

Slavery existed not only as a system of forced labor but also as a pattern of human relationships eventually legitimated by law. By the early eighteenth century, most provincial legislatures were enacting laws for controlling black rights and activities, known as "black codes." Slaves were forbidden to testify in court, engage in commercial activity, hold property, participate in the political process, congregate in public, travel without permission, or engage in legal marriage or parenthood. Nearly stripped of human status, they became defined as a form of property.

Eliminating all slave rights had both pragmatic and psychological dimensions. Every black man and woman in chains was a potential rebel. So the rapid increase in the slave population brought anxious demands to bring slaves under strict control. The desire to stifle black rebelliousness mingled with a need to justify brutal behavior toward slaves by defining

them as less than human. "The planters," wrote one Englishman in Jamaica, "do not want to be told that their Negroes are human creatures. If they believe them to be of human kind, they cannot regard them as no better than dogs or horses."

SLAVE CULTURE

Slave owners could set the external boundaries of existence for their slaves, controlling physical location, work roles, diet, and shelter. But the authority of the master class impinged far less on how slaves established friendships, fell in love, formed kin groups, raised children, worshiped their gods, buried their dead, and organized their leisure time.

In these aspects of daily life, slaves in America drew on their African heritage to shape their existence to some degree. In doing so, they laid the foundations for an African-American culture. At first, this culture had many variations because slaves came from many areas in Africa and lived under different conditions in the colonies. But common elements emerged, led by developments in the South, where about 90 percent of American slaves labored in the colonial period.

The Growth of Slavery

In contrast to other areas of the New World, in North America Africans reached a relatively healthy environment. In the southern colonies, where the ghastly mortality of the early decades had subsided by the time Africans were arriving in large numbers, their chances for survival were much better than in the West Indies or South America. This environmental advantage, combined with a more even sex ratio, led to a natural increase in the North American slave population that was unparalleled elsewhere.

In 1675, about 4,000 slaves were scattered across Virginia and Maryland. Most were men. A half century later, with the decline of white

The physical appearance of Africans captured the imaginations of some American artists. John Singleton Copley's Head of a Negro *depicts a slave in the eighteenth century.*

coastal low country they outnumbered whites three to one by 1760 and hence were able to maintain more of their African culture than slaves in the Chesapeake. Many slaves spoke Gullah, a "pidgin," or mixture, of several African languages. They often gave African names to their children, names like Cudjoe, Cuffe, Quashey, and Phibbi. And they kept alive their African religious customs.

In the northern colonies, slaves made up less than 10 percent of the population. Living in the same house as the master, slaves adapted to European ways much faster than in the South. Slavery was also less repressive in the North than in the South.

Slavery spread more extensively in the northern ports than across the countryside. Artisans, ship captains, and an emerging urban elite of merchants, lawyers, and landlords displayed their wealth and status by employing slaves. By the beginning of the eighteenth century, more than 40 percent of New York City's households owned slaves.

Resistance and Rebellion

While struggling to adapt to bondage in various regions of British America, slaves also rebelled in ways that constantly reminded their masters that slavery's price was eternal vigilance. "Saltwater" Africans fresh from their homelands often resisted slavery fiercely. "You would really be surprized at their perseverance," wrote one observer. "They often die before they can be conquered." Commonly this initial resistance took the form of escaping to the frontier to begin renegade settlements, to Indian tribes in the interior that sometimes offered refuge, or to Spanish Florida. Open rebellions, such as those in New York City in 1712 and at Stono, South Carolina, in 1739, mostly involved newly arrived slaves. There was no North American parallel, however, for the massive slave uprisings that erupted periodically in the West Indies and Brazil, where the slaves vastly outnumbered their masters.

servitude, 45,000 slaves labored on Chesapeake plantations. By 1760, when their number exceeded 185,000, the Chesapeake plantations relied almost entirely on black labor.

Although slave codes severely restricted the lives of slaves, the possibility for family life increased as the southern colonies matured. Larger plantations employed dozens and even hundreds of slaves, and the growth of roads and market towns permitted them greater opportunities to forge relationships beyond their own plantation. By the 1740s, a growing proportion of Chesapeake slaves were American-born, had established families, and lived in plantation outbuildings where from sundown to sunup they could fashion lives of their own.

In South Carolina, African slaves worked mostly on large plantations in swampy lowlands, and their knowledge of rice cultivation gave the colony a solid economic base. In the

In North America, slaves rarely outnumbered whites except in South Carolina, and the master class tried to cultivate tension between local Indians and slaves so that they would be "a check upon each other," as one worried planter explained. When rebellion did occur, white colonizers stopped at nothing to quell it. They tried to intimidate all slaves by torturing, hanging, dismembering, and even burning captured rebels at the stake.

Open rebelliousness often gave way to more subtle forms of resistance, such as dragging out the job, shamming illness, pretending ignorance, and breaking tools. Slaves also resisted through truancy, arson, crop destruction, pilfering to supplement their food supply, and direct assaults on masters, overseers, and drivers. In 1732, one South Carolina planter drove his slaves late into the night cleaning and barreling a rice crop. When he awoke in the morning, he found his barn, with the entire harvest in it, reduced to ashes.

Black Religion and Family

African-Americans struggled to find meaning and worth in their harsh existence. In this quest, religion and family played a central role—one destined to continue far into the post-slavery period.

Africans brought a complex religious heritage to the New World. No amount of desolation or physical abuse could wipe out these deeply rooted beliefs. Coming from cultures where the division between sacred and secular activities was less clear than in Europe, slaves made religion central to their existence. The black Christianity that emerged in the eighteenth century blended African religious practices with the religion of the master class. It laid the foundations for the black church that later became the central institution in African-American life.

The religious revival that began in the 1720s in the northern colonies and thereafter spread southward made important contributions to African-American religion. Evangelicalism stressed personal rebirth, used music and body motion, and caught individuals up in an intense emotional experience. The dancing, shouting, rhythmic clapping, and singing that came to characterize slaves' religious expression represented a creative mingling of West African and Christian religions.

Besides religion, the slaves' greatest refuge from their dreadful fate lay in their families. In West Africa, all social relations were centered in kinship lines, which stretched backward to include dead ancestors. Torn from their native societies, slaves placed great importance on rebuilding extended kin groups.

Most English colonies prohibited slave marriages. But in practice, domestic life was an area in which slaves and masters struck a bargain. Masters found that slaves would work harder if they were allowed to form families. Moreover, family ties stood in the way of escape or rebellion.

Slaves fashioned a family life only with difficulty, however. At first males outnumbered females, but as natural increase swelled the slave population in the eighteenth century, the sex ratio became more even.

The sale of either husband or wife could abruptly sever their fragile union. Young children usually stayed with their mothers until about age 8; then they were frequently torn from their families through sale, often to small planters needing only a hand or two. Few slaves escaped separation from family members at some time during their lives.

White male exploitation of black women represented another assault on family life. How many black women were coerced or lured with favors into sexual relations with white masters and overseers cannot be known. But the sizable mulatto (racially mixed) population at the end of the eighteenth century indicates that the number was large.

Not all interracial relationships were cruel. In some cases, black women sought the liaison to gain advantages for themselves or their children. These unions nonetheless threatened both the slave community and the white plantation ideal of separate racial categories.

While slave men struggled to preserve their family role, many black women assumed a position in the family that differed from that of white women. Plantation mistresses usually worked hard in helping to manage estates, but nonetheless the ideal grew that they should remain in the house to guard white virtue and set the standards for white culture. In contrast, the black woman remained indispensable to both the work of the plantation and the functioning of the slave quarters. She toiled in the fields and worked in the slave cabins. Paradoxically, black women's roles, which required constant labor, made them more equal to men than was the case of women in white society.

Above all, slavery was a set of power relationships designed to extract the maximum labor from its victims. Hence it regularly involved cruelties that filled family life with tribulation and uncertainty.

THE STRUGGLE FOR LAND

In the same period that slavery gained a permanent foothold in North America, both New England and Virginia fought major wars against Native Americans. The desire for land, a cause of both wars, produced a similar conflict somewhat later in South Carolina. The conflicts brought widespread destruction to the towns of both colonizers and Indians, inflicted heavy human casualties, and left a legacy of bitterness on both sides. For the coastal tribes, it was a disastrous time of defeat and decline.

King Philip's War in New England

Following the Pequot War of 1637 in New England, the Wampanoags and Narragansetts, whose fertile land lay within the boundaries of Plymouth and Rhode Island, attempted to maintain their distance from the New England colonists. But the New Englanders coveted Indian territories and gradually reduced the Indians' land base.

By the 1670s, when New England's population had grown to about 50,000, younger Indians began brooding over their situation. Their leader, Metacomet (named King Philip by the English), was the son of Massasoit, the Wampanoag who had allied himself with the first Plymouth settlers in 1620. As the Wampanoag leader, Metacomet faced one humiliating challenge after another. In 1671, for example, Plymouth forced Metacomet to surrender a large stock of guns and accept a treaty of submission acknowledging Wampanoag subjection to English law. Convinced that more setbacks would follow and humiliated by the discriminatory treatment of Indians brought before English courts, Metacomet began recruiting for a resistance movement.

The execution of three tribesmen in June 1675 was the catalyst for King Philip's War, but the root cause was the rising anger of the young Wampanoag males. As would happen repeatedly in the next two centuries as Americans pushed westward, these younger Native Americans refused to imitate their fathers, who had watched the colonizers erode their land base and compromise their sovereignty. Instead, they attempted a pan-Indian offensive against an intruder with far greater numbers and a much larger arsenal of weapons.

In the summer of 1675, the Wampanoags unleashed daring hit-and-run attacks on villages in the Plymouth colony. By autumn, many New England tribes, including the powerful Narragansetts, had joined King Philip's warriors. Towns all along the frontier reeled under Indian attacks. By the time the first snow fell in November, mobile Indian warriors had laid waste to the entire upper Connecticut River valley.

King Philip's offensive faltered in the spring

of 1676. Food shortages and disease sapped Indian strength, and the powerful Mohawks refused to support the New England tribes. By summer, groups of Indians were surrendering, while some moved westward seeking shelter among other tribes. King Philip fell in battle. His head was carried triumphantly back to Plymouth, where it remained on display for 25 years.

At war's end, several thousand colonists and perhaps twice as many Indians lay dead. Of some 90 Puritan towns, 52 had been attacked and 13 completely destroyed. Not for 40 years would the frontier advance beyond the line it had reached in 1675. Indian towns were devastated even more completely. Many of the survivors, including Metacomet's wife and son, were sold into slavery in the West Indies.

Bacon's Rebellion Engulfs Virginia

While New Englanders fought local tribes in 1675 and 1676, the Chesapeake colonies became locked in a struggle involving both a war between the red and white populations and civil war within the colonizers' society. This deeply tangled conflict was called Bacon's Rebellion after the headstrong Cambridge-educated planter Nathaniel Bacon, who arrived in Virginia at age 28.

Bacon and many other ambitious young planters detested the Indian policy of Virginia's royal governor, Sir William Berkeley. In 1646, at the end of the second Indian uprising against the Virginians, the Powhatan tribes had accepted a treaty granting them exclusive rights to territory north of the York River, beyond the limits of white settlement. Stable Indian relations suited the established planters, some of whom traded profitably with the Indians, but became obnoxious to new settlers arriving in the 1650s and 1660s. Nor did it please the white indentured servants who had served their time and were hoping to find cheap frontier land.

In the summer of 1675, a group of frontiersmen used an incident with a local tribe as an excuse to attack the Susquehannocks, whose rich land they coveted. Governor Berkeley denounced the attack, but few supported his position. He faced, he said, "a people where six parts of seven at least are poor, indebted, discontented, and armed."

Although badly outnumbered, the Susquehannocks prepared for war. They attacked during the winter of 1675–1676 and killed 36 Virginians. That spring, the hot-blooded Nathaniel Bacon became the frontiersmen's leader. Joined by hundreds of runaway servants and some slaves, he launched a campaign of indiscriminate warfare on friendly and hostile Indians alike. When Governor Berkeley declared Bacon a rebel and sent out 300 militiamen to drag him to Jamestown for trial, Bacon headed into the wilderness and recruited more followers, including many substantial planters. Frontier skirmishes with Indians had turned into civil war.

In the summer of 1676, Bacon and his followers captured the capital at Jamestown and put Governor Berkeley to flight across Chesapeake Bay.

Virginians at all levels had chafed under Berkeley's rule. High taxes, an increase in the governor's powers at the expense of local officials, and the monopoly that Berkeley and his friends held on the Indian trade were especially unpopular. Berkeley tried to rally public support by holding new assembly elections and extending the vote to all freemen, whether they owned property or not. The new assembly promptly turned on the governor, passing a set of reform laws intended to make government more responsive to the common people and to end rapacious officeholding. The assembly also made legal the enslavement of Native Americans.

Time was on the governor's side, however. Having crushed the Indians, Bacon's followers began drifting home to tend their crops. Meanwhile, Berkeley's reports of the rebellion brought the dispatch of 1,100 royal troops from England. By the time they arrived, in January 1677, Nathaniel Bacon lay dead of swamp fever and most of his followers had melted back into the frontier. After Bacon's death in October 1676, Berkeley rounded up 23 rebel leaders and hanged them without benefit of civil trial. Royal investigators who arrived in 1677 denounced Governor Berkeley as well as the rebels, whom they described as the "inconsiderate sort of men who so rashly and causelessly cry up a war and seem to wish and aim at an utter extirpation of the Indians."

The hatred of Indians did not die with the end of the rebellion. A generation later, in 1711, the Virginia legislature voted military appropriations of £20,000 "for extirpating all Indians without distinction of Friends or Enemys." The remnants of the once populous Powhatan Confederacy lost their last struggle for the world they had known. Now they moved farther west or submitted to a life on the margins of white society as tenant farmers, day laborers, or domestic servants.

After Bacon's Rebellion, an emerging planter aristocracy annulled most of the reform laws of 1676. But the war relieved much of the social tension among white Virginians. Newly available Indian land created fresh opportunities for small planters and former servants. Equally important, Virginians with capital to invest were turning to West Africa to supply their labor needs. A racial consensus, uniting whites of different ranks in the common pursuit of a prosperous, slave-based economy, began to take shape.

North and south of Virginia, Bacon's Rebellion caused insurrectionary rumblings. A dissident group in North Carolina's Albemarle County drove the governor from office and briefly seized the reins of power.

In Maryland, Protestant settlers chafed under high taxes, quitrents, and officeholders regarded as venal, Catholic, or both. Declining tobacco prices and a fear of Indian attacks increased their touchiness. A month after Bacon razed Jamestown, insurgent small planters tried to seize the Maryland government. Two of their leaders were hanged for the attempt. In 1681, another abortive uprising took place.

In all three southern colonies, the volatility of late-seventeenth-century life owed much to the region's peculiar social development. Where family formation was retarded by imbalanced sex ratios and fearsome mortality, and where geographic mobility was high, little social cohesion or attachment to community could grow. Missing in the southern colonies were mature local institutions, a vision of a larger purpose, and experienced and responsive political leaders.

AN ERA OF INSTABILITY

A dozen years after the major Indian wars in New England and Virginia, a series of insurrections and a major witchcraft incident rumbled through colonial society. The rebellions were triggered by the Revolution of 1688, known to Protestants in England thereafter as the Glorious Revolution because it ended forever the notion that kings ruled by a God-given "divine right" and marked the last serious Catholic challenge to Protestant supremacy. But these colonial disruptions also signified a struggle for social and political dominance in the expanding colonies, as did the Salem witchcraft trials in Massachusetts.

Organizing the Empire

From the earliest attempts at colonization, the English assumed that overseas settlements existed to promote the national interest at home. According to this mercantilist theory, colonies served as outlets for English manufactured goods, provided foodstuffs and raw materials, stimulated trade (and hence promoted a larger merchant navy), and contributed to the royal coffers by paying duties on exported commodities such as sugar and tobacco. Colonies benefited by the military protection and guaranteed markets provided from England.

England proceeded slowly in the seventeenth century to regulate its colonies accordingly. In 1621, the king's council forbade tobacco growers to export their crop to anywhere but England. Three years later, when the Virginia Company of London plunged into bankruptcy, the Crown made Virginia a royal colony, the first of many. In 1651, Parliament passed a navigation act requiring that English or colonial ships, manned by English or colonial sailors, carry all goods entering England, Ireland, and the colonies, no matter where those goods originated.

In 1660, after the monarchy was restored, Parliament passed a more comprehensive navigation act that listed colonial products (tobacco, sugar, indigo, dyewoods, cotton) that could be shipped only to England or to other English colonies. Like its predecessor, the act took dead aim at Holland's domination of Atlantic commerce while increasing England's revenues by imposing duties on the enumerated articles. In the following decades, other navigation acts closed loopholes in the 1660 law and added other enumerated articles. Nevertheless, this regulation bore lightly on the colonists because the laws lacked enforcement mechanisms.

After 1675, England tightened imperial control. That year marked the establishment of the Lords of Trade, a committee of the king's privy council vested with power to make and enforce decisions regarding the management of the colonies. Chief among their goals was the creation of more uniform governments in North America and the West Indies that would answer to the Crown's will. England was becoming the shipper of the world, and its state-regulated policy of economic nationalism, duplicating that of the Dutch, was essential to this rise to commercial greatness.

The Glorious Revolution in New England

When Charles II died in 1685, his brother, the duke of York, assumed the throne as James II. This set in motion a chain of events that nearly led to civil war. Like his brother, James II professed the Catholic faith. But unlike Charles II, who had disclosed this only on his deathbed, the new king announced his faith immediately upon assuming the throne. Consternation ensued. James proceeded to favor Catholics in various ways. When his wife gave birth to a son in 1688, a Catholic succession loomed.

Convinced that James was trying to seize absolute power and fearing a Catholic conspiracy, a group of Protestant leaders secretly plotted the king's downfall. In 1688, led by the earl of Shaftesbury, they invited William of Orange, a prince of the Netherlands, to invade England and take the throne with his wife, Mary, James's Protestant daughter. James abdicated rather than fight. It was a bloodless victory for Protestantism, for parliamentary power and the limitation of kingly prerogatives, and for the propertied merchants and gentry of England who stood behind the revolt.

The response of New Englanders to these events stemmed from their previous experience with royal authority and their fear of "papists." New England became a prime target for reform when the administrative reorganization of the empire began in 1675. In 1684, Charles II had annulled the Massachusetts charter. Two years later, James II appointed Sir Edmund Andros, former governor of New York, to rule over the newly created Dominion of New England that soon gathered under one government the colonies of New Hampshire, Massachusetts, Connecticut, Plymouth, Rhode Island, New York, New Jersey, and part of Maine. Puritans were now forced to swallow the bitter fact that they were subjects of London bureaucrats who cared more about shaping a disciplined empire than about the special religious vision of one group of overseas subjects.

At first, most New Englanders accepted Andros, but he soon earned their hatred. He imposed taxes without legislative consent, ended trial by jury, abolished the General Court of Massachusetts (which had met annually since 1630), muzzled Boston's town meeting, and challenged the validity of all land titles. He converted a Boston Puritan church into an Anglican chapel and rejected the Puritan practice of suppressing religious dissent.

When news reached Boston in April 1689 that William of Orange had landed in England, ending James II's hated Catholic regime, Bostonians streamed into the streets to the beat of drums. They imprisoned Andros, a suspected papist, and an interim government ruled Massachusetts for three years while the Bay colonists awaited a new charter and a royal governor.

Leisler's Rebellion in New York

In New York, the Glorious Revolution was similarly bloodless at first but far more disruptive. When news arrived of James II's abdication, the royal government simply melted away. A local militia captain, the German-born Jacob Leisler, appeared with his followers at Fort James at the lower tip of Manhattan. Governor Francis Nicholson made only a token show of resistance before quietly stepping down.

Leisler had come to New Amsterdam in 1660 as a common footsoldier of the Dutch West India Company, married into an established Dutch family, and become a successful merchant. After ousting Governor Nicholson, Leisler established an interim government and ruled with an elected Committee of Safety for 13 months, until a governor appointed by King William arrived.

Leisler's government enjoyed popularity among small landowners and urban laboring people. Most of the upper echelon, however, regarded him as an upstart commoner who had leapfrogged into the merchant class by marrying a wealthy widow. Leislerians were often labeled as people of "mean birth, and sordid education and desperate fortunes."

Much of this antipathy originated in the smoldering resentment lower- and middle-class Dutch inhabitants felt toward the town's English elite. Many Dutch merchants had readily adjusted to the English conquest of New Netherland in 1664, and many incoming English merchants had married into Dutch families. But beneath the upper class, incidents of Anglo-Dutch hostility were common. The feeling rose in the 1670s and 1680s among ordinary Dutch families that the English were crowding them out of the society they had built.

Leisler shared Dutch hostility toward New York's English elite, and his sympathy for the common people, mostly Dutch, earned him the hatred of the city's oligarchy. Leisler freed imprisoned debtors, planned a town-meeting system of government for New York City, and replaced merchants with artisans in important official posts. By the autumn of 1689, Leislerian mobs were attacking the property of some of New York's wealthiest merchants.

When a new English governor arrived in 1691, the anti-Leislerians embraced him and charged Leisler and seven of his assistants with treason for assuming the government without royal instructions. In the ensuing trial, Leisler and Jacob Milbourne, his son-in-law and chief lieutenant, were convicted of treason by an all-English jury and hanged. Leisler's popularity among the artisans of the city was evident when his wealthy opponents could find no carpenter in the city who would furnish a ladder to use at the scaffold. After his execution, peace gradually returned to New York, but for years provincial and city politics reflected the deep rift between Leislerians and anti-Leislerians.

Southern Rumblings

The Glorious Revolution also focused dissatisfactions in several southern colonies. Since Maryland was ruled by a Catholic proprietary family, the Protestant majority predictably seized on word of the Glorious Revolution and used it for their own purposes. Leading officials and planters formed a Protestant Association. Seizing control of the government in July 1689, they vowed to cleanse Maryland of its popish hue and to reform a corrupt customs service, cut taxes and fees, and extend the rights of the representative assembly. John Coode, formerly a fiery Anglican minister who had been involved in a brief rebellion in 1681, assumed the reins of government and held them until the arrival of Maryland's first royal governor in 1692.

In neighboring Virginia, the Catholic governor, Lord Howard of Effingham, had installed a number of Catholic officials. News of the revolution in England led a group of planters to attempt an overthrow of the governor. The uprising quickly faded when the governor's council asserted itself and took its own measures to remove Catholics from positions of authority.

The Glorious Revolution brought political changes to several colonies. The Dominion of New England was shattered. While Connecticut and Rhode Island were allowed to elect their own governors, Massachusetts and New Hampshire became royal colonies with governors appointed by the king. In Massachusetts, a new royal charter in 1691 eliminated church membership as a voting requirement. The Maryland proprietorship was abolished (to be restored in 1715 when the Baltimore family became Protestant), and Catholics were barred from office. Everywhere the liberties of Protestant Englishmen were celebrated.

The Social Basis of Politics

The colonial insurrections associated with the Glorious Revolution revealed social and political tensions in the immature societies. The colonial elite tried, of course, to foster social and political stability. The best insurance of this, they believed, was the maintenance of a stratified society where children were subordinate to parents, women to men, servants to masters, and the poor to the rich. In every settlement, leaders tried to maintain a system of social gradations and subordination. Churchgoers, for example, did not file into church on Sundays and occupy the pews in random fashion. Rather, the seats

were "doomed," or assigned according to customary yardsticks of respectability—age, parentage, social position, wealth, and occupation.

This social ideal proved difficult to maintain on North American soil, however. Regardless of previous rank, settlers rubbed elbows so frequently and faced such raw conditions together that those without pedigrees often saw little reason to defer to men of superior rank. "In Virginia," explained John Smith, "a plain soldier that can use a pickaxe and spade is better than five knights." Colonists everywhere learned that basic lesson. They gave respect not to those who claimed it by birth but to those who earned it by deed.

Ambitious men on the rise, such as Nathaniel Bacon and Jacob Leisler, rose up against the constituted authorities. When they gained power during the Glorious Revolution, in every case only briefly, the leaders of these uprisings linked themselves with a tradition of English struggle against tyranny and oligarchical power. They vowed to make government more responsive to the ordinary people, who composed most of their societies.

Witchcraft in Salem

The ordinary people in the colonies, for whom Bacon and Leisler tried to speak, could sometimes be misled, as the tragic events of the Salem witch hunts demonstrated. The deposing of Governor Andros in 1689 left the Massachusetts colony in political limbo for three years, and this allowed what might have been a brief outbreak of witchcraft in the little community of Salem to escalate into a bitter and bloody battle to which the provincial government, caught in transition, reacted only belatedly.

On a winter's day in 1692, 9-year-old Betty Parris and her 11-year-old cousin Abigail Williams began to play at magic in the kitchen of a small house in Salem, Massachusetts. They enlisted the aid of Tituba, the slave of Betty's father, Samuel Parris, the minister of the small community. Tituba told voodoo tales handed down from her African past and baked "witch cakes." The girls soon became seized with fits and began making wild gestures and speeches. Soon other young girls in the village were behaving strangely. Village elders extracted confessions that they were being tormented by Tituba and two other women, one a decrepit pauper, the other a disagreeable hag.

What began as the innocent play of young girls turned into a ghastly rending of a farm community capped by the execution of 20 villagers accused of witchcraft. In the seventeenth century, people still took literally the biblical injunction "Thou shalt not suffer a witch to live." In Massachusetts, more than 100 people, mostly older women, had been accused of witchcraft before 1692, and more than a dozen had been hanged.

In Salem, the initial accusations against three older women quickly multiplied. Within a matter of weeks, dozens had been charged with witchcraft, including several prominent members of the community. But formal prosecution of the accused witches could not proceed because neither the new royal charter of 1691 nor the royal governor to rule the colony had yet arrived. When Governor William Phips arrived from England in May 1692, he ordered a special court to try the accused, but by now events had careened out of control. All through the summer the court listened to testimony. By September it had condemned about two dozen villagers. The authorities hanged 19 of them on barren "Witches Hill" outside the town, and 80-year-old Giles Corey was crushed to death under heavy stones. The trials rolled on into 1693, but by then colonial leaders, including many of the clergy, recognized that a feverish fear of one's neighbors, rather than witchcraft itself, had possessed the little village of Salem.

Many factors contributed to the hysteria. Among them were generational differences between older Puritan colonists and the sometimes less religiously motivated younger generation, old family animosities, population growth and pressures on the available farmland, and tensions between agricultural Salem Village and the nearby commercial center called Salem Town. An outbreak of food poisoning may also have caused hallucinogenic behavior. The fact that most of the individuals charged with witchcraft were women underscores the relatively weak position of women in Puritan society. The witch-hunting fever produced the greatest internal conflict in late-seventeenth-century America. Probably nobody will ever fully understand the underlying causes, but the fact that the accusations of witchcraft kept spreading suggests the anxiety of this tumultuous era, marked by war, economic disruption, the political takeover of the colony by Andros and then his overthrow, and the erosion of the early generation's utopian vision.

CONTENDING FOR A CONTINENT

At the end of the seventeenth century, following an era of Indian wars and internal upheaval, the colonists for the first time confronted an extended period of international war. The struggle for mastery of the New World among four contending European powers—Holland, Spain, France, and England—now became more overt, marking the beginning of nearly 100 years of conflict.

Anglo-French Rivalry

In 1661, the French king, Louis XIV, determined to make his country the most powerful in Europe, regarded North America and the Caribbean with renewed interest. New France's timber resources would build the royal navy, its fish would feed the growing mass of slaves in the French West Indies, and its fur trade, if greatly expanded, would fill the royal coffers.

Under the leadership of able governors such as Count Frontenac, New France grew in population, economic strength, and ambition in the late seventeenth century. In the 1670s, Louis Jolliet and Father Jacques Marquette, a Jesuit priest, explored an immense territory watered by the Mississippi and Missouri rivers, previously unknown to Europeans. A decade later, military engineers and priests began building forts and missions, one complementing the other, throughout the Great Lakes region and the Mississippi valley. In 1682, René Robert de La Salle canoed down the Mississippi all the way to the Gulf of Mexico.

The growth of French strength and ambitions brought New England and New France into deadly conflict for a generation, beginning in the late seventeenth century. Religious hostility overlaid commercial rivalry. Protestant New Englanders regarded Catholic New France as a satanic challenge to their divinely sanctioned mission. When the European wars began in 1689, armed conflict between England and France quickly extended into every overseas theater where the two powers had colonies. In North America, the battle zone was New York, New England, and eastern Canada.

In two wars, from 1689 to 1697 and 1702 to 1713, the English and French, while fighting in Europe, also sought to oust each other from the New World. The zone of greatest importance was the Caribbean, where slaves produced huge sugar fortunes. In the North American zone, problems of weather, disease, transport, and supply were so great that only irregular warfare was possible.

The English struck three times at the centers of French power. In 1690, during King William's War (1689–1697), their small flotilla captured Port Royal, the hub of Acadia (which was returned to France at the end of the war). The English assault on Quebec, however, failed disastrously. In Queen Anne's War (1702–1713), New England attacked Port Royal three times before finally capturing it in 1710. A year later, when England sent a flotilla of 60 ships and 5,000 men to conquer Canada, the land and sea operations foundered before reaching their destinations.

When European-style warfare failed miserably in America, both England and France attempted to subcontract military tasks to their Indian allies. This policy occasionally succeeded, especially with the French, who gladly sent their own troops into the fray alongside Indian partners. The French and Indians wiped out the frontier outpost of Schenectady, New York, in 1690; razed Wells, Maine, and Deerfield, Massachusetts, in 1703; and battered other towns along the New England frontier during both wars. In retaliation, the Iroquois, supplied by the English, stung several French settlements. Too powerful to be dictated to by either France or England, the Iroquois sat out the second war in the early eighteenth century.

The Results of War

The Peace of Utrecht in 1713, which ended the war, capped the century-long rise of England and the decline of Spain in the rivalry for the sources of wealth outside Europe. England, the big winner, received Newfoundland and Acadia (renamed Nova Scotia), and France recognized English sovereignty over the fur-rich Hudson Bay territory. France retained Cape Breton Island, controlling the entrance to the St. Lawrence River. In the Caribbean, France yielded St. Kitts and Nevis to England. In Europe, Spain lost its provinces in Italy and the last of its holdings in the Netherlands to the Austrian Hapsburgs. Spain also surrendered Gibraltar and Minorca to the English and awarded England the lucrative privilege of supplying the Spanish empire in America with African slaves, a favor formerly enjoyed by the French Senegal Company.

The French were the big losers in these wars, but they did not abandon their ambitions in the New World. Soon after Louis XIV died in 1715, the Regency government of the duke of Orleans tried to regain lost time in America by mounting

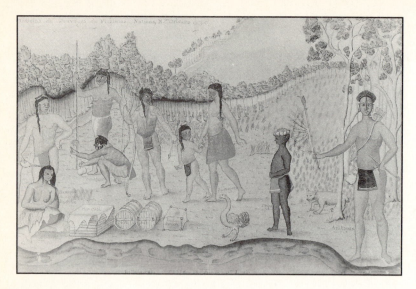

Visiting French Louisiana in 1735, Alexander de Batz painted members of the Illinois tribe who traded at New Orleans. Note the hatted African who apparently has been adopted by the Illinois.

a huge expedition to settle Louisiana. Because of mismanagement, however, this plan produced little result. French colonies expanded only in the Caribbean, where by 1750 the islands of Hispaniola, Martinique, and Guadeloupe counted 46,000 whites and 250,000 slaves.

At the Peace of Utrecht, Spain retained a vast empire in America. When France decided in 1762 that Louisiana was not worth the expense, Spain gladly accepted it and tried to make it a buffer against the British Americans migrating westward toward New Spain.

Though England had rebuffed France after a generation of war, New England suffered grievously. Massachusetts bore the brunt of the burden. Probably one-fifth of all able-bodied males in the colony participated in the Canadian campaigns, and of these about one-quarter never lived to tell of the terrors of New England's first major experience with international warfare. At the end of the first war in 1697, one leader bemoaned that Massachusetts was left "quite exhausted and ready to sink under the calamities and fatigue of a tedious consuming war." The war debt was £50,000 sterling in Massachusetts alone, a greater per capita burden than the na-

tional debt today. At the end of the second conflict in 1713, war widows were so numerous that the Bay Colony faced its first serious poverty problem.

The colonies south of New England were also affected by the wars. In Queen Anne's War, New York lost one of its best grain markets when Spain, allied with France, outlawed American foodstuffs in its West Indian colonies. The French navy plucked off nearly 30 New York merchant vessels, about one-quarter of the port's fleet, and disrupted the vital sea lanes between the mainland and the Caribbean, also to the detriment of Philadelphia's grain merchants.

One lesson of war, to be repeated many times in succeeding generations, was that the burdens and rewards fell unevenly on the participants. Some lowborn men could rise spectacularly. William Phips, the twenty-sixth child in his family, rose from sheep farmer and ship's carpenter in Maine to governor of Massachusetts in 1691. Other men, already rich, multiplied their wealth. Andrew Belcher of Boston, who had grown wealthy on provisioning contracts during King Philip's War in 1675 and 1676, combined patriotism with profit in King William's and Queen Anne's wars by supplying warships and outfitting the New England expeditions to Canada. However, most men, especially those who did the fighting, gained little, and many lost all.

CONCLUSION

CONTROLLING THE NEW ENVIRONMENT

By the second decade of the eighteenth century, the 12 English colonies on the eastern edge of North America had erected the basic scaffolding of colonial life. With the aid of England, they had ousted the Dutch, fought the French to a draw, and held their own against the Spanish. The coastal Indian tribes were reeling from disease and war. The settlers had overcome a scarcity of labor by copying the other European colonists in the hemisphere and importing slaves. Finally, the colonists had rebelled against what they viewed as arbitrary and tainted governments imposed by England.

Physically isolated from Europe, the colonists developed a large measure of self-reliance. Slowly, they began to identify themselves as the permanent inhabitants of a new land rather than transplanted English, Dutch, or Scots-Irish. The new land was a puzzling mixture of unpredictable opportunity and sudden turbulence, unprecedented freedom and debilitating wars, racial intermingling and racial separation. It was a New World in much more than a geographic sense, for the people of three cultures who now inhabited it had remade it; and, while doing so, they were remaking themselves.

Recommended Reading

The Atlantic slave trade is explored in Philip Curtin, *The Atlantic Slave Trade* (1969); and Martin Kilson and Robert I. Rotberg, eds., *The African Diaspora* (1976).

The origins and early history of slavery in the Americas are studied in H. Hoetink, *Slavery and Race Relations in the Americas* (1973); and Richard S. Dunn, *Sugar and Slaves* (1972).

For slavery in the American colonies, see Ira Berlin, "Time, Space, and the Evolution of Afro-American Society in British Mainland America," *American Historical Review* 85 (1980); Peter H. Wood, *Black Majority* (1974); and Daniel C. Littlefield, *Rice and Slaves* (1981).

Relations between colonizers and Native Americans after the founding period are examined in James Axtell, *The European and the Indian* (1981); Francis Jennings, *The Invasion of America* (1975); *The Ambiguous Iroquois Empire* (1984); J. Leitch Wright, *The Only Land They Knew: The Tragic Story of the American Indians in the Old South* (1981); and Gary B. Nash, *Red, White, and Black* (1974, 1982).

For the Glorious Revolution in America and the era of instability at the end of the seventeenth century, consult David Lovejoy, *The Glorious Revolution in America* (1972); Carol F. Karlsen, *The Devil in the Shape of a Woman* (1987); and Paul Boyer and Stephen Nissenbaum, *Salem Possessed* (1974).

Time Line

1600–1700	Dutch monopolize slave trade
1619	First Africans imported to Virginia
1637	Pequot War in New England
1640s	New England merchants enter slave trade
	Virginia forbids blacks to carry firearms
1650–1670	Judicial and legislative decisions in Chesapeake colonies solidify racial lines
1660	Parliament passes first Navigation Act
1664	English conquer New Netherland
1673–1685	French expand into Mississippi valley
1675–1676	King Philip's War in New England
1676	Bacon's Rebellion in Virginia

1682	La Salle sails down Mississippi River and claims Louisiana for France
1684	Massachusetts charter recalled
1686	Dominion of New England
1688	Glorious Revolution in England, followed by accession of William and Mary
1689	Overthrow of Governor Andros in New England
	Leisler's Rebellion in New York
1689–1697	King William's War
1690s	Transition from white indentured to black slave labor begins in Chesapeake
1692	Witchcraft hysteria in Salem
1702–1713	Queen Anne's War
1713	Peace of Utrecht

chapter 4

The Maturing of Colonial Society

Devereaux Jarratt was born in 1733 on the Virginia frontier, the third son of an immigrant yeoman farmer. In New Kent County, where Jarratt grew up, a farmer's "whole dress and apparel," he recalled later, "consisted in a pair of coarse breeches, one or two shirts, a pair of shoes and stockings, an old felt hat, and a bear skin coat." In a maturing colonial society that was six generations old by the mid–eighteenth century, such simple folk stepped aside and tipped their hats when prosperous neighbors went by.

As the colonies grew rapidly after 1700, economic development brought handsome gains for some, opened modest opportunities for many, but produced disappointment and privation for others. Jarratt was among those who advanced. His huge appetite for learning earned him some schooling. But at age 8, when his parents died, he had to take his place behind the plow alongside his brothers. Then, at 19, Jarratt was "called from the ax to the quill" by a neighboring planter's timely offer of a job tutoring his children.

Tutoring put Jarratt in touch with the world of wealth and status. Gradually he advanced to positions in the households of wealthy Virginia planters. His modest success also introduced him to the world of evangelical religion. In the eighteenth century, an explosion of religious fervor dramatically reversed the growing secularism of the settlers. Jarratt first encountered evangelicalism in the published sermons of George Whitefield, an English clergyman.

Later, at the plantation of John Cannon, he personally experienced conversion under the influence of Cannon's wife. Jarratt later became a clergyman in the Anglican church, but he never lost his religious zeal and desire to carry religion to the common people. In this, he was part of the first mass religious movement to occur in colonial society.

Colonial North America in the first half of the eighteenth century was a thriving, changing set of regional societies that had developed from turbulent seventeenth-century beginnings. New England, the mid-Atlantic colonies, the Upper and Lower

South, New France, and the northern frontier of New Spain were all distinct regions. Even within regions, diversity increased in the eighteenth century as newcomers, mostly from Africa, Germany, Ireland, and France, added new pieces to the emerging American mosaic.

Despite their bewildering diversity and lack of cohesion, the colonies along the Atlantic seaboard were affected similarly by population growth and economic development. Everywhere except on the frontier, class differences grew. A commercial orientation spread from north to south, especially in the towns, as local economies matured and forged links with the network of trade in the Atlantic basin. The exercise of political power of elected legislative assemblies and local bodies produced seasoned leaders, a tradition of local autonomy, and a widespread belief in a political ideology stressing the liberties that freeborn Englishmen should enjoy. All regions experienced a deep-running religious awakening that was itself connected to secular changes. All of these themes will be explored as we follow the way that scattered frontier settlements developed into mature provincial societies.

AMERICA'S FIRST POPULATION EXPLOSION

In 1680, some 150,000 colonizers clung to the eastern edge of North America. By 1750, they had swelled sevenfold to top one million. This growth rate, never experienced in Europe, staggered English policymakers. The population boom was fed from both internal and external sources. Natural increase accounted for much of the growth in all the colonies and nearly all of it in New England, where immigrants arrived only in a trickle in the eighteenth century. The black population also began to increase naturally by the 1720s. American-born slaves soon began to outnumber slaves born in Africa.

The Newcomers

While expanding through natural increase, the colonial population also received waves of newcomers. The eighteenth-century arrivals, who far outnumbered those who came before 1700, came overwhelmingly from Germany, Switzerland, Ireland, and Africa, and they were mostly indentured servants and slaves. Of all the groups arriving in the eighteenth century, the Africans were the largest. Numbering about 15,000 in 1690, they grew to 80,000 in 1730 and 325,000 in 1760.

German-speaking settlers, about 90,000 strong, flocked to the colonies in the eighteenth century. Most settled between New York and South Carolina, with Pennsylvania claiming the largest number of them.

Outnumbering the Germans were the Protestant Scots-Irish. Several thousand from Northern Ireland arrived each year after the Peace of Utrecht in 1713 reopened the Atlantic sea lanes. Mostly poor farmers, they streamed into the same backcountry areas where Germans were settling, though more of them followed the mountain valleys south into the Carolinas and Georgia. They washed over the ridges of Appalachia until their appetite for land brought

German Settlements, 1775

Scots-Irish Settlements, 1775

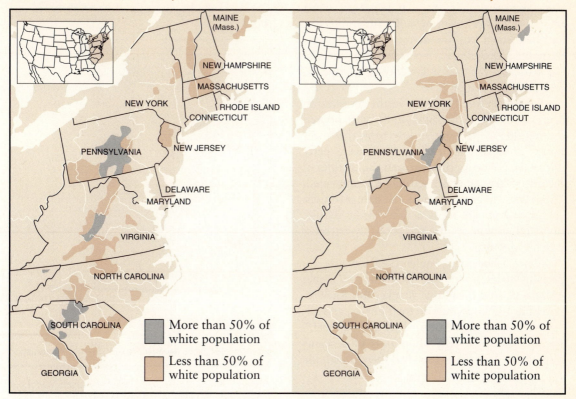

German Settlements, 1775 — map showing settlement areas across the eastern colonies.

More than 50% of white population

Less than 50% of white population

Scots-Irish Settlements, 1775 — map showing settlement areas across the eastern colonies.

More than 50% of white population

Less than 50% of white population

them face to face with the ancient occupiers of the land. No major Indian wars occurred between 1715 and 1754, but the frontier bristled with tension as the new settlers pushed westward.

In the enormous population growth occurring after 1715, New England nearly tripled in population, but the middle and southern colonies quadrupled, though in the South the fast-growing slave population accounted for much more of the growth than in the mid-Atlantic.

The social background of the new European immigrants differed substantially from that of their seventeenth-century predecessors. The early settlers included a number of men from the upper levels of the English social pyramid: university-trained Puritan ministers, sons of wealthy gentry, and merchants. The earlier immigrants had also included many from the middle rungs of the English social ladder—yeomen farmers, skilled craftsmen, and shopkeepers. But slaves and indentured servants made up most of the incoming human tide after 1713. The traffic in servants became a regular part of the commerce linking Europe and America.

Shipboard conditions for servants worsened in the eighteenth century and were hardly better than aboard the slave ships. Crammed between decks in stifling air, servants suffered from smallpox and fevers, rotten food, impure water, cold, and lice. "Children between the ages of one and seven seldom survive the sea voyage," bemoaned one German immigrant, "and parents must often watch their offspring suffer miserably, die, and be thrown into the ocean." The shipboard mortality rate of about 15 percent in the colonial era made this the most unhealthy of all times to seek American shores.

Like indentured servants in the seventeenth century, the servant immigrants who poured ashore after 1715 came mostly from the lower ranks of society. As earlier, some were petty criminals, political prisoners, and the castoffs of the cities. Yet, as one Englishman commented, "Men who emigrate are from the nature of their circumstances, the most active, hardy, daring, bold and resolute spirits, and probably the most mischievous also."

Once ashore, most indentured servants, especially males, found the labor system harsh. Merchants sold them, one shocked Britisher reported in 1773, "as they do their horses, and advertise them as they do their beef and oatmeal." Facing cruel treatment, thousands of servants ran away. Advertisements for them filled the colonial newspapers alongside notices for escaped slaves.

The goal of every servant was to secure a foothold on the ladder of opportunity. "The hope of buying land in America," a New Yorker noted, "is what chiefly induces people into America." However, many servants died before serving out their time. Others won freedom only to toil for years as poor day laborers and tenant farmers. Only a small proportion achieved the dream of becoming independent landholders. The chief beneficiaries of the system of bound white labor were not the laborers but their masters.

Africans in Chains

Among the thousands of ships crossing the Atlantic in the eighteenth century, the ones fitted out as seagoing dungeons for slaves were the

Population of European Colonies in North America, 1680–1770

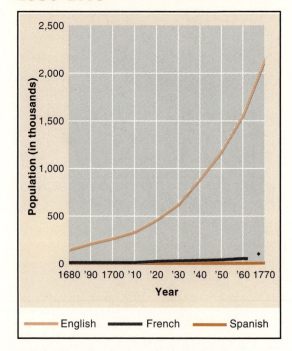

*France's North American colonies in Canada and Louisiana ceded to England and Spain, respectively, in 1763

most numerous. After the Peace of Utrecht, the slave trade to the southern colonies expanded sharply. The generation after 1730 witnessed the largest influx of African slaves in the colonial period, averaging about 5,000 a year. In the entire period from 1700 to 1775, more than 350,000 African slaves entered the American colonies.

Even as the traffic in slaves peaked, religious and humanitarian opposition to slavery arose. A few individuals, mostly Quaker, had objected to slavery on moral grounds since the late seventeenth century. But the idea grew in the 1750s that slavery contradicted the Christian concept of brotherhood and the Enlightenment notion of the natural equality of all humans. John Woolman, a Quaker tailor from New Jersey, dedicated his life in the 1750s to a crusade against slavery and planted the seeds of abolitionism.

BEYOND THE APPALACHIANS

By the mid–eighteenth century, the American colonists, though increasing rapidly in number, still occupied only a narrow strip of coastal plain in eastern North America. Of about 1.2 million settlers and slaves in 1750, only a tiny fraction lived farther than 100 miles from the shores of the Atlantic. Beginning in the 1750s, westward-moving colonists in pursuit of more land would encounter four other groups already established to their west: the populous interior Native American tribes, and smaller groups of French-Americans, Spanish-Americans, and African-Americans. Changes already occurring among these groups would affect settlers breaching the

Appalachian barrier and, in the third quarter of the eighteenth century, would even reach eastward to the original British settlements.

Cultural Changes Among Interior Tribes

During the first half of the eighteenth century, the inland tribes began to be affected by extensive contact with the French, Spanish, and English. The introduction of European trade goods, especially iron implements, textiles, firearms and ammunition, and alcohol, inescapably changed Indian lifeways. Subsistence hunting, limited to satisfying tribal food requirements, turned into commercial hunting, restricted only by the quantity of trade goods desired. Indian males spent far more time away from the villages trapping and hunting, and the increased importance of

The communalistic Moravian immigrants who came to Pennsylvania in the 1740s dedicated themselves, like the Quakers, to peaceful relations with the Indians. The Prussian John Jacob Schmick and his Norwegian wife Johanna were missionaries to the Delaware tribe

this activity to tribal life undermined the matrilineal basis of society. Women were also drawn into the new economic activities, helping to skin the beaver, marten, and fox, scrape and trim the pelts, and sew them into robes. Among some tribes, the trapping, preparation, and transporting of skins became so time-consuming that they had to procure food resources from other tribes.

Involvement in the fur trade altered the traditional Native American belief that the destinies of humans and animals were closely linked. In addition, the fur trade heightened intertribal tensions, often to the point of war. When a tribe depleted the furs in their hunting grounds, they could maintain their trade only by conquering more remote tribes with fertile hunting grounds or by forcibly intercepting the furs of other tribes as they were carried to European trading posts. The introduction of European weaponry, which Indians quickly mastered, further intensified intertribal conflict.

Tribal political organization among the interior tribes also changed in the eighteenth century. Most tribes had earlier been loose confederations of villages and clans, each exercising local autonomy. The Creek, Cherokee, and Iroquois gave primary loyalty to the village, not to the tribe or confederacy. But trade, diplomatic contact, and war with Europeans required more coordinated policies. To deal effectively with traders and officials, the villages gradually adjusted to more centralized leadership.

By 1750, the Cherokee, for example, had formed a more centralized tribal "priest state." When this proved inadequate, warriors began to assume the dominant role in tribal councils, replacing the civil chiefs. By this process the Cherokee reorganized their political structure so that dozens of scattered villages could amalgamate their strength.

While incorporating trade goods into their material culture and adapting their economies and political structures to new situations, the interior tribes held fast to tradition in many ways. They saw little reason to adopt the colonists' systems of law and justice, religion, education, family organization, or child rearing. Their refusal to accept the superiority of white culture frustrated English missionaries, eager to win Native Americans from "savage" ways. But a Carolinian admitted that "they are really better to us than we are to them. We look upon them with scorn and disdain, and think them little better than beasts in human shape, though if well examined, we shall find that, for all our religion and education, we possess more moral deformities and evils than these savages do."

Despite maintaining many cultural practices, the interior Indian tribes suffered from the contact with the British colonizers. Decade by decade, the fur trade spread epidemic diseases, raised the level of warfare, depleted their lands of game animals, and drew the Native Americans into a market economy where their trading partners gradually became trading masters.

France's Inland Empire

While the powerful Iroquois, Cherokee, Creek, and Choctaw tribes interacted with British colonists to their east, they also dealt with a growing French presence to their west. Between 1699 and 1754, the French developed a system of small forts, trading posts, and agricultural villages throughout the central area of the continent from French Canada to the Gulf of Mexico. The Indians retained sovereignty over the land but gradually succumbed to French diseases, French arms, and French-promoted intertribal wars. At the same time, however, because France's interior empire was organized primarily as a military and trading operation, soldiers, fur traders, and other men arriving without wives often exploited or married Indian women. French Louisiana had more mixed-race children and more white and black men who lived with Native Americans than any Anglo-American colony.

In 1718, France settled New Orleans at

France's Inland Empire, 1600–1720

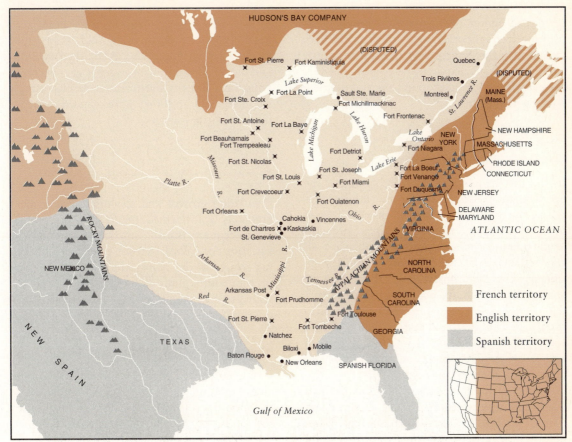

great cost by transporting almost 7,000 whites and 5,000 African slaves to the mouth of the Mississippi River. Disease rapidly whittled down these numbers, and an uprising of the powerful Natchez tribe in 1729 discouraged further French immigration. Most of the survivors settled around the little town of New Orleans and raised indigo, rice, and other crops.

In its economy and society, New Orleans much resembled early Charleston, South Carolina. What distinguished the people of New Orleans from those of Charleston, however, was that the French knew nothing of representative political institutions. Ruled by a governor, a commissary and chief judge, and a small appointed council, the people had no elections or assembly, no newspapers or taxes.

From its first introduction in Louisiana in 1719, French plantation slavery grew so that by 1765, blacks outnumbered whites. Most slaves and a majority of whites lived in the New Orleans area. The conditions of life for slaves differed little from those in the southern English colonies. But the French had a paternalistic black legal code that gave slaves some protection in courts. When the Spanish took over the colony in 1769, they instituted their law guaranteeing slaves the right to buy freedom with money earned in their free time. Soon a large free black class emerged, headed by substantial people like Simon Colfat, who ran various enterprises, helped other slaves pay for their freedom, and headed the company of free black militia. When Americans acquired the colony in 1803, they suppressed freedom purchase and discouraged manumission.

Spain's North America

In the first half of the eighteenth century, the Spanish still possessed by far the largest American empire. Even as Spanish power declined in Europe, it spread in America. Spain strengthened its Florida military posts to challenge English settlement of the Carolinas and French settlement of the Mississippi valley. Also to counter the French, the Spanish established permanent military posts in Texas and New Mexico for the first time. At the end of the eighteenth century, however, fewer than 50,000 Spanish and Hispanicized people of color inhabited Texas, New Mexico, and California.

As in New France, racial intermixture and social fluidity were more extensive in New Spain than in the English colonies. The Spanish never defined racial groups as distinctly as the English. The word *Spaniard* on a census might mean a white immigrant from Mexico or a part-Indian person who "lived like a Spaniard." Social mobility was considerable because the Crown was willing to raise even a common person to the status of *hidalgo* (minor nobleman) as an inducement to settle in New Spain's remote northern frontier. Most of the immigrants became small ranchers, producing livestock, corn, and wheat for export to other Spanish provinces to the south.

The Native Americans of New Mexico were more successful in resisting Spanish domination than the tribes of California. In the 1770s, the Spanish rapidly completed their western land and sea routes from San Diego to the new port of Yerba Buena (San Francisco) to block Russian settlement south of their base in northern California. The Spanish pioneers were Franciscan missionaries, accompanied by soldiers provided by the Crown. The priests established missions and induced local Indians to settle nearby. These "mission" Indians lived under an increasingly harsh regimen until they were reduced to a condition of virtual slavery.

A LAND OF FAMILY FARMS

Population growth and economic development gradually transformed the landscape of eighteenth-century British America. Three distinct variations of colonial society emerged: the farming society of the North, the plantation society of the South, and the urban society of the seaboard commercial towns.

Northern Agricultural Society

In the northern colonies, especially New England, tightknit farming families, organized in communities of several thousand people, dotted the landscape by the mid–eighteenth century. They based their mixed economy on timber, fish, cultivation, and livestock.

The farmers of the middle colonies—Pennsylvania, Delaware, New Jersey, and New York—set their wooden plows to much richer soils than New Englanders did. They enjoyed the additional advantage of settling an area cleared by Native Americans who had relied more on agriculture than New England tribes. Thus favored, mid-Atlantic farm families produced modest surpluses of corn, wheat, beef, and pork, which were sold not only to the West Indies but also to areas that could no longer feed themselves—England, Spain, Portugal, and even New England.

In the North, the broad ownership of land distinguished farming society from every other agricultural region of the Western world. In most communities before 1750, the truly rich and abjectly poor were few and the gap between them small compared with European society. Most men other than indentured servants lived to purchase or inherit a farm of at least 50 acres. Settlers valued land highly, for freehold tenure ordinarily guaranteed both economic independence and political rights.

Amid widespread property ownership, a rising population pressed against a limited land supply by the eighteenth century, especially in New England. Family farms could not be divided and subdivided indefinitely, for it took at least 50 acres (of which only a quarter could usually be cultivated) to support a single family. The decreasing fertility of the soil compounded the problem of dwindling farm size. When land had been plentiful, farmers planted crops in the same field for three years and then let it lie fallow in pasturage seven years or more until it regained its fertility. But on the smaller farms of the eighteenth century, farmers had reduced fallow time to only a year or two. Inevitably, such intense use of the soil reduced crop yields.

The diminishing size and productivity of family farms forced many New Englanders in the eighteenth century to move to the frontier or out of the area altogether. Some drifted south to New York and Pennsylvania. Others sought opportunities as artisans in the coastal towns or took to the sea. More headed for the colony's western frontier or north into New Hampshire and the eastern frontier of Maine. Several thousand New England families migrated even farther north, to the Annapolis valley of Nova Scotia.

Wherever they took up farming, northern cultivators engaged in agricultural work routines that were far less intense than in the South. The growing season was much shorter, and the cultivation of cereal crops required incessant labor only during spring planting and autumn harvesting. This less burdensome work rhythm led many northern cultivators to fill out their calendars with intermittent work as clockmakers, shoemakers, carpenters, and weavers.

Changing Values

On April 29, 1695, an unusually severe hailstorm struck Boston. Merchant Samuel Sewall dined that evening with Cotton Mather, New England's most prominent Puritan clergyman. As Mather wondered why "more ministers houses than others proportionately had been smitten with lightning," hailstones began to shatter the windows of Sewall's house. Sewall and Mather fell to their knees and broke into prayer together "after this awful Providence."

As these two third-generation Massachusetts Puritans understood it, God was angry with them as leaders of a people whose piety and moral rectitude were being overtaken by worldliness. The people of Massachusetts had become "sermon-proof," as one dejected minister put it.

In other parts of the North, the expansive environment and the Protestant emphasis on self-discipline and hard work were also breeding qualities that would become hallmarks of American culture: an ambitious outlook, individualistic behavior, and a love of material things. In Europe, most tillers of the soil expected little from life. In America, one colonist remarked, "Every man expects one day or another to be upon a footing with his wealthiest neighbor."

Commitment to religion, family, and community did not disappear in the eighteenth century. But fewer men and women saw daily existence as a preparation for the afterlife. A slender almanac, written by the twelfth child of a poor Boston candlemaker, captured the new outlook with wit and charm. Born in 1706, Benjamin Franklin had abandoned a declining Boston for a rising Philadelphia. By age 23, he had learned the printer's trade and was publishing the *Pennsylvania Gazette*. Three years later, he began *Poor Richard's Almanack,* next to the Bible the most widely read book in the colonies.

Franklin spiced his annual almanac—the ordinary person's guide to weather and useful information—with quips, adages, and home-spun philosophy. Eventually this homely material added up to a primer for success published in 1747 as *The Way to Wealth*. "The sleeping fox gathers no poultry" and "Lost time is never found again," advised Poor Richard, emphasizing that time is money. "It costs more to maintain one vice than to raise two children," he counseled, advocating not morality but practicality. Ever cocky, Franklin caught the spirit of the rising secularism of the eighteenth century. He embodied the growing utilitarian doctrine that the good is whatever is useful and the notion that the community is best served through individual self-improvement and accomplishment.

Women and the Family in Northern Colonial Society

In 1662, Elnathan Chauncy, a Massachusetts schoolboy, copied into his writing book that "the soul consists of two portions, inferior and superior; the superior is masculine and eternal; the feminine inferior and mortal." This lesson had been taught for generations on both sides of the Atlantic. It was part of a larger conception of a world, of God's design, that assigned degrees of status and stations in life to all persons. In such a world, the place of women was, by definition, subordinate to that of men. As daughters they were subject to their fathers, as wives, to their husbands.

European women usually accepted these narrowly circumscribed roles. Few complained, at least openly, that their work was generally limited to housewifery and midwifery. They remained silent about exclusion from the early public schools and laws that transferred to their husbands any property or income they brought into a marriage. Nor could women speak in their churches or participate in governing them, and

they had no legal voice in political affairs. Most women did not expect to choose a husband for love; parental guidance prevailed in a society in which producing legal heirs was the means of transmitting property. Once wed, women expected to remain so until death, for they could rarely obtain a divorce.

On the colonial frontier, women's lives changed in modest ways. In Europe, about one of ten women did not marry. But in the colonies, where men outnumbered women for the first century, a spinster was almost unheard of, and widows remarried with astounding speed. *Woman* and *wife* thus became nearly synonymous.

A second difference concerned property rights. Single women and widows in the colonies, as in England, could make contracts, hold and convey property, represent themselves in court, and conduct business. Under English common law, a woman forfeited these rights, as well as all property, when she married. In the colonies, however, legislatures and courts gave wives more control over property brought into marriage or left at their husband's death. They also enjoyed broader rights to act for and with their husbands in business transactions. In addition, young colonial women slowly gained the right of consenting to a marriage partner—a right that came by default to the thousands of female indentured servants who completed their labor contracts and had no parents within 3,000 miles to dictate to them.

Women had limited career choices in colonial society, but the work spaces and daily routines of husband and wife overlapped and intersected far more than today. Farm women as well as men worked at planting, harvesting, and milking cows. Women also made candles and soap, butter and cheese, and smoked meat; they made cloth and sometimes marketed farm products. A merchant's wife kept shop, handled accounts when her husband voyaged abroad, and helped supervise the servants and apprentices. "Deputy husbands" and "yoke mates" were re-

Childbirth was an oft-repeated event in the lives of most colonial wives. In this portrait of the Cheney family, the older woman is a nanny or mother-in-law; the younger woman holding a baby is Mr. Cheney's second wife.

vealing terms used by New Englanders to describe eighteenth-century wives.

Women held vital responsibilities as midwives. Until the late eighteenth century, the "obstetrick art" was almost entirely in women's hands. Midwives counseled pregnant women, delivered babies, supervised postpartum recovery, and participated in ceremonies of infant baptism and burial. Mrs. Phillips, an immigrant to Boston in 1719, delivered more than 3,000 infants in her 42-year career. Because childbirth was a recurring and dangerous crisis, the circle of female friends and relatives who attended childbirth created strong networks of mutual assistance.

In her role as wife and mother, the eighteenth-century northern colonial woman differed somewhat from her English counterpart. American women married earlier and produced more children (on average seven, two of whom died in infancy). But gradually, as the coastal plain filled up in the eighteenth century, marriage age crept up and the number of children per family inched down.

Northern child-rearing patterns differed considerably. In the seventeenth century, stern fathers dominated Puritan family life, and few were reluctant to punish unruly children. "Better whip'd than damn'd," advised Cotton Mather. In Quaker families, however, mothers played a more active role in child rearing. More permissive, they relied on tenderness and love rather than guilt to mold their children. Attitudes toward choosing a marriage partner also separated early Puritan and Quaker approaches to family life. Puritan parents usually arranged their children's marriages but allowed them the right to veto. Young Quaker men and women made their own matches, subject to parental veto.

Despite this initial diversity in child rearing, the father-dominated family of New England gradually declined in the eighteenth century. In its place rose the mother-centered family, in which affectionate parents encouraged self-expression and independence in their children. This "modern" approach was closer to the parenting methods of the coastal Native Americans, who initially had been widely disparaged for their lax methods of rearing their young.

ECOLOGICAL TRANSFORMATION

Wherever Europeans settled in the Americas, they brought with them not only social and family traditions but also animals, plant life, diseases, and ways of viewing the natural resources they found—all of which had enormous consequences for the ecosystems they were entering. In New Spain, the Spanish introduction of grazing animals—cattle, horses, pigs, sheep, and goats—profoundly altered the landscape. Breeding prolifically, pigs and cattle devoured the tall grasses and most palatable plant species and within half a century left huge areas with little or no ground cover.

In England's North American colonies, the rapid increase of settlers after 1715 led to a swift depletion of the forests near the coast. Just for heating and cooking, the typical northern farmhouse required an acre of trees each year, and with the population explosion of the eighteenth century, the price of a cord of firewood quickly rose as woodcutters ventured farther inland.

Rapid harvesting of the forests had many effects. As the colonists chopped down the forest canopy that had previously moderated the weather, the summers became hotter and the winters colder. In deforested areas the snow melted sooner, and, as the winter's melting snow ran off more quickly, watersheds emptied faster. This, in turn, caused soil erosion and periods of drought.

The second ecological transformation came about as the result of the replacement of the animals already in North America by those brought by Europeans. European colonists were a livestock people, skilled in mixed farming and herding of domesticated cattle, horses, pigs, sheep, and goats. Such animals provided food, leather, fibers for clothmaking, and the sheer pulling and carrying power relied upon by a people who had no other source of energy than their own muscles. Multiplying rapidly in a favorable environment, pigs and cattle "swarm like vermin upon the earth," reported one Virginia account as early as 1700. In some areas, the animals multiplied so rapidly and denuded the native grasses and shrubs so quickly that they actually ate themselves out of subsistence and began to die for lack of grazing land. While European livestock filled the land, the native fur-bearing animals—beaver, deer, bear, wolf, raccoon, and marten—rapidly became extinct in the areas of settlement.

All these environmental changes were linked not only to the numbers of Europeans arriving in North America but also to their ways of thinking about nature. Looking out over wooded hills and fertile valleys, transplanted Europeans could only imagine the possibility of raising valuable crops as if the ecosystem were composed of unconnected elements, each ripe for exploitation. Land, lumber, fish, and fur-bearing animals could be converted into sources of cash that would buy imported commodities that improved one's material condition. The New England writer Edward Johnson described the process perceptively as early as 1653: Who would have imagined, he mused, "that this wilderness should turn a mart for merchants in so short a space, Holland, France, Spain, and Portugal coming hither for trade." Supplying these Europeans were the farmers, woodcutters, and fishermen who consigned to the marketplace huge portions of the ecosystem.

The "rage for commerce" and for an improved life produced wasteful practices on farms and in forests and fisheries. "The grain fields, the meadows, the forests, the cattle, etc.," wrote a Swedish visitor in the 1750s, "are treated with equal carelessness." Accustomed to the natural abundance once the native peoples had been driven from the land, the colonists embarked on ecologically destructive practices that over a period of many generations profoundly altered the natural world around them.

THE PLANTATION SOUTH

Between 1680 and 1750, the white tidewater settlements of the southern colonies made the transition from a frontier society marked by a high immigration rate, a surplus of males, and an unstable social organization to a settled society composed mostly of native-born families. Between the piedmont region and the ocean, a mature southern culture took form.

The Tobacco Coast

Tobacco production in Virginia and Maryland expanded rapidly in the seventeenth century, but war in Europe and the Americas for the two decades bridging the turn of the century drove up transportation costs and dampened the demand for tobacco. Stagnation in the tobacco market lasted from the mid-1680s until about 1715.

Yet it was in this period that the Upper South underwent a profound social transformation. First, slaves replaced indentured servants so rapidly that by 1730 the unfree labor force was overwhelmingly black. Second, the planters responded to the dull tobacco market by diversifying their crops. They shifted some of their tobacco fields to grain, hemp, and flax; increased their herds of cattle and swine; and became more

self-sufficient by developing local industries to produce iron, leather, and textiles. By the 1720s, when a profitable tobacco trade with France created a new period of prosperity, their economy was much more diverse and resilient than it had been a generation before.

Third, the structure of the population changed rapidly. Black slaves grew from about 7 percent to 35 percent of the region's population between 1690 and 1750, and the drastic imbalance between white men and women disappeared.

Notwithstanding the influx of Africans, slave owning was far from universal. As late as 1750, a majority of families owned no slaves at all. Among slave owners, fewer than one-tenth held more than 20 slaves. Nonetheless, the common goal was the large plantation where black slaves made the earth yield up profits to support an aristocratic life for their masters.

The Chesapeake planters who acquired the best land and accumulated enough capital to invest heavily in slaves created a gentry life style that set them apart from ordinary farmers such as Devereaux Jarratt's father. Men such as Charles Carroll of Maryland and Robert "King" Carter and William Byrd of Virginia counted their slaves by the hundreds, their acres by the thousands, and their fortunes by the tens of thousands of pounds.

Ritual display of wealth marked southern gentry life. Racing thoroughbred horses and gambling on them recklessly became common sport for young gentlemen, who had often been educated in England. Planters began to construct stately brick Georgian mansions and fill them with imported furniture.

The emerging Chesapeake planter elite controlled the county courts, officered the local militia, ruled the parish vestries of the Anglican church, and made law in their legislative assemblies. To their sons they passed the mantle of political and social leadership.

For all their social display, southern planter squires were essentially agrarian businessmen. They spent their days obtaining credit, dealing in land and slaves, scheduling planting and harvesting routines, conferring with overseers, disciplining slaves, and arranging leases with tenants. A planter's reputation rose and fell with the quality of his crop. His wife also shouldered many responsibilities. She superintended cloth production and the processing and preparation of food while ruling over a household crowded with children, slaves, and occasional visitors. The farms were often so isolated from one another, however, that planter families lived a "solitary and unsociable existence," as one phrased it.

The Rice Coast

The plantation economy of the Lower South in the eighteenth century rested on the production of rice and indigo. Rice exports surpassed 1.5 million pounds per year by 1710 and reached 80 million pounds by the eve of the Revolution. Indigo, a blue dye obtained from plants for use in textiles, became a staple crop in the 1740s after Eliza Lucas Pinckney, a wealthy South Carolina planter's wife, experimented successfully with its cultivation. Within a generation, indigo production had spread into Georgia. It soon ranked among the leading colonial exports.

The expansion of rice production transformed the swampy coastal lowlands. In the rice-producing region radiating out from Charleston, planters imported thousands of slaves after 1720; by 1740, they composed nearly 90 percent of the region's inhabitants. White population declined as wealthy planters left their estates in the hands of resident overseers. At midcentury, a shocked New England visitor described local society as one "divided into opulent and lordly planters, poor and spiritless peasants, and vile slaves."

Throughout the plantation South, the courthouse became a central gathering place for men. Court day brought together men of all classes. They came to settle debts, dispute land boundaries, sue and be sued. When court was over, a multitude lingered on, drinking, gossiping, and staging horse races, cockfights, wrestling matches, footraces, and fiddling contests. Competition and assertiveness lay at the heart of all these demonstrations of male personal prowess.

The Backcountry

While the southern gentry matured along the tobacco and rice coasts, settlers poured into the upland backcountry. Thousands of land-hungry German and Scots-Irish settlers spilled into the interior valleys running along the eastern side of the Appalachians. Their enclaves of small farms remained isolated from the coastal region for several generations, which helped these pioneers cling fiercely to the folkways they had known on the other side of the Atlantic.

The crudity of backcountry life appalled many visitors from the more refined seaboard. In 1733, William Byrd described a large Virginia frontier plantation as "a poor, dirty hovel, with hardly anything in it but children that wallowed about like so many pigs." Charles Woodmason, a stiff-necked Anglican minister who spent three years tramping between settlements in the Carolina upcountry, wrote: "Many hundreds live in concubinage—swopping their wives as cattle and living in a state of nature more irregularly and unchastely than the Indians."

What Byrd and Woodmason were really observing was the poverty of frontier life and the lack of schools, churches, and towns. Most families lived in rough-hewn log cabins and planted their corn, beans, and wheat between the stumps of trees they had felled. Women toiled alongside men, in the fields, forest, and homestead. For a generation, these settlers endured a poor diet, endless work, and meager rewards.

By the 1760s, the southern backcountry began to emerge from the frontier stage. Small marketing towns became centers of craft activity, church life, and local government. Farms began producing surpluses for shipment east. Density of settlement increased. Class distinctions remained narrow compared with the older seaboard settlements, but many backcountry settlements acquired the look of permanence.

Family Life in the South

As the South emerged from the early era of withering mortality and stunted families, male and female roles gradually became more physically and functionally separated. In most areas, the white gender ratio reached parity by the 1720s. Women lost the leverage in the marriage market that scarcity had provided earlier. With the growth of slavery, the work role of white women also changed. The wealthy planter's wife became the domestic manager in the "great house."

The balanced sex ratio and the growth of slavery also brought changes for southern white males. The planter's son had always been trained in horsemanship, the use of a gun, and the rhythms of agricultural life. Ordering and disciplining slaves also became a part of his education. Bred to command, southern planters' sons also developed a self-confidence and authority that propelled many of them into leadership roles during the American Revolution.

On the small farms of the tidewater region and throughout the backcountry settlements, women's roles closely resembled those of northern women. Women labored in the fields alongside their menfolk. "She is a very civil woman," noted an observer of a southern frontierswoman, "and shows nothing of ruggedness or immodesty in her carriage; yet she will carry a gun in the woods and kill deer and turkeys, shoot down wild cattle, catch and tie hogs, knock down beeves with an ax, and perform the most manful exercises as well as most men in those parts."

Marriage and family life were also more informal in the backcountry. With vast areas unattended by ministers of any religion and courthouses out of reach, most couples married or "took up" with each other in matches unsanctioned by state or church until an itinerant clergyman passed through the area.

THE URBAN WORLD OF COMMERCE AND IDEAS

Only about 5 percent of the colonists lived in towns as large as 2,500, and none of the commercial centers boasted a population greater than 16,000 in 1750 or 30,000 in 1775. Yet the urban societies were at the leading edge of social change. Almost all the alterations associated with the advent of "modern" life occurred first in the seaport towns and radiated outward to the hinterland. In the seaboard centers, the transition first occurred from a barter to a commercial economy, from a social order based on assigned status to one based on achievement, from rank-conscious and deferential politics to participatory and contentious politics, and from small-scale craftsmanship to factory production. In addition, the cities were the centers of intellectual life and the conduits through which European ideas flowed into the colonies.

Sinews of Trade

In the half century after 1690, Boston, New York, and Philadelphia blossomed from urban villages into thriving commercial centers. This urban growth accompanied the development of the agricultural interior, to which the seaports were closely linked. Through the trade centers flowed colonial export staples such as tobacco, rice, wheat, timber products, and fish as well as the imported goods that colonists needed. The imports included manufactured and luxury goods from England such as glass, paper, iron implements, and cloth; wine, spices, coffee, tea, and sugar from other parts of the world; and the human cargo to fill the labor gap. In these seaports, the pivotal figure was the merchant. Frequently engaged in both retail and wholesale trade, the merchant was also moneylender (for no banks yet existed), shipbuilder, insurance agent, land developer, and often coordinator of artisan production.

By the eighteenth century, the American

economy was integrated into an Atlantic basin trading system that connected Great Britain, western Europe, Africa, the West Indies, and Newfoundland. The rulers of Great Britain, like those of other major trading nations of western Europe, pursued mercantilist trade policies. According to the principles of mercantilism, a country should strive to gain wealth by increasing its exports, levying duties on imports, regulating production and trade, and exploiting its colonies to its own advantage. The British followed these principles by controlling their colonies' trade, requiring the colonies to supply them with foodstuffs, lumber, and other non-manufactured products, and by selling the colonists British manufactured goods.

The colonists could never produce enough exportable raw materials to pay for the imported goods they craved, so they had to earn credits in England by supplying the West Indies and other areas with foodstuffs and timber products. They also accumulated credit by providing shipping and distributional services. New Englanders became the most ambitious participants in the carrying trade, sailing along the Atlantic seaboard, the Caribbean, and across the Atlantic.

The Artisan's World

Though merchants stood first in wealth and prestige in the colonial towns, artisans were far more numerous. About two-thirds of urban adult males, slaves excluded, labored at handicrafts. These "leather apron men" included not only the proverbial butcher, baker, and candlestick maker but also carpenters and coopers (who made barrels); shoemakers and tailors; silver-, gold-, pewter-, and blacksmiths; mast and sail makers; masons, plasterers, weavers, potters; and many more. They worked with hand tools, usually in small shops.

Work patterns for artisans were irregular, dictated by weather, hours of daylight, erratic delivery of raw materials, and shifting consumer demand. When ice blocked northern harbors,

mariners and dockworkers endured slack time. If prolonged rain delayed the slaughter of cows in the country or made impassable the rutted roads into the city, the tanner and the shoemaker laid their tools aside.

Urban artisans took fierce pride in their crafts. "Our professions rendered us useful and necessary members of our community," the Philadelphia shoemakers asserted. "Proud of that rank, we aspired to no higher." Yet the upperclass tended to view artisans as mere mechanics, part of the "vulgar herd."

In striving for respectability, artisans placed a premium on achieving economic independence. Every craftsman began as an apprentice, spending five or more teenage years learning the "mysteries of the craft" in the shop of a master "mechanick." After fulfilling his contract, the young artisan became a "journeyman." He sold his labor to a master craftsman and frequently lived in his house, ate at his table, and sometimes married his daughter. The journeyman hoped to complete within a few years the three-step climb from servitude to self-employment. After setting up his own shop, he could control his work hours and acquire the respect that came from economic independence. In trades requiring greater organization and capital, such as distilling and shipbuilding, the rise from journeyman to master proved impossible for many artisans. Nonetheless, the ideal of the independent craftsman prevailed.

In good times, urban artisans fared well. They expected to earn "a decent competency" and eventually to purchase a small house. But success was far from automatic, even for those following all of Poor Richard's advice about hard work and frugal living. An advantageous marriage, luck in avoiding illness, and the size of an inheritance were often the critical factors in whether an artisan moved up or down the ladder of success.

Urban Social Structure

Population growth, economic development, and a series of wars that punctuated the period from

1690 to 1765 altered the urban social structure. Stately townhouses rose as testimony to the fortunes acquired in trade, shipbuilding, war contracting, and urban land development. This last may have been the most profitable of all. "It is almost a proverb," a Philadelphian observed in the 1760s, "that every great fortune made here within these 50 years has been by land." By the late colonial era, some commercial titans had become America's first millionaires by accumulating estates of £10,000 to £20,000 sterling.

Alongside urban wealth grew urban poverty. From the beginning, every city had its disabled, orphaned, and widowed who required aid. But after 1720, poverty marred the lives of many more city dwellers. Boston was hit especially hard in the 1740s. The overseers of the poor groaned that their relief expenditures were double the outlays of any town of equal size "upon the face of the whole earth."

Burdened with mounting poor taxes, cities devised new ways of helping the needy. Rather than support the impoverished in their homes with "outrelief" payments, officials built large almshouses where the poor could be housed and fed more economically. Many of the indigent preferred "to starve in their homes."

The increasing gap between the wealthy and the poor in the colonial cities was recorded in the eighteenth-century tax lists. The top five percent of taxpayers increased their share of the cities' taxable assets between 1690 and 1770, while the bottom half of the taxable inhabitants saw their share of the wealth shrink. The urban middle classes, except in Boston, continued to make gains. But the growth of princely fortunes amid increasing poverty made some urban dwellers reflect that the conditions of the Old World seemed to be reappearing in the New.

The Entrepreneurial Ethos

As the cities grew, new values took hold. In the older, medieval, "corporate" view of society, economic life ideally operated according to what was equitable, not what was profitable. Citizens usually agreed that government should provide for the general welfare by regulating prices and wages, setting quality controls, licensing providers of service such as tavernkeepers and ferrymen, and supervising public markets where all food was sold. Such regulation seemed natural because a community was defined not as a collection of individuals, each entitled to pursue separate interests, but as a single body of interrelated parts where individual rights and responsibilities formed a seamless web.

In America, as in Europe, new ideas about economic life gathered support. The subordination of private interests to the commonweal became viewed as a lofty but unrealistic ideal. According to the new view, people should be allowed to pursue their own material desires competitively. The resulting impersonal market of producers and consumers would operate to everyone's advantage.

As the colonial port towns took their places in the Atlantic world of commerce, merchants became accustomed to making decisions according to the emerging commercial ethic that rejected traditional restraints on entrepreneurial activity. The underlying tension between the new economic freedom and the older concern for the public good erupted only with food shortages or galloping inflation.

Such a moment struck in Boston during Queen Anne's War. Merchant Andrew Belcher contracted to ship large quantities of wheat to the Caribbean, where higher prices would yield greater profit than in Boston. Ordinary neighbors, threatened with a bread shortage and angered that a townsman would put profit ahead of community needs, attacked one of Belcher's grain-laden ships in 1710. They sawed through the rudder and tried to run the vessel aground in order to seize the grain. Invoking the older ethic that the public welfare outweighed private interests, they took the law into their own hands. Even the grand jury, composed of substantial members of the community, hinted its approval of the violent action against Belcher by refusing to indict the rioters.

The two conceptions of community and economic life rubbed against each other for many decades. But by the mid–eighteenth century, the pursuit of a profitable livelihood, not the social compact of the community, animated most city dwellers.

The American Enlightenment

Ideas about not only economic life but also the nature of the universe and improving the human condition reached across the Atlantic to the colonies. In the eighteenth century, an American version of the European intellectual movement called the Enlightenment occurred, and the cities became centers for disseminating these new ideas.

European thinkers, in what is called the Age of Reason, rejected the pessimistic Calvinist concept of innate human depravity, replacing it with the optimistic notion that a benevolent God had blessed humankind with the supreme gift of reason. Thinkers like John Locke, in his influential *Essay Concerning Human Understanding* (1689), argued that God had not predetermined the content of the human mind but furnished it with the capacity to acquire knowledge. All Enlightenment thinkers prized this acquisition of knowledge, for it allowed humankind to improve its condition. As the great scientific thinker Isaac Newton demonstrated, systematic investigation could unlock the secrets of the physical universe. Moreover, scientific knowledge could be applied to human institutions in order to improve society.

Though only a small number of educated colonists read the Enlightenment authors, they began in the eighteenth century to make significant contributions to the advancement of science. Naturalists such as John Bartram of Philadelphia ranged the eastern part of the continent gathering and describing American plants as part of the transatlantic attempt to classify all plant life into one universal system of classification. Professor John Winthrop III of Harvard made an unusually accurate measurement of the earth's distance from the sun. Standing above them all was Benjamin Franklin, whose spectacular (and dangerous) experiments with electricity, the properties of which were just becoming known, earned him an international reputation.

Franklin's true genius as a figure of the Enlightenment came, however, in his practical application of scientific knowledge. Among his inventions were the lightning rod, which nearly ended the age-old danger of fires when lightning struck wooden buildings; bifocal spectacles; and an iron stove that heated rooms—in an age when firewood was a major item in the household budget—far more efficiently than the open fireplace commonly used. Franklin also made his adopted home of Philadelphia a center of the American Enlightenment. He played a leading role in founding America's first circulating library in 1731, an artisans' debating club for "mutual improvement" through discussion of the latest ideas from Europe, and an intercolonial scientific association that would emerge in 1769 as the American Philosophical Society.

The scientific and intellectual advances of the seventeenth- and eighteenth-century Enlightenment encouraged a belief in "natural law" and debate about the "natural" rights of human beings. In Europe issues of equality were explored by French philosophers François Voltaire and Denis Diderot. From 1750 to 1772, Diderot published his *Encyclopedia*, which treated such topics as equality, liberty, reason, and rights. The ideas of the Enlightenment spread in Europe and America and eventually found expression in movements for reform, democracy, and liberation. Though most American colonists were not educated enough to participate actively in the American Enlightenment, the efforts of men such as Franklin exposed thousands, especially in the cities, to new currents of thought. This led to the growing sense that the colonists, blessed by their abundant environment, might truly inhabit the part of the world where the Enlightenment ideal of achieving a perfect society might be fulfilled.

THE GREAT AWAKENING

Many of the social, economic, and political changes occurring in the eighteenth-century colonies converged in the Great Awakening, the first of many religious revivals that would sweep American society during the next two centuries. This quest for spiritual renewal challenged old sources of authority and produced patterns of thought and behavior that helped fuel a revolutionary movement in the next generation.

Fading Faith

Colonial America in the early eighteenth century remained an overwhelmingly Protestant culture. The Puritan, or Congregational, church dominated all of New England except Rhode Island. Anglicanism held sway in much of New York and throughout the South except the backcountry. In the mid-Atlantic and in the back settlements, a polyglot of German Mennonites, Dunkers, Moravians, and Lutherans; Scots-Irish Presbyterians; and English Baptists and Quakers mingled.

Yet these diverse groups commanded the allegiance of only about one-third of the colonists. Those who went to no church at all remained the majority. In many areas, ministers and churches were simply unavailable. In Virginia, the most populous colony, only 60 clergymen in 1761 served a population of 350,000—one parson for every 5,800 people.

In the eighteenth century, most colonial churches were voluntary or gathered ("congregated") groups, formed for reasons of conscience, not because of government compulsion. Catholics, Jews, and nonbelievers could not vote or hold office. But the persecution of Quakers and Catholics had largely passed, and some dissenting groups had gained the right by 1720 to use long-obligatory church taxes to support their own congregations.

The clergy often administered their congregations with difficulty. For example, Anglican ministers had to be ordained in England and make regular reports to the bishop of London. But once installed in Chesapeake parishes, Anglican priests faced wealthy planters who controlled the vestry (the local church's governing body), set the minister's salary, and drove out ministers who challenged them too forcefully.

Though governing their churches frustrated many clergymen, religious apathy was a far more pressing problem in the early eighteenth century. As early as 1662, the Congregational clergy of New England had attempted to return wandering sheep to the fold by adopting the Half-Way Covenant. It specified that children of church members, if they adhered to the "forms of godliness," might join the church even if they could not demonstrate that they had undergone a conversion experience. But despite compromises and innovations, most church leaders saw creeping religious apathy when they surveyed their towns.

The Awakeners' Message

The Great Awakening was not a unified movement but rather a series of revivals that swept different regions between 1720 and 1760 with varying degrees of intensity. The first stirrings came in the 1720s in New Jersey and Pennsylvania. Theodore Frelinghuysen, a Dutch Reformed minister, excited his congregation through emotional preaching. Avoiding theological abstractions, he concentrated on arousing among his parishioners a need to be "saved." A neighboring Presbyterian, Gilbert Tennent, soon took up the Dutchman's techniques, with similar success.

From New Jersey the Awakening spread to Pennsylvania in the 1730s, especially among Presbyterians, and then broke out in the Connecticut River valley. There it was led by Jonathan Edwards, pastor in Northampton. Edwards later became a philosophical giant in the colonies. But as a young man, he gained renown by lambasting his parishioners: "God and your

Jonathan Edwards (1703–1758) was the first major philosopher in the American colonies. A leader of the Great Awakening in Massachusetts, he was ousted by his congregation for reprimanding the children of church members for reading The Midwife Rightly Instructed, *an obstetric guide that was as close as curious children could come to learning about sex.*

own consciences know what abominable lasciviousness you have practised in things not fit to be named, when you have been alone; when you ought to have been reading, or meditating, or on your knees before God in secret prayer." After cataloging his parishioners' sins, Edwards drew such graphic pictures of the hell awaiting the unrepentant that his Northampton neighbors were soon preparing frantically for the conversion experience by which they would be "born again."

In 1739, these regional brushfires of evangelicalism began to spread. Instrumental in drawing together the separate local revivals and in inspiring a more scorching religious enthusiasm was George Whitefield, a 24-year-old Anglican priest from England. Whitefield made seven barnstorming tours along the American sea-

board, the first in 1739 and 1740. Thousands turned out to see him, and with each success his fame and influence grew. In Boston, Whitefield preached to 19,000 in three days. Then, at a farewell sermon, he left 25,000 writhing in fear of damnation. In his wake came American preachers, mostly young men like Devereaux Jarratt, whom he had inspired.

The Awakeners preached that the established, college-trained clergy was too intellectual and tradition-bound to bring faith and piety to a new generation. Congregations were dead, Whitefield declared, "because dead men preach to them." "The sapless discourses of such dead drones," cried another Awakener, were worthless. The fires of Protestant belief could be reignited only if individuals assumed responsibility for their own conversion.

An important form of individual participation was "lay exhorting." In this personal religious testimony, any person—young or old, female or male, black or white—might spontaneously recount a conversion experience and preach "the Lord's truth." This horrified most established clergymen. Lay exhorting shattered the trained clergy's monopoly on religious discourse and permitted ordinary men and women, and even children, servants, and slaves, to defy traditionally assigned roles.

How religion, social change, and politics became interwoven in the Great Awakening can be seen by examining two regions swept by revivalism. Both Boston, the heartland of Puritanism, and interior Virginia, a land of struggling small planters and slave-rich aristocrats, experienced the Great Awakening, but in different ways and at different times.

The Urban North

In Boston, revivalism ignited in the midst of political controversy about remedies for the severe depreciation of the province's paper currency. Paper bills had been issued for years to finance military expeditions against French Canada. The

English government insisted that Massachusetts retire all paper money by 1741. Searching for a substitute circulating medium, one group proposed a land bank to issue private bills of credit backed by land. Another group proposed a silver bank to distribute bills of credit backed by silver. Large merchants preferred the fiscally conservative silver bank, while local traders, artisans, and the laboring poor preferred the land bank.

Whitefield's arrival in Boston coincided with the currency furor. At first, Boston's elite applauded Whitefield's ability to call the masses to worship. The master evangelist, it seemed, might restore social harmony by redirecting people from earthly matters such as the currency dispute to concerns of the soul.

When Whitefield left Boston in 1740, he was succeeded by others who were more critical of the "unconverted" clergy and the self-indulgent accumulation of wealth. Among them was James Davenport, who arrived in 1742. Finding every church closed to him, Davenport preached daily on Boston Common, aroused religious ecstasy among thousands, and stirred up feeling against Boston's leading figures. Respectable people grew convinced that revivalism had gotten out of hand, for by this time ordinary people were verbally attacking opponents of the land bank in the streets as "carnal wretches, hypocrites, fighters against God, children of the devil, cursed Pharisees." A revival that had begun as a return to religion now threatened polite culture, which stressed order and discipline from ordinary people.

The Rural South

The Great Awakening was ebbing in New England and the middle colonies by 1744, although aftershocks continued for years. But in Virginia, the movement rippled through society from the mid-1740s onward. As in Boston, the Awakeners challenged and disturbed the gentry-led social order.

Whitefield stirred some religious fervor during his early trips through Virginia. Traveling "New Light" preachers, led by the brilliant orator Samuel Davies, were soon gathering large crowds both in the backcountry and in the traditionally Anglican parishes of the older settled areas. By 1747, worried Anglican clergymen persuaded the governor to issue a proclamation restraining "strolling preachers." As one critic put it in 1745, the wandering preachers "have turned the world upside down."

New Light Presbyterianism, which challenged the religious monopoly of the gentry-dominated Anglican church, continued to spread in the 1750s. The evangelical cause advanced further with the rise of the Baptists in the 1760s. Renouncing finery and addressing one another as "brother" and "sister," the Baptists reached out to thousands of unchurched people. Like northern revivalists, they focused on the conversion experience. Many of their preachers were uneducated farmers and artisans who called themselves "Christ's poor." They stressed equality in human affairs, and their message penetrated deeply among Virginia's 140,000 slaves and other poor. As in New England, social changes had weakened the cultural authority of the upper class and, in the context of religious revival, produced a vision of a society drawn along more equal lines.

Legacy of the Awakening

By the time George Whitefield returned to America for his third tour in 1745, the revival had burned out in the North. Its effects, however, were long-lasting. The Awakening promoted religious pluralism and nourished the idea that all denominations were equally legitimate; none had a monopoly on the truth. The Great Awakening gave competing Protestant churches a theory for living together in relative harmony. From this framework of denominationalism came a second change—the separation of church and state. Once a variety of churches gained legitimacy, it was impossible for any one church to claim special privileges. This undermining of the church-state tie would be completed during the Revolutionary era.

A third effect of the revival was to bolster the view that diversity within communities, for better or worse, could not be prevented. Almost from the beginning. Rhode Island, the Carolinas, and the middle colonies had recognized this. But in Massachusetts and Connecticut, people learned through church schism caused by the Awakening that the fabric of community could be woven from threads of many hues.

New eighteenth-century colonial colleges reflected the religious pluralism symbolized by the Great Awakening. Before 1740 there existed only three. Puritans had founded Harvard in 1636 and Yale in 1701 to provide New England with educated ministers, and Anglicans had chartered William and Mary in 1693. To these small seats of higher education were added six new colleges between 1746 and 1769. But none of the new colleges were controlled by an established church, all had governing bodies composed of men of different faiths, and all admitted students regardless of religion.

Last, the Awakening nurtured a subtle change in values that crossed over into politics and daily life. Especially for ordinary people, the revival experience created a new feeling of self-worth. People assumed new responsibilities in religious affairs and became skeptical of dogma and authority. By learning to oppose authority and to take part in the creation of new churches, thousands of colonists unknowingly rehearsed for revolution.

POLITICAL LIFE

"Were it not for government, the world would soon run into all manner of disorders and confusions," wrote a Massachusetts clergyman early in the eighteenth century. Few colonists, wherever they lived, would have disagreed. A much less easily resolved matter was how political power should be divided within each colony. American colonists naturally drew heavily on in- herited political ideas and institutions. These were almost entirely English because English charters sanctioned settlement, English governors ruled the colonies, and English common law governed the courts. But in a new environment, where they met unexpected circumstances, the colonists modified familiar political forms to suit their needs.

Structuring Colonial Governments

In England, the notion of the God-given supreme authority of the monarch was crumbling even before the planting of the colonies. In its place arose the belief that stable and enlightened government depended on balancing the interests of monarchy, aristocracy, and democracy. The Revolution of 1688 in England, by thwarting the king's pretensions to greater power, seemed to most colonists a vindication and strengthening of a carefully balanced political system.

In colonial governments, political balance was achieved somewhat differently. The governor was the king's agent or, in proprietary colonies, the agent of the king's delegated authority. The council, composed of wealthy appointees of the governor in most colonies, was a pale equivalent of the English House of Lords. The assembly, elected by white male freeholders, functioned as a replica of the House of Commons.

Bicameral legislatures developed in most of the colonies in the seventeenth century. The lower houses, or assemblies, represented the local interests of the people at large. The upper houses, or councils (which usually also sat as the highest courts), represented the nascent aristocracy. Except in Rhode Island and Connecticut, every statute required the governor's assent, and all colonial laws required final approval from the king's privy council. But during the months it took to receive such approval, the laws set down in the colonies took force.

Behind the formal structure of politics stood the rules governing who could participate in the

Table 4.1
Colonial Foundations of the American Political System

1606	Virginia companies of London and Plymouth granted patents to settle lands in North America.
1619	First elected colonial legislature meets in Virginia.
1634	Under a charter granted in 1632, Maryland's proprietor is given all the authority "as any bishop of Durham" ever held—more than the king possessed in England.
1635	The council in Virginia deports Governor John Harvey for exceeding his power, thus asserting the rights of local magistrates to contest authority of royally appointed governors.
1643	The colonies of Massachusetts, Plymouth, Connecticut, and New Haven draw up articles of confederation and form the first intercolonial union, the United Colonies of New England.
1647	Under a charter granted in 1644, elected freemen from the Providence Plantations draft a constitution establishing freedom of conscience, separating church and state, and authorizing referenda by the towns on laws passed by the assembly.
1677	The Laws, Concessions and Agreements for West New Jersey provide for a legislature elected annually by virtually all free males, secret voting, liberty of conscience, election of justices of the peace and local officeholders, and trial by jury in public so that "justice may not be done in a corner."
1689	James II deposed in England in the Glorious Revolution, and royal governors, accused of abusing their authority, ousted in Massachusetts, New York, and Maryland.
1701	First colonial unicameral legislature meets in Pennsylvania under the Frame of Government of 1701.
1735	John Peter Zenger, a New York printer, acquitted of seditious libel for printing attacks on the royal governor and his faction, thus widening the freedom of the press.
1754	First congress of all the colonies meets at Albany (with seven colonies sending delegates) and agrees on a Plan of Union (which is rejected by the colonies and the English government).
1765	The Stamp Act Congress, the first intercolonial convention called outside England's authority, meets in New York.

political process. In England since the fifteenth century, the ownership of land had largely defined electoral participation (women and non-Christians were uniformly excluded). Only those with property sufficient to produce an annual rental income of 40 shillings could vote or hold office. The colonists usually followed this principle closely, except in Massachusetts, where it took until 1691 to break the requirement of church membership for suffrage.

Whereas in England the 40-shilling freehold requirement was intended to restrict the size of the electorate, in the colonies, because of the cheapness of land, it conferred the vote on a large proportion of adult males. Between 50 and 75 percent of the adult free males could vote in most colonies. As the proportion of landless colonists increased in the eighteenth century, however, the franchise slowly became more limited.

Though voting rights were broadly based, the upper class assumed that only the wealthy and socially prominent were entitled to hold positions of political power. Lesser men, it was held, ought to defer to their betters. Balancing the elitist conception of politics, however, was the notion that the entire electorate should periodically judge the performance of those they entrusted with political power and reject those who represented them inadequately. Unlike the members of the English House of Commons, who by the seventeenth century thought of themselves as representing the entire nation, the colonial representatives were expected to reflect the views of those who elected them locally. Believing this, their constituents judged them accordingly. The people also felt justified in badgering their leaders, protesting openly, and, in extreme cases of abuse of power, assuming control.

The Crowd in Action

What gave special power to the common people when they assembled to protest oppressive authority was the general absence of effective police power. In the countryside, where most colonists lived, only the county sheriff, with an occasional deputy, insulated civil leaders from angry farmers. In the towns, police forces were still unknown. Only the sheriff, backed up by the night watch, safeguarded public order. Under these conditions, crowd action, frequently effective, gradually achieved a kind of legitimacy. The assembled people came to be perceived as the watchdog of government, ready to chastise or drive from office those who violated the collective sense of what was right and proper.

Boston's impressment riot of 1747 vividly illustrates the people's readiness to fight oppression. It began when Commodore Charles Knowles brought his Royal Navy ships to Boston for provisioning—and to replenish the ranks of mariners thinned by desertion. When Knowles sent press gangs out on a chill November evening with orders to fill the crew vacancies from Boston's waterfront population, they scooped up artisans, laborers, servants, and slaves, as well as merchant seamen from ships riding at anchor in the harbor.

But before the press gangs could hustle their victims back to the British men-of-war, a crowd of angry Bostonians seized several British officers, surrounded the governor's house, and demanded the release of their townsmen. When the sheriff and his deputies attempted to intervene, the crowd mauled them. The militia, called to arms by the governor, refused to respond. By dusk, a crowd of several thousand defied the governor's orders to disperse, stoned the windows of the governor's house, and dragged a royal barge from one of the British ships into the courtyard of his house, where they burned it amid cheers. After several days of negotiations amid further tumult, Knowles released the impressed Bostonians.

The Growing Power of the Assemblies

Incidents such as the impressment riot of 1747 demonstrated the touchiness of England's colonial subjects. But a more gradual and restrained change—the growing ambition and power of the legislative assemblies—was far more important. For most of the seventeenth century, royal and proprietary governors had exercised greater power in relation to the elected legislatures than did the king in relation to Parliament. The governors could dissolve the lower houses and delay their sitting, control the election of their speakers, and in most colonies initiate legislation with their appointed councils. Colonial governors also had authority to appoint and dismiss judges at all levels of the judiciary and to create chancery courts, which sat without juries. Governors also controlled the expenditure of public monies and had authority to grant land to individuals and groups, which they sometimes used to confer vast estates on their favorites.

In the seventeenth century, Virginia, Massachusetts, and New York had become royal colonies, with governors appointed by the Crown. By the 1730s, royal governments had replaced many of the proprietary governments, including New Jersey (1702), South Carolina (1719), and North Carolina (1729). Some of the royal governors were competent military officers or bureaucrats, but most were mediocre.

In the eighteenth century, elected colonial legislatures challenged the swollen executive powers of these colonial governors. Bit by bit, the representative assemblies won new rights—to initiate legislation, to elect their own speakers, to settle contested elections, to discipline their membership, and to nominate provincial treasurers who controlled the disbursement of public funds. The most important gain of all was acquiring the "power of the purse"—the authority to initiate money bills, which specified how much money should be raised by taxes and how it should be spent. Originally thought of as advisory bodies, the elected assemblies gradually transformed themselves into governing bodies reflecting the interests of the electorate.

Local Politics

Binding elected officeholders to their constituents became an important feature of the colonial political system. In England, the House of Commons was filled with representatives from "rotten boroughs," ancient places left virtually uninhabited by population shifts, and with men whose vote was in the pocket of the ministry because they had accepted Crown appointments, contracts, or gifts. The American assemblies, by contrast, contained mostly representatives sent by voters who often instructed them on particular issues and held them accountable for serving local interests. The voters mostly sent merchants, lawyers, and substantial planters and farmers to represent them in the lower houses, and by the mid–eighteenth century in most colonies, these men had formed political elites.

Local government was usually more important to the colonists than provincial government. In the North, local political authority generally rested in the towns. The New England town meeting decided a wide range of matters, striving for consensus, searching and arguing until it could express itself as a single unit. "By general agreement" and "by the free and united consent of the whole" were phrases denoting a decision-making process that sought participatory assent rather than a democratic competition among differing interests and points of view.

In the South, the county constituted the primary unit of government. No equivalent of the town meeting existed for placing local decisions before the populace. The planter gentry ruled the county courts and the legislature, while substantial farmers served in minor offices such as road surveyor and deputy sheriff. At court sessions, usually convened four times a year, deeds were read aloud and then recorded, juries impaneled and justice dispensed, elections held, licenses issued, and proclamations read aloud. On election days, gentlemen treated their neighbors (on whom they depended for votes) to "bumbo," "kill devil," and other alcoholic treats. By the mid–eighteenth century, a landed squirearchy of third- and fourth-generation families had achieved political dominance.

The Spread of Whig Ideology

Whether in local or provincial affairs, a political ideology called Whig or "republican" had spread widely by the mid–eighteenth century. The canons of this body of thought, inherited from England, flowed from the belief that concentrated power was historically the enemy of liberty and that too much power lodged in any person or group inevitably produced corruption and tyranny. The best defenses against concentrated power were balanced government, elected legislatures adept at checking executive authority, prohibition of standing armies (almost always controlled by tyrannical monarchs to oppress the people), and vigilance by the people for telltale signs of corruption in their leaders.

Much of this Whig ideology reached the people through the newspapers that began appearing in the seaboard towns in the early eighteenth century. The first was the *Boston News-Letter,* founded in 1704. By the 1730s, newspapers had become an important conduit of Whig political thought.

The new importance of the press was vividly illustrated in the Zenger case in New York. Young John Peter Zenger, a printer's apprentice, had been hired in 1733 by the antigovernment faction of Lewis Morris to start a newspaper that would publicize the tyrannical actions of Governor William Cosby. In Zenger's *New-York Weekly Journal,* the Morris faction fired salvos at Cosby's interference with the courts and his alleged corruption in giving important offices to his henchmen.

These charges led to Zenger's arrest for seditious libel. He was brilliantly defended by Andrew Hamilton, a Philadelphia lawyer. Although the jury acquitted Zenger, the libel laws remained very restrictive. But the acquittal did reinforce the notion that the government was the people's servant, and it brought home the point that public criticism could keep people with political authority responsible to the people they ruled. Such ideas about liberty and corruption, raised in the context of local politics, would shortly achieve a much broader significance.

CONCLUSION

AMERICA IN 1750

The American colonies, robust and expanding, matured rapidly between 1700 and 1750. Churches, schools, and towns—the visible marks of the receding frontier—appeared everywhere. A balanced sex ratio and stable family life had been achieved throughout the colonies. Seasoned political leaders and familiar political institutions functioned from Maine to Georgia.

Yet the sinew, bone, and muscle of American society had not yet fully knit together. One-fifth of the population was bound in chattel slavery, and the Native American component was still unassimilated and uneasily situated on the frontier. Full of strength yet marked by awkward incongruities, colonial Americans in 1750 approached an era of strife and momentous decisions.

Recommended Reading

James A. Henretta and Gregory Nobles provide a good introduction to the growth and development of eighteenth-century colonial society in *Evolution and Revolution: American Society: 1620–1820* (1986). On immigration and immigration groups, see Jon But-ler, *The Huguenots in Colonial America* (1983); Ned Landsman, *Scotland and Its First American Colony* (1985); and Bernard Bailyn, *Voyagers to the West* (1986).

On the development of the northern colonies,

rich material can be found in Laurel T. Ulrich, *Good Wives* (1982); and Sung Bok Kim, *Landlord and Tenant in the Colony of New York* (1976).

The transformation of eighteenth-century southern society is the subject of Allan Kulikoff, *Tobacco and Slaves* (1986); T. H. Breen, *Tobacco Culture: The Mentality of the Great Tidewater Planters on the Eve of the Revolution* (1985); and Mechal Sobel, *The World They Made Together: Black and White Values in Eighteenth-Century Virginia* (1987).

Much can be learned about commercial and intellectual life in the cities from Gary M. Walton and James F. Shepherd, *The Economic Rise of Early America* (1979); and Gary B. Nash, *The Urban Crucible* (1979).

Henry May addresses the American Enlightenment in *The American Enlightenment* (1976).

Excellent treatments of religious life and the Great Awakening include Harry S. Stout, *The New England Soul: Preaching and Religious Life in Colonial New England* (1986); and Patricia Bonomi, *Under the Cope of Heaven: Religion, Society, and Politics in Colonial America* (1986).

On the maturing colonial political systems, see Bernard Bailyn, *The Origins of American Politics* (1968); Edward M. Cook, Jr., *The Fathers of the Towns* (1976); and Patricia Bonomi, *A Factious People: Politics and Society in Colonial New York* (1977).

Time Line

1662	Half-Way Covenant in New England		1739–1740	Whitefield's first American tour spreads Great Awakening Slaves compose 90 percent of population on Carolina rice coast
1685–1715	Stagnation in tobacco market			
1704	*Boston News-Letter,* first regular colonial newspaper, published		1740s	Indigo becomes staple crop in Lower South
1713	Beginning of Scots-Irish and German immigration		1747	Benjamin Franklin publishes first *Poor Richard's Almanack* Impressment riot in Boston
1715–1730	Volume of slave trade doubles		1760	Africans compose 20 percent of American population
1718	French settle New Orleans			
1720s	Black population begins to increase naturally		1760s–1770s	Spanish establish California mission system
1734–1736	Great Awakening begins in Northampton, Massachusetts		1769	American Philosophical Society founded at Philadelphia
1735	Zenger acquitted of seditious libel in New York			

chapter 5

Bursting the Colonial Bonds

In 1758, when he was 21 years old, Ebenezer MacIntosh of Boston laid down his shoemaker's awl and enlisted in the Massachusetts expedition against the French on Lake Champlain. He contributed his mite to the climactic Anglo-American struggle that drove the French from North America.

But a greater role lay ahead for the poor Boston shoemaker. Two years after the Peace of Paris ended the Seven Years' War in 1763, England imposed a stamp tax on the American colonists. In the massive protests that followed, MacIntosh emerged as the street leader of the Boston crowd. In two nights of violent attacks on private property, a Boston crowd nearly destroyed the houses of two of the colony's most important officials. On August 14, they tore through the house of Andrew Oliver, a wealthy merchant and the appointed distributor of stamps for Massachusetts. Twelve days later, MacIntosh led the crowd in attacking the mansion of Thomas Hutchinson, a wealthy merchant who served as lieutenant governor and chief justice of Massachusetts. "The mob was so general," wrote the governor, "and so supported that all civil power ceased in an instant."

On November 5, 2,000 townsmen followed MacIntosh in an orderly march through the crooked streets of Boston to demonstrate their solidarity in resisting the hated stamps. Five weeks later, a crowd forced stamp distributor Oliver to announce his resignation publicly at the "Liberty Tree," which had become a symbol of resistance to England's new colonial policies. Few colonists in 1750 wanted to break the connection with England. Yet in a whirlwind of events, two million colonists moved haltingly toward a showdown with mighty England. Little-known men like Ebenezer MacIntosh as well as historically celebrated Samuel Adams, John Hancock, and John Adams were part of the struggle. Collectively, ordinary persons such as MacIntosh influenced—and in fact sometimes even dictated—the revolutionary movement in the colonies. Though we read and speak mostly of a small group of "founding fathers," the wellsprings of the American Revolution can be fully discovered only among a variety of people from different social groups, occupations, regions, and religions.

This chapter addresses the tensions in late colonial society, the imperial crisis that followed the Seven Years' War (in the colonies often called the French and Indian War), and the tumultuous decade that led to the "shots heard around the world" fired at Concord Bridge in April 1775. It portrays the origins of a dual American Revolution. Ebenezer MacIntosh, in leading the Boston mob against Crown officers and their colonial collaborators, helped set in motion a revolutionary movement to restore ancient liberties thought by the Americans to be under deliberate attack in England. This movement eventually escalated into the War of American Independence.

But MacIntosh's Boston followers were also venting years of resentment at the accumulation of wealth and power by Boston's aristocratic elite. Calls for the reform of a colonial society that had become corrupt, self-indulgent, and elite-dominated thus accompanied the movement to sever the colonial bond. As distinguished from the War for Independence, this was the American Revolution.

THE CLIMACTIC SEVEN YEARS' WAR

After a brief period of peace following King George's War (1744–1748), France and England fought the fourth, largest, and by far most significant of the wars for empire that had begun in the late seventeenth century. Known variously as the Seven Years' War, the French and Indian War, and the Great War for Empire, this global conflict in part represented a showdown for control of North America between the Atlantic Ocean and the Mississippi River. In North America, the Anglo-American forces ultimately prevailed, and their victory dramatically affected the lives of the great variety of people living in the huge region east of the Mississippi.

War and the Management of Empire

After the Glorious Revolution of 1688, England began constructing a more coherent imperial administration. In 1696, a professional Board of Trade replaced the old Lords of Trade; the Treasury strengthened the customs service; and Parliament created overseas vice-admiralty courts, which functioned without juries to prosecute smugglers who evaded the trade regulations set forth in the Navigation Acts. Royal governors received greater powers and more detailed instructions and came under more insistent demands from the Board of Trade to enforce British policies. England was quietly installing the machinery of imperial management and a corps of colonial bureaucrats.

The best test of an effectively organized state was its ability to wage war. Four times between 1689 and 1763, England matched its strength against France, its archrival in North America and the Caribbean. During this period, the English king and Parliament also increased their control over colonial affairs.

Parliament added new articles such as furs, copper, hemp, tar, and turpentine to the list of items produced in North America that had to be shipped to England before being exported to another country. Parliament also curtailed colonial production of articles important to England's economy: woolen cloth in 1699, beaver hats in 1732, finished iron products in 1750. Most important, Parliament passed the Molasses Act in

1733. Attempting to stop the trade between New England and the French West Indies, where Yankee traders exchanged fish, beef, and pork for molasses to convert into rum, Parliament imposed a prohibitive duty of six pence per gallon on molasses imported from the French islands. This turned many of New England's largest merchants, distillers, and ship captains and crews into smugglers.

The generation of peace ended abruptly in 1739 when England declared war on Spain. The cause of the war was England's determination to continue its drive toward commercial domination of the Atlantic basin. Five years after the war with Spain began in 1739, it merged into a much larger conflict between England and France, in Europe called the War of Austrian Succession, that lasted until 1748. The scale of King George's War (1744–1748) far exceeded previous conflicts. As military priorities became paramount, England pressed for increased discipline within the empire and larger colonial revenues. England asked its West Indian and American colonies to share in the costs of defending—and extending—the empire and to tailor their behavior to the needs of the home country.

Outbreak of Hostilities

The tension between English and French colonists in North America was intensified by the spectacular growth of the English colonies: from 0.25 million in 1700 to 1.25 million in 1750 and to 1.75 million in the next decade. Three-quarters of the increase came in the colonies south of New York. Such growth propelled thousands of land-hungry settlers toward the mountain gaps in the Appalachians in search of farmland.

Promoting this westward rush were eastern fur traders and speculators. But the farther west the settlement line moved, the closer it came to the western trading empire of the French and their Indian allies. Colonial pene-

tration of the Ohio valley in the 1740s established the first English outposts in the continental heartland. This challenged the French where their interest was vital. While the English controlled most of the eastern coastal plain of North America, the French had nearly encircled them to the west by building a chain of trading posts and forts along the St. Lawrence River, through the Great Lakes, and southward into the Ohio and Mississippi valleys all the way to New Orleans. The French attempted to block further English expansion by constructing new forts in the Ohio valley and by prying some tribes loose from their new English connections.

By 1755, the French had driven the English traders out of the Ohio valley and established forts as far east as the forks of the Ohio River, near present-day Pittsburgh. It was there, at Fort Duquesne, that the French smartly rebuffed an ambitious young Virginia militia colonel named George Washington, dispatched by his colony's government to expel them from the region.

Men in the capitals of Europe, not in the colonies, made the decision to force a showdown in the interior of North America. Urged on by England's powerful merchants, who were eager to destroy French overseas trade, the English ministry ordered several thousand troops to America in 1754; in France, 3,000 regulars embarked to meet the English challenge.

With war looming, the colonial governments attempted to coordinate their efforts. Representatives of seven colonies met with 150 Iroquois chiefs at Albany, New York, in June 1754. The twin goals were to woo the powerful Iroquois out of their neutrality and to perfect a plan of colonial union. Both failed. "Everyone cries a union is necessary," sighed Benjamin Franklin, "but when they come to the manner and form of the union, their weak noodles are perfectly distracted."

With his British army and hundreds of American recruits, General Edward Braddock slogged his way across Virginia in the summer of

1755, cutting a road through forests and across mountains at a few miles a day. A headstrong professional soldier, Braddock had contempt for the woods-wise French regiments and their stealthy Indian allies.

As Braddock neared Fort Duquesne, the entire French force and the British suddenly surprised each other in the forest. The French had 218 soldiers and militiamen and 637 Indian allies, while Braddock commanded twice that many men but few Indians. After an initial standoff, the French redeployed their Indian allies along both sides of the road in the trees. Unseen, the Indians poured murderous fire into Braddock's tidy lines of men. Braddock was mortally wounded, and two-thirds of his forces were killed or wounded. The Anglo-American force beat a hasty, ignominious retreat.

Throughout the summer, French-supplied Indian raiders put the torch to the Virginia and Pennsylvania backcountry. "The roads are full of starved, naked, indigent multitudes," observed one officer. One French triumph followed another during the next two years, and almost every tribe north of the Ohio River joined the French side.

The turning point in the war came after the energetic William Pitt became England's prime minister in 1757. Proclaiming "I believe that I can save this nation and that no one else can," he abandoned Europe as the main theater of action against the French and threw his nation's military might into the American campaign. About 23,000 British troops landed in America in 1757 and 1758, and the huge naval fleet that arrived in the latter year included 14,000 mariners. But even forces of this magnitude, when asked to engage the enemy in the forests of North America, were not necessarily sufficient to the task without Indian support, or at least neutrality.

Tribal Strategies

Anglo-American leaders knew that in a war fought mainly in the northern colonies, the support of the Iroquois Confederacy and their tributary tribes was crucial. Iroquois allegiance could be secured in only two ways, through purchase or by a demonstration of power that would convince the tribes that the English would prevail with or without their assistance. The Iroquois understood that their interest lay in playing off one European power against the other.

In 1758, the huge English military buildup began to produce victories. After a failed British and American assault on Fort Ticonderoga on Lake Champlain in June 1758, the tide turned. Troops under Sir Jeffrey Amherst captured Louisbourg, on Cape Breton Island, and Fort Duquesne fell to an army of 6,000 led by General John Forbes. The resolute Pitt had mobilized the fighting power of the English nation and put more men in the field than existed in all of New France. The colonists, in turn, had put aside intramural squabbling long enough to overwhelm the badly outnumbered French.

The victories of 1758 finally moved the Iroquois to join the Anglo-American side. In the South, however, back country skirmishes with the Cherokee from Virginia to South Carolina turned into a costly war from 1759 to 1761.

Other Anglo-American victories in 1759, the "year of miracles," decided the outcome of the bloodiest war yet known in the New World. The culminating stroke came with a dramatic victory at Quebec. Led by 32-year-old General James Wolfe, 5,000 troops scaled a rocky cliff and overcame the French on the Plains of Abraham. The capture of Montreal late in 1760 completed the shattering of French power in North America. The theater of operations shifted to the Caribbean, where fighting continued, as in Europe, for three years longer. But in the American colonies, the "Gallic menace" was gone.

Consequences of War

For the interior Indian tribes, the Treaty of Paris ending the Seven Years' War in 1763 dealt a harsh blow. Unlike the coastal Native Americans, whose population and independence had ebbed rapidly through contact with the colonizers, the inland tribes had maintained their strength and sometimes even grown more unified through relations with settlers. Although they came to depend on European trade goods, Native Americans had turned this commercial connection to their advantage so long as more than one source of trade goods existed.

The Indian play-off system ended with the French defeat. By the terms of the Treaty of Paris, France ceded Canada and all territory east of the Mississippi, except for New Orleans, to England. To Spain went New Orleans and France's trans-Mississippi empire. Spain yielded Florida to England. For the interior tribes, only one source of trade goods remained. Two centuries of European rivalry for control of eastern North America ended abruptly. Iroquois, Cherokee, Creek, and other interior peoples were now forced to adjust to this reality.

After concluding peace with the French, the English government launched a new policy in North America designed to separate Native Americans and colonizers by creating a racial boundary roughly following the crestline of the Appalachian Mountains from Maine to Georgia. The Proclamation of 1763 ordered the colonial governors to reserve all land west of the line for Indian nations. White settlers already living beyond the Appalachians were charged to withdraw to the east.

Though well intended, this attempt to legislate interracial accord failed completely. Even before the proclamation was issued, the Ottawa chief Pontiac was organizing a pan-Indian movement to drive the British out of the Ohio valley. Although his plan collapsed in 1764, it served notice that the interior tribes would fight for their lands.

The English government could not enforce its racial separation policy. Staggering under an immense wartime debt, England decided to maintain only small army garrisons in America to regulate the interior. Nor could royal governors stop land speculators and settlers from privately purchasing land from trans-Appalachian tribes or from simply encroaching on their land. Under such circumstances, the western frontier seethed with tension after 1763.

While the Seven Years' War marked an epic victory of Anglo-American arms over the French and redrew the map of North America, it also had important social and economic effects on colonial society. The war convinced the colonists of their growing strength yet left them debt-ridden and weakened in manpower. The wartime economy spurred economic development and poured British capital into the colonies yet rendered them more vulnerable to cyclic fluctuations in the British economy.

Military contracts, for example, brought prosperity to most colonies during the war years. Huge orders for ships, arms, uniforms, and provisions enriched northern merchants and provided good prices for farmers as well.

The war, however, required heavy taxes and took a huge human toll. The magnitude of the human losses in Boston indicates the war's impact. The wartime muster lists show that nearly every working-class Bostonian tasted military service at some point during the long war. When peace came, Boston had a deficit of almost 700 men in a town of about 2,000 families. The high rate of war widowhood produced a feminization of poverty and required expanded poor relief for the maintenance of husbandless women and fatherless children.

Peace ended the casualties but also brought depression. After the British forces left the American theater in 1760, the economy slumped badly, especially in the coastal towns. The greatest hardships fell on laboring people, although even some wealthy merchants went bankrupt. In Philadelphia, many poor people, unable to pay their property taxes, were "disposing of their huts and lots to others more wealthy than themselves." A New York artisan expressed a common lament in 1762. Although he still had employment, he had fallen into poverty and found it "beyond my ability to support my family . . . [which] can scarcely appear with decency or have necessaries to subsist." His situation, he added, "is really the case with many of the inhabitants of this city."

In spite of its heavy casualties and economic repercussions, the Seven Years' War paved the way for a far larger conflict in the next generation. The legislative assemblies, for example, which had been flexing their muscles at the expense of the governors in earlier decades, accelerated their bid for political power. During wartime, knowing that their governors must obtain military appropriations, they extracted concessions as the price for raising revenues. The war also trained a new group of military and political leaders. In carrying out military operations on a scale unknown in the colonies and in shouldering heavier political responsibilities, men such as George Washington, Samuel Adams, Benjamin Franklin, Patrick Henry, and Christopher Gadsden acquired the experience that would serve them well in the future.

The Seven Years' War, in spite of the severe costs, left many of the colonists with a sense of buoyancy. New Englanders rejoiced at the final victory over the "Papist enemy of the North." Frontiersmen, fur traders, and land speculators also celebrated the French withdrawal, for the West now appeared open for exploitation. The colonists also felt a new sense of their identity after the war. Surveying a world free of French and Spanish threats, they could not help but reassess the advantages and disadvantages of subordination to England.

THE CRISIS WITH ENGLAND

George Grenville became the chief minister of England's 25-year-old king, George III, at the end of the Seven Years' War. Struggling to reduce the large national debt, Grenville proposed new taxes in England and others in North America, where the colonists were asked to bear their share of running the empire. Grenville's particu-

lar concern was financing the 10,000 British regulars left in North America after 1763 to police French-speaking Canada and the frontier. His revenue program initiated a rift between England and its colonies that a dozen years later would culminate in revolution.

Sugar, Currency, and Stamps

In 1764, Grenville pushed through Parliament several bills that in combination pressed hard against the economic system of the colonies. First came the Revenue Act (or Sugar Act) of 1764, which imposed new taxes on the colonies and tightened up enforcement of old taxes. The new law reduced the tax on imported French molasses from six to three pence per gallon and added a number of colonial products to the list of commodities that could be sent only to England. It required American shippers to post bonds guaranteeing observance of the trade regulations before loading their cargoes. Finally, it strengthened the vice-admiralty courts, where violators of the trade acts were prosecuted.

Many of the colonial legislatures grumbled about the Sugar Act because a strictly enforced duty of three pence per gallon on molasses pinched more than the loosely enforced six-pence duty. But only New York objected that *any* tax by Parliament to raise revenue (rather than to control trade) violated the rights of overseas English subjects who were unrepresented in Parliament. On the heels of the Sugar Act came the Currency Act, which forbade the colonies to issue paper money as legal tender. In a colonial economy chronically short of hard cash, this constricted trade.

The move to tighten up the machinery of empire confused the colonists because many of the new regulations came from Parliament, which had heretofore been content to allow the king, his ministers, and the Board of Trade to run overseas affairs. In a world where history taught that power and liberty were perpetually at war, generations of colonists had viewed Parliament as a bastion of English liberty, the bulwark against despotic political rule. The Parliament on which colonial legislatures had modeled themselves now began to seem like a violator of colonial rights.

After Parliament passed the Sugar Act in 1764, Grenville announced his intention to extend to America the stamp duties that had already been imposed in England. However, he gave the colonies a year to suggest alternative ways of raising revenue. The colonies objected strenuously to the proposed stamp tax, but none provided another plan. The Stamp Act, effective November 1765, required revenue stamps on every newspaper, pamphlet, almanac, legal document, liquor license, college diploma, pack of playing cards, and pair of dice.

Colonial reaction to the Stamp Act ranged from disgruntled submission to mass defiance. In many cases, resistance involved not only discontent over England's tightening of the screws on the American colonies but also internal resentments born out of the play of local events. Especially in the cities, the defiance of authority and destruction of property by people from the middle and lower ranks redefined the dynamics of politics, setting the stage for a ten-year internal struggle for control among the various social elements alarmed by the new English policies.

Stamp Act Riots

The Virginia House of Burgesses was the first legislature to react to the news of the Stamp Act, which arrived in April 1765. In May, led by 29-year-old Patrick Henry, a fiery lawyer newly elected from a frontier county, the House of Burgesses debated seven strongly worded resolutions. Old-guard burgesses regarded some of them as treasonable. The legislature finally adopted the four more moderate resolves, including one proclaiming Virginia's right to impose taxes. They rejected the other resolves,

which declared it "illegal, unconstitutional, and unjust" for anybody outside Virginia to lay taxes, asserted that Virginians did not have to obey any externally imposed tax law, and labeled as "an enemy to this, his Majesty's colony," anyone denying Virginia's exclusive right to tax its inhabitants. But within a month, all seven resolutions were broadcast in the newspapers of other colonies.

Governor Francis Bernard of Massachusetts called the Virginia resolves "an alarm bell for the disaffected." The events in Boston in August 1765 amply confirmed his view. On August 14, Bostonians reduced the luxurious mansion of stamp distributor Andrew Oliver to a shambles. Twelve days later, the shoemaker Ebenezer MacIntosh led the crowd again in attacks on the handsomely appointed homes of two British officials and Lieutenant-Governor Thomas Hutchinson. Military men "who have seen towns sacked by the enemy," one observer reported, "declare they never before saw an instance of such fury."

In attacking the property of men associated with the stamp tax, the Boston crowd demonstrated its opposition to parliamentary policy. But the crowd was also expressing hostility toward a local elite that for years had disdained lower-class political participation and had publicly denounced the working poor for their supposed lack of industry and frugality. For decades, ordinary Bostonians had aligned politically with the Boston "caucus," which led the colony's "popular party" against conservative aristocrats such as Hutchinson and Oliver. But the "rage-intoxicated rabble" had suddenly broken away from the leaders of the popular party and gone further than they had intended. The more cautious political leaders knew that they would have to struggle to regain control of the protest movement.

Violent protest against the Stamp Act also wracked New York and Newport, Rhode Island. Leading the resistance were groups calling themselves the Sons of Liberty, composed mostly of

From the time of his election to the Virginia House of Burgesses at the age of 29, Patrick Henry was an outspoken proponent of American rights. In this portrait, he pleads a case at a county courthouse crowded with local planters.

artisans, shopkeepers, and ordinary citizens. Protest took a more dignified form at the Stamp Act Congress, called by Massachusetts and attended by representatives of nine colonies, who met in New York in October 1765. The delegates formulated 12 restrained resolutions that accepted Parliament's right to legislate for the colonies but denied its right to tax them directly unless they had representation in the law-making body.

All over America by late 1765, effigy-burning crowds had convinced stamp distributors to resign their commissions. Some colonists defied

English authority even more directly by forcing most customs officers and court officials to open the ports and courts for business after November 1 without using the hated stamps required after that date. In March 1766, Parliament bowed to expediency and repealed the hated Stamp Act. The crisis had passed, yet nothing was really solved.

In the course of challenging parliamentary authority, the Stamp Act resisters politicized their communities as never before. The established leaders, generally cautious in their protests, were often displaced by those beneath them on the social ladder. Scribbled John Adams in his diary: "The people have become more attentive to their liberties, . . . and more determined to defend them."

An Uncertain Interlude

Ministerial instability in England hampered the quest for a coherent, workable American policy. Attempting to be a strong king, George III chose ministers who commanded little respect in Parliament. This led to strife between Parliament and the king's chief ministers; that in turn led to a shuffling of chief ministers and to a chaotic political situation at the very time that the king was attempting to overhaul the administration of the empire.

To manage the colonies more effectively, the Pitt-Grafton ministry that the king appointed in 1767 obtained new laws to reorganize the customs service, establish a secretary of state for American affairs, and install three new vice-admiralty courts in the port cities. Still hard pressed for revenue, the ministry also pushed through Parliament the Townshend duties on paper, lead, painters' colors, and tea. A final law suspended New York's assembly until that body ceased its noncompliance with the Quartering Act of 1765. This law not only required public funds for support of British troops garrisoned in the colonies but also spelled out how the colonial assemblies should allocate public funds for that purpose. Many colonists resented these new regulations, which they saw as more taxation without representation, but only the Massachusetts and New York assemblies refused to vote the mandated supplies to the troops.

Colonial reaction to the Townshend Acts, centered in Massachusetts, was more restrained than in 1765. New York buckled under to the Quartering Act rather than see its assembly suspended. But the Massachusetts House of Representatives sent a circular letter to each colony objecting to the new Townshend duties, small though they were. Written by Samuel Adams, the letter attacked as unconstitutional the plan to underwrite salaries for royal officials in America from customs duties.

"The Americans have made a discovery," declared Edmund Burke before Parliament, "that we mean to oppress them; we have made a discovery that they intend to raise a rebellion. We do not know how to advance; they do not know how to retreat."

While most of the colonists only grumbled and petitioned, Bostonians protested angrily. In the summer of 1768, after customs officials seized a sloop owned by John Hancock for a violation of the trade regulations, an angry crowd mobbed them. They fled to a British warship in Boston harbor and remained there for months. The newspapers warned of new measures designed "to suck the life blood" from the people and predicted that troops would be sent "to dragoon us into passive obedience."

Troops indeed came. The attack on the customs officials brought a resolute response from England. The ministry dispatched two regiments from England and two more from Nova Scotia. On October 1, 1768, red-coated troops marched into Boston without resistance.

After the troops occupied Boston, the colonists' main tactic of protest against the Townshend Acts became economic boycott. First in Boston and then in New York and Philadelphia, merchants and consumers adopted nonimportation and nonconsumption agreements. They pledged neither to import nor to use British articles. These measures promised to bring the politically influential English merchants to their aid, for half of British shipping was engaged in commerce with the colonies, and one-quarter of all English exports were consumed there.

Many colonial merchants, however, did not wish to support the boycott and had to be persuaded to comply by street brigades. Crowd action welled up again in the seaports, as determined patriot bands attacked the homes and warehouses of offending merchants and "rescued" incoming contraband goods seized by zealous customs officials. When the southern colonies also adopted nonimportation agreements in 1768, a new step toward intercolonial union had been taken.

England's attempts to discipline its American colonies and oblige them to share the costs of governing an empire lay in shambles by the end of the 1760s. The Townshend duties had failed miserably, yielding less than £21,000 by 1770 while costing British business £700,000 through the colonial nonimportation movement.

In London, on March 5, 1770, Parliament repealed all the Townshend duties except the one on tea. On that same evening in Boston, British troops fired on an unruly crowd of heckling citizens. When the smoke cleared, five bloody bodies lay dead in the snow-covered street. Among them were Ebenezer MacIntosh's brother-in-law and Crispus Attucks, a runaway slave who may have been the first black to lose his life in the American struggle against British authority. Bowing to furious popular reaction, Thomas Hutchinson, recently appointed governor, ordered the British troops out of town and arrested the commanding officer and the soldiers involved. They were later acquitted, with two young local lawyers, John Adams and Josiah Quincy, Jr., providing a brilliant defense.

The Growing Rift

After the "Boston massacre," opposition to English policies subsided for a time. From 1770 to 1772, relative quiet descended over the colonies. Not until June 1772 did England provide another inflammatory issue. Then, by announcing that it would pay the salaries of the royal governor and superior court judges in Massachusetts rather than allow the provincial legislature to continue supporting these positions, the Crown created a new furor. Even though the measure saved the colony money, it was seen as a dangerous innovation because it undermined a right set forth in the colony's charter. Judges paid from London, it was assumed, would respond to London.

Boston's town meeting protested loudly and created a Committee of Correspondence "to state the rights of the colonists . . . and to communicate and publish the same to the several towns and to the world." Crown supporters called the committee "the foulest, sublest, and most venomous serpent ever issued from the egg of sedition." By the end of 1772, another 80 towns in Massachusetts had created committees. In the next year, all but three colonies established Committees of Correspondence in their legislatures.

Samuel Adams was by now the leader of the Boston radicals. A man with deep roots among the laboring people despite his Harvard degree, he organized the working ranks through the taverns, clubs, and volunteer fire companies and also secured the support of wealthy merchants such as John Hancock. In England, Adams became known as one of the most dangerous firebrands in America.

In 1772, a band of Rhode Island colonists gave Adams new material to work with when they attacked a royal warship. The British commander of the *Gaspee* was roundly hated for hounding the fishermen and small traders of Narragansett Bay. When his ship ran aground, Rhode Islanders boarded the stranded vessel and burned it to the water's edge. A Rhode Island court then convicted the *Gaspee*'s captain of illegally seizing what he was convinced was smuggled sugar and rum. The government in London reacted with cries of high treason. Finding the lips of Rhode Islanders sealed regarding the identity of the arsonists, an investigating committee could do little. The event was tailor-made for Samuel Adams, who used it to "awaken the American colonies, which have been too long dozing upon the brink of ruin."

In early 1773, Parliament's passage of the Tea Act precipitated the final plunge into revolution. The act allowed the East India Company, which was on the verge of bankruptcy, to ship its tea directly to America. By eliminating English middlemen and English import taxes, this pro-

British Exports to North America, 1756-1775

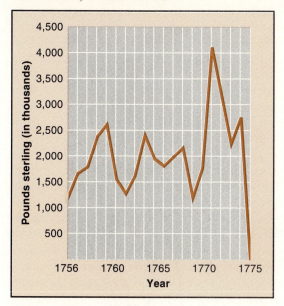

Source: U.S. Bureau of the Census.

vided Americans with the opportunity to buy their tea cheaply from the company's agents in the colonies. Even with the small tax to be paid in the colonies, Indian tea would now undersell smuggled Dutch tea.

Parliament monumentally miscalculated the American response. For several years, merchants in Philadelphia and New York had been flagrantly smuggling Dutch tea. As a consequence, imports of English tea plummeted. The merchants bitterly denounced the new act for giving the East India Company a monopoly on the North American tea market. Many colonists also objected that the government was shrewdly trying to gain implicit acceptance of Parliament's taxing power by offering tea at a new reduced rate. When Americans drank the taxed tea, they would also be swallowing the English right to impose taxes. Mass meetings in the port towns soon forced the resignation of the East India

Company's agents, and citizens vowed to stop the obnoxious tea at the water's edge.

Governor Hutchinson of Massachusetts brought the tea crisis to a climax. The popular party led by Samuel Adams wanted to send the tea back to England, but Hutchinson refused to grant the tea ships clearance papers to return to England with their cargoes. Finally, a band of Bostonians, dressed as Indians, boarded the tea ships at nightfall, broke open the chests of tea, and flung £10,000 worth of the East India Company's property into Boston harbor. Lord North, the king's chief minister, now argued that the dispute was no longer about taxes but about whether England had any authority at all over the colonies.

Thoroughly aroused by the Boston Tea Party, Parliament passed the Coercive Acts, which Bostonians promptly labeled the "Intolerable Acts." The acts closed the port of Boston to all shipping until the colony paid for the destroyed tea. They declared British soldiers and officials immune from local court trials for acts committed while suppressing civil disturbances. Parliament amended the Massachusetts charter to transform the council from an upper legislative chamber, elected by the lower house, to a body appointed by the governor. The acts also authorized the governor to prohibit all town meetings except for one annual meeting in each town to elect local officers of government. Finally, General Thomas Gage, commander in chief of British forces in America, replaced Thomas Hutchinson as governor. The Americans now found their maneuvering room severely narrowed.

When the Intolerable Acts arrived in May 1774, Boston's town meeting reacted belligerently. It dispatched a circular letter to all the colonies urging an end to trade with England. This met with faint support. But a second call, for a meeting in Philadelphia of delegates from all colonies, received a better response. The Continental Congress, as it was called, now began to transform a ten-year debate on constitutional rights conducted by separate colonies into a unified American cause.

Fifty-five delegates from all the colonies except Georgia converged on Carpenter's Hall in Philadelphia in September 1774. None were advocating American independence at this time. The discussions centered not on how to prepare for a war that many sensed was inevitable but on how to resolve differences that most delegates feared were irreconcilable.

Some delegates, led by cousins Samuel and John Adams from Massachusetts and Richard Henry Lee and Patrick Henry of Virginia, argued for outright resistance to Parliament's Coercive Acts. Moderate delegates from the middle colonies, led by Joseph Galloway of Pennsylvania and James Duane of New York, urged restraint and further attempts at reconciliation. After weeks of debate, the delegates agreed to issue a restrained Declaration of Rights and Resolves, which attempted to define American grievances and to justify the colonists' defiance of English policies and laws by appealing to the "immutable laws of nature, the principles of the English constitution, and the several [colonial] charters and compacts" under which they lived. More concrete was the Congress's agreement on a plan of resistance. If England did not rescind the Intolerable Acts by December 1, 1774, a ban on all imports and exports between the colonies and Great Britain, Ireland, and the British West Indies would take effect. Some exceptions were made for the export of southern staple commodities in order to keep reluctant southern colonies in the fold.

By the time the Congress adjourned in late October, Boston's cause had been transformed into a national movement. Patrick Henry declared, "The distinctions between Virginians, Pennsylvanians, New Yorkers, and New Englanders are no more. I am not a Virginian, but an American." Many of Henry's fellow delegates were more bound to their provincial identities, but in adjourning, the Congress agreed to reconvene in May 1775.

Even before the Second Continental Con-

Liberty always had to struggle against power, as American colonists saw it; in this cartoon, England (power) forces Liberty (America in the form of a woman) to drink the "Bitter Draught" of tea. Uncompliant, America spits the tea into England's face while another corrupt Englishman peeks under her petticoat.

gress met, the fabric of government had been badly torn in most colonies. Revolutionary committees, conventions, and congresses, entirely unauthorized by law, were replacing legal governing bodies. Assuming authority in defiance of royal governors, these extralegal bodies created and armed militia units, promoted observance of boycotts, levied taxes, operated the courts, and obstructed the work of English customs officials. By the end of 1774, all but three colonies defied their own charters by appointing provincial assemblies without royal authority. In the next year, this independently created power became evident in the nearly complete cessation of trade with England.

The Final Rupture

The final spark to the revolutionary powder keg was struck in early 1775. General Thomas Gage had assumed the governorship of Massachusetts 11 months earlier and occupied Boston with 4,000 troops—one for every adult male in the town. Ordered to arrest the leaders of the Boston insurrection, Gage sent 700 redcoats under cover of night to seize colonial arms and ammunition in nearby Concord. But Americans learned of the plan. When the troops reached Lexington at dawn, 70 "Minutemen"—townsmen available on a minute's notice—occupied the village green. In the skirmish that ensued, 18 Massachusetts farmers fell, 8 of them mortally wounded.

Marching six miles west, the British entered Concord, where another firefight broke out. Withdrawing, the redcoats made their way back to Boston, harassed by militiamen firing from farmhouses and barns and from behind stone walls. Before the bloody day ended, 273 British and 95 Americans lay dead or wounded. News of the bloodshed swept through the colonies. Within weeks, thousands of men besieged the British troops in Boston. One colonist reported that wherever one traveled, "you see the inhabitants training, making firelocks, casting mortars, shells, and shot."

The outbreak of fighting vastly altered the debates of the Second Continental Congress, which assembled in Philadelphia in May 1775. New delegates included Boston's wealthy merchant, John Hancock; a tall, young planter-lawyer from Virginia, Thomas Jefferson; and the much-applauded Benjamin Franklin, who had arrived from London only four days before the Congress convened.

The Congress had no power to legislate or command; it could only request and recommend. But setting to work, it authorized a continental army of 20,000 and chose George Washington as commander in chief. It issued a "Declaration of Causes of Taking-up Arms," sent the king an "Olive Branch Petition" humbly begging him to remove the obstacles to reconciliation, made moves to secure the neutrality of the interior Indian tribes, issued paper money, erected a postal system, and approved plans for a military hospital.

While debate continued over whether the colonies ought to declare themselves independent, military action grew hotter. The hotheaded Ethan Allen and his Green Mountain boys from eastern New York captured Fort Ticonderoga, controlling the Champlain valley, in May 1775. On New Year's Day in 1776, the British shelled Norfolk, Virginia. In March 1776, Washington's army forced the British to evacuate Boston. Hope for reconciliation with England crumbled at the end of 1775 when news arrived that the king, rejecting the Olive Branch Petition, had dispatched 20,000 additional British troops to quell the American insurrection and had proclaimed the colonies in "open and avowed rebellion." Those fatal words made all the Congress's actions treasonable and turned all who obeyed them into traitors.

By the time Thomas Paine's hard-hitting pamphlet *Common Sense* appeared in Philadelphia on January 9, 1776, members of the Congress were talking less gingerly about independence. Paine's blunt words and compelling rhetoric smashed through the remaining reserve. "O ye that love mankind! Ye that dare oppose not only the tyranny, but also the tyrant, stand forth!" wrote Paine. Within weeks the pamphlet was in bookstalls all over the colonies. "The public sentiment which a few weeks before had shuddered at the tremendous obstacles, with which independence was envisioned," declared Edmund Randolph of Virginia, now "overleaped every barrier."

The Continental Congress continued to debate independence during the spring of 1776, even as the war became bloodier. When an American assault on Quebec failed in May 1776, England embargoed all trade to the colonies and ordered the seizure of American ships. That convinced the Congress to declare its ports open to all countries. "Nothing is left now," Joseph Hewes of North Carolina admitted, "but to fight it out." On June 9 the Congress ordered a committee chaired by Jefferson to begin drafting a declaration of independence.

The declaration was not a highly original statement. It drew heavily on the addresses that the Congress had been issuing to justify American resistance, and it presented a theory of government that was embedded in the scores of pamphlets that had issued from the colonial presses over the previous decade. Jefferson's committee brought its handiwork before the Congress on June 28. On July 2, twelve delegations voted for the declaration, with New York's abstaining, thus allowing the Congress to say that the vote for independence was unanimous. Two days more were spent cutting and polishing the document.

In eloquent terms, the document declared that "all men are created equal" and "are endowed by their Creator with certain inalienable rights," including "life, liberty, and the pursuit of happiness." Governments rule by consent of the governed, and if a government becomes unjust and oppressive, the citizens have a right to "alter or abolish" it. After enumerating the many injuries inflicted on the colonies by the unjust British king, who was termed "unfit to be the ruler of a free people," the document finally declared the united colonies, or "United States of America," totally independent of Great Britain. On July 4, Congress sent the Declaration of Independence to the printer.

THE IDEOLOGY OF REVOLUTIONARY REPUBLICANISM

In the years after 1763, the colonists pieced together a political ideology, borrowed partly from English political thought, partly from the theories of the Enlightenment, and partly from their own experiences. Historians call this new ideology "revolutionary republicanism." But it is important to understand that because the colonists varied widely in interests and experiences, there was never a single coherent ideology to which they all subscribed.

A Plot Against Liberty

Many American colonists subscribed to the notion advanced by earlier English Whig writers that corrupt and power-hungry men were slowly extinguishing the lamp of liberty in England. The so-called "country" party represented by these Whig pamphleteers proclaimed itself the guardian of the true principles of the English constitution and opposed the "court" party representing the king and his appointees.

Every ministerial policy and parliamentary act in the decade after the Stamp Act appeared as a subversion of English liberties. The belief that England was carrying out "a deep-laid and desperate plan of imperial despotism . . . for the extinction of all civil liberty," as the Boston town meeting expressed it in 1770, spread rapidly in the next few years. By 1774, John Adams was writing of "the conspiracy against the public liberty [that] was first regularly formed and begun to be executed in 1763 and 1764." From London, America's favorite writer, Benjamin Franklin, described the "extreme corruption prevalent among all orders of men in this old rotten state."

Among many Americans, especially merchants, the attack on constitutional rights blended closely with the threats to their economic interests contained in the tough new trade policies. Merchants perceived a coordinated attack on their "lives, liberties, and property," as they frequently phrased it. Others saw in revolution an opportunity to restore and strengthen virtue in American life.

Revitalizing American Society

Many colonists believed that the growing commercial connection with the decadent and corrupt mother country was injecting deadly fluids into the American bloodstream. They worried about the luxury and vice they saw around them and came to believe that the resistance to England would return American society to a state of civic virtue, spartan living, and godly purpose.

The fervent support of the patriot movement by much of the colonial clergy, especially in New England, helped give a high-toned moral character to colonial protest. The notion of moral regeneration through battle against a corrupt enemy ennobled the cause.

The growth of a revolutionary spirit among common people also owed much to the plain style of polemical writers such as Thomas Paine and Patrick Henry. Paine's *Common Sense* attacked the idea of monarchy itself. Its astounding popularity—it sold more copies than any printed piece in colonial history—stemmed not only from its argument but also from its style. Paine wrote for the common people, using plain language and assuming their knowledge of nothing more than the Bible. He appealed to millennial yearnings: "We have it in our power to begin the world over again," if only the Americans would stand up for liberty, the goddess whom "Europe regards . . . like a stranger, and England hath given . . . warning to depart." Many Whig leaders denounced Paine as "crack-

brained," but thousands who read or listened to *Common Sense* were radicalized by it and came to believe not only that independence could be wrested from England but also that a new social and political order could be created in North America.

THE TURMOIL OF REVOLUTIONARY SOCIETY

The long struggle with England over colonial rights between 1764 and 1776 did not occur in a unified society. Social and economic change, which accelerated in the late colonial period, brought deep unrest and calls for reform from many quarters.

As agitation against English policy intensified, previously acquiescent people took a more active interest in politics. Groups emerged— slaves, urban laboring people, backcountry farmers, evangelicals, women—who enunciated goals of their own that were sometimes only loosely connected to the struggle with England. The stridency and potential power of these groups raised for many upper-class leaders the frightening specter of a radically changed society. Losing control of the protests they had initially led, many of them would abandon the resistance movement against England.

Urban People

Although the cities contained only about 5 percent of the colonial population, they formed the vital cores of revolutionary agitation. They led the way in protesting English policy, and they soon contained the most politicized citizens in America. Local politics could be rapidly transformed as the struggle against England became enmeshed with calls for internal reform.

In Philadelphia, for example, economic difficulties in the 1760s and 1770s led craftsmen to band together within their craft and their community. Artisans played a central role in forging

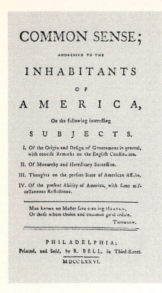

In Common Sense, *Thomas Paine dared to articulate, in plain but muscular language, the thoughts of rebellion and independence that others had only alluded to.*

a nonimportation agreement in 1768, calling public meetings, publishing newspaper appeals, organizing secondary boycotts against foot-dragging merchants, and ferreting out and tarring and feathering opponents to their policies. By 1772, artisans were filling elected municipal positions and insisting on their right to participate equally with their social superiors in nominating assemblymen and other important office-holders.

By 1774, working-class intermeddling in state affairs had taken a bold new step—the de facto assumption of governmental powers by committees called into being by the people at large. Craftsmen had first clothed themselves in such extralegal authority in policing the nonimportation agreement in 1769. Five years later, in response to the Intolerable Acts, they put forward a radical slate of candidates for a committee to enforce a new economic boycott. Their ticket drubbed one nominated by the city's conservative merchants.

The political mobilization of laboring Philadelphians continued as the impasse with England reached a climax in 1775. Many pacifist Quaker leaders of the city had abandoned politics by this time, and other conservative merchants had also concluded that mob rule had triumphed. Into the leadership vacuum stepped a group of radicals from the middling ranks: the fiery Scots-Irish doctor Thomas Young, who had agitated in Boston and Albany before migrating to Philadelphia; Timothy Matlack, a hardware retailer who was popular with the lower class for matching his prize bantam cocks against those of New York's aristocratic James Delancy; James Cannon, a young schoolteacher; Benjamin Rush, whose new medical practice took him into the garrets and cramped rooms of the city's poor; and Thomas Paine, a recent immigrant seeking something better in America than he had found as an ill-paid excise officer in England.

The political support of the new radical leaders was centered in the 31 companies of the Philadelphia militia, composed mostly of laboring men, and in the extralegal committees now controlling the city's economic life. Their leadership helped to overcome the conservatism of the regularly elected Pennsylvania legislature, which was resisting the movement of the Continental Congress toward independence. In addition, the new radical leaders demanded internal reforms: opening up opportunity; curbing the accumulation of wealth by "our great merchants" who were "making immense fortunes at the expense of the people"; abolishing the property requirement for voting; allowing militiamen to elect their officers; and imposing stiff fines, to be used for the support of the families of poor militiamen, on men who refused militia service.

Mobilization among artisans, laborers, and mariners, in other cities as well as Philadelphia, became part of the chain of events that led toward independence. Whereas most of the patriot elite fought only to change English colonial policy, the populace of the cities also struggled for internal reforms and raised notions of how an independent American society might be reorganized.

Women

Women also played a vital role in the relentless movement toward revolution, and they drew upon revolutionary arguments to define their own goals. Women signed nonimportation agreements, harassed noncomplying merchants, and helped organize "fast days," during which communities prayed for deliverance from English oppression. But the women's most important role was in facilitating the economic boycott of English goods. The success of the nonconsumption pacts depended on substituting homespun cloth for English textiles on which colonists of all classes had always relied. From Georgia to Maine, women and children began spinning yarn and weaving cloth. In 1769, the women of tiny Middletown, Massachusetts, set the standard by weaving 20,522 yards of cloth, about 160 yards each. After the Tea Act in 1773, patriotic women boycotted their favorite drink as well.

Women's perception of their role was also changed by colonial protests and petitions against England's arbitrary uses of power. The more male leaders talked about England's intentions to "enslave" the Americans and England's callous treatment of its colonial "subjects," the more American women began to rethink their own domestic situations. Many American women felt that they too were badly treated "subjects" of their husbands. If there was to be independence, new laws must be passed, Abigail Adams reminded her husband, John, in March 1776. Choosing words and phrases that had been used over and over in the protests against England, she wrote: "Do not put such unlimited power into the hand of the husbands. . . . Put it out of the power of the vicious and the lawless to use us with cruelty and indignity," she insisted. "Remember, all men would be tyrants if they could." Abigail Adams warned that American women "will not hold ourselves bound by any laws in which we have no voice, or representation" and even promised that women would "foment a rebellion" if men did not heed their rightful claims.

Nothing came of Abigail Adams's plea on behalf of women, for there was no women's movement to take up her cause. The issues she raised about women's lack of power in society and in the family were largely ignored until the middle of the next century.

Protesting Farmers

In most of the agricultural areas of the colonies, where many settlers made their livelihoods, passions concerning English policies were aroused only slowly. After about 1740, farmers had benefited from a sharp rise in the demand for foodstuffs in England, southern Europe, and the West Indies. Living far from harping English customs officers, impressment gangs, and occupying armies, the colonists of the interior had to be drawn gradually into the resistance movement by their urban cousins. Even in Concord, Massachusetts, only a dozen miles from the center of colonial agitation, townspeople found little to protest in English policies until England closed the port of Boston in 1774.

Yet some parts of rural America seethed with social tension in the prewar era. The dynamics of conflict, shaped by the social development of particular regions, eventually became part of the momentum for revolution. In three western counties of North Carolina and in the Hudson River valley of New York, for example, widespread civil disorder marked the pre-Revolutionary decades. The militant rhetoric and tactics small farmers used to combat exploitation formed rivulets that fed the main stream of revolutionary consciousness.

For years, the small farmers of western North Carolina had suffered exploitation by corrupt county court officials appointed by the governor and a legislature dominated by eastern planter interests. Sheriffs and justices, allied with land speculators and lawyers, seized property when farmers could not pay their taxes and sold it, often at a fraction of its worth, to their cronies. In the mid-1760s, frustrated at getting no satisfaction from legal forms of protest, the farmers formed associations of so-called Regulators that forcibly closed the courts, attacked the property of their enemies, and whipped and publicly humiliated judges and lawyers. When their leaders were arrested, the Regulators stormed the jails and released them.

In 1768 and again in 1771, Governor William Tryon led troops against the Regulators, who were finally defeated. Seven leaders were executed in the ensuing trials. Though the Regulators lost on the field of battle, their protest against the self-interested behavior of a wealthy elite became part of the larger revolutionary struggle.

Rural insurgency in New York flared up in the 1750s and again in 1766 over land rights. The Hudson River valley had long been controlled by a few wealthy families with enormous landholdings, which they leased to small tenant farmers. The Van Rensselaer manor totaled a million acres, the Phillipses' manor nearly half as much. When tenants resisted rent increases or purchased land from Indians who swore that manor lords had extended the boundaries of their manors by fraud, the landlords began evicting their leaseholders.

The landlords had the power of government, including control of the courts, on their side, so the tenants, like the Carolina Regulators, went outside the law. By 1766, while New York City was absorbed in the Stamp Act furor, tenants led by William Prendergast began resisting sheriffs who tried to evict tenants from lands they claimed. The militant tenants threatened landlords with death and broke open jails to rescue their friends. British troops from New York were used to break the tenant rebellion. Prendergast was tried and sentenced to be hanged, beheaded, and quartered. Although he was pardoned, the bitterness of the Hudson River tenants endured through the Revolution, when most of them, unlike the Carolina Regulators, fought with the British because their landlords had joined the patriot cause.

CONCLUSION

FORGING A REVOLUTION

The Seven Years' War nurtured the colonists' sense of separate identity. Yet it left them with difficult economic adjustments, heavy debts, and growing social divisions. The Treaty of Paris in 1763 led to a reorganization of England's triumphant yet debt-torn empire that had profound repercussions in North America.

In the pre-Revolutionary decade, a dual disillusionment penetrated ever deeper into the colonial consciousness. Pervasive doubt arose concerning both the colonies' role, as assigned by England, in the economic life of the empire and the sensitivity of the government in London to the colonists' needs. At the same time, the colonists began to perceive British policies—instituted by Parliament, the king, and his advisers—as a systematic attack on the fundamental liberties and natural rights of British subjects in America.

The fluidity and diversity of colonial society and the differing experiences of Americans during and after the Seven Years' War evoked varying responses to the disruption that accompanied the English reorganization of the empire. In the course of resisting English policy, many previously inactive groups entered public life to challenge gentry control of political affairs. Often occupying the most radical ground in the opposition to England, they simultaneously challenged the growing concentration of economic and political power in their own communities.

When the Congress turned the 15-month undeclared war into a formally declared struggle for national liberation in July 1776, it steered its compatriots onto turbulent and unknown seas.

Recommended Reading

Further knowledge of the long, exhausting wars of empire that embroiled the colonies for four generations before 1763 can be derived from Douglas E. Leach, *Arms for Empire* (1973); and William Eccles, *The Canadian Frontier,* rev. ed. (1983).

The administration of the British Empire and the advent of the Seven Years' War are addressed in Michael Kammen, *Empire and Interest* (1970); and Francis Jennings, *Empire of Fortune: Crown, Colonies, and Tribes in the Seven Years' War in America* (1988).

For different points of view on the origins of the American Revolution, see Bernard Bailyn, *The Ideological Origins of the American Revolution* (1967);

Gary B. Nash, *The Urban Crucible* (1979); Joseph A. Ernst, *Money and Politics in America, 1755–1775* (1973); David Ammerman, *In the Common Cause* (1974); and Pauline Maier, *From Resistance to Rebellion* (1972).

Rich local studies of the Revolutionary crisis include Dirk Hoerder, *Crowd Action in Revolutionary Massachusetts* (1977); and Edward Countryman, *A People in Revolution* (1981). Excellent essays on various aspects of the coming of the Revolution can be found in Alfred F. Young, ed., *The American Revolution* (1976); and Jeffrey J. Crow and Larry E. Tise, eds., *The Southern Experience in the American Revolution* (1978).

Time Line

1696	Parliament establishes Board of Trade
1701	Iroquois set policy of neutrality
1702–1713	Queen Anne's War
1713	Peace of Utrecht
1733	Molasses Act
1744–1748	King George's War
1754	Albany conference
1755	Braddock defeated by French and Indian allies
1756–1763	Seven Years' War
1759	Wolfe defeats the French at Quebec
1759–1761	Cherokee War against the English
1760s	Economic slump
1763	Treaty of Paris ends Seven Years' War Proclamation line limits westward expansion
1764	Sugar and Currency acts
1764	Pontiac's Rebellion in Ohio valley
1765	Colonists resist Stamp Act Virginia House of Burgesses issues Stamp Act resolutions
1766	Declaratory Act Tenant rent war in New York Slave insurrections in South Carolina
1767	Townshend duties imposed
1768	British troops occupy Boston
1770	"Boston Massacre" Townshend duties repealed (except on tea)
1771	North Carolina Regulators defeated
1772	*Gaspee* incident in Rhode Island
1773	Tea Act provokes Boston Tea Party
1774	"Intolerable Acts" First Continental Congress meets
1775	Second Continental Congress meets Battles of Lexington and Concord
1776	Thomas Paine publishes *Common Sense* Declaration of Independence

part 2

A Revolutionary People

1775-1828

The American Revolution not only marked an epic military victory over the powerful mother country but also set the course of national development in ways that still affect American society. Members of the Revolutionary generation were inspired by the idea of building a model society based on principles of freedom and equality. Their attempt to construct a *novus ordo seclorum,* a new order of the ages, continued beyond the Revolutionary era and continues yet today.

Chapter 6, "A People in Revolution," traces the impact of the Revolutionary call to arms on the various groups—male and female, white, black, and Native American—that made up American society and traces the exhilarating yet divisive efforts to fashion a new, republican political order. Chapter 7, "Consolidating the Revolution," examines the critical years of the 1780s, when the new nation struggled to forge national unity following the Revolutionary War and to find security in a hostile Atlantic world. Out of that struggle and the continuing competition for political power in the states emerged a great debate over the new nation's government. That debate led to the replacement of the Articles of Confederation with a new constitution. Learning to live under the new constitution during the 1790s is the focus for Chapter 8, "Creating a Nation."

Chapter 9, "Society and Politics in the Early Republic," delves into the political developments, foreign relations, and Indian-white relations of the first three decades of the nineteenth century.

chapter 6

....

A People in Revolution

Among the Americans wounded and captured at the Battle of Bunker Hill in the spring of 1775 was Lieutenant William Scott of Peterborough, New Hampshire. Asked by his captors how he had come to be a rebel, "Long Bill" Scott replied:

> *The case was this Sir! I lived in a Country Town; I was a Shoemaker, & got [my] living by my labor. When this rebellion came on, I saw some of my neighbors get into commission, who were no better than myself. . . . I was asked to enlist, as a private soldier. My ambition was too great for so low a rank. I offered to enlist upon having a lieutenant's commission, which was granted. I imagined my self now in a way of promotion. If I was killed in battle, there would be an end of me, but if my Captain was killed, I should rise in rank, & should still have a chance to rise higher. These Sir! were the only motives of my entering into the service. For as to the dispute between Great Britain & the colonies, I know nothing of it; neither am I capable of judging whether it is right or wrong.*

People fought in America's Revolutionary War for many reasons: fear, ambition, principle. We have no way of knowing whether Long Bill Scott's motives were typical. Certainly many Americans knew more than he about the colonies' struggle with England. But many did not.

In the spring of 1775, the Revolutionary War had just begun. So, as it turned out, had Long Bill's adventures. When the British evacuated Boston a year later, they transported Scott as a prisoner to Halifax, Nova Scotia. After more than a year's captivity, he managed to escape and make his way home to fight once more. He was recaptured near New York City when its garrison fell to a surprise British assault. Again Scott escaped, this time by swimming the Hudson River at night with his sword tied around his neck and his watch pinned to his hat.

During the winter of 1777, he returned to New Hampshire to recruit his own militia company. It included two of his sons. In the fall, he joined in the defeat of Burgoyne's army near Saratoga, New York, and later took part in the fighting around Newport, Rhode Island. In early 1778, Scott's health broke, and he was permitted to resign from the army. After only a few months, however, he was at it again. During the last year of the war, he served as a volunteer on a navy frigate.

For seven years, the war held Scott in its harsh grasp. Scott's oldest son died of camp fever after six years of service. In 1777, Long Bill sold his New Hampshire farm to meet family expenses. The note he took in exchange turned into a scrap of paper when the dollar of 1777 became worth less than two cents by 1780. He lost a second farm, in Massachusetts, when his military pay depreciated similarly. After his wife died, he helplessly turned their younger children over to his oldest son and set off to beg a pension or job from the government. He was employed by the government as a surveyor when he died of a fever in 1796, near Sandusky in the Ohio country.

American independence and the Revolutionary War that accompanied it were not as hard on everyone as they were on Long Bill Scott, yet together they transformed the lives of countless Americans. The war lasted for seven years, longer than any other of America's wars until Vietnam nearly two centuries later. And unlike the nation's twentieth-century contests, it was fought on American soil, among the American people. It called men by the thousands from shops and fields, disrupted families, killed civilians, spread diseases, and made a shambles of the economy.

While carrying on this struggle for independence, the American people also mounted a political revolution of profound importance. Politics, government, and elections were transformed in keeping with republican principles and the rapidly changing circumstances of political life. What did republican liberty mean? How should governmental power be organized? How democratic should American politics be? These were among the questions with which the American people wrestled at the nation's beginning.

Faced with the twin pressures of war and revolution, people turned increasingly to politics to solve their problems and achieve their goals. As the tempo of political activity increased, they clashed repeatedly over such explosive issues as slavery, the separation of church and state, paper money and debt relief, the regulation of prices, and the toleration of political dissent. They argued as well over the design of new state constitutions and the shape of a new national government. Seldom has America's political agenda been fuller or more troubled.

The American Revolution dominated the lives of all who lived through it. But it had different consequences for men than for women, for black slaves than for their white masters, for Native Americans than for frontier settlers, for overseas merchants than for urban workers, for northern businessmen than for southern planters. Our understanding of the experience out of which our nation emerged must begin with the Revolutionary War, for liberty came at a high cost.

THE WAR FOR AMERICAN INDEPENDENCE

As we know, the war began in Massachusetts in 1775. Within a year, the center of fighting shifted to the middle states. After 1779, the South was the primary theater. Why did this geographic pattern develop, what was its significance, and why did the Americans win?

The War in the North

For a brief time following Lexington and Concord, British officials thought of launching forays out from Boston into the surrounding countryside. They soon reconsidered, however, for the growing size of the continental army and the absence of significant Loyalist strength in the New England region urged caution. Even more important, American artillery on the strategic Dorchester Heights overlooking the city made its continued occupation untenable. On March 7, 1776, the British commander, General William Howe, decided to evacuate.

For a half dozen years after Boston's evacuation, British ships prowled the New England coast, attacking American commerce, confiscating supplies, and destroying towns. Yet away from the coast there was little fighting at all. Most New Englanders had reason to be thankful for their good fortune.

After evacuating Boston, British officials established their military headquarters in New York City, which offered important advantages over Boston. New York was more centrally located, and its spacious harbor lay at the mouth of the Hudson River, the major water route northward into the interior. Control of New York would, in addition, ensure access to the abundant grain and livestock of the Middle Atlantic states. Finally, Loyalist sentiment ran wide and deep among the inhabitants of the city and its environs.

In the summer of 1776, Washington tried to challenge the British for control of Manhattan, but he was outmaneuvered and badly outnumbered. By late October, the city was firmly in British hands. It would remain so until the war's end.

In the fall of 1776, King George III instructed his military commanders in North America to make one last effort at reconciliation with the colonists. When the British demanded that Congress revoke the Declaration of Independence, however, the negotiations collapsed.

For the next two years, the war swept back and forth across New Jersey and Pennsylvania. Reinforced by German mercenaries hired in Europe, the British moved virtually at will. Neither the state militias nor the continental army offered serious opposition. At Trenton in December 1776 and again at Princeton the following month, Washington surprised the British and scored victories that prevented the Americans' collapse. For the rebels, however, survival remained the primary goal.

American efforts during the first year of the war to invade Canada and bring that British colony into the rebellion also fared badly. In November 1775, American forces under General Richard Montgomery had taken Montreal. But the subsequent assault against Quebec ended with almost 100 Americans killed or wounded and more than 300 taken prisoner. The American cause could not survive many such losses.

At New York, Washington had learned the painful lesson that his troops were no match for the British in frontal combat. Thus he adopted a strategy of caution and delay. He would harass the British but avoid major battles. For the remainder of the war, Washington's posture was primarily defensive and reactive.

As a consequence, the war's middle years turned into a deadly chase that neither side proved able to win. In September 1777, the British took Philadelphia, sending the Congress fleeing into the countryside, but then failed to press their advantage. In October, the Americans won a victory at Saratoga, New York, where

Europeans were fascinated by news of the colonies' rebellion against England. Here a French artist offers a dramatic portrayal of the fateful encounter at Lexington in April 1775.

General Burgoyne surrendered with 5,700 British soldiers.

Congress and the Articles of Confederation

As the war erupted around them, members of the Continental Congress turned anxiously to the task of creating a more permanent and effective national government. It was a daunting assignment, for the American people had little experience working together across state lines.

Prior to independence, the colonies had repeatedly quarreled over territory, settlers, control of the fur trade, and commercial advantage within the British Empire. The crisis with England, however, forced them together, and the Continental Congress was the first embodiment of that union. The First Continental Congress sent resolutions of protest to England and functioned as a temporary assembly.

The Second Continental Congress, however, meeting in May 1775, in the midst of a war crisis, began to exercise some of the most basic responsibilities of a sovereign government: raising an army and conducting diplomatic relations. Its powers, though, were unclear, its legitimacy uncertain. As independence and the prospects of an extended war loomed, pressure grew to establish the Congress on a more sound footing. On June 20, 1776, shortly before independence was declared, Congress appointed a committee, chaired by John Dickinson of Pennsylvania, to draw up a plan of perpetual union. It was called the Articles of Confederation. While the war erupted around them, the delegates struggled with the new and difficult problem of creating a permanent government. They clashed over whether to form a strong, consolidated regime or a loosely joined confederation of sovereign states.

The final "Articles of Confederation" represented a compromise. Article 9 gave the Congress sole authority to regulate foreign affairs, declare war, mediate boundary disputes between the states, manage the post office, and administer relations with Indians living outside state boundaries. The Articles also stipulated that the citizens of each state were to enjoy "the privileges and immunities" of the citizens of every other state. Embedded in that clause was the basis for national, as distinguished from state, citizenship.

At the same time, the Articles sharply limited what Congress could do and reserved broad governing powers to the states. For example, the Congress could not raise troops or levy taxes on its own authority. Perhaps most important, Article 2 stipulated that each of the states was to "retain its sovereignty, freedom and independence, and every power, jurisdiction, and right which is not by this confederation expressly delegated to the United States in Congress assembled."

Though the Congress sent the Articles to the states for approval in November 1777, they were not ratified until March 1781. This was primarily because of disputes over the control of lands west of the Appalachian Mountains between states such as Virginia, South Carolina, and New York, which had western claims tracing back to their colonial charters, and states such as Maryland and New Jersey, which had none.

For several years, ratification hung in the balance while politicians and speculators jockeyed for advantage. A breakthrough finally came in 1780, when New York and Virginia agreed to transfer their western lands to the Congress. In early 1781, Maryland became the final state to approve the Articles, and their ratification was assured.

The war did not wait during the struggle over ratification. The Congress did the best it could, using the unratified Articles as a guide. Events, however, quickly proved the inadequacy of the powers allotted to the Congress, since it could do little more than pass resolutions and ask the states for support. If they refused, as they frequently did, the Congress could only protest and urge cooperation. Its ability to function was further limited by the stipulation that each state's delegation cast but one vote. On a number of occasions, disagree-

ments within state delegations prevented them from voting at all. That could paralyze the Congress, since most important decisions required a nine-state majority.

During the war, Washington repeatedly criticized the Congress for its failure to support the army adequately. In 1778, acknowledging its own ineffectiveness, the body temporarily granted Washington extraordinary powers and asked him to manage the war on his own.

The War Moves South

As the war in the North bogged down in a costly stalemate, British officials adopted another strategy: invasion and pacification of the South. Royal officials in the South encouraged the idea with the promise that thousands of Loyalists would rally to the British standard. The southern coastline with its numerous rivers, moreover, offered maximum advantage to British naval strength. Then there were the slaves, that vast but imponderable force in southern society. If they could be lured to the British side, the balance might tip in Britain's favor. Persuaded by these arguments, British policymakers made the southern states the primary theater of military operations during the final years of the war.

Georgia—small, isolated, and largely defenseless—was the initial target. In December 1778, the British took Savannah, Georgia's major port, and on May 12, 1780, they occupied Charleston, South Carolina, after a month's siege. At a cost of only 225 casualties, the British captured the entire 5,400-man American garrison. It was the costliest American defeat of the war. The British then quickly extended their control north and south along the Carolina coast.

Their successes, however, proved deceptive, for British officers quickly learned the difficulty of extending their control into the interior. The distances were too large, the problems of supply too great, the reliability of Loyalist troops too problematic, and support for the Revolutionary cause among the people too strong.

Military Operations in the North, 1776-1780

In October 1780, Washington sent Nathanael Greene south to lead the continental forces, for Greene knew the region and the kind of war that had to be fought. Dividing his army into small, mobile bands, he employed what today would be called guerrilla tactics, harassing the British and their Loyalist allies at every op-portunity, striking by surprise and then disap-pearing into the interior. Bands of private ma-rauders, roving the land and seizing advantage from the war's confusion, compounded the chaos.

In time, the tide began to turn. At Cowpens, South Carolina, in early 1781, American troops

Western Land Claims Ceded by the States, 1782-1802

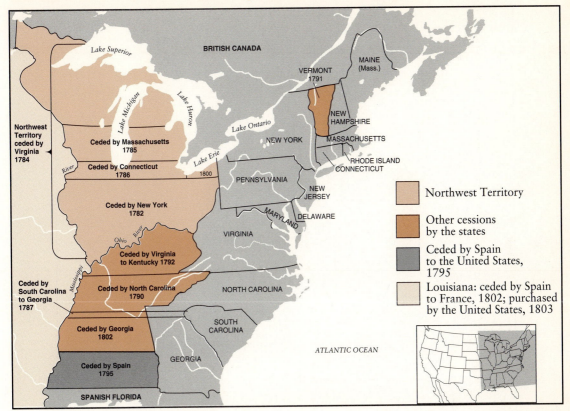

Northwest Territory

Other cessions by the states

Ceded by Spain to the United States, 1795

Louisiana: ceded by Spain to France, 1802; purchased by the United States, 1803

under General Daniel Morgan won a decisive victory. In April 1781, convinced that British authority could not be restored in the Carolinas while Virginia remained a supply and staging area for the rebels, British Commander Cornwallis moved north out of the Carolinas. With a force of 7,500, he raided deep into Virginia. In June, his forces sent Governor Jefferson and the Virginia legislature fleeing from Charlottesville into the mountains. But again Cornwallis had to turn toward the coast for protection and resupply. His goal was Yorktown, where he arrived on August 1.

So long as the British fleet controlled the waters of Chesapeake Bay, his position was secure. That advantage, however, did not last. In 1778, the French government, still smarting from its defeat by England in the Seven Years' War and buoyed by the American victory at Saratoga in 1777, had signed a treaty of alliance with the American Congress, promising to send its naval forces into the war. On August 30, 1781, the French admiral Comte de Grasse arrived off Yorktown. Reinforced by a second French squadron from the North, de Grasse established naval superiority in the region. Cut off from the sea and caught on a peninsula between the York and James rivers by 17,000 French and American troops, Cornwallis found that his fate was sealed. On October 17, 1781, he opened negotiations for surrender.

In Philadelphia, upon hearing of the British surrender, citizens poured into the streets to celebrate while the Congress assembled for a solemn

Military Operations in the South, 1778-1781

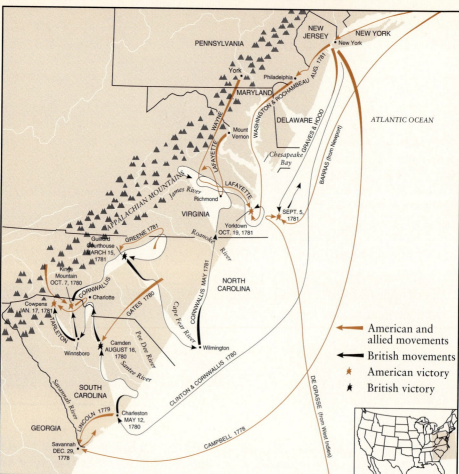

ceremony of thanksgiving. Sporadic fighting continued for another several months; not until November 1782 were the preliminary articles of peace signed. But everyone knew after Yorktown that the war was over. Americans had won their independence.

Native Americans in the Revolution

The Revolutionary War involved more than Englishmen and colonists, for it drew in countless Na-

tive Americans as well. It could hardly have been otherwise, for the lives of all three peoples had been intimately connected since the first white settlements more than a century and a half before.

By the time of the Revolution, the coastal tribes were mostly gone, victims of white settlement and the ravages of European diseases. Between the Appalachian Mountains and the Mississippi River, however, powerful tribes remained. The Iroquois Six Nations, formed into a confederation numbering 15,000 people, controlled the area from Albany, New York, to the

Ohio country and dominated the "western" tribes of the Ohio valley—the Shawnee, Delaware, Wyandotte, and Miami. In the Southeast, five tribes—the Choctaw, Chickasaw, Seminole, Creek, and Cherokee, together numbering 60,000 people—occupied the interior.

When the Revolutionary War began, British and American officials urged neutrality on the Indians. But by the spring of 1776, both sides were actively seeking Indian alliances. Recognizing their immense stake in the Anglo-colonial conflict, Native Americans up and down the interior debated their options. Alarmed by the westward advance of white settlement and eager to take advantage of the colonists' troubles, a band of Cherokee, led by the warrior Dragging Canoe, launched a series of raids in July 1776

against white settlements in what is today eastern Tennessee. In a quick and devastating response, the Virginia and Carolina militias laid waste a group of Cherokee towns.

During the winter of 1780–1781, American militias again attacked the Cherokees. Though the Cherokees raided sporadically throughout the war, they never again mounted a sustained military effort against the patriots. Seeing what had become of their neighbors, the Creek stayed aloof. Their time for resistance would come decades later, when white settlers began to push aggressively onto their lands.

In the Ohio country—the home of the Shawnee, Delaware, Wyandotte, and Miami— white encroachment had begun several decades before the Revolution, with explorers such as

Indian Battles and the War in the West, 1775–1783

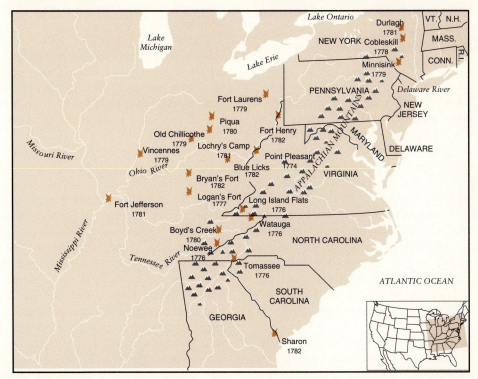

Though most battles were fought along the coastal plain, the British and their Indian allies opened a second front far to the west.

Mohawk chief Joseph Brant (Tayadaneega) played a major role in the Iroquois's decision to enter the war on the side of Britain.

Daniel Boone. The Revolution intensified conflict over control of the land. In February 1778, George Rogers Clark led a ragtag body of Kentuckians through icy rivers and across 180 miles of forbidding terrain to attack an English fort at Vincennes, in present-day Indiana. Though outnumbered nearly four to one by the 500 British regulars and their Indian allies, Clark fooled the British into believing that his force was much larger, and the fort's commander surrendered without a shot. Indians continued to fight sporadically for several years against English and American forces in the region, but Clark's victory tipped the balance in the western theater of the war.

To the northeast, a similar but more deadly scenario unfolded. A council of representatives of the Iroquois Six Nations, meeting at Albany, New York, at first opted for neutrality, but as the war spread and American troops raided deep into Mohawk territory west of Albany in the summer of 1777, most of the Iroquois abandoned neutrality and joined the struggle against the Americans. They did so at the urging of Joseph Brant, a Mohawk warrior who had visited England several years before and argued England's value as an ally against American expansion.

It was a fateful decision for Indians and whites alike. Over the next several years, the Iroquois and their English allies devastated large areas in central New York and Pennsylvania. The Americans' revenge came swiftly. During the summer of 1779, General John Sullivan led a series of raids into Iroquois country, burning the Iroquois villages, killing men, women, and children, and destroying fields of corn. The Iroquois recovered sufficiently to conduct punishing counter-raids during the final years of the war, but their losses in human lives and property were great.

At the peace talks that ended the Revolutionary War, the British entirely ignored the interests of their Indian allies. They received neither compensation for their losses nor any guarantees of their land, for the boundary of the United States was set far to the west, at the Mississippi River.

Negotiating Peace

In September 1781, formal peace negotiations began in Paris between the British commissioner and the American emissaries, Benjamin Franklin, John Adams, and John Jay. The negotiations were complicated by the fact that several European countries, seeking opportunity to weaken Great Britain, had become involved. France had entered the war in February 1778. Eight months later, Spain declared war on England, though it declined to recognize American independence. Between 1780 and 1782, Russia, the Netherlands, and six other European countries joined in a League of Armed Neutrality aimed at protecting their maritime trade against British efforts to control it. America's Revolutionary War had quickly become internationalized.

Dependent on French economic and military support, the Congress instructed the American commissioners to follow the advice of Vergennes, the French foreign minister. As the treaty talks began, the Americans learned to their distress that Vergennes was prepared to let the exhausting war continue in order to weaken England further and tighten America's dependence on France.

In the end, the American commissioners ignored their instructions and, without a word to Vergennes, arranged a provisional peace agreement with the British emissaries. In the Treaty of Paris, signed in September 1783, England agreed to recognize American independence. Moreover, Britain promised that U.S. fishermen would have the "right" to fish the waters off Newfoundland and that British forces would evacuate American territory "with all convenient speed" once hostilities had ceased. In return, the Congress agreed to recommend that the states restore the rights and property of the Loyalists. Both sides agreed that prewar debts owed the citizens of one country by the citizens of the other would remain valid. Each of these issues would trouble Anglo-American relations in the decades ahead, but for the moment it seemed a splendid outcome to a long and difficult struggle.

The Ingredients of Victory

How were the weak and disunited American states able to defeat Great Britain, the most powerful nation in the Atlantic world? Certainly the Dutch and French loans, war supplies, and military forces were crucially important. More decisive, though, was the American people's determination not to submit. Often the Americans were disorganized and uncooperative. As the war progressed, however, the people's estrangement from England and their commitment to the "glo-

rious cause" increased. To subdue the colonies, England would have had to occupy the entire eastern third of the continent, and that it could not do.

The American victory also owed much to the administrative and organizational talents of Washington. Against massive odds, he held the continental army together, often by the sheer force of his will. Had he failed, the Americans could not possibly have defeated the British.

In the end, however, it is as accurate to say that Britain lost the war as that the United States won it. With vast economic and military resources, Britain enjoyed clear military superiority over the American states and, until the closing months of the contest, naval superiority as well.

Britain had difficulty, however, extending its command structures and supply routes across several thousand miles of ocean. Because information flowed erratically back and forth across the water, strategic decisions made in London were often based on faulty or outdated intelligence. Given the difficulties of supply over such distances, British troops often had to live off the land. This reduced their mobility and antagonized the Americans whose crops and animals they commandeered. Faced with these circumstances, British leaders were often overly cautious.

British commanders also generally failed to adapt their battlefield tactics to the realities of the American war. They continued to fight in the European style, during specified times of the year and using set formations of troops deployed in formal battlefield maneuvers. Much of the American terrain, however, was rough and wooded and thus better suited to the use of smaller units and irregular troops. Washington and Greene were more flexible, often employing a patient strategy of raiding, harassment, and strategic retreat. Over time the costs of continuing the war became greater than the British government could bear. As a much later American war in Vietnam would also reveal, a guerrilla force can win if it does not lose; a regular army loses if it does not consistently win.

THE EXPERIENCE OF WAR

In terms of loss of life and destruction of property, the Revolutionary War pales by comparison with America's more recent wars. Yet modern comparisons are misleading, for the War for American Independence was terrifying to the people caught up in it and destructive of lives and property.

Recruiting an Army

Estimates vary, but on the American side as many as 250,000 men may at one time or another have borne arms. That would amount to about one out of every two or three adult males.

Tens of thousands served in the state militias. At the time of independence, however, the militia in most of the states was not an effective fighting force. This was especially true in the South, where Nathanael Greene complained that the men came "from home with all the tender feelings of domestic life" and were not "sufficiently fortified . . . to stand the shocking scenes of war, to march over dead men, [or] to hear without concern the groans of the wounded."

The militia did serve as a convenient recruiting system. Given its grounding in local community life, it also served to secure people's commitment to the Revolutionary cause. What better way to separate the Patriots (those who supported the cause of independence) from the Loyalists (those who supported England) than by mustering the local militia company and seeing who turned out?

During the first year of the war, when enthusiasm ran high, men of all ranks volunteered to fight the British. But as the war progressed, it gradually became a battle by conscripts. Eventually it was transformed, as wars so often are, into a poor man's fight. Middle- and upper-class men increasingly hired substitutes to replace them, and communities filled their militia quotas with strangers lured by the promise of enlistment bonuses. This social transformation was even more evident in the continental army, where terms were longer, discipline was stiffer, and battlefields were more distant from the soldiers' homes.

For the poor and the jobless, whose ranks the war rapidly expanded, bonus payments and the promise of board and keep proved attractive. But often the bonuses failed to materialize, and pay was long overdue. Moreover, life in the camps was harsh, and soldiers frequently heard from their wives about their families' distress at home. Faced with such trials, soldiers often became disgruntled and insubordinate. As the war dragged on, Washington imposed harsher discipline on the continental troops in an effort to hold them in line.

Throughout the war, soldiers suffered from severe shortages of supplies. At Valley Forge during the terrible winter of 1777–1778, men hobbled about without shoes or coats. "I am sick, discontented, and out of humour," declared one despairing soul. "Poor food, hard lodging, cold weather, fatigue, nasty cloathes, nasty cookery, vomit half my time, smoked out of my senses. The Devil's in't, I can't Endure it. Why are we sent here to starve and freeze?"

The states possessed food and clothing enough but were often reluctant to strip their own people of wagons and livestock, blankets and shoes for use elsewhere. Moreover, mismanagement and difficulties in transportation stood in the way. Wagon transport was slow and costly, and the presence of the British fleet made water transportation along the coast perilous. Though many individuals served honorably as supply officers, others took advantage of the army's distress. Washington commented bitterly on the "speculators, various tribes of money makers, and stock-jobbers of all denominations"

The American rifleman, even as idealized in this engraving, lacked the pomp and formality—and often the discipline—of the British soldier.

whose "avarice and thirst for gain" threatened the country's ruin.

The Casualties of Combat

The death that soldiers dispensed to one another on the battlefield was intensely personal. Because the effective range of muskets was little more than 100 yards, combat was typically at close quarters. According to eighteenth-century military conventions, armies formed on the battlefield in ranks and fired in unison. After massed volleys, the lines often closed for hand-

to-hand combat with knives and bayonets. The partisan warfare in the South, with its emphasis on ambush and small group actions, shocked British officers used to more distanced and dispassionate styles of warfare. One attributed to the American troops "a sort of implacable ardor and revenge."

The Americans' fervor in battle may be explained by the fact that this was in part a civil war. As many as 50,000 colonists fought for the king and engaged in some of the war's most bitter encounters. They figured importantly in Burgoyne's invasion from Canada and in the attacks on Savannah and Charleston. Benedict Arnold led a force of Loyalists on raids through the Connecticut and James river valleys, and Loyalist militia joined Indian allies in destructive sweeps through the Carolina backcountry. Throughout America, communities and families were divided against one another. The war's violent temper reflected this civil conflict.

Moreover, the war was fought in the midst of American society. Soldiers often found themselves fighting for the survival of their family and community. Finally, Americans believed fervently in the Revolutionary cause. The struggle, as they understood it, was for their own liberty. In such a crusade, against such a foe, nothing was to be spared that might bring victory.

Medical treatment, whether for wounds or diseases such as smallpox, dysentery, and typhus that raged through the camps, did little to help. Casualties poured into hospitals, overcrowding them beyond capacity. Dr. Jonathan Potts, the attending physician at Fort George in New York, reported that "we have at present upwards of one thousand sick crowded into sheds & labouring under the various and cruel disorders of dysentaries, bilious putrid fevers and the effects of a confluent smallpox: to attend to this large number we have four seniors and four mates, exclusive of myself."

Surgeons, operating without anesthetics and

with the crudest of instruments, as readily threatened life as preserved it. Doctoring consisted mostly of bleeding, blistering, inducing vomiting, and administering laxatives. Mercury, a highly toxic chemical, was a commonly administered drug.

How many soldiers actually died we do not know, but the most conservative estimate runs to more than 25,000, a higher percentage of the total population than for any other American conflict except the Civil War. About 12 percent of American soldiers died of wounds or disease, a rate virtually the equivalent of the Civil War and higher than any of America's other conflicts.

Civilians and the War

Noncombatants also suffered, most of all in the densely settled areas along the coast, where England focused its military efforts. At one time or another, British troops occupied every major port—Boston, New York, Philadelphia, Charleston, and Savannah. The resulting disruptions of urban life were profound.

The chaos in New York was typical. In September 1776, a fire consumed 500 houses, nearly a quarter of the city's dwellings. About half the town's inhabitants fled when the British occupation began and were replaced by an almost equal number of Loyalists who streamed in from the surrounding countryside. Ten thousand British and German troops added to the crowding. The growing numbers of poor erected makeshift shelters of sailcloth and timbers.

In Philadelphia, the occupation was shorter and the disruptions were less severe, but the shock of invasion was no less real. Elizabeth Drinker, living alone after local Patriots had exiled her Quaker husband, found herself the unwilling landlady of a British officer, Major Crammond, and his friends. Constantly anxious, she confided to her journal that "I often feel afraid to go to Bed." During the occupation, British soldiers frequently took what they wanted, tore down fences for their campfires,

and confiscated food to supplement their own tedious fare. Even the Loyalists commented on the "dreadful consequences" of occupation.

Along the entire coastal plain, British landing parties descended without warning to capture supplies or terrorize inhabitants. In 1780 and 1781, the British mounted a sustained attack along the Connecticut coast. Over 200 buildings in Fairfield were burned, and much of nearby Norwalk was destroyed.

The southern coast, with its broad rivers, was even more vulnerable. In December 1780, Benedict Arnold ravaged the James River valley, uprooting tobacco, confiscating slaves, and creating panic among the white population. Similar devastation befell the coasts of Georgia and the Carolinas. Such punishing attacks sent civilians fleeing into the interior. During the first years of the war, the port cities lost nearly half their population, while inland communities strained to cope with the thousands of migrants who streamed into them.

Not all the traffic was inland, away from the coast. In New York, Pennsylvania, Virginia, and the Carolinas, numerous frontier settlements collapsed in the face of British and Indian assaults. By 1783, the white population along the Mohawk River west of Albany, New York, had declined from 10,000 to 3,500. According to one observer, after nearly five years of warfare in Tryon County, 12,000 farms had been abandoned, 700 buildings burned, hundreds of thousands of bushels of grain destroyed, nearly 400 women widowed, and perhaps 2,000 children orphaned.

Wherever the armies went, they generated a swirl of refugees, who spread vivid tales of the war. This refugee traffic, added to the constant movement of soldiers back and forth between army and civilian life, brought the war home even to people who did not experience it at first hand. As they moved across the countryside, the armies lived off the land, commandeering the supplies they needed. During the desperate winter of 1777–1778, in an effort to protect the sur-

In September 1776, as American troops fought unsuccessfully for control of New York, nearly a quarter of the city was destroyed by fire. Not until the war ended did reconstruction and cleanup of the ruins begin.

rounding population, Washington issued an order prohibiting his troops from roaming more than a half mile from camp. In New Jersey, Britain's German mercenaries generated special fears among the citizenry. The Patriot press was filled with lurid stories of attacks on American civilians, especially women.

The Loyalists

No Americans suffered greater losses than those who remained loyal to the Crown. On September 8, 1783, Thomas Danforth, formerly a lawyer from Cambridge, Massachusetts, appeared in London before the King's Commission of Enquiry into the Losses and Services of the American Loyalists. Danforth was there to seek compensation for losses he had suffered at the hands of the American Revolutionaries. He explained that

> ...now he finds himself near his fortieth year, banished under pain of death, to a distant country, where he has not the most remote family connection ... cut off from his profession—from every hope of importance in life, and in a great degree from social enjoyments.

The commission's response is unknown, but few of the several thousand Loyalists who appeared before it were reimbursed for more than one-third of their losses.

Though no count of the colonists who remained loyal to England can be exact, as many as 80,000 men, women, and children may have departed from the new nation, while several hundred thousand more remained in the United

States. These are substantial numbers when set against the total American population, black and white, of about 2.5 million. The incidence of loyalism differed dramatically from region to region. There were fewest Loyalists in New England and most in and around New York City, where British authority was most stable.

Why did so many Americans remain loyal, often at the cost of personal danger and loss? Customs officers, members of the governors' councils, and Anglican clergymen—all appointed to office in the King's name—often remained with the Crown. Loyalism was common as well among groups dependent on British authority— for example, settlers on the Carolina frontier who believed themselves mistreated by the planter elite along the coast; ethnic minorities, such as the Germans in the middle states, who feared domination by the Anglo-American majority; or tenants on some of the large estates along the Hudson River, who had struggled for years with their landlords over the terms of their leaseholds.

For many Loyalists, the prospect of confronting English military power proved sufficiently daunting. Others doubted the ability of a new, weak nation to survive in an Atlantic world dominated by competing empires, even if independence could be won.

William Eddis wondered what kind of society independence would bring when Revolutionary crowds showed no respect for the rights of Loyalist dissenters such as he. "If I differ in opinion from the multitude," he asked, "must I therefore be deprived of my character, and the confidence of my fellow-citizens; when in every station of life I discharge my duty with fidelity and honour?"

Whatever their motives, the Loyalists believed themselves advocates of reason and the rule of law in the midst of revolutionary passion. Tens of thousands of Americans believed strongly enough in their position to sacrifice home, community, and personal safety on its behalf.

Many who faced exile successfully established new lives in other parts of the empire. The majority settled in the Maritime Provinces of Canada. But even under the best of circumstances, forced resettlement was traumatic.

Loyalists came from all social classes but were most numerous among the upper and middle ranks of society, where individuals were most likely to have direct political and social connections with English officials and to fear the social consequences of revolution. Given their adherence to monarchical government and its values of hierarchy and subordination, their loss weakened the forces of social conservatism in America and facilitated the progress of revolutionary reform.

African-Americans and the Revolutionary War

American blacks were deeply involved in the Revolution. In fact, the conflict provoked the largest slave rebellion in American history prior to the Civil War. Once the war was under way, blacks found a variety of ways to turn events to their own advantage. For some, this meant applying Revolutionary principles to their own lives and calling for their personal freedom. For others, it meant seeking liberty behind English lines or in the continent's interior.

During the pre-Revolutionary decade, as their white masters talked excitedly about liberty, increasing numbers of black Americans questioned their own oppression. In the North, some slaves petitioned legislatures to set them free. In the South, pockets of insurrection appeared. In 1765, more than 100 South Carolina slaves fled to the interior, where they tried to establish a colony of their own. The next year, slaves paraded through the streets of Charleston, chanting, "Liberty, liberty!"

In November 1775, Lord Dunmore issued a proclamation offering freedom to all Virginia slaves and servants, "able and willing to bear arms," who would leave their masters and join the British forces in Norfolk. Within weeks, 500 to 600 slaves had responded. Among them was

Thomas Peters, from Wilmington, North Carolina.

Kidnapped from the Yoruba tribe in what is now Nigeria and brought to America by a French slave trader, Peters had been first purchased in Louisiana about 1760. He resisted enslavement so fiercely that his master sold him into the English colonies. By 1770, Peters belonged to William Campbell, an immigrant Scots planter on North Carolina's Cape Fear River, where he toiled while the storm brewed between England and the colonies. Four months after Dunmore issued his dramatic proclamation, Thomas Peters escaped and joined the British-officered Black Pioneers.

Many blacks saw in England the promise of freedom, not tyranny. From the Virginia slaves who responded to Dunmore's proclamation, a regiment of black soldiers was formed and marched into battle, their chests covered with sashes on which was emblazoned "Liberty to Slaves." At the war's end, several thousand former slaves were evacuated with the British to Nova Scotia, where they established their own settlements. Their reception by the white inhabitants there, however, was generally hostile. By the end of the century, most had left Canada to found the free black colony of Sierra Leone on the west coast of Africa. Thomas Peters was a leader among them.

Many of the slaves who fled behind English lines never won their freedom. In keeping with the terms of the peace treaty, hundreds were returned to their American owners. Several thousand others were transported to the West Indies and the harsher slavery of the sugar plantations.

Other blacks took advantage of the war's confusion to drift away in pursuit of a new life. Some sought refuge among the Indians. Some made their way north, following rumors that slavery had been abolished there.

Fewer blacks fought on the American side than on England's, because the Americans were not eager to see blacks armed. Of the blacks who served the Patriot cause, many received the freedom they were promised. The patriotism of untold others, however, went unrewarded.

THE FERMENT OF REVOLUTIONARY POLITICS

The Revolution altered people's lives in countless ways that reached beyond the sights and sounds of battle. No areas of American life were more powerfully changed than politics and government. What were the basic principles of the new republican ideology? How would the constitutions being written in each of the states balance the need for order against competing needs for democratic openness and accountability? Who among the American people would have political voice in revolutionary politics, and who would be excluded? These were some of the questions with which the revolutionaries wrestled.

Other explosive issues threatened to overwhelm Congress and the states—controlling the Loyalist "menace," deciding whether to abolish or retain slavery, arguing over religious freedom and the separation of church and state, apportioning taxes, regulating prices, issuing paper money and providing debt relief. Seldom has American politics been more heated, seldom has it struggled with a more daunting agenda, and seldom has it proved more creative than during the years of the nation's founding.

Mobilizing the People

Under the pressure of Revolutionary events, politics absorbed people's energies as never before. Newspapers multiplied in number, and between 1750 and 1783, more than 1,500 pamphlets joined the debate. Declared one contemporary in amazement, "Never . . . were [political pamphlets] . . . so cheap, so universally diffused, so easy of access." Pulpits rocked with political exhortations as well. Religion and politics had never been sharply separated in colonial America, but the Revolution drew them more tightly together. Some believed that God intended America as the place of Christ's Second Coming and that independence foretold that glorious day. Others thought of America as a New Israel, a covenanted people specially chosen by God to preserve liberty in a threatening world.

The belief that God sanctioned their Revolution strengthened American resolve. It also encouraged Americans to equate national interest with divine intent and thus offered convenient justification for whatever they believed necessary to do. This was not the last time Americans would make that dangerous equation.

Belief in the momentous importance of what they were doing intensified politics as well. In a letter from Philadelphia to his wife, Abigail, John Adams exalted independence as "the greatest question . . . which ever was debated in America."

As independence was declared, people in towns and hamlets throughout the land raised toasts to the great event: "Liberty to those who have the spirit to preserve it." "May the Crowns of Tyrants be crowns of thorns." They called themselves the Patriots of '76, a generation of Americans fused together by the searing experience of rebellion, war, and nation building and persuaded that they held in their hands the future of human liberty. Small wonder that they took politics so seriously.

The most dramatic evidence of America's expanding Revolutionary politics appeared in the array of extralegal committees and spontaneous gatherings that erupted across the states during the 1770s and 1780s. Electoral politics simply could not contain the political energies or resolve the political conflicts generated by the Revolution, and so people devised more direct forms of political action. Artisans, workingmen, and farmers, people formerly on the margins of political life, took seriously the talk about liberty, natural rights, and government by consent and applied those principles to their own lives.

The result was a growing demand for access to the political process. In addition, Patriot leaders, recognizing the need for popular support in the desperate struggle against England, organized committees of safety and correspondence to stimulate popular participation.

A Republican Ideology

Throughout history, as people have moved from colonial subordination to independence, they have struggled to define themselves as a free and separate nation. It was no different with the Revolutionary generation. No longer English, they were now Americans; but what exactly did that mean? "Our style and manner of thinking," observed Thomas Paine in amazement, "have undergone a revolution. . . . We see with other eyes, we hear with other ears, and think with other thoughts than those we formerly used." The ideology of revolutionary republicanism, pieced together from English political thought, theories of the Enlightenment, and people's own experience, constituted a revolution in thought.

The rejection of monarchy was one basic component of America's new republican faith. "The word *republic*," explained Paine, "means the public good of the whole, in contradistinction to the despotic form which makes the good of the sovereign, or of one man, the only object of government." It was Paine's unsparing rejection of monarchy that made his pamphlet *Common Sense* so radical. "Of more worth is one honest man to society, and in the sight of God," he scoffed, "than all the crowned ruffians that ever lived."

Limiting governmental power on behalf of preserving individual liberty was another basic postulate of republican belief. Those who wielded power, went the common refrain, inevitably used it for their own advantage rather than for the general good. It followed then that ways had to be found of controlling governmental power and maximizing liberty.

Given the dangers of governmental power,

how could political order be maintained? The Revolutionary generation offered an extraordinary answer to that question. Order was not to be imposed from above but would flow upward from the self-regulated behavior of the people, especially from their willingness to put the public good ahead of their own interests. The term for this extraordinary self-denial was "public virtue." It formed the core of republican ideology.

If public virtue provided the essential strength of republican politics, "faction," that is, organized self-interest, constituted its most dangerous enemy. Faction, or "party" as it was sometimes called, was the "mortal disease under which popular governments have everywhere perished." Given a republic's openness, factional conflict could easily spin out of control. It thus followed that republics could survive only in small territories, where society was homogeneous and where serious economic or religious conflicts were absent. This fear of party faction did not preclude political conflict in Revolutionary America, but it raised the ideological stakes and inclined people to question the basic motives of their political opponents.

Few Patriots were so naive as to believe that the American people were altogether virtuous. During the first years of independence, when Revolutionary enthusiasm ran high, however, many believed that public virtue was sufficiently widespread to support republican government. More than that, the American people would learn virtue by its practice. It was an extraordinarily hopeful but risk-filled undertaking.

The principle of political equality was another controversial touchstone of republicanism. Virtually everyone agreed that republican governments must be grounded in popular consent, that elections should be frequent, and that citizens must be vigilant in defense of their liberties. There, however, agreement often ended.

Some Americans took the principle of political equality literally, arguing that all citizens should have equal voice and that public office should be open to all. This position was argued most forcefully by individuals often excluded from the political process—farmers and tenants in the interior, workers and artisans in the coastal cities. More cautious citizens talked about the need for order as well as liberty and argued that stable republics depended on leadership by an "aristocracy of talent"—men of ability, wisdom, and experience. Merchants, planters, and large commercial farmers saw no need to alter radically the existing distribution of political power. These differences of principle and self-interest generated much of the conflict that lay at the heart of revolutionary politics.

Creating Republican Governments

With their English ties dissolved, the Revolutionaries set about the difficult task of creating new state governments. Connecticut and Rhode Island continued under their colonial charters, simply deleting all references to the British Crown. The other 11 states, however, set their charters aside and started anew. Within two years, all but Massachusetts had completed the task. By 1780, it had done so as well.

It was hard going, for the American people had no experience with government making on such a scale; they were embroiled in war, and they were sharply divided over the kind of government they wished to create.

In most states, the provincial congresses, extralegal successors to the defunct colonial assemblies, wrote the first constitutions. As the process went along, however, people became increasingly uneasy. Constitutions were intended to define and control government, but if governmental bodies wrote the documents, they could change them as well. If they could do that, what would guarantee against the abuse of governmental power? Some way had to be found of grounding the constitutions directly in the people's sovereign will.

Massachusetts was the first state to perfect

Occupational Composition of Several State Assemblies in the 1780s

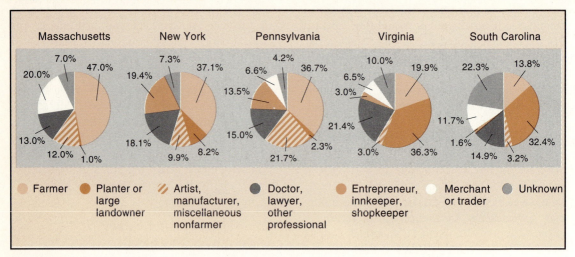

Membership in the Revolutionary assemblies reflected differences in the economies and societies of the various states. Those differences often generated political conflict throughout the Revolutionary era.
Source: Main, *Political Parties Before the Constitution, 1973.*

the new procedures. In 1779, its citizens formed a special convention for the sole purpose of preparing a new constitution. The convention did its work, and the resulting constitution was returned to the people for ratification.

Through trial and argumentation, the Revolutionary generation worked out a practical understanding of what a constitution was and how it should be developed. In the process, it established some of the most basic doctrines of American constitutionalism: that sovereignty resides in the people; that written constitutions, produced by specially elected conventions and then ratified by the people, embody their sovereign will; and that government functions within constitutional limits. No doctrines have been more important to the preservation of American liberty.

The new state constitutions redefined American government in fundamental and lasting ways. For one thing, the new governments were considerably more democratic than the colonial

regimes had been. Most officials were now elected, many of them annually rather than every two or three years as before.

Most of the new constitutions also sharply reduced the governors' powers and increased the powers of the assemblies. Above all, the documents sharply reduced the governors' powers of appointment. "He who has the giving of . . . places in the government," went the common refrain, "will always be master."

The assemblies absorbed most of the powers stripped from the governors. Not only were the assemblies more powerful, but they were larger and more representative as well. Reflecting the spirit of republican reform as well as the demands of farmers and artisans for a larger voice in public affairs, the assemblies grew in size by half or more.

At the same time, constitution making generated heated conflicts over political principles and the competition for political power. Two examples, Pennsylvania and Massachusetts, illustrate how controversial the process was and how different the outcomes could be.

In Pennsylvania, a coalition of western farmers, Philadelphia artisans and shopkeepers, and radical leaders such as Thomas Paine, Timothy Matlack, and Thomas Young pushed through the most democratic state constitution of all. Drafted in 1776, during the most intense period of republican reform, it rejected the familiar English model of two legislative houses and an independent executive. Instead, the constitution provided for a single, all-powerful legislative house, its members annually elected, its debates open to the public. There was to be no governor. Legislative committees would assume executive duties. A truly radical assumption underlay this design: that only the "common interest of society" and not "separate and jarring private interests" should be represented in public affairs. Property-holding requirements for public office were abolished, and the franchise was opened to every male over 21 who paid taxes. The bill of rights introducing the document guaranteed every citizen religious freedom, trial by jury, and freedom of speech.

The most radical proposal of all called for the redistribution of property within the state, a step described as essential to preserving republican liberty. This was narrowly defeated.

Debate over the constitution divided the state deeply. Men of wealth led the opposition, but in 1776, the radicals had their way. The Pennsylvania constitution—together with its counterparts in Vermont and Georgia—represented the most radical thrust of Revolutionary republicanism. Its guiding principle, declared Thomas Young, was that "the people at large [are] the true proprietors of governmental power." The struggle for control of the Revolution in Pennsylvania was not over, for in 1790 a new and more moderate constitution would be approved. For the moment, however, the lines of political power had been decisively redrawn.

In Massachusetts, constitution making followed a more cautious course. There, the disruptions of the war were less severe and the continuity of political leadership was much greater. The main architect of the constitution, John Adams, readily admitted that the new government must be firmly grounded in the people. No principle was more fundamental to America's new republican faith. Yet Adams saw danger in reckless experimentation. A balance between two legislative houses and an independent executive was essential to preserving liberty, he believed, for "power must be opposed to power, force to force, . . . interest to interest, . . . and passion to passion."

Believing that society was inescapably divided between "democratic" and "aristocratic" forces, he sought to isolate them in separate legislative houses where they could guard against each other. The lower house, he explained, should be "an exact portrait, in miniature," of the people; it should "think, feel, act, and reason" like them. The senate, by contrast, should constitute a "natural aristocracy" of wealth, talent, and good sense intended to balance the popular excesses of the assembly and look after the interests of property. Following Adams's advice, the Massachusetts convention provided for a popular, annually elected assembly and a senate based on wealth, its members apportioned according to the amount of taxes paid in special senatorial districts. The constitution also provided for an independent governor with the power to veto legislation, make appointments, serve as commander in chief of the militia, and oversee state expenditures.

When the convention sent the document to the town meetings for approval in March 1779, farmers as well as artisans and working people attacked it as "aristocratic," too much like the old colonial regime. But when the convention reconvened in July 1779, it declared the constitution ratified. It went into effect the following year.

Two states, two very different outcomes to the politics of constitution making.

Women and the Limits of Republican Citizenship

Revolutionary leaders defined the boundaries of republican politics too narrowly to include all white Americans. Only people with property could vote in state elections. Most states reduced property requirements for the franchise, but nowhere were they abolished altogether.

Even more significant, republican citizenship did not encompass women. Except on scattered occasions, women had neither voted nor held public office during the colonial period. Nor, with rare exceptions, did they do so in Revolutionary America. The New Jersey constitution of 1776 opened the franchise to property-owning women, but the experiment did not last long. Declared one political leader: "It is evident that women, generally, are neither by nature, nor habit, nor education . . . fitted to perform this duty with credit to themselves, or advantage to the public." In 1807, the New Jersey assembly passed a bill specifically disenfranchising women. Its author, John Condict, had several years earlier narrowly escaped defeat when a number of women voted for his opponent. In no other state did women even temporarily secure the vote.

Most women did not press for political equality, for the idea flew in the face of long-standing social convention, and its advocacy often exposed a person to public ridicule. Some women did make the case, most often with one another or their husbands. "I cannot say, that I think you are very generous to the ladies," Abigail Adams chided her husband, John. "For whilst you are proclaiming peace and good will to men, emancipating all nations, you insist upon retaining an absolute power over all wives."

Prior to independence, most women had accepted the principle that political debate fell outside the feminine sphere, but the Revolution changed that. Women felt the urgency of the Revolutionary crisis as much as men. "How shall I impose a silence upon myself," wondered Anne Emlen in 1777, "when the subject is so very interesting, so much engrossing conversation—& what every member of the community is more or less concerned in?" With increasing

frequency, women wrote and spoke to one another about public events, especially as they affected their own lives.

As the war progressed, increasing numbers of women ventured their opinions publicly. A few, such as Esther DeBerdt Reed of Philadelphia, published essays explaining women's urgent need to contribute to the Patriot cause. In her 1780 broadside, "The Sentiments of an American Woman," she called on women to renounce "vain ornament" as they had earlier renounced tea and English finery. The money no longer spent on clothing and hairstyles would be "the offering of the Ladies" to Washington's army. In Philadelphia, women responded by collecting $300,000 in continental currency from more than 1,600 individuals. Refusing Washington's proposal that the money be mixed with general funds in the national treasury, they insisted on using it to purchase materials for shirts so that each soldier might know he had received a contribution specifically from the women.

In the Revolutionary context, traditional female roles took on new political resonance. With English imports cut off and the army badly in need of clothing, spinning and weaving assumed increased importance. Often coming together as Daughters of Liberty, women made shirts, stockings, and other items of clothing. Charity Clarke, a New York teenager who knitted "stockens" for the soldiers, acknowledged that she "felt Nationaly."

Finally, the most traditional of female roles, the care and nurture of children, also took on political overtones during the Revolutionary era. Once independence was won, the republic would have to be sustained by the upcoming generation of republican citizens schooled in the principles of public virtue. They would have to be taught their responsibilities as citizens during their earliest years by their republican mothers, the women of the Revolution.

In a variety of ways, women developed new connections with the public realm during the Revolutionary years. Those connections re-

Abigail Adams, like many women of the Revolutionary generation, protested the contradiction in men's subordination of women while they extolled the principles of liberty and equality.

mained limited, for the assumption that politics and government belonged to men did not die easily. But challenges to that assumption would come, and when they did, women found guidance in the principles that the women of the Revolution had helped to define.

THE AGENDA OF REVOLUTIONARY POLITICS

Revolutionary politics followed different paths in different states. In Pennsylvania political change ran deep, while in other states, such as Connecticut and Virginia, change was more muted. In each of the states, though, citizens struggled with a bewildering and often intractable array of issues that revealed the clash of conflicting ideologies, interests, and ambitions.

Separating Church and State

Among the most explosive questions was the proper relationship between church and state in a republican order. In most of the colonies prior to the Revolution, one religious group had enjoyed the benefits of endorsement by the government and public tax support for its clergy. At the time of independence, however, "dissenting" groups such as the Methodists and the Baptists were growing in numbers, especially among the lower classes of city and countryside, and were grudgingly tolerated by colonial authorities.

With independence, pressure built for severing church and state completely. Even before independence, Rhode Island, New Jersey, Pennsylvania, and Delaware had established full religious liberty. In five additional states, the Anglican church collapsed when English support was withdrawn.

In Massachusetts, Connecticut, and New Hampshire, the Congregationalists fought to retain their long-established privileges. Isaac Backus, the most outspoken of the New England Baptists, protested that "many, who are filling the nation with the cry of *liberty* and against oppressors are at the same time themselves violating that dearest of all rights, *liberty of conscience.*"

Massachusetts's new constitution guaranteed everyone the right to worship God "in the manner and season most agreeable to the dictates of his own conscience." But as Backus pointed out, it also empowered the legislature to require towns to lay taxes for "the public worship of *God,* and for the support and maintenance of public protestant teachers of piety, religion, and morality." During the decades following independence, New England's Congregational establishment continued to weaken. But not until the early nineteenth century—in Massachusetts not until 1833—were the laws linking church and state finally repealed.

In Virginia, the Baptists pressed their cause against the Protestant Episcopal church, successor to the Church of England. In 1786, the adoption of Thomas Jefferson's Bill for Establishing Religious Freedom, rejecting all connections between church and state and removing all religious tests for public office, finally settled the issue. Three years later, that statute served as a model for the First Amendment to the new federal Constitution.

Legal disestablishment did not end religious discrimination. But it did implant firmly the principle of religious liberty in American constitutional law.

Loyalists and the Public Safety

Emotions ran high between Patriots and Loyalists in Revolutionary America. "The rage of civil discord," lamented one individual, "hath advanced among us with an astonishing rapidity. The son is armed against the father, the brother against the brother, family against family." The security, perhaps the very survival, of the republic required stern measures against counterrevolutionaries. More than security was involved, however, for the Patriots were also determined to exact revenge against those who had rejected the Revolutionary cause.

During the war, each of the states passed a series of laws designed to deprive Loyalists of the vote, confiscate their property and banish them from their homes. In 1776, the Connecticut assembly passed a remarkably punitive law threatening anyone who criticized either the assembly or the Continental Congress with immediate fine and imprisonment. Probably not more than a few dozen Tories died at the hands of the Revolutionary regimes, but many others died in combat, and thousands found their livelihoods destroyed, their families ostracized, and themselves subject to physical attack.

Punishing Loyalists—or persons accused of loyalism—was a popular activity, especially since Loyalists were most numerous among the upper classes. Yet many of the more conservative Patriots wondered how safe their property was if others' property could be confiscated and sold.

Caught up in the Revolution's turmoil, many argued that the Loyalists had put themselves outside the protection of American law. Others worried about the implications of setting aside the protections of the law, even for Loyalists. Republics, after all, were supposed to be "governments of law, and not of men." Once that distinction disappeared, no one would be safe.

After the war ended and passions cooled, most states repealed their anti-Tory legislation. In the midst of the Revolution, however, no issue raised more clearly the troubling question of how to balance individual liberty against the needs of public security.

Slavery Under Attack

The place of human slavery in a republican society also vexed the Revolutionary generation. During the several decades preceding the imperial crisis, the trade in human chattels had flourished. Though several northern colonies abolished the slave trade, the 1760s witnessed the largest importations of slaves in colonial history.

The Revolution halted that trade almost completely. Once the war ended, southern planters sought to replace their lost slaves. But Revolutionary principles, a reduced need for fieldhands in the depressed tobacco economy, continuing natural increase in the slave population, and post-Revolutionary anxiety over black rebelliousness argued for the slave trade's extinction. By 1790, every state except South Carolina and Georgia had outlawed slave importations. Termination of the slave trade reduced the infusion of new Africans into the black population. This meant that over time an ever higher proportion of blacks were American-born, thus speeding the process of cultural transformation by which Africans became African-Americans.

Slavery itself came under attack during the Revolutionary era. As the crisis with England heated up, catchwords such as *liberty* and *tyranny,* employed by colonists protesting British policies, reminded citizens that one-fifth of the colonial population was in chains. Samuel Hopkins, a New England clergyman, chided his compatriots for "making a vain parade of being advocates for the liberties of mankind, while … you at the same time are continuing this lawless, cruel, inhuman, and abominable practice of enslaving your fellow creatures." Following independence, the attacks intensified.

In Georgia and South Carolina, where blacks outnumbered whites more than two to one, slavery escaped significant challenge. In Virginia and Maryland, by contrast, whites argued openly over slavery's incompatibility with republicanism, and change did occur. The depression in the tobacco economy made the debate easier. Though neither state abolished slavery, both passed laws making it easier for owners to free their slaves. Moreover, increasing numbers of blacks petitioned for their own freedom, purchased it from their masters, or simply fled. By 1800, more than one of every ten blacks in the Chesapeake region were free, a dramatic increase over 30 years before. For many blacks in the Chesapeake region, the conditions of life slowly changed for the better.

The most dramatic breakthroughs occurred in the North, where slavery was either abolished or put on the road to extinction. Abolition was easier in the North because there were fewer slaves. In most areas, they constituted no more than 4 percent of the population.

Northern blacks joined in the attack on slavery. Following independence, they frequently petitioned state assemblies for their freedom. "Every Principle from which America has acted in the course of their unhappy difficulties with Great Britain," declared one group of Philadelphia blacks, "pleads stronger than a thousand arguments in favor of our petition." In 1780, the Pennsylvania assembly passed a law stipulating that all newborn blacks were to be free when they reached age 28. It was a cautious but decisive step. In the following decades, other northern states adopted similar policies of gradual emancipation.

Freed blacks continued to encounter pervasive discrimination. Still, remarkable progress had been made. Prior to the Revolution, slavery had been an accepted fact of northern life; after the Revolution, it no longer was. In addition, there now existed a coherent and publicly proclaimed antislavery argument, one closely linked in Americans' minds with the nation's founding. The first antislavery organizations had been created as well. Although another half century would pass before antislavery became a force in national political life, the groundwork for slavery's final abolition had been laid.

Politics and the Economy

The economic disruptions of independence and war also generated political conflict. The cutoff of long-established patterns of overseas trade sent American commerce into a tailspin from which it didn't recover for nearly 20 years. While English men-of-war prowled the coast, American ships rocked idly at empty wharves, as communities whose livelihood depended on the sea sank into depression. Virginia tobacco planters, their English markets gone and their plantations open to seaborne attack, struggled to survive. Farmers in the middle and New England states often prospered while hungry armies were nearby but saw their profits plummet when the armies moved on.

The war's impact on American manufacturing was uneven. With British goods excluded and wearing homespun deemed patriotic, American artisans and other producers took up the slack. (The familiar slogan "Buy American" has a long tradition.) Handsome profits were to be

Exports and Imports, 1768–1783

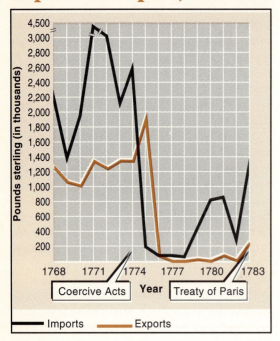

Source: U.S. Bureau of the Census.

made from government contracts by people with the right connections.

But even as some prospered, the war devastated major sectors of the economy. New England's booming shipbuilding industry virtually ceased production. The consequences for sailmakers, shipwrights, and blacksmiths were disastrous.

As major sectors of the economy fell into disarray and the costs of the war escalated, state governments struggled to cope. Price and wage inflation, skyrocketing taxation, mushrooming private and public debt—all demanded attention and often set people against one another. Debates raged, for example, over whether the public debt should be funded at face value or at some reduced rate. In support of full value were merchants and other people of wealth who had loaned the states money and had bought up large amounts of securities at deep discounts.

Others spoke out against full funding, arguing that speculators should reap no advantage from public distress.

The issue of taxation, seared into Americans' consciousness by their troubles with England, generated even greater controversy. As the costs of the war mounted, so did the tax burden. Between 1774 and 1778, Massachusetts levied a total of £408,976 in taxes, a dramatic increase over colonial days. Taxes, complained one anguished soul, equaled nearly one-third of the inhabitants' incomes. And Massachusetts was not unique.

As taxes rose, so did clashes over tax policy. Farmers, artisans, and others of modest means argued that taxes should be payable in depreciated paper money or government securities rather than only in specie, as some state laws required. In the New York assembly, men of property urged continuing dependence on the poll tax, a uniform assessment levied on all males 16 years of age and older. Working people, however, insisted that taxes should bear some relationship to people's ability to pay. As the demand for public revenue increased, pressure for taxing property rather than people grew.

Controversy swirled around the states' efforts to control soaring prices as well. Each of the states experimented with price controls at one time or another. Seldom were such efforts effective; always they generated political storms. In general, the poor and those not yet integrated into the market economy supported price controls. For merchants, shopkeepers, and others caught up in the commercial economy, however, the exchange of goods was an economic transaction that should be controlled by the laws of supply and demand.

Paper money was a final issue that energized state politics. Faced with the uncontrollable escalation of wartime expenses, Congress and the states did what colonial governments had done before and American governments have done ever since: They printed money. In the first year of the war alone, they issued more than $400 million in various kinds of paper, and that was only the beginning. Nothing supported the paper's value but the citizens' willingness to accept it in their dealings with the government and one another.

That willingness rapidly disappeared as the flood of paper grew and efforts lagged to draw it out of circulation through taxation. The result was a headlong collapse of the currency's value. Congressional bills of credit that in 1776 were pegged against gold at the ratio of 1.5 to 1 had slipped five years later to 147 to 1. State currencies depreciated even more alarmingly.

The flood of depreciated paper brought wild inflation of prices. In Massachusetts, a bushel of corn that sold for less than a dollar in 1777 went for nearly $80 two years later, while in Maryland the price of wheat increased several thousand-fold. In Boston, a crowd of women, angered by the escalating costs of food, tossed a merchant suspected of monopolizing commodities into a cart and dragged him through the city's streets while "a large concourse of men stood amazed."

In general, the poor and those not yet integrated into the market economy supported price controls. Faced with escalating prices, they had difficulty simply making ends meet. They also believed that goods should be sold for a "just price," one deemed fair to buyer and seller alike. In keeping with these principles, a crowd in New Windsor, New York, in 1777 seized a shipment of tea bound for Albany and sold it for what they deemed a fair price.

Merchants, shopkeepers, and others caught up in the commercial economy, however, believed that economic transactions should be controlled by the laws of supply and demand. "It is contrary to the nature of commerce," declared Benjamin Franklin, "for government to interfere in the prices of commodities." Attempts to regulate prices only created a disincentive to labor, which was "the principal part of the wealth of every country."

There were no ready solutions to the problems of debt, taxation, and price control. Thus they continued on the public agenda through the 1780s, heightening political tensions.

CONCLUSION

THE CRUCIBLE OF REVOLUTION

Independence and war redrew the contours of American life and changed the destinies of the American people. Though the Revolutionary War ended in victory, independence had its costs. Lives were lost, property was destroyed, local economies were deranged. The war changed relationships between Indians and whites, for it left the Iroquois and Cherokee severely weakened and opened the floodgates of western expansion. For black Americans, the Revolution had paradoxical results. It produced an ideology that decried slavery of all sorts and marked the first general debate over abolishing the oppressive institution. Yet the Revolutionary generation took steps to eradicate slavery only where it was least important, in the North, while preserving it in the South, where it was most important.

By 1783, a new nation had come into being, a nation based on the doctrines of republican liberty. That was the greatest change of all. The years immediately ahead would determine whether the republican experiment, launched with such hopefulness in 1776, would succeed.

Recommended Reading

Standard accounts of the Revolutionary War can be found in Don Higginbotham, *The War of American Independence* (1971); and Robert Middlekauff, *The Glorious Cause* (1982). Charles Royster, *A Revolutionary People at War* (1979), explains how the continental army embodied the Revolution's social and ideological goals. Jonathan Dull, *A Diplomatic History of the American Revolution* (1985), offers skillful discussion of Revolutionary War diplomacy.

The most vivid description of Native American involvement in the Revolution can be found in Anthony Wallace, *The Death and Rebirth of the Seneca* (1969). James O'Donnell discusses the situation in the Southeast in *Southern Indians in the American Revolution* (1973). Books that deal with the tangled history of slavery, race, and the Revolution include Duncan MacLeod, *Slavery, Race, and the American Revolution* (1974); and Ira Berlin and Ronald Hoffman, eds., *Slavery and Freedom in the Age of the American Revolution* (1983).

Linda Kerber, *Women of the Republic* (1980), examines the Revolutionary experience of women. Robert Calhoon, *The Loyalists in Revolutionary America, 1760–1781* (1973), deals with the experiences of Loyalist Americans. On daily life in the period, see Robert Gross, *The Minutemen and Their World* (1976); Jeffrey Crow and Larry Tise, eds., *The Southern Experience in the American Revolution* (1987); and Barbara Smith, *After the Revolution: The History of Everyday Life in the Eighteenth Century* (1985). Thomas Doerflinger, *A Vigorous Spirit of Enterprise* (1986), describes the Revolution's economic impact on Philadelphia.

For further information about the ideology of Revolutionary republicanism, see Bernard Bailyn, *The Ideological Origins of American Revolution* (1967).

State constitution making is discussed in Gordon Wood, *The Creation of the American Republic, 1776–1787* (1969). On Revolutionary state politics see Ronald Hoffman, *A Spirit of Dissension: Economics, Politics and the Revolution in Maryland* (1987); and Eric Foner, *Tom Paine and Revolutionary America* (1976).

Among many readable biographical accounts are Pauline Maier, *The Old Revolutionaries: Political Lives in the Age of Samuel Adams* (1980); Fawn Brodie, *Thomas Jefferson: An Intimate History* (1974); Claude Lopez and Eugenia Herbert, *The Private Franklin: The Man and His Family* (1975); and Marcus Cunliffe, *George Washington: Man and Monument* (1958).

Time Line

1775	Lord Dunmore's proclamation to slaves and servants in Virginia Iroquois Six Nations pledge neutrality Continental Congress urges "states" to establish new governments	**1779**	Massachusetts state constitutional convention Sullivan destroys Iroquois villages in New York
1776	British evacuate Boston and seize New York City Declaration of Independence Eight states draft constitutions Cherokee raids and American retaliation	**1780**	Massachusetts constitution ratified Charleston surrenders to British Pennsylvania begins gradual abolition of slavery
		1780s	Virginia and Maryland debate abolition of slavery Destruction of Iroquois Confederacy
1777	British occupy Philadelphia Most Iroquois join the British Americans win victory at Saratoga Washington's army winters at Valley Forge	**1781**	Cornwallis surrenders at Yorktown Articles of Confederation ratified by states
1778	War shifts to the South Savannah falls to British French treaty of alliance and commerce	**1783**	Peace Treaty with England signed in Paris Massachusetts Supreme Court abolishes slavery King's Commission on American Loyalists begins work

chapter 7

....

Consolidating the Revolution

Timothy Bloodworth of New Hanover County, North Carolina, knew what the American Revolution was about, for he had experienced it firsthand. A man of humble origins, Bloodworth had worked hard as an innkeeper and ferry pilot, self-styled preacher and farmer. By the mid-1770s, he owned nine slaves and 4,200 acres of land, considerably more than most of his neighbors.

His unpretentious manner and commitment to political equality earned Bloodworth the confidence of his community. In 1758, at the age of 22, he was elected to the North Carolina colonial assembly. Over the next three decades, he remained deeply involved in North Carolina's political life.

When the colonies' troubles with England drew toward a crisis, Bloodworth spoke ardently of American rights and mobilized support for independence. In 1784, shortly after the war ended, the North Carolina assembly named Bloodworth one of the state's delegates to the Confederation Congress. There he learned for the first time about the problems of governing a new nation. As the Congress struggled through the middle years of the 1780s, Bloodworth shared the growing conviction that the Articles of Confederation were too weak. He supported the Congress's call for a special convention to meet in Philadelphia in May 1787 to address this problem.

Like thousands of Americans, Bloodworth eagerly awaited the convention's work, but he was stunned by the result, for the proposed constitution seemed to him designed not to preserve republican liberty but to endanger it. Once again sniffing political tyranny on the breeze, he resigned his congressional seat in August 1787 and hurried back to North Carolina, where, over the next several years, he worked tirelessly to prevent its ratification.

A national government as strong as the one described in the proposed constitution, Bloodworth feared, would gobble up the states and destroy individual liberties. Alarmed by the provisions giving Congress the power of taxation as well as by the absence of explicit guarantees of trial by jury, Bloodworth demanded the addition of a federal bill of rights to protect individual liberties.

Bloodworth also feared the sweeping authority Congress would have "to make all laws which shall be necessary and proper for carrying into execution . . . all other powers vested . . . in the government of the United States." That language, he insisted, threatened the integrity of the states.

In North Carolina, the arguments of Bloodworth and his Anti-Federalist colleagues carried the day. By a vote of 184 to 84, the state ratifying convention declared that a bill of rights "asserting and securing from encroachment the great Principles of civil and religious Liberty, and the unalienable rights of the People" must be approved before North Carolina would concur. Not until November 1789—well after the new government had gotten under way and Congress had forwarded a national bill of rights to the states for approval—did North Carolina enter the new union.

As a member of the Confederation Congress, Timothy Bloodworth confronted the continuing vestiges of colonialism—the patronizing attitudes of England and France, their continuing imperial ambitions in North America, and the republic's ongoing economic dependence on Europe. He also observed the Congress's inability to reduce the war debt, open foreign ports to American commerce, and persuade the states to cooperate in solving the new nation's problems.

By 1786, Bloodworth, like countless other Americans, was caught up in the escalating debate between the Federalists, who believed that the Articles of Confederation were fatally deficient, and the Anti-Federalists, committed to retaining America's traditional localism and still deeply impressed by the dangers posed to individual liberties by consolidated power.

That debate came to a focus in the momentous Philadelphia convention of 1787, which produced not reform but revolutionary change in the national government and opened a portentous new chapter in the history of the American people.

STRUGGLING WITH THE PEACETIME AGENDA

As the war ended, difficult problems of demobilization and adjustment to the conditions of independence troubled the new nation. Whether the Confederation Congress could effectively deal with the problems of the postwar era remained unclear.

Demobilizing the Army

Demobilizing the army presented the Confederation government with some difficult moments, for when the fighting stopped, many of the troops refused to disband and go home until the Congress redressed their grievances. Trouble first arose in January 1783, when officers at the continental army camp in Newburgh, New York, sent a delegation to the Congress to complain about arrears in pay and other promised benefits. The Congress responded by calling for the army to be decommissioned. Almost immediately, an anonymous document circulated among the officers, attacking the "coldness and severity" of the Congress and hinting darkly at direct action if their grievances were not addressed. Washington urged the officers not to tarnish the victory they had so recently won. His efforts succeeded, for the officers reaffirmed their confidence in the Congress and agreed to disband.

In June, several hundred disgruntled continental soldiers and Pennsylvania militiamen gathered to express their frustrations in front of Independence Hall, causing Congress to flee to Princeton, New Jersey. Again, the crisis was eventually smoothed over, but the Congress's authority had been seriously challenged. During the mid-1780s, the Congress shuffled between Princeton and Annapolis, Trenton and New York, its transiency visible evidence of its steadily eroding position.

Opening the West

The Congress was not without important accomplishments during the postwar years. Most notable were the two great land ordinances of 1785 and 1787. The first provided for the systematic survey and sale of the region west of New York and Pennsylvania and north of the Ohio River. The area was to be laid out in townships six miles square, which were in turn to be subdivided into lots of 640 acres each. Thus began the rectangular grid pattern of land survey and settlement that to this day characterizes the nation's Midwest and distinguishes it so markedly from the irregular settlement patterns of the older colonial areas to the east.

Two years later, the Congress passed the Northwest Ordinance. It provided for the political organization of the same interior region, first with congressionally appointed officials, then with popularly elected assemblies, and ultimately as new states to be incorporated into the Union "on an equal footing with the original states in all respects whatsoever." Together these two pieces of legislation provided the legal mechanism for the nation's dramatic territorial expansion during the nineteenth century.

Despite its success in providing the legal framework for settlement of the trans-Appalachian frontier, however, Congress could neither secure removal of the British troops from the western posts after 1783 nor guarantee free navigation of the Mississippi. Nor could it clear the tribes of the Ohio region out of the white settlers' way.

During the immediate postwar years, the Congress operated as if the Native Americans of the interior were "conquered" peoples. The Treaty of Paris, American officials insisted, gave the United States political sovereignty over the tribes east of the Mississippi as well as ownership of their land.

For a few years the conquest strategy seemed to work. During the mid-1780s, the Congress negotiated several important land treaties with the interior tribes. At the Treaty of Fort Stanwix in 1784, the first congressional treaty with an Indian tribe, the Iroquois Six Nations made peace, ceded much of their land to the United States, and retreated to small reservations where they struggled for survival against disease and poverty, their traditional lifeways gone, their self-confidence broken.

The Iroquois were not the only tribes to lose their land. In January 1785, representatives of the Wyandotte, Chippewa, Delaware, and Ottawa tribes relinquished claim to most of present-day Ohio. The treaties with the Indians, however, were often exacted under the threat of force and generated widespread resentment. At Fort Stanwix, for example, negotiations were held at gunpoint, and hostages were taken to coerce the Indian delegates. Two years later, the Iroquois openly repudiated the treaty, asserting that they were still sovereigns of their own soil and "equally free as . . . any nation under the sun."

The Revolution, moreover, left behind a legacy of bitterness for both Indians and whites: for Indians because they had suffered betrayal and defeat, for white Americans because the Indians had sided with England and thus threatened the success of the Revolutionary cause. This bitterness would trouble Indian-white relations for years to come.

By the mid-1780s, tribal groups both above and below the Ohio River were actively resisting

Areas of White Settlement and Frontier in 1787

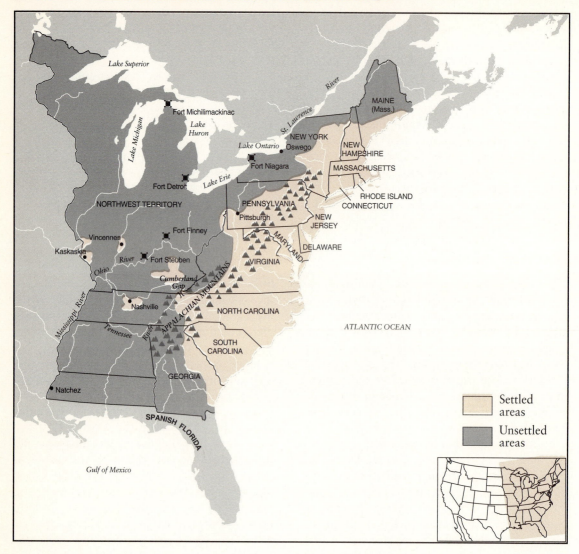

white expansion onto their land. In the summer of 1786, the Creek resumed hostilities in the backcountry of Georgia, while north of the Ohio, the Shawnee, Delaware, Wyandotte, and Miami moved to strengthen their Western Confederacy, reject the conquest theory, and prepare for the defense of their common homeland. When white settlers continued to press into the region, Native Americans launched a series of devastating raids, virtually halting white settlement. By 1786, the entire region from the Great Lakes to the Gulf of Mexico was embroiled in warfare. With the continental army disbanded and the nation in no position to raise a new one, there was little that Congress could do.

Settling the interior also involved relations

with other nations, and here, too, the Congress proved ineffective. In June 1784, Spain—still in possession of Florida, the Gulf Coast, and the trans-Mississippi West—closed the outlet of the Mississippi River at New Orleans to American shipping. Spain's action raised a storm of protest, especially among settlers in the West, who counted on the interior river system to float their produce downstream to outside markets. Land speculators from Virginia to South Carolina were aroused as well, for closure of the Mississippi would discourage development of the southern backcountry. Rumors spread that Spanish agents were urging backcountry American settlers to break away and seek affiliation with Spain. When Foreign Secretary John Jay offered to relinquish American claims to free transit of the Mississippi in return for a new commercial treaty opening Spanish ports to American shipping, the northern states supported the bargain. The southern states, however, angry at Jay's betrayal of their interests, refused. Thus stalemated, the Congress could take no action at all.

Wrestling with the National Debt

The Congress's inability to deal effectively with the massive war debt offered further evidence of the Confederation government's weakness. The public debt stood at about $35 million, much of it held abroad by French and Dutch bankers. Not only was the Congress unable to make regular payment against the loan's principal, but it had to borrow additional money abroad simply to pay the accumulating interest.

At home, things were no better. In response to the incessant demands of its creditors, the government could only delay and try to borrow more. Lacking the power to tax, the Congress continued to depend on the states' willingness to honor their obligations. This arrangement proved unworkable. By 1786, total federal revenue amounted to no more than $370,000 a year—not a sufficient amount, as one official lamented, to provide for "the bare maintenance of the federal government [even] on the most economical establishment, and in a time of profound peace."

Not all Americans were alarmed. Some pointed out approvingly that several state governments were beginning to assume responsibility for portions of the national debt. Others saw that as additional evidence of the Congress's weakening condition and wondered how a government unable to maintain its credit could long endure.

Surviving in a Hostile World

The Congress's difficulties in countering Spain's decision to close the Mississippi River to American commerce and in dealing with its creditors overseas pointed to a broader problem in American foreign relations. Even after the United States had formally won independence, England, France, and Spain continued to harbor imperial ambitions in North America. France had lost its North American possessions following the Seven Years' War, but before the century was over, it would gain title to most of the continent west of the Mississippi River. England's Union Jack continued to fly over eastern Canada, while English troops retained possession of strategic outposts on American soil—at Detroit, Michilimackinac, and Niagara. Spain, in control of New Orleans and Florida, still conjured up grim memories of past New World conquests. The reason for America's diplomatic troubles was clear: The country was new, weak, and republican in a world dominated by monarchical governments and divided into warring empires.

Nothing revealed more starkly the difficulties of national survival than the Congress's largely futile efforts to rebuild America's overseas commerce. A flourishing overseas trade, across the Atlantic to markets in England and down the coast to the Caribbean, had been the foundation of colonial economic prosperity.

British and Spanish Possessions in Eastern North America, 1783

Military and administrative centers ✳

British Canada

United States

Spanish possessions

Once the war was over, American traders sought eagerly to rebuild this trade. It proved a difficult task because the Congress could give them little support.

When the war ended, familiar English goods flooded American markets. Few American goods, however, flowed the other way, for English officials could command American markets without needing to grant trade concessions in return. Meanwhile, France and Spain gradually withdrew the special wartime trading privileges they had extended and returned to their policy of mercantile restrictions.

In an effort to rebuild American commerce, the Congress tried to secure the states' cooperation in a program of economic recovery. In 1784, however, it failed to obtain authorization

from the states to regulate foreign commerce; each state wanted to channel its own trade for its own advantage. As a result, the Congress was unable to negotiate satisfactory commercial agreements abroad, and overseas trade continued to languish.

By the late 1780s, the per capita value of American exports had fallen a startling 30 percent from two decades earlier. In an Atlantic world divided into exclusive, imperial trading spheres, the United States stood outside and alone, lacking both the political unity and the economic power to protect its interests.

POLITICAL TUMULT IN THE STATES

As the Confederation Congress struggled to chart the nation's postwar course, controversy again embroiled state politics. Two issues carried over from the Revolutionary agenda came together with particularly explosive force: problems of debt relief and paper money on the one hand, and continuing arguments over political equality and the sharing of political power on the other.

The Limits of Republican Experimentation

In a pattern that would frequently recur in American history, the postwar era witnessed growing social and political conservatism. Popular voting declined, while leadership in the state governments fell increasingly to people convinced that republican experimentation had gone too far, that order had to balance liberty, and that the "better sort" of men, not democratic newcomers, should be in charge. The repeal of anti-Loyalist legislation and the occasional reappearance of Loyalists in public life provided evidence of the changing political climate.

In 1790, Pennsylvania replaced its radical constitution of 1776 with a more conservative document that provided for a strong governor with power to veto legislation and control the militia and a senate intended to balance the more democratic assembly. Gaining a majority in the assembly as early as 1786, the conservatives dismantled much of the radicals' program, repealing the revolutionary test oaths and thus reenfranchising thousands of conservatives, stopping the issuance of paper money, and rechartering the Bank of North America.

Shays's Rebellion

In other states, popular opposition to hard money and high-tax policies, problems still festering from the Revolution, provoked vigorous protest. The controversy that erupted in Massachusetts in 1786 echoed strongly of equal rights and popular consent, staples of the rhetoric of 1776.

The war vastly expanded the burden of debt among Massachusetts' citizens. By the mid-1780s, increasing numbers of people had to borrow money just to pay their taxes or support their families, while others borrowed to speculate in western land or government securities. Because there were no commercial banks in the state, people borrowed from one another in a complicated and vulnerable pyramid of credit and debt.

A crisis began to build shortly after the war's end. As English goods once again flooded the American market, American importers borrowed heavily in England to expand their purchases, which they sold to local retailers at a handsome profit. Some of those profits they loaned back to the retailers so that they could sell even more goods. The retailers in turn extended credit to their customers.

In time the flood of English goods glutted the American market and forced prices down. By 1785, a number of English banking houses, heavily overcommitted in the American trade, were in trouble. When they called in their American loans, American merchants in turn tried to collect the debts due them, sending a credit crisis surging through the economy.

The crisis was most acute among the small farmers and laboring people of country and town. Caught in a tightening bind, they turned to their state governments for "stay laws" suspending the collection of private debts. If not granted relief, they faced foreclosure and the loss of shops and farms. They also pressed for new issues of paper money so that they would have something with which to pay both private debts and public taxes.

The largest creditors, however, most of whom lived in commercial areas along the coast, fought these relief proposals, because they wanted to collect sums owed them in hard currency.

By 1786, Massachusetts farmers, made desperate by private debt and a lingering agricultural depression, petitioned the Massachusetts assembly for relief. Peter Wood, tax collector for the town of Marlborough, reported that "there was not . . . the money in possession or at command among the people . . . to discharge taxes." Between 1784 and 1786, fully 29 towns declared themselves unable to meet their tax payments. The farmers' appeals, however, fell on deaf ears, for commercial and creditor interests now controlled the government.

As frustrated citizens had done before and would do again when the law proved unresponsive to their needs, Massachusetts farmers stepped outside the law and took matters into their own hands. A Hampshire County convention of 50 towns condemned the state senate, lawyers, court fees, and the tax system. It advised against violence, but crowds soon began to form.

The county courts drew much of the farmers' wrath because they issued the writs of property foreclosure that state and private creditors demanded. On August 31, 1786, armed men prevented the county court from sitting at Northampton, and on September 5, angry citizens closed down the court at Worcester. When farmers threatened similar actions elsewhere, an alarmed Governor James Bowdoin dispatched 600 militiamen to protect the Supreme Court, then on circuit at Springfield.

About 500 insurgents had gathered near there under the leadership of Daniel Shays, a popular Revolutionary War captain recently fallen on hard times. Most of the men who gathered around Shays were also debtors and veterans. Worried about a possible raid on the federal arsenal at Springfield, the Continental Congress authorized 1,300 troops to be readied for use against Shays and his rebels. For a few weeks, Massachusetts seemed poised on the brink of civil war.

In late November, the insurrection collapsed in eastern Massachusetts, but things were far from over in the west. When several insurgent groups refused to disband at Governor Bowdoin's command, he called out a force of 4,400 men, financed and led by worried eastern merchants. On January 26, 1787, Shays led 1,200 men toward the federal arsenal. Frightened by the siege, its defenders opened fire, killing four of the attackers and sending the Shaysites into retreat.

Over the next several weeks, the militia chased the remnants of Shays's followers across the state and sent Shays himself fleeing into Vermont for safety. By the end of February, the rebellion was over. In March, the legislature pardoned all but Shays and three other leaders; in another year, they too had been forgiven.

Similar challenges to public authority, fired by personal troubles and frustration over unresponsive government, erupted in South Carolina in May 1785, in Maryland in June 1786, and in several other states. Across the nation, state politics was in turmoil.

TOWARD A NEW NATIONAL GOVERNMENT

By 1786, as a result of Shays's Rebellion and other rumbles of discontent, belief was spreading among members of the Congress and other political leaders that the nation was in crisis. Attention focused increasingly on the inadequacies of the Articles of Confederation. Within two years, following a raucous political struggle, a new and far more powerful constitution replaced the Articles. That outcome would change forever the course of American history.

The Rise of Federalism

The supporters of a stronger national government called themselves Federalists (leading their opponents to adopt the name Anti-Federalists). Led by men such as Washington, Hamilton, Madison, and Jay, they believed that the nation was in the midst of a social and political crisis that threatened its very survival. Such men had never been comfortable with the more radical impulses of the Revolution. While supporting the principles of moderate republicanism, they continued to believe in an aristocracy of talent and to place high value on social order and the rights of property.

They were now persuaded that social and political change had carried too far. The Revolution, Jay lamented, "laid open a wide field for the operation of ambition," especially for "men raised from low degrees to high stations and rendered giddy by elevation." It was time, he insisted, to find better ways of protecting "the worthy against the licentious." In 1776, American liberty had needed protection against English power. Danger now, however, came from too much liberty threatening to degenerate into license. "We have probably had too good an opinion of human nature," wrote Washington. "Experience has taught us, that men will not adopt and carry into execution measures the best calculated for their own good, without the intervention of a coercive power." In the Federalists' minds, America needed "a strong government, ably administered" by the "better sort."

Congressional inability to handle the national debt, establish public credit, and restore

James Madison of Virginia worked tirelessly between 1786 and 1788 to replace the Articles of Confederation with a new and more effective national constitution.

overseas trade also troubled the Federalists. They stressed the need for a new national government capable of extending American trade, spurring economic recovery, and protecting national interests against Anglo-European designs.

Beyond that, the Federalists shared a vision of an expanding commercial republic, its people spreading across the rich lands of the interior, its merchant ships connecting America with the markets of Europe and beyond. That vision, so rich in national promise, seemed also at risk.

The Grand Convention

The first step toward governmental reform came in September 1786, when delegates of five states, who had gathered in Annapolis, Maryland, to discuss interstate commerce, prepared an address to all 13 states. Written by the ardent nationalist Alexander Hamilton, it called for a new convention to gather in Philadelphia in May 1787. In February, the Confederation Congress cautiously endorsed the idea of a convention to revise the Articles of Confederation. Before long, however, it became clear that more dramatic changes were in store.

During May, delegates representing every state except Rhode Island began assembling in Philadelphia. Eventually 55 delegates would participate in the convention's work, though daily attendance was usually between 30 and 40. The city bustled with excitement as they gathered, for the Grand Convention's roster read like an honor roll of the Revolution. From Virginia came the distinguished lawyer George Mason, chief author of Virginia's trailblazing bill of rights, and the already legendary George Washington. James Madison was there as well. No one, with perhaps the single exception of Alexander Hamilton, was more committed to nationalist reform. Madison brought to Philadelphia his own design for a new national government. That design, presented in the convention as the Virginia Plan, would serve as the basis for the new constitution. Nor did anyone rival the diminutive Madison's contributions to the convention's work. Tirelessly he took the convention floor to argue the nationalist cause or buttonhole wavering delegates to strengthen their resolve. In addition, he somehow found the energy to keep extensive notes in his personal shorthand. Those notes constitute our essential record of the convention's proceedings.

Two distinguished Virginians were conspicuously absent. Thomas Jefferson was abroad serving as minister to France, while the old patriot Patrick Henry, an ardent champion of state supremacy, wanted no part of the convention.

Other distinguished delegates included the venerable Benjamin Franklin, the erudite lawyer James Wilson, and the wealthy Robert Morris from Pennsylvania; Elbridge Gerry and Rufus King from Massachusetts; John Rutledge and Charles Pinckney from South Carolina; and Roger Sherman from Connecticut.

The New York assembly sent a deeply divided delegation that included Alexander Hamilton. Determined to protect New York's autonomy and his own political power, Governor George Clinton saw to it that several Anti-Federalist skeptics also made the trip to Philadelphia. They were no match for Hamilton, whose immense intelligence and ingratiating charm had enabled him to rise rapidly in the world. In 1777, while still in his early twenties, he became Washington's wartime aide-de-camp. That relationship served Hamilton well for the next 20 years. Returning from the war, Hamilton wooed and won the wealthy Elizabeth Schuyler, thereby securing his personal fortune and strengthening his political support. At Philadelphia, he was determined to drive his own nationalist vision ahead.

Meeting in Independence Hall, where the Declaration of Independence had been proclaimed little more than a decade before, the convention elected Washington its presiding officer, adopted rules of procedure, and, after spirited debate, voted to close the doors and conduct the convention's business in secret.

Debate focused first on Madison's Virginia Plan, which outlined a powerful national government and effectively set the convention's agenda. According to its provisions, there would be a bicameral congress, with the lower house elected by the people and the upper house, or senate, elected by the lower house from nominees proposed by the state legislatures. The plan also called for a president to be chosen by the congress, a national judiciary, and a council of revision, whose task was to review the constitutionality of legislation.

The smaller states quickly objected to the Virginia Plan's provision for proportional rather than equal representation. On June 15, William Paterson introduced a counterproposal, the New Jersey Plan, which would retain the Articles of Confederation while granting Congress the powers to tax and regulate both foreign and interstate commerce. After three days of heated debate, the delegates by a vote of seven states to three adopted the Virginia Plan as the basis for further discussions. It was now clear that the convention would set aside the Articles for a much stronger national government. Over the next four months, the convention struggled to shape that new government.

At times it seemed that the Grand Convention would collapse under the weight of its own disagreements and the oppressive summer heat as delegates wrestled over the sharply conflicting interests of large and small states, the balance of power between national and state governments, and the volatile issue of slavery. The delegates wrangled as well over the knotty problem of how to fashion an executive branch strong enough to govern but not so strong as to endanger republican liberty.

At one extreme was Hamilton's audaciously conservative proposal, made early in the convention's deliberations, for a congress and president elected for life and a national government so powerful that the states would survive as little more than administrative agencies. Finding his plan under attack and his influence among the delegates rapidly eroding, a disillusioned Hamilton withdrew from the convention in late June. He would return a month later but make few additional contributions.

At the other extreme stood the ardent Anti-Federalist Luther Martin of Maryland. Rude and unkempt, Martin voiced his uncompromising opposition to anything that threatened state sovereignty or smacked of aristocracy. Increasingly isolated by the convention's nationalist inclinations, Martin also returned home, in his case to warn of the convention's doings.

By early July, with tempers frayed and frustrated over the apparent deadlock, the delegates agreed to recess, ostensibly in recognition of Independence Day but actually to enable Franklin, Roger Sherman, and others to mount a final effort at compromise. All agreed that only a bold stroke could save the convention from collapse.

That stroke came on July 12, as part of what has become known as the Great Compromise.

The reassembled delegates agreed that representation in the lower house should be based on the total of each state's white population plus three-fifths of its black population. Though blacks were not accorded citizenship and could not vote, the southern delegates argued that they should be fully counted for this purpose. Delegates from the northern states, where relatively few blacks lived, did not want them counted at all, but the bargain was struck. As part of this compromise, the convention agreed that direct taxes would also be apportioned on the basis of population and that blacks would be counted similarly in that calculation as well. On July 16, the convention accepted the principle that each state should have an equal vote in the senate. The compromise thus accommodated the interests of both large and small states.

The convention then submitted its work to a committee of detail for drafting in proper constitutional form. That group reported on August 6, and for the next month the delegates hammered out the exact language of the document's seven articles.

Determined to give the new government the stability the state governments lacked, the delegates created an electoral process designed to bring only persons of standing and experience into national office. An electoral college of wise and experienced leaders would meet to choose the president. The process functioned exactly that way during the first several presidential elections.

Selection of the new Senate would be similarly indirect, for its members were to be named by the state legislatures. (Not until 1913, when the Seventeenth Amendment to the Constitution was ratified, would the people elect their senators.) Even the House of Representatives, the only popularly elected branch of the new government, was to be filled with persons of standing and wealth, for the Federalists were confident that only experienced and well-known leaders would be able to attract the necessary votes.

The delegates' final set of compromises touched the fate of black Americans. At the insistence of southerners, the convention agreed that the slave trade would not formally end for another 20 years. The delegates never used the words *slavery* or *slave trade* but spoke more vaguely about not prohibiting "the migration or importation of such persons as any of the states now existing shall think proper to admit." Their meaning, however, was clear.

More than that, they guaranteed slavery's protection, writing in Section 2 of Article 4 of the Constitution: "No person held to service or labour in one state, . . . [and] escaping into another, shall, in consequence of any law . . . therein, be discharged from such service, but shall be delivered up on claim of the party to whom such service or labour may be due." The delegates thus provided federal sanction for the capture and return of runaway slaves. This fugitive slave clause would return to haunt northern consciences in the years ahead, but at the time it seemed a small price to pay for sectional harmony and a new government. Northern accommodation to the demands of the southern delegates was eased, however, by knowledge that southerners in the Confederation Congress had recently agreed to prohibit the entry of new slaves into the Northwest Territory.

The document that emerged from the Philadelphia Convention, then, represented compromises between large states and small, as well as between North and South. Some of those compromises came at the expense of black Americans, who had no voice in the Constitution's drafting or ratification.

The Constitution decisively strengthened the national government, for Congress would now have authority to levy and collect taxes, regulate commerce, devise uniform rules for naturalization, and control the federal district in which it would eventually be located. Conspicuously missing was any statement reserving to the states all powers not explicitly conferred on the central government, which had been a crippling limitation of the Articles. On the contrary, the Constitution contained a number of clauses bestowing general grants of power on the new government. A final measure of the Federalists' determination to make the new government supreme over the states was the assertion in Article 6 that the Constitution and all laws passed under it were to be regarded as "the supreme Law of the Land."

When the convention had finished its business, 3 of the 42 remaining delegates refused to sign the document. The other 39, however, affixed their names and forwarded it to the Confederation Congress along with their request that it be sent on to the states for approval. On September 17, the Grand Convention adjourned.

Federalists Versus Anti-Federalists

Ratification presented the Federalists with more difficult problems than they had faced at Philadelphia. Now the debate shifted to the states, where sentiment was sharply divided and the situation was more difficult to control. Recognizing the unlikelihood of gaining quick agreement from all 13 states, the Federalists provided that the Constitution should go into effect when any nine agreed to it. Other states could then enter the Union as they were ready. They arranged for ratification by specially elected conventions rather than the state assemblies, since under the Constitution the assemblies would lose substantial amounts of power. Ratification by convention was also more constitutionally sound, since it would give the new government its own grounding in the people and free it from dependence on the state governments.

Word of the dramatic changes being proposed spread rapidly. In each state, Federalists and Anti-Federalists prepared to debate the new articles of government. Some critics feared that a stronger central government would threaten state interests or their own political power. Others, like Timothy Bloodworth, charged the Federalists with betraying Revolutionary republicanism. Like all "vigorous" and "energetic" governments, they warned, the new one would be corrupted by its own power.

The Anti-Federalists were aghast at the Federalists' vision of an expanding "republican empire." "The idea of . . . [a] republic, on an average of 1000 miles in length, and 800 in breadth, and containing 6 millions of white inhabitants all reduced to the same standards of morals, . . . habits . . . [and] laws," exclaimed one critic incredulously, "is itself an absurdity, and contrary to the whole experience of mankind." Such an attempt, the argument went, would guarantee factional conflict and disorder. Nor did the Anti-Federalists believe that the proposed separation of executive, legislative, and judicial powers or the balancing of state and national governments would prevent power's abuse. Government, they insisted, must be kept simple. Republican liberty could be preserved only in simple, homogeneous societies, where faction was absent and public virtue guided citizens' behavior.

Federalist spokesmen moved quickly to counter the criticism. The Federalists' most important effort was a series of essays penned by James Madison, Alexander Hamilton, and John Jay and published in New York under the pseudonym "Publius." Madison, Hamilton, and Jay moved systematically through the proposed constitution, explaining its virtues and responding to the Anti-Federalists' attacks. In the process, they described a political vision fundamentally different from that of their Anti-Federalist opponents.

Power, the Federalists now argued, was not the enemy of liberty but its guarantor. Nothing was more dangerous than the "mischievous effects of unstable government." Where government was not "energetic" and "efficient" (these were favorite Federalist words), demagogues and disorganizers did their work.

The *Federalist Papers* also countered the Anti-Federalists' warning that a single, extended republic encompassing the country's economic and social diversity would lead inevitably to factional warfare and the end of republican liberty. Factional divisions, they explained, could never be avoided, even in the smallest societies, because they were the inevitable by-products of economic and social development. Faction, moreover, was the necessary accompaniment of human liberty. Wrote Madison in *Federalist* No. 10: "Liberty is to faction what air is to fire, an ailment without which it instantly expires." To suppress faction would be to destroy liberty itself. Out of the clash and accommodation of social and economic interests would emerge public order and the best possible approximation of the public good.

The Federalist's arguments left the Anti-Federalists sputtering in amazement. What would become of public virtue in a system built on the notion of competing factional interests? They also accused their opponents of elitism, of wishing to join the government to wealth and privilege. Not all the Antis were democrats, but they were more consistently sympathetic to democratic principles than were their Federalist opponents. Certainly they believed more firmly that for government to be safe, it must be tied intimately to the people.

As the ratification debate revealed, the Federalists and Anti-Federalists held sharply contrasting visions of the new republic. The Antis remained much closer to the original republicanism of 1776, with its suspicion of power and wealth, its emphasis on the primacy of local government, and its fears of centralization. The Federalists, arguing that America's situation had changed dramatically since 1776, embraced the idea of nationhood and looked forward with anticipation to the development of a rising "republican empire" based on commercial development and led by men of wealth and talent. Both Federalists and Anti-Federalists claimed to be heirs of the Revolution, yet they differed dramatically on what the Revolution had meant.

The Struggle over Ratification

No one knows with certainty what most Americans thought of the proposed constitution. No national plebiscite on the Constitution was ever taken. A majority of the people probably opposed the document, either out of indifference or alarm. Fortunately for the Federalists, they did not have to persuade most Americans; they

needed only secure majorities in nine of the state ratifying conventions, a much less formidable task.

It took less than a year from the time the document left Congress to secure approval of the necessary nine states. Delaware, Pennsylvania, and New Jersey ratified first, in December 1787. Approval came a month later in Georgia and Connecticut. Massachusetts was next to ratify, but only after Federalist leaders forwarded a set of amendments outlining a federal "bill of rights" along with notice of ratification. Maryland and South Carolina were the seventh and eighth states to approve. The honor of being ninth and putting the Constitution over the top went to New Hampshire, which ratified on June 21.

Two massive gaps in the new Union remained—Virginia and New York. Clearly, the nation could not endure without them. In Virginia, careful politicking by Madison and other Federalist leaders made the difference. On June 25, the Virginia convention voted to ratify by the narrow margin of ten votes.

The New York convention met on June 17 at Poughkeepsie, with the Anti-Federalist followers of Governor Clinton firmly in command. Hamilton worked for delay, hoping that news of the results in New Hampshire and Virginia would turn the tide. For several weeks, approval hung in the balance while the two sides maneuvered for support. On July 27, approval squeaked through, 30 to 27. That left two states still uncommitted. North Carolina (with Timothy Bloodworth's cautious approval) finally ratified in November 1789. The final state, Rhode Island, did not enter the Union until May 1790, more than a year after the new government had gotten under way.

The Social Geography of Ratification

A glance at the geographic pattern of Federalist and Anti-Federalist strength indicates their different sources of political support. Federalist strength was concentrated along the coast and

Federalist and Anti-Federalist Areas, 1787–1788

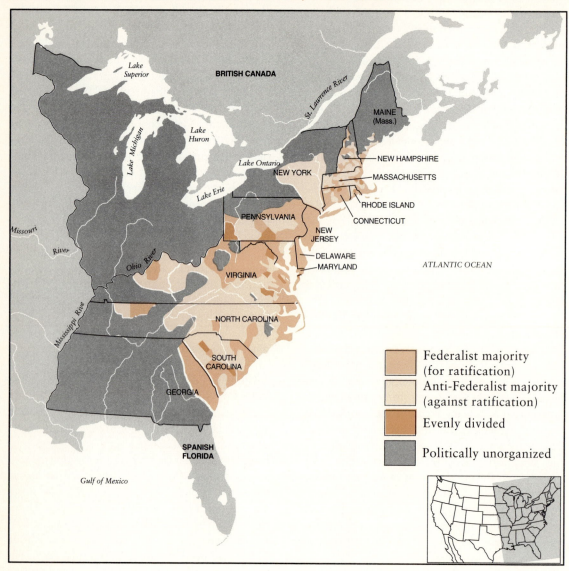

Federalist majority
(for ratification)

Anti-Federalist majority
(against ratification)

Evenly divided

Politically unorganized

navigable rivers and was strongest in cities and towns. The centers of Anti-Federalist support lay away from the coast, in the interior of New England, upstate New York, the Virginia piedmont and southside, and the western regions of the Carolinas.

Merchants and businessmen supported the Constitution most ardently. Enthusiasm also ran high among urban laborers, artisans, and shopkeepers, who believed that a stronger government could better promote the overseas trade on which their prosperity depended and protect

American artisans from foreign competition. The Constitution also found support in the countryside, especially among commercial farmers and southern planters eager for profit and anxious about overseas markets. But Federalist enthusiasm waned and Anti-Federalist sentiment increased in the interior. Among most ordinary farmers living outside the market economy and immersed in their own localities, the republicanism of 1776 outweighed their interests in national affairs. They found the Federalist vision of an "American empire" both strange and alarming.

Why were the Federalists finally successful? Their task was simplified by the widespread perception that the Articles needed strengthening. In light of the obvious troubles of the Confederation, the Federalists could argue that the Revolution was doomed to failure unless dramatic action was taken.

Most of all, however, the Federalists succeeded because of their determination and political skill. Most of the Revolution's major leaders were Federalists. Time and again these heroes spoke out for the Constitution in the state ratifying debates, and time and again their support proved decisive. Their experience as army officers and as members of the Continental and Confederation congresses caused them to identify with the nation and what it might become. They brought their vision to the ratification process and asked others to share it. With their success, the Federalists turned the American republic in a new and fateful direction.

CONCLUSION

COMPLETING THE REVOLUTION

Only five years had passed between England's acknowledgment of American independence in 1783 and ratification of the new national Constitution, yet to many Americans it seemed far longer. By war's end, the difficulties of sustaining American liberty were evident. The experience of the next half decade added to them. Americans continued to argue about their experiment in republicanism and to wonder whether it would actually work.

At the same time, the American people retained an immense reservoir of optimism about the future. Much would depend, of course, on their new constitution and the government soon to be created under it. As the ratification debate subsided and Congress prepared for the transition, the American people looked eagerly and anxiously ahead.

Recommended Reading

Among the major works dealing with the Articles of Confederation and the 1780s are Jack Rakove, *The Beginnings of National Politics: An Interpretive History of the Continental Congress* (1979); and Peter Onuf, *The Origins of the Federal Republic* (1983).

On the Philadelphia convention see Richard

Morris, *Witnesses at the Creation: Hamilton, Madison, Jay and the Constitution* (1985); Christopher Collier and James Collier, *Decision in Philadelphia* (1986); and J. Jackson Barlow et al., *The American Founding: Essays on the Formation of the Constitution* (1988). Robert Rutland's *James Madison, the*

Founding Father (1987) is a readable biography of the most important constitution maker.

For postwar political and economic problems, see Ronald Hoffman and Peter Albert, eds., *Sovereign States in an Age of Uncertainty* (1918); and David Szatmary, *Shays's Rebellion: The Making of an Agrarian Rebellion* (1980).

Though several decades old, Jackson Main, *The*

Anti-Federalists: Critics of the Constitution, 1781–1788 (1961), is still important for an understanding of the Anti-Federalist opposition. See also Steven Boyd, *The Politics of Opposition: Antifederalists and the Acceptance of the Constitution* (1979). Dumas Malone et al., *Rhetoric and the Founding* (1987), examines the relationship between language and meaning in the constitutional debates.

Time Line

1784	Treaty of Fort Stanwix with the Iroquois Spain closes Mississippi River to American navigation	1786	Annapolis convention calls for revision of the Articles of Confederation
1785	Land Ordinance for the Northwest Territory Jay-Gardoqui negotiations	1786–1787	Shays's Rebellion
1786	Virginia adopts "Bill for Establishing Religious Freedom"	1787	Northwest Ordinance Constitutional Convention *Federalist Papers* published by Hamilton, Jay, and Madison
		1788	Constitution ratified

chapter 8

....

Creating a Nation

In October 1789, David Brown arrived in Dedham, Massachusetts. Born about 50 years before in Bethlehem, Connecticut, Brown served in the Revolutionary army and after the war shipped out on an American merchantman to see the world. His travels, as he later reported, took him to "nineteen different . . . Kingdoms in Europe, and nearly all the United States."

Though Brown had little formal schooling, he was a man with powerful opinions and considerable natural ability. His reading and personal experience had persuaded him that government was a conspiracy of the rich to exploit farmers, artisans, and other common folk, and he was quick to make his opinions known. "The occupation of government," Brown declared bluntly in one of his numerous pamphlets, "is to plunder and steal." The object of his wrath was the central government recently established under the new national constitution. The leaders of government, he charged, were engrossing the nation's western lands for themselves. "Five hundred [people] out of the union of five millions receive all the benefit of public property and live upon the ruins of the rest of the community."

In the highly charged political climate of the 1790s, Brown's attacks on the new government's leaders brought a sharp response. In 1798, John Davis, the federal district attorney in Boston, issued a warrant for Brown's arrest on charges of sedition. Brown fled to Salem on the Massachusetts coast but was caught and charged with intent to defame the government and aid the country's enemies. For want of $400 bail, he was clapped in prison.

In June 1799, Brown came before the U.S. Circuit Court, Justice Samuel Chase presiding. Determined to make Brown an example of what criticism of the government would bring, Chase sentenced him to a fine of $480 and 18 months in jail. For nearly two years, Brown languished in prison. Not until the Federalist party was defeated in the election of 1800 and the Jeffersonian Republicans had taken office was he freed.

David Brown discovered how easy it was for critics of the government to get into trouble during the 1790s, a decade of extraordinary political controversy. Even though the Revolutionary War was long past, the debate over Revolutionary principles and the struggle to create a republican political order continued. As Benjamin Rush, Philadelphia physician and Revolutionary patriot, explained: "The American War is over, but this is far from being the case with the American revolution. On the contrary, nothing but the first act of the great drama is closed. It remains . . . to establish and perfect our new forms of government."

As we have seen, the contest for ratification of the new Constitution had generated fierce debate over the familiar concerns about power, political equality, and the proper role of the central government in a republican society. As the new government got under way during the 1790s, that debate heated up once again, drawing countless people like David Brown into the struggle.

As the decade proceeded and the political debate escalated, Americans divided into two opposing political camps. The Federalists supported the presidential administrations of George Washington and John Adams; the Jeffersonian Republicans were the Federalists' increasingly vocal critics. Seldom has American political discourse been so virulent, and rarely has the survival of the republic seemed to hang more clearly in the balance.

In this chapter, we examine the new government's beginnings, and the domestic and foreign issues that polarized political divisions between Federalists and Jeffersonian Republicans during the administration of John Adams. The chapter ends with the election of 1800, which brought Federalist defeat and Thomas Jefferson's election to the presidency.

LAUNCHING THE NATIONAL REPUBLIC

Once ratification of the Constitution was achieved, many Anti-Federalists seemed ready to give the new experiment a chance. They determined, however, to watch it closely and raise the alarm at the first sign of danger. It was not many months before those alarms were sounded.

Beginning the New Government

On April 16, 1789, George Washington started north from Virginia toward New York City to be inaugurated as the first president of the United States. The first electoral college had convened under the Constitution and unanimously elected him to the nation's highest office. His feelings were mixed as he set forth. "I bade adieu to Mount Vernon, to private life, and to domestic felicity," he confided to his diary, "and with a mind oppressed with more anxious and painful sensations than I have words to express, set out for New York . . . with the best disposition to render service to my country in obedience to its call, but with less hope of answering its expectations."

Washington's journey through the countryside resembled a royal procession, for he was the object of constant adulation along the way. When he reached New York City, throngs of citizens and newly elected members of Congress greeted the weary traveler. Over the streets of the city stretched gaily decorated arches. During the parade uptown to the governor's mansion, young women in white flowing robes preceded him, strewing flowers in his path. That night, bonfires illuminated the city.

Already the transition from the old Confed-

This imaginative scene of President-elect Washington's reception in Trenton, New Jersey, during his trip from Virginia to New York City for his first inauguration depicts the popular adulation that surrounded him as well as the sharply different political roles of men and women.

eration Congress to the new government was under way. On October 10, the old Congress adjourned *sine die* after setting March 4, 1789, as the day for the new Congress to assemble.

Inaugural day was April 30. Shortly after noon, on a small balcony overlooking a Wall Street thronged with people, Washington took the oath of office. With the crowd roaring approval and 13 guns booming in the harbor, the president bowed his way off the balcony and into Federal Hall. The rest of the day and late into the night, celebrations filled the air.

The Bill of Rights

Among the new government's first items of business were the amendments that several states had made conditions of their ratification. After considerable debate Congress reached agreement on 12 amendments and sent them on to the states, which ratified ten of them. These ten became the Bill of Rights. Among other things, they guaranteed freedom of speech, press, and religion; pledged the right of trial by jury, the right to bear arms, and the right to due process of law; forbade "unreasonable searches and seizures"; and protected individuals against self-

incrimination in criminal cases. These constitutional amendments have protected individuals' basic rights throughout the nation's history.

During its first months in office, Washington's administration enjoyed almost universal support, both in Congress and among the people. The honeymoon, however, did not last long. Within a year criticism began, and by the middle of the decade, opposition groups came together in a political coalition known as the Jeffersonian Republicans. By 1800, the Jeffersonians had gained control of the government. The political conflict of this first decade revealed the fragility but also the resilience of this new government.

The People Divide

Disagreement began in January 1790, when Secretary of the Treasury Alexander Hamilton submitted the first of several major policy statements, the "Report on the Public Credit," to Congress. Seldom in the nation's history has a single official so dominated public affairs as Hamilton did during these years. A man of extraordinary intelligence and ambition, Hamilton was both a nationalist and a proponent of America's economic development. Perhaps more clearly than anyone else among the nation's founders, he foresaw the country's future strength and was determined to promote its growth. The United States, he was fond of saying, was "a Hercules in the cradle."

He believed that the proper role of the new government was to promote economic enterprise. The people he most admired were men of wealth, ambitious entrepreneurs eager to tie their own fortunes to America's rising empire. Hamilton regarded a close alliance between these people and government officials as essential to achieving American greatness.

If Hamilton's economic policies were liberal in looking forward to enhanced economic opportunity, his politics were profoundly conservative. He distrusted the people and doubted their

Alexander Hamilton used both the office of secretary of the treasury and his personal relationship with President Washington to shape national policy during the early 1790s.

wisdom. "The people," he asserted, "are turbulent and changing; they seldom judge or determine right." That stark belief guided much of what he did.

With the Constitution now in place, Hamilton set about to give it proper direction. His opportunity came when Washington named him secretary of the treasury. Hamilton had five objectives: stabilize the government's finances and establish its credit, build and demonstrate its power, tie the interests of the rich and well-born to the national government, promote the country's commercial expansion overseas and its economic development at home, and anchor the nation's foreign relations in a commercial and diplomatic alliance with England. All were essential to the nation's survival; each, he believed, was closely tied to the others.

In his first "Report on the Public Credit,"

Hamilton recommended funding the remaining Revolutionary War debt by encouraging the government's creditors to exchange their badly depreciated securities at full face value for new interest-bearing government bonds. The foreign debt, held chiefly in France and the Netherlands, Hamilton set at $11.7 million. The domestic debt, including back interest, he fixed at $40.4 million. Second, he proposed that the federal government assume responsibility for the $21.5 million in remaining state war debts. By these actions, he hoped to revive confidence in the government at home and abroad and tie business and commercial interests, which held most of the outstanding securities, firmly to the new government.

The proposal to fund the foreign debt aroused little controversy, but Hamilton's plans for handling the government's domestic obligations generated immediate opposition. In the House of Representatives, James Madison protested the unfairness of funding depreciated securities at their face value, especially since speculators, anticipating Hamilton's proposals, had acquired most of them at a fraction of their initial worth. In addition, Madison and many of his southern colleagues knew that northern businessmen held most of the securities and that funding would little benefit the South. After a bit of grumbling, Congress endorsed the funding plan.

Federal assumption of the remaining state debts aroused even greater criticism. States with the largest remaining unpaid obligations, such as Massachusetts, thought assumption a splendid idea. But others, such as Virginia and Pennsylvania, which had already retired much of their debt, were opposed. Critics also pointed out that assumption would strengthen the central government at the expense of the states, for wealthy individuals would now look to it rather than the states for a return on their investments. Moreover, with its increased need for revenue, the federal government would now have reason to exercise its newly acquired power of taxation. That was exactly what Hamilton intended.

Once again, Congress supported Hamilton's bill. Both Madison and Jefferson approved it as part of an agreement to move the seat of government from New York, first to Philadelphia and then, after 1800, to a special federal district on the Potomac River.

While the southern states continued to complain about the funding and assumption schemes, Hamilton introduced the second phase of his financial program in December 1790. He proposed a national bank capable of handling the government's financial affairs and pooling private investment capital for economic development. Though he was careful not to mention it publicly, he had the example of the Bank of England and its ties with the royal government clearly in mind.

Congressional opposition to the bank came almost entirely from the South. It seemed obvious that the bank would serve the needs of northern merchants and manufacturers far better than those of southern agrarians. Still, in February 1791, Congress approved the bank bill.

Before signing it, Washington asked his cabinet for advice. Following the constitutional doctrine of "implied powers"—the principle that the government possessed the authority to make any laws "necessary and proper" for exercising the powers specifically granted to it—Hamilton argued that Congress could charter such a bank under its power to collect taxes and regulate trade. Secretary of State Jefferson disagreed, maintaining that since the Constitution said nothing at all about chartering banks, the bill was unconstitutional and should be rejected.

Jefferson also opposed the bank because he feared it would promote a commercial republic filled with merchants and a dependent laboring class. He sought instead an agrarian republic populated by yeoman farmers committed to economic and political equality. To Jefferson's distress, Washington followed Hamilton's advice and signed the bank bill into law.

In December 1790, in his second "Report on the Public Credit," Hamilton broached the issue of federal taxation. He proposed a series of excise taxes, including one on the manufacture of distilled liquor. The power to tax and spend, Hamilton knew, was the power to govern. The Whiskey Tax became law in March 1791.

Finally, in his "Report on Manufactures," issued in December 1791, Hamilton called for a system of protective tariffs for American industry, bounties to encourage the expansion of commercial agriculture, and a network of federally sponsored internal improvements such as roadways and lighthouses. Neither the agrarian South nor northern seaport districts, however, wanted tariffs that might reduce trade and raise the cost of living. As a result, Congress never endorsed this report.

All the while, criticism of Hamilton's policies continued to grow, reaching a climax in January 1793 when Representative William Branch Giles of Virginia introduced a series of resolutions calling for an inquiry into the condition of the Treasury and urging censure of the secretary's conduct. None of Giles's accusations passed the House, but the debate was now spreading beyond the circle of governing officials in Philadelphia.

Among ordinary Americans, Hamilton's financial program drew a mixed response. In northern towns and cities, artisans and other working people generally approved. Closely dependent on the expansion of commerce and manufacturing, they supported efforts to improve credit and stimulate economic development. With their own economic circumstances improving, they seemed undisturbed by the special benefits that funding, assumption, and the bank brought to a few. Within several years, many of them would move into political opposition, but for the moment their support of the government was secure.

The Whiskey Rebellion

The farmers of western Pennsylvania provided the most dramatic expression of popular discontent with government policies. Their anger focused on the Whiskey Tax, for their livelihood depended on their ability to transport surplus grain eastward across the mountains to market. To ship it in bulk was prohibitively expensive, so they distilled the grain and moved it in the more cost-efficient form of whiskey. Hamilton's tax threatened to make this practice unprofitable. He knew that but cared little what the farmers thought.

Trouble was brewing by the summer of 1792 as angry farmers and their supporters gathered in mass meetings across western Pennsylvania. In August, a convention at Pittsburgh drew up a series of resolutions denouncing the tax and declaring that the people would prevent its collection. The convention's pronouncements echoed the Anti-Federalists' warnings against the centralizing and taxing tendencies of a national government. Like opponents of the Stamp Act in 1765, they decided that repression would follow if resistance did not soon begin.

Alarmed by the convention's resolutions, Washington quickly issued a proclamation warning against such "unlawful" gatherings and insisting on the enforcement of the excise. In July 1794, federal marshal David Lennox, in company with John Neville, a local excise inspector, attempted to serve papers on several western farmers, commanding their appearance in court at Philadelphia. An angry crowd gathered and stood in the way. Soon 500 armed men surrounded Neville's home just outside Pittsburgh and demanded his resignation. Learning that Neville had left, they ordered the dozen soldiers trapped in the house to lay down their arms and come out. The soldiers refused, and for several hours the two sides exchanged rifle fire. After several men had been wounded, the soldiers finally surrendered, whereupon Neville's house was put to the torch. Similar episodes involving angry crowds and the erection of Liberty Poles reminiscent of the Revolution erupted across the state. At Parkinson's Ferry, a convention of over 200 delegates debated both armed resistance and secession from the United States.

Alarmed that the protests might spread through the entire whiskey-producing backcountry from New York to Georgia, Washington ordered the insurgents home and called out troops from eastern Pennsylvania and surrounding states to restore order. Hamilton viewed the insurrection not as evidence of an unjust policy needing change but as a test of the administration's ability to govern. Suppressing the rebellion, Hamilton explained, "will . . . add to the solidity of everything in this country." He eagerly volunteered to accompany a federal army west.

In late August, a force of nearly 13,000 men, larger than the average strength of the continental army during the Revolutionary War, moved toward western Pennsylvania. At its center was Colonel William McPherson's "Pennsylvania Blues," an upper-class and strongly Federalist cavalry regiment. At its head rode the president of the United States and the secretary of the treasury. Washington soon returned to Philadelphia, persuaded by his aides of the danger to his safety, but Hamilton pressed ahead. The battle that Hamilton had anticipated never materialized, for as the federal army approached, the "Whiskey Rebels" dispersed. The army managed to take 20 prisoners, two of whom were convicted of high treason and sentenced to death. Later, in a calmer mood, Washington pardoned them both.

As people quickly realized, the "Whiskey Rebellion" had never threatened the government's safety. Even as ardent a Federalist as Fisher Ames was uneasy at the sight of federal troops marching against American citizens. Though a government "by overcoming an unsuccessful insurrection becomes stronger," he noted, "elective rulers can scarcely ever employ the physical force of a democracy without turning the moral force, or the power of public opinion, against the government." Americans would soon have additional reason to ponder Ames's warning.

THE REPUBLIC IN A THREATENING WORLD

Because the nation was so new and the outside world so threatening, issues of foreign policy during the 1790s generated extraordinary excitement. In the arguments over the French Revolution and its implications for the new American republic, the American people revealed once again how sharply they differed in values and beliefs.

The Promise and Peril of the French Revolution

France's revolution began in 1789 as an effort to reform an arbitrary monarchy weakened by debt and administrative decay. Pent-up demands for social justice, however, quickly outran the initial attempts at moderate, constitutional reform. By the early 1790s, France was embroiled in a radical social revolution. In January 1793, the monarch, Louis XVI, was beheaded. While the rest of Europe watched in horror and fascination, the forces of revolution and reaction struggled for the nation's soul.

As the revolution grew, the forces of conservatism across the Continent gathered in opposition. In response, France's revolutionary government launched a series of military thrusts into Belgium and Prussia. By the end of 1793, Europe was locked in a deadly war between revolutionary France and a counterrevolutionary coalition led by Prussia and Great Britain.

For more than a decade, the French Revolution dominated European affairs. It also cut like a plowshare through the surface of American politics, dividing Americans more deeply against one another.

The outbreak of European war posed a number of thorny problems for Washington's administration. Both England and France wanted America's raw materials, and each was determined to prevent them from reaching the other. Both nations attempted to control American trade for their own advantage by stopping American ships headed for the other's ports and confiscating American cargoes.

America's relations with England were further complicated by its practice of impressing American sailors into service aboard ships of the Royal Navy to meet its growing demand for seamen. Washington faced the problem of upholding the country's neutral rights and protecting its citizens without getting drawn into the European war.

The old French alliance of 1778 compounded the government's dilemma. If still in effect, it seemed to require the United States to aid France, much as France had assisted the American states a decade and a half before. But some insisted that the old treaty had been dissolved when the French monarchy collapsed.

The American people's intense reaction to the European drama further complicated the situation. At first, virtually everyone supported the French Revolution, viewing it as an extension of their own struggle for liberty. Even the swing toward social revolution did not immediately dampen American enthusiasm.

By the mid-1790s, however, especially after France's revolutionary regime launched its attacks on organized Christianity, many Americans pulled back in alarm. This certainly did not resemble their own revolution. What connection could there possibly be between the principles of 1776 and the chaos of revolutionary France? "There is a difference between the French and the American Revolution," insisted the *Gazette of the United States,* a Federalist newspaper. "In America no barbarities were perpetrated—no men's heads were stuck upon poles—no mangled ladies bodies were carried thro' the streets in triumph.... Whatever blood was shed, flowed gallantly in the field." The writer ignored the violence meted out by the supporters of monarchy in France and betrayed a selective memory of America's own revolution. But the differences were indeed profound.

For the Federalists, revolutionary France now symbolized social anarchy. With increasing vigor, they castigated the revolution and championed England as the defender of European stability and civilization.

Many Americans, however, continued to support France. While decrying the revolution's excesses, they believed that republican liberty would ultimately emerge from the turmoil. Jefferson wrote that although he regretted the shedding of innocent blood, he believed it necessary if true liberty were to be achieved.

Citizen Genêt and the Democratic-Republican Societies

Popular associations known as the Democratic-Republican societies provided the most vocal support for revolutionary France. As early as 1792, ordinary citizens began to establish "constitutional societies" dedicated to "watching over the rights of the people, and giving an early alarm in case of governmental encroachments." During the government's first years, several dozen such societies, modeled after the Sons of Liberty of 30 years before, formed to oppose Hamilton's financial program.

It was the French Revolution, however, that kindled democratic enthusiasm and stimulated the societies' growth. The arrival in April 1793 of Citizen Edmund Genêt, minister from the French republic to the United States, provided the spark. Genêt landed first at Charleston, South Carolina, to a tumultuous reception. His instructions were to woo public support and negotiate a commercial treaty with Washington's administration. However, he soon began commissioning American privateers to prey on British shipping in the Caribbean and enlisting American seamen for expeditions against Spanish Florida, both clear violations of American neutrality.

Later, despite a warning by Secretary of State Jefferson, Genêt, in open defiance of diplomatic protocol, urged Congress to reject Washington's recently issued neutrality proclamation and side with revolutionary France. That was the final straw. On August 2, the president demanded Genêt's recall, charging that his conduct threatened "war abroad and anarchy at home."

Although Genêt had little success as a diplomat, instead of returning to France, where the political situation was changing rapidly, he remained in the United States, fanning popular enthusiasm for the French revolution. In June 1793, with his open encouragement, the largest and most influential of the new societies, the Democratic Society of Pennsylvania, had been founded in Philadelphia. About 40 similar organizations scattered from Maine to Georgia sprang up during the next several years. Working people—mechanics, artisans, and laborers in the cities, small farmers and tenants in the countryside—provided the bulk of membership. The leaders, however, were doctors, lawyers, tradesmen, and landowners. All were united by a common dedication to what they called the "principles of '76" and a determination to preserve those principles against the "royalizing" tendencies of Washington's administration. They labeled Washington's proclamation of neutrality a "pusillanimous truckling to Britain." Declared the New York society: "We firmly believe that he who is an enemy to the French revolution cannot be a firm republican; and therefore . . . ought not to be entrusted with the guidance of any part of the machine of government." Several of the societies openly urged the United States to enter the war on France's behalf.

In western areas, local societies agitated against the continuing British occupation of the frontier posts around the Great Lakes and berated Spain for closing the Mississippi. In the East, they castigated England for its "piracy" against American shipping. In the Carolinas, they demanded fuller representation for the growing backcountry in the state's assembly. And almost to a person they protested the Excise Tax, opposed the administration's overtures to

England, and demanded that public officials, state and federal alike, attend to the people's wishes. Finally, they campaigned for a press free from the political control of Federalist "aristocrats." "The greater part of the American newspapers," they protested, "seem to be lock, stock, and barrel in the hands of the anti-democrats."

President Washington and his supporters were incensed by the societies' support of Genêt and their criticism of the government's domestic program. The "real design" of the societies, thundered the staunch Federalist Fisher Ames, was "to involve the country in war, to assume the reins of government and tyrannize over the people." Writing in the *Virginia Chronicle* of January 17, 1794, "Xantippe" berated Kentucky's Democratic Society as "that horrible sink of treason, that hateful synagogue of anarchy, that odious conclave of tumult, that frightful cathedral of discord, that poisonous garden of conspiracy, that hellish school of rebellion and opposition to all regular and well-balanced authority!" Such polemics illustrated how inflamed public discourse had become.

Jay's Controversial Treaty

Controversy over Jay's Treaty with England further heightened tensions at mid-decade. Alarmed by the worsening relations with England, Washington sent Chief Justice John Jay to London in the spring of 1794 with instructions to negotiate on a wide range of troublesome issues, including continued British occupation of the western posts, British interference with American neutral shipping, and impressment of American seamen.

Early in 1795, Jay returned home with a treaty that resolved almost none of America's grievances. England finally agreed to vacate the western posts, but not for another year and then only if it had uninterrupted access to the fur trade on American soil south of the Great Lakes. Jay failed to secure compensation for American slaves carried off by the British at the end of the Revolution. Nor would the British foreign minister offer guarantees against the future impress-

ment of American seamen, compromise on the issue of neutral rights, or open the British West Indies to American shipping.

When the terms of the treaty were made public, they triggered an explosion of protest. Southern planters were angry because the agreement brought no compensation for their slaves. Westerners complained that the British were not evacuating the posts, while merchants and sailors railed against Jay's capitulation on the West Indies trade and impressment. After a long and acrimonious debate, however, the Senate ratified the treaty by the narrowest of margins.

The administration made better progress on the still-volatile issue of free transit out the mouth of the Mississippi River. In the Treaty of San Lorenzo, negotiated by Thomas Pinckney in 1795, Spain for the first time recognized the United States' boundaries under the peace treaty of 1783 and thus gave up all claim to U.S. territory. Spain also granted free navigation of the Mississippi and the right of American merchants to unload their goods on shore for transshipment for the next three years.

By mid-decade, political harmony had disappeared, and the American people stood sharply divided on almost every significant issue of foreign and domestic policy. Increasingly estranged from administration policy, Jefferson resigned as secretary of state in July 1793 and soon joined politicians such as Madison and Albert Gallatin of Pennsylvania in open opposition to the Federalist administration.

In September 1796, Washington announced that he would not accept a third term. He had long been contemplating retirement, for he was now 64 and was exhausted by the political controversy swirling about him.

FEDERALISTS VERSUS JEFFERSONIANS

By 1796, bitter controversy surrounded the national government. That controversy intensified

As one of the first true elder statesmen of the early republic, Thomas Jefferson almost became the second president in the 1796 election after Washington declined to run for a third term. John Adams won that election by only three votes, and Jefferson—as the nominal leader of many of those in opposition to the Federalists—represented a powerful voice against many of Adams's policies

during the last half of the 1790s until it seemed to threaten the very stability of the country.

The Election of 1796

The presidential election of 1796 reflected the political storms buffeting the nation. In 1792, Washington and Adams had been reelected president and vice president, respectively, without significant opposition. Four years later, the situation was vastly different.

With Washington out of the picture, the presidential contest quickly narrowed to John Adams and Thomas Jefferson. Both were now

elder statesmen. Both had played distinguished roles during the Revolution, when they had become friends and earned each other's respect. Though they had worked closely together, Adams and Jefferson differed in many ways. Short, round, and self-consciously neat, Adams contrasted sharply in physical appearance with the tall and frequently disheveled Jefferson. Intensely ambitious, Adams struggled self-consciously with his public career. Jefferson, by contrast, charted his course more quietly and repeatedly sought the solace of private life.

They differed in intellect and vision as well. Jefferson's mind was more expansive and his interests far more encompassing. Politician and political theorist, he was also an avid naturalist, architect, and philosopher. Adams's interests were more tightly focused on legal and constitutional affairs. By the mid-1790s, they differed as well in their visions of the new republic.

Adams, a committed Federalist, was appalled by the French Revolution and longed for political and social order. Jefferson, while firmly supporting the Constitution, was alarmed by Hamilton's financial program, viewed France's revolution as a logical if chaotic extension of America's struggle for freedom, and sought to expand political democracy. By 1796, he had become the vocal leader of an increasingly articulate political opposition, the Jeffersonian Republicans.

The election of that year bound Jefferson and Adams in a strained alliance. With Washington gone, Adams became the Federalists' candidate. He received 71 electoral votes and was declared president. Jefferson came in second with 68 and therefore, as specified in the Constitution, became vice president. The narrowness of Adams's majority gave indication of the Federalists' weakness and the growing strength of the Jeffersonians.

The War Crisis with France

Adams had no sooner taken office than he confronted a deepening crisis with France. Hoping to ease diplomatic relations between the two countries, he sent off a three-person commission to try to negotiate an accord.

When the commissioners arrived in Paris, agents of the French foreign minister, Charles Maurice de Talleyrand-Périgord, visited them and made it clear that the success of the negotiations depended on a prior loan to the French government and a $240,000 gratuity for them. The two staunchly Federalist commissioners, John Marshall and Charles Pinckney, indignantly rejected the demands and sailed home. The third commissioner, Elbridge Gerry, stayed behind, still hoping for an accommodation and alarmed by Talleyrand's intimation that if all three Americans left, France would declare war.

When Adams submitted a report to Congress on this incident, he substituted the letters X, Y, and Z for the names of the French agents involved, so the matter became known as the "XYZ affair." Americans were outraged at the French demands. Federalist congressmen thundered against the insult to American honor and demanded action. "Millions for defense, but not one cent for tribute" became their rallying cry. Adams now found himself an unexpected hero. Caught up in the anti-French furor, the president lashed out at "enemies" at home and abroad. "In the last extremity," he declared, "we shall find traitors who will unite with the invading enemy and fly within their lines."

For the moment, the Republicans were in disarray. Publicly they deplored the French government's behavior and pledged to uphold the nation's honor. But among themselves they talked with alarm about the Federalists' intentions. They had good reason for concern, because the Federalists quickly mounted a crash program to repel foreign invaders and roust out traitors in the country's midst.

The Alien and Sedition Acts

In May 1798, Congress created the Navy Department and called for the rapid development of a naval force to defend the American coast against French attack. In July, Congress unilaterally repeated the treaty of 1778, thus moving closer to an open breach with France, and then approved a 10,000-man army. The army's stated mission was to defend the country against an expected French invasion. The Jeffersonians, however, feared otherwise, for they remembered the speed with which the Federalists had used force against the Whiskey Rebels.

As criticism of the army bill mounted, Adams had second thoughts. He was still enough of a revolutionary to worry about the domestic dangers of standing armies. "This damned army," he burst out, "will be the ruin of the country." To the dismay of hard-line Federalists, he issued only a few of the officers' commissions that Congress had authorized. Without officers, the troops could not be mobilized.

Fearful of foreign subversion and aware that French immigrants were active in the Jeffersonian opposition, the Federalist-dominated Congress moved in the summer of 1798 to curb the flow of aliens into the country. The Naturalization Act extended from 5 to 14 years the residence requirement for citizenship, and the Alien Act authorized the president to expel "all such aliens as he shall judge dangerous to the peace and safety of the United States." Another bill, the Alien Enemies Act, empowered the president in time of war to arrest, imprison, or banish the subjects of any hostile nation without specifying charges against them or providing opportunity for appeal.

The implications of these acts for basic political liberties were ominous enough, but the Federalists had not yet finished. In July 1798, Congress passed the Sedition Act, aimed directly at the Jeffersonian opposition. The bill made it a high misdemeanor, punishable by fine and imprisonment, for anyone, citizen or alien, to conspire in opposition to "any measure or measures of the government" or to aid "any insurrection, riot, unlawful assembly, or combination." Fines and imprisonment were provided as well for persons who "write, print, utter, or publish . . . any false, scandalous and malicious writing" bringing the government, Congress, or the president into disrepute. The Federalists now equated preservation of their own political power with national survival. The Federalist moves stunned the Jeffersonians, for they threatened to smother political opposition.

Under the terms of the Alien Act, Secretary of State Timothy Pickering launched investigations intended to force the registration of all foreigners. The act's chilling effects were widespread. In July, Pickering noted approvingly that large numbers of aliens, especially persons of French ancestry, were leaving the country. Prosecutions under the Sedition Act were numerous. Twenty-five people, including David Brown of Dedham, were arrested and charged with violating the act. Fifteen were indicted, and ten were ultimately convicted, the majority of them Jeffersonian printers and editors.

Passage of the Alien and Sedition acts generated a firestorm of protest. The Virginia and Kentucky assemblies directly challenged the Federalist laws. The Kentucky Resolutions, drafted by Jefferson and passed on November 16, 1798, declared that the national government had violated the Bill of Rights. Faced with the arbitrary exercise of federal power, the resolutions continued, each state "has an equal right to judge by itself . . . infractions . . . [and] the mode and measure of redress." Nullification (declaring a law invalid within a state's borders) was the "rightful remedy" for unconstitutional laws. The Virginia Resolutions, written by Madison and passed the following month, asserted that when the central government threatened the people's liberties, the states "have the right and are in duty bound to interpose for arresting the progress of the evil." It would not be the last time that state leaders would claim authority to set aside a federal law.

The Kentucky and Virginia resolutions received little support elsewhere, but they indicated the depth of popular opposition to the Federalists' program. In Philadelphia, armed Federalist patrols walked the streets to protect government officials from angry crowds. As 1799 began, the country seemed on the brink of upheaval.

Within a year, however, the cycle turned again, this time decisively against the Federalists. The break came with Adams's dramatic decision to send a new emissary to France. From Europe, Adams's son, John Quincy Adams, sent assurances that Talleyrand was ready to negotiate an honorable accord. The president seized the opening, fearing that war with France "would convulse the attachments of the country." "The end of war is peace," Adams explained, "and peace was offered me." Moreover, he had concluded that his only chance of reelection lay in fashioning a peace coalition out of both parties.

Adams's cabinet strongly disapproved, for the entire Federalist war program depended on the credibility of the French crisis. But by year's end, the president's emissaries had secured an agreement providing for the restoration of peaceful relations between the two nations.

The "Revolution of 1800"

As the election of 1800 approached, the Federalists were bitterly divided. The Hamiltonians were furious at Adams's "betrayal" and demanded that he not seek reelection. When Adams did not withdraw, the Hamiltonians plotted his defeat.

Both sides believed that the republic's survival hung in the balance. Jefferson declared that this election would "fix our national character" and "determine whether republicanism or aristocracy" would prevail. The Federalists saw the choice as between republicanism and "anarchy." In Virginia, rumors of a slave insurrection briefly interrupted the feuding. But the scare passed quickly, and Federalists and Jeffersonians were soon at each others' throats once again.

Though election day was tense throughout the nation, it passed without serious interruption. As the results were tallied, it became clear that the Jeffersonians had handed the Federalists a decisive defeat. Jefferson, the Republicans' preferred candidate for president, and Aaron Burr, their other nominee, each had 73 votes. Adams followed with 65.

Presidential Election of 1800

NEW HAMPSHIRE (6)
VERMONT (4)
MAINE (Mass.)
NEW YORK (12)
MASSACHUSETTS (16)
RHODE ISLAND (4)
CONNECTICUT (9)
NEW JERSEY (7)
DELAWARE (3)
MARYLAND (10)
INDIANA TERRITORY
NORTHWEST TERRITORY
PENNSYLVANIA (15)
VIRGINIA (21)
KENTUCKY (4)
TENNESSEE (3)
NORTH CAROLINA (12)
MISSISSIPPI TERRITORY
SOUTH CAROLINA (8)
GEORGIA (4)

Electoral Votes:
Jefferson (Republican)
Adams (Federalist)
Vote divided

elsewhere, loyalty to Jefferson, strong anti-British and pro-French sentiment, and suspicion of the commercially oriented Federalists kept power in the hands of the Jeffersonians.

In the middle states, Federalists and Jeffersonians were more evenly balanced and the election was more fiercely contested because economic and social differences were greater and issues of foreign and domestic policy cut across society in more complicated ways. This sectional pattern would continue to shape American politics.

The distinctions between the Federalists and Jeffersonians were grounded in socioeconomic divisions as well. The Federalists were strongest among merchants, manufacturers, and commercial farmers located within easy reach of the coast—groups that had supported the Constitution in 1787 and 1788. In both New York City and Philadelphia, the Federalists' main strength was in the wards where assessments were highest and addresses most fashionable.

By contrast, the Jeffersonians included most of the old Anti-Federalists, agriculturalists in both North and South, and countless urban workers and artisans who resented Federalist arrogance. They also attracted people such as Irish and French immigrants and religious minorities—Baptists, Jews, and Catholics—restive under the lingering religious establishments.

The political alignment of 1800 resembled but did not exactly duplicate the Federalist–Anti-Federalist division of 1786–1788. The Jeffersonian coalition was much broader than the Anti-Federalists' had been, for it included countless individuals, from urban workers to leaders such as Madison and Jefferson, who had supported the Constitution and helped set the new government on its feet. Unlike the Anti-Federalists, the Jeffersonians were ardent supporters of the Constitution who called for the new government to be grounded in the principles of liberty, political equality, and a strong dependence on state authority. Nationally, the Jeffersonians now enjoyed a clear political majority. Their coalition would dominate American politics well into the nineteenth century.

Because of the tie vote, the election was thrown into the House of Representatives, where a deadlock quickly developed. After a bitter struggle, the House finally elected Jefferson, ten states to four, on the thirty-sixth ballot. (Seeking to prevent a recurrence of such a crisis, the new Congress soon passed, and the states ratified, the Twelfth Amendment, providing for separate electoral college ballots for president and vice president.) The magnitude of the Federalists' defeat was even more evident in the congressional elections, where they lost their majorities in both House and Senate.

The election's outcome revealed the strong sectional divisions now evident in the country's politics. The Federalists remained dominant in New England because of regional loyalty to Adams, the importance of the area's commercial ties with England, and fears that the Jeffersonians intended to import social revolution. From Maryland south, Jeffersonian control was almost as complete. In South Carolina, whites' fears of the black majority smothered every tendency toward political division, and the Federalists remained solidly in control. But

CONCLUSION

TOWARD THE NINETEENTH CENTURY

The election of 1800 provided a remarkable outcome to more than a decade of political crisis. The series of events had begun in the late 1780s with the intensifying debate over the Articles of Confederation and the movement toward a stronger central government. Under the new Constitution, divisions began to form, first in Congress, then, increasingly, among the people. Hamilton's domestic policies first generated opposition, but it was foreign affairs—the French Revolution, the European war, Jay's Treaty, and the prospect of a war with France—that galvanized political energies and set the Federalists and Jeffersonians against each other.

After the election of 1800, control of the federal government passed for the first time from one political party to another, not easily but peacefully and legally. The Jeffersonians called it "The Revolution of 1800." The future would show whether the Jeffersonians were correct.

Recommended Reading

On politics in the states during the 1790s see Richard Beeman, *The Old Dominion and the New Nation, 1788–1801* (1972); Norman Risjord, *Chesapeake Politics, 1781–1800* (1978); and Charles Steffen, *The Mechanics of Baltimore: Workers and Politics in the Age of Revolution, 1763–1812* (1984).

For cogent discussions of the ideological debates between Federalists and Jeffersonians, see Joyce Appleby, *Capitalism and a New Social Order: The Republican Vision of the 1790s* (1984); and Lance Banning, *The Jeffersonian Persuasion: The Evolution of a Party Ideology* (1978).

Party development during the 1790s can be followed in John Hoadley, *Origins of American Political Parties, 1789–1803* (1986); and Merrill Peterson, *Thomas Jefferson and the New Nation* (1970).

The Bill of Rights and the problem of civil liberties are treated by Bernard Schwartz, *The Great Rights of Mankind* (1977); and Leonard Levy, *Legacy of Suppression: Freedom of Speech and Press in Early American History* (1960).

For a fuller understanding of foreign policy issues, turn to Harry Ammon, *The Genêt Mission* (1973); Jerald Combs, *The Jay Treaty* (1970); and Daniel Lang, *Foreign Policy in the Early Republic* (1985).

Thomas Slaughter explains the character of backwoods revolt in *The Whiskey Rebellion: Frontier Epilogue to the American Revolution* (1986). Aleine Austin, *Matthew Lyon: "New Man" of the Democratic Revolution, 1749–1822* (1981), traces the meaning of political equality in the life of an ardent Jeffersonian.

Time Line

1789	George Washington inaugurated as first president Outbreak of French Revolution
1790	Slave trade outlawed in all states except Georgia and South Carolina Hamilton's "Reports on the Public Credit"
1791	Bill of Rights ratified Whiskey tax and national bank established Hamilton's "Report on Manufactures"
1792	Washington reelected
1793	Outbreak of war in Europe Washington's Neutrality Proclamation Jefferson resigns from cabinet
1793	Controversy over Citizen Genêt's visit
1794	Whiskey Rebellion in Pennsylvania
1795	Controversy over Jay's Treaty with England
1796	Washington's Farewell Address John Adams elected president
1797	XYZ affair in France
1798	Naturalization Act; Alien and Sedition Acts Virginia and Kentucky resolutions
1798–1800	Undeclared naval war with France
1801	Jefferson elected president by House of Representatives

chapter 9

Society and Politics in the Early Republic

In May 1809, Mary and James Harrod gathered their five children, loaded a few belongings (tools, seeds for the summer planting, and several prized pieces of furniture) on a wagon, closed the door on their four-room cabin, fell in line with a dozen other families, and headed west from Spotsylvania County, Virginia, toward a new life in Kentucky. They left behind 10 acres of marginal upland, 15 years of wearying effort at trying to wring a modest living from it, and a family cemetery holding two of their other children and Mary's parents.

The first years in central Kentucky would be especially hard for James and Mary as they "opened up" the land, planted the first crops, and erected a cabin. They would be lonesome as well, for the Harrods would be unlikely to see even the chimney smoke from their nearest neighbors. James and Mary were hopeful, though, and that sustained them as they trudged west.

In April 1795, Ben Thompson started north from Queen Anne's County, Maryland, for New York City. Ben knew little beyond farming, but he was ambitious and listened carefully to the ship's captains who talked about life at sea while they recruited men for their crews. Sailors were in demand, and pay was good. For five years, Ben sailed the seas. Having enough of travel, he returned to New York and hired out as an apprentice to a ship's carpenter.

About the same time, Phyllis Sherman left her home in Norwalk, Connecticut. She also headed for New York, where she took a job as a maid. As fate would have it, Phyllis and Ben met, fell in love, and in the spring of 1802 they were married.

There is little of note in this, except that Ben and Phyllis were former slaves and were married in the African Methodist Episcopal Zion church. Ben had purchased his freedom just as cotton production began to grow through the Chesapeake region. In another decade, he would have faced greater difficulty securing his freedom. Phyllis had been freed as a child when slavery ended in Connecticut. As she grew up, she tired of living as a servant with her former owner's family and longed for the companionship of other blacks. She had heard that there were people of color in New York City, and she was correct. In 1800, it contained 6,300 African-Americans, more than half of them free.

Though life in New York was better than either Ben or Phyllis had known before, it was hardly easy. They shared only marginally in the city's commercial prosperity. In 1804, they watched helplessly as yellow fever carried off their daughter and many of their friends. And while they found support in the expanding black community, they had to be on guard because slave ships still moved in and out of the port, and slave catchers pursued runaways from the South in the city's streets.

During the early years of the nineteenth century, thousands of people like Mary and James and Ben and Phyllis seized whatever opportunities they could find to improve their lives. Like countless others, they knew little about political theories or congressional debates between Federalists and Jeffersonians. Still they valued America's revolutionary origins and sought ways to make republican notions of opportunity and equality fit their lives. In the process, they helped shape the new republic.

The Jeffersonian Republicans, after their victory over the Federalists in 1800, implemented their vision of an expanding agrarian republic. At the local level, this meant increasing democratization of political life. Nationally, these years brought the collapse of the Federalist-Jeffersonian party system of the 1790s and set the stage for the dramatically new political era that Andrew Jackson's election to the presidency in 1828 would usher in. The Jeffersonians also reconstructed America's relationship with Europe, finally breaking free of a centuries-long pattern of dependence.

In 1800 one could speak of two Americas—one evolving via the decisions made by ordinary people in communities across the land, the other centered in the halls of Congress. In the early nineteenth century, political change would bring those two Americas closer together. In that gradual convergence is to be found much of the nation's history during those years.

RESTORING REPUBLICAN LIBERTY

The Jeffersonians entered office in March 1801 with several objectives in mind: calming the political storms that had threatened to rend the country, consolidating their recent victory, purging the government of Federalist holdovers, and setting it on a proper republican course.

The Jeffersonian Republicans Take Control

The government had moved from Philadelphia to the new capital in the District of Columbia in November 1800, while John Adams was still president. When the politicians arrived in Washington, they were stunned by its primitiveness and isolation, for the new capital was little more than a swampy clearing, holding about 5,000 residents, on the banks of the Potomac River.

In keeping with his desire to rid the government of Federalist embellishments, Jefferson planned a simple inauguration. Shortly before noon on March 4, 1801, the president-elect walked to the Capitol from his temporary lodgings at a nearby boardinghouse. "His dress," noted one observer, "was, as usual, that of a plain citizen, without any distinctive badge of office." Chief Justice John Marshall, a Virginian but a staunch Federalist as well, administered the oath of office, and a company of militia fired a 16-gun salute.

Though simple, the inauguration was filled with significance. This was the first time in the nation's brief history that control of the government had shifted from one political party to another. Mrs. Samuel Harrison Smith, Washington resident and political observer, described the occasion's drama: "I have this morning witnessed one of the most interesting scenes a free people can ever witness," she wrote a friend. "The changes of administration, which in every . . . age have most generally been epochs of confusion, villainy, and bloodshed, in this our happy country take place without any species of distraction or disorder." Many Americans shared her sense of relief and pride.

In his inaugural speech, Jefferson enumerated "the essential principles of republican government" that would guide his administration: "equal and exact justice to all," support of the states as "the surest bulwarks against anti-republican tendencies," "absolute acquiescence" in the decisions of the majority, supremacy of civil over military authority, reduction of government spending, "honest payment" of the public debt, freedom of the press, and "freedom of the person under the protection of the *habeas corpus*." Though Jefferson never mentioned the Federalists by name, his litany of principles reverberated with the dark experience of the 1790s.

The president spoke also of political reconciliation. "Every difference of opinion," he explained, "is not a difference of principle. We

have called by different names brethren of the same principles. We are all republicans—we are all federalists."

Not all his followers welcomed that final flourish, for many were eager to root out the Federalists and scatter them to the political winds. Jefferson's goal, however, was to absorb the moderate Federalists, isolate the extremists, and destroy the Federalist Party as a political force. His strategy worked, for never again did the Federalists regain control of the national government.

Having swept both houses of Congress as well as the presidency in 1800, the Jeffersonians claimed a mandate to rid the government of Federalist officeholders. They were especially outraged by a flurry of last-minute appointments President Adams had pushed through the lame-duck Federalist Congress during the closing days of his administration in an effort to reward party loyalists and deny the Jeffersonians full control of the government.

Under pressure from party supporters, Jefferson reluctantly agreed that "a general sweep" of Federalist officeholders was necessary. By the time Jefferson left office in 1809, virtually all government personnel were solid Republicans.

Politics and the Federal Courts

Late in Adams's administration, the Federalists had introduced a new Judiciary Act calling for more circuit courts and judges with their attendant array of federal marshals, attorneys, and clerks. Congress passed the bill in February 1801, just before adjourning. This blatant effort to pack the judiciary aroused the Jeffersonians' wrath. "The Federalists," observed Jefferson bitterly, "defeated at the polls, have retired into the Judiciary, and from that barricade . . . hope to batter down all the bulwarks of Republicanism." Something had to be done.

In January 1802, Senator John Breckinridge of Kentucky introduced a bill calling for repeal of the Judiciary Act of 1801. "The time will never arrive," Breckinridge naively asserted, "when America will stand in need of 38 federal judges."

The resulting controversy centered on the independence of the judiciary from political attack and the doctrine of judicial review, the notion that it was the federal courts' responsibility to judge the constitutionality of congressional laws and executive behavior. Gouverneur Morris, Federalist senator from New York, declared that an independent judiciary was necessary "to save the people from their most dangerous enemy, themselves." The Jeffersonians argued that each branch of the government—executive and legislative as well as judicial—must have the right to decide on the validity of an act. Congressional debate over repeal of the Judiciary Act drew wide public attention, for it offered a vivid contrast between Federalist and Jeffersonian notions of republican government. In February 1802, by a strict party vote, Congress repealed the Judiciary Act.

The Jeffersonians also sought to purge several highly partisan Federalist judges from the bench. In March 1803, the House of Representatives voted to impeach Federal District Judge John Pickering of New Hampshire. The grounds were not "high crimes and misdemeanors" as the Constitution required, but the Federalist diatribes with which Pickering regularly assaulted defendants and juries. The Senate convicted Pickering, by a strict party vote.

Spurred on by success, the Jeffersonians brought impeachment charges against Supreme Court Justice Samuel Chase, one of the most notorious Republican baiters. The trial, however, revealed that Chase had committed no impeachable offense. He was acquitted on every count and returned triumphantly to the bench.

After that defeat, the Jeffersonians pulled back, content to allow time and the regular turnover of personnel to cleanse the courts of Federalist control.

In several trailblazing decisions, the Supreme Court, led by Chief Justice John Marshall, soon established some of the most basic principles of American constitutional law. In *Marbury* v. *Madison* (1803), Marshall laid down in unmistakable terms the principle of judicial review. "It is emphatically the province and duty of the judicial department," he declared, "to say what the law is." This decision nullified the Judiciary Act of 1789, by which Congress had granted the Supreme Court certain powers. The Court decided that its powers, which were based on the Constitution, could not be extended by Congress. In so doing, the Court laid down a precedent for judicial review of laws as cases challenging specific laws came before it.

In another landmark decision, *McCulloch* v. *Maryland* (1819), the Court struck down a Maryland law taxing the Baltimore branch of the Second Bank of the United States. No state, explained Marshall, possessed the right to tax a nationally chartered bank, for "the power to tax involves the power to destroy." By affirming the constitutionality of the bank's congressional charter, Marshall laid down the constitutional argument for broad congressional authority. Let congressional intent "be within the scope of the Constitution," he wrote, "and all means which are appropriate . . . which are not prohibited, but consist with the letter and spirit of the Constitution, are constitutional."

Dismantling the Federalist War Program

The Jeffersonians had regarded the Federalists' war program as a threat to republican liberty, so they moved quickly to dismantle it. Jefferson stopped prosecutions under the hated Sedition Act and freed its victims. In 1802, the act silently lapsed. The Jeffersonians, though not thoroughgoing civil libertarians, never duplicated the Federalists' campaign to stifle dissent.

Jefferson handled the Alien acts similarly, not bothering to seek their repeal but dismantling the Federalists' inspection system and allowing enforcement to lapse. In 1802, Congress passed a new and more liberal naturalization law, restoring the requirement of 5 rather than 14 years of residence for citizenship. The Federalists' provisional army was also reduced by 1802, to only 3,400. No longer would federal troops intimidate American citizens.

Finally, the Jeffersonians sought ways to reduce the size and operations of the federal government. The central government, Jefferson declared in his first message to Congress in 1801, was "charged with the external and mutual relations only of these states. The principal care of our persons, our property, and our reputation, constituting the great field of human concerns," should be left to the states.

The government inherited by the Jeffersonians was tiny by modern standards. In 1802, it had fewer than 3,000 civilian employees. In terms of domestic policy, it did little more than deliver the mail, deal with Native Americans, and administer the public lands. As the nation grew, however, so did pressures for a federal program of internal improvements. That reflected in part the growing political influence of the West, for the new states forming beyond the Appalachians sought closer ties of trade and communication with the East. The government responded by launching construction of several western routes, including the National Road (in 1811) connecting Cumberland, Maryland, with Wheeling on the Ohio River. The states, however, carried the major responsibility for internal improvements.

The Jeffersonians also reduced the national debt. In spite of the extraordinary costs of the Louisiana Purchase (1803), the debt dropped from $83 million in 1801 to $57 million a decade later. Though the Jeffersonians may not have "revolutionized" the government as they claimed, they clearly changed its character and direction.

BUILDING AN AGRARIAN REPUBLIC

The Jeffersonians worked vigorously to implement their vision of an expanding, agrarian republic. That vision was mixed and inconsistent, for the Jeffersonian party was an amalgam of different and often conflicting groups: southern patricians determined to maintain a privileged, slavery-based agrarian order; lower- and middle-class southern whites generally committed to black slavery though resentful of the patricians' social pretensions, and ardent proponents of political equality; northern artisans dedicated to honest toil and their own economic interests; and western farmers devoted to working the land and living free. In time, this diversity would splinter the Jeffersonian party. For the moment, however, these groups found unity not only against their common Federalist enemies but also in a set of broadly shared principles. Those principles guided Jeffersonian policies for over two decades, through the presidential administrations of Jefferson (1801–1809), James Madison (1809–1817), and James Monroe (1817–1825).

The Jeffersonian Vision

Political liberty, the Jeffersonians believed, could survive only under conditions of broad economic and social equality. The central task of Jeffersonian statecraft was thus to maintain an open and roughly equal society. The task was believed difficult because as societies grew in wealth and power, equality eroded and liberty was snuffed out. England's efforts to destroy colonial liberties had offered ample evidence of that.

The Jeffersonians, however, continued to believe that America, if properly guided, could escape England's fate. Their strategy centered on the independent yeoman farmer—self-reliant, secure in person and possessions, industrious and yet filled with concern for the public good. Such people exemplified the qualities essential to republican citizenship.

The Jeffersonian vision threatened to become clouded, however, because industriousness generated wealth, and wealth bred inequality. In short, economic and social development threatened to destroy the social bases of republicanism.

The solution to the problem of economic and social development, the Jeffersonians believed, lay in rapid territorial expansion. Land, constantly expanding and readily available to the nation's yeoman citizens, would offer opportunity to a restless people, draw them out of the cities and off the crowded lands of the East, and preserve the social equality that republican liberty required. The republic's growth across the North American continent would delay, perhaps even prevent, the cyclic process of growth, maturity, and decay through which all past societies had traveled.

Calls for expanding America's land base were strengthened by the arguments of an English clergyman and political economist named Thomas Malthus. In 1798, Malthus published an essay that jolted Europeans and Americans alike. Given the remarkable fecundity of human beings, Malthus argued, population increased more rapidly than agricultural production. Enlightenment notions of the steadily improving quality of human life, he warned, were a delusion, for the future would be filled with increasing misery and exploitation as population outran food. The future was most clear in Europe, where land was limited and poverty widespread, but the same fate awaited America.

Jefferson believed that America's vast reservoir of land would enable its people to escape Europe's fate. Rapid and continuing national expansion was thus indispensable to the Jeffersonian vision of the agrarian republic. Occupation of the West was also essential to secure America's borders against continuing threats from England, France, and Spain. The rapid sale of new public lands would in addition provide revenue for reducing the national debt. Finally, the Jeffersonians calculated that the creation of new western states would strengthen their political control and assure the Federalists' demise.

A Nation of Regions: The Northeast and the South

The growing young country continued to exhibit striking regional differences. While the long-established differences between Northeast and South that had originated during the colonial period persisted and even increased, an entirely new region of white settlement began to take shape beyond the Appalachians, in the nation's interior.

In the Northeast, a broad region stretching from eastern Pennsylvania through New England, family farms dominated the landscape. Because much of New England's land was poor, farmers there often turned their fields from tillage into pasture to take advantage of more profitable dairying and livestock raising. On the richer agricultural lands of New York and Pennsylvania, by contrast, farmers cultivated their land intensively, planting it in grain year after year rather than following the time-honored custom of allowing worn-out fields to lie fallow and recover their fertility.

Many northeastern farmers, especially in southern New England, along the Hudson River in New York, and in southeastern Pennsylvania, produced an agricultural surplus, which they exchanged in nearby towns for commodities such as tea, sugar, window glass, and tools. Many farm families, however, consumed nearly all they produced. As late as 1820, no more than 25 percent of agricultural output was available for export.

Across much of the rural Northeast, cash played only a small part in economic exchanges. "Instead of money going incessantly backwards and forwards into the same hands," declared an observant Frenchman, people "supply their

Although the cotton gin, invented in 1793, simplified one step of cotton processing, much of the work on a plantation continued to be done with rudimentary tools by slave labor. Here Benjamin Latrobe sketches An Overseer Doing His Duty.

needs in the countryside by direct reciprocal exchanges. The tailor and the bootmaker go and do the work of their calling at the home of the farmer ... who most frequently provides the raw material for it and pays for the work in goods. . . . They write down what they give and receive on both sides, and at the end of the year they settle a large variety of exchanges with a very small quantity of coin."

Most farms were not large. By 1800, the average farm in the longer-settled areas of New England and the mid-Atlantic states was no more than 100 to 150 acres, down substantially from half a century before, as a result of the continued division of farm property across generations of fathers and sons. Economic opportunity was also declining. Long and continuous cropping had robbed the soil of its fertility, forcing farmers to bring more marginal land under cultivation.

Though the vast majority of northeasterners made their living from the land, growing numbers worked as artisans or day laborers in the cities or labored in the small-scale manufactories—grain and saw mills, potash works, and iron forges—that dotted the rural landscape.

By 1800, the standard of living of many northeastern families was higher than it had been 30 years earlier, but for the countless families still outside the market system, life went on much as it had generations before.

Life was very different in the South. As the nineteenth century began, southern agriculture was in disarray. Falling prices, worn-out land, and the destruction wrought by the Revolutionary War had left the Chesapeake's tobacco economy in shambles. The extensive loss of slaves added to the region's economic woes.

Southern planters had experimented with wheat and other grains in an effort to bolster their sagging fortunes, but regional recovery began when they turned to a new staple crop—cotton. The fibers of the long-staple variety were highly valued and could easily be separated from the cotton's seeds. The delicate long-staple plant, however, grew only where soil and climate were right—on the sea islands off the coast of Georgia and South Carolina. The hardier short-staple variety could be cultivated across large areas of the South, but its fibers clung tenaciously to its sticky, green seeds. A slave could clean no more than a pound of short-staple cotton a day.

Demand for cotton of all sorts was growing, especially in England, where new textile factories created an insatiable appetite for the crop. In 1793 Eli Whitney, a Yankee schoolteacher seeking employment in the South, set his mind to the problem of short-staple cotton and its seeds. Within a few days, he had designed a "cotton gin," a box containing a roller, equipped with wire teeth, designed to pull the fibers through a comblike barrier, thus stripping them from the seeds. A hand crank activated the mechanism. The implications of Whitney's invention were immediately apparent, for with this crude device a laborer could clean up to 50 pounds of short-staple cotton per day.

During the next several decades, southern cotton production soared. In 1805, cotton accounted for 30 percent of the nation's agricultural exports; by 1820, it exceeded half. Across both the old coastal South and the newly developing states of Alabama, Mississippi, and Tennessee, cotton was becoming king.

As we shall see in later chapters, the swing to cotton marked a momentous turning point for the South and the nation, for it increased the demand for fieldhands and breathed new life into the institution of slavery. Some of the escalating demand was met from overseas, but much would be met by the internal slave trade that moved African-Americans from the worn-out lands of the Chesapeake to the booming cotton lands of the Deep South.

Trans-Appalachia

A third region, west of the Appalachian Mountains, was forming as the nineteenth century began. New, raw, repeatedly embroiled in warfare between Indian inhabitants and white intruders, Trans-Appalachia constituted a broad and shifting zone of cultural, political, economic, and military interaction between Native American and European-American peoples. It extended, east to west, from the Appalachian Mountains to the Mississippi River and from the Great Lakes on the north to the Gulf of Mexico. In 1790, scarcely 100,000 white settlers lived beyond the Appalachians. By 1800, their number had swollen to nearly a million; by 1820, fed by people like Mary and James Harrod, there were over a million more.

"The woods are full of new settlers," wrote an observer near Batavia, New York, in 1805. "Axes are resounding, and the trees literally falling around us as we passed." By 1812, some 200,000 souls lived in the western part of the state, where scarcely 30,000 whites had lived 20 years before. "America is breaking up and going west!" exclaimed the British traveler Morris Birkbeck.

Settlers were drawn by the promotions of land speculators. Between 1790 and 1820, land companies hawked vast areas of New York, Ohio, and Kentucky to prospective settlers such

as James and Mary Harrod. Individual settlers shared in the speculative fever, going into debt to buy extra land so they might sell it at a premium when population increased and land prices rose.

North of the Ohio River, settlement followed the grid pattern prescribed in the Land Ordinance of 1785, while south of the Ohio people distributed themselves more randomly across the land, much as their ancestors had done back east. Above the Ohio, mixed, free-labor agriculture took hold. Towns such as Columbus and Cincinnati emerged to provide services and cultural amenities for the surrounding population. In Kentucky and Tennessee, free-labor agriculture also developed but was soon challenged by the spread of slave-based cotton.

As people continued to spill into the region, they established churches, schools, and even colleges (Transylvania University, founded in Lexington, Kentucky, in 1780, was the first college west of the Appalachians). Even so, Trans-Appalachia retained a reputation for its rough and colorful ways. No characters were more famous in popular folklore than westerners like Daniel Boone. None were more colorful than the mythical riverman Mike Fink, "half man, half alligator," who could "whip his weight in grizzly bears."

As the settlers came, they began the long process of transforming the region's heavily forested land. In the mountainous areas of western Pennsylvania, entire hillsides were denuded of trees by anxious travelers who cut them down to drag behind their wagons as makeshift brakes during the jolting rides downhill. Regarding the unforested "oak openings" scattered through the woods of Ohio and southern Michigan as "barren" and infertile, many farmers staked their claims where the trees grew thickest and set about clearing the land.

Farmers followed the long-established practice of cutting a girdle of bark off the trees and leaving them to die in place, while planting crops around the decaying hulks. By this method, a family could clear from 3 to 5 acres a year for cultivation. The relentless demands for wood—for log cabins and barns, fences and fuel, potash and turpentine—added to the assault on the region's forests.

The Windfall Louisiana Purchase

The strategy of securing the agrarian republic by territorial expansion explains Jefferson's most dramatic accomplishment, his purchase of the Louisiana Territory in 1803. In 1800, Spain ceded the vast trans-Mississippi region known as Louisiana to France. When Jefferson learned of the secret agreement in 1801, he was profoundly disturbed. Especially upsetting were rumors that Spain would soon transfer New Orleans, the major outlet for western agricultural produce, to France. His fears were well grounded, for in October 1802 the Spanish commander at New Orleans, which Spain had retained, once again closed the Mississippi River to American commerce.

In January 1803, the president sent his young associate James Monroe to Paris with instructions to purchase New Orleans and West Florida, which contained Mobile, the only good harbor on the Gulf Coast, and the mouths of several rivers that drained the southern interior. When Monroe arrived, he found French Foreign Minister Talleyrand unwilling to sell West Florida but ready to sell all of Louisiana, a huge territory of nearly 830,000 square miles.

In April, the deal was struck. For $15 million, the United States obtained all of Louisiana, in one stroke doubling the nation's size. The public's response was overwhelmingly favorable, and Congress readily approved the purchase.

The Federalists reacted with alarm, fearing with good reason that the new states to be carved from Louisiana would be staunchly Jeffersonian and worrying that rapid expansion of the frontier would "decivilize" the nation. In New England, Federalist extremists talked of forming a northern confederacy and seceding from the Union.

National expansion did not stop with Louisiana. In 1810, American adventurers fomented a revolt in Spanish West Florida, proclaimed an independent republic, and sought annexation by the United States. In May 1812, over vigorous Spanish objections, Congress formally annexed the area. In 1819, in the Adams-Onis treaty, Spain ceded East Florida as well. As part of that agreement, the United States for the first time extended its territorial claims beyond Louisiana to include the Pacific Northwest. These impressive accomplishments set the stage for the final surge of continental expansion during the 1840s.

Opening the Trans-Mississippi West

If America's vast new domain was to serve the needs of the agrarian republic, it would have to be explored and made ready for settlement. In the summer of 1803, Jefferson dispatched an expedition led by his personal secretary, Meriwether Lewis, and William Clark, a young army officer, to explore the Far Northwest. For nearly 2½ years, the intrepid band of explorers, assisted by the Shoshoni woman Sacajawea, made its way across thousands of miles of unmapped terrain—up the Missouri River, through the Rockies via the Bitterroot Valley and Lolo Pass, down the Columbia to the Pacific coast, and back again, finally reemerging at St. Louis in September 1806. Lewis and Clark's reports of their journey fanned American interest in the trans-Mississippi West, established an American presence in the region, and demonstrated the feasibility of an overland route to the Pacific.

In 1805 and 1806, Lieutenant Zebulon Pike explored the sources of the Mississippi as far as Leech Lake in northern Minnesota. He followed that trek with an equally bold venture into New Mexico and Colorado, where he explored and named the peak that bears his name. In the

Important Routes Westward

decade after 1815, the government established a string of military posts from Fort Snelling, at the confluence of the Minnesota and Mississippi rivers, to Fort Atkinson on the Missouri and Fort Smith on the Arkansas. They were intended to secure the American frontier, promote the fur trade, and support white settlement.

The Jeffersonians' agrarian vision also guided changes in land policy. The primary objective of Federalist land policy had been to produce government revenue. The Jeffersonians were more interested in encouraging people to settle on the land.

The Land Act of 1801 reduced the minimum purchase of federal land to 320 acres, established a four-year credit system, and provided 8 percent discounts for cash sales. Over the next year and a half, settlers, speculators, and land

companies purchased nearly 400,000 acres of federal land, more than four times as much as during the entire 1790s. The amounts increased geometrically in the following decade.

In succeeding years, Congress established the principles of preemption, which enabled squatters to secure title to land, and pricing graduation, whereby lands that did not readily sell were offered at less than the established price or were even given away. All were efforts to speed the transfer of public land into private hands.

PERFECTING REPUBLICAN SOCIETY

During the Revolutionary era, politics and government had preoccupied the American people.

Exploring the Trans-Mississippi West, 1804–1807

BRITISH POSSESSIONS

OREGON COUNTRY

1805 Fort Clatsop

LEWIS
1806
Fort Mandan

CLARK
1806

ROCKY MOUNTAINS

PIKE

LEWIS & CLARK

GREAT PLAINS

Great Salt Lake

Pikes Peak

1806–1807

Santa Fe

SPANISH

POSSESSIONS

Rio Grande

San Antonio

Red River

Arkansas River

FREEMAN

Natchitoches

Fort Adams

New Orleans

Mobile

SPANISH FLORIDA

NEW HAMPSHIRE
VERMONT
MAINE

MASSACHUSETTS
NEW YORK
RHODE ISLAND
CONNECTICUT

MICHIGAN TERRITORY

PENNSYLVANIA
NEW JERSEY

DELAWARE
MARYLAND

OHIO

INDIANA TERRITORY

St. Louis

VIRGINIA

KENTUCKY

NORTH CAROLINA

TENNESSEE

SOUTH CAROLINA

MISSISSIPPI TERRITORY

GEORGIA

☐ Louisiana Purchase, 1803

In the early republic, there was increasing concern about fashioning a social order capable of supporting republican government. Spurred by that concern, Americans launched various projects of social reform intended to implement republican ideals.

The Principles of Reform

The first of these ideals was social equality. In part this meant equality of opportunity, the notion that people should have a chance to rise as far as ability and ambition would carry them. Privilege should be set aside, and everyone should have an equal chance.

Promises of equal opportunity had limited relevance for many Americans. Slaves, women, and working-class men understood all too well the limits of opportunity in preindustrial America. But the principle was bold and inspiring for countless others.

Social equality also had a powerful moral dimension, because it implied an equality of social worth among individuals, no matter what their wealth or social standing might be. That attitude showed up vividly in an episode that took place in New York City in 1795. Thomas Burke and Timothy Crady, two recent Irish immigrants, operated a ferry across the East River between lower Manhattan and Brooklyn. One day in early November, Gabriel Furman, a merchant and Federalist alderman, arrived on the Brooklyn shore a bit before the scheduled departure time and instructed the ferrymen to leave early. When they refused, he upbraided the "rascals" for their disrespect and threatened to have them arrested. Crady was especially angered by the alderman's arrogance. He and Burke, Crady exploded, "were as good as any buggers." When the ferry landed on the Manhattan shore, Furman had the two arrested.

Both Crady and Burke were eventually hauled before Mayor Richard Varick and three other Federalist aldermen, sitting as the Court of General Sessions. There was no jury. The judges quickly decided to make examples of the two insolent Irishmen. "You rascals, we'll trim you," Varick allegedly said; "we'll learn you to insult men in office." The magistrates quickly found the two guilty on charges of insulting an alderman and threatening the constable, sentenced them to two months at hard labor, and ordered 25 lashes for Crady as well.

Within a month, the two ferrymen had bolted from jail and disappeared into Pennsylvania, never to be heard from again. The episode, however, was not yet over, for a young Jeffersonian lawyer named William Keteltas took up the case and in time carried it all the way to the New York assembly. In a two-column newspaper account signed "One of the People," he castigated "the tyranny and partiality of the court" and concluded that Burke and Crady had been punished to "gratify the pride, the ambition and insolence of men in office." That, he argued, was intolerable in a republican society. The assembly, he charged, was protecting the mayor to save his reputation. But what of the ruined reputations of the ferrymen? Were they not just as important?

Before it was over, the incident generated wide public anger, and Keteltas earned a jail sentence for his efforts. When released, however, he was paraded through the streets by a throng carrying American and French flags and a banner inscribed "What, you rascal, insult your superi-

ors?" In the early republic, notions of equal social worth spread rapidly.

The doctrine of individualism was a second basic element of the new social faith. It asserted the primacy of individuals' needs and interests. During the colonial years, that idea had been carefully balanced by the opposing view that individuals must subordinate themselves to the general good. The Revolutionary experience, however, shifted the balance in favor of an emphasis on the primacy of the free and unfettered individual.

Patterns of Wealth and Poverty

In the early republic, as at other times in the nation's history, ideals jarred awkwardly against social reality. In that tension is to be found the primary impulse for social reform.

As the nineteenth century began, property was unequally distributed across gender and racial lines. Women continued to hold far less property than men. The large majority of blacks, moreover, were slaves; for them, ownership of anything more than the smallest items of personal property was beyond reach. Though the condition of free blacks such as Ben Thompson and his wife, Phyllis, was better, they too held little of the country's wealth.

Among white males, property was most broadly shared in rural areas of the North, where free labor and family-farm agriculture predominated, and least so in the South, where control of slave labor and the best land permitted tobacco, rice, and cotton planters to monopolize the region's wealth.

The class structure was also sharply drawn in the port cities where merchant capitalists controlled the sources of commercial and manufacturing wealth, while small artisans, sailors, and unskilled workers lived at the margins of the economy, their lives dominated by a relentless struggle for survival. The most even distribution of wealth existed on the edges of white settlement in the trans-Appalachian frontier, but that was an equality of want.

Taking the country as a whole, the pattern of wealth distribution had not changed much from pre-Revolutionary times. In 1800, the top 10 percent of property holders controlled about 42 percent of the nation's wealth, very close to what the situation had been 50 years before.

Though America contained no large destitute underclass such as could be found in the cities and countryside of Europe, poverty was real and was increasing. In the South, it was most evident among slaves and poor whites living on the sandy pine barrens of the backcountry. In the North, the port cities held growing numbers of the poor. In Boston, artisans and shopkeepers, who together had owned 20 percent of the city's wealth in 1700, held scarcely half as much a century later. During the winter of 1805, New York's mayor DeWitt Clinton worried publicly about the fate of 10,000 impoverished New Yorkers and asked the state legislature for help. During the winter of 1814–1815, relief agencies assisted nearly one-fifth of the city's population.

Even in rural New England and southeastern Pennsylvania, a lower class of transient and propertyless people was growing. The "strolling poor," they were called—landless men, and sometimes women, forced to roam the countryside searching for work.

Three other groups were conspicuous among the nation's poor. One consisted of old Revolutionary War veterans like Long Bill Scott, who had found poverty as well as adventure in the war. The others were women and children. Annual censuses of almshouse residents in New York City from 1816 to 1821 consistently listed more women and children than men.

Poverty was a continuing reality in the early republic. And for every American who actually suffered its effects, there were several others living just beyond its reach, their margin of safety alarmingly thin.

Just how thin became clear during the depression of 1819–1822. Triggered by a financial panic created by the unsound practices of hundreds of newly chartered state banks, a deep depression settled over the land, generating bankruptcies and sending unemployment soaring. In upstate New York, the pay of turnpike workers sank from 75 cents to 12 cents a day. In the South, farms and plantations stood abandoned as cotton and tobacco exports fell. By the early 1820s, the depression was lifting, but it left behind broken fortunes and shattered dreams.

Alleviating Poverty and Distress

Alleviating poverty was one goal of the early social reformers. In New York City during the early decades of the century, private and public authorities established more than 100 charitable and relief agencies to aid orphans and widows, aged females and young prostitutes, immigrants and imprisoned debtors, juvenile delinquents and poverty-stricken seamen. Across the nation as a whole, a "charitable revolution" increased benevolent institutions from 50 to nearly 2,000 by 1820.

Most of these ventures attempted to distinguish between the "worthy poor," respectable folk who were victims of circumstance and merited assistance, and the "idle" or "vicious poor," who were deemed to lack character and therefore deserved their fate.

Poverty was not the only object of public and private reform. Municipal authorities and private charities established orphanages for children, asylums for the insane, and hospitals for the sick. Most of these institutions were small and short-lived, but they provided a base for the more ambitious reform efforts to come several decades later.

Women's Lives

Though women's lives were not markedly altered during these years, changes that helped set the stage for later, more dramatic breakthroughs did occur. Divorce was one area where women achieved more equal treatment. When a neighbor asked John Backus, a silversmith in Great Barrington, Massachusetts, why he kicked and struck his wife, John replied that it was partly owing to the fact that his father had often treated his mother in the same way. We don't know whether John's mother tolerated such abuse, but his wife did not. She complained of cruelty and obtained a divorce. Her reaction was not unique, for more and more women were following her example.

Thomas and Sarah Mifflin, a well-to-do Quaker couple, sat for this portrait by John Singleton Copley. Note that Mrs. Mifflin's hands are busy weaving thread into a strip of fringe, while her husband marks his place in the book he is reading. Their activities suggest the different social roles men and women were expected to play.

The process of divorce was not easy. Most states allowed it only on the ground of adultery, while South Carolina did not permit it at all. Moreover, women typically had to present detailed evidence of their husbands' infidelities and face the discomfort of an all-male court, while accusations of a wife's transgressions could be more easily proven in court. Short of divorce, many women demonstrated their unwillingness to stay with a bad marriage by walking out. We know this from the increasing number of newspaper notices filed by deserted husbands announcing that their wives had left bed and board.

Changes also occurred in women's education. This was part of the general enthusiasm for educational reform, but it reflected a special concern for women's place in the new republic. Given women's role as keepers of public morality and nurturers of future citizens, their education was a subject of general concern. If the republic was to fulfill its destiny, young women would have to prepare for the responsibilities that motherhood would bring. During the 1790s, Judith Sargeant Murray published a series of essays, gathered under the title *The Gleaner,* in which she criticized parents who "pointed their daughters" toward marriage and dependence. "I would give my daughters every accomplishment which I thought proper," Murray wrote. "They should be enabled to procure for themselves the necessaries of life; independence should be placed within their grasp."

Between 1790 and 1820, a number of female academies were established, most of them in northeastern cities. Timothy Dwight, the future president of Yale, opened his academy at Greenfield Hill in Connecticut to girls and taught them the same subjects he taught boys, at the same time and in the same room; but he was the exception. Benjamin Rush, in his essay "Thoughts upon Female Education" (1787), prescribed bookkeeping, reading, grammar, penmanship, geography, natural philosophy, vocal music ("because it soothes cares and is good for the lungs"), and history. Traditionalists such as the Boston minister John Gardiner were decidedly less sympathetic. "Women of masculine minds," he warned, "have generally masculine manners, and a robustness of person ill calculated to inspire the tender passions."

The prediction that intellect would unsex women was accompanied by the warning that educated women would abandon their proper sphere as mothers and wives. Even the most ardent supporters of female learning insisted that they seek education so that they might function more effectively within their traditional sphere.

Race, Slavery, and the Limits of Reform

As we have seen (Chapter 7), the Revolution initiated the end of slavery in the northern states and raised challenges to its continued existence in the Upper South. As the new century began, however, antislavery sentiment was declining, while private manumission slowed as well. The reasons were several. The gradual abolition of slavery in the North soothed many consciences, while in the South, the spread of cotton increased the value of slave labor. Equally important were two slave rebellions that generated intense alarm.

Panic-stricken whites fleeing Hispaniola for their lives in 1791 carried word to the North American mainland of the black Haitians' successful rebellion against a French colonial army of 25,000. The news spread terror, especially through the South, where southern whites immediately tightened their black codes, cut the importation of new slaves from the Caribbean, and quizzed their slaves in an effort to root out suspected Haitian revolutionaries. The bloody rebellion and the prospect of a nearby island nation governed by blacks frightened northern whites as well.

A second shock followed in the summer of 1800, when a rebellion just outside Richmond, Virginia, was nipped in the bud. Gabriel Prosser,

a 24-year-old slave, had devised a plan to arm 1,000 slaves for an assault on the city. Betrayed by several black house servants, Prosser's plan failed. No white lives were lost, but scores of slaves and free blacks were arrested, and 25 suspects, including Prosser, were hanged at the personal order of Governor James Monroe.

In the early nineteenth century, antislavery appeals all but disappeared from the South, while proslavery arguments increased.

In the North, antislavery attitudes were increasingly conciliatory toward slave owners and unsympathetic toward blacks. Most of slavery's critics assumed that private manumission was the only safe approach, that it should be gradual so as to avoid social turmoil, and that freed blacks should be relocated to colonies in Africa. The American Colonization Society, founded in 1816, typified these attitudes. The Society never sent many blacks abroad, but it did help allay white anxieties.

Nor did free blacks living in the North find their lives much improved by the first stirrings of republican reform. During the half century following independence, strong and growing black communities appeared in the northern ports, notably in Boston, New York, Philadelphia, and Baltimore. Their growth was fed by people like Phyllis Sherman coming in from the northern countryside and Ben Thompson making his way up from the South. On the eve of independence, 4,000 slaves and a few hundred free blacks had called the four port cities home; 50 years later, more than 30,000 free blacks did so.

The men who came sought employment as laborers or sailors, the women as domestics. They sought as well the companionship of other people of color. The development of black neighborhoods was a result both of white discrimination and the black desire for community. In rural areas, free blacks lived in relative isolation and were largely defenseless against white hostility. In the cities, however, numbers provided some protection and greatly improved the chances of finding a marriage partner, establishing a family,

Blacks and Slavery, 1790–1820

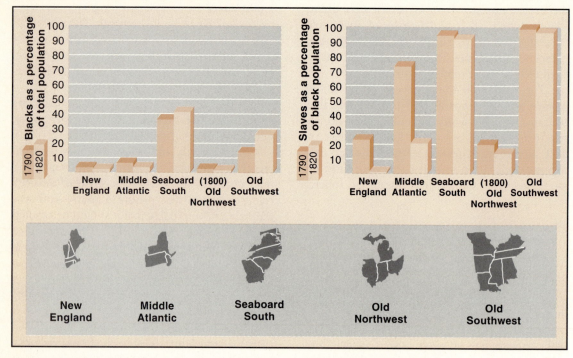

Though regions had differed in the importance of slavery and the number of blacks in their population as the Revolutionary era ended, those differences increased significantly over the next 30 years. Source: U.S. Bureau of the Census.

and participating in community activities. Family formation was eased by the fact that many of the migrants were women, thus correcting a long-standing gender imbalance.

As their numbers increased, blacks organized community institutions. In 1794, Richard Allen and Absalom Jones founded the first two black churches in Philadelphia. By 1813, the two congregations had over 1,800 members. "African" schools, mutual-aid societies, and fraternal associations followed, first in Philadelphia and Boston, more slowly in New York and Baltimore, where slavery lingered longer.

By 1820, a rich institutional and cultural life had taken root in the black neighborhoods of the port cities. White hostility, however, re-

mained. Slavery's abolition actually increased rather than diminished white enmity in the North, in part because it pitted free blacks more directly against white laborers for employment and cheap housing. Race, as well as gender and class, continued to separate Americans from one another and reveal the limits of America's new social faith.

A FOREIGN POLICY FOR THE AGRARIAN REPUBLIC

During the early decades of the nineteenth century, the Jeffersonians struggled to fashion a foreign policy appropriate for the expanding agrarian republic. They had several major goals: protecting American interests on the high seas, clearing America's western territories of foreign troops and influence, and breaking free from the country's historic dependence on Europe. Those goals were not easily accomplished; yet by the 1820s, aided by changes taking place across the Atlantic, the Jeffersonians had fashioned a new relationship with Europe. In the Monroe Doctrine of 1823, they also projected a momentous new role for the United States within the Americas.

Jeffersonian Principles

Jeffersonian foreign policy was based on the doctrine of "no entangling alliances" with Europe that Washington had articulated in his Farewell Address of 1796. In the Jeffersonians' minds, England was still the prime enemy, but France was now suspect as well. By the time the Jeffersonians took office, the French Revolution had run its course and ended in the consulate of Napoleon. Second, the Jeffersonians emphasized the importance of overseas commerce to the security and prosperity of the agrarian republic, for trade provided markets for America's agricultural produce and fetched back manufactured goods in return. Third, they sought to maintain peace, because they feared war's effects on republican liberty. Not only did war kill people and destroy property, but it also inflamed politics, stifled freedom of speech, disrupted the economy, increased the public debt, and expanded governmental power.

The Jeffersonians' handling of the crisis leading into the War of 1812 against Great Britain illustrates how eagerly, and in this case how futilely, they sought to avoid conflict.

Struggling for Neutral Rights

After a brief interlude of peace, European war resumed in 1803. Once again England and

France seized American shipping. England's overwhelming naval superiority made its attacks especially serious. British impressment of American seamen and continued occupation of the Great Lakes posts also increased tension between the two nations.

In response to increasing British seizures of American shipping, in April 1806 Congress passed the Non-Importation Act, prohibiting the importation of English goods that could be produced domestically or acquired elsewhere. On May 16, Britain replied by declaring a full blockade of the European coast. Threatened by Britain's action, Napoleon answered with the Berlin Decree, forbidding all commerce and communication with the British Isles. Americans were further angered by Britain's refusal to deal in good faith on issues of impressment and the reopening of the West Indian trade.

Tension between England and the United States reached the breaking point in June 1807, when the British warship *Leopard* stopped the American frigate *Chesapeake* off the Virginia coast. The British captain claimed that four *Chesapeake* crew members were British deserters and demanded their surrender. When the American commander refused, the *Leopard* opened fire, killing 3 men and wounding 18, and removed the alleged deserters. After the *Chesapeake* limped back into port with the story, cries of outrage rang across the land.

Fearing war and recognizing that the United States was not prepared to confront England, Jefferson decided to withdraw American ships from the Atlantic. In December 1807, Congress passed the Embargo Act, forbidding all American vessels from sailing for foreign ports. It was one of Jefferson's most ill-fated decisions.

The embargo had relatively little effect on England. British shipping actually profited from the withdrawal of American competition. The embargo's domestic impact, however, was far-reaching. American exports fell 80 percent in a year, and imports dropped by more than half.

New England ports were hardest hit, but up and down the coast, communities dependent on overseas commerce openly challenged the embargo. At Plattsburgh, New York, on Lake Champlain, federal officials declared martial law and sent in federal troops in an effort to stop smuggling into Canada. The result was guerrilla skirmishing as local citizens fired on U.S. revenue boats and recaptured confiscated goods. Throughout the largely Federalist Northeast, bitterness threatened to escalate into open rebellion. Connecticut's governor, in words reminiscent of the Virginia and Kentucky resolutions, warned that whenever Congress exceeded its authority, the states were duty-bound "to interpose their protecting shield between the rights and liberties of the people and the assumed power of the general government."

In the election of 1808, the Federalists rebounded after nearly a decade of decline. James Madison handily succeeded Jefferson in the presidency, but the Federalist candidates, C. C. Pinckney and Rufus King, garnered 47 electoral votes. Their party also made gains in Congress and recaptured several state legislatures.

Faced with the embargo's ineffectiveness abroad and its disastrous political consequences at home, Congress repealed the measure in 1809. In that year and the next, Congress tried more limited trade restrictions aimed at reducing English and French attacks on American shipping, but these strategies also failed, and American war fever continued to grow.

The War of 1812

The most vocal calls for war came from the West and the South. The election of 1810 had brought to Congress a new group of western and southern leaders, firmly Republican in their party loyalty but impatient with the Madison administration's bumbling policy and convinced of the need for tougher measures. The War Hawks, they were called, and an impressive group they proved to be: Henry Clay and Richard Johnson

of Kentucky, John Calhoun and Langdon Cheves from South Carolina, Felix Grundy of Tennessee, and Peter Porter from western New York.

For too long, the War Hawks cried, the United States had tolerated Britain's presence on American soil, encouragement of Tecumseh's confederation, and attacks on American commerce. Their language echoed as well with talk of territorial expansion north into Canada and south into Florida. Their overriding goals were to secure the republic from European threats and demonstrate the Republican party's ability to govern.

Responding to the growing pressure, President Madison finally asked Congress for a declaration of war on June 1, 1812. Opposition came entirely from the New England and Middle Atlantic states—ironically, the regions British policies affected most adversely—while the South and West voted solidly for war. Seldom had sectional alignments been sharper.

The war itself was a curious affair, for its causes were uncertain and its goals unclear. England successfully fended off several American forays into Canada. The British navy once again blockaded American coastal waters, while British landing parties launched punishing attacks up and down the East Coast. On August 14, a British force occupied Washington, torched the Capitol and the president's house (which became known as the White House after being repaired and whitewashed), and sent the president, Congress, and a panic-stricken American army fleeing into Virginia. England, however, did not press its advantage, for it was preoccupied with Napoleon's armies in Europe and wanted to end the American quarrel.

On the American side, emotions ran high among both the war's Federalist critics and Republican supporters. In Baltimore, on the night of June 22, 1812, a Republican crowd demolished the printing office of the *Federal-Republican*, a local Federalist newspaper.

In late July, after copies of the *Federal-Republican* again appeared on Baltimore's

The War of 1812

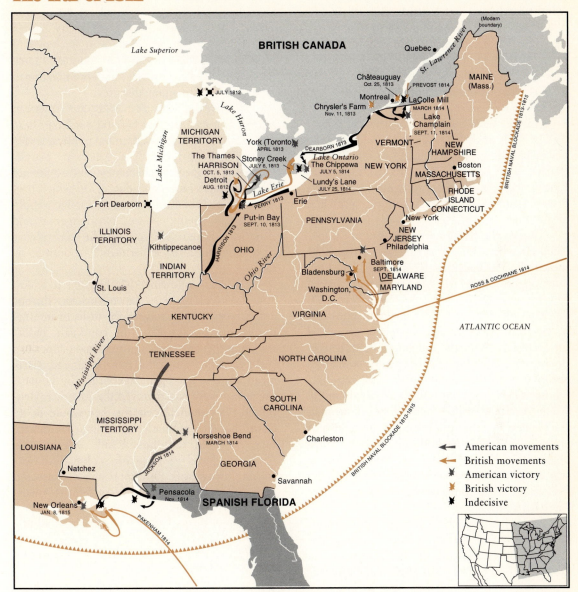

The War of 1812 scarcely touched the lives of most Americans, but areas around the Great Lakes, Lake Champlain, Chesapeake Bay, and the Gulf Coast witnessed significant fighting.

streets, a thousand men and women once more surrounded the paper's office. This time, 50 armed Federalists were there to defend it. When the Federalist defenders opened fire, the crowd rolled up a cannon and sent a round of grapeshot into the building. Several people lay dead on both sides before the militia finally arrived to cart the Federalists off to the safety of jail.

On the following night, a crowd reassembled in front of the city jail and seized ten prisoners, including James Lingan, an old Revolutionary War general. The enraged mob beat Lingan and several others to death and left the bodies, stripped of their fine clothing, sprawling in the street.

Though the Baltimore riots were not duplicated elsewhere, emotions ran high throughout the country. In Federalist-dominated New England, opposition to "Mr. Madison's War" veered toward outright disloyalty. In December 1814, delegates from the five New England states met at Hartford, Connecticut, to debate proposals for secession. With the outcome of the war in doubt, some New England Federalists wanted to separate from the seemingly doomed republic, whose policies and administration they opposed. Cooler heads prevailed, but before adjourning, the Hartford Convention asserted the right of a state "to interpose its authority" against "unconstitutional" acts of the government. As the war dragged on, Federalist fortunes soared in the Northeast, while elsewhere bitterness grew over New England's disloyalty.

Before the war ended, American forces won several impressive victories, among them Commander Oliver Hazard Perry's defeat of the British fleet on Lake Erie in 1813. The most dramatic American triumph was Andrew Jackson's smashing victory in 1815 over an attacking British force at New Orleans. It occurred, however, after preliminary terms of peace had already been signed.

The treaty signed on Christmas Eve in 1814, at Ghent, Belgium, resolved almost nothing, for it ignored impressment, blockades, neutral rights, and American access to Canadian fisheries. England did agree to evacuate the western posts, but other than that, the treaty simply ended the conflict, provided for an exchange of prisoners and the restoration of conquered territory, and called for several joint commissions to deal with the remaining disputes.

The war did leave its mark on the American nation. It made Andrew Jackson a military hero and established him as a national political leader of major importance. The American people, moreover, regarded the contest as a "Second War of American Independence," in which they had whipped the British once again. The republic seemed finally secure. No longer would Americans have to worry about the vulnerability of their republican "experiment" to outside attack.

The years following 1815 brought an end to America's colonial-like dependence on Europe and a reorientation toward the tasks of internal development—occupying the continent, industrializing the economy, and reforming American society. At the same time, Europe entered nearly a century free from general conflict. In the past, European wars had involved the American people; in the twentieth century, they would do so again. For the remainder of the nineteenth century, however, that fateful link was missing. Also, the focus of European colonialism was shifting away from the Americas to Africa and Asia. From the 1820s on, Europe left the Americas relatively alone.

The United States and the Americas

While disengaging from Europe, the Jeffersonians fashioned new policies for Latin America that would guide the United States hemispheric relations for years to come. Although the American people gave little thought to Europe's Latin American colonies prior to 1800, when those colonies began their struggles for independence from Spain and Portugal in 1808, Americans voiced support. In the early 1820s, the United States recognized the new Latin American republics of Colombia, Mexico, Chile, and Argentina.

In November 1822, the Quadruple Alliance (France, Austria, Russia, and Prussia) talked of a plan to help Spain regain its American colonies, alarming both the United States and Great Britain. The British foreign secretary, George Canning, broached the idea of Anglo-American cooperation to thwart Spain's intentions.

Secretary of State John Quincy Adams opposed the idea. Son of the former Federalist president, Adams had joined the Jeffersonian camp some years before as part of the continuing exodus from the Federalist party. In the new spirit of nationalism so evident following the War of 1812, Adams declared that the United States should not "come in as a cockboat in the wake of the British man-of-war." He urged independent action based on two principles: a sharp separation between the Old World and the New, and the United States' dominance in the Western Hemisphere.

President Monroe, elected to a second term in 1820, soon agreed that the United States should issue its own policy statement. In his annual message of December 1823, he outlined a new Latin American policy. Though known as the Monroe Doctrine, its content was of Adams's devising.

Monroe asserted four basic principles: (1) the American continents were closed to new European colonization, (2) the political systems of the Americas were separate from those of Europe, (3) the United States would consider as dangerous to its peace and safety any attempts to extend Europe's political influence into the Western Hemisphere, and (4) the United States would neither interfere with existing colonies in the New World nor meddle in the internal affairs of Europe.

When Monroe issued his doctrine, the United States had neither the economic nor military power to enforce it. By the end of the nineteenth century, however, when the country's power had increased, it would become clear

what a fateful turning point in the history of the Americas Monroe's declaration had been.

INDIAN-WHITE RELATIONS IN THE EARLY REPUBLIC

The young country's power grew as it expanded westward. As white settlers surged across the interior, however, they found a land already occupied by Native American peoples. By 1800, white settlement, disease, and warfare had decimated Native Americans along the Atlantic coast. Powerful tribes, however, still controlled much of the trans-Appalachian interior. North of the Ohio River, the Shawnee, Delaware, Miami, and Potawatomi were allied in a Western confederacy capable of mustering several thousand warriors. South of the Ohio lived five major tribal groups: the Cherokee, Creek, Choctaw, Chickasaw, and Seminole. Together these southern tribes totaled nearly 60,000 people.

The years from 1790 to the 1820s brought a decisive shift in Indian-white relations throughout the trans-Appalachian interior. In 1790, the region was aflame with raids and warfare. As the pressures of white expansion increased, tribal groups devised various strategies of resistance and survival. The Cherokee followed a path of peaceful accommodation. Others, like the Shawnee and the Creek, rose in armed resistance. Neither strategy was altogether successful, for by the 1820s the balance of power in the interior had shifted, and the Indians faced a future of continued acculturation, military defeat, or forced migration to lands west of the Mississippi.

The Goals of Indian Policy

Between 1790 and 1820, the government established policies that would guide Indian-white relations for much of the nineteenth century.

Indian Land Cessions, 1750-1830

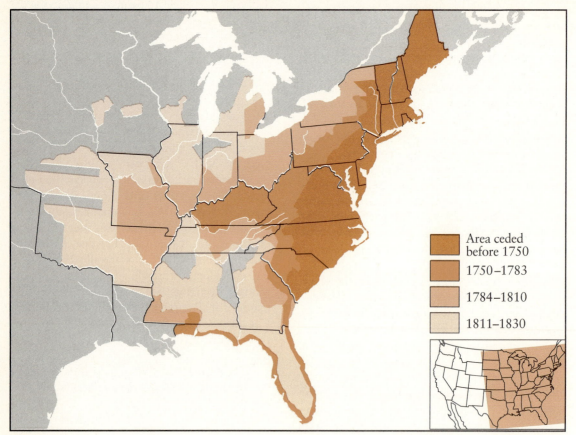

Area ceded before 1750

1750–1783

1784–1810

1811–1830

Though federal policymakers attempted to protect Native Americans from unscrupulous traders and aggressive settlers and to Christianize and civilize them in preparation for their admission into white society, the pace of territorial expansion created irresistible pressure to move the Indians out of the white settlers' way.

The acquisition of Native American land became the main objective of federal Indian policy. By 1790, the government had given up its earlier "conquest" theory, recognized Indian rights to the soil, and declared that land transfers would henceforth be accomplished through treaty agreements.

Responsibility for the management of Indian affairs rested with the War Department.

Henry Knox, Washington's first secretary of war, laid out the government's basic positions in 1789. The Indians, he said, "being the prior occupants of the soil, possess the right of the soil." It should not be taken from them "unless by their free consent, or by the right of conquest in case of just war." Few of the land treaties negotiated after 1789 represented the "free consent" of Native American people. Still, Knox had established a new, more humane principle, the acquisition of Native American land by formal treaty agreement.

The new treaty-based strategy was effective. Native American leaders were frequently willing to cede land in return for trade goods, yearly annuity payments, and assurances that no further

Sequoyah, who sat for this portrait in 1838, devised the Cherokee alphabet, which formed the basis for the first written Indian language in North America.

demands would be made on them. When tribal leaders proved reluctant, they could often be persuaded to cooperate by warnings about the inevitable spread of white settlement, or more tractable chieftains could be found. In these ways, state and national governments gained title to vast areas of tribal land throughout the trans-Appalachian interior. The continuing loss of land disastrously affected Native Americans, altering the balance of tribal power and forcing many to migrate west.

The fur trade was also a major concern of federal Indian policy. By 1790, most trans-Appalachian tribes served as intermediaries for hunters farther to the west. Both Native Americans and whites entered willingly into the trade. In return for furs, which they had in abundance, the Indians secured highly valued goods such as blankets, guns, rum, and ironware. White traders acquired valuable furs in exchange for relatively inexpensive trade items. Both sides also used the trade to cement diplomatic relations with each other.

The fur trade served white society very well. It had severe costs, however, for Native Americans, who fell victim to deadly diseases such as smallpox and measles and became dependent on renewed supplies of rum, firearms, and other goods. As the demand for furs and pelts increased, moreover, Native Americans overtrapped their hunting grounds, forcing them to reach farther west for fresh sources of supply. That process disturbed long-standing tribal patterns of trade and diplomatic relations.

A third objective of federal Indian policy was to civilize and Christianize the Native Americans and ultimately assimilate them into white society. In the trans-Appalachian West, where whites and Native Americans struggled openly for survival, most people believed that Indians would always remain "savage" and regarded them as impediments to be moved out of white settlement's way. Different attitudes, however, were evident in the East, where clergymen and government officials, newspaper editors and ordinary citizens displayed greater sympathy for the Native Americans' well-being.

A policy of assimilation seemed to offer hope for the Indians' survival in the face of continuing warfare, disease, and white expansion. Although the assimilationists cared deeply about the physical and spiritual fate of Native American people, they had little sympathy for Indian culture, for they demanded that Native Americans cease being Indian and adopt the ways of white society instead. Assimilation or continuing destruction were the alternatives posed by even the most benevolent whites.

Education and Christianization were the major instruments of assimilationist policy. Together Moravian, Quaker, Baptist, Congregationalist, and Dutch Reformed churches sent scores of missionaries to live among the Indians, preach the gospel, and teach the benefits of white civilization. Baptist missionary Isaac

McCoy ministered to the Shawnee tribe in Indiana from 1817 to 1829. John Stewart, a free-born mulatto who was part Indian, preached to the Wyandotte near Sandusky, Ohio, from 1815 to his death in 1821. Among the most selfless were the Quaker missionaries who labored with the Iroquois in New York.

The missionaries' greatest success occurred where Indians had succumbed to white control or when missionaries blended Indian beliefs with the basic tenets of Christianity. Even so, most Native Americans remained aloof, for the chasm between Christianity and their own religions was wide (see Chapter 1), and the missionaries' denigration of Indian culture was obvious.

Education was the other weapon of the assimilationists. In 1793, Congress appropriated $20,000 to promote literacy, agriculture, and vocational instruction. Church groups established schools as well, and in 1819, the government handed over to the churches full responsibility for Indian education. Because federal officials thought that Christianity and civilization went hand in hand, they encouraged missionaries to teach their Indian students religious doctrine as well as reading, writing, and vocational skills.

Strategies of Survival: The Iroquois and the Cherokee

Faced with the steady loss of land and tribal autonomy, Native Americans devised various strategies of resistance and survival. Among the Iroquois, a prophet named Handsome Lake, who had fought with England during the Revolutionary War but who had succumbed to the despair of military defeat and reservation life, led his people through a process of cultural revitalization. In 1799, in a series of religious and social gospels, he preached a combination of Indian and white ways that included temperance, peace, land retention, and the rituals of Gaiwiio, a new religion joining elements of Christianity and traditional Iroquois belief. His vision, a new definition of "Indianness," offered hope and renewed pride for the Iroquois in their dramatically changed world.

Far to the south, the Cherokee followed a different path of accommodation. As the nineteenth century began, the Cherokee still controlled millions of acres in Tennessee, Georgia, and the western Carolinas. Their land base, however, was shrinking. By 1800, more than 40 Cherokee towns had disappeared, and over two-thirds of all Cherokee families had been forced to move into the increasingly crowded settlements that remained.

In 1801, the Tennessee legislature unilaterally expanded the boundaries of several counties to include Cherokee land and then claimed that the Indians fell under the authority of state law. The Cherokee, declaring that they had their own system of justice and distrusting the state courts with their all-white juries and exclusion of Indian testimony, rejected white demands.

In Cherokee councils, a group of full-blood leaders argued for armed resistance. Others, however, including mixed-bloods such as John Ross, pointed out the futility of fighting and argued that accommodation offered the only hope for survival. In the early 1800s, following a bitter struggle for tribal control, the accommodationists won out.

Their first goal was to bring the tribe's scattered villages under a common government. In 1808, the Cherokee National Council adopted a written legal code combining elements of white and Indian law, and in July 1827, the Cherokee devised a written constitution patterned after those of nearby states, complete with executive, legislative, and judicial branches of government. They accompanied it with a bold declaration of their standing as an independent nation. In 1829, the Cherokee government formalized the "blood law," making it an offense punishable by death for any tribe member to transfer land to white ownership without the consent of tribal authorities.

Meanwhile, the process of social and cultural accommodation went forward. Missionaries opened a school for Cherokee youth on the Hiwanee River in 1804 and established a boarding school near present-day Chattanooga 12 years later. They stepped up their religious activities as well, baptizing Cherokee into the Christian faith.

As the Cherokee changed from a mixed hunting, gathering, and farming economy to one based predominantly on settled agriculture, many of them moved from traditional town settlements onto individual farmsteads. The majority continued to inhabit crude log cabins and live a hand-to-mouth existence. However, some prospered, especially mixed-bloods who learned English and understood how to deal with white society. A few of the most successful lived as well as upper-class whites. Joseph Vann, known as "Rich Joe," accumulated hundreds of acres of fertile land, scores of black slaves, and an assortment of mills, stores, and river ferries.

Changes in the Cherokee economy altered relations with blacks as well. Since the mid–eighteenth century, the Cherokee had held a few blacks in slavelike conditions. During the early nineteenth century, however, Cherokee slavery expanded and became more harsh. By 1820, there were nearly 1,300 black slaves in the Cherokee nation. Such changes came about primarily because the spread of cotton cultivation increased the demand for slave labor among Cherokee as well as whites.

By 1820, the strategy of peaceful accommodation had brought obvious rewards. Tribal government was stronger, the standard of living higher, and the sense of Cherokee identity reasonably secure. In the end, however, the Cherokee's success proved their undoing, for as their self-confidence grew, so did the hostility of southern whites, who were increasingly impatient to get them out of the way. That hostility would soon erupt in a final campaign to remove the Cherokee from their land forever (see Chapter 12).

Patterns of Armed Resistance: The Shawnee and the Creek

Not all tribes of the interior proved so accommodating to white expansion. Faced with growing threats to their political and cultural survival, the Shawnee and Creek nations rose in armed resistance during the War of 1812.

In the late 1780s, the tribes of the Old Northwest had launched a series of devastating raids across Indiana, Ohio, and western Pennsylvania, creating panic among white settlers. In September 1790, a force of 1,500, dispatched by President Washington to quell the uprising, fell into an ambush in northwestern Ohio, losing nearly 200 men. The following year, another army of 6,000 troops met a similar fate. Buoyed by their victories, the Shawnee and their allies followed up with a furious assault, virtually clearing northern and central Ohio of white settlement.

Faced with two humiliating defeats, Washington determined to smash the Indians' resistance. In the autumn of 1793, General Anthony Wayne led a third army of conquest into the Ohio wilderness. The following year, his army won a complete victory in the decisive Battle of Fallen Timbers. After the smoke of battle had cleared, the assembled chiefs ceded the southern two-thirds of Ohio in return for $20,000 in trade goods and a $10,000 annual annuity. It was the largest single transfer of Indian land yet, and it opened the heart of the Old Northwest to white control.

In subsequent years, additional treaties further reduced the Indians' land base, driving the Shawnee and Delaware, the Miami and Wyandotte more tightly in upon each other. In the early years of the nineteenth century, two Shawnee leaders, the brothers Tecumseh and Elskwatawa, the latter known to whites as "the Prophet," began to forge an alliance of the region's tribes against the invading whites. In 1809, they established headquarters at an ancient Indian town named Kithtippecanoe in northern Indiana.

Between 1809 and 1811, Tecumseh carried his message of Indian nationalism and military resistance south to the Creek and the Cherokee, calling for "a war of extermination against the paleface." The southern tribes refused to join, but by 1811, over 1,000 fighting men had gathered at Kithtippecanoe.

Alarmed by the Indians' growing militancy, the governor of the Indiana Territory, William Henry Harrison, mustering a force of 1,000 soldiers, attacked and burned Kithtippecanoe.

Over the next several months, Tecumseh's followers, taking advantage of the recent outbreak of the War of 1812 between the United States and England and aided by British troops from Canada, carried out devastating raids across Indiana and southern Michigan. Together they crushed American armies at Detroit and Fort Nelson. At the Battle of the Thames near Detroit, the tide finally turned, for there Harrison inflicted a grievous defeat on a combined British and Indian force. Among those slain was Tecumseh.

The American victory at the Thames signaled the end of Indian resistance in the Old Northwest. Beginning in 1815, American settlers surged once more across Ohio and Indiana and pressed on unimpeded into Illinois and Michigan.

To the south, the Creek challenged white intruders with similar militancy. As the nineteenth century began, white settlers were pushing onto Creek lands in northwestern Georgia and central Alabama. While some Creek leaders urged accommodation, others, called Red Sticks, prepared to fight. The embers of this smoldering conflict were fanned into flame by an aggressive Tennessee militia commander named Andrew Jackson. Citing Creek atrocities, Jackson urged President Jefferson in 1808 to endorse a campaign against the Creek.

Bristling at their treatment by Georgia and Alabama, the Red Sticks carried out a series of violent frontier raids in the spring and summer of 1813. They capped their campaign with an assault on Fort Mims on the Alabama River, where they killed as many as 500 people, women and children among them. News of that tragedy raised bitter cries for revenge. At the head of 5,000 Tennessee and Kentucky militia, augmented by Cherokee, Choctaw, and Chickasaw warriors eager to punish their traditional Creek enemies, Jackson launched his long-

awaited attack. As he moved south, the ferocity of the fighting grew.

The climactic battle of the Creek War came in March 1814 at Horseshoe Bend, on the Tallapoosa River in central Alabama. There, in the fortified town of Tohopeka, 1,000 Creek warriors made a futile stand against 1,400 state troops and 600 Indian allies. Over 800 Native Americans died, more than in any other single battle in the history of Indian-white warfare. With no hope left, Red Eagle, one of the few remaining Red Stick leaders, walked alone into Jackson's camp and addressed the American commander:

> General Jackson, I am not afraid of you. . . . for I am a Creek warrior. . . . You can kill me if you desire. But I come to beg you to send for the women and children of the war party, who are now starving in the woods. . . . If I could fight you any longer I would most heartily do so. Send for the women and children. They never did you any harm. But kill me, if the white people want it done.

The war against the Creek was finished, and Jackson allowed Red Eagle to return home.

But the general was not quite done. He built Fort Jackson on the Hickory Ground, the most sacred spot of the Creek nation, and seized 22 million acres of land, nearly two-thirds of their domain. Before his Indian-fighting days were over, Jackson would acquire through treaty and military conquest nearly three-fourths of Alabama and Florida, a third of Tennessee, and a fifth of both Georgia and Mississippi.

The Creek's defeat at Horseshoe Bend broke the back of Indian defenses in the South. With all possibility of armed resistance gone, the Native Americans of the Old Southwest gave way before the swelling tide of white settlement.

POLITICS IN TRANSITION

For two decades following Jefferson's election in 1800, the Jeffersonian Republicans monopolized the presidency and dominated Congress, while the Federalist Party, its reputation damaged by charges of disloyalty during the War of 1812 and by its continuing "aristocratic" image, gradually collapsed. By the 1820s, however, the Jeffersonian ascendancy was coming to an end as political changes ushered in a new era of American politics.

A New Style of Politics

By the 1820s, basic patterns of political behavior were changing. Most evident was the surge of voter participation in state and local elections. Women, blacks, and Native Americans continued to be excluded, but white men flocked to the polls in unprecedented numbers. The flood of voters resulted in part from removal of property-holding and taxpaying restrictions on the franchise in some states.

Equally important were the growing strength of democratic beliefs among the people and the appearance of a new generation of political leaders skilled in the techniques of mass, electoral politics.

Division Among the Jeffersonians

With the Federalists in disarray following the War of 1812, the Jeffersonian Republicans stood triumphant, their ranks swollen by fresh recruits in the East and the admission of new states in the West. The Jeffersonians' success, however, proved their undoing, for no single party could contain the nation's growing diversity of economic and social interests, sectional differences, and individual ambitions.

Following the War of 1812, largely in response to growing pressures from the West and Northeast, the government launched a Federalist-like program of national economic development. Wartime disorganization of the currency demonstrated the need for a new national bank to replace the First Bank of the United States,

whose charter had expired in 1811. In March 1816, President Madison signed a bill creating a second bank, intended to stimulate economic expansion and regulate the loose currency-issuing practices of the country's countless state-chartered banks. In his final message to Congress in December 1816, Madison called for a tariff to protect the country's infant industries. Congress responded with the first truly protective tariff in American history, a set of duties on imported woolen and cotton goods, iron, leather, hats, paper, and sugar.

The administration's program of national economic development drew sharp criticism from so-called Old Republicans, a group of southern politicians who regarded themselves as keepers of the Jeffersonian conscience. Thirty-three Old Republicans voted against the bank bill. Over the next decade, their strength dwindled, even as their cries of alarm became increasingly shrill. By the early 1820s, Henry Clay and others, taking up the name National Republicans, were proposing an ambitious "American system" of tariffs and internal improvements.

The Specter of Sectionalism

In spite of the postwar surge of national spirit, Federalist talk of disunion had illustrated just how uncertain national unity continued to be. Congressional debates over the tariff, internal improvements, and the national bank reverberated with the clash of state and sectional interests. The Missouri crisis of 1819–1820 revealed how deep-seated sectional rivalries had become.

Ever since 1789, politicians had labored to keep the explosive issue of slavery tucked safely beneath the surface of political life, for they recognized how quickly it could jeopardize national unity. Their fears were borne out in 1819 when Missouri applied for admission to the Union and raised anew the question of slavery's expansion. In the Northwest Ordinance of 1787, Congress had limited slavery north of the Ohio River while allowing its expansion to the south. But

Missouri Compromise of 1820

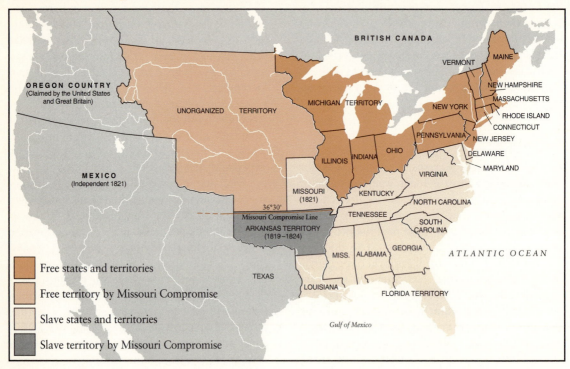

what about the vast new territory west of the Mississippi River?

Seizing the opportunity to deal with that question, Senator Rufus King of New York demanded that Missouri prohibit slavery before entering the Union. His proposal triggered a fierce debate over Congress's authority to prevent slavery's spread. Southerners were adamant that Congress could not close the trans-Mississippi West to their slave property and were determined to maintain the Senate's balance between slave and free states. Already by 1819, the North's more rapidly growing population had given it a 105-to-81 advantage in the House of Representatives. Equality in the Senate offered the only sure protection of southern interests. Northerners vowed to keep the trans-Mississippi West open to free labor. That meant closing it to slavery.

For nearly three months, Congress debated the issue. During much of the time, free blacks listening intently to northern antislavery speeches filled the House gallery. "This momentous question," worried the aged Jefferson, "like a fire-bell in the night, [has] awakened and filled me with terror." Northerners were similarly alarmed. The Missouri question, declared the editor of the New York *Daily Advertiser*, "involves not only the future character of our nation, but the future weight and influence of the free states. If now lost—it is lost forever."

In the end, compromise prevailed. Missouri gained admission as a slave state, while Maine came in as a counterbalancing free state, and a line was drawn west from Missouri at latitude 36°30′ to the Rocky Mountains dividing the lands that would be open to slavery from those that would not. For the moment, the explosive issue of slavery's expansion had again been put to rest.

Collapse of the Federalist-Jeffersonian Party System

The final collapse of the Federalist-Jeffersonian party system came with the presidential election of John Quincy Adams in 1824. For the first time since 1800, when the "Virginia dynasty" of Jefferson, Madison, and Monroe began, there was competition for the presidency from every major wing of the Jeffersonian Party. Of the five candidates, Adams of Massachusetts and Henry Clay of Kentucky advocated strong federal programs of economic development. William Crawford of Georgia and Andrew Jackson of Tennessee clung to traditional Jeffersonian principles of limited government, agrarianism, and states' rights. In between stood John Calhoun of South Carolina, just beginning his fateful passage from nationalism to southern nullification.

A medical problem eliminated Crawford from the campaign, while Calhoun, attracting limited support, withdrew to become the vice-presidential partner of both Adams and Jackson. When none of the remaining candidates received an electoral majority, the election, as in 1800, moved into the House of Representatives. There, an alliance of Adams and Clay supporters gave the New Englander the election, even though he had trailed Jackson in electoral votes, 84 to 99. The Jacksonians' charges of a "corrupt bargain" gained credence when Adams appointed Clay secretary of state.

Adams's ill-fated administration revealed the disarray in American politics. His stirring calls for federal road and canal building, standardization of weights and measures, establishment of a national university, promotion of commerce and manufacturing, and government support for science and the arts quickly fell victim to sectional conflicts, political factionalism, and his own open scorn for the increasingly democratic politics of the day. Within a year of Adams's inauguration, his administration had foundered. For the rest of his term, politicians jockeyed for position in the political realignment that was under way.

CONCLUSION

THE PASSING OF AN ERA

During the first quarter of the nineteenth century, Americans saw their nation's territory more than double in size while the Jeffersonians labored to set the government on a proper republican course. They promoted agrarian expansion and transformed the country's relations with Europe and the Americas. They also sought, less successfully, to reconcile Native American rights with national expansion.

The 1820s brought an end to the era of founding, a turning point that was dramatized on July 4, 1826, the fiftieth anniversary of American independence, when two of the remaining Revolutionary patriarchs, John Adams and Thomas Jefferson, died within a few hours of each other. "The sterling virtues of the Revolution are silently passing away," wrote George McDuffie of South Carolina, "and the period is not distant when there will be no living monument to remind us of those glorious days of trial." A new and different era was at hand.

Recommended Reading

Drew McCoy, *The Elusive Republic* (1980), describes the importance of agrarian expansion for the Jeffersonians. For Jeffersonian politics and government, see also Noble Cunningham, *The Process of Government Under Jefferson* (1978); Daniel Jordan, *Political Leadership in Jefferson's Virginia* (1983); and Andrew Cayton, *The Frontier Republic: Ideology and Politics in the Ohio Country, 1780–1825* (1986). Discussions of the Federalists can be found in James Broussard, *The Southern Federalists, 1800–1816* (1978); and Linda Kerber, *Federalists in Dissent* (1970). Steven Watts, *The Republic Reborn: War and the Making of Liberal America, 1790–1820* (1987), traces the change from Revolutionary republicanism to liberal capitalism.

Robert Berkhofer discusses white attitudes toward Indians in *The White Man's Indian* (1978). See also William McLoughlin, *Cherokees and Missionaries, 1789–1839* (1984).

Foreign policy issues and the politics surrounding them are portrayed by Reginald Horsman, *The Diplomacy of the New Republic, 1776–1815* (1986); and Ernest May, *The Making of the Monroe Doctrine* (1975).

On politics and the Supreme Court, see Richard Ellis, *The Jeffersonian Crisis: Courts and Politics in the Young Republic* (1971).

Donald Jackson, *Thomas Jefferson and the Stony Mountains: Exploring the West from Monticello* (1981), discusses Jefferson's fascination with the West. For problems of cultural nationalism, see Joseph Ellis, *After the Revolution: Profiles of Early American Culture* (1979); Emory Elliott, *Revolutionary Writers: Literature and Authority in the New Republic, 1725–1810* (1985); and David Simpson, *The Politics of American English* (1986).

Time Line

1789	Treaty of Fort Harmar Knox's reports on Indian affairs
1794	Battle of Fallen Timbers
1795	Treaty of Greenville
1796	Congress establishes Indian Factory System
1800	Capital moves to Washington Thomas Jefferson elected president
1801	Judiciary Act New Land Act
1802	Judiciary Act repealed
1803	*Marbury* v. *Madison* Louisiana Purchase
1803–1806	Lewis and Clark expedition
1803–1812	Napoleonic Wars resume British impress American sailors
1804	Jefferson reelected
1805–1807	Pike explores the West
1806	Non-Importation Act
1807	Embargo Act *Chesapeake-Leopard* affair Congress prohibits slave trade
1808	James Madison elected Cherokee legal code established
1809	Tecumseh's confederacy formed Non-Intercourse Act

1810	Macon's Bill No. 2
1811	Battle of Kithtippecanoe
1812	Madison reelected West Florida annexed War declared against Great Britain
1813	Battle of the Thames
1813–1814	Creek War
1814	Treaty of Ghent Battle of Horseshoe Bend
1814–1815	Hartford Convention
1815	Battle of New Orleans U.S. establishes military posts in trans-Mississippi West
1816	James Monroe elected president Second United States Bank chartered
1819	Adams-Onis Treaty with Spain Spain cedes East Florida to U.S. *McCulloch* v. *Maryland*
1820	Land Act Missouri Compromise Monroe reelected
1822	Diplomatic recognition of Latin American republics
1823	Monroe Doctrine proclaimed
1824	John Quincy Adams elected president
1827	Cherokee adopt written constitution

part 3

An Expanding People

1820-1877

During the first half of the nineteenth century, the young nation expanded rapidly. As Americans surged west, and, in the 1840s, pushed on to the Pacific coast, the population soared and became more diverse. Expansion also sharpened regional differences, particularly between the North and the South, and the period ended with the most devastating conflict the nation has ever experienced.

Chapters 10, 11, and 12 cover roughly the same time period. Chapter 10, "Currents of Change in the Northeast and the Old Northwest," investigates the economic and social transformations that affected everyday life in these two regions. Chapter 11, "Slavery and the Old South," considers the South's distinctive economic and social system, which, based as it was on slavery, raised questions about the special virtue of the nation and the meaning of justice and equality.

In Chapter 12, "Shaping America in the Antebellum Age," we focus on economic and social changes that sharpened the familiar tension between narrowly defined self-interest and social concerns. The election of Andrew Jackson as president marked the advent of the second American party system and of a lively political culture firmly rooted in new economic and social conditions.

Chapter 13, "Moving West," shows the power of American expansionism and the limited meaning many Americans gave to terms like *liberty* and *equality*. During the 1840s, as settlers to new frontiers sought to re-create familiar institutions and patterns, the earlier inhabitants, mostly Mexicans and Native Americans, found themselves excluded from most of the promises of American life.

The expansion of slavery into the West threatened the political balance of power between the North and the South and raised the question of where power and authority lay to decide the future of the West.

Chapter 14, "The Union In Peril," traces the disintegration of the second party system and the eruption of civil war in Kansas. Secession and civil war soon followed. Chapter 15, "The Union Severed," examines the Civil War and the unanticipated results of the conflict. Chapter 16, "The Union Reconstructed," explores how Americans tried to resolve the many dilemmas of the postwar period.

chapter 10

....

Currents of Change in the Northeast and the Old Northwest

For her first eighteen years, Susan Warner was little touched by the far-reaching economic and social changes that were transforming the character of the country and her own city of New York. While some New Yorkers toiled to make a living by taking in piecework and others responded to unsettling new means of producing goods by joining trade unions to agitate for wages that would enable them to "live as comfortable as others," Susan was surrounded by luxuries and privilege. Much of the year was spent in the family's townhouse on St. Mark's Place, not far from the home of the enormously rich real estate investor and fur trader John Jacob Astor. There Susan acquired the social graces and skills appropriate for a girl of her position and background. She had dancing and singing lessons, studied Italian and French, and learned the etiquette involved in receiving visitors and making calls. When the hot weather made life in New York unpleasant, the Warners escaped to the cooler airs of Canaan, where they had a summer house.

All this changed after Susan's father, heretofore so successful a provider and parent, lost most of his fortune during the financial Panic of 1837. Like others experiencing a sharp economic reversal, the Warners had to make radical adjustments. The fashionable home on St. Mark's Place was exchanged for a more modest one on an island in the Hudson River. Susan turned "housekeeper" and learned how to do tasks once relegated to others: sewing and making butter, pudding sauces, and johnny cake. Prized possessions eventually went up for auction. "When at last the men and the confusion were gone," Susan's younger sister, Anna, recalled, "then we woke up to life."

Waking up to life meant facing the necessity of making money. But what could Susan do to reverse sliding family fortunes? True, some women labored as factory operatives, domestics, seamstresses, or schoolteachers, but it was doubtful Susan could even imagine herself in any of these occupations.

On the advice of her Aunt Fanny, Susan decided to try her hand at writing fiction. She constructed a story around the trials of a young orphan girl, Ellen Montgomery. As Ellen suffered one reverse after another, she learned the lessons that allowed her to survive and eventually triumph over adversity: piety, self-denial, discipline, and the power of a mother's love. Entitled *The Wide, Wide World,* the novel was accepted for publication only after the mother of the publisher, George Putnam, read it and told her son, "If you never publish another book, you must make *The Wide, Wide World* available for your fellow men." Much to Putnam's surprise, *The Wide, Wide World* became the first American novel to sell more than a million copies. It was one of the best-sellers of the century.

Susan Warner's second novel described the spiritual and intellectual life of a young girl thrust into poverty after an early life of luxury in New York. Entitled *Queechy,* this novel was also a great success.

The popularity of Susan's books suggested how well they spoke to the concerns and interests of a broad readership. The background of social and financial uncertainty, with its sudden changes of fortune, captured the reality and fears of a fluid society in the process of transformation. Pious heroines like Ellen Montgomery, who struggled to master their passions and urges toward independence, were shining exemplars of the new norms for middle-class women. Their successful efforts to mold themselves heartened readers who believed that the future of the nation depended on virtuous mothers and who struggled to live up to new ideals. Susan's novels validated their efforts and affirmed the importance of the domestic sphere.

This chapter explores the economic changes in the Northeast and Old Northwest that not only transformed the economy between 1820 and 1860, as Susan Warner discovered, but also shaped social, cultural, and political life. Though most Americans still lived in rural settings rather than in factory towns or cities, economic growth and the new industrial mode of production affected them through the creation of new goods, opportunities, and markets. In urban communities and factory towns, the new economic order ushered in new forms of work, new class arrangements, and new forms of social strife.

After discussing the factors that fueled antebellum growth, the chapter turns to the industrial world, where so many of the new patterns of work and life appeared. An investigation of urbanization reveals shifting class arrangements and values as well as rising social and racial tensions. Finally, an examination of rural communities in the East and on the frontier in the Old Northwest highlights the transformation of these two sections of the country. Between 1840 and 1860, industrialization and economic growth increasingly knit them together.

ECONOMIC GROWTH

Between 1820 and 1860, the American economy moved away from its reliance on agriculture as the major source of growth toward an industrial and technological future. Real per capita output of goods and services grew an average of 2 percent annually between 1820 and 1840 and slightly less between 1840 and 1860. But the economy, though expanding, was also unstable, lurching from periods of boom (1822–1834, mid-1840s–1850s) to periods of bust (1816–1821, 1837–1843). As never before, Americans faced dramatic shifts in the availability of jobs and goods and in prices and wages. Moreover, because regional economies were increasingly linked, problems in one area tended to affect conditions in others.

Factors Fueling Economic Development

What accounted for this new phase of growth and economic development? The United States, of course, had abundant natural resources, enormously increased by the Louisiana Purchase in 1803. An expanding population, soaring from 9 million in 1820 to over 30 million in 1860, represented the new workers, new households, and new consumers so essential to economic development. Until the 1840s, most of the growth in population came from natural increase. But as the size of American families gradually shrank—in 1800, the average white woman bore seven children; by 1860, the number had declined to five—foreign immigration took up the slack.

Improved transportation played a key role in bringing about economic and geographic expansion. Early in the century, high freight rates discouraged production for distant markets, and primitive transportation hindered western settlement. During the 1820s and 1830s, however, canal-building projects revolutionized travel and commerce and made migration much easier. The Erie Canal, completed in 1825, stretched 363 miles between Albany and Buffalo, New York. The canal was the last link in the chain of waterways binding New York City to the Great Lakes and the Northwest.

The Erie Canal and hundreds of other newly constructed canals fostered strong economic and social ties between the Northwest and the East.

Even at the height of the canal boom, politicians, promoters, and others, impressed with Britain's success with railways, also supported the construction of railroads. Only 73 miles of track were laid between 1828 and 1830, but by 1840, there were 3,000 miles of track, most in the Northeast. By the end of the 1850s, total mileage soared to 30,000. Like the canals, the new railroads strengthened the links between the Old Northwest and the East.

Improved transportation had such a profound influence on American life that some historians use the term *transportation revolution* to refer to its impact. Canals and railroads provided cheap and reliable access to distant markets and goods and encouraged Americans to settle the frontier and cultivate virgin lands. Eventually, the strong economic and social ties the waterways and then the railways fostered between the Northwest and the East led people living in the two regions to share political outlooks.

Especially in terms of the pattern of western settlement, railroads exerted enormous influence. Their routes could determine whether a city, town, or even homestead survived. The railroad transformed Chicago from a small settlement into a bustling commercial and transportation center. In 1850, the city contained not 1 mile of track, but within five years, 2,200 miles of track serving 150,000 square miles terminated in Chicago.

Improved transportation stimulated agricultural expansion and regional specialization. Farmers began to plant larger crops for the market, concentrating on those most suited to their soil and climate. By the late 1830s, the Old Northwest had become the country's granary, while New England farmers turned to dairy or produce farming. By 1860, American farmers

Growth of the Railroads, 1850-1860

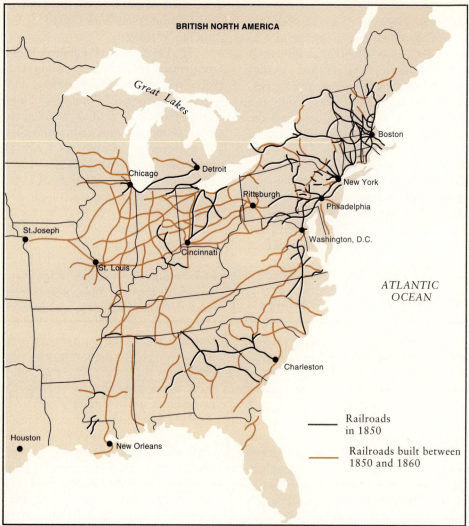

were producing four to five times as much wheat, corn, cattle, and hogs as they had in 1810.

Capital and Government Support

Internal improvements, the exploitation of natural resources, and the cultivation of new lands all demanded capital. Much of it came from European investors. Between 1790 and 1861, over $500 million flowed into the United States from Europe. Foreign investors from Europe, adding to funds brought by immigrant families, financed as much as a third of all canal construction and bought about a quarter of all railroad bonds.

American mercantile capital fueled growth

as well. The merchant class prospered in the half century after the Revolution, and merchants invested in schemes ranging from canals to textile factories. Many ventured into the production of goods and became manufacturers themselves.

Prosperous Americans eagerly sought opportunities to put their capital to work. Two New Yorkers, Arthur Bronson and Charles Butler, made a careful tour of the Northwest in 1833. Despite primitive conditions, both men saw wonderful opportunities. Detroit, Butler concluded, "is destined to be a very great city," while Chicago "presents one of the finest fields in America for industry & enterprise." Each man channeled funds into western projects. Bronson's investments ranged from Ohio banks to farmland in Wisconsin Territory, Illinois, Michigan, Ohio, and Indiana to real estate in Chicago and Detroit, all in addition to his holdings in New York ironworks and banks.

Local and state government played their part by enthusiastically supporting economic growth. States often helped new ventures raise capital by passing laws of incorporation, by awarding entrepreneurs special privileges such as tax breaks or monopolistic control, by underwriting bonds for improvement projects (which increased their investment appeal), and by providing loans for internal improvements. New York, Pennsylvania, Ohio, Indiana, Illinois, and Virginia publicly financed almost 75 percent of the canal systems in their states between 1815 and 1860.

The national government assisted some internal improvements such as the National Road linking Maryland and Illinois. Federal tariff policy shielded American products, and the second U.S. Bank provided the financial stability investors required. The line separating the public sector from the private often became unclear.

The law also helped to promote aggressive economic growth. The case of *Palmer* v. *Mulligan,* decided by the New York State Supreme Court in 1805, laid down the principle that property ownership included the right to develop property for business purposes. A series of important Supreme Court decisions between 1819 and 1824 clarified contract law, establishing the basic principle that contracts were binding.

A New Mentality

As the discussion of the links between law and economic growth suggests, economic expansion depends on intangible factors as well as more obvious ones such as improved transportation. The entrepreneurial mentality that encouraged investment, new business ventures, and land speculation was an important component of antebellum economic development. Another factor was American energy and openness to change. As one Frenchman explained in 1834, "All here is circulation, motion, and boiling agitation. Experiment follows experiment; enterprise succeeds to enterprise."

Others described an American mechanical "genius." The American was "a mechanic by nature," one Frenchman insisted. "In Massachusetts and Connecticut, there is not a labourer who had not invented a machine or tool." This observer exaggerated, but Americans did develop a number of efficient and productive tools and machines. The McCormick harvester, the Colt revolver, Goodyear vulcanized rubber products, and the sewing machine were developed, refined, and developed further. Such improvements cut labor costs and increased efficiency.

While the shortage of labor in the United States stimulated technological innovations that replaced humans with machines, the rapid spread of education after 1800 also contributed to innovation and increased productivity. By 1840, most whites were literate. In that year, public schools nationwide were educating 38.4 percent of white children between the ages of 5 and 19.

The belief that education spurred economic growth helped to foster enthusiasm for public education, particularly in the Northeast. Massachusetts moved first toward mass education by mandating in 1827 that taxes pay the whole cost of the state's public schools. At first, the Massachusetts school system did not function well. School buildings were often run-down and even unheated. Because school curricula were virtually nonexistent, students often lounged idly at their desks.

Under the leadership of Horace Mann, the reform of state education for white children began in 1837. Mann advocated graded schools, uniform curricula, teacher training, and reduced the power of local districts over schools. His campaigns made the Massachusetts system a model for reformers everywhere.

Mann believed that education promoted inventiveness. It "had a market value." Businessmen often agreed. Prominent industrialists in the 1840s believed that education produced workers who could handle complex machinery without undue supervision and were superior employees—reliable, punctual, industrious, and sober.

Ambivalence Toward Change

While supporting education as a means to economic growth, many Americans also firmly believed in its social value. Public schools could mold student character and promote "virtuous habits" and "rational self-governing" behavior. Students learned facts by rote because memory work and recitation taught them discipline and concentration. Nineteenth-century schoolbooks reinforced the classroom message. "It is a great sin to be idle," children read in one 1830 text, while another warned, "Poverty is the fruit of idleness."

The concern with education and character indicate that as much as Americans welcomed economic progress, they also feared social and economic change. Schools, which taught students to be deferential, obedient, and punctual, could counter the worst by-products of change. Schools served as much as a defense against change as its agents.

The touted virtues of diligence, punctuality, temperance, and thrift probably did assist economic growth, but the success of early nineteenth-century economic ventures frequently depended on the ability to take risks, to think daringly. The emphasis given to the safe but stolid virtues suggests that the fear of social disintegration ran through antebellum society.

The Advance of Industrialization

Significant economic growth between 1820 and 1860 resulted from the reorganization of production. Factory production reorganized work by breaking down the manufacture of an article into discrete steps. At first, manufacturers often relied on the putting-out system. Eventually, they centralized all the steps of production under one roof, where hand labor gradually gave way to power-driven machinery such as wooden "spinning jennies." Often they sought the help of British immigrants who had the practical experience and technical know-how no American possessed.

As factory workers replaced artisans and home manufacturers, the volume of goods rose, and prices dropped dramatically. The price of a yard of cotton cloth fell from 18 cents to 2 cents over the 45 years preceding the Civil War.

Between 1820 and 1860, textile manufacturing became the country's leading industry. Textile mills sprang up across the New England and the Middle Atlantic states, regions that contained swift-flowing streams to power the mills, capitalists eager to finance the ventures, children and women to tend the machines, and numerous cities and towns with ready markets for cheap textiles. Early mills were small affairs, containing only the machines for carding and spinning. The thread was then put out to home workers to be woven into cloth. The early mechanization of cloth production did not replace home manufacture but supplemented it.

Already underway in 1813, however, were experiments that would lead to the development

This calico factory, located in Manchester, New Hampshire, produced colorful fabrics for American consumers. In 1854, fully 1,250 of the 2,000 workers were female.

of the power loom. Eventually, the loom devised by Francis Cabot Lowell and Paul Moody was installed in a mill at Waltham, Massachusetts.

The most important innovation of the Waltham operation was Lowell's decision to bring all the steps of cotton cloth production together under one roof. By centralizing the entire manufacturing process and work force in one factory, cloth for the mass market could be produced more cheaply and more profitably. In 1823, the Boston Associates expanded their operations to East Chelmsford on the Merrimack River, a town they renamed Lowell.

Most New England mills followed the Lowell system. The cumulative impact of the rise of the textile industry was to supplant the home production of cloth, even though some women would continue to spin and weave for their families for some years to come, and hand-loom weavers would survive for another generation. In the process, Americans were transformed from a people clad in earth-colored homespun into a nation decked out in gayer, more colorful clothing.

Textile mills helped to account for the increasingly industrial character of the Northeast. By 1860, fully 71 percent of all manufacturing workers lived in this region of the country.

Other important manufacturing operations reached west and south from New England. The processing of wheat, timber, and hides using power-driven machinery was common in most communities of 200 families or more. Paper mills were widespread, although a third of them were clustered in Philadelphia. The iron and metalworking industry stretched from Albany, New York, south to Maryland and west to Cincinnati.

Environmental Consequences

The impact of this economic growth on the environment was far-reaching and often harmful. Steamboats and early railroads, for example, depended on wood for fuel. So too did the heating stoves that were keeping American families warm. Armed with new steel axes, lumbermen and farmers kept up with the increased demand for wood, and the eastern forest and the wildlife that lived there rapidly disappeared. Better transportation, which encouraged western settlement, also promoted forest clearance as individual settlers cleared land for crops and cut wood for housing. Sawmills and milldams interfered with spawning habits of fish, clogged their gills with sawdust, and even changed the flow of rivers. The process of ecological change, spurred by the desire for wood, recurred as lumber companies and entrepreneurs moved from the East to exploit the forests of the Great Lakes and of the Gulf states.

As late as 1840, wood was the main source for the country's energy needs. But the high price of wood and the discovery of anthracite coal in Pennsylvania signaled the beginning of a shift to coal as the major source of power. While the East gradually regained some of its forest cover, the heavy use of coal resulted in air pollution. Steam engines and heating stoves poured out dirty fumes into the air. In New York City, one could see the evidence of pollution everywhere—in the gray cloud hanging over the city, in the smoke rising from its machine shops, refineries, and private houses, in the acrid smells and black soot that were a part of daily life.

Some Americans were aware of the environmental consequences of rapid growth and change. Author James Fenimore Cooper had one of his characters in his novel *The Pioneers* condemn those who destroyed nature "without remorse and without shame." Yet most Americans accepted the changing environment as an inevitable part of progress.

EARLY MANUFACTURING

Industrialization created a more efficient means of producing more goods at much lower cost than had been possible in the homes and small shops of an earlier day. Philadelphian Samuel Breck's diary reveals some of the new profusion and range of goods. "Went to town principally to see the Exhibition of American Manufactures

at the Masonic Hall," he noted in 1833. "More than 700 articles have been sent. Among this great variety, I distinguished the Philadelphia porcelains, beautiful Canton cotton, made at York in this state, soft and capacious blankets, silver plate, . . . chymical drugs, hardware, saddlery, and the most beautiful black broadcloth I ever saw."

The Impact of Industrialization

Two examples illustrate how industrialization transformed American life. Before the nineteenth century, local printing shops depended on manual labor to produce books, newspapers, and journals. The cost of reading material was high enough to make a library a sign of wealth.

Between 1830 and 1850, however, adoption and improvement of British inventions, together with managerial and marketing innovations, revolutionized the printing and publishing industries.

As books and magazines dropped in cost and grew in number, far more people could afford them. No longer dependent solely on the words of the "better sort" for information, people could now form their views on the basis of what they read. The proliferation of printed matter had an enormous impact on people's stock of information, values, tastes, and use of leisure time. It also contributed to the rising literacy rate among white Americans.

Just as printed materials wrought great changes in American life, the making of inexpensive timepieces affected its pace and rhythms. Before the 1830s, when few Americans could afford a clock, it was difficult to make exact plans. But the production of timepieces soared in the 1830s, and by midcentury, inexpensive, mass-produced ones could be found everywhere. Clocks encouraged a more disciplined use of time and undergirded the economic changes taking place. Timepieces, for example, were essential for the successful operation of railroads, which ran on schedules. Clocks also imposed a new rhythm in many workplaces.

A New England Textile Town

To understand the process of industrialization and its impact on work and the work force, let us examine Lowell, the "model" Massachusetts textile town, and Cincinnati, a bustling midwestern industrial center.

Lowell was a new town, planned and built expressly for industrial purposes in the 1820s. Regarded as a model factory community, in 1836 Lowell, with 17,000 inhabitants, aspired to become the "Manchester of America," Manchester being the center of England's textile industry. Lowell was America's most important textile center.

By 1830, women composed nearly 70 percent of the Lowell textile work force. The women who came to Lowell for jobs were the first American women to labor outside their homes in large numbers. They were also among the first Americans to experience the full impact of the factory system.

Working and Living in a Mill Town

Mary Paul was typical of the young women drawn to work in Lowell and other New England textile towns. As the planners had anticipated, most were unmarried and young. In 1830, more than 63 percent of Lowell's population was female, and most were between the ages of 15 and 29.

These women, from New England's middling rural families, came to the mills for a variety of reasons ranging from the desire for economic independence to the decline of home manufacturing. As Sally Rice from Vermont explained, "I am almost nineteen years old. I must of course have something of my own before

many more years have passed over my head. And where is that something coming from if I go home and earn nothing." Mill work paid women relatively well in the 1820s and 1830s. Domestic servants' weekly wages hovered around 75 cents and seamstresses' 90 cents, while in the mid-1830s women could make between $2.40 and $3.20 a week in the mill.

Few of the women considered their decision to come to Lowell a permanent commitment. They came to work for a few years, felt free to go home or to school for a few months, and then returned to mill work. Once married, they left the mill work force forever.

New manufacturing work was regimented and exhausting. The standard schedule was 12 hours a day, six days a week, with only a half hour for breakfast and lunch.

Within the factory, the organization of space facilitated production. In the basement was the waterwheel, the source of power. Above, successive floors were completely open, each containing the machines necessary for the different steps of cloth making: carding, spinning, weaving, and dressing. Elevators moved materials from one floor to another. On a typical floor, rows of machines stretched the length of the low room, tended by operatives who might watch over several machines at the same time. From his elevated desk at the end of the room, the overseer watched the workers.

Involving an adaptation to a completely new work situation, mill work also entailed an entirely new living situation for women operatives. The companies provided substantial quarters for their overseers and housing for male workers and their families. Hoping to attract respectable females to Lowell, the mill owners also constructed company boardinghouses where women workers had to live, usually four to six to a room. Headed by female housekeepers, the boardinghouse maintained strict rules, including a 10 o'clock curfew. Amid such intimate working and living conditions, young women formed close ties with one another and developed a strong sense of community.

Female Responses to Work

Although mill work offered better wages than other occupations open to women, all female workers had limited job mobility, because only men could hold supervisory positions. Most female operatives accepted such sexual discrimination as part of life. But the sense of sisterhood supported open protest when trouble arose.

Trouble broke out when hard times hit Lowell in February 1834. Falling prices, poor sales, and rising inventories prompted managers to announce a 15 percent wage cut. This was their way of protecting profits—at the expense of their employees. The mill workers sprang into action. Petitions circulated, threatening a strike. Meetings followed. At one lunchtime gathering, the company agent, hoping to end the protests, fired an apparent ringleader. But, as the agent re-

Work in textile mills was often tedious and repetitive. Although women were paid less than men, they often welcomed the opportunity to live independently and to earn their own money.

ported, "she declared that every girl in the room should leave with her," then "made a signal, and . . . they all marched out & few returned the ensuing morning." The strikers roamed the streets appealing to other workers and visited other mills. In all, about a sixth of the town's work force turned out.

Though this work stoppage was brief and failed to prevent the wage reduction, it demonstrated women workers' concern about the impact of industrialization on the labor force. Strikers, taunted as unfeminine for their "amazonian display," refused to agree that workers were inferior to bosses. Pointing out that they were daughters of free men, strikers called the bosses "Tories in disguise" and sought to link their protest to their fathers' and grandfathers' efforts to throw off the bonds of British oppression during the Revolution. Revolutionary rhetoric that once held only political meaning took on economic overtones as Lowell women confronted industrial work.

During the 1830s, wage cuts, long hours, increased work loads, and production speed-ups, mandated by owners' desires to protect profits, constantly reminded Lowell women and other textile workers of the possibility of "wage slavery." In Dover, New Hampshire, 800 women turned out and formed a union in 1834 to protest wage cuts. In the 1840s, women in several New England states agitated for the ten-hour day, while petitions from Lowell prompted the Massachusetts legislature to hold the first government hearing on industrial working conditions.

The Changing Character of the Work Force

Most protest efforts met with limited success. The short tenure of most women mill workers prevented permanent labor organizations. In addition, the waves of immigration that deposited so many penniless foreigners in northeastern cities in the 1840s and 1850s created a new pool of labor. The newcomers were desperate for jobs and would accept lower wages than New England farm girls. Gradually, the Irish began to replace Yankee women in the mills. Representing only 8 percent of the Lowell work force in 1845, the Irish composed nearly half the workers by 1860. As the ethnic makeup of the work force changed, so did its gender composition. More men came to work in the mills. By 1860, some 30 percent of the Lowell workers were male. All these changes made the women expendable and increased the costs of going "against the mill."

Lowell itself changed as the Irish crowded into the city and New England women gradually left the mills. With owners no longer feeling the need to continue paternalistic practices, boardinghouses disappeared. A permanent work force, once a nightmare to owners, had become a reality by 1860, and Lowell's reputation as a model factory town faded away.

Factories on the Frontier

Cincinnati, a small Ohio River settlement of 2,540 in 1810, grew to be the country's third largest industrial center by 1840. With a population of 40,382, it contained a variety of industries at different stages of development. Cincinnati manufacturers who turned out machines, machine parts, hardware, and furniture were quick to mechanize for increased volume and profits. Other trades like carriage making and cigar making moved far more slowly toward mechanization before 1860. Alongside these concerns, artisans like coopers, blacksmiths, and riverboat builders still labored in small shops using traditional hand tools. The new and the old ways coexisted in Cincinnati, as they did in most manufacturing communities.

In 1850, most Cincinnati workers worked in small or medium-size shops, but almost 20 percent labored in factories with over 100 employees. Some craftsmen continued to use a wide array of skills as they produced goods in time-honored ways. Others worked in new factories, performing more specialized and limited tasks. In furniture factories, for example, some artisans worked exclusively as varnishers, others as carpenters, and still others as finishers. No single worker made a chair from start to finish. But all used some of their skills and earned steady wages. Though in the long run machines threatened to replace them, these skilled factory workers often had reason in the short run to praise the factory's opportunities. Less fortunate was the new class of unskilled factory laborers, who received low wages and had little job security.

Many of Cincinnati's female residents were "outworkers" who worked in small shops or at home as seamstresses for the city's growing ready-to-wear clothing industry. Manufacturers purchased the cloth, cut it into basic patterns, and then contracted the work out to be finished.

Paid by the piece, female outworkers were among the most exploited of Cincinnati's workers. The successful marketing of sewing machines in the 1850s contributed to worsening working conditions and lower pay. Since the sewing machine made stitching easier, the pool of potential workers increased and the volume of work that bosses expected grew.

Cincinnati employers claimed that the new industrial order offered great opportunities to most of the city's male citizens. Manufacturing work encouraged the "manly virtues" so necessary to the "republican citizen." Not all Cincinnati workers agreed. Like workers in Lowell and other manufacturing communities, Cincinnati's laborers rose up against their bosses in the decades before the Civil War.

The workingman's plight, as Cincinnati labor leaders analyzed it, stemmed from his loss of independence. The new industrial order was changing the nature of the laboring class itself. A new kind of worker had emerged. Rather than selling the products of his skills, he had only his raw labor to sell. His "wage slavery," or dependence on wages, promised to be lifelong. The reorganization of work signaled the end of the progression from apprentice to journeyman to master and undermined traditional skills. Few workers could expect to rise to the position of independent craftsman. Most would labor only for others, just as slaves labored for their mas-

In 1848, an unknown photographer took this picture of Cincinnati. The prominence of steamboats in the picture suggests the role location and improvements in transportation played in the city's growth. Although the countryside is visible in the background, the rows of substantial commercial and industrial buildings make Cincinnati's status as a bustling urban center clear.

ters. Nor would wages bring to most that other form of independence, the ownership of shop and home. The expression "wage slavery" contained a deep truth about the changed conditions of many American workingmen.

Workers also resented the masters' attempts to control their lives. In the new factories, owners insisted on a steady pace of work and uninterrupted production. Artisans who were used to working in spurts, stopping for a few moments of conversation or a drink, disliked the new routines.

The fact that workers' wages in Cincinnati, as in other cities, rose more slowly than food and housing costs compounded discontent over changing working conditions. The working class sensed it was losing ground at the very time the city's rich were visibly growing richer. In 1817, the top tenth of the city's taxpayers owned over half the wealth, while the bottom half possessed

only 10 percent. In 1860, the share of the top tenth had increased to two-thirds, while the bottom half's share had shrunk to 2.4 percent.

In the decades before the Civil War, Cincinnati workers formed unions, turned out for fair wages, and rallied in favor of the ten-hour day. Like the Lowell mill women, they cloaked their protest with the mantle of the Revolution. Striking workers staged parades with fifes and drums and appropriated patriotic symbols to bolster their demands for justice and independence. They insisted that masters were denying them a fair share of profits, thereby dooming them to economic dependency. Since the republic depended on a free and independent citizenry, the male workers warned that their bosses' policies threatened to undermine the republic itself.

Only in the early 1850s did Cincinnati workers begin to suspect that their employers formed a distinct class of parasitic "nonproducers." Although most strikes still revolved around familiar issues of better hours and wages, signs appeared of the more hostile labor relations that would emerge after the Civil War.

As elsewhere, skilled workers were in the forefront of Cincinnati's labor protest and union activities. But Cincinnati workers did not readily unite with them. The uneven pace of industrialization meant that these workers, unlike the Lowell mill women, had no common working experience. Moreover, growing cultural and ethnic diversity compounded differences in the workplace. By 1850, almost half the people in the city were foreign-born, most of them German, compared with 22 percent in 1825. Protestant workers frequently felt that they had more in common with their Protestant bosses than with Catholic Irish or German fellow workers.

These tensions exploded in Cincinnati in the spring of 1855. Americans attacked barricades erected in German neighborhoods, crying out death threats. Their wrath visited the Irish as well. In many cases, labor disunity served economic progress by undermining workers' efforts for higher pay, shorter hours, and better working conditions, thus favoring businesses.

URBAN LIFE

Americans experienced the impact of economic growth most dramatically in the cities. In the four decades before the Civil War, the rate of urbanization in the United States was faster than ever before or since. In 1820, about 9 percent of the American people lived in cities (defined as areas containing a population of 2,500 or more). Forty years later, almost 20 percent of them did.

The Process of Urbanization

Three distinct types of cities—commercial centers, mill towns, and transportation hubs—emerged during these years of rapid economic growth. Commercial seaports like Boston,

Philadelphia, and Baltimore expanded steadily and developed diversified manufacturing to supplement the older functions of importing, exporting, and providing services and credit. New York replaced Philadelphia as the country's largest and most important city. With the completion of the Erie Canal, New York merchants gained control of much of the trade with the West. By 1840, they had also secured the largest share of the country's import and export trade.

Access to waterpower fueled the development of a second kind of city like Lowell, Massachusetts; Trenton, New Jersey; and Wilmington, Delaware. Situated inland along the waterfalls and rapids that provided the power to run their mills, these cities burgeoned in the decades before the Civil War.

West of the Appalachian Mountains, a third type of city arose. Louisville, Cleveland, and St. Louis were typical of cities that had served as transportation service and distribution centers from the earliest days of frontier settlement. Chicago acted as "grand depot, exchange, counting-house, and metropolis" for its hinterlands.

As the number of urban dwellers grew, their needs helped to generate economic growth. Cities provided a growing market for farm products and manufactured goods such as shoes, clothing, furniture, carriages, cast-iron stoves, and building materials.

Until 1840, the people eagerly crowding into cities came mostly from the American countryside. Then a growing number of immigrants arrived in the seaport cities. Many moved on to the interior, but the penniless had little choice but to remain in eastern cities and search for work there. By 1860, fully 20 percent of the people living in the Northeast were immigrants. The Irish, fleeing famine and poverty at home, were the largest foreign group in the Northeast.

A look at Philadelphia reveals the character and tensions of urban life during the antebellum period. An inland port, Philadelphia stood second only to New York. Though William Penn's "green country town" boasted an attractive appearance and an orderly plan, the expanding nineteenth-century city merited little praise. Speculators interested only in profit relied on the grid pattern as the cheapest and most efficient way to divide land for development. They built monotonous miles of new streets, new houses, new alleys, with "not a single acre left for public use, either for pleasure or health," as merchant Samuel Breck observed.

Overwhelmed by rapid growth, city governments provided few of the services we consider essential today, and usually only to those who paid for them. Water is a case in point. Only by paying a special fee could Philadelphians have water brought into their homes, so most of the city's residents went without. An inspection carried out by Mathew Carey in 1837 had pointed to an even more basic problem: 253 persons crowded into 30 tenements without even one privy. The ability to pay for services determined not only comfort but health.

Class Structure in the Cities

The drastic differences in the quality of urban life reflected the growing economic inequality that characterized Philadelphia and other American cities. In sharp contrast to the colonial period, the first half of the nineteenth century witnessed a dramatic rise in the concentration of wealth in the United States. The pattern was most extreme in cities. By the late 1840s, the wealthiest 4 percent of Philadelphia's population (merchants, brokers, lawyers, bankers, and manufacturers) held about two-thirds of the wealth. The economic pattern was similar in other American cities.

This widening gap between the upper class and the working class did not translate into mass suffering because more wealth was being generated. But the growing inequality hardened class lines, nourished social tensions, and contributed to the labor protests of the antebellum period.

Between 1820 and 1860, Philadelphia's working class, like Cincinnati's, was transformed. As preindustrial ways yielded to factory production, some former artisans and skilled workers climbed into the middle class, becoming businessmen, factory owners, mill supervisors, and shopkeepers. But downward occupational mobility also increased. Fed by waves of immigrants, the lower class was growing at an accelerating rate. Moreover, within the working class itself, the percentage of unskilled wage earners living in poverty or on its brink increased.

The Urban Working Class

As with so much else in urban life, housing reflected social and economic divisions. The poorest rented quarters in crowded, flimsily constructed shacks, shanties, and two-room houses. The urban working class faced not just poverty but the transformation of family life. Men could no longer be sure of supporting their wives and children, even when they were employed, and they felt that they had lost much of their authority and power in the family. Some found their wives no longer subservient or seemingly careless with their hard-earned money. Family violence that spilled out onto the streets was not uncommon in working-class quarters.

Middle-Class Life and Ideals

Members of the comfortable middle class profited from the dramatic increase in wealth in antebellum America. The houses of the city's elite were spacious and filled with new conveniences. Samuel Breck's house in 1839 was elegant and luxurious, with "parlours 14 feet high, . . . furnaces, water closet and shower and common bath up stairs, marble mantels and fireplaces in dressing rooms."

For the urban middle and upper class, the rewards of economic success included residential comfort, choice, and stability. But working-class renters moved often, from one cramped lodging to another. This common pattern of repeated mobility made it difficult to create close-knit neighborhoods in urban settings.

As the gap between classes widened, new

middle-class norms emerged, nourished by the changing economy. Better transportation, new products, and the rise of factory production and large businesses changed family life. Falling prices for processed and manufactured goods made it unnecessary for women to continue making these items at home. As men increasingly involved themselves in a money economy, women's and children's contributions to the family economy became relatively less significant. Even the rhythm of their lives, oriented to housework rather than the demands of the clock, separated them from the bustling commercial world where their husbands now labored. By 1820, the notion emerged that the sexes occupied separate spheres.

While men pursued success in the public world, what were women's responsibilities? Sarah Hale, editor of the popular magazine *Godey's Lady's Book,* and Catharine Beecher, well-known lecturer and writer, argued that woman's sphere was at home, keeping house and creating a clean, wholesome, and private setting for family life.

Women also served as their families' moral and cultural guardians. Arguing that women had different characters from men, that they were innately pious, virtuous, unselfish, and modest, publicists maintained that mothers would train future citizens and workers to be obedient, moral, patriotic, and hardworking. Just as important, they would preserve important values in a time of rapid change. As one preacher explained, a wife was the guardian angel who "watches over" her husband's interests, "warns him against dangers, comforts him under trial; and by . . . pious, assiduous, and attractive deportment, constantly endeavors to render him more virtuous, more useful, more honourable, and more happy."

This view, characterizing women as morally superior to and different from men, had important consequences for many women's lives. The physical separation of the male and female worlds and the shift in women's status often meant that women shared more with one another than with men, even their husbands. Similar social experiences and perspectives made female friendships central for many women, the source of comfort, security, and happiness.

They also experienced both pleasure and frustration in their role as housekeepers. Now that most domestic production had disappeared from the household, the task of creating a comfortable and attractive home became primary. But new standards of cleanliness, order, and beauty were often impossible to achieve. Moreover, efforts to create a perfect home often worked against harmonious family life.

Although the concept of domesticity seemed to confine women to the domestic sphere, it actually prompted women to take on activities in the outside world. If women were the guardians of morality, why should they not carry out their tasks in the public sphere? This reasoning lay behind the tremendous growth of voluntary female associations in the early decades of the nineteenth century. Initially, most involved religious and charitable activities. In the 1830s, as we shall see in Chapter 12, women added specific moral concerns like the abolition of slavery to their missionary and benevolent efforts, often clashing with men and with social conventions about "woman's place."

Domesticity described norms, not the actual conduct of middle-class women. Obviously not all women were pious, disinterested, selfless, virtuous, cheerful, and loving. But these ideas influenced how women thought of themselves. The new norms, effectively spread by the publishing industry, influenced rural women and urban working women. The insistence on marriage and service to family discouraged married women from entering the work force. Those who had to work often bore a burden of guilt. Though the new feminine ideal may have seemed noble to middle-class women in cities and towns, it created difficult tensions in the lives of working-class women.

As family roles were reformulated, a new view of childhood emerged. Working-class children still worked or scavenged for goods to sell or use at home, but middle-class children were no longer expected to contribute economically to the family. Middle-class parents now came to see childhood as a special stage of life, a period of preparation for adulthood.

Children were to spend their early years learning important values from their mothers and through schooling. Children's fiction also presented dutiful, religious, loving, and industrious youngsters as role models.

The growing publishing industry helped to spread new ideas about family roles and appropriate family behavior. Novels, magazines, etiquette and child-rearing manuals, and schoolbooks all carried the message from northern and midwestern centers of publishing to the South, to the West, and to the frontier. Probably few Americans lived up to the new standards established for the model parent or child, but the standards increasingly influenced them.

New notions of family life supported the widespread use of contraception for the first time in American history. Since children required so much loving attention and needed careful preparation for adulthood, many parents desired smaller families. The declining birthrate was evident first in the Northeast, particularly in cities and among the middle class. Contraceptive methods included abortion, which was legal in many states until 1860. This medical procedure terminated perhaps as many as a third of all pregnancies. Other birth control methods included coitus interruptus and abstinence. The success of these methods for family limitation suggests that many men and women adopted the new definitions of the female sex as naturally affectionate but passionless and sexually restrained.

Mounting Urban Tensions

The social and economic changes transforming American cities in the half century before the Civil War produced urban violence on a scale never before witnessed in America, not even during the Revolution. Festering ethnic and racial tensions often triggered mob actions that lasted for days.

Racial tensions contributed to Philadelphia's disorders. An unsavory riot in August 1834 revealed other important sources of social antagonism as well as the inability of its police force to control disorder.

One hot August evening, several hundred white Philadelphians wrecked a building on South Street that contained the "Flying Horses," a merry-go-round patronized by both blacks and whites. A general melee followed. As the *Philadelphia Gazette* reported, "At one time it is supposed that four or five hundred persons were engaged in the conflict, with clubs, brickbats, paving stones, and the materials of the shed in which the flying horses were kept." Spurred by the taste of blood, the white mob moved into the center of the crowded, racially mixed neighborhood, where they continued their orgy of destruction, looting, and intimidation of black residents.

An investigation following the riots revealed that the white mob had caused at least $4,000 of damage to two black churches and more than 36 private homes. At least one black had been killed, and numerous others had been injured.

Many rioters bragged that they were "hunting the nigs." Riots, however, are complicated events, and this racial explanation does not reveal the range of causes underlying the rampage of violence and destruction.

The mob's composition hints at some of the reasons for participation. Many of the rioters were young and at the bottom of the occupational and economic ladder, competing with blacks for jobs. This was particularly true of the newly arrived Irish immigrants, who were attempting to replace blacks in low-status jobs. Subsequent violence against blacks suggested that economic rivalry was an important component of the riot. "Colored persons, when engaged in their usual vocations," the *Niles Register* observed, "were repeatedly assailed and maltreated. . . . Parties of white men have insisted that no blacks shall be employed in certain departments of labor."

Some rioters were skilled workers who had experienced the negative impact of a changing economic system that was undermining the small-scale mode of production. To them, blacks were scapegoats, but the real but intangible villain was the economic system itself. Trade union organizing and a general strike a year later would highlight the grievances of this group.

Rapid urban expansion also figured as a factor in the racial violence. Most of the rioters lived either in the riot area or nearby. All had experienced the overcrowded and inadequate living conditions caused by the city's rapid growth. The racial tensions generated by squalid surroundings and social proximity go far to explain the outbreak of violence. The same area would later become the scene of race riots and election trouble and became infamous for harboring criminals and juvenile gangs.

The city's small, newly formed police force proved unable to control the mob, thus prolonging the violence. Philadelphia, like other eastern cities, was in the midst of creating its police force. Only continued rowdiness, violence, and riots would convince residents and city officials in Philadelphia (and in other large cities) to support an expanded, quasi-military, preventive police force in uniforms. By 1855, most sizable eastern cities had established such forces.

Finally, the character of the free black community itself was a factor in producing those gruesome August events. Not only was the community large and visible, but it had also created its own institutions and its own elite. Whites resented "dressy blacks." The mob targeted the solid brick houses of middle-class blacks, robbing them of silver and watches.

The Black Underclass

Events in Philadelphia showed how hazardous life for free blacks could be. Northern whites, like southerners, believed in black inferiority and depravity and feared black competition for jobs and resources. Although northern states had passed gradual abolition acts between 1780 and 1803 and the national government had banned slaves from entering new states to be formed out of the Northwest Territory, nowhere did any government extend equal rights and citizenship or economic opportunities to free blacks in their midst.

For a time in the early nineteenth century, some blacks living in the North were permitted to vote, but they soon lost that right. Beginning in the 1830s, Pennsylvania, Connecticut, and New Jersey disenfranchised blacks. New York allowed only those with three years' residence and property valued at $250 or more to vote. Only the New England states (with the exception of Connecticut), which had tiny black populations, preserved the right to vote regardless of color. By 1840, fully 93 percent of the northern free black population lived in states where law or custom prevented them from voting.

Other black civil rights were also restricted. In five northern states, blacks could not testify against whites or serve on juries. In most states, the two races were thoroughly segregated. Blacks increasingly endured separate and inferior facilities in railway cars, steamboats, hospitals, prisons, and other facilities. They sat in "Negro pews" in churches and took communion only after whites had left the church. Although most Protestant religious denominations in the antebellum period split into northern and southern branches over the issue of slavery, most northern churches were not disposed to welcome blacks as full members.

As the Philadelphia riot revealed, whites were driving blacks from their jobs. In 1839, *The Colored American* blamed the Irish. "These impoverished and destitute beings . . . are crowding themselves into every place of business . . . and driving the poor colored American citizen out." Increasingly after 1837, these "white niggers" became coachmen, stevedores, barbers, cooks, house servants—all occupations blacks had once held.

Educational opportunities for blacks were also severely limited. Only a few school systems admitted blacks, in separate facilities. The case of Prudence Crandall illustrates the lengths to which northern whites would go to maintain racial segregation. In 1833, Crandall, a Quaker schoolmistress in Canterbury, Connecticut, announced that she would admit "young colored ladies and Misses" to her school. The outraged townspeople, unable to persuade her to abandon her project, harassed and insulted students and teachers and finally demolished the school. Crandall was arrested, and after two trials—in which free blacks were declared to have no citizenship rights—she finally gave up and moved to Illinois.

Crandall would not have found the Old Northwest much more hospitable. The fast-growing western states were intensely committed to white supremacy and black exclusion. As an Indiana newspaper editor observed in 1854, informal customs made life dangerous for blacks. They were "constantly subject to insults and annoyance in traveling and the daily avocations of life; [and] are practically excluded from all social privileges, and even from the Christian communion."

RURAL COMMUNITIES

Although the percentage of families involved in farming fell from 72 to 60 percent between 1820 and 1860, Americans remained a rural people. Agriculture persisted as the country's most significant economic activity, and farm products still made up most of the nation's exports. The small family farm still characterized eastern and western agriculture.

Farming remained the dominant way of life, but agriculture changed in the antebellum period. Vast new tracts of land came under cultivation in the West. Railroads, canals, and better roads pulled rural Americans into the orbit of the wider world. Some crops were shipped to regional markets; others, like grain, hides, and

pork, stimulated industrial processing. Manufactured goods, ranging from cloth and tools to books and periodicals, flowed in return to farm families. Commercial farming encouraged different ways of thinking and acting and lessened the isolation so typical before 1820.

Farming in the East

During the antebellum period, economic changes created new rural patterns in the Northeast. Marginal lands in New England, New York, and Pennsylvania, cultivated as more fertile lands ran out, yielded discouraging returns. Gradually after 1830, farmers abandoned these farms, often to move westward. By 1860, almost 40 percent of people who had been born in Vermont had left their native state.

Farmers who did not migrate west had to transform their production. Realizing that they could not compete with western grain, they sought new agricultural opportunities created by better transportation and growing urban markets. One of the demands was for fresh milk. By the 1830s, some eastern cities had grown so large that milk was turning sour before it reached central marketplaces. To meet the desire for milk, several cities, including New York City, started urban dairies. As railroad lines extended into rural areas, however, farmers living as far away as Vermont and upper New York state discovered that they could ship cooled milk to urban centers. City residents had fresher and cheaper milk and drank more of it as a result.

Urban appetites encouraged other farmers to cultivate fruit and vegetables for sale in city markets. With fresh produce in regular supply, cookbooks began to include recipes calling for fresh ingredients.

As northern farmers adopted new crops, they began to consider farming as a scientific endeavor. After 1800, northern farmers started using manure as fertilizer rather than disposing of it as a smelly nuisance. By the 1820s, some

This 1856 print titled Preparing for Market *shows the farm as a center of human and animal activity. The goods this farmer is loading in his wagon suggest the shifts in agriculture that took place in the East as competition from the Midwest encouraged farmers to raise new crops for the market.*

farmers were rotating their crops and planting new grasses and clover to restore fertility to the soil. By 1860, American farmers had developed thousands of special varieties of plants for local conditions. Many improvements resulted from experimentation, but farmers also enjoyed more and better information, which they found in new journals like the *New England Farmer,* the *Farmers' Register,* and the *Cultivator.* Following New York's lead in 1819, many states established agricultural agencies to propagate new ideas. A "scientific" farmer in 1850 could often produce two to four times as much per acre as in 1820.

Farmers in the fertile area around Northampton, Massachusetts, illustrate the American farmer's adjustment to new economic conditions. As roads and canals improved, markets became more accessible. Farmers started to cultivate crops "scientifically" in order to increase profits. Farming was becoming a business. At home, women found themselves freed from many of their traditional tasks. Peddlers brought goods to the door. The onerous duty of making cloth and clothing disappeared with the coming of inexpensive ready-made cloth and even ready-made clothes in the 1820s. Daughters liberated from the chores of home manufacturing went off to the mills or earned money by taking in piecework from local merchants. Cash transactions replaced the exchange of goods. Country stores became more reluctant to accept wood, rye, corn, oats, and butter as payment for goods instead of cash.

Some farmers prospered as they became involved in the market economy; others just got along. Wealth inequality increased near Northampton, as it did elsewhere in the rural Northeast.

Frontier Families

Many people who left the North during these years headed for the Old Northwest, where they raised corn and pork, sending their products down the Ohio and Mississippi rivers to southern buyers. In 1820, less than one-fifth of the American population lived west of the Appalachians; by 1860, almost half did, and Ohio and Illinois had become two of the nation's most populous states.

In 1830, Chicago had only 250 residents. Conditions were often primitive, as Charles Butler and Arthur Bronson discovered during their 1833 trip. Their hotel in Michigan City, Indiana, was "a small log house, a single room, which answered the purpose of drawing room, sitting room, eating room & sleeping room; in this room some eleven or twelve persons lodged in beds & on the floor."

During the 1830s, land sales and settlement boomed in the Old Northwest. Eastern capital contributed to the boom with loans, mortgages, and speculative buying. Internal improvement schemes after 1830 also influenced new settlement patterns and tied the Old Northwest firmly to the East. Erasmus Gest, who as a 17-year-old had worked on canal projects in Indiana, recalled the settlers' enthusiasm for improvements: "We Engineers were favorites with the People wherever we went."

Wheat for the eastern market rather than corn and hogs for the southern market became increasingly important with the transportation links eastward. Between 1840 and 1860, Illinois, southern Wisconsin, and eastern Iowa turned into the country's most rapidly growing grain regions. In the 1850s, these three states accounted for 70 percent of the increase in national wheat production.

Settling in the Old Northwest required hard work and at least some money. Catharine Skinner, who moved from New York to Indiana with her husband when she was 24, wrote to her sister in 1849: "We have got 80 acres of land in the woods of Indiana, a very level country; we have got two acres cleared and fenced and four more pirty well under way; we have got about five acres of wheat in the ground; we raised corn enough for our use and to fat our pork . . . we have a cow so that we have milk and butter and plenty of corn bread but wheat is hard to be got in account of our not having mony."

The Skinners probably spent $500 to $600 to start farming. They invested perhaps $100 for 80 acres of government land, $300 for basic farming equipment, and another $100 or $150 for livestock. To buy an already "improved" farm cost more. Once farmers moved onto the prairies of Indiana and Illinois, they needed an initial investment of about $1,000 since they had to buy materials for fencing, housing, and expensive steel plows. If farmers invested in the new horse-drawn reapers, they could cultivate more land, but all their costs also increased.

Opportunities in the Old Northwest

It was possible to begin farming with less, however. Some farmers borrowed from relatives, banks, or insurance companies like the Ohio Life Insurance and Trust Company. Others rented land from farmers who had bought more acres than they could manage. Tenants who furnished their own seeds and animals could expect to keep about a third of the yield. Within a few years, some saved enough to buy their own farms. Even those without any capital could work as hired hands. Since labor was scarce, they earned good wages. Probably about a quarter of the western farm population consisted of young men laboring as tenants or hired hands.

Rural communities, unlike the cities, had no growing class of propertyless wage earners, but inequalities nevertheless existed in the Old Northwest. In Butler County, Ohio, for example, 16 percent of people leaving wills in the 1830s held half of the wealth. By 1860, the wealthiest 8 percent held half of the wealth. While wealth was not as concentrated in rural areas as in the cities, a few residents benefited more from rapid economic development than others. Nevertheless, the Northwest offered many American families the chance to become independent producers and to enjoy "a pleasing competence."

Agriculture and the Environment

Shifting agricultural patterns in the East and expanding settlement into the Old Northwest contributed to the changing character of the American landscape. As naturalist John Audubon mused in 1826, "a century hence," the rivers, swamps, and mountains "will not be here as I see them. Nature will have been robbed of many brilliant charms, the rivers will be tormented and turned astray from their primitive course, the hills will be levelled with the swamps, and perhaps the swamps will have become a mount surmounted by a fortress of a thousand guns."

When eastern farmers changed their agricultural practices as they became involved in the market economy, their decisions left an imprint on the land. As forests disappeared, so too did their wildlife. Even using mineral manures like gypsum or lime or organic fertilizers like guano to revitalize worn-out soil and increase crop yields meant the depletion of land elsewhere.

When farmers moved into the old Northwest, they used new steel plows, like the one developed in 1837 by Illinois blacksmith John Deere. Unlike older eastern plows, the new ones could cut through the dense, tough prairie cover. Deep plowing and the intensive cultivation of large cash crops had immediate benefits. But these practices could result in robbing the soil of necessary minerals like phosphorous, carbon, and nitrogen. When farmers built new timber houses as frontier conditions receded, they helped fuel the destruction of the country's forests.

CONCLUSION

THE CHARACTER OF PROGRESS

Between 1820 and 1860, the United States experienced tremendous growth and economic development. Visitors constantly remarked on the amazing bustle and rapid pace of American life. The United States was, in the words of one Frenchman, "one gigantic workshop, over the entrance of which there is the blazing inscription 'NO ADMISSION HERE, EXCEPT ON BUSINESS.' "

Although the wonders of American development dazzled foreigners and Americans alike, economic growth had its costs. Expansion was cyclic, and financial panics and depression punctuated the era. Industrial profits were based partly on low wages to workers. Time-honored routes to economic independence disappeared, and a large class of unskilled, impoverished workers appeared in American cities. Growing inequality characterized urban and rural life, prompting some labor activists to criticize new economic and social arrangements. But workers, still largely unorganized, did not speak with one voice. Ethnic, racial, and religious diversity divided Americans in new and troubling ways.

During these decades, many also noted that the paths between the East, Northwest, and South seemed to diverge. The rise of King Cotton in the South, where slave rather than free labor formed the foundation of the economy, created a new kind of tension in American life, as the next chapter will show.

Recommended Reading

Two useful introductions to economic change during this period are Stuart Bruchey, *The Roots of American Economic Growth, 1607–1861* (1965), and Albert W. Niemi, *U.S. Economic History: A Survey of the Major Issues* (1975).

Thomas C. Cochran provides an overview of industrial development in *Frontiers of Change: Early Industrialism in America* (1981), while technological innovation is the subject of David J. Jeremy, *Transatlantic Industrial Revolution: The Diffusion of Textile Technology Between Britain and America, 1790–1830* (1981).

On economic change in individual communities, see Thomas Dublin, *Women at Work: The Transformation of Work and Community in Lowell, Massachusetts, 1826–1860* (1979), and (as editor) *Farm to Factory: Women's Letters, 1830–1860* (1981); Allen F. Davis and Mark H. Haller, eds., *The Peoples of Philadelphia: A History of Ethnic Groups and Lower-Class Life, 1790–1940* (1973); and Steven J. Ross, *Workers on the Edge: Work, Leisure, and Politics in Industrializing Cincinnati, 1788–1890* (1985). See also Gary B. Nash, *Forging Freedom: The Formation of Philadelphia's Black Community, 1720–1840* (1988).

Alexis de Tocqueville analyzes American society in the 1830s in *Democracy in America* (1957 ed.). Edward Pessen shows the growth of inequality in four cities in *Riches, Class, and Power Before the Civil War* (1973). Mary P. Ryan focuses on the middle-class family in *Cradle of the Middle Class: The Family in Oneida County, New York, 1790–1865* (1981), while Christine Stansell focuses on lower-class urban women in *City of Women: Sex and Class in New York, 1789–1860* (1986). On family life see also Robert V. Wells, *Revolutions in Americans' Lives: A Demographic Perspective of the History of Americans, Their Families, and Their Society* (1982). Immigrant life is described in Stephan Thernstrom, ed., *Harvard Encyclopedia of American Ethnic Groups* (1980).

On the midwestern frontier, see Clarence Danhof, *Changes in Agriculture: The Northern United States, 1820–1870* (1969); Don H. Doyle, *The Social Order of a Frontier Community: Jacksonville, Illinois, 1825–1870* (1978); and John Mack Faragher, *Sugar Creek: Life on the Illinois Prairies* (1986).

Time Line

1805	*Palmer* v. *Mulligan*	**1830s**	Boom in the Old Northwest
1816	Second U.S. Bank chartered		Increasing discrimination against free blacks
1819– 1824	Supreme Court decisions establish the principle that contracts are binding.		Public education movement spreads
		1833	Philadelphia establishes small police force
1820	Lowell, Massachusetts, founded by Boston Associates The expression "woman's sphere" becomes current	**1834**	Philadelphia race riots Lowell work stoppage
		1837	Horace Mann becomes secretary of Massachusetts Board of Education
1824– 1850	Construction of canals in the Northeast	**1837– 1844**	Financial panic and depression
1825– 1856	Construction of canals linking the Ohio, the Mississippi, and the Great Lakes	**1840**	Agitation for ten-hour day
		1840s– 1850s	Rising tide of immigration
1828	Baltimore and Ohio Railroad begins operation		

chapter 11

Slavery and the Old South

As a young slave boy, Frederick Douglass was sent by his master to live in Baltimore. When he first met his mistress, Sophia Auld, she appeared to be "a woman of the kindest heart and finest feelings." He was "astonished at her goodness" as she began to teach him to read. Her husband, however, ordered her to stop because Maryland law forbade teaching slaves to read. In the seven years he lived with the Aulds, young Frederick had to use "various strategems" to teach himself to read and write, the key to his later escape to freedom.

Slaves and masters were inextricably bound to each other. After her husband's interference, Sophia Auld, Douglass observed, was transformed from an angel into a demon by the "fatal poison of irresponsible power." Her formerly tender heart turned to "stone" when she ceased teaching him. "Slavery proved as injurious to her," Douglass wrote, "as it did to me."

Such was also the case in Douglass's relationship with Mr. Covey, a slavebreaker to whom he was sent in 1833 to have his will broken. Covey succeeded for a time, Douglass reported, in breaking his "body, soul, and spirit" by brutal hard work and discipline. But one hot August day in 1833, the two men fought a long, grueling battle, which Douglass won. His victory, he said, "rekindled the few expiring embers of freedom, and revived within me a sense of my own manhood." Although it would be four more years before his escape to the North, the young man never again felt like a slave. The key to Douglass's successful resistance to Covey's power was not just his strong will, but rather his knowledge of how to jeopardize Covey's reputation and livelihood as a slavebreaker. The oppressed survive by knowing their oppressors.

As Sophia Auld and Covey discovered, as long as some people were not free, no one was free. After quarreling with a house servant, one plantation mistress complained that she "exercises dominion over me—or tries to do it. One would have thought . . . that I was the Servant, she the mistress." Many whites lived in constant fear of a slave revolt, sometimes sleeping with "a brace of loaded pistols at their sides."

Slavery, then, was an intricate web of human relationships as well as a labor system. After showing the economic growth and development of the Old South, in which slavery and cotton played vital roles, this chapter will emphasize the daily lives and relationships of masters and slaves who, like Douglass and the Aulds, lived, loved, learned, worked, and struggled with one another in the years before the Civil War.

Perhaps no issue in American history has generated quite as many interpretations or as much emotional controversy as slavery. As American attitudes toward that institution have changed over the years, three interpretive schools have developed, each adding to our knowledge of the "peculiar institution." The first saw slavery as a relatively humane and reasonable institution in which plantation owners took care of helpless, childlike slaves. The second depicted slavery as a harsh and cruel system of oppressive exploitation. The third, and most recent, interpretation described the slavery experience from the perspective of the slaves, who did indeed suffer brutal treatment in slavery but who also survived with individual self-esteem and a sense of community and culture.

The first and second interpretive schools emphasized workaday interactions among masters and slaves, while the third focused on life in the slave quarters from sundown to sunup. In a unique structure, this chapter follows these masters and slaves through their day, from morning in the Big House through hot afternoon in the fields to the slave cabins at night. But although slavery was the crucial institution in defining the Old South, many other social groups and patterns contributed to the tremendous economic growth of the South from 1820 to 1860. We will look first at these diverse aspects of antebellum southern life.

BUILDING THE COTTON KINGDOM

The vast region of the antebellum South was not a monolithic society filled only with large cotton plantations worked by hundreds of slaves. The realities of the South and slavery were much more complex. Large-plantation agriculture was dominant, but most southern whites were not even slaveholders, much less large planters. Most southern farmers lived in dark, cramped, two-room cabins. Cotton was a key cash crop in the South, but it was not the only crop grown there. Some masters were kindly, but many were not; some slaves were contented, but most were not.

There were many Souths, encompassing several geographic regions, each with different economic bases and social structures. The older Upper South of Virginia, Maryland, North Carolina, and Kentucky grew different staple crops from those grown in the newer, Lower or "Black Belt" South that stretched from South Carolina to eastern Texas. Within each state, moreover, the economies differed between flat, coastal areas and inland, up-country forests and pine barrens. A still further diversity existed between these areas and the Appalachian highlands of northern Alabama and Georgia, eastern Tennessee and Kentucky, and western Virginia and North Carolina. Finally, the cultural and economic life of New Orleans, Savannah,

Charleston, and Richmond differed dramatically from that of rural areas of the South. But although the South was diverse, agriculture dominated its industry and commerce.

Economic Expansion

In the 20 years preceding the Civil War, the South's economy grew slightly faster than the North's. Personal income in 1860 was 15 percent higher in the South than in the prosperous states of the Old Northwest. The cotton gin was fundamental to this economic growth, wedding the southern economy to cotton production for a century and stimulating the expansion of slavery into vast new territories.

As we learned in Chapter 9, most cotton farmers planted "long staple" cotton prior to the invention of Eli Whitney's cotton gin in 1793. After the cotton gin, the "short staple" variety, which could grow anywhere in the South, predominated. But only large-plantation owners could afford to buy gins and purchase the fertile bottomlands of the Gulf states. Thus the plantation system and slavery spread with the rise of cotton.

Although corn was a larger crop than cotton in total acreage, cotton was the largest cash crop and for that reason was called "king." In 1820, the South became the world's largest producer of cotton, and from 1815 to 1860 cotton represented more than half of all American exports. Cotton was not only the mainstay of the southern economy but also a crucial link in the national economy.

The supply of cotton from the South grew at an astonishing rate, soaring from 461,000 bales in 1817 to 1.35 million bales in 1840, 2.85 million bales in 1849, and 4.8 million bales in 1860. In the period from 1817 to 1860, cotton production jumped over tenfold. This rapid growth was stimulated by world demand, especially from English textile mills. The availability of new lands, a self-reproducing supply of cheap slave labor, and low-cost steamboat transportation down the Mississippi River to New Orleans helped to keep cotton king.

White and Black Migrations

Southerners migrated southwestward in huge numbers between 1830 and 1860 to grow more and more cotton. They pushed the southeastern Indians and the Mexicans in Texas out of the way and were still moving into Texas as the Civil War began. The migration process made many planters rich.

By the 1830s, the center of cotton production had shifted from South Carolina and Georgia to Alabama and Mississippi. This process continued in the 1850s as southerners forged into Arkansas, Louisiana, and eastern Texas. As they moved, they carried their values and institutions, including slavery, with them.

Not only were these migrating southern families attracted by the pull of fresh land and cheap labor, but they were also pushed westward by worsening economic conditions and other pressures in the older Atlantic states. Beginning in the 1820s, the states of the Upper South underwent a long depression affecting tobacco and cotton prices. Moreover, years of constant use had exhausted their lands. Those who stayed in the Upper South continued to shift to grains, mainly corn and wheat. Because these crops required less labor than tobacco, slave owners began to sell some of their slaves.

The internal slave trade from Virginia "down the river" to the Old Southwest thus became a multimillion-dollar "industry" in the 1830s. Between 1830 and 1860, an estimated 300,000 Virginia slaves were transported south for sale. Although most southern states attempted occasionally to outlaw or control the traffic in slaves, these efforts were poorly enforced and usually short-lived. Besides, the reason for outlawing the slave trade was generally not humanitarian but rather originated in a fear of a rapid increase in the slave population, especially of "wicked" slaves sent south because they

The Varied Economic Life in the South

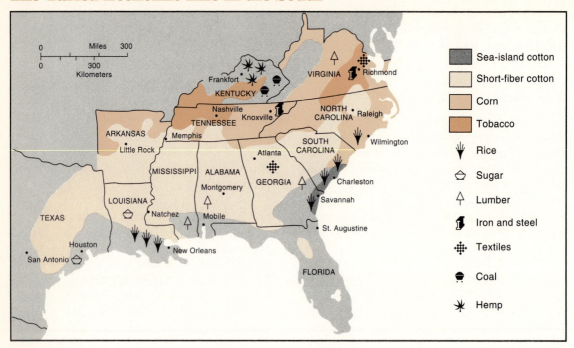

were considered unmanageable. Alabama, Mississippi, and Louisiana all banned the importation of slaves after the Nat Turner revolt in Virginia in 1831 (described later in this chapter). But all three states permitted the slave trade again during the profitable 1850s.

Congress formally ended the external slave trade on January 1, 1808, the earliest time permitted by the Constitution. Although many thousands of blacks continued to be smuggled to North America until the end of the Civil War, the tremendous increase in the slave population was the result not of this illegal trade but of natural reproduction, often encouraged by slaveowners eager for more laborers and salable human property.

The Dependence on Slavery

The rapid increase in the number of slaves, from 1.5 million in 1820 to 4 million in 1860, paral-

leled the growth of the southern economy and its dependence on the slave labor system. Economic growth and migration southwestward changed the geographic distribution of slaves, thus hindering the cause of abolition.

Although most slaves worked on plantations and medium-size farms, they could be found in all segments of the southern economy. In 1850, some 75 percent of all slaves were engaged in agricultural labor. The 300,000 slaves in 1850 who were not domestics or agricultural laborers worked as lumberjacks and turpentine producers in Carolina and Georgia forests; gold, coal, and salt miners in Virginia and Kentucky; boiler stokers and deckhands on Mississippi River steamships; toilers on road and railroad construction gangs in Georgia and Louisiana; textile laborers in Alabama cotton mills; dockworkers in Savannah and Charleston; and tobacco and iron workers in Richmond factories.

Southern Cotton Production, 1821-1859

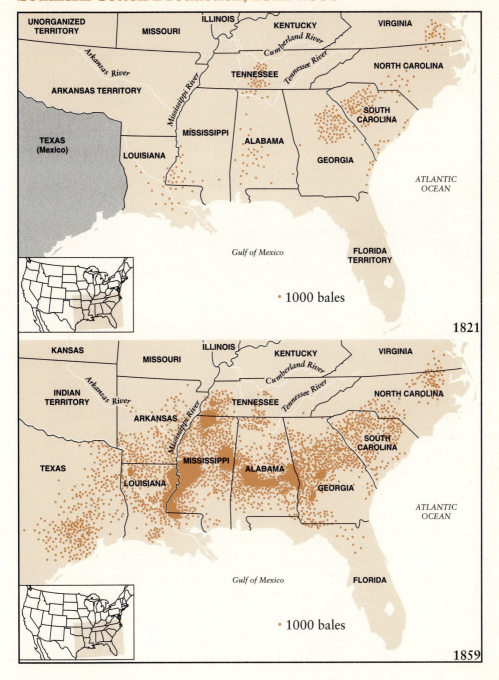

Concentration of Slavery, 1820-1860

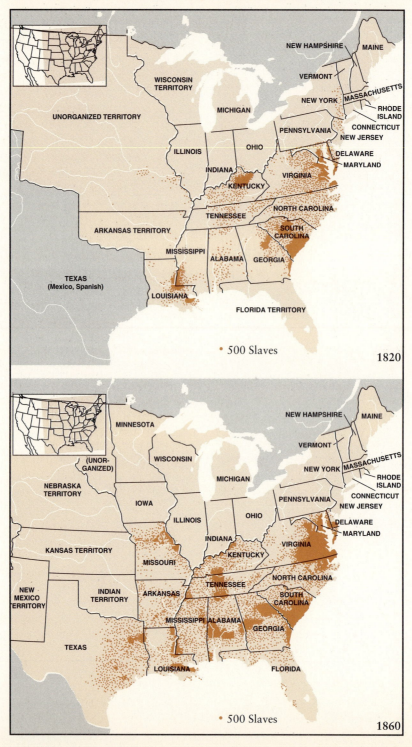

Slaves were also used in the industrial sector. The Tredegar Iron Company of Richmond decided in 1847 to shift from white labor "almost exclusively" to slave labor in order to destroy the potential power of organized white workers to strike. Tredegar's decision, though local, had enormous future implications. Although black and white workers have sometimes been able to agree on class issues, racial animosities based on white perceptions of threats to their job security by black workers continue to this day.

Whether in iron factories, coal mines, or cotton fields, slavery was profitable to owners. In 1859, the average plantation slave produced $78 in cotton earnings for his master annually while costing only about $32 to be fed, clothed, and housed. Slaves were also a good investment. In 1844, a "prime field hand" sold for $600. A cotton boom beginning in 1849 raised this price by 1860 to $1,800.

The economic growth of the slaveholding South was impressive, but it was limited because of the dependence on slavery. Generally, agricultural growth leads to the rise of cities and industry, facilitating sustained economic growth. In the planter-dominated antebellum South, however, agricultural improvements did not lead to industrialization and urbanization. On the eve of the Civil War, one southerner in 14 was a city dweller, compared with one of every three people in the North. The South would be economically backward as long as the whites with capital insisted on putting all their business energies toward cotton production.

Slavery and Class in the South

Slavery was more than an economic institution, for it also served social purposes. Although the proportion of southern white families that owned slaves slowly declined from 40 to 25 percent as some families sold off their slaves to cotton planters, the ideal of slave ownership still permeated all classes and determined the hierarchical character of the southern social structure. At the top stood the planter aristocracy, much of

it new wealth. Some 10,000 rich families owned 50 or more slaves in 1860; about 3,000 of these owned over 100. Below them was a slightly larger group of small planters who held from 10 to 50 slaves. But the largest group, 70 percent of all slaveholders in 1860, comprised 270,000 middle-level farm families with fewer than ten slaves. The typical slaveholder worked a small family farm of about 100 acres with eight or nine slaves, perhaps members of the same family. The typical slave, however, was more likely to be in a group of 20 or more other slaves on a large farm or small plantation.

In 1841, a young, white North Carolinian, John Flintoff, went to Mississippi to fulfil his dream of wealth and prestige. Beginning as an overseer managing an uncle's farm, he bought "a negro boy 7 years old" even before he owned any land. After several years of unrewarding struggle, Flintoff married and returned to North Carolina. There he finally bought 124 acres and a few more cheap, young blacks, and by 1860 he had a modest farm with several slaves growing corn, wheat, and tobacco. Although he never became as prosperous as he had dreamed, his son went to college, and his wife, he reported proudly, "has lived a *Lady*."

Like Flintoff, most southerners supported slavery for reasons of upward economic mobility, social prestige, and political influence. But they also defended the institution because it gave them a sense of superiority over at least one group and a sense of kinship, if not quite equality, with other whites. Although there was always a small element of southern society that believed in emancipation, most southerners did not. A small Alabama farmer told a northern visitor in the 1850s that if the slaves were given their freedom, "they'd all think themselves just as good as we. . . . How would you like to hev a nigger feelin' just as good as a white man?"

The Nonslaveholding South

Below Flintoff and other middling farmers lived the majority of white southerners, who owned no slaves but were equally, or even more, anti-black. Newton Knight, for example, worked a harsh piece of land cut out of the pines of southern Mississippi. He and his wife lived in a crude log cabin, scratching out their livelihood by growing corn and sweet potatoes and raising chickens and hogs. A staunch Baptist given to fits of violence, Knight had once killed a black.

The 75 percent of southern whites who owned no slaves were scattered throughout the South. Many were Scots-Irish. Most lived in the foothills of the mountains and worked generally poorer land than the large planters. Largely self-sufficient, they raised mostly corn and wheat, hogs, enough cotton for their own clothes and a little cash, and subsistence vegetable crops. They lived in two-room log houses separated by a "dog run." Families gathered at corn huskings and quilting parties, logrolling and wrestling matches, and political stump and revivalist camp meetings. In many ways the yeoman farmers were the solid backbone of the South. Fiercely proud of their independence, they had a share of political power, voting overwhelmingly for Andrew Jackson.

Another little-known group of southern whites were the herdsmen who raised hogs and other livestock. They supplied bacon and pork to local slaveholders (who often thought hog growing was beneath their dignity) and drove herds of hogs to stockyards in Nashville, Louisville, and Savannah. The South raised two-thirds of the nation's hogs. In 1860, the value of southern livestock was $500 million, twice that of cotton. However valuable the total size of the hog business, individual hog herdsmen did not stand very high on the southern social ladder.

Below them were the poor whites of the South, about 10 percent of the population. Often sneeringly called "hillbillies," "dirt eaters," "crackers," or "poor white trash," they eked out a living from the poor soil of pine barrens, sand hills, and marshes. Although they grew a little corn and vegetables, their livelihood came mostly from fishing, hunting small game,

and raising a few pigs. Some made corn whiskey, and many hired themselves out as farmhands for an average wage, with board, of about $14 per month. Because of poor diet and bad living conditions, these poor whites often suffered from diseases such as hookworm and malaria.

The poor whites were kept poor in part because the slave system allowed the planter class to accumulate a disproportionate amount of land and political power. High slave prices made entry into the planter class increasingly difficult, thus increasing class tensions within the South. Because the larger planters dominated southern life and owned the most slaves, an understanding of the character of slavery and the relationships between masters and slaves is best accomplished by looking at plantation life during a typical day from morning to night.

MORNING: MASTER IN THE BIG HOUSE

It is early morning on the southern plantation. Imagine three scenes. In the first, on the South Carolina plantation of James Hammond, the horn blows an hour before daylight to awaken the slaves for work in the fields. Hammond rises soon after, ever aware that "to continue" as a wealthy master, he must "draw the reign tighter and tighter" to hold his slaves "in complete check." He is as good as his word, recommending that "in general 15 to 20 lashes will be sufficient flogging" for most offenses but that "in extreme cases" the punishment "must not exceed 100 lashes in one day."

On an Alabama plantation, Hugh Lawson is up early, writing a sorrowful letter to Susanna Clay, telling her of the death of a "devotedly attached and faithful" slave, Jim. "I feel desolate," Hugh writes. "My most devoted friend is gone and *his place* can never be supplied by another." As Lawson pens his letter, a female slave has already awakened and "walked across a frosty field in the early morning and gone to the big house to build a fire" for her mistress. As the mistress wakes up to a warming house, she says to the slave, a grown woman responsible for the welfare of two families, "Well, how's my little nigger today?"

In a third household, this one a medium-size farm in up-country Georgia, not far from Hammond's huge plantation, Charles Brock wakes up at dawn and joins his two sons and four slaves to work his modest acreage of grains and sweet potatoes, while Brock's wife and a female slave tend the cows that provide milk and butter. On small and medium-size family farms with five or fewer slaves, blacks and whites commonly worked together, as one observer noted, with "the axe of master and man [slave] falling with alternate strokes . . . [and] ploughing side by side."

As these scenes suggest, slavery thoroughly permeated the lives of southern whites. For the slaves, morning was a time for getting up and going to work. But for southern whites, morning involved contact with slaves in many ways: as burdens of figuring profit and loss, as objects to be kept obedient and orderly, as intimates and fellow workers, and as ever-present reminders of fear, hate, and uncertainty.

The Burdens of Slaveholding

Robert Francis Withers Allston (1801–1864) was a major rice planter in a low, swampy, mosquito-infested tidal area of South Carolina. It was a perfect spot for growing rice, but so unhealthy that few whites wanted to live there. The death rate among slaves was appallingly high. In 1840, a total of 18,274 slaves toiled in the Georgetown district, but only 2,193 whites, many for only part of the year. By 1860, Allston owned seven plantations along the Peedee River, totaling some 4,000 acres. He held nearly 600 slaves, 236 of whom worked at the home plantation, Chicora Wood. Rich in land and labor, he nevertheless had large mortgages and outstanding debts.

Allston was an educated, talented, public-spirited man. He served in the South Carolina state senate for 24 years and as governor from 1856 to 1858. His political creed, he wrote in 1838, was one of "virtue and purity" based on "the principles of Thomas Jefferson." Allston was active in the Episcopal church and an ardent reformer, advocating liberalization of South Carolina's poor laws; an improved system of public education open to rich and poor alike; humanitarian care of the deaf, blind, insane, and other disabled persons; and the improvement of conditions on the reservations of the Catawba Indians.

In 1832, Allston married Adele Petigru, an equally enlightened and hardworking person. She participated fully in the management of the plantation and ran it while Robert was away on politics. After Robert's death during the Civil War, she assumed control of the Allston plantations, which had been abandoned when Union troops moved through the area.

State politics lured Robert from his land for part of each year, but he was by no means an absentee owner. Managing thousands of acres of rice required careful supervision of both the slaves and an elaborate irrigation system.

Allston's letters frequently expressed the serious burdens of owning slaves. Although he was careful to distribute enough cloth, blankets, and shoes to his slaves and to give them sufficient rest, the sickness and death of slaves, especially young field-workers, headed his list of concerns. "I lost in one year 28 negroes," Allston complained, "22 of whom were task hands." He tried to keep slave families together but sold slaves when necessary.

Other planters shared Allston's concerns, seeing slavery as both a duty and a burden. Many planters insisted that they worked harder than their slaves to feed and clothe them and to make their lives "as comfortable as possible." R. L. Dabney of Virginia exclaimed that "there could be no greater curse inflicted on us than to be compelled to manage a parcel of Negroes." Curse or not, Dabney and other planters profited from their burdens, a point they seldom admitted.

Adele and Robert F. W. Allston shared the work and burdens of managing their rice plantations.

Their wives experienced other kinds of burdens. "The mistress of a plantation," wrote Susan Dabney Smedes, "was the most complete slave on it." Plantation mistresses were expected to act as chaste ladies, while their husbands had virtually unrestricted sexual access to slave women. "God forgive us, but ours is a monstrous system," Mary Boykin Chestnut wrote in her diary. "Like the patriarchs of old, our men live all in one house with their wives and their concubines; and the mulattoes one sees in every family partly resemble the white children. Any lady is ready to tell you who is the father of all the mulatto children in everybody's household but her own. Those, she seems to think, drop from the clouds."

Chestnut called the sexual dynamics of slavery "the sorest spot." There were others. Southern white women had to tend to the food, clothing, health, and welfare not just of their husbands and children but of the plantation slave population as well. The plantation mistress, then, served many roles: as a potential hu-

manizing influence on men; as a tough, resourceful, responsible manager of numerous plantation affairs; as a coercer of slaves and perpetuator of the system; and sometimes as a victim herself.

Justifying Slavery

As slavery was increasingly attacked as immoral, slaveholders felt compelled to justify their institution. Until the 1830s, their defense explained slavery as a "necessary evil." After the abolitionists stepped up their attack in that decade, however, the justification shifted to defending slavery, in John C. Calhoun's words, as "a positive good." Various arguments were used: biblical, historical, constitutional, scientific, and sociological.

The biblical justification was based in part (incorrectly) on the curse of Canaan, the son of Ham, who was condemned to eternal servitude because his father had looked on Noah's nakedness. Furthermore, in various places both the Old and New Testaments admonished servants to obey their masters and accept their earthly lot.

Southern apologists also cited historical arguments. Slavery had existed throughout history. In fact, the greatest civilizations—Egypt, Greece, and Rome—had all built their strength and grandeur in part on slave labor.

A third argument justified slavery on legal grounds. Southerners pointed out (correctly) that the United States Constitution clearly sanctioned slavery.

A fourth justification was "scientific." Southern ethnologists argued that blacks had been created separately (a theory called "polygenesis") and were an inherently inferior race with inferior brains. Therefore, the destiny of the inferior Africans was to serve the superior Caucasians (the "Adamic race") in work.

In a paternalistic defense of slavery based on racism and social control, George Fitzhugh argued that "the Negro is but a grown child and must be governed as a child." Social chaos would result if the slaves were freed. Emancipation, therefore, would be heartless and unthinkable, a burden to both blacks and whites.

Southern apologists for slavery faced the difficult intellectual task of justifying a system that ran counter to the main ideological directions of nineteenth-century American society: the expansion of individual liberty, mobility, economic opportunity, and democratic political participation. Moreover, the southern defense of slavery had to take into account the 75 percent of white families who owned no slaves and who envied those who did. Because of the potential for class anatagonisms among whites, wealthy planters developed a justification of slavery that deflected class differences by maintaining that all whites were superior to all blacks but equal to one another. The theory of democratic equality among whites, therefore, was made consistent with racism and the holding of slaves.

As the southern defense of slavery intensified in the 1840s and 1850s, it aroused greater opposition from northerners and from slaves themselves. Although slavery was cruel in many ways, perhaps its worst feature was not physical but psychological: to be enslaved at all and barred from economic advancement in a nation that put a high value on freedom and equality of opportunity.

NOON: SLAVES IN HOUSE AND FIELDS

It is two o'clock on a hot July afternoon on the plantation. The midday lunch break is over, and the slaves are returning to their work in the fields. Lunch was the usual nutritionally deficient fare of cornmeal and pork. Douglass remembered that "we worked all weathers. . . . It was never too hot, or too cold" for toiling in the fields.

Daily Toil

The daily work schedule for most slaves, whether in the fields or the Big House, was long and demanding. Aroused by a bell or horn before daybreak, they worked on an average day 14 hours in the summer and 10 hours in the winter. During harvest time, it was not uncommon to work for 18 hours. Depending on the size of the work force and the crop, the slaves were organized either in gangs or according to tasks. The gangs, usually of 20 to 25, worked their way along the cotton rows under the watchful eye and quick whip of a driver. Ben Simpson, a Georgia slave, remembered vividly how his master would use a "great, long whip platted out of rawhide" to hit a slave in the work gang who would "fall behind or give out."

Under the task system, each slave had a specific task to complete daily. This system gave slaves the incentive to work hard enough to finish early, but it meant that the quality of their work was scrutinized constantly. An overseer's weekly report to Robert Allston in 1860 noted that he had "flogged for hoeing corn bad Fanny 12 lashes, Sylvia 12, Monday 12, Phoebee 12, Susanna 12, Salina 12, Celia 12, Iris 12."

An average slave was expected to pick 130 to 150 pounds of cotton per day. The work on sugar and rice plantations was even harder. Sugar demanded constant cultivation and the digging of drainage ditches in snake-infested fields. At harvest time, cutting, stripping, and carrying the cane to the sugar house for boiling was exhausting. In addition, huge quantities of firewood had to be cut and carried. Working in the low-country rice fields was worse: Slaves spent long hours standing in water up to their knees.

House slaves, most of them women, had relatively easier assignments than the field slaves, though they were usually called on to help with the harvest. They also ate and dressed better than their fellow slaves in the fields. But house slaves were watched more closely, were on call at all hours of the day and night, and were more often involved in personality conflicts in the white household. The most feared punishment for a house slave, other than sale to the Deep South, was to be sent to the fields.

Slave Health

Although slave owners had an interest in keeping their slaves healthy by providing adequate care, slaves led sickly lives. Home was a crude, one-room log cabin with a dirt floor. Most cabins had a fireplace for heat and cooking, a table, some stools or boxes to sit on, an iron pot and wooden dishes, and perhaps a bed. The cabins were crowded, with usually more than one family living in each. Slave clothing was shabby and uncomfortable.

Studies on the adequacy of slave diet disagree, some showing that the food most slaves ate was deficient in calories and vitamins, others claiming that the energy value of the slave diet exceeded that of free whites in the general population. Compared with Latin American slaves, American slaves were well fed, receiving weekly rations of cornmeal, salt pork or bacon, molasses, and perhaps sweet potatoes. This bland fare was supplemented for some slaves, with the master's permission, by vegetables grown in a small garden and by fishing or hunting small game.

Most slaves, however, rarely enjoyed fresh meat, dairy products, fruits, or vegetables. To make up for these deficiencies, they sometimes stole from the master's kitchen, gardens, and barnyard. Inadequate diet led some slaves to become dirt eaters, which gave them worms and "swollen shiny skin, puffy eyelids, pale palms and soles." Others suffered regularly from skin disorders, cracked lips, and sore eyes. Many slaves, like poor whites, came down with vitamin deficiency diseases such as rickets, pellagra, beriberi, scurvy, and even mental illness.

Women slaves especially suffered weaknesses caused by vitamin deficiency, hard work, and disease, as well as those associated with the menstrual cycle and childbirth. Women were expected to do the same tasks in the fields as the men, in addition to cooking, sewing, child care, and traditional female jobs in the quarters when the fieldwork was finished. "Pregnant women," the usual rule stated, "should not plough or lift but must be kept at moderate work until the last hour" and were given a three-week recovery period after giving birth. But these guidelines were more often violated than honored. Infant mortality of slave children under 5 years of age was twice as high as for white children.

Life expectancy for American slaves was longer than for those in Latin America and the Caribbean, but not very high for either blacks or whites in the antebellum South (21.4 for blacks and 25.5 for whites in 1850). In part because of poor diet and climate, slaves were highly susceptible to disease. Many died from malaria, yellow fever, cholera, intestinal ailments, and respiratory diseases.

The relatively frequent incidence of whippings and other physical punishments aggravated the poor physical condition of the slaves. The slave William Wells Brown reported that on his plantation the whip was used "very frequently and freely" for inadequate or uncompleted work, stealing, running away, and even insolence and lying. Former slaves described a good owner as one who did not "whip too much" and a bad owner as one who "whipped till he'd bloodied you and blistered you." Other forms of punishment included isolation and confinement in stocks and jails during leisure hours, chains, muzzling, salting lash wounds, branding, burning, and castration.

Slave Law and the Family

Complicating master-slave relationships was the status of slaves as both persons and property, a legal and psychological ambiguity the South never resolved. On the one hand, the slaves had names, personalities, families, and wills of their own. This required dealing with them as fellow humans. On the other hand, they were items of property, purchased and maintained to perform specific profit-making tasks. As a Kentucky court put the problem, "Although the law of this state considers slaves as property, . . . it recognizes their personal existence, and, to a qualified extent, their natural right."

This ambiguity in the laws changed after the challenges to slavery in the early 1830s. As a result of Nat Turner's revolt and William Lloyd Garrison's publication of the abolitionist *Liberator* in 1831 (discussed later), the South tightened up the slave system. Laws prohibiting manumission were passed, but at the same time, laws protecting slaves from overly severe treatment were strengthened, and material conditions generally improved.

But whatever the law said, the practice was always more telling. Treatment varied with individual slaveholders. This was especially true with regard to the slave family. Most planters, like Robert Allston, generally encouraged their slaves to marry and did all they could to keep families intact. They believed that families made black males more docile and less inclined to re-

volt or run away. But some masters failed to respect slave marriages or broke them up because of financial problems. This tendency was supported by southern courts and legislatures, which did not legally recognize slave marriages or the right to family unity.

Adding to the pain of forced breakup of the slave family was the sexual abuse of black women. Although the frequency of such abuse is unknown, the presence of thousands of mulattoes in the antebellum era is testimony to this practice. White men in the South abused black slave women in several ways: by offering gifts for sexual "favors," by threatening those who refused with physical punishment or the sale of a child or loved one, by purchasing concubines, or by rape. As Frederick Douglass put it, the "slave woman is at the mercy of the fathers, sons or brothers of her master."

Because of the need to obtain cheap additional slaves for the work force, slaveholders encouraged young slave women to bear children, whether married or not. If verbal prodding and inducements such as less work and more rations did not work, masters would choose mates and foist them on slave women. More often, slaves chose their own mates on the basis of mutual attraction during an uneasy courtship complicated by the threat of white interferences. As among poor whites, premarital intercourse was frequent, but promiscuous behavior was rare. Most couples maintained affectionate, lasting relationships.

Although motherhood was the key event in a slave woman's life, bearing children and the double burden of work and family responsibilities challenged her resourcefulness. New mothers often had to choose between taking their babies into the fields to be fed or leaving them with others. Some masters would provide time off for nursing mothers, but the more common practice was for them to work in the fields with their newborn infants lying nearby, wrapped in cloth to protect them from the sun. Women developed networks of mutual support, looking after one another's children, meeting together to

Despite separation, sale, and sexual abuse by white masters, many slave families endured and provided love, support and self-esteem to their members. This 1862 photograph shows five generations of a slave family, all born on the plantation of J. J. Smith of Beaufort, South Carolina.

sew, quilt, cook, or do laundry, and attending births, caring for the sick and dying, and praying together.

The most traumatic problem for slaves was the separation of families, a haunting fear rarely absent from slave consciousness. The separation of husbands and wives (one-third according to one study of three Deep South states) challenged the couples to maintain contact. When Abream Scriven informed his wife, Dinah, of his sale to a trader in New Orleans, he had no idea where he would be sold but promised to "write and let you know where I am. . . . My Dear Wife for you and my Children my pen cannot Express the griffe I feel to be parted from you all."

There was much basis in fact for the abolitionists' contention that slavery was a harsh, brutal system. Yet, despite the travail of slavery, whether under relatively kind or cruel masters, the slaves endured with dignity, communal sensitivity, and even some joy. If daytime in the fields describes a view of slavery at its worst, nighttime in the quarters, as examined from the black perspective, reveals the slaves' survival powers and their capacity to mold an African-American culture under slavery.

NIGHT: SLAVES IN THEIR QUARTERS

It is near sundown, and the workday is almost over. Some of the slaves begin singing the gentle spiritual "Steal Away to Jesus," and others join in. Or perhaps they sing, "Dere's a meeting here tonight." To the unwary overseer or master, the humming, soothing sound of the song suggests happy slaves, content with their earthly lot and looking forward to deliverance in heaven, "in the sweet bosom of Jesus." To the slaves, however, the songs are a signal that, as an ex-slave, Wash Wilson, put it, they are to "steal away to Jesus" because "dere gwine be a 'ligious meetin' dat night." When evening arrived on the plantation, after a hard day of work in the hot sun or in the Big House, the slaves returned to their own quarters. There, as Wilson said, "sometimes us sing and pray all night."

In the slave quarters, away from white masters, overseers, and the burdens of daily work, an elaborate black community helped the slaves make sense out of their lives. In family life, religion, song, dance, the playing of musical instruments, and the telling of stories, the slaves both described their experiences and sought release from hardship and suffering. However burdensome their lives from sunup to sundown, after work the slaves experienced enjoyment and a sense of self-worth, hope, and group identity in their quarters.

Black Christianity

As suggested by the scene Wash Wilson described, Christian worship was an indispensable part of slave life in the quarters. The revivals of the early nineteenth century led to an enormous growth of Christianity among black Americans. Some independent black Baptist and Methodist churches, especially in border states and cities, served both slaves and free blacks and occasionally even whites. These separate churches had to steer a careful path to maintain their freedom and avoid white interference. But the vast majority of southern blacks were slaves, attending plantation missions set up by their masters.

For the slaveholders, religion often represented a form of social control. Black religious gatherings were usually forbidden unless white observers were present or white preachers led them. Whether in slave or white churches (where blacks sat in the back), preachers often delivered sermons from the biblical text "Servants, obey your masters."

Although some slaves accommodated themselves to the master's brand of Christianity and patiently waited for heavenly deliverance, others rebelled and sought earthly liberty. Douglass had an illegal Sabbath school on one plantation, where he and others risked being whipped while learning about Christianity and how to read. "The work of instructing my dear fellow-slaves," he wrote, "was the sweetest engagement with which I was ever blessed." Sarah Fitzpatrick, an Alabama slave, recalled that the slaves wanted so much to "go to church by de'selves" that they were willing to sit through the "white fo'ks' . . . service in de mornin'." But when evening came, "a'ter dey clean up, wash de dishes, an' look a'ter ever'thing," the slaves would "steal away" to the nearby woods for their own service. Long into the night they would sing, dance, shout, and pray.

Although many of the expressive forms were African, the message reiterated over and over in the slave church was the Christian theme of suffering and deliverance from bondage. Slaves identified with the children of Israel and with the Exodus story, as well as with the suffering of Jesus and the inner turmoil of an unconverted "trebbled spirit." Nothing illustrated both the communal religious experience and these mixed Christian themes of suffering and redemption better than slave spirituals.

The Power of Song

A group of slaves gathers in the dark of night in the woods behind their quarters to sing and shout together.

O brothers, don't get weary
O brothers, don't get weary
O brothers, don't get weary
We're waiting for the Lord.
We'll land on Canaan's shore

We'll land on Canaan's shore
When we land on Canaan's shore
We'll meet forever more.

Music was a crucial form of expression in the slave quarters on both secular and religious occasions. The slaves were adept at creating a song, as one slave woman recalled, "on de spurn of de moment."

Although the spirituals were composed for many purposes, they reiterated one basic Christian theme: A chosen people, the children of God, were held captive in bondage but would be delivered. The titles and lyrics reveal the message: "We Are de People of de Lord," "To the Promised Land I'm Bound to Go," "Go Down, Moses," "Who Will Deliver Po' Me?" What they meant by "deliverance" was not always clear and often had a double meaning: freedom in heaven and freedom in the North.

"The songs of the slave," Douglass wrote, "represent the sorrows of his heart." Although they often expressed the sadness of broken families and the burdens of work, they also expressed joy, triumph, and deliverance. Slave songs did not always contain hidden meanings. Sometimes slaves gathered simply for music, to play fiddles, drums, and other instruments fashioned by local artists in imitation of West African models. Sacred and secular events such as weddings, funerals, holiday celebrations, family reunions, and a successful harvest were all occasions for a communal gathering, usually with music. So too was news of external events that affected their lives— a crisis in the master's situation, a change in the slave code, the outcome of a battle during the Civil War, or emancipation itself.

The Enduring Family

The role of music in births, weddings, funerals, and other milestones of family life suggests that the family was central to life in the slave quarters. Although the pain of sexual abuse and fam-

ily separation was a real or potential part of the experience of all slaves, so was the hope for family continuity.

The benefits of family cohesion were those of any group: love, protection, education, moral guidance, the transmission of culture, and the provision of status, role models, and basic support. All of these existed in the slave quarters. As the slaves gathered together at the end of the working day, parents passed on to their children the family story, language patterns and words, recipes, folktales, religious and musical traditions, and strong impressions of strength and beauty. In this way they preserved cultural tradition, which enhanced the identity and self-esteem of parents and children alike. Parents taught their children how to survive in the world and how to cope with life under slavery. As the young ones neared the age when they would work full time in the fields, their parents instructed them in the best ways to pick cotton or corn, how to avoid the overseer's whip, whom to trust and learn from, and ways of fooling the master.

The love and affection that slaves had for one another was sometimes a liability. Many slaves, women especially, were reluctant to run away because they did not want to leave their families. The slave family, though constantly endangered, played a crucial role in helping blacks adapt to slavery and achieve a sense of self-esteem.

RESISTANCE AND FREEDOM

Songs, folktales, and other forms of cultural expression enabled slaves to articulate their resistance to slavery. For example, Old Jim was going on a "journey" to the "kingdom" and, as he invited others to "go 'long" with him, he taunted his owner: "O blow, blow, Ole Massa, blow de cotton horn / Ole Jim'll neber wuck no mo' in de cotton an' de corn." From refusal to work it was a short step to outright revolt. In another song,

"Samson," the slaves clearly stated their determination to abolish the house of bondage: "An' if I had-'n my way / I'd tear the buildin' down! / . . . And now I got my way / And I'll tear this buildin' down." Every hostile song, story, or event, like Douglass's victory over Covey, was an act of resistance by which the slaves asserted their dignity and gained a measure of freedom. Some escaped slavery altogether to achieve such autonomy as was possible for free blacks in the antebellum South.

Forms of Black Protest

One way slaves protested the burdensome demands of continuous forced labor was in various "day to day" acts of resistance. These ranged from breaking or misplacing tools to burning crops, barns, and houses, from stealing or destroying animals and food to defending fellow slaves from punishment, from self-mutilation to deliberate work slowdowns, and from poisoning masters to feigning illness.

Overseers also suffered from these acts of disobedience, for their job depended on productivity, which in turn depended on the goodwill of the slave workers. No one knew this better than the slaves themselves, who adeptly played on the frequent struggle between overseer and master. Often the conflicts were ended by firing a bad overseer and hiring a more suitable replacement. Many slave-holders eventually resorted to using black drivers rather than overseers, but this created other problems.

The slave drivers were "men between," charged with the tricky job of getting the master's work done without alienating fellow slaves or compromising their own values. Although some drivers were as brutal as white overseers, many became leaders and role models for other slaves. A common practice of the drivers was to appear to punish without really doing so. Solomon Northrup reported that he "learned to handle the whip with marvellous dexterity and precision, throwing the lash within a hair's breadth of the back, the ear, the nose, without, however, touching either of them." As he did this, the "punished" slave would howl in pretended pain and complain loudly to his master about his harsh treatment.

Another form of resistance was to run away. The typical runaway was a young male, who ran off alone and hid out in a nearby wood or swamp. He left to avoid a whipping or because he had just been whipped, to protest excessive work demands, or, as one master put it, for "no cause" at all. But there was a cause—the need to experience a period of freedom away from the restraints and discipline of the plantation.

Some slaves left again and again. Remus and his wife, Patty, ran away from their master, James Battle, in Alabama. They were caught and jailed three times, but each time they escaped again. Battle urged the next jailer to "secure Remus well." Some runaways, called "Maroons," hid out for months and years at a time in communities of runaway slaves. Several Maroon colonies were located in the swamps and mountains of the South, especially in Florida, where Seminole and other Indian groups befriended them. In these areas, blacks and Indians, sharing a common hostility to local whites, frequently intermarried, though sometimes Indians were hired to track down runaway slaves.

The underground railroad, organized by abolitionists, was a series of safe houses and stations where runaway slaves could rest, eat, and spend the night before continuing. Harriet Tubman, who led some 300 slaves out of the South on 19 separate trips, was the railroad's most famous "conductor." It is difficult to know exactly how many slaves actually escaped to the North and Canada, but the numbers were not large. One estimate suggests that in 1850 about a thousand slaves (out of over three million) attempted to run away, and most of them were returned. Nightly patrols by white militiamen, an important aspect of southern life, reduced the chances for any slave to escape and probably deterred many slaves from even trying to run away.

Slave Revolts

The ultimate act of resistance, of course, was rebellion. Countless slaves committed individual acts of revolt. In addition, there were hundreds of conspiracies whereby slaves met to plan a group escape and often the massacre of whites. Most of these conspiracies never led to action, either because circumstances changed or the slaves lost the will to follow through or, more often, because some fellow slave—perhaps planted by the master—betrayed the plot. Such spies thwarted the elaborate conspiracies of Gabriel Prosser (Richmond, Virginia, 1800) and Denmark Vesey (Charleston, South Carolina, 1822). Both resulted in severe reprisals by whites, including mass executions of leaders and the random killing of innocent blacks.

Only a few organized revolts, in which slaves threatened white lives and property, ever actually took place. Latin American slaves challenged their masters more often than their North American counterparts. Weaker military control, easier escape to rugged interior areas, the greater imbalance of blacks to whites, and the continued dependence of Latin American slaveholders on the African slave trade for their supply of mostly male workers explain this pattern. The imbalance of males to females (156 to 100 in Cuba in 1860, for example, compared with a near one-to-one ratio in the United States) weakened family restraints on violent revolts.

The most famous slave revolt in North America, led by Nat Turner, occurred in Southampton County, Virginia, in 1831. Turner was an intelligent, skilled, unmarried, religious slave who had experienced many visions of "white spirits and black spirits engaged in bat-

tle." He believed that he was "ordained for some great purpose in the hands of the Almighty."

On a hot August night, Turner and a small band of fellow slaves launched their revolt. They intended, as Turner said, "to carry terror and devastation" throughout the country. They crept into the home of Turner's master, Joseph Travis, who Nat said was "a kind master" with "the greatest confidence in me," and killed the entire family. Before the revolt was finally put down, 55 white men, women, and children had been murdered and twice as many blacks killed in the aftermath. Turner hid in a hole in the woods for two weeks before he was apprehended and executed, but not before dictating a chilling confession to a white lawyer. Rarely thereafter would slaveholders go to sleep without the Southampton revolt in mind.

Free Blacks: Becoming One's Own Master

No matter how well they coped with their bondage, the slaves obviously preferred freedom. As Frederick Douglass said of the slave, "Give him a *bad* master, and he aspires to a *good* master; give him a good master, and he wishes to become his *own* master." Between 1820 and 1860, the number of free blacks in the United States doubled, from 233,500 to 488,000. This rise resulted from natural increase, successful escapes, "passing" as whites, purchasing freedom, and a continuation of some manumissions despite legal restriction in most states after the 1830s.

However freedom was achieved, what was life like for the 11 percent of the total black population who in 1860 were not slaves? More than half the free blacks lived in the South, most (85 percent in 1860) in the Upper South, where the total number of slaves had declined slightly. Free blacks generally lived away from the dense plantation centers, scattered on impoverished rural farmlands and in small towns and cities. One-

Frederick Douglass, photographed here in about 1855, spent his life working for freedom and improved opportunities for blacks after his own escape to freedom as a young man in 1838.

third of southern free blacks lived in cities such as Baltimore, Richmond, Charleston, and New Orleans. In part because it took a long time to buy their freedom, they tended to be older, more literate, and more skilled than other blacks. A great many were light-skinned women, reflecting the favored privileges these blacks received from slaveholders.

Most southern free blacks were poor, laboring as farmhands, day laborers, or woodcutters. In the cities, they lived in appalling poverty and worked in factories. A few skilled jobs, such as barbering, shoemaking, and plastering, were reserved for black men; they were barred from more than 50 other trades. Women worked as cooks, laundresses, and domestics. The 15 percent of free blacks who lived in the Lower South were divided into two distinct castes. Most were poor. But in New Orleans, Charleston, and other southern cities, a small, mixed-blood class of free blacks emerged as an elite group, closely connected to white society and removed from the mass of poor blacks. A handful even owned land and slaves.

Most free blacks, however, had no such privileges. In most states, they could not vote, bear arms, buy liquor, assemble, speak in public, form societies, or testify against whites in court. In Richmond, efforts were also made to confine the free blacks to certain sections of the city or, increasingly by the 1850s, to compel them to leave the city, county, or state altogether. Those who stayed had trouble finding work, were required to carry licenses and freedom papers to be surrendered on demand, and often needed a white guardian to approve their actions. Nevertheless, free blacks and slaves often worked together in factories and fields, attended the same churches and places of entertainment, and sometimes even married.

The center of urban black community was the church. Martin Delaney wrote to Douglass in 1849 that "among our people ... the Church is the Alpha and Omega of all things." The church not only performed the usual religious functions but also provided and promoted education, social insurance, fraternal associations, and picnics, concerts, and other forms of recreation. Besides the church, black community identity and pride revolved around the African schools and various burial and benevolent societies for self-help and protection against poverty, illness, and other disasters. Like their counterparts among whites, these societies grew and took on a new and significant social importance in the two decades before the Civil War.

Free blacks faced a crisis of extinction in the 1850s, especially when pressures increased late in the decade either to deport the free blacks or to enslave them. In the wake of increasing threats to their already precarious free status, some black leaders not surprisingly began to look more favorably on migration to Africa. That quest was interrupted, however, by the outbreak of the Civil War, rekindling in Douglass and others the "expiring embers of freedom."

CONCLUSION

DOUGLASS'S DREAM OF FREEDOM

Frederick Douglass won his freedom by forging a free black sailor's pass and escaping through Chesapeake Bay to New York. In a real sense, he wrote himself into freedom. The *Narrative of the Life of Frederick Douglass,* "written by himself" in 1845, was a way both of exposing the many evils of slavery and of creating his own identity, even to the point of choosing his own name. Ironically, Douglass had learned to value reading and writing, we recall, from his Baltimore masters, the Aulds. This reminds us again of the intricate and subtle ways in which the lives of slaves and masters were tied together in the antebellum South.

In a poignant moment in his *Narrative,* Douglass described his dreams of freedom as he looked out at the boats on the waters of Chesapeake Bay as a boy. As we will see later, southern white planters also bemoaned their lack of freedom relative to the North and made their own plans to achieve independent status through secession. Meanwhile, as that struggle brewed beneath the surface of antebellum life, many other Americans were dismayed by various evil aspects in their society, slavery among them, and sought ways of shaping a better America. We turn to these other dreams in the next chapter.

Recommended Reading

Gavin Wright provides a difficult but thorough analysis of the economic development of the Old South in *The Political Economy of the Cotton South: Households, Markets, and Wealth in the Nineteenth Century* (1978). On the economics of slavery, see Paul David et al., *Reckoning with Slavery: A Critical Study of the Quantitative History of American Negro Slavery* (1976). Nonagricultural slaves are dealt with in Robert Starobin, *Industrial Slavery in the Old South* (1970). The most readable story of the lives of nonslaveholding whites in the South is an old one, Frank Owsley's *Plain Folk in the Old South* (1949).

A brilliant study of racism in America, including excellent chapters on the southern justification of slavery, is George Fredrickson, *The Black Image in the White Mind: The Debate on Afro-American Character and Destiny, 1817–1914* (1971). For a stunning portrayal of female slaves in the plantation South, see Deborah Gray White, *Arn't I a Woman?* (1985). A remarkable work that treats both white and slave women is Elizabeth Fox-Genovese, *Within the Plantation Household* (1988).

Of the many collections of primary source documents about slavery, the best is Willie Lee Rose, *A Documentary History of Slavery in North America* (1976). Among the best surveys of slavery are Nathan I. Huggins, *Black Odyssey: The Afro-American Ordeal in Slavery* (1977); and John Blassingame, *The Slave Community,* rev. ed. (1979). Slave culture and life in the quarters are treated brilliantly in Charles Joyner, *Down by the Riverside: A South Carolina Slave Community* (1984); and Lawrence Levine, *Black Culture and Black Consciousness: Afro-American Folk Thought from Slavery to Freedom* (1977). Frederick Douglass's experiences are told in three separate autobiographies, including *My Bondage and My Freedom* (1855), and *Life and Times of Frederick Douglass* (1881). A superb biography is *Frederick Douglass* (1990) by William S. McFeely.

The definitive work on free blacks in the South is Ira Berlin, *Slaves Without Masters: The Free Negro in the Antebellum South* (1976). Slave resistance and revolt are described in Vincent Harding, *There Is a River: The Black Struggle for Freedom in America* (1981), but a superb way to experience both slavery and the struggle for freedom is by reading an old classic, Harriet Beecher Stowe's *Uncle Tom's Cabin* (1852).

Time Line

1787	Constitution adopted with pro-slavery provisions
1793	Eli Whitney invents cotton gin
1800	Gabriel Prosser conspiracy in Virginia
1808	External slave trade prohibited by Congress
1820	South becomes world's largest cotton producer
1822	Denmark Vesey's conspiracy in Charleston
1830s	Southern justification of slavery changes from a necessary evil to a positive good

1831	Nat Turner's slave revolt in Virginia
1845	*Narrative of the Life of Frederick Douglass* published
1850s	Cotton boom
1851	Indiana state constitution excludes free blacks
1852	Harriet Beecher Stowe publishes best-selling *Uncle Tom's Cabin*
1860	Cotton production and prices peak

chapter 12

....

Shaping America in the Antebellum Age

On November 19, 1836, 30-year-old Marius Robinson and Emily Rakestraw were married near Cincinnati, Ohio. Two months after their wedding, he went on the road to speak against slavery and to organize abolitionist societies throughout Ohio. Emily stayed in Cincinnati to teach in a school for free blacks. During their ten-month separation, they exchanged affectionate letters that reflected their love and work. Marius, who had experienced a series of conversions inspired by the revivalist Charles G. Finney and his abolitionist disciple Theodore Dwight Weld, described the reason for their separation: "God and humanity bleeding and suffering demand our services apart." Thus motivated by a strong religious commitment to serve others, these two young reformers dedicated themselves to several social causes: the abolition of slavery, equal rights and education for free blacks, temperance, and women's rights.

Their commitments cost more than separation. Emily's parents disapproved of Marius and of their reformist activities. Teaching at the school in Cincinnati was demanding, and the white citizens of the city resented the school and the young abolitionists in their midst. But Emily persisted in the work of "our school" while worrying about the health and safety of her husband on the road.

She had good reason for concern, for Marius's letters were full of reports of mob attacks, disrupted meetings, stonings, and narrow escapes. In June, he was dragged from the home of his Quaker host and beaten, tarred, and feathered. Never quite recovering his health, Marius spent half a year in bed, weak and dispirited. For nearly ten years after that, the Robinsons lived quietly on an Ohio farm, only slightly involved in the abolitionist movement. Despite the joyous birth of two daughters, they felt lonely, restless, and guilt-ridden, "tired of days blank of benevolent effort and almost of benevolent desires."

The work of Emily and Marius Robinson represents one response by the American people to the rapid social and economic changes of the antebellum era described in Chapters 10 and 11. In September 1835, a year before the Robinsons' marriage, the

Niles Register commented on some 500 recent incidents of mob violence and social upheaval. *"Society seems everywhere unhinged,* and the demon of 'blood and slaughter' has been let loose upon us. . . . [The] character of our countrymen seems suddenly changed." How did Americans adapt to these changes and maintain some sense of control over their lives?

One way was to embrace the changes fully. Thus some Americans became entrepreneurs in new industries; invested in banks, canals, and railroads; bought more land and slaves; and invented new machines. Others went west or to the new textile mills, enrolled in common schools, joined trade unions, specialized their labor both in the workplace and the home, and celebrated the practical benefits that resulted from modernization. Marius Robinson eventually went into life insurance, though he and Emily never fully abandoned their reformist efforts and idealism.

But many Americans were uncomfortable with the character of the new era. Some worried about the unrestrained power and selfish materialism symbolized by the slavemaster's control over his slaves. Others feared that institutions like the U.S. Bank represented a "monied aristocracy" capable of undermining the country's honest producers. Seeking positions of leadership and authority, these critics of the new order tried to shape a nation that retained the benefits of economic change without sacrificing humane principles of liberty, equality of opportunity, and community virtue. This chapter examines four ways in which the American people responded to change by attempting to influence their country's development: party politics, religious revivalism, utopian communitarianism, and social reform.

THE POLITICAL RESPONSE TO CHANGE

At the heart of American politics was the concern for the continued health of the republican experiment. As American society changed, so too did the understanding of political measures necessary to maintain that health. The economic dislocations after 1819 and in the late 1830s and the spirited presidential campaigns of Andrew Jackson helped to create widespread interest in politics in the era between 1820 and 1840.

Changing Political Culture

The presidency of Andrew Jackson was a crucial factor in bringing politics to the center of many Americans' lives. Styling himself as the people's candidate in 1828, Andrew Jackson derided the Adams administration as corrupt and aristocratic and promised a more democratic political system with the interests of the people at its center. Then as today, many Americans believed the campaign rhetoric. Four times more men turned out to vote in the election of 1828 than had gone to the polls four years earlier. They gave Jackson a resounding 56 percent of their ballots. No other president in the century would equal that percentage of popular support.

Despite campaign rhetoric, Jackson was not personally very democratic, nor did the era he symbolized involve any significant redistribution of wealth. Jackson himself owned slaves, defended slavery, and condoned mob attacks on abolitionists like Marius Robinson in the mid-1830s. And belying promises of widening opportunity, the rich got richer during the Jacksonian era, and most farming and urban laboring families did not prosper.

But the nation's political life had changed in important ways. The old system of politics based on elite coalitions and the deference of voters to their "betters" largely disappeared. In its place emerged a competitive party system, begun early in the republic but now oriented toward widespread voter participation in state and local politics. Political parties sponsored conventions, rallies, and parades. In the North, even women turned out for political rallies and speeches and rode on floats at party parades. Party-subsidized newspapers regularly indulged in scurrilous attacks on political candidates.

As depicted in this Robert Cruikshank lithograph, All Creation Going to the White House, *the first inauguration of Andrew Jackson in 1829 was the scene of wild festivities, a harbinger of the excesses in American life and politics in the ensuing years.*

Jackson's Path to the White House

Andrew Jackson's personality suited the new era. Orphaned at 14, young Jackson was rowdy, indecisive, and often in trouble. As a law student he was described as a "most roaring, rollicking, game-cocking, horse-racing, card-playing, mischievous fellow." He passed the bar and set out at the age of 21 to seek his fortune in the West. Settling in the frontier town of Nashville, the tall, red-headed young man built up a successful law practice in Tennessee and went on to become public prosecutor (called attorney general). Eventually, he became a substantial landowner and a prominent citizen of Nashville.

Jackson's national reputation stemmed mainly from his military exploits against American Indians and from his victory over the British at New Orleans in 1815. Careful political maneuvering in Tennessee in the early 1820s brought him election as U.S. senator and nomination for the presidency in 1824.

In the 1824 election, Jackson won both the popular and electoral votes but lost in the House of Representatives to John Quincy Adams.

When Henry Clay threw his support to Adams and was named secretary of state, Jackson condemned this deal as a "corrupt bargain." Jackson's loss convinced him of the importance of having an effective political organization. He organized his campaign by setting up loyal committees and newspapers in many states and by encouraging efforts to undermine Adams and Clay.

The loose coalition promoting Jackson's candidacy, which began to call itself the Democratic Party, was a mixed lot, drawing in politicians of diverse views from all sections of the country. Jackson played down his position on controversial issues, but he made clear his intentions of reforming government by throwing out of office anyone who was incompetent or who failed to represent the will of the people. Democratic newspapers picked up this theme and presented Jackson as a politician who would cleanse government of corruption and privileged interests.

The campaign between Jackson and Adams

in 1828 degenerated into a nasty but entertaining contest. Both sides engaged in slanderous personal attacks. Supporters of Adams and Clay, who called themselves National Republicans, claimed that Jackson was "an adulterer, a gambler, a cockfighter, a brawler, a drunkard, and a murderer." The Jacksonians in turn described Adams as a "stingy, undemocratic" aristocrat determined to destroy the people's liberties. Worse yet, Adams was an intellectual, "a man who can write." Jackson, by contrast, was the hero of the Battle of New Orleans, "a man who can fight." The efforts of Jackson and his party paid off as he won an astonishing 647,286 ballots, about 56 percent of the total.

Jackson's inauguration on a mild March 4 horrified many Americans. Washington was packed for the ceremonies. When Jackson appeared on the steps of the Capitol to take the oath of office, wild and unrestrained cheering broke out. After making a short address and taking the oath, Jackson was all but mobbed as he tried to make his way to his horse.

The White House reception soon got completely out of hand. A throng of people poured into the White House with muddy boots to overturn furniture in a rush for food and punch. The inauguration, according to Justice Joseph Story, illustrated "the reign of King Mob." Another observer called it "a proud day for the people." These contrasting views on the events of the inauguration captured the essence of the Jackson era. For some they symbolized the excesses of democracy; for others they represented democratic fulfillment.

Old Hickory's Vigorous Presidency

President Jackson's decisions, often controversial, helped to sharpen what it meant to be a Democrat and what it meant to be democracy's opponent. A few key convictions—the principle of majority rule, the limited power of the national government, the obligation of the national government to defend the interests of the nation's average people against the machinations of the "monied aristocracy"—guided Jackson's political behavior as president. Because he saw himself as the people's most authentic representative (only the president was elected by all the people), Jackson intended to be an effective, vigorous executive. More than any previous president, Jackson used presidential power in the name of the people and justified his actions by popular appeals to the electorate.

Jackson asserted his power most dramatically through use of the veto. The six preceding presidents had used the veto only nine times, most often against measures that they had believed unconstitutional. Jackson vetoed 12 bills during his eight years in office.

One of the abuses Jackson had promised to correct was what he described as an undemocratic and corrupt system of government officeholding. Too often "unfaithful or incompetent" men held onto their offices for years, making a mockery of the idea of representation. In the first year and a half of his presidency, Jackson removed 919 officeholders of a total of 10,093, fewer than one in ten. Most of these were for good reason—corruption or incompetence. The new Democratic appointees were not much better than their predecessors.

Jackson's similarly controversial Indian policy of forcible removal and relocation westward defined white American practice for the rest of the century. In the opening decades of the nineteenth century, the vast landholdings of the five "civilized nations" of the Southeast (the Cherokee, Choctaw, Chickasaw, Seminole, and Creek) had been seriously eroded by the pressures of land-hungry whites supported by successful military campaigns led by professional Indian fighters such as General Jackson. Land cessions to the government and private sales accounted for huge losses of Indian lands. In his first annual message to Congress in 1829, Jackson urged removal of the southeastern tribes. He argued that because the Indians were "surrounded by the whites with their arts of civilization," it was inevitable that the "resources of the savage" would be destroyed, dooming the Indians to "weakness and decay." Removal was justified, Jackson claimed, by both "humanity and national honor." He also endorsed the paramount right of state laws over the claims of either Indians or the federal government.

With the president's position clear, the crisis soon came to a head in Georgia. In 1829, the Georgia legislature declared the Cherokee tribal council illegal and its laws null and void in Cherokee territories and announced that the state had jurisdiction over both the tribe and its lands. Without legal recourse on the state level, the Cherokee carried their protests to the Supreme Court. In 1832, Chief Justice Marshall supported their position in *Worcester* v. *Georgia,* holding that the Georgia law was "repugnant to the Constitution" and did not apply to the Cherokee nation.

With Jackson's blessing, however, Georgians defied the Court ruling. By 1835, harassment, intimidation, and bribery had persuaded a minority of chiefs to sign a removal treaty. But most Cherokee refused to leave their lands. Therefore, in 1837 and 1838, the United States Army searched and seized the terrified Indians and gathered them in stockades prior to herding them west to the "Indian Territory" in Oklahoma. An eyewitness described how the Cherokee trek began:

> Families at dinner were startled by the sudden gleam of bayonets in the doorway and rose to be driven with blows and oaths along the weary miles of trail that led to the stockade. Men were seized in their fields, or going along the road, women were taken from their [spinning] wheels and children from their play. In many cases, on turning for one last look as they crossed the ridge they saw their homes in flames, fired by the lawless rabble that followed on the heels of the soldiers to loot and pillage.

The removal, the $6 million cost of which was deducted from the $9 million awarded the tribe for its eastern lands, brought death to perhaps a quarter of the 15,000 who set out. The Cherokee remember this event as the "Trail of Tears." Other southern and some northwestern tribes between 1821 and 1840 shared a similar fate. Although both Jackson and the Removal Act of 1830 had promised to protect and forever guarantee the Indian lands in the west, within a generation those promises, like others before and since, would be broken.

Indian removal left the eastern United States open for the enormous economic expansion described in Chapters 10 and 11. On the question of internal improvements to support that expansion, Jackson also imposed his enormous will.

When proposals for federal support for internal improvements seemed to rob local and state authorities of their proper function, Jackson, a firm believer in states' rights, opposed them. But projects of national significance, like the building of lighthouses or river improvements, were different matters. In fact, Jackson supported an annual average of $1.3 million in internal improvements while he was in office.

In a period of rapid economic change, tariffs were a matter of heated debate. New England and the Middle Atlantic states, the center of manufacturing operations, favored protective tariffs. But the South had long opposed such tariffs because they made it more expensive for southerners to buy manufactured goods from the North or abroad. Feelings against the high protective "Tariff of Abominations" were particularly strong in South Carolina, which was suffering from an economic depression.

Vice President John C. Calhoun, a brilliant political thinker from South Carolina, who aimed to defend southern agrarian interests against the more industrialized North, argued that minority rights could be protected by seeing the nation as "a confederacy of equal and sovereign states." In 1828, the same year as the hateful tariff, Calhoun published an anonymous essay, *Exposition and Protest,* which presented the doctrine of nullification as a means by which the southern states could protect themselves from harmful national action. According to this doctrine, when federal laws were deemed to overstep the limits of constitutional authority, a state had the right to declare that legislation null and void within its borders and refuse to enforce it.

In 1830, at a Jefferson birthday dinner, President Jackson declared himself on the issue. Despite his support of states' rights, Jackson did not believe that any state had the right to reject the will of the majority or to destroy the Union. He rose for a toast, held high his glass, and said, "Our Union—it must be preserved." Not to be outdone, Calhoun followed with his toast: "The Union—next to our liberty most dear." The split between them widened, and in 1833 Calhoun resigned as vice president. Final rupture came in a collision over the tariff and nullification.

In 1832, following Jackson's recommendation of a "middle course" for tariff revisions, Congress modified the tariff of 1828 by retaining high duties on goods such as wool, woolens, iron, and hemp and lowering other rates to an earlier level. Many southerners felt injured. In a special convention later that year in South Carolina, the delegates adopted an Ordinance of Nullification, declaring that the offending tariffs of 1828 and 1832 were null and void in that state. None of the duties would be collected. Furthermore, South Carolina threatened secession if the federal government should try to force the state to comply.

South Carolina's actions represented a direct attack on the concepts of federal union and majority rule. Jackson responded with a proclamation which stated emphatically that "the laws of the United States must be executed.... The Union will be preserved and treason and rebellion promptly put down."

Jackson's proclamation stimulated an outburst of patriotism and popular support all over the country. No other southern states supported nullification, and several state legislatures denounced it. South Carolina stood alone. When

Jackson asked Congress for legislation to enforce tariff duties (the Force Bill of 1833), the crisis neared resolution. Tariff revisions, engineered by Henry Clay and supported by Calhoun, called for reductions over a ten-year period. South Carolina quickly repealed its nullification of the tariff laws but saved face by nullifying the Force Bill at the same time, an act that Jackson ignored. The crisis was over, but left unresolved were the constitutional issues it raised.

Jackson's Bank War and "Van Ruin's" Depression

As the people's advocate, Jackson could not ignore the Second Bank of the United States, which had been chartered for 20 years in 1816. Jackson believed that the bank threatened the people's liberties and called it a "monster." But the bank was not as irresponsible as Jacksonians imagined.

Guided since 1823 by the aristocratic Nicholas Biddle, the Philadelphia bank and its 29 branches performed many useful financial services and generally played a responsible economic role in an expansionary period. As the nation's largest commercial bank, the U.S. Bank was able to shift funds to different parts of the country as necessary and to influence state banking activity. It restrained state banks from making unwise loans by insisting that they back their notes with specie (gold or silver coin) and by calling in its own loans to these institutions. The bank accepted federal deposits, made commercial loans, and bought and sold government bonds. Businessmen, state bankers needing credit, and nationalist politicians such as Daniel Webster and Henry Clay, who were on the bank's payroll, all favored the bank.

Other Americans, however, led by the president, distrusted the bank. Jackson had long opposed the bank both for personal reasons (a near financial disaster in his own past) and because he and his advisers believed it was the chief example of a special privilege monopoly that hurt the common man—farmers, craftsmen, and debtors.

Aware of Jackson's persisting hostility, Clay and Webster persuaded Biddle to ask Congress to recharter the bank in 1832, four years ahead of schedule. They reasoned that in an election year, Jackson would not risk a veto. The bill to recharter the bank swept through Congress and landed on the president's desk one hot, muggy day in July. "The bank . . . is trying to kill me," he told his running mate, Martin Van Buren, *"but I will kill it."*

Jackson determined not only to veto the bill but also to carry his case to the public. His veto message condemned the bank as undemocratic, un-American, and unconstitutional. He denounced the bank as a dangerous monopoly that helped the rich and harmed "the humble members of society."

The furor over the bank helped to clarify party differences. In the election of 1832, the National Republicans, now becoming known as Whigs to show their opposition to "King Andrew," nominated Henry Clay. Democratic campaign rhetoric pitted Jackson, the people, and democracy against Clay, the bank, and aristocracy. A popular movement known as Anti-Masonry had formed in the 1820s and had become the first third party in American political life and the first to hold a nominating convention. The Anti-Masons' efforts revealed real issues more clearly than the two major parties. The anti-Masonic movement, which began in upstate New York, expressed popular resentments against the elitist Masonic order (Jackson was a member) and other secret societies. At a deeper level, anti-Masonry reflected tensions over commercialization as new groups vied with old families for political power.

When the ballots were counted, Jackson had once again won handsomely, garnering 124,000 more popular votes than the combined total for Clay and the Anti-Mason candidate, William Wirt, who said of Jackson, "He may be President for life if he chooses."

Although the election results suggest that the bank issue actually harmed Jackson, he interpreted the election as a victory for his bank policy and made plans to finish his war with Biddle. The bank still had four years before the charter expired, so Jackson and his advisers decided to weaken the bank by transferring $10 million in government funds to state banks. Although two secretaries of the treasury balked at the removal request as financially unsound, Jackson persisted until he found one, Roger Taney, willing to remove the funds. And when Chief Justice John Marshall, a Whig, died in 1835, Jackson replaced him with Taney.

Jackson's war with Biddle and the bank had serious economic consequences. A wave of speculation in western lands and ambitious new state internal improvement schemes in the mid-1830s led to rising land prices and a flood of paper money. Determined to curtail irresponsible economic activity, in July 1836 Jackson issued the Specie Circular, announcing that the government would accept only gold and silver in payment for public lands. Panicky investors rushed to change paper notes into specie, while banks started to call in loans. The result was the Panic of 1837. Although Jackson was blamed for this rapid monetary expansion followed by sudden deflation in the mid-1830s, international trade problems with Britain and China probably contributed more to the panic and to the ensuing seven years of depression than Jackson's erratic policies.

Whatever the primary cause, Jackson stuck his successor, Martin Van Buren, who was elected in 1836 over a trio of Whig opponents, with an economic crisis. Van Buren had barely taken the oath of office in 1837 when banks and businesses began to collapse. His term as president was marked by a depression so severe that it brought him the unfortunate nickname "Martin Van Ruin." As New York banks suspended credit and began calling in loans, an estimated $6 million was lost on defaulted debts.

By the fall of 1837, one-third of America's

workers were unemployed, and thousands of others found only sporadic, part-time work. Wages fell, while the price of necessities like flour, pork, and coal nearly doubled.

The pride of workers was damped as soup kitchens and bread lines grew faster than jobs. Moreover, the depression destroyed the trade union movement begun a decade earlier, leaving laboring families isolated and defenseless. In 1842, when Philadelphia textile employers lowered wages below subsistence levels, angry handloom weavers broke machinery, destroyed cloth, and wrecked the homes of Irish strike-breakers. Job competition, poverty, and ethnic animosities led to violent clashes in other eastern cities as well, as we saw in Chapter 10.

"How is it," a Philadelphia mechanic asked in 1837, that in a country as rich as the United States so many people were "pinched for the common necessaries of life?" President Van Buren's responses to the social misery behind this question were sympathetic but limited and inadequate. Political participation, as well as church membership, reached new heights during the depression, as Americans sought to alleviate their "gloom and despair."

The Second American Party System

By the mid-1830s, a new two-party system and a lively participatory national political culture had emerged in the United States. Although both parties included wealthy and influential, even despotic leaders, the Democrats had the better claim that they were the party of the common man with strength in all sections of the country.

Whigs represented greater wealth than Democrats and were strongest in New England and in areas settled by New Englanders across the Upper Midwest. Whigs generally favored a national bank, federally supported internal improvements, and tariff protection for industry. Artisans and laborers belonged equally to each party, making it difficult to draw clear regional

or class distinctions between Whigs and Democrats. This blurring of party lines among social groups suggests that other factors, such as ethnic, religious, and cultural background, also influenced party choice.

In the Jeffersonian tradition, the Democrats espoused liberty and local rule. They wanted freedom from legislators of morality, from special privilege, and from too much government. Those who wanted to maintain religious or ethnic traditions found a home in the Democratic party. The Scots-Irish, German, French, and Irish Catholic immigrants, as well as free thinkers and labor organizers, tended to be Jacksonians. They were less moralistic than Whigs, especially on matters like temperance and slavery. Democrats sought to keep politics separate from moral issues.

By contrast, for many Whigs the line between reform and politics was hazy. Old-stock New England Yankee Congregationalists and Presbyterians were usually Whigs. So were Quakers and evangelical Protestants, who believed that positive government action could change moral behavior and eradicate sin. Whigs supported a wide variety of reforms, such as temperance, antislavery, public education, and strict observance of the Sabbath, as well as government action to promote economic development.

The election of 1840 illustrated the new style of political culture. Passing over Henry Clay, the Whigs nominated William Henry Harrison of Indiana, the aging hero of the Battle of Tippecanoe (Kithtippecanoe), fought nearly 30 years earlier. A Virginian, John Tyler, was nominated for vice president to underline the regional diversity of the party. The Democrats had no choice but to renominate Van Buren, who conducted a quiet campaign. The Whig campaign, however, featured every form of popularized appeals for votes—barbecues, torchlight parades, songs, and cartoons. Harrison (who lived in a mansion) was depicted in front of a rural log cabin with a barrel of hard cider, while the

Whigs labeled Van Buren an aristocratic dandy. Harrison reminded voters of General Jackson, and they swept him into office, 234 electoral votes to Van Buren's 60. In one of the largest turnouts in American history, over 80 percent of eligible voters marched to the polls. Commenting on the defeat, a Democratic party journal acknowledged that the Whigs had out-Jacksoned the Jacksonians: "We taught them how to conquer us."

Concern over the new politics outlasted Harrison, who died only a month after taking office. For many Americans, usually Whigs and often women, it was precisely the excesses of Jacksonian politics, most notably intemperance and the inherent violence of slavery, that led them to seek other ways than politics of imposing order and morality on American society. To gain a measure of control over their lives and reshape their changing world, the American people turned also to religion, social reform, and utopianism.

RELIGIOUS REVIVAL AND REFORM PHILOSOPHY

When the Frenchman Alexis de Tocqueville visited the United States in 1831 and 1832, he observed that he could find "no country in the whole world in which the Christian religion retains a greater influence over the souls of men than in America." What de Tocqueville was describing was a new and powerful religious enthusiasm among the American people.

Finney and the Second Great Awakening

From the late 1790s until the late 1830s, a wave of religious revivals that matched the intensity of the Great Awakening in the 1730s and 1740s swept through the United States. The camp meeting revivals of the frontier at the turn of the century and the New England revivals sparked by Lyman Beecher took on a new emphasis and location after 1830. Led by the spellbinding Charles G. Finney, revivalism shifted to upstate New York and the Old Northwest. Both areas had been experiencing profound economic and social changes, as the example of Rochester, New York, suggests.

By the 1830s, Rochester, like Lowell and Cincinnati, was a rapidly growing American city. Its location on the recently completed Erie Canal changed Rochester from a sleepy little village of 300 in 1815 to a bustling commercial and milling city of nearly 20,000 inhabitants by 1830. Saloons and unions sprang up in workingmen's neighborhoods, and workers became more transient, following the canal and other opportunities westward.

Prominent Rochester citizens, sensing a widening gulf between laborers and their masters, invited Charles Finney to come to town in 1830 to deliver some sermons. What followed was one of the most successful revivals of the Second Great Awakening. For six months Rochester went through a citywide prayer meeting in which one conversion led to another. The Rochester revival was part of the wave of religious enthusiasm in America that contributed to the tremendous growth of the Methodists, the Baptists, and other evangelical sects in the first half of the nineteenth century.

Most revivalists, especially in the South, sought individual salvation. The Finney revivals, however, were unique in that they nourished collective reform. Finney taught that humans were not passive objects of God's predestined plan but moral free agents who could choose good over evil, convince others to do the same, and thereby eradicate sin from the world. Conversion and salvation were not the end of religious experience but the beginning. Finney's idea of the "utility of benevolence" meant not only individual reformation but also the commitment to reform society. The Bible commanded humans, "Be ye therefore perfect even as your Father in heaven is perfect," and mid-nineteenth-century reformers took the challenge seriously.

Reform and Politics

The reform impulse ultimately involved antebellum activists in the broader politics of the Jacksonian era. Reformers and party politicians, especially Whigs, both faced timeless dilemmas about how best to effect change. Does one, for example, try to change attitudes first and then behavior, or the reverse? Which is more effective, to appeal to people's minds and hearts in order to change bad institutions or to change institutions first, assuming that altered behavior will change hearts and attitudes? Reformers, moreover, have to decide whether to attempt to improve on a partly defective system or tear down the entire system in order to build a utopian new one; whether to use or recommend force; and whether to enter into coalitions with less principled potential allies.

Advocates of change also experience enormous pressures, recriminations, and persecution, as Marius and Emily Robinson learned. Nevertheless, their duty to themselves, their society, and God sustains their commitment.

The Transcendentalists

No one knew this better than Ralph Waldo Emerson, a Concord, Massachusetts, essayist who was the era's foremost intellectual figure. The small but influential group of New England intellectuals who lived near Emerson were called Transcendentalists because of their belief that truth was found beyond experience in intuition. Casting off the European intellectual tradition, Emerson urged Americans to look inward and to nature for self-knowledge, self-reliance, and the spark of divinity burning within all persons. "To acquaint a man with himself," he wrote, would inspire a "reverence" for self and others, which would then lead outward to social reform.

"What is man born for," Emerson wrote, "but to be a Reformer?"

The Transcendentalists questioned not only slavery, an obvious evil, but also the obsessive competitive pace of economic life, the overriding concern for materialism, and the restrictive conformity of social life.

Although not considered Transcendentalists, Nathaniel Hawthorne and Herman Melville, two giants of midcentury American literature, also reflected these concerns in their fiction. In his greatest novel, *The Scarlet Letter* (1850), Hawthorne sympathetically told the story of a courageous Puritan woman's adultery and her eventual loving triumph over the narrowness of both cold intellect and intolerant social conformity.

Herman Melville's epic novel *Moby Dick* (1851), at one level a rousing story of pursuit of the great white whale, was actually an immense allegory of good and evil, bravery and weakness, innocence and experience. Like Emerson, Hawthorne and Melville mirrored the tensions of the age as they explored issues of freedom and control.

When Emerson wrote, "Whoso would be a man, must be a nonconformist," he described his friend Henry David Thoreau. On July 4, 1845, Thoreau went to live in a small hut by Walden Pond, near Concord, to confront "the essential facts of life." When Thoreau left Walden two years later, he protested against slavery and the Mexican War by refusing to pay his taxes. He went to jail briefly and wrote an essay, "On Civil Disobedience" (1849), and a book, *Walden* (1854), which are still considered classic statements of what one person can do to protest unjust laws and wars and live a life of principle.

UTOPIAN COMMUNITARIANISM

Thoreau tried to lead an ideal solitary life. Other reformers sought to create perfect communities. Emerson noted in 1840 that he hardly met a thinking, reading man who did not have "a draft of a new community in his waistcoat pocket."

Oneida and the Shakers

One such man was John Humphrey Noyes of Putney, Vermont, an instant, if unorthodox, convert of Charles Finney. Noyes believed that the act of final conversion led to absolute perfection and complete release from sin. Among those who were perfect, he argued, all men and women belonged equally to one another. For Noyes, complete sharing in family relationships was a step toward perfect cooperation and shared wealth in socioeconomic relationships. Others called his heretical doctrines "free love" and socialism. Noyes married a loyal follower, and when she delivered four stillborn children within six years, he revised even further his unconventional ideas about sex.

In 1848, Noyes and 51 devoted followers founded a "perfectionist" community at Oneida, New York. Sexual life at the commune was subject to many regulations, including sexual restraint and male continence except under carefully prescribed conditions. In a system of planned reproduction, only certain spiritually advanced males (usually Noyes) were allowed to father children. Other controversial practices included communal child rearing, sexual equality in work, the removal of the competitive spirit from both work and play, and an elaborate program of "mutual criticism" at community meetings presided over by "Father" Noyes.

The Oneida community grew and prospered through manufacturing. Oneida specialized at first in the fabrication of steel animal traps and later diversified into making silverware. Eventually abandoning religion to become a joint-stock company in which individual members held shares, Oneida thrived for many years and continues today as a silverware company.

Noyes greatly admired another group of communitarians, the Shakers, who also believed in perfectionism, the surrender of all worldly property to the community, and the devotion of one's labor and love to bringing about the millennial kingdom of heaven. But unlike the Oneidans, Shakers viewed sexuality as a sin and believed in absolute chastity, trusting in conversions to perpetuate their sect. They believed that God had a dual personality, male and female, and that their founder, Mother Ann Lee, was the female counterpart to the masculine Christ. The Shaker worship service featured frenetic dancing intended to release (or "shake") sin out through the fingertips. Shaker communities, some of which still survive, were characterized by communal ownership of property, the equality of women and men, simplicity, and beautifully crafted furniture.

Other Utopias

In an era of disruptive economic and social change, over 100 utopian communities like Oneida and the Shaker colonies were founded. Some were religiously motivated; others were secular. Most were small and lasted only a few months or years. All eventually failed.

Pietist German-speaking immigrants founded the earliest utopian communities in America to preserve their language, spirituality, and ascetic life style. The most notable of these were the Ephrata colonists in Pennsylvania, the Harmonists in Indiana, the Zoar community in Ohio, and the Amana Society in Iowa. In 1840, Adin Ballou founded Hopedale in Massachusetts as "a miniature Christian republic" based on the ethical teachings of Jesus. Hopedale's newspaper, *The Practical Christian,* advocated temperance, pacifism, women's rights, and other reforms.

The secular communities responded more directly to the social misery and wretched working conditions accompanying the industrial revolution. They believed that altered environments rather than new morals would eliminate or reduce poverty, ignorance, intemperance, and other ugly by-products of industrialism.

In 1824, Robert Owen, a Scottish industrialist, founded New Harmony in Indiana. But

In this sacred Shaker dance, sin is being shaken out of the body through the fingertips. Note the separation of women and men.

problems rather than harmony prevailed. Overcrowding, lazy and uncooperative members, Owen's frequent absences, splintered goals, and financial mismanagement ruined New Harmony within three years.

Brook Farm, founded by two Concord friends of Emerson, Bronson Alcott and George Ripley, was an experiment in integrating "intellectual and manual labor." Residents would hoe in the fields and shovel manure for a few hours each day and then study literature and recite poetry. The colony lasted less than three years.

Whether secular or religious, the utopian communities all failed for similar reasons. Americans seemed ill-suited to communal living and work responsibilities and were unwilling to share either their property or their spouses with others. Nor was celibacy greeted with much enthusiasm. Other recurring problems included unstable leadership, financial bickering, the hostility of local citizens, the indiscriminate admission of members, and a waning of enthusiasm after initial settlement. Emerson pinned the failure of the communities on their inability to confront the individualistic impulses of human nature. As he said of Brook Farm, "It met every test but life itself." That could serve as an epitaph for all the utopian communities.

Millerites and Mormons

If utopian communities failed to bring about the millennium, an alternative hope was to leap directly past the thousand years of peace and harmony to the Second Coming of Christ. William Miller, a shy farmer from upstate New York, became so absorbed with the idea of the imminent coming of Christ that he figured out mathematically the exact time of the event: 1843, probably in March. A religious sect, the Millerites, gathered around him to prepare for Christ's return and the Day of Judgment. When 1843 passed without the expected end, Miller and his followers recalculated and set a series of alternative dates. Each new disappointment diminished Miller's followers, and he died in 1848 a discredited man.

Other groups that emerged from the same religiously active area of upstate New York were more successful. As Palmyra, New York, was being swept by Finney revivalism, young Joseph Smith, a recent convert, claimed to be visited by the angel Moroni. According to Smith, Moroni led him to golden tablets buried in the ground near his home. On these plates were inscribed more than 500 pages of *The Book of Mormon,* which described the one true church and a "lost tribe of Israel" missing for centuries. The book also predicted the appearance of an American prophet who would establish a new and pure kingdom of Christ in America. Smith published his book in 1830 and soon founded the Church of Jesus Christ of Latter-day Saints.

Smith and a steadily growing band of converts migrated successively to Ohio and Missouri and then back to Illinois. Despite ridicule, persecution, and violence, the Mormons prospered and increased. By the mid-1840s, Nauvoo, Illinois, with a thriving population of nearly 15,000, was the showplace of Mormonism. Smith petitioned Congress for separate territorial status and ran for the presidency in 1844. This was too much for the citizens of nearby towns. Violence escalated and culminated in Smith's trial for treason and his murder by a mob. Under the brilliant leadership of Smith's successor, Brigham Young, the Mormons headed westward in 1846 in their continuing search for the "land of promise."

REFORMING SOCIETY

Most Americans sought to bring about "the promised land" by focusing in a practical way on a specific social evil rather than by embracing whole new religions or joining utopian colonies.

"We are all a little wild here," Emerson wrote in 1840, "with numberless projects of social reform." The reformers, including thousands of women, created and joined all kinds of societies for social betterment. They addressed such issues as alcohol consumption; diet and health; sexuality; institutional treatment of the mentally ill, the disabled, paupers, and criminals; education; the rights of labor; slavery; and women's rights.

Temperance

On New Year's Eve in 1831, a Finney disciple, Theodore Dwight Weld, delivered a four-hour temperance lecture in Rochester. In graphic detail he described the awful fate of those who refused to stop drinking and urged his audience not only to cease their tippling but to stop others as well. Several were converted to abstinence on the spot. The next day, Elijah and Albert Smith, the largest providers of whiskey in Rochester, rolled their barrels out onto the sidewalk and smashed them. Cheering Christians applauded as the whiskey ran out into Exchange Street.

Americans in the nineteenth century drank heavily. One man observed that "a house could not be raised, a field of wheat cut down, nor could there be a log rolling, a husking, a quilting, a wedding, or a funeral without the aid of alcohol." The corrosive effects of drinking were obvious: poverty, crime, illness, insanity, battered and broken families, and corrupt politics.

Religion, Reform, and Utopian Activity, 1830–1850

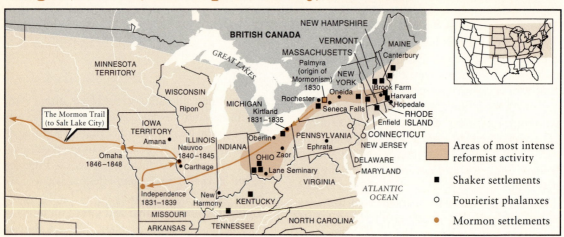

Early efforts at curbing alcohol consumption emphasized moderation. But the American Temperance Society, founded in 1826, was dedicated to total abstinence. Within a few years, thousands of local and state societies had formed, though some refused to prohibit drinking of hard cider and communion wine.

Temperance advocates copied successful revival techniques. Fiery lecturers expounded on the evil consequences of drink and distributed a deluge of graphic and sometimes gory temperance tracts.

By 1840, disagreements over goals and methods split the temperance movement into many separate organizations. The Washington Temperance Society, founded in a Baltimore tavern in 1840, was enormously popular with unemployed young workers and grew to an estimated 600,000 members in three years. The Washingtonians, arguing that alcoholism was a disease rather than moral failure, changed the shape of the temperance movement. They replaced revivalist techniques with those of the new party politics by organizing parades, picnics, melodramas, and festivals to encourage people to take the pledge.

Tactics in the 1840s also shifted away from moral suasion to political action. Temperance societies lobbied for local option laws, which allowed communities to prohibit the sale, manufacture, and consumption of alcohol. The Maine law in 1851 was the first in the nation. Fifteen other states followed with similar laws before the Civil War. Despite weak enforcement, the per capita consumption of alcohol declined dramatically in the 1850s. Interrupted by the Civil War, the movement did not reach its ultimate objective until passage of the Eighteenth Amendment to the Constitution in 1919.

The temperance crusade reveals the many practical motivations that attracted Americans to join reform societies. For some, as in Rochester, temperance provided an opportunity for the Protestant middle classes to exert some control over laborers, immigrants, and Catholics. For perfectionists, abstinence was a way of practicing self-control and reaching moral perfection. For many young men, especially after the onset of the depression of 1837, a temperance society provided entertainment, fellowship, and contacts to help their careers. In temperance societies as in political parties, Americans found jobs, purpose, support, spouses, and relief from the loneliness and uncertainty of a changing world.

For many women, the temperance effort was a respectable way to control the behavior of drunken men who beat wives and daughters. The movement also educated some women about their own political weakness. Women such as Susan B. Anthony, who worked as an organizer in the temperance movement, found a wall of prejudice against women's active participation. She also became aware that women could not provide effective financial support to a cause as long as their husbands controlled their earnings. (Several more decades elapsed before

the founding in 1874 of the Women's Christian Temperance Union. See Chapter 19.)

Health and Sexuality

It was a short step from the physical and psychological ravages of drink to other potentially harmful effects on the body. Reformers were quick to attack excessive eating, use of stimulants of any kind, and, above all, the evils of too much sexual activity. Many endorsed a variety of special diets and exercise programs for maintaining good health. Some promoted panaceas for all ailments. One of these was hydropathy:

The temperance movement of the 1830s and 1840s used the tactics of religious revivalists to scare drinkers into taking the "teetotal" pledge. Who could resist this poignant 1846 portrayal of The Drunkard's Progress?

Clients sojourned at one of 70 special resorts for bathing and water purges of the body.

Another movement concerned sexual purity. In 1834, Sylvester Graham, a promoter of proper diet and hygiene, delivered a series of lectures on chastity, later published as a manual of advice. To those "troubled" by sexual desire, the inventor of the Graham cracker recommended taking "more active exercise in the open air" and using "the cold bath under proper circumstances." Women were advised to remain pure and to "have intercourse only for procreation."

The authors of antebellum "health" manuals advocated abstinence from sexual activity as vehemently as they recommended abstinence from alcohol. Semen was to be saved for reproductive purposes and should not be used for pleasure in either masturbation or intercourse. Such use, maintained the manuals on sexual purity, would lead to enervation, disease, insanity, and death. Some argued further that the "expenditure" of sperm meant a loss of needed energy from the economy. One doctor argued that women ought not to be educated because blood needed for the womb would be diverted to the head, thus breeding "puny men."

Humanizing the Asylum

In their effort to restore order to American society, some reformers preferred to work not for private influence over individuals but toward public changes in institutions. They wanted to transform such social institutions as asylums, almshouses, prisons, schools, and even factories. In many ways, Horace Mann, who led the struggle for common schools in Massachusetts (see Chapter 10), was a typical antebellum reformer. He blended dedicated idealism with a canny, practical sense of how to institutionalize educational improvements in one state: teacher training schools, higher teachers' salaries, and compulsory attendance laws.

Other reformers were less successful in achieving their goals. This was especially true of

the treatment of society's outcasts. In 1843, Dorothea Dix, a frail New Englander, horrified the Massachusetts legislature with her famous report that imprisoned insane persons in the state were subject to "the extremest state of degradation and misery." They were confined in "cages, closets, stalls, pens! Chained, naked, beaten with rods, and lashed into obedience!" Dix recommended special hospitals or asylums where the insane could be "humanly and properly controlled" by trained attendants.

Many perfectionist reformers like Dix believed that special asylums could reform society's outcasts. But all too often, results were disappointing. Prison reformers believed that a properly built and administered penitentiary could bring a hardened criminal "back to virtue." Some assumed that by putting "penitents" into isolated cells to study the Bible and reflect on their wrongdoing, they would eventually decide to become good citizens. In practice, many criminals simply went mad or committed suicide. The institutions built by well-intentioned reformers became dumping places for society's outcasts. By midcentury, American prisons and mental asylums had become the impersonal, understaffed, overcrowded institutions we know today.

Working-Class Reform

For working-class Americans, the social institution most in need of transformation was the factory. Workers, many of whom were involved in other issues such as temperance, peace, and abolitionism, took it upon themselves to improve their own lives. As labor leader Seth Luther told a meeting of New England mechanics and laborers, "We must take our business into our own hands. Let us awake." And awake they did, forming both trade unions and workingmen's parties as Andrew Jackson neared the presidency.

Between 1828 and 1832, dozens of workingmen's parties were formed, advocating such programs as free, tax-supported schools, free public lands in the West, equal rights for the poor, and the elimination of all monopolistic privilege. Trade union activity began in Philadelphia in 1827 as skilled workers organized journeymen carpenters, plasterers, printers, weavers, tailors, and other tradesmen. That same year, 15 unions combined into a citywide federation, a process followed in other cities. The National Trades Union, founded in 1834, was the first attempt at a national labor organization.

The trade unions called for shorter hours, wages that would keep pace with rising prices, and ways (such as the closed shop) of warding off the competitive threat of cheap labor. In addition, both workers and their middle-class interlocutors called for the abolition of imprisonment for debt and of compulsory militia duty, both of which often cost workers their jobs; free public education; improved living conditions in workers' neighborhoods; and the right to organize.

With union membership of near 300,000, workers struck some 168 times between 1834 and 1836, usually for higher wages. The Panic of 1837 and the ensuing depression dashed the hopes and efforts of American workers. But the organizational work of the 1830s promised that the labor movement would reemerge with greater strength later in the century.

ABOLITIONISM AND WOMEN'S RIGHTS

As American workers struggled in Lowell and other eastern cities for better wages and hours in 1834, Emily and Marius Robinson arrived in Cincinnati to fight for their causes. They had been attracted there, along with scores of other young idealists, by the newly founded Lane Seminary, a school to train abolitionist leaders. Lane soon became a center of reformist activity. When nervous local residents persuaded President Lyman Beecher to crack down on the students,

40 "Lane rebels," led by Theodore Weld, fled to Oberlin in northern Ohio. As the Robinsons remained in southern Ohio, the group in the north turned Oberlin College into the first institution in the United States open equally to women and men, blacks and whites. Thus the movements to abolish slavery and to grant equal rights to women and free blacks were joined. Whether seeking to eliminate coercion in the cotton fields or in the kitchen, reformers faced the dual challenge of pursuing distant and elusive goals while at the same time achieving practical changes in everyday life.

Tensions Within the Antislavery Movement

Although the antislavery movement had a smaller membership than temperance reform, it revealed more clearly the difficulties of trying to achieve significant social change in America. On January 1, 1831, eight months before Nat Turner's revolt, William Lloyd Garrison published the first issue of *The Liberator,* soon to become the leading antislavery journal in the United States. "I am in earnest," he wrote. "I will not equivocate—AND I WILL BE HEARD." After first organizing the New England Anti-Slavery Society with a group of blacks and whites in a church basement in Boston, in 1833 Garrison and 62 others established the American Anti-Slavery Society.

Until Garrison's publication, most people opposed to slavery, other than blacks, had advocated gradual emancipation by individual slave owners and colonization of the freed blacks on the west coast of Africa. Garrison opposed the moderation and gradualism of the colonizationists, declaring that compromise was unthinkable. There would be "no Union with slaveholders," he cried, condemning the Constitution that perpetuated slavery as *"a covenant with death, an agreement with Hell."* The American Anti-Slavery Society called for the immediate and total abolition of slavery. But the abolitionists did not always agree, splitting into factions over ideological differences between colonizationists, gradualists, and immediatists.

Abolitionists also differed over the tactics of ending slavery. Their primary method was moral suasion, by which they sought to convince slaveholders and their supporters that slavery was a sin. In an outpouring of sermons, petitions, resolutions, pamphlets, and speeches, abolitionists tried to overwhelm slaveholders with moral guilt to get them to free their slaves as an act of repentance. In 1839, Weld published *American Slavery As It Is,* which described in gory detail every conceivable form of inhumane treatment of the slaves.

Other abolitionists preferred more direct methods. Some brought antislavery petitions before Congress or formed third parties. Another tactic was to boycott goods made by slave labor. A fourth approach, although rare, was to call for slave rebellion, as did two northern blacks, David Walker in a pamphlet in 1829 and Henry Highland Garnet in a speech at a convention of black Americans in 1843.

Disagreement over tactics helped to splinter the abolitionist movement. Class differences and race further divided abolitionists. Northern workers, though fearful of the job competition implications of emancipation, nevertheless saw their "wage slavery" as similar to chattel slavery. Strains between northern labor leaders and middle-class abolitionists, who minimized the seriousness of workingmen's concerns, were similar to those between white and black antislavery forces. Whites like Wendell Phillips decried slavery as a moral blot on American society, while blacks like Douglass were more concerned with the effects of slavery and discrimination on black people. Moreover, white abolitionists tended to see slavery and freedom as absolute moral opposites: A person was either slave or free. Blacks, however, knew that there were degrees of freedom and that discriminatory restrictions on freedom existed for blacks in the North just as did relative degrees of servitude in the South.

Furthermore, black abolitionists themselves experienced prejudice, not just from ordinary northern citizens but also from their white abolitionist colleagues, many of whom refused to hire black workers. One free black described a white abolitionist as one who hated slavery, "especially that slavery which is 1000 to 1500 miles away," but who hated even more "a man who wears a black skin."

The celebrated conflict between Garrison and Douglass reflected these tensions. The famous runaway slave was one of the most effective orators in the movement. But after a while, rather than simply describing his life as a slave, Douglass began skillfully to analyze abolitionist policies. Garrison warned him that audiences would not believe he had ever been a slave, and other whites told him to stick to the facts and let them take care of the philosophy. Douglass gradually moved away from Garrison's views, endorsing political action and sometimes even slave rebellion.

Moving beyond Garrison, a few black nationalists, like the fiery Martin Delany, totally rejected white American society and advocated emigration and a new destiny in Africa. Most blacks, however, agreed with Douglass to work to end slavery and discrimination in the United States, which, for better or worse, was their home. These black leaders organized a National Negro Convention Movement, which began annual meetings in 1830. They met not only to condemn slavery but also to discuss concrete issues of discrimination facing free blacks in the North.

Flood Tide of Abolitionism

Black and white abolitionists, however, agreed more than they disagreed and usually worked together well. They supported each other's publications, stayed in each other's homes when they traveled, and cooperated on the underground railroad.

The two races worked together fighting discrimination as well as slavery. When David Ruggles was dragged from the "white car" of a New Bedford, Massachusetts, railway in 1841, Garrison, Douglass, and 40 other protesters organized what may have been the first successful integrated "sit-in" act of civil disobedience in American history. Blacks and whites also worked harmoniously in protesting segregated schools. In 1855, Massachusetts became the first state to outlaw segregated public education.

White and black abolitionists united in defending themselves against the attacks of people who regarded them as dangerous fanatics. Mob attacks like the one on Marius Robinson in Ohio in 1836 occurred frequently in the mid-1830s. Abolitionists were stoned, dragged through streets, ousted from their jobs and homes, and reviled by northern mobs, often led or encouraged by leading citizens. Theodore Weld, known as "the most mobbed man in the United States," could hardly finish a speech without disruption. In 1837, an antislavery editor in Illinois, Elijah Lovejoy, was murdered and his printing press destroyed.

Antiabolitionists were as fervid as the abolitionists themselves and equally determined to publicize their cause. "I warn the abolitionists, ignorant and infatuated barbarians as they are," growled one South Carolinian, "that if chance shall throw any of them into our hands, they may expect a felon's death." President Jackson denounced the abolitionists in his annual message in 1835 as "incendiaries" who deserved to have their "unconstitutional and wicked" activities broken up by mobs. The president went on to urge Congress to ban antislavery literature from the U.S. mails. A year later, southern Democratic congressmen, with the crucial support of Van Buren, succeeded in passing a "gag rule," which stopped the flood of abolitionists petitions in Congress until the rule was repealed in 1844.

By the 1840s, many northerners, including many workers otherwise unsympathetic to the goal of ending slavery, decried the mob violence, supported the right of free speech, and denounced the South and its northern defenders as undemocratic. The gag rule, interference with the mails, and the killing of Lovejoy seemed proof of the growing pernicious influence of slave power.

Women's Rights

Another important source of tension within the antislavery movement was disagreement over the participation of women. In an age when women were not supposed to speak in public, those who dared to do so encountered rude and humiliating treatment. The reception women experienced in the antislavery movement directly inspired some of them to launch a campaign for women's rights.

Abby Kelley, a young teacher in Massachusetts in 1836, circulated petitions for the local antislavery society. She came to reform from revivalism and in 1837 wrote, " 'Tis a great joy to see the world grow better. . . . Indeed I think endeavors to improve mankind is the only object worth living for." A year later, she braved the threats of an angry crowd in Philadelphia by delivering an abolitionist speech to a convention of antislavery women. Her speech was so eloquent that Weld told her that if she did not join the movement full time, "God will smite you." Before the convention was over, a mob, incensed by both abolitionists and women speaking in public, attacked with stones and torches and burned the hall to the ground.

After a soul-searching year, Kelley left teaching to devote all her efforts to antislavery and women's rights. When she married Stephen Foster, she retained her own name and went on lecture tours of the West while her husband stayed home to care for their daughter.

Angelina and Sarah Grimké, two demure but outspoken Quaker sisters from Philadelphia who had grown up in slaveholding South Carolina, went to New England in 1837 to lecture to disapproving audiences on behalf of abolitionism and the rights of women. After the tour, Angelina married Theodore Weld and stopped her public speaking to show that she could also be a good wife and mother.

Young couples like Grimké and Weld, the Robinsons, and Kelley and Foster, while pursuing reform, experimented with equal private relationships in an age that assigned distinctly unequal roles to husbands and wives.

Catharine Beecher argued that it was by accepting marriage and the home as woman's sphere and by mastering domestic duties there that women could best achieve moral power and autonomy. In another form of "domestic feminism," American wives exerted considerable control over their own bodies by convincing their husbands to practice abstinence, coitus interruptus, and other forms of birth control. Some women found an outlet for their role as moral guardians by attacking the sexual double standard. They worked to convert prostitutes to evangelical Protestantism and to close houses of prostitution.

Women reformers sought more legally protected equal rights with men. Campaigns to secure married women control of their property and custody of their children involved many women, who discovered striking similarities between their own oppression and that of slaves. American women "have good cause to be grateful to the slave," Kelley wrote, for in "striving to strike his iron off, we found most surely, that we were manacled *ourselves.*"

Activist antislavery women encountered hostility, especially from clergymen, who quoted the Bible to justify female inferiority and servility. Sarah Grimké struck back in 1837 with a series called *Letters on the Condition of Women and the Equality of the Sexes,* claiming that "men and women were CREATED EQUAL" and that "whatever is *right* for man to do, is *right* for woman."

Male abolitionists were divided about women's rights. At the World Anti-Slavery Con-

vention in 1840, attended by many American abolitionists, the delegates refused to let women participate. Two upstate New Yorkers, Elizabeth Cady Stanton and Lucretia Mott, were compelled to sit behind curtains and not even be seen, much less be permitted to speak. When they returned home, they resolved to "form a society to advocate the rights of women." In 1848, in Seneca Falls, New York, their intentions, though delayed, were fulfilled in one of the most significant protest gatherings of the antebellum era.

In preparing for the meeting, Mott and Stanton drew up a list of women's grievances. They discovered that even though some states had awarded married women control over their property, they still had none over their earnings. Modeling their Declaration of Sentiments on the Declaration of Independence, the women at Seneca Falls proclaimed it a self-evident truth that "all men and women are created equal," and that men had usurped women's freedom and dignity. A man, the Declaration of Sentiments charged, "endeavored in every way he could, to destroy [woman's] confidence in her own powers, to lessen her self-respect, and to make her willing to lead a dependent and abject life." The remedy was expressed in 11 resolutions calling for equal opportunities in education and work, equality before the law, and the right to appear on public platforms. The most controversial resolution called for women's "sacred right to the elective franchise." The convention approved Mott and Stanton's list of resolutions.

Throughout the 1850s, led by Stanton and Susan B. Anthony, women continued to meet in annual conventions, working by resolution, persuasion, and petition campaign to achieve equal political, legal, and property rights with men. The right to vote, however, was considered the cornerstone of the movement. It remained so for 72 years of struggle until 1920, when passage of the Nineteenth Amendment made woman suffrage part of the Constitution. The Seneca Falls convention was crucial in beginning the cam-

Elizabeth Cady Stanton (1815–1902) and Lucretia Mott (1793–1880) were the leaders of the 1848 gathering for women's rights at Seneca Falls, New York.

paign for equal public rights. The seeds of gaining psychological autonomy and self-respect, however, were sown in the struggles of countless women like Abby Kelley, Sarah Grimké, and Emily Robinson. The struggle for that kind of liberation continues today.

CONCLUSION

PERFECTING AMERICA

Advocates for women's rights and temperance, abolitionists, and other reformers carried on very different crusades from those waged by Andrew Jackson against Indians, nullificationists, and the U.S. Bank. In fact, Jacksonian politics and antebellum reform were often at odds. Most abolitionists and temperance reformers were anti-Jackson Whigs. Jackson and most Democrats repudiated the passionate moralism of reformers.

Yet both sides shared an abiding faith in change and the idea of progress. Whether inspired by religious revivalism or political party loyalty, both believed that by stamping out evil forces, they could shape a better America.

As the United States neared midcentury,

slavery emerged as the most divisive issue. Although both major political parties tried to evade the question, westward expansion and the addition of new territories to the nation would soon make avoidance impossible. Would new states be slave or free? The question increasingly aroused the deepest passions of the American people. For the pioneer family, the driving force behind the westward movement, however, questions involving their fears and dreams seemed more important. We turn to this family and that movement in the next chapter.

Recommended Reading

Richard McCormick, *The Second Party System: Party Formation in the Jacksonian Era* (1966); and Richard Latner, *The Presidency of Andrew Jackson: White House Politics, 1829–1837* (1979), are the definitive works on those topics. See also Richard Ellis, *The Union at Risk: Jacksonian Democracy, States' Rights, and The Nullification Crisis* (1987); Ronald Formisano, *The Transformation of Political Culture* (1983); and Jean Baker, *Affairs of Party* (1983). On Jackson's popular appeal, see two books by Robert Remini, *Andrew Jackson and the Course of American Freedom, 1822–1832* (1981), and *Andrew Jackson and the Course of American Democracy* (1984). Jackson's political opponents are best understood by reading biographies of his major rivals: Clement Eaton, *Henry Clay and the Art of American Politics* (1957); Irving H. Bartlett, *Daniel Webster* (1978); and Margaret Coit, *John P. Calhoun: American Portrait* (1950).

The best single volume on antebellum religion and reform is Ronald Walters, *American Reformers, 1815–1860* (1978). A fascinating account of revivalism is William McLoughlin, *Modern Revivalism: From Charles G. Finney to Billy Graham* (1959). Paul Johnson, *A Shopkeeper's Millennium: Society and Revivals in Rochester, New York, 1815–1837* (1978), details the social impact of both economic change and revivalism in one community. To understand the Transcendentalists, read Perry Miller, ed., *The Transcendentalists* (1957), or Thoreau's *Walden*.

The standard work on utopian communities is Arthur Bestor, *Backwoods Utopias* (1950); but John Humphrey Noyes's *History of American Socialisms* (1870) is indispensable.

On the temperance crusade, see Ian Tyrrell, *Sobering Up: From Temperance to Prohibition in Antebellum America, 1800–1860* (1979). The experience of most efforts at institutional reforms is superbly analyzed in David Rothman, *The Discovery of the Asylum: Social Order and Disorder in the New Republic* (1971). Working-class reformers are the focus in Edward Pessen, *Most Uncommon Jacksonians: The Radical Leaders of the Early Labor Movement* (1967). On women's suffrage, see Eleanor Flexner, *Century of Struggle: The Woman's Rights Movement in the United States*, rev. ed. (1975).

Time Line

1824	New Harmony established
1825	John Quincy Adams chosen president by the House of Representatives
1826	American Temperance Society founded
1828	Calhoun publishes *Exposition and Protest*
	Jackson defeats Adams for the presidency
	Tariff of Abominations
1828–1832	Rise of workingmen's parties
1830	Webster-Hayne debate and Jackson-Calhoun toast
	Joseph Smith publishes *The Book of Mormon*
	Indian Removal Act
1830–1831	Charles Finney's religious revivals
1831	Garrison begins publishing *The Liberator*
1832	Jackson vetoes U.S. Bank charter
	Jackson reelected
	Worcester v. Georgia
1832–1833	Nullification crisis
1832–1836	Removal of funds from U.S. Bank to state banks
1833	Force Bill
	Compromise tariff
	Calhoun resigns as vice president
	American Anti-Slavery Society founded
1834	National Trades Union founded
	Whig Party established
1835–1836	Countless incidents of mob violence

1836	"Gag rule"
	Specie circular
	Van Buren elected president
1837	Financial panic and depression
	Sarah Grimké publishes *Letters on the Equality of the Sexes*
	Emerson's "American Scholar" address
1837–1838	Cherokee "Trail of Tears"
1840	William Henry Harrison elected president
	American Anti-Slavery Society splits
	World Anti-Slavery Convention
	Ten-hour day for federal employees
1840–1841	Transcendentalists found Hopedale and Brook Farm
1843	Dorothea Dix's report on treatment of the insane
1844	Joseph Smith murdered in Nauvoo, Illinois
1846–1848	Mormon migration to the Great Basin
1847	First issue of Frederick Douglass's *North Star*
1848	Oneida community founded
	First women's rights convention at Seneca Falls, New York
1850	Nathaniel Hawthorne, *Scarlet Letter*
1851	Maine prohibition law
	Herman Melville, *Moby Dick*
1853	Children's Aid Society established in New York City
1854	Thoreau publishes *Walden*
1855	Massachusetts bans segregated public schools

chapter 13

Moving West

By the 1840s, the frontier was retreating across the Mississippi. As Americans contemplated the lands west of the great river, they debated the question of expansion. Some, like Michigan's senator Lewis Cass, saw the Pacific Ocean as the only limit to territorial expansion. Cass believed that the West represented not only economic opportunity for Americans but political stability for the nation as well. People crowded into cities and confined to limited territories endangered the republic, he told fellow senators in a speech. But if they headed west to convert "the woods and forests into towns and villages and cultivate[d] fields" and to extend "the dominion of civilization and improvement over the domain of nature," they would find rewarding personal opportunities that would ensure political and social harmony.

Thousands of men seconded Cass's sentiments by volunteering to join American forces in the war against Mexico in the summer of 1845. Largely untrained, the companies hurried south. But before long these supporters of expansion saw the ugly side of territorial adventures: insects, bad weather, poor food, unsanitary conditions, and illnesses such as the "black vomit" (yellow fever), dysentery, and diarrhea. As a member of the American occupying army, Henry Judah also experienced the hostility of conquered peoples. In his diary, he reported, "It is dangerous to go out after night. . . . Four of our men were stabbed today."

Thomas Gibson, a captain of Indiana volunteers, described a battlefield "still covered with [Mexican] dead" where "the stench is most horrible." Indiana friends had been killed, and Gibson himself had narrowly escaped. His wife, Mary, had not escaped the heady propaganda for national expansion. She had heard that Indiana soldiers had "shode themselves great cowards by retreating during battle," and she disapproved. "We all would rather you had stood like good soldiers," she told her husband.

Lewis Cass, Henry Judah, Thomas and Mary Gibson, and thousands of other Americans played a part in the nation's expansion into the trans-Mississippi West. The differences and similarities in their perspectives and in their responses to territorial growth unveil the complex nature of the western experience. Lewis Cass's speech illustrates the hold the West had on people's imagination and how some Americans linked expansion to individual opportunity and national progress. Yet his assumption that the West was vacant points to the costs of white expansion for Mexican-Americans and Native Americans.

This chapter concerns movement into the trans-Mississippi West between 1830 and 1865. First, we will consider how and when Americans moved west, by what means the United States acquired the vast territories that in 1840 belonged to other nations, and the meaning of "Manifest Destiny," the slogan used to defend the conquest of the continent west of the Mississippi River. Then, we explore the nature of life on the western farming, mining, and urban frontiers. Finally, the chapter examines responses of Native Americans and Mexican-Americans to expansion and illuminates the ways in which different cultural traditions intersected in the West.

PROBING THE TRANS-MISSISSIPPI WEST

Until the 1840s, most Americans lived east of the Mississippi. The admission of new states between 1815 and 1840 symbolized the steady settlement of the eastern half of the continent. By 1860, some 4.3 million Americans had moved west of the great river.

Foreign Claims and Possessions

With the exception of the Louisiana Territory, Spain held title to most of the trans-Mississippi region in 1815. Spanish holdings stretched south to Mexico and west to the Pacific and included present-day Texas, Arizona, New Mexico, Nevada, Utah, western Colorado, California, and small parts of Wyoming, Kansas, and Oklahoma. When Mexico won its independence from Spain in 1821, it inherited these lands and the 75,000 Spanish-speaking inhabitants and numerous Native Americans living there.

To the north of California was the Oregon country, a vaguely defined area extending from California to Alaska. Both Great Britain and the United States claimed the Oregon country on the basis of explorations in the late eighteenth cen-

tury and fur trading in the early nineteenth. Joint occupation, agreed on in the Convention of 1818 and the Occupation Treaty of 1827, temporarily deferred settling the boundary question.

Traders, Trappers, and Cotton Farmers

Americans made commercial forays into the trans-Mississippi West long before the migrations of the 1840s and 1850s and became familiar with some of its people and terrains. As early as 1811, Americans engaged in the fur trade in Oregon, and within ten years, fur trappers and traders were exploiting the resources of the Rocky Mountain region. By the mid-1830s, trappers had almost exterminated the beaver, but trade in bison robes prepared by the Plains tribes flourished in the area around the upper Missouri River and its tributaries until after 1860.

With the collapse of the Spanish Empire in 1821, American traders were able to penetrate the Southwest. Each year, caravans from "the States" followed the Santa Fe Trail over the plains and mountains, loaded with weapons, tools, and brightly colored calicoes, which they traded for metals and furs.

To the south, in Texas, land for cotton

rather than trade attracted settlers and squatters in the 1820s. By 1835, almost 30,000 Americans were living in Texas, the largest group of Americans living outside the nation's boundaries at that time.

On the Pacific, New England traders acquired California cowhides and tallow in exchange for clothes, boots, hardware, and furniture manufactured in the East.

Among the earliest easterners to settle in the trans-Mississippi West were tribes from the South and the Old Northwest whom the American government forcibly relocated in present-day Oklahoma and Kansas. Ironically, some of these eastern tribes acted as agents of white civilization by introducing cotton, the plantation system, and schools. Other tribes triggered conflicts that weakened the western tribes with whom they came into contact. The Cherokee, Shawnee, and Delaware forced the Osages out of their Missouri and Arkansas hunting grounds, while tribes from the Old Northwest claimed hunting areas long used by Kansas plains tribes. These disruptions foreshadowed white incursions later in the century.

The facts that much of the trans-Mississippi West lay outside U.S. boundaries and that the government had guaranteed Indian tribes permanent possession of some western territories did not curtail American economic activities. By the 1840s, a growing volume of published information fostered dreams of possession. Lansford Hastings's *Emigrants' Guide to Oregon and California* (1845) provided not only the practical information that emigrants would need but also the encouragement that heading for the frontier was the right thing to do.

In his widely read guide, Hastings minimized the importance of Mexican and British sovereignty. His belief that Americans would obtain rights to foreign holdings in the West came true within a decade. In the course of the 1840s, the United States acquired the Southwest and Texas as well as the Oregon country up to the 49th parallel. Later, with the Gadsden Purchase

in 1853, the total area of all these new lands amounted to over 1,500,000 square miles.

Manifest Destiny

Bursts of rhetoric accompanied territorial growth and its slogan, "Manifest Destiny." The phrase, coined in 1845 by the editor of the *Democratic Review,* suggests that the country's superior institutions and culture gave Americans a God-given right to spread their civilization across the entire continent.

This sense of a unique mission was a legacy of early Puritan utopianism and revolutionary republicanism. By the 1840s, however, an argument for territorial expansion merged with the belief that the United States possessed a unique civilization. States could successfully absorb new territories. Publicists of Manifest Destiny proclaimed that the nation must.

WINNING THE TRANS-MISSISSIPPI WEST

Manifest Destiny justified expansion but did not cause it. Concrete events in Texas triggered the national government's determination to acquire territories west of the Mississippi River.

The Texas question originated in the years when Spain held most of the Southwest. Although some settlements such as Santa Fe, founded in 1609, were almost as old as Jamestown, the Spanish considered the sparsely populated and underdeveloped Southwest primarily a buffer zone for Mexico. In the Adams-Onis treaty with Spain in 1819, the United States accepted a southern border excluding Texas, to which the Americans had vague claims stemming from the Louisiana Purchase.

Annexing Texas, 1845

By the time the treaty was ratified in 1821, Mexico had won its independence from Spain. The

United States Territorial Expansion by 1860

Ceded by Great Britain, 1818

Oregon Territory (Treaty of 1846 with Great Britain)

CANADA

NEW HAMPSHIRE

VERMONT

MAINE

MASSACHUSETTS

WISCONSIN

Louisiana Purchase (from France, 1803)

NEW YORK

RHODE ISLAND

MICHIGAN

CONNECTICUT

Mexican Cession (acquired from Mexico, 1848)

ILLINOIS

INDIANA

OHIO

PENNSYLVANIA

NEW JERSEY

Original colonies

DELAWARE

United States after Peace of Paris, 1783

VIRGINIA

MARYLAND

KENTUCKY

NORTH CAROLINA

TENNESSEE

PACIFIC OCEAN

MISSISSIPPI

SOUTH CAROLINA

ATLANTIC OCEAN

Texas Annexation (1845)

ALABAMA

GEORGIA

Gadsden Purchase (from Mexico, 1853)

Louisiana (1810–1813)

Florida Territory (purchased from Spain, 1819)

MEXICO

Gulf of Mexico

---

new nation inherited the borderlands, their people, and their problems. Mexicans soon had reason to fear American expansionism, after several attempts by the United States to buy Texas and continuing aggressive American statements.

In 1823, the Mexican government determined to strengthen border areas by increasing population. To attract settlers, it offered land in return for token payments and pledges to become Roman Catholics and Mexican citizens. Stephen F. Austin, who gained rights to bring 300 families into Texas, was among the first of the American *empresarios,* or contractors, to take advantage of this opportunity. By the end of the decade, some 15,000 white Americans and 1,000 slaves lived in Texas, far outnumbering the 5,000 Mexican inhabitants.

Mexican officials soon questioned their invitation. Few American settlers became Catholics, and they remained more American than Mexi-

can. Some of the settlers disliked Mexican laws and customs, and in late 1826, a small group raised the flag of rebellion and declared the Republic of Fredonia. Although settlers like Austin assisted in putting down the brief uprising, American newspapers hailed the rebels as "apostles of democracy" and called Mexico "an alien civilization."

Mexican anxiety grew apace. In 1829, the Mexican government, determined to curb American influence, abolished slavery in Texas. The next year, it forbade further American immigration, and officials began to collect customs duties on goods crossing the Louisiana border. But little changed in Texas. American slave owners freed their slaves and forced them to sign life indenture contracts. Emigrants still crossed the border and continued to outnumber Mexicans.

Tensions escalated to the brink of war. In October 1835, a skirmish between the colonial militia and Mexican forces signaled the beginning of hostilities. Sam Houston, onetime governor of Tennessee and army officer, became commander in chief of the Texas forces.

Mexican dictator and general Antonio López de Santa Anna hurried north to crush the rebellion with an army of 6,000 conscripts. Santa Anna and his men won the initial engagements of the war: The Alamo at San Antonio fell to him, taking Davy Crockett and Jim Bowie with it. So too did the fortress of Goliad, to the southeast.

As he pursued Houston and the Texans toward the San Jacinto River, carelessness proved Santa Anna's undoing. When the Mexican general and his men settled down to their usual siesta on April 21, 1836, without posting an adequate guard, the Americans attacked. With cries of "Remember the Alamo! Remember Goliad!" the Texans overcame the army, captured its commander in his slippers, and won the war within 20 minutes. Their casualties numbered only two, while 630 Mexicans lay dead.

With the victory at San Jacinto, Texas gained its independence. But although Texans immediately sought admission to the Union, their request failed. Many northerners violently opposed annexation of another slave state. The Union was precariously balanced, with 13 free and 13 slave states. Texas would upset that equilibrium in favor of the South.

For the next few years, the Lone Star Republic led a precarious existence. Mexico refused to recognize its independence, and Texans skirmished with Mexican bands. Financial ties with the United States increased, however, as trade grew and many Americans invested in Texas bonds and lands.

Texas became headline news again in 1844, when President John Tyler (who had assumed office after William Henry Harrison's death one month into his term) reopened the question of annexation, hoping that Texas would ensure his reelection. The issue exploded, however, bringing to life powerful sectional, national, and political tensions. Southern Democrats insisted that the South's future hinged on the annexation of Texas.

Democrats Lewis Cass, Stephen Douglas of Illinois, and Robert Walker of Mississippi vigorously supported annexation, not because it would expand slavery, a topic they avoided, but because it would spread the benefits of American civilization. Their arguments, classic examples of the tenets of Manifest Destiny, put the question into a national context of expanding American freedom. So successfully did they link Texas to Manifest Destiny and avoid sectional issues that their candidate, James Polk of Tennessee, secured the Democratic nomination in 1844. Polk called for "the reannexation of Texas at the earliest practicable period" and the occupation of the Oregon Territory. Manifest Destiny had come of age.

Polk won a close election in 1844. But by the time Polk took the oath of office in March 1845, Tyler, in his last months in office, had pushed through Congress a joint resolution admitting Texas to the Union. Nine years after its revolution, Texas finally became part of the Union. The agreement gave Texas the unusual right to divide into five states if it chose to do so.

War with Mexico, 1846–1848

When Mexico learned of Texas's annexation, it promptly severed diplomatic ties with the United States. It was easy for Mexicans to interpret the events from the 1820s on as part of a gigantic American plot to steal Texas. Now that the Americans had gained Texas, would they want still more?

Polk, like many other Americans, failed to appreciate how the annexation of Texas humiliated Mexico and increased pressures on its government to respond belligerently. Aware of its weakness, the president anticipated that Mexico would grant his grandiose demands: a Texas bounded by the Rio Grande rather than the Nueces River 150 miles to its north, as well as California and New Mexico.

Even before the Texans could accept the

The Mexican-American War, 1846–1848

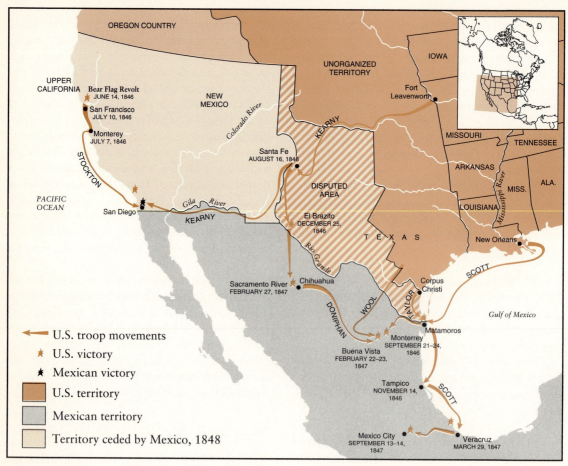

Legend:
- ← U.S. troop movements
- ★ U.S. victory
- ★ Mexican victory
- U.S. territory
- Mexican territory
- Territory ceded by Mexico, 1848

Map labels: OREGON COUNTRY; IOWA; UNORGANIZED TERRITORY; UPPER CALIFORNIA; NEW MEXICO; Bear Flag Revolt JUNE 14, 1846; San Francisco JULY 10, 1846; Monterey JULY 7, 1846; Fort Leavenworth; MISSOURI; TENNESSEE; ARKANSAS; Santa Fe AUGUST 16, 1846; KEARNY; MISS.; ALA.; PACIFIC OCEAN; San Diego; KEARNY; STOCKTON; Gila River; Colorado River; DISPUTED AREA; LOUISIANA; El Brazito DECEMBER 25, 1846; T E X A S; New Orleans; Rio Grande; Sacramento River FEBRUARY 27, 1847; Chihuahua; Corpus Christi; SCOTT; Gulf of Mexico; DONIPHAN; WOOL; TAYLOR; Matamoros; Monterrey SEPTEMBER 21–24, 1846; Buena Vista FEBRUARY 22–23, 1847; Tampico NOVEMBER 14, 1846; SCOTT; Mexico City SEPTEMBER 13–14, 1847; Veracruz MARCH 29, 1847

long-awaited invitation to join the Union, rumors of a Mexican invasion were afloat. As a precautionary move, Polk ordered General Zachary Taylor to move "on or near the Rio Grande." By October 1845, Taylor and 3,500 American troops had reached the Nueces River. In November, the president sent his secret agent, John L. Slidell, to Mexico City with instructions to secure the Rio Grande border and to buy Upper California and New Mexico. When the Mexican government refused to receive Slidell, an angry Polk decided to force Mexico into accepting American terms. He ordered Taylor

south of the Rio Grande. To the Mexicans, who insisted that the Nueces River was the legitimate boundary, their presence constituted an act of war.

In late April, the Mexican government declared a state of defensive war. Two days later, a skirmish broke out between Mexican and American troops, resulting in 16 American casualties. When Polk received Taylor's report, he quickly drafted a war message for Congress. The president claimed that Mexico had "passed the boundary of the United States ... invaded our territory and shed American blood upon American soil." "War exists," he claimed and, he added untruthfully, "notwithstanding all our efforts to avoid it, exists by act of Mexico."

Although Congress declared war, the conflict bitterly divided Americans. Many Whigs, including Abraham Lincoln, questioned the accuracy of Polk's initial account of the events, and their opposition grew more vocal as time passed. In 1847, a month after General Winfield Scott took Mexico City, Philadelphian Joseph Sills wrote in his diary, "There is a widely spread conviction ... that it is a wicked & disgraceful war."

Yet Polk enjoyed the enthusiastic support of expansionists. Thomas Gibson's men, like most other soldiers, were eager volunteers. Some expansionists even urged permanent occupation of Mexico.

In the end, chance helped draw hostilities to a close. Mexican moderates approached Polk's diplomatic representative, Nicholas Trist, who accompanied the American army in Mexico. In Trist's baggage were detailed, though out-of-date, instructions outlining Polk's requirements: the Rio Grande boundary, Upper California, and New Mexico. Although the president had lost confidence in Trist and had ordered him home in chains, Trist stayed in Mexico to negotiate an end to the war. Having obtained most of Polk's objectives, Trist returned to Washington to an ungrateful president. Apparently Polk had wanted more territory from Mexico for less money. Firing him from his job at the State Department, Polk denounced Trist as an "impudent and unqualified scoundrel."

California and New Mexico

Polk made it clear from the early days of his presidency that California and New Mexico were part of any resolution of the Mexico crisis. Serious American interest in California dated only from the late 1830s. A few Americans had settled in California during the 1820s and 1830s. But gradual recognition of California's fine harbors, its favorable position for the China trade, and the suspicion that other countries, especially Great Britain, had designs on the region nourished the conviction that it must become part of the United States. As more Americans poured into California in the early 1840s, one resident realized, "The American population will soon be sufficiently numerous to play the Texas game."

Polk tried to purchase California, but Santa Anna, who bore the burden of having lost Texas, was in no position to sell. Thus in 1846, a few armed American settlers rose up against Mexican "tyranny" and established the "Bear Flag Republic."

New Mexico was also on Polk's list. Ties with the United States began in the 1820s, when American traders began to bring their goods to Santa Fe. New Mexicans had little desire for annexation, however, and the unsuccessful attempt by the Texans to capture Santa Fe in 1841 and border clashes in the following two years did not enhance the attractiveness of their Anglo neighbors. But standing awkwardly in the path of American westward expansion, New Mexico faced an uncertain future.

In June 1846, shortly after the declaration of war with Mexico, the Army of the West, led by Colonel Stephen W. Kearny, left Fort Leavenworth, Kansas, for New Mexico. Two months later, the army took Santa Fe without a shot. New Mexico's upper class, who had already begun to intermarry with American merchants and send some sons to colleges in the United States, readily accepted the new rulers. However, ordinary Mexicans and Pueblo Indians did not take conquest so lightly. After Kearny departed, resistance erupted in New Mexico. Californians also fought the American occupation force. Kearny was wounded, and the first appointed American governor of New Mexico was killed. In the end, however, superior American military strength won the day. By January 1847, both California and New Mexico were firmly in American hands.

The Treaty of Guadalupe Hidalgo, 1848

Negotiated by Trist and signed on February 2, 1848, the Treaty of Guadalupe Hidalgo dictated the fate of most people living in the Southwest. The United States absorbed the region's 75,000 Spanish-speaking inhabitants and its 150,000 Native Americans and increased its territory by 529,017 square miles, almost a third of Mexico's extent. Mexico received $15 million and in 1853 would receive another $10 million for large tracts of land in southern Arizona and New Mexico (the Gadsden Purchase). In the treaty, the United States guaranteed the civil and political rights of former Mexican citizens and their rights to land and also agreed to satisfy all American claims against Mexico. The war had cost the United States 13,000 American lives, lost mostly to diseases such as measles and dysentery, and $97 million expended for military operations.

The Oregon Question, 1844–1846

Belligerence and war secured vast areas of the Southwest and California for the United States. In the Pacific Northwest, the presence of mighty Great Britain rather than the weak, crisis-ridden Mexican government suggested more cautious tactics. There diplomacy became the means for territorial gains.

Despite the disputed nature of claims to the Oregon Territory, Polk assured the inauguration day crowd huddled under umbrellas that "our title to the country of Oregon is 'clear and unquestionable,' . . . already our people are preparing to perfect that title by occupying it with their wives and children." Polk's words reflected American confidence that settlement carried the presumption of possession. But the British did not agree.

Between 1842 and 1845, the number of Americans in Oregon grew from 400 to over 5,000. Most located south of the Columbia River in the Willamette valley. By 1843, these settlers had written a constitution and soon after elected a legislature. At the same time, British interests in the area were declining as the fur trade dwindled.

The Democratic platform and the slogan that had helped elect Polk laid claim to a boundary of 54°40′. In fact, Polk was not willing to go to war with Great Britain for Oregon. Privately, he considered reasonable a boundary at the 49th parallel, which would extend the existing Canadian-American border to the Pacific and secure the harbors of Puget Sound for the United States. But Polk could hardly admit this to his Democratic supporters, who had so enthusiastically shouted "Fifty-four forty or fight" during the recent campaign.

Soon after his inaugural, Polk offered his compromise to Great Britain. But his tone offended the British minister, who rejected the offer at once. However, most Americans did not want to fight for Oregon and preferred to resolve the crisis diplomatically. As war with Mexico loomed, this task became more urgent.

The British, too, were eager to settle. In June 1846, the British agreed to accept the 49th parallel boundary if Vancouver Island remained British. With overwhelming Senate approval, Polk ended the crisis just a few weeks before the declaration of war with Mexico.

As these events show, Manifest Destiny was an idea that supported and justified expansionist policies. It corresponded, at the most basic level, to what Americans believed, that expansion was both necessary and right.

GOING WEST

After diplomacy and war clarified the status of the western territories, Americans lost little time in moving there. A trickle of emigrants became a flood. During the 1840s, 1850s, and 1860s, thousands of Americans left their homes for the frontier. By 1860, California alone had 380,000 settlers.

Some chose to migrate by sea, sailing around South America to the West Coast or taking a ship to Panama, crossing the isthmus by land, and then continuing by sea. Most emigrants, however, chose land routes. In 1843, the first large party succeeded in crossing the plains and mountains to Oregon. More followed. Between 1841 and 1867, some 350,000 traveled over the overland trails to California or to Oregon, while others trekked part of the way to intermediate points like Colorado and Utah.

The Emigrants

Most of the emigrants who headed for the Far West, where slavery was prohibited, were white and American-born. They came from the Midwest and the Upper South. A few free blacks made the trip as well. Pioneer Margaret Frink remembered seeing "a Negro woman . . . tramping along through the heat and dust, carrying a cast iron black stove on her head, with her provisions and a blanket piled on top . . . bravely pushing on for California." Emigrants from the Deep South usually selected Arkansas or Texas as their destination, and many brought their slaves with them. By 1840, over 11,000 slaves toiled in Texas and 20,000 in Arkansas.

The many pioneers who kept journals during the five- to six-month overland trip captured the human dimension of emigrating. One migrant, Lodisa Frizzell, described her feelings of parting in 1852:

> Who is there that does not recollect their first night when started on a long journey, the well known voices of our friends still ring in our ears, the parting kiss feels still warm upon our lips, and that last separating word FAREWELL! sinks deeply into the heart. It may be the last we ever hear from some or all of them, and to those who

start . . . there can be no more solemn scene of parting only at death.

Most emigrants traveled with family and relatives. Only during the gold rush years did large numbers, usually young men, travel independently. Migration was a family experience, mostly involving men and women from their late twenties to early forties. A sizable number of them had recently married, and many had moved before. The difference was the vast distance to this frontier and the seemingly final separation from home.

Migrants' Motives

What led so many Americans to sell most of their possessions and embark on an unknown future thousands of miles away? Many believed that frontier life would offer rich opportunities. Thousands sought riches in the form of gold. Others anticipated making their fortune as merchants, shopkeepers, peddlers, land speculators, or practitioners of law or medicine.

Most migrants dreamed of bettering their life by cultivating the land. Federal and state land policies made the acquisition of land increasingly alluring. Preemption acts during the 1830s and 1840s gave "squatters" the right to settle public lands before the government offered them for sale and then allowed them to purchase these lands at the minimum price once they came on the market. At the same time, the amount of land a family had to buy shrank to only 40 acres. In 1862, the Homestead Act went further by offering 160 acres of government land free to citizens or future citizens over 21 who lived on the property, improved it, and paid a small registration fee. Oregon's land policy, which predated the Homestead Act, was even more generous. It awarded a single man 320 acres of free land and a married man 640 acres provided he occupied his claim for four years and made improvements.

Some emigrants hoped the West would restore them to health. Others pursued religious or cultural missions in the West. Missionary couples like David and Catherine Blaine, who settled in Seattle when it was a frontier outpost, determined to bring Protestantism and education west. Stirred by the stories they had heard of the "deplorable morals" on the frontier, they left the comforts of home to evangelize and educate westerners. Still others, like the Mormons, made the long trek to Utah to establish a society in conformity with their religious beliefs.

Not everyone who dreamed of setting off for the frontier could do so. The trip to the Far West involved considerable expense. The sea route around Cape Horn came to perhaps $600 per person. For the same sum, four people could make the overland trip. And if the emigrants sold their wagons and oxen at the journey's end, the final expenses might amount to only $220. Clearly, however, the initial financial outlay was considerable enough to rule out the trip for the very poor. Despite increasingly liberal land policies, migration to the Far West (with the exception of group migration to Utah) was a movement of middle-class Americans.

The Overland Trails

The trip started for most emigrants in the late spring, when they left their homes and headed for starting points in Iowa and Missouri: Council Bluffs, Independence, Westport, St. Joseph. There companies of wagons gathered, and when grass was up for the stock, usually by the middle of May, they set out. Emigrant trains first followed the valley of the Platte River. Making only 15 miles a day, they slowly wound their way through the South Pass of the Rockies, heading for destinations in California or Oregon.

Emigrants found the first part of the trip novel and even enjoyable. The Indians, one woman noted, "proved better than represented." Men drove and repaired the wagons,

Overland Trails to the West

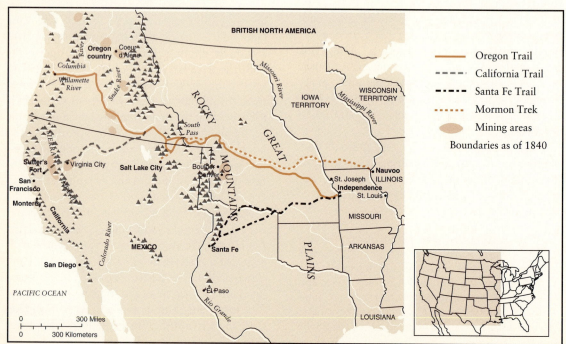

This undated photograph of two emigrant wagons and their occupants gives a good idea of the family character of emigration and the limited space that the wagons had for family possessions and items needed at the end of the trip. Note that the children are barefoot.

ferried cattle and wagons across rivers, hunted, and stood guard at night. Women labored at domestic chores, caring for children, cooking meals, and washing clothes. Many of the children later remembered the trip as an exciting adventure.

As the trip lengthened, difficulties multiplied. Cholera often took a heavy toll. Conflict with Indians became a problem only in the 1850s and made emigrants jumpy during the second half of the trip. (Between 1840 and 1860, Indians killed about 400 emigrants, most during the second half of the trip; the emigrants themselves killed at least that many Indians.) Traveling grew more arduous as deserts and mountains replaced rolling prairies.

Since emigrants had to cross the final mountain ranges of the Sierras and the Cascades before the first snowfall, there was a pressing need to push ever onward. Animals weakened by constant travel, poor feed, and bad water sickened, collapsed, and often died. As families faced the harsh realities of travel, they had to lighten their wagons by throwing out possessions lovingly brought from home. Food grew scarce.

Finally, five or six months after setting out, emigrants arrived, exhausted and often penniless, in Oregon or California. As one wrote on a September day in 1854, her journey had ended "which for care, fatigue, tediousness, perplexities and dangers of various kinds, can not be excelled."

LIVING ON THE FRONTIER

When emigrants finally reached their destinations and began building a new life, they naturally drew on their experiences back east. "Pioneers though we are, and proud of it, we are not content with the wilds . . . with the idleness of the land, the rudely construct[ed] log cabin," one Oregon settler explained. "Pioneers are not that kind of folks."

The Agricultural Frontier

Pioneer farmers faced the urgent task of establishing their homesteads and beginning farming. First, the family had to locate a suitable claim. Clearing the land and constructing a crude shelter followed. Only then could crops be planted. Since emigrants brought few of their possessions west, their work was more difficult. A young Oregon bride who set up housekeeping in the

1840s with only a stew kettle and three knives was not unusual.

After months of intense interaction with other travelers, families were now alone on their claims. The typical frontier household consisted of parents with one to four children. For several years, isolation was the rule. One pioneer remembered, "We were ... 'all told,' eleven families within a radius of six or eight miles, widely separated by our holdings and three hundred and twenty acres to each family. In those days anyone residing within twenty miles was considered a neighbor." But the isolation usually ended within a few years as most areas attracted new emigrants and old settlers seeking better claims.

In Oregon, the pioneers set up a political system based on eastern models before the status of the territory was resolved. Before permanent schools or churches existed, men resumed the familiar political rituals of voting, electioneering, and talking politics. They were also going to court to resolve controversies and to ensure law and order. Although modern movies and novels suggest that violence was a part of everyday life on the frontier, this was not true on the farming frontier. Courts, rather than rough-and-ready vigilante groups, usually handled the occasional violence.

The chronic shortage of cash on the frontier retarded the growth of both schools and churches. Until farmers could send their goods to market, they had little cash to spare. Geographic mobility also contributed to institutional instability. Up to three-quarters of the population of a frontier county might vanish within a ten-year period as emigrants left to seek better land. Some farmed in as many as four locations until they found a satisfactory claim. Institutions relying on continuing personal and financial support suffered accordingly.

Yet even if their efforts to re-create familiar institutional life often faltered, settlers did not lose sight of their goals. Newspapers, journals, and books, which circulated early on the frontier, reinforced familiar values and norms and kept determination strong. As more and more

settlers arrived, the numbers willing to support educational, religious, and cultural institutions grew. In the end, as one pioneer pointed out, "We have a telegraph line from the East, a daily rail road train, daily mail and I am beginning to feel quite civilized. And here ended my pioneer experience." Only 16 years had passed since she had crossed the Plains.

Although the belief in the frontier's special economic and social opportunities encouraged emigration, the dream was often illusory. The appearance of workers for hire and tenant farmers also pointed to real economic differences and hinted at the difficulties those on the bottom would face as they tried to improve their situation. Their widespread geographic mobility also indicates that many found it difficult to capitalize on the benefits of homesteading. Census data show that those who moved were generally less successful than the core of stable residents.

The Mining Frontier

On the mining frontier, tales of prospectors who had reportedly struck it rich fueled the fantasies of fortune hunters. News of the discovery of gold in 1848 in California swept the country like wildfire. Thousands raced to cash in on the bonanza. Within a year, California's population ballooned from 14,000 to almost 100,000. By 1852, that figure had more than doubled.

The forty-niners were mostly young, unmarried, predominantly male, and heterogeneous. Of those pouring into California in 1849, about 80 percent came from the United States, 8 percent from Mexico, and 5 percent from South America. The rest came from Europe and Asia. Few were as interested in settling the West as they were in extracting its precious metals and returning home rich.

California was the first and most dramatic of the western mining frontiers. Later gold strikes drew prospectors to the Pacific Northwest and British Columbia, Colorado, and Montana in the 1850s and 1860s. In the mid-1870s, yet another discovery of gold, this time in the

Black Hills of South Dakota, attracted hordes of fortune seekers.

The discovery of gold or silver spurred immediate, if usually short-lived, growth. Merchants, saloonkeepers, cooks, druggists, gamblers, and prostitutes hurried into boom areas as fast as prospectors. Usually about half of the residents of any mining camp were there to relieve the miners of their profits, not to prospect themselves.

Life in the mining boomtowns was often disorderly. Racial antagonism between American miners and foreigners, whom they labeled "greasers" (Mexicans), "chinks" (Chinese), "keskedees" (Frenchmen), and lesser "breeds," led to ugly riots and lynchings. Fistfights, drunkenness, and murder occurred often enough to become part of the lore of the gold rush. Wrote one woman, "In the short space of twenty four days, we have had murders, fearful accidents, bloody deaths, a mob, whippings, a hanging, an attempt at suicide, and a fatal duel."

Although the lucky few struck it rich or at least made enough money to return home with pride intact, miners' journals and letters reveal that many made only enough to keep going. The problem was that easily mined silver and gold deposits soon ran out. The remaining rich deposits lay deeply embedded in rock or gravel.

Extraction required cooperative efforts, capital, technological experience, and expensive machinery. Eventually, mining became a corporate industrial concern, with miners as wage earners. As early as 1852, the changing nature of mining in California had transformed most of the shaggy miners into wage workers.

Probably 5 percent of early gold rush emigrants to California were women and children. Many of the women also anticipated getting "rich in a hurry." Because there were so few of them, the cooking, nursing, laundry, and hotel services women provided had a high value. Yet it was wearying work, and some wondered if the money compensated for the exhaustion. As Mary Ballou thought it over, she decided, "I would not advise any Lady to come out here and suffer to toil and fatigue I have suffered for the sake of a little gold." As men's profits shrank, so too did those of the women who served them.

Some of the first women to arrive on the mining frontier were prostitutes, who may have made up as much as 20 percent of California's female population in 1850. During boom days, they made good money and sometimes won a recognized place in society. But they were more often the victims of murder and violence than the recipients of courtesy.

The Mexicans, South Americans, Chinese,

Although there were only a few women on the early mining frontier, they often found that the predominantly male environment offered them good opportunities to earn money.

and small numbers of blacks seeking their fortunes in California soon discovered that racial discrimination flourished vigorously in the land of golden promise. At first, American miners hoped to force foreigners out of the gold fields altogether. But an attempt to declare mining illegal for all foreigners failed. A high tax on foreign miners proved more successful. Thousands of Mexicans and Chinese left the mines. As business stagnated in mining towns, however, white miners had second thoughts about the levy and reduced it. In 1870, the tax was declared unconstitutional.

Black Americans found that color placed them in a situation akin to that of foreigners. Deprived of the vote, forbidden to testify in civil or criminal cases involving whites, excluded from the bounties of the state's homestead law, blacks led a precarious existence. When news arrived of the discovery of gold in British Columbia in the late 1850s, hundreds of blacks as well as thousands of Chinese left the state hoping that the Canadian frontier would be more hospitable than California.

Although men's and women's fantasies of dazzling riches rarely came true, gold had a huge impact on the West as a whole. Between 1848 and 1883, California mines supplied two-thirds of the country's gold. This gold transformed San Francisco from a sleepy town into a bustling metropolis. It fueled the development of California and Oregon, and it built harbors, railroads, and irrigation systems all over the West.

The Mormon Frontier

In the decades before 1860, many emigrants heading for the Far West stopped to rest and buy supplies in Salt Lake City, the heart of the Mormon state of Deseret. There they encountered a society that seemed familiar and orderly, yet foreign and shocking. Visitors admired the attractively laid out town with its irrigation ditches, gardens, and tidy houses, but they deplored

polygamy. They were amazed that so few Mormon women seemed interested in escaping from the bonds of plural marriage.

Violent events had driven the Mormons to the arid Great Basin area. Joseph Smith's murder in 1844 marked no end to the persecution of his followers. By the fall of 1846, angry mobs had chased the last of the "Saints" out of Nauvoo, Illinois. Smith's successor, Brigham Young, realized that flight from the United States represented the best hope for survival.

Young selected the Great Basin area, technically part of Mexico, as the best site for his future kingdom. It was arid and remote, 1,000 miles from its nearest "civilized" neighbors. But if irrigated, Mormon leaders concluded, it might prove as fertile as the fields and vineyards of ancient Israel.

In April 1847, Young led an exploratory expedition of 143 men, three women, and two children to this promised land. By September 1847, fully 566 wagons and 1,500 of the Saints had made the arduous trek to Salt Lake City. By 1850, the Mormon frontier had attracted over 11,000 settlers. Missionary efforts in the United States and abroad, especially in Great Britain and Scandinavia, drew thousands of converts to the Great Basin. By the end of the decade, over 30,000 Saints lived in Utah. Though hardship marked these early years, the Mormons thrived. As one early settler remarked, "We have everything around us we could ask."

Non-Mormon or "Gentile" emigrants passing through Utah found much that was recognizable but also perceived profound differences, for the heart of Mormon society was not the individual farmer living on his own homestead but the cooperative village. Years of persecution had nourished a strong sense of group identity and acceptance of church leadership. Organized by the church leaders, who made the essential decisions, farming became a collective enterprise. All farmers were allotted land. All had irrigation rights, for water did not belong to individuals but to the community. During Sunday services, the local bishop might give farming instructions to his congregation along with his sermon.

The church was omnipresent in Utah; in fact, nothing separated church and state. When it became clear that Utah would become a territory, Mormon leaders drew up a constitution that divided religious and political power. But once in place, powers overlapped. As one Gentile pointed out, "This intimate connection of church and state seems to pervade everything that is done. The supreme power in both being lodged in the hands of the same individuals, it is difficult to separate their two official characters, and to determine whether in any one instance they act as spiritual or merely temporal officers."

The Treaty of Guadalupe Hidalgo officially incorporated Utah into the United States but little affected political and religious arrangements. Brigham Young became territorial governor. Local bishops continued to act as spiritual leaders as well as civil magistrates in Mormon communities.

Other aspects of the Mormon frontier were distinctive. Mormon policy toward the Indian tribes was remarkably enlightened. As one prominent Mormon pointed out, "It has been our habit to shoot Indians with tobacco and bread biscuits rather than with powder and lead, and we are most successful with them." After two expeditions against the Timpanagos and Shoshone in 1850, Mormons concentrated on converting rather than killing Native Americans. Mormon missionaries learned Bannock, Ute, Navajo, and Hopi languages in order to bring the faith to these tribes. They also encouraged Native Americans to ranch and farm.

While most Gentiles could tolerate some of the differences they encountered on the Mormon frontier, few could accept polygamy and the seemingly immoral extended family structure that plural marriage entailed. Although Joseph Smith and other church leaders had secretly practiced polygamy in the early 1840s, Brigham Young publicly revealed the doctrine only in 1852, when the Saints were safely in Utah.

Actually, relatively few families were polygamous. During the 40-year period in which Mormons practiced plural marriage, only 10 to 20 percent of Mormon families were polygamous. Few men had more than two wives. Because of the expense of maintaining several families and the personal strains involved, usually only the most successful and visible Mormon leaders practiced polygamy. To the shock of outsiders, Mormon women defended polygamy to the outside world. Polygamy was preferable to monogamy, which left the single woman without the economic and social protection of family life and forced some of them into prostitution.

Although the Mormon frontier seemed alien to outsiders, it succeeded in terms of its numbers, its growing economic prosperity, and its group unity. Long-term threats loomed for this community, however, once the area became part of the United States. Attacks on Young's power as well as heated verbal denunciations of polygamy proliferated. Efforts began in Congress to outlaw polygamy. In the years before the Civil War, Mormons withstood these assaults on their way of life. But as Utah became more connected to the rest of the country, the tide would turn against them.

The Urban Frontier

Many emigrants went west to settle in cities like San Francisco, Denver, and Portland. There they hoped to find business and professional opportunities or, perhaps, the chance to make a fortune by speculating in town lots.

Cities were an integral part of frontier life and sometimes preceded agricultural settlement. Some communities turned into bustling cities as they catered to the emigrant trade. St. Joseph, Missouri, outfitted families setting out on the overland journey. Salt Lake City offered pioneers headed for California an opportunity to rest and restock. Portland was the destination of many emigrants and became a market and supply center for homesteaders.

Some cities, like San Francisco and Denver, sprang up almost overnight. In a mere 12 years, San Francisco's population zoomed from 812 to 56,802.

Young, single men seeking their fortunes made up a disproportionate share of the urban population. Frontier Portland had more than three men for every woman. Predictably, urban life was often noisy, rowdy, and occasionally violent. Eventually the sex ratio became balanced, but as late as 1880, fully 18 of the 24 largest western cities had more men than women.

Although western cities began with distinctive characters, they soon resembled eastern cities. As a western publication boasted, "Transport a resident of an Eastern city and put him down in the streets of Portland, and he would observe little difference between his new surroundings and those he beheld but a moment before in his native city."

The history of Portland suggests the common pattern of development. In 1845, Portland was only a clearing in the forest. By the early 1850s, it had grown into a small trading center. As farmers poured into Oregon, the city became a regional commercial center. More permanent structures were built, giving the city an "eastern" appearance.

The belief that urban life in the West abounded with special opportunities initially drew many young men to Portland and other western cities. Many of them did not find financial success there. Opportunities were greatest for newcomers who brought assets with them. These residents became the elite of the community.

CULTURES IN CONFLICT

Looking at westward expansion through the eyes of white emigrants provides only one view of the frontier experience. An entry from an Oregon Trail journal suggests other perspectives. On May 7, 1864, Mary Warner, a bride of only a few months, described a frightening event. That day, a "fine-looking" Indian had visited the wagon train and tried to buy her. Mary's husband, probably uncertain how to handle the situation, played along, agreeing to trade his wife for two ponies. The Indian generously offered three. "Then," wrote Mary, "he took hold of my shawl to make me understand to get out [of the wagon]. About this time I got frightened and really was so hysterical [that] I began to cry." Everyone laughed at her, she reported, though surely the Indian found the whole incident no more amusing than she had. This ordinary encounter on the overland trail only begins to hint at the social and cultural differences separating white Americans moving west and the peoples with whom they came into contact.

Confronting the Plains Tribes

During the 1840s, white Americans first came into extensive contact with the powerful Plains tribes. Probably a quarter million Native Americans occupied the area from the Rocky Mountains to the Missouri River and from the Platte River to New Mexico. Nearest the Missouri and Iowa frontier lived the "border" tribes—the Pawnee, Omaha, Oto, Ponca, and Kansa. These Indians, unlike other Plains tribes, lived in villages and raised crops, though they supplemented their diet with buffalo meat during the summer months. On the Central Plains lived the Brulé and Oglala Sioux, the Cheyenne, the Shoshone, and the Arapaho, aggressive tribes that followed the buffalo and often raided the border tribes. In the Southwest were the Comanche, Ute, Navajo, and some Apache bands, while the Kiowa, Wichita, Apache, and southern Comanche claimed northern and western Texas as their hunting grounds.

Although there were differences among these tribes, they shared certain characteristics. Most had adopted a nomadic way of life after the introduction of horses in the sixteenth century increased their seasonal mobility from 50

Artists were fascinated by Plains Indian life, which they captured in sketches and paintings. Most anticipated that native culture would disappear with the coming of whites to the West.

miles to 500 miles. Horses allowed Indian braves to hunt the buffalo with such success that tribes (with the exclusion of the border groups) came to depend on the beasts for food, clothing, fuel, tepee dwellings, and trading purposes. Because women were responsible for processing buffalo products, some men had more than one wife to tan skins for trading.

Mobility also increased tribal contact and conflict. War played a central part in the lives of the Plains tribes. But tribal warfare was not like the warfare of white men. Indians sought not to exterminate their enemies or to claim territory but rather to steal horses and to prove individual prowess. They considered it braver to touch an enemy than to kill or scalp him.

The Plains tribes, though disunified, posed a fearsome obstacle to white expansion. They had signed no treaties with the United States and had

few friendly feelings toward whites. Their contact with white society had brought gains through trade in skins, but the trade had also brought alcohol and destructive epidemics.

When the first emigrants drove their wagons across the plains and prairies in the early 1840s, relations between Indians and whites were peaceable. But the intrusion of whites set in motion an environmental cycle that eventually drew the two groups into conflict. Indian tribes depended on the buffalo and slaughtered only what they needed. Whites, however, adopted the "most exciting sport," the buffalo hunt. As the great herds began to shrink, Native American tribes began to battle one another for hunting grounds and food. In an 1846 petition to President Polk, the Sioux requested compensation for damages caused by whites. When the president denied their request, they tried to extract taxes

Indian Tribes in 1840

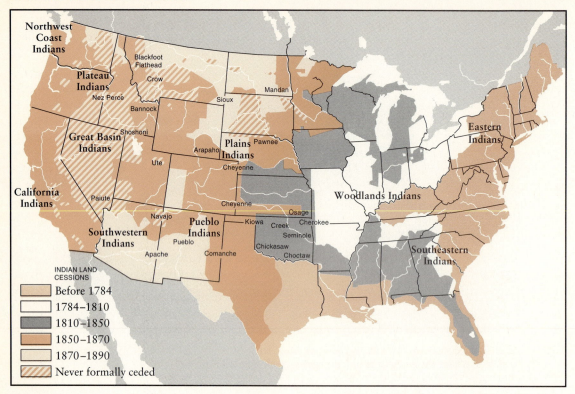

Northwest Coast Indians

Blackfoot
Flathead

Crow

Plateau Indians

Nez Perce

Bannock

Sioux

Mandan

Great Basin Indians

Shoshoni

Eastern Indians

Ute

Arapaho

Plains Indians

Pawnee

Cheyenne

California Indians

Paiute

Cheyenne

Woodlands Indians

Navajo

Osage

Pueblo Indians

Kiowa

Creek

Cherokee

Southwestern Indians

Pueblo

Seminole

Chickasaw

Apache

Comanche

Choctaw

Southeastern Indians

INDIAN LAND CESSIONS

Before 1784
1784–1810
1810–1850
1850–1870
1870–1890
Never formally ceded

from the emigrants passing over their lands. Emigrants were outraged.

The discovery of gold in California, which lured over 20,000 across the Plains in 1849 alone, became the catalyst for federal action. The vast numbers of gold seekers and their animals wrought such devastation in the Platte valley that it rapidly became a wasteland for the Indians. The dreaded cholera that whites carried with them spread to the Indians, killing thousands.

To meet the crisis, government officials devised a two-pronged plan. The government would construct a chain of forts to protect emigrants and, simultaneously, call the tribes to a general conference. Officials expected that in return for generous presents, Indians would end tribal warfare and limit their movements to prescribe areas. They instructed tribes to select chiefs to speak for them at the conference.

The Fort Laramie Council, 1851

In 1851, the council convened at Fort Laramie. As many as 10,000 Indians, hopeful of ending the destruction of their way of life and eager for the promised presents, gathered at the fort. Tribal animosities simmered, however. Skirmishes occurred on the way to the fort, and the border tribes, fearful of the Sioux, declined to participate. The Comanche, Kiowa, and Apache also refused to come since their enemies, the Sioux and the Crow, were to be there.

At the conference, whites told the gathered tribes that times had changed. In the past, "you had plenty of buffalo and game ... and your Great Father well knows that war has always been your favorite amusement and pursuit. He then left the question of peace and war to yourselves. Now, since the settling of the districts West of you by the white men, your condition has changed." There would be compensation for the destruction of their grass, timber, and buffalo and annual payments of goods and services. But in return, the tribes had to give up their rights of free movement. The government drew tribal boundaries, and chiefs made promises to stay within them. In most cases, some tribal lands were sold.

The Fort Laramie Treaty was the first agreement between the Plains tribes and the United States government. It expressed the conviction of whites that Indians must stay in clearly defined areas apart from white civilization.

But ominous signs appeared that more trouble would precede any "resolution" of Indian-white affairs. Sioux chief Black Hawk told whites, "You have split the country and I do not like it." His powerful tribe refused to be restricted to lands north of the Platte. In the following years, it would become evident that Americans and Sioux had conflicting interests south of the Platte. Elsewhere in the trans-Mississippi West, other tribes, like the fierce Navajo of New Mexico, also resisted white attempts to confine them.

Overwhelming the Mexicans

In the Southwest, in Texas, and in California, Americans contended with a Spanish-speaking population. Americans regarded Mexicans as lazy, ignorant, and cunning, the "dregs of society." Although Mexicans easily recognized such cultural arrogance, they lacked the numbers to fend off American aggression.

Although Anglo-Mexican interaction differed from place to place, few Anglos heeded the Treaty of Guadalupe Hidalgo's assurances that Mexicans would have citizens' rights and the "free enjoyment of their liberty and property." The greatest numbers of Spanish-speaking people lived in New Mexico, and, of all former Mexican citizens, they probably fared the best. Most were of mixed blood, living marginally as ranch hands for rich landowners or as farmers and herdsmen in small villages dominated by a *patron* or headman. As the century wore on, Americans produced legal titles and took over lands long occupied by peasant farmers and stock raisers. But despite economic reversals, New Mexicans survived, carrying their rural culture well into the twentieth century.

Light-skinned, upper-class landowners fared better. When the United States annexed New Mexico, this substantial and powerful class contracted strategic marriage and business alliances with the Anglo men who slowly trickled into the territory. During the 1850s, they maintained their influence and prestige and their American connections. Only rarely did they bother with the plight of their poor countrymen. Class outweighed ethnic or cultural considerations.

In Texas, the Spanish-speaking residents, only 10 percent of the population in 1840, shrank to a mere 6 percent by 1860. Although the upper class also intermarried with Americans, they lost most of their power as Germans, Irish, French, and Americans poured into the state. Poor, dark-skinned Hispanics clustered in low-paying and largely unskilled jobs.

In California, the discovery of gold radically changed the situation for Hispanic-Americans. In 1848, there were 7,000 Californios and about twice as many Anglos. By 1860, the Anglo population had ballooned to 360,000. Hispanic-Americans were hard pressed to cope with the rapid influx of outsiders.

In 1851, Congress passed the Gwin Land Law, which forced California landowners to defend what was already theirs and encouraged squatters to settle on land in the hopes that the Californios' titles would prove false. It took an average of 17 years to establish clear title to land. A victory at court often turned into a defeat when legal expenses forced owners to sell their lands to pay debts. In the south, where Anglos judged land less valuable than in the mining north, the process of dispossession was slower. But by the early 1860s, the ranching class there had also lost most of its extensive holdings.

Many working-class Hispanic-Americans lived marginal existences in California's growing towns and cities. Others became cowboys on American ranches or lived on their own small ranches in the backcountry. For them, the coming of the Anglos presented not opportunity but oppression. By 1870, the average Hispanic-American worker's property was worth only about a third of its value of 20 years earlier.

As the career of Tiburcio Vásquez, a notorious *bandido* in southern California, suggests, some Hispanics felt that they could protest events only through violence:

> My career grew out of the circumstances by which I was surrounded. . . . As I grew to manhood I was in the habit of attending balls and parties given by the native Californians, into which the Americans, then beginning to become numerous, would force themselves and shove the native born men aside, monopolizing the dance and the women. This was about 1852. A spirit of hatred and revenge took possession of me. I had numerous fights in defense of my countrywomen. The officers were continually in pursuit of me. I believed we were unjustly and wrongfully deprived of the social rights that belonged to us.

What Anglos called crime, Vásquez called self-defense.

CONCLUSION

FRUITS OF MANIFEST DESTINY

Like Lewis Cass, many nineteenth-century Americans were convinced that the country had merely gained western territories to which it was entitled. The expanding nation did gain vast natural wealth in the trans-Mississippi West. But only a small fraction of the hopeful emigrants heading for the frontier realized their dreams of success. And the move west had a dark side as Americans clashed with Mexicans and Native Americans in their drive to fulfill their "Manifest Destiny."

Recommended Reading

Ray Allen Billington gives an overview of the move west in *America's Frontier Heritage* (1966). Gilbert C. Fite treats agriculture in *The Farmer's Frontier, 1865–1900* (1966). The cities of the West are the subject of *The Urban West at the End of the Frontier* (1978) by Lawrence H. Larson.

Frederick Merk explores Manifest Destiny in *Manifest Destiny and Mission in American History* (1963). Robert W. Johanssen treats the Mexican War in *To the Halls of Montezuma: The Mexican War in the American Imagination* (1985). George Pierre Castile treats cultural conflict in

North American Indians: An Introduction to the Chichimeca (1979). Peter Nabakov has edited a collection of Indian responses, *Native American Testimony: An Anthology of Indian and White Relations* (1978).

Julie Roy Jeffrey compensates for the neglect of women in older frontier studies in *Frontier Women: The Trans-Mississippi West, 1840–1880* (1979). Sandra Myres edited women's diaries in *Ho for California! Women's Overland Diaries from the Huntington Library* (1980). See also John D. Unruh, Jr., *The Plains Across: The Overland Emigrants and the Trans-Mississippi West, 1840–1860* (1979). For details of

the mining frontier, consult Rodman W. Paul, *California Gold: The Beginning of Mining in the Far West* (1974). Although there were not many blacks on the frontier, William Loren Katz studies them in *The Black West* (1971). As for the Mormons, see Richard L. Bushman's *Joseph Smith and the Beginnings of Mormonism* (1984). Studies of Mexicans include Leonard Pitt, *The Decline of the Californios: A Social History of the Spanish-Speaking Californians, 1846–1890* (1970); M. S. Meir and Feliciano Rivera, *The Chicanos: A History of Mexican-Americans* (1972); and Alfredo Mirande and Evangeline Enriquez, *La Chicana: The Mexican-American Woman* (1979).

Time Line

1803–1806	Lewis and Clark expedition	1844	James Polk elected president
1818	Treaty on joint U.S.-British occupation of Oregon	1845	"Manifest Destiny" coined United States annexes Texas and sends troops to the Rio Grande Americans attempt to buy Upper California and New Mexico
1819	Spain cedes Spanish territory in United States and sets transcontinental boundary of Louisiana Purchase, excluding Texas	1846	Mexico declares defensive war United States declares war and takes Santa Fe Resolution of Oregon question
1821	Mexican independence Opening of Santa Fe Trail Stephen Austin leads American settlement of Texas	1847	Attacks on Veracruz and Mexico City Mormon migration to Utah begins
1821–1840	Indian removals	1848	Treaty of Guadalupe Hidalgo
1829	Mexico abolishes slavery in Texas	1849	California gold rush begins
1836	Texas declares independence Battles of the Alamo and San Jacinto	1850	California admitted to the Union
		1851	Fort Laramie Treaty
1840s	Emigrant crossings of Overland Trail	1853	Gadsden Purchase
		1862	Homestead Act

chapter 14

The Union in Peril

The election of 1860 confronted Abraham Lincoln and the American people with the most serious crisis since the founding of the Republic. Feeling deeply "the responsibility that was upon me," Lincoln won an unusual four-party election with only 39 percent of the popular vote. He had appealed almost exclusively to northern voters in a blatantly sectional campaign, defeating his three opponents by carrying every free state except New Jersey.

Other Americans sensed the mood of crisis that fall and faced their own fears and responsibilities. A month before the election, plantation owner Robert Allston wrote his oldest son, Benjamin, that "disastrous consequences" would follow from a Lincoln victory. After the election, Allston corresponded with a southern colleague about the need for "an effective military organization" to resist "Northern and Federal aggression." In this shift from sewing machines to military ones, Robert Allston prepared for what he called the "impending crisis."

Frederick Douglass, however, greeted the election with characteristic optimism. "Slaveholders," he said, "know that the day of their power is over when a Republican President is elected." But no sooner had Lincoln's victory been determined than Douglass's hopes turned sour. He noted that Republican leaders, in their desire to keep southern border states from seceding, sounded more antiabolitionist than antislavery. Slavery would, in fact, Douglass bitterly concluded, "be as safe, and safer" with Lincoln than with a Democrat.

Michael Luark, an Iowa farmer, was not so sure. Born in Virginia, Luark was a typically mobile nineteenth-century American. After growing up in Indiana, he followed the mining booms of the 1850s to Colorado and California before returning to the Midwest to farm. Writing in his diary on the last day of 1860, Luark looked ahead to 1861 with a deep sense of fear. "Startling" political changes would occur, he predicted, perhaps even the "Dissolution of the Union and Civil War with all its train of horrors." Within four months of this diary entry, the guns of the Confederate States of America fired on a federal fort in South Carolina, and the Civil War began.

Such a calamitous event had numerous causes, large and small. But as Douglass understood, by 1860 it was clear that "slavery is the real issue, the single bone of contention between all parties and sections."

This chapter analyzes how the momentous issue of slavery disrupted the political system and eventually the Union itself. We will look at how four major developments between 1848 and 1861 contributed to the Civil War: first, a sectional dispute over the extension of slavery into the western territories; second, the breakdown of the political party system; third, growing cultural differences in the views and life styles of southerners and northerners; and fourth, intensifying emotional and ideological polarization between the two regions over losing their way of life and sacred republican rights at the hands of the other. All four of these developments were tied to the central issue of slavery, and the election of Lincoln, the antislavery candidate, was the spark that touched off the conflagration.

SLAVERY IN THE TERRITORIES

The North and the South had managed to contain their differences over slavery, with only occasional difficulties, during the 60 years after the Constitutional Convention. Political compromise in 1787 had resolved the questions of the slave trade and how to count slaves for congressional representation. In 1820, the Missouri Compromise had established a workable way of balancing the admission of free and slave states to the Union and had also defined a geographic line (36°30′) to determine future decisions. In 1833, compromise had defused South Carolina's nullification of the tariff, and the gag rule in 1836 had kept divisive abolitionist petitions to end slavery off the floor of Congress.

One reason these compromises were temporarily successful was the existence of a two-party system with intersectional membership. Whigs and Democrats lived on both sides of the Mason-Dixon line. This changed in the late 1840s with territorial expansion, and the change would prove catastrophic to the Union.

Free Soil or Constitutional Protection?

When the Mexican War broke out in 1846, it seemed likely that the United States would acquire new territories in the Southwest. Would they be slave or free? To an appropriations bill to pay for the war, David Wilmot, a congressman from Pennsylvania, added a short amendment declaring that "neither slavery nor involuntary servitude shall ever exist" in any territories acquired from Mexico. The debates in Congress over the Wilmot Proviso were significant because legislators voted not as Whigs and Democrats but as northerners and southerners.

When the Mexican War ended, several solutions were presented to deal with this question of slavery in the territories. The first was the "free soil" idea of preventing any extensions of slavery. Supporters of "free soil" had mixed motives. For some, slavery was a moral evil. But for many northern white farmers looking to move westward, the threat of economic competition with an expanding system of large-scale slave labor was even more serious. Nor did they wish to compete for land with free blacks. As Wilmot put it, his proviso was intended to preserve the area for "the sons of toil, of my own race and own color." Other northerners resented the "insufferable arrogance" of the "spirit and demands of the Slave Power."

Opposed to the free-soil position were the arguments of Senator John C. Calhoun of South Carolina, expressed in several resolutions introduced in the Senate in 1847. Not only did Congress lack the constitutional right to exclude slavery from the territories, Calhoun argued, but it had a positive duty to protect it. The Wilmot Proviso, therefore, was unconstitutional, as was the Missouri Compromise and any other federal act that prevented slaveholders from taking their slave property into the territories of the United States.

Economic, political, and moral considerations stood behind the Calhoun position. Many southerners hungered for new cotton lands in the West and Southwest. Politically, southerners wanted to protect their institutions against destructive abolitionists. Southern leaders saw the Wilmot Proviso as a moral issue that raised questions about basic republican principles. Senator Robert Toombs of Georgia warned that if Congress passed the proviso, he would favor disunion rather than "degradation."

Popular Sovereignty and the Election of 1848

With such divisive potential, it was natural that many Americans sought a compromise solution to keep slavery out of politics. "Popular sovereignty," as promulgated by Senator Lewis Cass, left the decision of whether to permit slavery in a territory to the local territorial legislature. The Democratic Party, attracted to the idea that popular sovereignty could mean all things to all people, nominated Cass for president in 1848. He denounced abolitionists and the Wilmot Proviso but otherwise avoided the issue of slavery.

The Whigs found an even better way to evade the slavery issue. They nominated the Mexican War hero General Zachary Taylor, a Louisiana slaveholder, who compared himself to Washington as a "no party" man above politics. This was nearly the only thing he stood for. Southern Whigs supported Taylor because they thought he might understand the burdens of slave-holding, while northern Whigs were pleased that he took no stand on the Wilmot Proviso.

The evasions of the two major parties disappointed Calhoun, who tried to create a new unified southern party. Threatening secession, Calhoun called for a united effort against further attempts to interfere with the southern right to extend slavery, but his effort failed.

Warnings also issued from the North. Disaffected Democrats in New York and "conscience" Whigs from Massachusetts met in Buffalo, New York, to form the Free-Soil party and nominate Martin Van Buren as president. The platform of the new party, composed of an uneasy mixture of ardent abolitionists and racist opponents of free black mobility into western lands, pledged to fight for "free soil, free speech, free labor and free men."

General Taylor won the election largely because defections from Cass in New York and Pennsylvania to the Free-Soilers cost the Democrats the electoral votes from those states. Although weakened, the two-party system survived, and purely sectional parties were prevented.

The Compromise of 1850

Taylor won the election by avoiding slavery issues, but as president he could no longer do so. As he was inaugurated in 1849, four compelling issues faced the nation. The rush of some 80,000 unruly gold miners to California qualified that territory for admission to the Union. But California's entry as a free state would upset the balance between slave and free states in the Senate that had prevailed since 1820.

The unresolved status of the Mexican cession in the Southwest posed a second problem. The boundary between Texas and the New Mexico Territory was also in dispute, with Texas claiming lands all the way to Santa Fe. This increased northern fears that Texas might be divided into five or six slave states.

The existence of slavery and one of the largest slave markets in North America in the nation's capital was a third problem, especially to abolitionists. Fourth, Southerners resented the lax federal enforcement of the Fugitive Slave Act of 1793. They called for a stronger act that would end the protection northerners gave runaway slaves as they fled along the underground railroad to Canada.

Early in 1850, therefore, the old compromiser Henry Clay introduced a series of resolutions in an omnibus package intended to settle these issues once and for all. Despite some 70 speeches on behalf of the compromise, however, the Senate defeated Clay's Omnibus Bill, and the tired and disheartened 73-year-old Clay left Washington. Into the gap stepped a new compromiser, Senator Stephen Douglas of Illinois, who understood that Clay's resolutions had a better chance of passing if voted on individually rather than as a package. Under Douglas's leadership, and with the support of Millard Fillmore, who succeeded to the presidency upon Taylor's untimely death, a series of bills was finally passed.

The so-called Compromise of 1850 put Clay's resolutions, slightly altered, into law. First, California entered the Union as a free state, upsetting the balance of free and slave states, 16 to 15. Second, the territorial governments of New Mexico and Utah were organized by letting the people of those territories decide for themselves whether to permit slavery. The Texas–New Mexico border was settled in a compromise that denied Texas the disputed area. In turn, the federal government compensated Texas with $10 million to pay off debts owed to Mexico. Third, the slave trade, but not slavery itself,

The Compromise of 1850

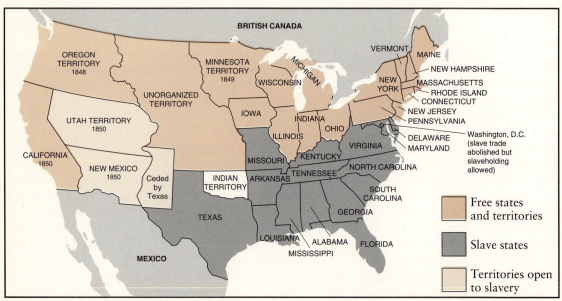

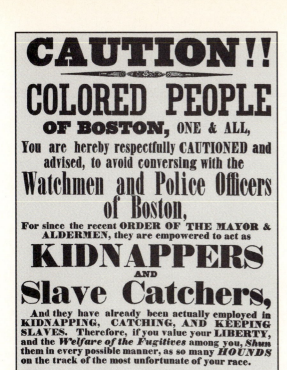

CAUTION!!
COLORED PEOPLE
OF BOSTON, ONE & ALL,

You are hereby respectfully CAUTIONED and advised, to avoid conversing with the

Watchmen and Police Officers of Boston,

For since the recent ORDER OF THE MAYOR & ALDERMEN, they are empowered to act as

KIDNAPPERS
AND
Slave Catchers,

And they have already been actually employed in KIDNAPPING, CATCHING, AND KEEPING SLAVES. Therefore, if you value your LIBERTY, and the *Welfare of the Fugitives* among you, *Shun* them in every possible manner, as so many *HOUNDS* on the track of the most unfortunate of your race.

Keep a Sharp Look Out for KIDNAPPERS, and have TOP EYE open.
APRIL 24, 1851.

THEODORE PARKER'S PLACARD

Placard written by Theodore Parker and printed and posted by the Vigilance Committee of Boston after the rendition of Thomas Sims to slavery in April, 1851.

The dangers of the Fugitive Slave Act are evident in this 1851 broadside published by Boston abolitionist Theodore Parker, which alerted the city's black community to the dangers posed by the new law.

was abolished in the District of Columbia. Fourth, a strengthened Fugitive Slave Act went into effect; it contained many provisions that offended northerners.

Consequences of Compromise

The Compromise of 1850 was the last attempt to keep slavery out of politics. The intersectional party system was severely tested but for a while was preserved. Douglas celebrated the acts of 1850 as a "final settlement" of the slavery question.

The Compromise, however, only delayed more serious sectional conflict. It added two new ingredients to American politics. The first hinted at the realignment of parties along sectional lines. Second, although repudiated by most ordinary citizens, ideas like secessionism, disunion, and a "higher law" than the Constitution entered more and more into political discourse.

The new fugitive slave law angered many northerners because it brought the evils of slavery right into their midst, compelling northerners to turn in runaways. The owners of escaped slaves hired agents, labeled "kidnappers" in the North, to hunt down fugitives. Ralph Waldo Emerson said it was "a filthy law" that he would not obey.

Frederick Douglass would not obey it either. As a runaway slave himself, he was threatened with arrest and return to the South until friends overcame his objections and purchased his freedom. Arguing the "rightfulness of forcible resistance," he urged free blacks to arm themselves and even wondered whether it was justifiable to kill kidnappers. Douglass raised money for black fugitives, hid runaways in his home, and helped hundreds escape to Canada. Other northerners, white as well as black, increased their work for the underground railroad in response to the fugitive slave law.

Douglass and others also spoke out on the wrongs of slavery. In an Independence Day speech in 1852, Douglass wondered, "What, to the American slave, is your 4th of July?" It was, he said, the day that revealed to the slave "the gross injustice and cruelty to which he is the constant victim." To a slave, the American claims of national greatness were vain and empty; the "shouts of liberty and equality" were "hollow mockery." Douglass's speeches, like those of another ex-slave, Sojourner Truth, took on an increasingly strident tone in the early 1850s.

At a women's rights convention in Akron, Ohio, in 1851, Truth made one of the decade's boldest statements for minority rights. The convention was attended by clergymen, who kept interrupting the proceedings to heckle female speakers. Up stood Sojourner Truth. She pointed to her many years of childbearing and hard, backbreaking work as a slave, crying out in a repetitive refrain, "And ar'n't I a woman?" Referring to Jesus, she asked where he came from: "From God and a woman: Man had nothing to do with Him." Referring to Eve, she concluded, "If the first woman God ever made was strong enough to turn the world upside down all alone, these women together ought to be able to turn it back, and get it right side up again! And now they is asking to do it, the men better let them." Her brief speech silenced the hecklers.

As Truth spoke, another American woman, Harriet Beecher Stowe, was finishing a novel, *Uncle Tom's Cabin*. Stowe's novel gave readers an absorbing indictment of the horrors of slavery and its immoral impact on both northerners and southerners. The book was published initially in serial form, and each month's chapter ended at a nail-biting dramatic moment. Readers throughout the North cheered Eliza's daring escape across the ice floes on the Ohio River, cried over Uncle Tom's humanity and Little Eva's death, suffered under the lash of Simon Legree, and rejoiced in the reuniting of black family members. When published in full in 1852, *Uncle Tom's Cabin* became one of the all-time best-sellers in American history.

POLITICAL DISINTEGRATION

The response to *Uncle Tom's Cabin* and the Fugitive Slave Act indicated that politicians had congratulated themselves too soon for saving the Republic in 1850. Political developments, not all dealing with slavery, were already weakening the ability of political parties—and ultimately the

nation—to withstand the passions slavery aroused.

The Apathetic Election of 1852

Political parties must convince voters that their party stands for moral values and economic policies crucially different from those of the opposition. In the period between 1850 and 1854, these differences were blurred, thereby undermining party loyalty. First, both parties scrambled to convince voters that they had favored the Compromise of 1850. In addition, several states rewrote their constitutions and remodeled their laws in the early 1850s, standardizing many political and economic procedures. One effect of these changes was to reduce the number of patronage jobs available for party victors to dispense. Another effect was to regularize the process, begun in the 1830s, for securing banking, railroad, and other corporate charters, removing the role formerly played by the legislature. Both of these weakened the importance of the party in citizens' lives.

The third development that weakened parties was economic. During the prosperity of the early 1850s, party distinctions over economic policies seemed less important. Economic issues persisted, but the battles were fought at the local rather than national level. Around such issues as temperance, free blacks, taxes for internal improvements, and a ten-hour working day, local politicians formed fleeting alliances. As a Baltimore businessman said, "The two old parties are fast melting away."

The election of 1852 illustrated the lessening significance of political parties. After 52 ballots, the Whigs nominated General Winfield Scott, another Mexican War hero. Democrats had their own problems deciding on a candidate. After 49 ballots, in which Cass, Douglas, and James Buchanan each held the lead for a time, the party turned to the lackluster Franklin Pierce of New Hampshire as a compromise candidate.

The two parties offered little choice. The

Baltimore *Sun* remarked that "there is no issue that much interests the people." Democratic prospects were aided by thousands of new Catholic immigrants from Ireland and Germany. Party officials often bought their votes with bribes and drinks. Internal conflicts and defections seriously weakened the Whigs, and Pierce won easily, 254 to 42 electoral votes.

The Kansas-Nebraska Act

The Whig party's final disintegration came on a February day in 1854 when southern Whigs stood to support Stephen Douglas's Nebraska bill, thus choosing to be more southern than Whig. The Illinois senator had many reasons for introducing a bill organizing the Nebraska Territory (which included Kansas). As an ardent nationalist and chairman of the Committee on Territories, he was concerned for the continuing development of the West. As an Illinoisan in a period of explosive railroad building, he wanted the eastern terminus for a transcontinental railroad in Chicago rather than in rival St. Louis. This meant organizing the lands west of Iowa and Missouri. Douglas also wanted to recapture the party leadership he had held when he led the fight to pass the Compromise of 1850, and he harbored presidential ambitions.

The entire Nebraska Territory lay north of the line where slavery had been prohibited by the Missouri Compromise. But Douglas's bill, introduced early in 1854, recommended using the principle of popular sovereignty in organizing the Kansas and Nebraska territories. This meant that inhabitants could vote slavery in, thereby violating the Missouri Compromise. Douglas reasoned, however, that the climate and soil of the prairies in Kansas and Nebraska would never support slavery-based agriculture, and the people would decide to be a free state. Therefore, he could win the votes he needed for the railroad without also getting slavery.

Douglas miscalculated. Northerners from his own party immediately attacked him and his bill as a "criminal betrayal of precious rights."

The outrage among Whigs and abolitionists was even greater.

But Stephen Douglas was a fighter. The more he was attacked, the harder he fought. Eventually his bill passed, but not without seriously damaging the political party system. What began as a railroad measure ended in reopening the question of slavery in the territories that Douglas and others had thought finally settled in 1850. What began as a way of avoiding conflict ended up in violence. What began as a way of strengthening party lines ended up destroying one party (the Whigs), planting deep, irreconcilable divisions in another (the Democrats), and creating two new ones (Know-Nothings and Republicans).

Expansionist "Young America"

The Democratic Party was weakened in the early 1850s not only by the Kansas-Nebraska Act but also by an ebullient, expansive energy that led Americans to adventures far beyond Kansas. As republican revolutions erupted in Europe in 1848, Americans greeted them as evidence that the American model of free republican institutions was the wave of the future. Those dedicated to the idea of this continuing national mission, which ironically included the spread of slavery, were called "Young America."

President Pierce's platform in 1852 recalled the successful expansionism of the Polk years, declaring that the Mexican War had been "just and necessary." Many Democrats took their overwhelming victory as a mandate to continue adding territory to the Republic. Pierce's ambassador to Mexico, for example, James Gadsden, tried without success to purchase large parts of Mexico. But he did manage to purchase a strip of desert along the southwest border in order to build a transcontinental railroad linking the Deep South with the Pacific Coast.

The failure to acquire more territory from Mexico legally did not discourage expansionist Americans from pursuing illegal means. During the 1850s, Texans and Californians staged dozens of raids (called "filibusters") into Mexico. The most daring adventurer of the era was William Walker, a 100-pound Tennesseean with a zest for danger and power. After migrating to southern California, Walker made plans to add slave lands to the country. In 1853, he invaded Lower California with fewer than 300 men and declared himself president of the independent Republic of Sonora. Although eventually arrested and tried in the United States, he was acquitted after eight minutes of deliberation. He later took it upon himself to invade Nicaragua. Walker came to a fitting end in 1860 when he was captured and shot by a Honduran firing squad after invading that country.

Undaunted by failures in the Southwest, the Pierce administration looked more seriously to the acquisition of Cuba, a Spanish colony many Americans thought destined to be a part of their country. Secretary of State William Marcy instructed the emissary to Spain, Pierre Soulé, to offer $130 million for Cuba. If that failed, Marcy suggested stronger measures. In 1854, the secretary arranged for Soulé and the American ministers to France and England to meet in Belgium to consider options. The result was the Ostend Manifesto, a document intended to pressure Spain to sell Cuba to the United States.

The manifesto argued that Cuba "belongs naturally" to the United States. Both geographically and economically, the fortunes and interests of Cubans and southerners were so "blended" that they were "one people with one destiny." Trade and commerce in the hemisphere would "never be secure" until Cuba was part of the United States.

If Spain refused to sell the island, the ministers threatened a revolution in Cuba with American support. If that should fail, the manifesto warned, "we should be justified in wresting it from Spain." Even Secretary Marcy was shocked when he received the document from Belgium, and he quickly rejected it. Like the Kansas-Nebraska Act, the Ostend Manifesto was urged

most by Democrats who advocated the expansion of slavery. The outraged reaction of northerners in both cases divided and further weakened the Democratic Party.

Nativism, Know-Nothings, and Republicans

Foreign immigration damaged an already enfeebled Whig Party and created concern among many native-born Americans. To the average hard-working Protestant American, the foreigners pouring into the cities and following the railroads westward spoke unfamiliar languages, wore funny clothes, drank alcohol freely in grogshops, and increased crime and pauperism. Still worse, they attended Catholic churches, sent children to their own schools, and worked for lower wages in worse conditions than American workers. Perhaps worst of all, these nativists said, the new immigrants corrupted American politics.

Catholic immigrants preferred the Democratic Party out of traditional loyalties and because Democrats were less inclined than Whigs to interfere with religion, schooling, drinking, and other aspects of personal behavior. It was mostly former Whigs, therefore, who in 1854 founded the American Party to oppose the new immigrants. Members wanted a longer period of naturalization and pledged themselves never to vote for Irish Catholics for public office since it was assumed that their highest loyalty was to the pope in Rome. They also agreed to keep information about their order secret. If asked, they would say, "I know nothing." Hence, they were dubbed the Know-Nothing Party.

The Know-Nothings were overwhelmingly a party of the middle and lower classes, workers who worried about their jobs and wages, and farmers and small-town Americans who worried about disruptive new forces in their lives. In the 1854 and 1855 elections, the Know-Nothings gave anti-Catholicism a national political focus for the first time. They did so well that they

The American (Know-Nothing) Party campaign against the immigrants is dramatically shown in this cartoon of a whiskey-drinking Irishman and beer-barreled German stealing the ballot box while native-born Americans fight at the election poll in the background.

threatened to replace the Whigs as the second major party.

Meanwhile, a group of ex-Whigs and Free-Soilers met and formed the nucleus of another new party, called the Republican Party. Its first challenge was to respond to popular sentiments by mobilizing sectional fears and ethnic and religious concerns.

Composed almost entirely of northerners, former "conscience" Whigs, and disaffected Democrats, the Republican Party combined four main elements. The first group sought to prohibit slavery in the territories and to repeal the Fugitive Slave Act. A more moderate and larger group, typified by Abraham Lincoln of Illinois, opposed slavery in the western territories but indicated that they would not interfere with it where it already existed.

A third element of the party was anti-Catholic, reflecting the traditional Whig position. The fourth element wanted the federal government to promote commercial and industrial development and the dignity of labor. This fourth group, which Lincoln was in as well, believed that a system of free labor led to progress. As the Springfield *Republican* said in 1856, the Republican Party's strength came from "those who work with their hands, who live and act independently, who hold the stakes of home and family, of farm and workshop, of education and freedom—these as a mass are enrolled in the Republican ranks."

The strengths of the Republican and Know-Nothing (American) parties were tested in 1856. Which party could best oppose the Democrats? The American Party nominated Fillmore, who had strong support in the Upper South and border states. The Republicans chose John C. Frémont, a Free-Soiler from Missouri with virtually no political experience. The Democrats nominated James Buchanan of Pennsylvania, commonly known as "a northern man with southern principles." Frémont won several free states, while Fillmore won only Maryland. Buchanan, taking advantage of the divided opposition, won the election, but with only 45 percent of the popular vote. After 1856, the Know-Nothings died out, but nativism did not.

KANSAS AND THE TWO CULTURES

As slaveholders sought ways of expanding slavery westward across the Plains and south into Cuba in the mid-1850s, Republicans wanted to halt the advance of slavery. In 1854, Lincoln worried that it was slavery that "deprives our republican example of its just influence in the world."

Competing for Kansas

Lincoln was concerned about the passage of the Kansas-Nebraska Act in 1854, which opened the way for proslavery and antislavery forces to meet physically and to compete over whether Kansas would become a slave or free state. No sooner had the bill passed Congress than Eli Thayer founded the Massachusetts Emigrant Aid Society to recruit Free-Soil settlers to go to Kansas. From New York, Frederick Douglass called for "companies of emigrants from the free states . . . to possess the goodly land." By the summer of 1855, about 1,200 New England colonists had migrated to Kansas.

David Atchison, Democratic senator from Missouri, believed that Congress had an obligation to protect slavery in the territories, thereby permitting Missouri slaveholders to move into Kansas. He described New England migrants as "negro thieves" and "abolition tyrants." He recommended to fellow Missourians that they defend their property and interests "with the *bayonet* and with *blood*" and, if need be, "to kill every God-damned abolitionist in the district."

Under Atchison's inflammatory leadership, secret societies sprang up in the Missouri counties adjacent to Kansas. They vowed to combat the Free-Soilers. Rumors of 20,000 Massachusetts migrants spurred Missourians to action. Thousands poured across the border late in 1854 to vote in the first territorial election. Twice as many ballots were cast as the number of registered voters, and in one polling place only 20 of over 600 voters were legal residents.

In March 1855, a second election was held to select a territorial legislature. The pattern of border crossings, intimidation, and illegal voting was repeated. Atchison himself, drinking "considerable whiskey" along the way, led a band of armed men across the state line to vote and frighten would-be Free-Soil voters away. Not surprisingly, a small minority of eligible voters elected a proslavery territorial legislature. Free-Soilers, meanwhile, staged their own constitutional convention in Lawrence and created a Free-Soil government at Topeka. It banned blacks from the state. The proslavery legislature settled in Lecompton, giving Kansas two governments.

Neither President Pierce nor Congress could do anything except send an investigating committee, which further inflamed passions. Throughout 1855, the call to arms grew more strident. One proslavery newspaper invited southerners to bring their weapons and "send the scoundrels" from the North "back to whence they came, or . . . to hell, it matters not which." At Yale University, the noted minister Henry Ward Beecher presented Bibles and rifles to young men who would go fight for the Lord in Kansas. Missourians dubbed the rifles "Beecher's Bibles" and vowed, as one newspaper put it, "Blood for Blood! . . . for each drop spilled, we shall require one hundred fold!"

"Bleeding Kansas"

Inevitably, blood flowed in Kansas. In May 1856, supported by a prosouthern federal Marshall, a mob entered Lawrence, smashed the offices and presses of a Free-Soil newspaper, fired several cannonballs into the Free State Hotel,

"Bleeding Kansas"

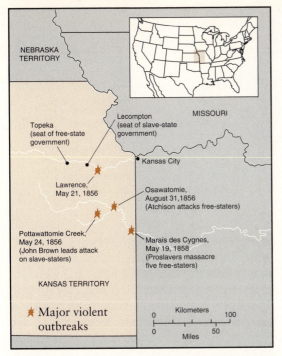

NEBRASKA TERRITORY

MISSOURI

Topeka
(seat of free-state
government)

Lecompton
(seat of slave-state
government)

Kansas City

Lawrence,
May 21, 1856

Osawatomie,
August 31,1856
(Atchison attacks free-staters)

Pottawattomie Creek,
May 24, 1856
(John Brown leads attack
on slave-staters)

Marais des Cygnes,
May 19, 1858
(Proslavers massacre
five free-staters)

KANSAS TERRITORY

★ Major violent outbreaks

Kilometers
0   100
0   50
Miles

and destroyed homes and shops. Three nights later, motivated by vengeance and a feeling that he was doing God's will, John Brown led a small New England band, including four of his sons, to a proslavery settlement near Pottawatomie Creek. There they dragged five men out of their cabins and despite the terrified entreaties of their wives, hacked them to death with swords.

Violence also entered the halls of Congress. That same week, abolitionist senator Charles Sumner accused proslavery Senate leaders, especially Atchison and Andrew Butler of South Carolina, of cavorting with "the harlot, Slavery." Two days later, Butler's nephew, Congressman Preston Brooks, avenged the honor of his colleague by beating Sumner senseless with his cane as he sat at his Senate desk.

The sack of Lawrence, the massacre at Pottawatomie Creek, and the caning of Sumner set off a minor civil war, which historians have called "Bleeding Kansas." It lasted throughout the summer. Crops were burned, homes were destroyed, fights broke out in saloons and streets, and night raiders tortured and murdered their enemies. For residents like Charles Lines, who just wanted to farm his land in peace, it was impossible to remain neutral. Lines hoped his neighbors near Lawrence would avoid "involving themselves in trouble." But when proslavery forces seized a mild-mannered neighbor, bound him, tortured him, and left him to die, Lines joined the battle. He wrote to a friend that "blood must end in the triumph of the right."

Even before the bleeding of Kansas began, the New York *Tribune* warned, "We are two peoples. We are a people for Freedom and a people for Slavery. Between the two, conflict is inevitable." The competing visions of two separate cultures for the future destiny of the United States were at stake.

Northern Views and Visions

The North saw itself as a prosperous land of bustling commerce and expanding, independent agriculture. Northern farmers and workers were typically self-made men who believed that individualism, equality of opportunity, and government support for free labor and industrial growth would lead to economic progress. Although the North contained many growing cities, northerners revered the values of the small towns that spread from New England across the Upper Midwest. These values included a respect for the rights of the people, tempered by the rule of law; individual enterprise, balanced by a concern for one's neighbors; and a fierce morality rooted in Calvinist Protestantism. Many northerners would regulate morality—by persuasion if possible but by legislation if necessary—to remove the sins of irreligion, illiteracy, and intemperance from American society. It was no accident that the ideas of universal public education and laws against the sale and consumption of alcohol both began in New England.

BORDER RUFFIANS "GOING OVER TO WIPE OUT LAWRENCE."

Led by Senator David Atchison, thousands of gun-toting Missourians crossed into Kansas in 1854 and 1855 in order to vote illegally for a proslavery territorial government. The ensuing bloodshed made Kansas a preview of the Civil War.

Most northerners also believed that only free men could achieve economic progress and moral society. Therefore, the worst sin in the northerner's view was the loss of one's freedom. Slavery was the root of all evil, and for many, the South represented the antithesis of everything that northerners saw as good. Northern migrants to Kansas described southerners as subhuman, unclean, and uncivilized. They were, as one put it, "drunken ourang-outans," "wild beasts" who drank whiskey, ate dirt, uttered oaths, raped slave women, and fought or dueled at the slightest excuse. In the popular language of the day, they were known as "Pukes."

The Southern Perspective

Epithets aside, southerners were a diverse people who, like northerners, shared certain broad values, generally those of the planter class. If in the North the values of economic enterprise were most important, southerners revered social values most. Like the English gentry they sought to emulate, they saw themselves as courteous, refined, hospitable, and chivalrous. By contrast, they saw northerners as coarse, ill-mannered, aggressive, materialistic "Yankees." In a society

where one person in three was a black slave, racial distinctions and paternalistic relationships were crucial in maintaining order and white supremacy. Fear of slave revolt was ever present. The South had five times more military schools than the North. Northerners educated the many for economic utility, but southerners educated the few for grace and character. In short, the South saw itself as a genteel, ordered society guided by the aristocratic code of the gentleman planter.

Southerners believed that the democratic principle of self-government was best preserved in local political units such as the state. They cherished the Union but preferred the loose confederacy of the Jeffersonian past to the centralized nationalism New York senator William Seward kept invoking.

Two images dominated the South's view of northerners: either they were stingy, hypocritical, moralizing Puritans, or they were grubby, slum-dwelling, Catholic immigrants.

Each side, then, saw the other threatening its freedom and infringing on its view of a proper republican society. As hostilities increased, the views each section had of the other grew steadily more rigid and conspiratorial. Northerners saw the South as a "slave power," determined to foist the slave system on free labor throughout the land. Southerners saw the North as full of "black Republicanism," determined to destroy the southern way of life.

POLARIZATION AND THE ROAD TO WAR

Because of the national constituencies of the two major political parties, northern and southern cultural stereotypes and conspiratorial accusations had been largely held in check. But events in Kansas solidified the image of the Republicans as a northern party and seriously weakened the Democrats. Further events, still involving the question of slavery in the territories, soon split the Democratic Party irrevocably into sectional halves: the *Dred Scott* decision of the Supreme Court (1857), the constitutional crisis in Kansas (1857), the Lincoln-Douglas debates in Illinois (1858), John Brown's raid in Virginia (1859), and Lincoln's election (1860). These incidents also further polarized the two cultures and set the nation on the final road to civil war.

The *Dred Scott* Case

The events of 1857 reinforced the arguments of those who believed in a slave power conspiracy. Two days after James Buchanan's inauguration, the Supreme Court finally ruled in *Dred Scott* v. *Sandford*. The case had been pending before the Court for nearly three years, but the slave family of Dred Scott had been waiting longer for the decision. In 1846, Dred and Harriet Scott had filed suit in Missouri for their freedom. They argued that their master had taken them into Minnesota, Wisconsin, and other territories where the Missouri Compromise prohibited slavery, and therefore they should be freed.

When the Court, which had a majority of southern judges, issued its decision, by a vote of 7 to 2, it made three rulings. First, since blacks were, as Chief Justice Roger Taney put it, "be-

ings of an inferior order [who] had no rights which white men were bound to respect," Dred Scott was not a citizen and had no right to sue in federal courts. The second ruling stated that the Missouri Compromise was unconstitutional because Congress did not have the power to ban slavery in a territory. And third, the fact that the Scotts had been taken in and out of free states did not affect their status. Despite two eloquent dissenting opinions, Dred and Harriet Scott remained slaves.

The implications of these decisions went far beyond the Scotts' personal freedom. The arguments about black citizenship insulted and infuriated many northerners. Even more troublesome was the possibility hinted at in the decision that slavery might be permitted in the free states of the North, where it had long been banned. One issue that remained unresolved by the Court was whether or not a territorial legislature could write a constitution that permitted the introduction of new slaves.

Douglas and the Democrats

The *Dred Scott* decision, endorsed by Buchanan, fed northern suspicions of a slave power conspiracy to impose slavery everywhere. Events in Kansas, which still had two governments, heightened these fears. In the summer of 1857, Kansas had still another election, called by the proslavery legislature at Lecompton. Free-Soilers refused to vote, charging gross irregularities in drawing district boundaries, so that only 2,000 out of a possible 24,000 voters participated. They elected a proslavery slate of delegates to a constitutional convention meeting at Lecompton as a preparation for statehood. The convention decided to exclude free blacks from the state, to guarantee the property rights of the few slaveholders in Kansas, and to ask voters to decide in a referendum whether to permit more slaves.

The proslavery Lecompton constitution,

clearly unrepresentative of the wishes of the majority of the people of Kansas, was sent to Congress for approval. Eager to retain the support of southern Democrats, Buchanan endorsed it. Stephen Douglas, a northern Democrat, opposed it. Congress sent the Lecompton constitution back to the people of Kansas for another referendum. This time they defeated it, which meant that Kansas remained a territory rather than becoming a slave state. While Kansas was left in an uncertain status, the larger political effect of the struggle was to split the Democratic party almost beyond repair.

Lincoln and the Illinois Debates

No sooner had Douglas settled the Lecompton question than he faced reelection in Illinois in 1858. Opposing him was Abraham Lincoln, who had emerged to challenge William Seward for leadership of the Republican Party. Lincoln's character was shaped on the midwestern frontier, where he had educated himself, developed antislavery views, and dreamed of America's greatness.

Since Douglas was clearly the leading Democrat, the Senate election in Illinois appeared to be a preview of the presidential election of 1860. The Illinois campaign featured a series of seven debates between Lincoln and Douglas in different cities. With a national as well as a local audience, the debates provided a remarkable opportunity for the two men to state their views on the heated racial issues before the nation.

Lincoln set a solemn tone when he accepted the Republican senatorial nomination in Chicago in June. The American nation, he said, was in a "crisis" and building toward a worse one: "A House divided against itself cannot stand. I believe this government cannot endure, permanently half *slave* and half *free*." Lincoln said he did not expect the Union "to be dissolved" or "the house to fall" but rather that "it will become *all* one thing, or *all* the other." In

the ensuing debates with Douglas, Lincoln skillfully staked out a moral position not only in advance of Douglas but well ahead of his time.

Lincoln was also very much a part of his time. He believed that whites were superior to blacks and opposed equal rights for free blacks. He believed, furthermore, that the physical and moral differences between whites and blacks would "forever forbid the two races from living together on terms of social and political equality." However, he not only believed that blacks were "entitled to all the natural rights . . . in the Declaration of Independence" but also that they had many specific economic rights as well, like "the right to put into his mouth the bread that his own hands have earned." In these rights, blacks were, Lincoln said, "my equal and the equal of Judge Douglas, and the equal of every living man."

Unlike Douglas, Lincoln hated slavery. At Galesburg, he said, "I contemplate slavery as a moral, social, and political evil." In Quincy, he said that the difference between a Republican and a Democrat was quite simply whether one thought slavery wrong or right. Douglas advocated "popular sovereignty," the doctrine that the people of a territory should have the right to determine whether they wanted to permit slavery or not. Douglas's moral indifference to slavery was clear in his admission that he did not care if a territorial legislature voted it "up or down." Republicans did care, Lincoln affirmed, sounding a warning that by stopping the expansion of slavery, the course toward its "ultimate extinction" had begun.

Douglas won the election. When he and Lincoln met again two years later, the order of their finish would be reversed. Elsewhere in 1858, however, Democrats did poorly, losing 18 congressional seats to the Republicans.

John Brown's Raid

The slavery issue grew more heated on October 16, 1859, when John Brown and a band of 22

This 1860 photograph of Lincoln shows him without the look of strain and overwhelming stress commonly seen in photographs taken during the Civil War.

men attacked a federal arsenal at Harpers Ferry, Virginia (now West Virginia). He hoped that the action might provoke a general uprising of slaves throughout the Upper South or at least provide the arms by which slaves could make their way to freedom. Although he seized the arsenal, federal troops soon overcame him. Nearly half his men were killed, including two sons. Brown himself was captured, tried, and hanged for treason. So ended a lifetime of failures.

In death, however, he was not a failure. Brown's daring if foolhardy raid, and his impressively dignified behavior during his trial and speedy execution, unleashed powerful passions, further widening the gap between North and South. Northerners responded to his death with an outpouring of admiration and sympathy, for both the man and his cause. But many southerners concluded that northerners would stop at nothing, including armed force, to free the slaves. Brown's raid stimulated a wave of fear and suspicion. In response to the Brown raid, southerners also became more convinced, as the governor of South Carolina put it, that a "black Republican" plot in the North was "arrayed against the slaveholders."

The Election of 1860

The conflict between Buchanan and Douglas took its toll on the Democratic Party. When the nominating convention met in Charleston, South Carolina, a hotbed of secessionist sentiments, it met for a record ten days without being able to name a presidential candidate. The Democrats went through 59 ballots, adjourned, and then met again, acknowledging their irreparable division by naming two candidates. Douglas represented northern Democrats, and John C. Breckinridge, Buchanan's vice president, carried the banner of the proslavery South. The Constitutional Union Party, made up of former southern Whigs and border-state nativists, claimed the middle ground of compromise and nominated John Bell, a slaveholder from Tennessee with mild views.

With Democrats split in two and a new party in contention, the Republican strategy aimed at keeping the states carried by Frémont in 1856 and adding Pennsylvania, Illinois, and Indiana. Lincoln, a moderate midwesterner with widespread appeal, won his party's nomination.

The Republican platform also reflected moderation, reducing attacks on slavery to oppose only its extension. Most of the platform spoke to the concerns of the several elements of the party: tariff protection, subsidized internal improvements, free labor, and a homestead bill. Above all, the Republicans, like southern Democrats, defended their view of what republican values meant for America's future. It did not include the kind of society of equal rights envisioned by Frederick Douglass. An English traveler in 1860 observed that in America "we see, in effect, two nations—one white and another black—growing up together within the same political circle, but never mingling on a principle of equality."

The Republican strategy for electoral victory worked exactly as planned, as Lincoln swept the entire Northeast and Midwest. Although he received less than 40 percent of the popular vote nationwide, his triumph in the North was decisive. Even a united Democratic Party could not have defeated him. With victory assured, Lincoln prepared for the consequences and awesome responsibilities of his election. They came even before his inauguration.

THE DIVIDED HOUSE FALLS

The Republicans overestimated the extent of Unionist sentiment in the South. They could not believe that the secessionists would prevail after Lincoln's victory. A year earlier, some southern congressmen had walked out in protest of the selection of an antislavery speaker of the House. A Republican leader, Carl Schurz, recalling this act, said that the southerners had taken a drink and then come back. After Lincoln's election, Schurz predicted, they would walk out, take two drinks, and come back again. He was wrong.

Secession and Uncertainty

On December 20, 1860, South Carolina seceded from the Union, declaring the "experiment" of putting people with "different pursuits and institutions" under one government a failure. By February 1, the other six Deep South states (Mississippi, Florida, Alabama, Georgia, Louisiana, and Texas) had seceded. A week later, delegates met in Montgomery, Alabama, created the Confederate States of America, adopted a consti-

tution, and elected Jefferson Davis, a Mississippi senator and cotton planter, its provisional president. The divided house had fallen, as Lincoln had predicted it would.

The nation waited and watched, wondering what Virginia and the border states would do, what outgoing President Buchanan would do, and what Congress would do. Buchanan did nothing, and so the entire nation waited for Abraham Lincoln.

Frederick Douglass waited too, without much hope. Seeing northern politicians and businessmen "granting the most demoralizing concessions to the Slave Power," Douglass began to explore possibilities for emigration and colonization in Haiti, an idea he had long opposed. In February, Douglass said, "Let the conflict come." He opposed all compromises, hoping that with Lincoln's inauguration in March it would "be decided, and decided forever, which of the two, Freedom or Slavery, shall give law to this Republic."

Lincoln and Fort Sumter

As Douglass penned these thoughts, Lincoln began a long, slow train ride from Springfield, Illinois, to Washington, writing and rewriting his inaugural address. Lincoln was firmly opposed to secession and to any compromises with the principle of stopping the extension of slavery. He would neither conciliate secessionist southern states nor force their return.

But Lincoln believed in his constitutional responsibility to uphold the laws of the land, and on this significant point he would not yield. The focus of his attention was a federal fort in the harbor of Charleston, South Carolina. Major Robert Anderson, the commander of Fort Sumter, was running out of provisions and had requested new supplies from Washington. Lincoln would enforce the laws and protect federal property at Fort Sumter.

Table 14.1
Major Causes of and Events Leading to the Civil War

Date	Event	Impact or Effect as Cause of Civil War
1600s–1860s	Slavery in the South	Major underlying pervasive cause
1700s–1860s	Development of two distinct socioeconomic systems and cultures	Further reinforced slavery as fundamental socioeconomic, cultural, moral issue
1787–1860s	States' rights, nullification doctrine	Ongoing political issue, less fundamental as cause
1820	Missouri Compromise (36°30′)	Background for conflict over slavery in territories
1828–1833	South Carolina tariff nullification crisis	Background for secession leadership in South Carolina
1831–1860s	Antislavery movements, southern justification	30 years of emotional preparation for conflict
1846–1848	Mexican War (Wilmot Proviso, Calhoun, popular sovereignty)	Options for slavery in territories issue
1850	Compromise of 1850	Temporary and unsatisfactory "settlement" of divisive issue
1851–1854	Fugitive slaves returned and rescued in North; personal liberty laws passed in North; Harriet Beecher Stowe's *Uncle Tom's Cabin*	Heightened northern emotional reactions against the South and slavery
1852–1856	Breakdown of Whig Party and national Democratic Party; creation of a new party system with sectional basis	Made national politics an arena where sectional and cultural differences over slavery were fought
1854	Ostend Manifesto and other expansionist efforts in Central America	Reinforced image of Democratic Party as favoring slavery
	Formation of Republican party	Major party identified as opposing the expansion of slavery
	Kansas-Nebraska Act	Reopened "settled" issue of slavery in the territories
1856	"Bleeding Kansas"; Senator Sumner physically attacked in Senate	Foretaste of civil war (200 killed, $2 million in property lost) inflamed emotions and polarized North and South

(continued)

Table 14.1 (continued)
Major Causes of and Events Leading to the Civil War

DATE	EVENT	IMPACT OR EFFECT as CAUSE OF CIVIL WAR
1857	*Dred Scott* decision; proslavery Lecompton constitution in Kansas	Made North fear a "slave power conspiracy," supported by President Buchanan and the Supreme Court
1858	Lincoln-Douglas debates in Illinois; Democrats lose 18 seats in Congress	Set stage for election of 1860
1859	John Brown's raid and reactions in North and South	Made South fear a "black Republican" plot against slavery; further polarization and irrationality
1860	Democratic party splits in half; Lincoln elected president; South Carolina secedes from Union	Final breakdown of national parties and election of "northern" president; no more compromises
1861	Six more southern states secede by February 1; Confederate constitution adopted February 4; Lincoln inaugurated March 4; Fort Sumter attacked April 12	Civil War begins

As the new president rose to deliver his inaugural address on March 4, he faced a tense and divided nation. Federal troops, fearing a Confederate attack on the nation's capital, were everywhere. Lincoln asserted his unequivocal intention to enforce the laws of the land, arguing that the Union was constitutionally "perpetual" and indissoluble. He reminded the nation that the "only substantial dispute" was that "one section of our country believes slavery is *right,* and ought to be extended, while the other believes it is *wrong,* and ought not to be extended." Still hoping to appeal to Unionist strength among southern moderates, Lincoln indicated that he would make no attempts to interfere with existing slavery or the law to return fugitive slaves. He urged against rash actions and put the burden of initiating a civil war on the "dissatisfied fellow-countrymen" who had seceded. His deepest hope was that

> the mystic chords of memory, stretching from every battlefield, and patriot grave, to every living heart and hearthstone, all over this broad land, will yet swell the chorus of the Union, when again touched, as surely they will be, by the better angels of our nature.

On April 6, Lincoln notified the governor of South Carolina that he was sending "provisions only" to Fort Sumter. No effort would be made "to throw in men, arms, or ammunition" unless the fort were attacked. On April 10, Jefferson Davis directed General P. G. T. Beauregard to demand the surrender of Fort Sumter. Davis told Beauregard to reduce the fort if Major Anderson refused.

On April 12, as Lincoln's relief expedition neared Charleston, Beauregard's batteries began shelling Fort Sumter, and the Civil War began. Frederick Douglass was about to leave for Haiti when he heard the news. He immediately changed his plans: "This is no time . . . to leave the country." He announced his readiness to help end the war by aiding the Union to organize freed slaves "into a liberating army" to "make war upon . . . the savage barbarism of slavery." Benjamin Allston, who was in Charleston, described the events to his father. On April 14, he reported exuberantly "the glorious, and astonishing news that Sumter has fallen." With it fell America's divided house.

CONCLUSION

THE "IRREPRESSIBLE CONFLICT"

Lincoln had been right. The nation could no longer endure half slave and half free. The collision between North and South, William Seward said, was not an "accidental, unnecessary" event but "an irrepressible conflict between opposing and enduring forces." Those forces had been at work for many decades but developed with increasing intensity after 1848 in the conflict over the question of the extension of slavery into the territories. Although economic, cultural, political, constitutional, and emotional forces all contributed to the developing opposition between North and South, slavery was the fundamental, enduring force that underlay all others, causing what poet Walt Whitman called "the red blood of civil war."

Recommended Reading

Easily the finest overall account of the political history of the 1850s is David Potter's superb narrative, *The Impending Crisis, 1848–1861* (1976), completed by Donald Fehrenbacher after Potter's death. See also James McPherson, *Ordeal by Fire: The Civil War and Reconstruction* (1982). Essay collections on recent Civil War scholarship are Eric Foner, ed., *Politics and Ideology in the Age of the Civil War* (1980); and William E. Gienapp, Thomas B. Alexander, Michael F. Holt, Stephen E. Mazlish, and Joel H. Silbey, *Essays on American Antebellum Politics, 1840–1860* (1982). Kenneth Stampp has compiled the most useful combination of primary and secondary sources representing differences of opinion, *The Causes of the Civil War*, rev. ed. (1974), a good book in which to explore various historical interpretations.

Michael F. Holt, *The Political Crisis of the 1850s* (1978), is the best overall work of "new politics" showing the breakdown of political parties as a major cause of the Civil War. On ethnic and religious politics and the effects of nativism on political behavior, see Paul Kleppner, *The Third Electoral System, 1853–1892: Parties, Voters, and Political Cultures* (1979). For a monumental new synthesis and interpretation, see William E. Gienapp, *The Origins of the Republican Party, 1852–1856* (1987). Specialized works on the effects of the issue of slavery in the territories on sectional rivalry and political parties are William J. Cooper, *The South and the Politics of Slavery* (1978); and Richard Sewell, *Ballots for Freedom: Antislavery Politics in the United States, 1837–1865* (1976).

On racism in the West, see James Rawley, *Race and Politics: "Bleeding Kansas" and the Coming of the Civil War* (1969). The definitive work on the *Dred Scott* case is Donald Fehrenbacher, *Slavery, Law, and Politics: The* Dred Scott *Case in Historical Perspective* (1981). The final road to war after Lincoln's election in 1860 is detailed in William Barney, *The Road to Secession* (1972); and Steven Channing, *Crisis of Fear: Secession in South Carolina* (1970).

Among biographies of major figures see Robert Johannsen, *Stephen Douglas* (1973); Stephen Oates, *To Purge This Land with Blood: A Biography of John Brown* (1970) and *With Malice Toward None: The Life of Abraham Lincoln* (1982). The emotional flavor of the decade is captured in Harriet Beecher Stowe's novel *Uncle Tom's Cabin* (1852); and Walt Whitman's poetry in *Leaves of Grass* (any edition).

Time Line

1832	Nullification crisis
1835–1840	Intensification of abolitionist attacks on slavery Violent retaliatory attacks on abolitionists
1840	Liberty party formed
1846	Wilmot Proviso
1848	Free-Soil party founded Zachary Taylor elected president
1850	Compromise of 1850, including Fugitive Slave Act
1850–1854	"Young America" movement
1851	Women's rights convention in Akron, Ohio
1852	Harriet Beecher Stowe publishes *Uncle Tom's Cabin* Franklin Pierce elected president
1854	Ostend Manifesto Kansas-Nebraska Act nullifies Missouri Compromise Republican and Know-Nothing parties formed

1855	Walt Whitman publishes *Leaves of Grass*
1855–1856	Thousands pour into Kansas, creating months of turmoil and violence
1856	John Brown's massacre in Kansas Sumner-Brooks incident in Senate James Buchanan elected president
1857	*Dred Scott* decision legalizes slavery in territories Lecompton constitution in Kansas
1858	Lincoln-Douglas debates
1859	John Brown's raid at Harpers Ferry
1860	Democratic Party splits Four-party campaign Abraham Lincoln elected president
1860–1861	Seven southern states secede
1861	Confederate States of America founded Attack on Fort Sumter begins Civil War

chapter 15

The Union Severed

We cannot escape history," Abraham Lincoln reminded Congress in 1862. "We of this Congress and this administration will be remembered in spite of ourselves." Lincoln's conviction that Americans would long remember him and other major actors of the Civil War—Jefferson Davis, Robert E. Lee, Ulysses S. Grant—was correct. Whether seen as heroes or villains, these great men have dominated the story of the Civil War.

Yet from the earliest days, the war touched the lives of even the most uncelebrated Americans. From Indianapolis, 20-year-old Arthur Carpenter wrote to his parents in Massachusetts begging for permission to enlist in the volunteer army: "I have always longed for the time to come when I could enter the army and be a military man, and when this war broke out, I thought the time had come, but you would not permit me to enter the service . . . now I make one more appeal to you." The pleas worked, and Carpenter enlisted, spending most of the war fighting in Kentucky and Tennessee.

In that same year, in Tennessee, George and Ethie Eagleton faced anguishing decisions. Though not an abolitionist, George, a 30-year-old Presbyterian preacher, was unsympathetic to slavery and opposed to secession. But when his native state left the Union, George felt compelled to follow and enlisted in the 44th Tennessee Infantry. Ethie, his 26-year-old wife, despaired over the war, George's decision, and her own forlorn situation:

> *Pres. Lincoln has done what no other Pres. ever dared to do—he has divided these once peaceful and happy United States. And Oh! the dreadful dark cloud that is now hanging over our country—'tis enough to sicken the heart of any one. . . . Mr. E. is gone. . . . What will become of me, left here without a home and relatives, a babe just nine months old and no George?*

Both Carpenter and the Eagletons survived the war, but the conflict transformed all of their lives. Carpenter had difficulty settling down to civilian life. Filled with bitter memories of the war years in Tennessee, the Eagletons moved to Arkansas.

For thousands of Americans, from Lincoln and Davis to Carpenter and the Eagletons, war was both a profoundly personal and a major national event. Its impact reached far beyond the four years of hostilities. The war that was fought to conserve two political, social, and economic visions ended by changing familiar ways of political, social, and economic life in both North and South. War was a transforming force, both destructive and creative in its effect on the structure and social dynamics of society and on the lives of ordinary people. This theme underlies this chapter's analysis of the war's three stages: the initial months of preparation, the years of military stalemate between 1861 and 1865, and, finally, resolution.

ORGANIZING FOR WAR

The Confederate bombardment of Fort Sumter on April 12, 1861, and the surrender of Union troops the next day ended the uncertainty of the secession winter. The North's response to Fort Sumter was a virtual declaration of war as President Lincoln called for state militia volunteers to crush southern "insurrection." His action pushed several slave states (Virginia, North Carolina, Tennessee, Arkansas) off the fence and into the southern camp. Other states (Maryland, Kentucky, and Missouri) agonizingly debated which way to go. The "War Between the States" was now a reality.

Many Americans were unenthusiastic about the course of events. Southerners like George Eagleton only reluctantly followed Tennessee out of the Union. Robert E. Lee of Virginia was initially hesitant to resign his federal commission. Many southern whites and residents of border states were dismayed at secession and war. Many would eventually join the Union forces.

In the North, large numbers had supported neither the Republican Party nor Lincoln. Nevertheless, the days following Fort Sumter and Lincoln's call for troops saw an outpouring of support on both sides, fueled in part by relief at decisive action, in part by patriotism and love of adventure, in part by unemployment. Sisters, wives, and mothers set to work making uniforms. A New Yorker, Jane Woolsey, described the drama of those early days "of terrible excitement."

> Outside the parlor windows the city is gay and brilliant with excited crowds, the incessant movement and music of marching regiments and all the thousands of flags, big and little, which suddenly came fluttering out of every window and door.

The war fever produced so many volunteers that neither northern nor southern officials could handle the throng. Northern authorities turned aside offers from blacks to serve. Both sides sent thousands of white would-be soldiers home. The conviction that the conflict would rapidly come to a glorious conclusion fueled the eagerness to enlist. Lincoln's call for 75,000 state militiamen for only 90 days of service and a similar enlistment term for Confederate soldiers supported the notion that the war would be short.

The Balance of Resources

Despite the bands, parades, cheers, and confidence, the outcome of the approaching civil conflict was much in doubt. The military stalemate in 1861 and 1862 proved that in the short term, North and South were not unevenly matched. Almost 187,000 Union troops bore arms in July 1861, while just over 112,00 men marched under Confederate colors.

Secession of the Southern States

First secession

Second secession

Border states

Free states and territories

The Union, however, enjoyed impressive economic advantages. In the North, one million workers in 110,000 manufacturing concerns produced goods valued at $1.5 billion annually, while 110,000 southern workers in 18,000 manufacturing concerns produced goods valued at only $155 million a year. The North had one factory for every southern industrial worker, and 70 percent of the nation's railroad tracks were in the North. Producing 17 times as much cotton cloth and woolen goods, 32 times as many firearms, and 20 times as much pig iron as the South, the North could clothe and arm troops and move them and their supplies on a scale that the South could not match. But to be effective, northern industrial resources had to be mobilized for war. Furthermore, the depleted northern treasury made the government's first task the raising of funds to pay for military necessities.

The South traditionally depended on imported manufactured goods from the North and from Europe. If Lincoln cut off that trade, the South would face the enormous task of creating its industry almost from scratch. Moreover, its railroad system was organized to move cotton, not armies and supplies. Yet the agricultural South did have important resources of food, draft animals, and, of course, cotton, which southerners believed would secure British and French support. Finally, in choosing to wage a defensive war, the South could tap regional loyalty and would enjoy protected lines of supply and support, while Union forces, embarked on an expensive war of conquest, would have extended supply lines vulnerable to attack.

The Border States

When the seven states of the Deep South seceded during the winter of 1860–1861, the strategically important border states adopted a wait-and-see attitude. Delaware identified with the Union camp, but the others vacillated. Lincoln's call for troops precipitated decisions in several states, however. Between April 17 and May 20, 1861, Virginia, Arkansas, Tennessee, and North Carolina joined the Confederacy.

In Maryland, sympathies were divided, but

Confederate enthusiasts abounded in Baltimore. On April 19, the 6th Massachusetts Regiment arrived in Baltimore headed for Washington. Because the regiment had to change railroad lines, the soldiers set out across the city on foot and in horsecars. As they marched through the streets, a mob of some 10,000 southern sympathizers, flying Confederate flags, attacked them with paving stones, then bayonets and bullets. The soldiers fought back, but would-be secessionists burned the railroad bridges connecting Baltimore to the North and to the South. Washington found itself cut off from the rest of the Union, an island in the middle of hostile territory.

Lincoln took stern measures to secure Maryland. Hundreds of southern sympathizers, including 19 state legislators and Baltimore's mayor, were arrested and languished in prison without trial. Although the chief justice of the United States, Roger B. Taney, challenged the legality of the president's action, Lincoln ignored him. A month later, Taney ruled in *Ex parte Merryman* that if the public's safety was endangered, only Congress had the right to suspend a writ of habeas corpus. By then, Lincoln had secured Maryland for the Union.

Though Lincoln's quick and harsh response ensured Maryland's loyalty, he was more cautious elsewhere, for any hasty action would push border states into the waiting arms of the Confederacy. In the end, after some fighting and much maneuvering, Kentucky and Missouri, like Maryland, stayed in the union.

Challenges of War

During the tense weeks after Fort Sumter, both the North and the South faced enormous organizational problems as they readied for war. The South had to create everything from a constitution and governmental departments to a flag and postage stamps.

In February 1861, the original seceding states sent delegates to Montgomery, Alabama, to begin work on a provisional framework and to select a provisional president and vice president. The delegates swiftly wrote a constitution, much like the federal constitution of 1787 except in its emphasis on the "sovereign and independent character" of the states and its explicit recognition of slavery. The provisional president, Jefferson Davis of Mississippi, put together a geographically and politically balanced cabinet, but it had few men of political stature. As time passed, it turned out to be unstable as well. In a four-year period, 14 men held six positions.

Davis's cabinet appointees faced the formidable challenge of creating government departments from scratch. The president's office was in a hotel parlor. The Confederate Treasury Department was housed in a room in an Alabama bank "without furniture of any kind." Treasury Secretary Christopher G. Memminger bought furniture with his own money; operations lurched forward in fits and starts. Other departments faced similar difficulties.

Lincoln never had to set up a postal system or decide whether laws passed before 1861 were valid, but the new president also faced organizational problems. The treasury was empty. The Republicans had won their first presidential election, and floods of office seekers who had worked for Lincoln now thronged into the White House looking for rewards.

Not knowing many of the "prominent men of the day," Lincoln appointed important Republicans from different factions of the party to cabinet posts whether they agreed with him or not. Most were almost strangers to the president. Several scorned him as a bumbling backwoods politician.

Lincoln and Davis

A number of Lincoln's early actions illustrated that he was no malleable backcountry bumbler. After Sumter, he swiftly called up the state militias, expanded the navy, and suspended habeas corpus. He ordered a naval blockade of the South and approved the expenditure of funds for military purposes, all without congressional sanction, since Congress was not in session. As Lincoln told legislators later, "The dogmas of the quiet past are inadequate to the stormy present. . . . As our case is new, so must we think anew, and act anew . . . and then we shall save our country." This willingness to "think anew" was a valuable personal asset, even though some critics called his expansion of presidential power despotic.

By coincidence, Lincoln and his rival, Jefferson Davis, had been born only 100 miles apart in Kentucky. However, the course of their lives had diverged radically. Lincoln's father had migrated north and eked out a simple existence as a farmer in Indiana and Illinois. Abraham had only a rudimentary formal education and was largely self-taught. Davis's family, however, had moved south to Mississippi and become cotton planters. Davis grew up in comfortable circumstances, went to Transylvania University and West Point, fought in the Mexican War before his election to the U.S. Senate, and served as secretary of war under Franklin Pierce (1853–1857). Tall and distinguished-looking, he appeared every inch the aristocratic southerner.

Davis reassured southerners in his inaugural address that his aims were conservative, "to preserve the Government of our fathers in spirit." Yet under the pressure of events, he moved toward creating a new kind of South.

CLASHING ON THE BATTLEFIELD, 1861-1862

The Civil War was the most brutal and destructive conflict in American history. Much of the bloodshed resulted from the application of the theories of Henri Jomini, a French military historian, to the battlefield. Jomini argued that an army seized victory by concentrating its infantry attack at the weakest point in the enemy's defenses. At the time Jomini wrote, this offensive strategy made military sense. The artillery, sta-

tioned well outside the range of enemy fire, could prepare the way for the infantry attack by bombarding enemy lines. By 1861, however, the range of rifles had increased from 100 yards to 500 yards. It was no longer possible to position the artillery close enough to the enemy to allow it to soften up the opposing line in preparation for the infantry charge. During the Civil War, then, enemy fire mowed down attacking infantry soldiers as they ran the 500 fatal yards to the front lines. Battles based on Jomini's theories produced a ghastly crop of dead men.

War in the East

The war's brutal character only gradually revealed itself. The Union commanding general, 70-year-old Winfield Scott, at first pressed for a cautious, long-term strategy, known as the Anaconda Plan. Scott proposed weakening the South gradually through blockades on land and at sea. The excited public, however, hungered for action and quick victory. So did Lincoln, who knew that the longer the war lasted, the more embittered the South and the North would both become, making reunion ever more difficult. Under the cry of "Forward to Richmond!" 35,000 partially trained men led by General Irwin McDowell headed out from Washington in sweltering July weather.

On July 21, 1861, only 25 miles from the capital at Manassas Creek, or Bull Run, as it is also called, inexperienced northern troops confronted 25,000 raw Confederate soldiers commanded by Brigadier General P.G.T. Beauregard, a West Point classmate of McDowell's. Although sightseers, journalists, and politicians accompanied the Union troops, expecting only a Sunday outing, the encounter at Bull Run was no picnic. The course of battle swayed back and forth before the arrival of 2,300 fresh Confederate troops, brought by trains, decided the day. Union soldiers and sightseers fled toward Washington in terror and confusion.

Yet inexperienced Confederate troops failed

Eastern Theater of the Civil War, 1861–1862

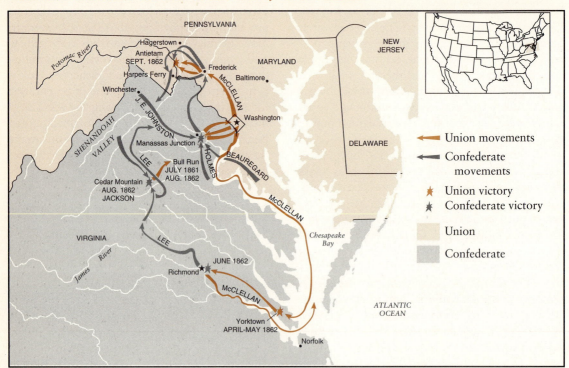

to turn the rout into the quick and decisive victory they sought. As General Joseph E. Johnston pointed out, his men were disorganized, confused by victory, and not well enough supplied with food to chase the Union army back toward Washington.

In many ways, the Battle of Bull Run was prophetic. Victory would be neither quick nor easy. As the disorganization and confusion of both sides suggested, the armies were unprofessional.

For the Union the loss at Bull Run was sobering. Replacing McDowell with 34-year-old General George McClellan, Lincoln began his search for a northern commander capable of winning the war. McClellan, formerly an army engineer, confronted the task of transforming the Army of the Potomac into a fighting force. Short-term militias went home. When Scott re-

tired in the fall of 1861, McClellan became general in chief of the Union armies.

McClellan had considerable organizational ability but no desire to be a daring leader on the battlefield. Convinced that the North must combine military victory with efforts to persuade the South to return to the Union, he sought to avoid unnecessary and embittering loss of life and property. He intended to win the war "by maneuvering rather than fighting."

Pushed by an impatient Lincoln, in June 1862 McClellan advanced with 130,000 troops toward Richmond, now the Confederate capital, but failed to take it. Other Union defeats followed in 1862 as commanders came and went. In September, the South boldly invaded Maryland but suffered a costly defeat at Antietam in which more than 5,000 soldiers were slaughtered and another 17,000 wounded on the grisli-

Trans-Mississippi Campaign of the Civil War

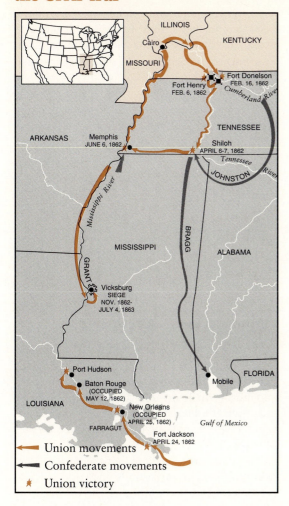

ILLINOIS

KENTUCKY

Cairo

MISSOURI

Fort Donelson
FEB. 16, 1862

Fort Henry
FEB. 6, 1862

Cumberland River

TENNESSEE

ARKANSAS

Memphis
JUNE 6, 1862

Shiloh
APRIL 6-7, 1862

Tennessee River

JOHNSTON

Mississippi River

BRAGG

GRANT

MISSISSIPPI

ALABAMA

Vicksburg
SIEGE
NOV. 1862-
JULY 4, 1863

Port Hudson

FLORIDA

Baton Rouge
(OCCUPIED
MAY 12, 1862)

Mobile

LOUISIANA

New Orleans
(OCCUPIED
APRIL 25, 1862)

Gulf of Mexico

FARRAGUT

Fort Jackson
APRIL 24, 1862

➤ Union movements

➤ Confederate movements

★ Union victory

vital river trade and its great port, New Orleans. Here both George Eagleton and Arthur Carpenter served. Beyond lay the trans-Mississippi West—Louisiana, Arkansas, Missouri, Texas, and the Great Plains—where Native American tribes joined the conflict on both sides.

In the western theater, the Union had two strategic objectives: the domination of Kentucky and eastern Tennessee, the avenues to the South and West, and control of the Mississippi River in order to split the South in two. Major campaigns sought strategic points along rivers and railroads.

It was in the western theater that Ulysses S. Grant rose to prominence. He had attended West Point and served creditably in the Mexican War. Soon after Fort Sumter, Grant enlisted as a colonel in an Illinois militia regiment. Within two months, he was a brigadier general.

Grant realized that the Tennessee and Cumberland rivers were the paths for the successful invasion of Tennessee. Assisted by gunboats, he was largely responsible for the capture of Fort Henry and Fort Donelson, key points on the rivers, in February 1862. His army was nearly destroyed, however, by a surprise Confederate attack at Shiloh Church in Tennessee. The North won this battle but suffered over 13,000 casualties, while 10,000 Confederates lay dead or wounded. More men fell in this single battle than in the American Revolution, the War of 1812, and the Mexican War combined. Because neither army offered sufficient care on the battlefield, many men died of untreated wounds and exposure.

The war in the trans-Mississippi West was a sporadic, far-flung struggle for the control of this vast area. California was one prize that lured both armies into the Southwest. Confederate troops from Texas held Albuquerque and Santa Fe briefly in 1862. Volunteer soldiers from the Colorado mining fields, joined by Mexican-Americans and other soldiers, drove the Texas Confederates from New Mexico. A Union force recruited in California arrived after the Confederates were gone. They spent the remainder of

est day of the war. Lee withdrew to Virginia, and the war in the East was stalemated.

War in the West

The East was only one of three theaters of actions. Between the Appalachian Mountains and the Mississippi lay the western theater, the states of Kentucky, Tennessee, Mississippi, and Alabama. At its edge lay the Mississippi, with its the Civil War years fighting the Apache and the Navajo and with brutal competence crushed both Native American nations.

Farther east was another prize, the Missouri River, which flowed into the Mississippi River, bordered Illinois, and affected military campaigns in Kentucky and Tennessee. Initially, Confederate troops were successful here, but in March 1862, at Pea Ridge in northern Arkansas, the Union forces defeated a Confederate army of 16,000 that included a brigade of Native Americans from the Five Civilized Nations. Missouri entered the Union camp for the first time in the war, and fierce guerrilla warfare continued in the region.

Naval Warfare

Lincoln's naval blockade of southern ports was not immediately effective. With no more than 33 ships, the Union navy tried to close up 189 ports along a 3,500-mile coastline. In 1861, the navy intercepted only about one blockade runner in ten and in 1862, one in eight. In the short run, the blockade did little damage to the South.

More successful were operations to gain footholds along the southern coast. In November 1861, a Union expedition took Port Royal Sound, where it freed the first slaves, and the nearby South Carolina Sea Islands. A few months later, the navy defeated a Confederate force on Roanoke Island. But the Union's greatest naval triumph in the early war years was the capture of New Orleans, the South's most important port, in 1862.

The Confederate leadership, recognizing that the South could not match the Union fleet, concentrated on developing new weapons like torpedoes and formidable ironclad vessels. They raised the *Merrimac,* a sunken U.S. warship, and covered it with heavy iron armor. Rechristened the *Virginia,* the ship steamed out of Norfolk in March 1862, heading directly for the Union ships blocking the harbor. Using its 1,500-pound ram and guns, the *Virginia* drove a third of the

ships aground and destroyed the squadron's largest ships. Victory was short-lived. The next day, the *Virginia* confronted the *Monitor,* a newly completed Union iron vessel. Their duel was inconclusive, and the *Virginia* withdrew. It was burned during the evacuation of Norfolk that May.

The Confederate navy's policy of harming northern commerce was moderately successful. Confederate raiders wreaked havoc on northern shipping. In its two-year career, the raider *Alabama* destroyed 69 Union merchant vessels valued at more than $6 million.

Throughout the first two years of conflict, both sides achieved victories, but the war remained deadlocked. The costs in manpower and supplies far exceeded what either side had anticipated. The need to replace lost men and supplies thus loomed ever more serious at the end of 1862.

Cotton Diplomacy

Both sides in the Civil War realized that attitudes in Europe could be critical. The Confederacy hoped to gain European diplomatic recognition and European loans and assistance. The European powers, however, consulted their own national interests and one by one declared a policy of neutrality.

Southerners were sure that the need of English and French textile mills for cotton would eventually force recognition of the Confederacy and an end to the North's blockade. But European industrialists found new sources for cotton in India and Egypt, and Southern hopes were dashed.

Union Secretary of State Seward sought above all else to prevent diplomatic recognition of the Confederacy. He daringly threatened Great Britain with war if it interfered in what he insisted was an internal matter. Some called his boldness reckless, even mad. Nevertheless, his policy succeeded. Even though England allowed the construction of Confederate raiders in its

Many deaths resulted from inadequate care for the wounded and sick soldiers of both armies. This wounded soldier receives water from a canteen rather than medical attention.

ports, it did not intervene in American affairs in 1861 or 1862. Nor did the other European powers.

Common Problems, Novel Solutions

As the conflict dragged on into 1863, unanticipated problems appeared in both the Union and the Confederacy, and leaders devised novel approaches to solve them.

Both treasuries had been empty initially, and the war was proving extraordinarily expensive. Eventually both sides initiated taxation on a small scale. Ultimately taxes financed 21 percent of the North's war expenses (but only one percent of southern expenses). Both treasuries also tried borrowing. Northerners bought over $2 billion worth of bonds, but southerners proved reluctant to buy their government's bonds.

Finally, both sides resorted to printing paper money. In August 1861, the Confederacy put into circulation $100 million in crudely engraved bills. Millions more followed the next year. Five months later, the Union issued $150 million in paper money, soon nicknamed "greenbacks" because of their color. The resulting inflation was particularly troublesome in the Confederacy, but it also caused an 80 percent increase in food prices for Union city families.

Both sides confronted manpower problems as initial enthusiasm for the war evaporated. Young men were shocked at the deadliness of diseases that accompanied the army wherever it went, and they were unprepared for the boredom of camp life. Those in the service longed to go home. The swarm of volunteers disappeared. Rather than fill their military quotas from within, rich northern communities began offering bounties of $800 to $1,000 to outsiders who would join up.

Arthur Carpenter's letters reveal growing disillusionment with the war as his regiment moved into Kentucky and Tennessee in the winter of 1862. "Soldiering in Kentucky and Tennessee," he complained, "is not so pretty as it was in Indianapolis.... We have been half starved, half frozen, and half drowned." Soldiering often meant marching over rutted roads carrying 50 or 60 pounds of equipment with insufficient food, water, or supplies. One blanket was not enough in the winter. In the summer, stifling woolen uniforms attracted lice and other vermin. Poor food, bugs, inadequate sanitation, and exposure invited disease. Carpenter marched through Tennessee suffering from diarrhea and then fever. His regiment left him behind in a convalescent barracks in Louisville, which he fled as soon as he could. He feared the hospital at least as much as the sickness. "[Ninety-nine] Surgeons out of a hundred," he wrote his parents, "would not know whether his patient had the horse distemper, lame toe, or any other disease."

Confederate soldiers, even less well supplied

than their northern counterparts, complained similarly. In 1862, a Virginia captain wrote:

> During our forced marches and hard fights, the soldiers have been compelled to throw away their knapsacks ... Hundreds of men are perfectly barefooted and there is no telling when they can be supplied with shoes.

Desertion was common, and as the manpower problems became critical, both governments resorted to the draft. Ultimately, over 30 percent of the Confederate army and six percent of the Union forces were draftees.

The Confederacy relied more heavily on the draft than the Union did because the North's initial manpower pool was larger and growing. During the war, 180,000 foreigners of military age poured into the northern states. Some came specifically to claim bounties and fight. Immigrants made up at least 20 percent of the Union army.

The draft laws were very unpopular. The first Confederate conscription declared all able-bodied men between 18 and 35 eligible for military service but allowed numerous exemptions and the purchase of substitutes. Critics complained that the provision entitling every planter with more than 20 slaves to one exemption from military service favored rich slave owners. The legislation fed class tension and encouraged disloyalty and desertion among the poorer classes, particularly among southern mountaineers. One woman shouted after her husband as he was dragged off to the army, "You desert again, quick as you kin. . . . Desert, Jake!"

The northern draft law of 1863 also allowed the hiring of substitutes, and $300 bought exemption from military service. Workers resented the ease with which moneyed citizens could avoid army duty. In July 1863, the resentment boiled over in New York City in the largest civil disturbance of the nineteenth century. Several Irish draftees destroyed draft records and the Enrollment Office. Events then spun out of control as a mob also burned the armory, plundered the

houses of the rich, and looted jewelry stores. Blacks, whom the Irish hated as economic competitors and the cause of the war, became special targets. Mobs beat and lynched blacks and even burned the Colored Orphan Asylum. More than 100 people died in the three days of rioting. There was much truth in the accusation that the war on both sides was a rich man's war but a poor man's fight.

Political Dissension, 1862

As the war continued, rumbles of dissension grew louder. In the South, criticism of Confederate leaders mounted. Wrote one southerner to a friend, "Impeach Jeff Davis for incompetency & call a convention of the States. . . . West Point is death to us & sick Presidents & Generals are equally fatal." Because the South had no party system, dissatisfaction with Davis and his handling of the war tended to be factional, petty, and personal.

Although Lincoln has since become a folk hero, at the time many northerners derided his performance and hoped for a new president in 1864. Peace Democrats, called Copperheads, claimed that Lincoln betrayed the Constitution and that working-class Americans bore the brunt of his policy of conscription. Immigrant workers had little sympathy for abolitionism or blacks, and they supported the antiwar stance of the Copperheads. Even Democrats favoring the war effort found Lincoln arbitrary and tyrannical, while some Republicans judged him indecisive and inept.

Republicans split gradually into two factions. The moderates favored a cautious approach toward winning the war and feared the possible consequences of emancipating the slaves, confiscating Confederate property, or arming blacks. The radicals, however, urged Lincoln to make emancipation a wartime objective. The reduction of the congressional Republican majority in the fall elections of 1862 made it imperative that Lincoln listen not only to both factions but also to the Democratic opposition.

THE TIDE TURNS, 1863-1865

Hard political realities made Lincoln delay an emancipation proclamation until 1863. Like congressional Democrats, many northerners supported a war for the Union but not one for emancipation. Many, if not most, whites saw blacks as inferior. They also suspected that emancipation would trigger a massive influx of former slaves who would steal white men's jobs and political rights. Race riots in New York, Brooklyn, Philadelphia, Buffalo, and Cincinnati dramatized white attitudes.

The Emancipation Proclamation, 1863

If the president moved too fast on emancipation, he risked losing the allegiance of people like Carpenter, offending the border states, and increasing the Democrats' chances for political victory. But if he did not move at all, he would alienate abolitionists and lose the support of radical Republicans, which he could ill afford.

For these reasons, Lincoln proceeded cautiously. In the early spring of 1862, he urged Congress to pass a joint resolution offering federal compensation to states beginning a "gradual abolishment of slavery." Border-state opposition killed the idea. Abolitionists and northern blacks, however, greeted Lincoln's proposal with "a thrill of joy."

That summer, Lincoln told his cabinet he intended to emancipate the slaves. Secretary of State Seward urged the president to delay any general proclamation until the North won a decisive military victory. Otherwise, he warned, Lincoln would appear to be urging racial insurrection behind the Confederate lines to compensate for northern military bungling.

Lincoln followed Seward's advice, using that summer and fall to prepare the North for the shift in the war's purpose. In August, Horace Greeley, the influential abolitionist editor of the New York *Tribune,* printed an open letter to Lincoln attacking him for failing to act on slavery. In his reply, Lincoln linked the idea of emancipation to military necessity. His primary goal, he wrote, was to save the Union:

> If I could save the Union without freeing *any* slave, I would do it; and if I could save it by freeing *all* the slaves, I would do it; and if I could do it by freeing some and leaving others alone, I would also do that. What I do about Slavery and the colored race, I do because I believe it helps to save this Union.

In September 1862, the Union victory at Antietam gave Lincoln the opportunity to issue a preliminary emancipation proclamation. It stated that unless rebellious states (or parts of states in rebellion) returned to the Union by January 1, 1863, the president would declare their slaves "forever free." Although supposedly aimed at bringing the southern states back into the Union, Lincoln never expected the South to lay down arms after two years of bloodshed. Rather, he was preparing northerners to accept the eventuality of emancipation on the grounds of necessity. Frederick Douglass greeted the president's action with jubilation. "We shout for joy," he wrote, "that we live to record this righteous decree."

Cautious cabinet members begged Lincoln to forget about emancipation, but on New Year's Day, 1863, he issued the final Emancipation Proclamation. It was "an act of justice, warranted by the Constitution upon military necessity." Thus what had started as a war to save the Union now also became a struggle that, if victorious, would free the slaves. Yet the proclamation had no immediate impact on slavery. It affected only slaves living in the unconquered portions of the Confederacy. It was silent about slaves in the border states and in parts of the

Black soldiers, some from southern states, were accepted for combat duty in the Union army as the war progressed. Here the First Carolina Volunteers gather to celebrate emancipation on January 1, 1863.

South already in northern hands. These limitations led Elizabeth Cady Stanton and Susan B. Anthony to establish the women's Loyal National League to lobby Congress to emancipate all southern slaves.

Though the Emancipation Proclamation did not immediately liberate southern slaves from their masters, it had a tremendous symbolic importance. Blacks realized that the proclamation had changed the nature of the war. For the first time, the government had committed itself to freeing slaves. Jubilant blacks could believe only that the president's action heralded a new era for their race. More immediately, the proclamation sanctioned the policy of accepting blacks as soldiers into the military.

Diplomatic concerns also lay behind the Emancipation Proclamation. Lincoln and his advisers anticipated that the commitment to abolish slavery would favorably impress foreign powers. European statesmen, however, did not abandon their cautious stance toward the Union. The English prime minister called the proclamation "trash." But important segments of the English public who opposed slavery now came to regard any attempt to help the South as immoral.

Unanticipated Consequences of War

The Emancipation Proclamation was but one example of the war's surprising consequences. Innovation was necessary for victory, and one of the Union's experiments involved using black troops for combat duty. Blacks had offered themselves as soldiers in 1861 but had been turned away. They were serving as cooks, laborers, teamsters, and carpenters in the army, however, and composed as much as a quarter of the navy. But as white casualties mounted, so did the interest in black service on the battlefield. The Union government allowed states to escape draft quotas if they enlisted enough volunteers and allowed them to count southern black enlistees on their state rosters.

Black leaders like Frederick Douglass pressed for military service. "Once let the black man get upon his person the brass letter, U.S., let him get an eagle on his button, and a musket on his shoulder and bullets in his pocket," Douglass believed, "there is no power on earth that can deny that he has earned the right to citizenship." By the war's end, 186,000 blacks (10 percent of the army) had served the Union cause, 134,111 of them escapees from slave states.

Enrolling blacks in the Union army was an important step toward citizenship and acceptance of blacks by white society. But the black experience in the army highlighted some of the obstacles to racial acceptance. Black soldiers, usually led by white officers, were second-class soldiers for most of the war, receiving lower pay ($10 a month as compared to $13), poorer food, often more menial work, and fewer benefits than whites. "If we are good enough to fill up white men's places and fight, we should be treated then, in all respects, the same as the white man," one black soldier protested.

The faith in Jomini's military tactics was another wartime casualty. The infantry charge, so valued at the war's beginning, resulted in horrible carnage. Military leaders came to realize the importance of the strong defensive position. Although Confederate soldiers criticized General Lee as "King of Spades" when he first ordered them to construct earthworks, the epithet evolved into one of affection as it became obvious that earthworks saved lives. By the end of 1862, both sides were digging defensive earthworks and trenches.

Gone, too, was the courtly idea that war involved only armies. Early in the war, many officers tried to protect civilians and their property, but such restraint soon vanished, and along with it went chickens, corn, livestock, and, as George Eagleton noted with disgust, even the furnishings of churches. War touched all of society, not just the battlefield participants.

Changing Military Strategies, 1863–1865

In the early war years, the South's military strategy combined defense with selective maneuvers. This policy, however, did not change the course of the war, and Lee concluded that the South had to win victories in the North in order to gain the peace it so desperately needed and European recognition.

In the summer of 1863, Lee led the Confederate Army of Northern Virginia across the Potomac into Maryland and southern Pennsylvania. His goal was a victory that would threaten both Philadelphia and Washington.

At Gettysburg on a hot and humid July 1, Lee came abruptly face to face with a Union army led by General George Meade. During three days of fighting, the fatal obsession with the infantry charge returned as Lee ordered costly assaults that probably lost him the battle. On July 3, Lee sent three divisions, about 15,000 men in all, against the Union center. The assault, known as Pickett's Charge, was as futile as it was gallant. At 700 yards, the Union artillery opened

fire. One southern officer described the scene: "Pickett's division just seemed to melt away in the blue musketry smoke which now covered the hill. Nothing but stragglers came back."

Lee's dreams of victory died that hot week, with grave consequences for the southern cause. Gettysburg marked the turn of the military tide in the East.

Despite the Gettysburg victory, Lincoln was dissatisfied with General Meade, who had failed to finish off Lee's demoralized and exhausted army as it retreated. His disappointment soon faded with news of a great victory at Vicksburg in the western theater on July 4. The commander, Ulysses S. Grant, completed the Union campaign to gain control of the Mississippi River and to divide the South.

Grant's successful capture of Vicksburg illustrated the boldness and flexibility that Lincoln sought in a commander, and in March 1864, Lincoln appointed him general in chief of the Union armies. Grant planned for victory within a year. "The art of war is simple enough," he reasoned. "Find out where your enemy is. Get at him as soon as you can. Strike at him as hard as you can, and keep moving on."

Grant proposed a grim campaign of annihilation, using the North's superior resources of men and supplies to wear down and defeat the South. He aimed "to consume everything that could be used to support or supply armies." Following this new policy of "total war," he set out after Lee's army in Virginia. General William Tecumseh Sherman, who pursued Confederate General Joseph Johnston from Tennessee toward Atlanta, further refined this plan.

Sherman wanted to make southerners "fear and dread" their foes. Therefore, his campaign to seize Atlanta and his march to Savannah spread destruction and terror. A Georgia woman described in her diary the impact of Sherman's march:

There was hardly a fence left standing all the way from Sparta to Gordon. The fields were trampled

The Tide Turns, 1863–1865

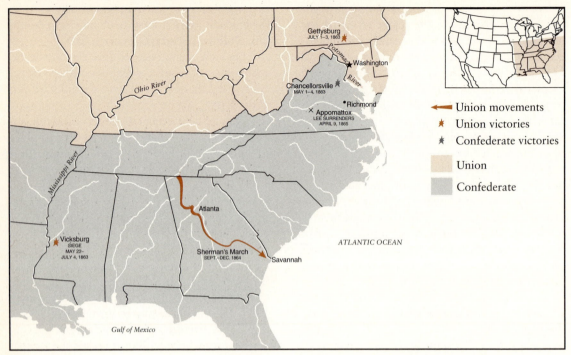

down and the road was lined with carcasses of horses, hogs and cattle that the invaders, unable either to consume or to carry away with them, had wantonly shot down, to starve out the people.... The dwellings that were standing all showed signs of pillage, and on every plantation we saw ... charred remains.

This destruction, with its goal of total victory, showed once more how conflict produced the unexpected. The war that both North and South had hoped would be quick and relatively painless was ending after four long years with great cost to both sides.

CHANGES WROUGHT BY WAR

As bold new tactics emerged both on and off the battlefield, both governments took steps that changed their societies in surprising ways. Of the two, the South, which had left the Union to conserve a traditional way of life, experienced the more radical transformation.

A New South

The expansion of the central government's power in the South, starting with the passage of the 1862 Conscription Act, continued in the last years of the war. Secession grew out of the concept of states' rights, but, ironically, winning the war depended on central direction and control. Many southerners denounced Davis as a tyrant and a despot because he recognized the need for the central government to take the lead. Despite the accusations, the Confederate Congress cooperated with him and established important precedents. In 1863, it enacted a comprehensive tax law and an impressment act that allowed government agents to requisition food, horses, wagons, and other necessary war materials, often for only about half their market price. These were prime examples of the central government's power to interfere with private property. Government impressment of slaves for war work in 1863 affected the very form of private property that had originally driven the South from the Union.

The Conscription Act of 1862 was followed in 1864 by an expanded conscription measure that made all white males between the ages 17 and 50 subject to the draft. By 1865, the necessities of war had led to the unthinkable: arming slaves as soldiers. Black companies were recruited in Richmond and other southern towns. However, because the war soon ended, no blacks actually fought for the Confederacy.

Southern agriculture also changed under the pressure of war. Earlier, the South had imported food from the North, concentrating on the production of staples such as cotton and tobacco for market. Now, more and more land was turned over to food crops. Cotton production declined from 4.5 million bales in 1861 to 300,000 bales in 1864, but food remained in short supply.

The war also triggered the expansion of military-related industries in the South. The war and navy offices directed industrial development, awarding contracts to private manufacturing firms like Richmond's Tredegar Iron Works and operating other factories themselves. The number of southerners working in industry rose dramatically. In 1861, the Tredegar Iron Works employed 700 workers; two years later, it employed 2,500, more than half of them black. At the end of the war, the soldiers were better supplied with arms and munitions than with food.

Although the war did not transform the southern class structure, relations between the classes began to change. Draft resistance and desertion reflected growing alienation from a war perceived as serving only the interests of upper-class plantation owners. More and more yeoman families suffered grinding poverty as the men went off to war and government officials and armies requisitioned needed resources. This new poverty was an ominous hint of the decline of the yeoman farming class in postwar years.

The Victorious North

Although changes in the South were more noticeable, the Union's government and economy also responded to the demands of war. Like Davis, Lincoln was accused of being a dictator. Although he rarely tried to control Congress, veto its legislation, or direct government departments, Lincoln did use executive power freely. He violated the writ of habeas corpus by suspending the civil rights of over 13,000 northerners, who languished in prison without trials; curbed the freedom of the press because of supposedly disloyal and inflammatory articles; established conscription; issued the Emancipation Proclamation; and removed army generals. Lincoln argued that this vast extension of presidential power was temporarily justified because, as president, he was responsible for defending and preserving the Constitution.

Many of the wartime changes in government proved more permanent than Lincoln had imagined. The financial necessities of war helped to revolutionize the country's banking system. Ever since Andrew Jackson's destruction of the Bank of the United States, state banks had served American financial needs. Treasury Secretary Salmon P. Chase found this banking system inadequate and chaotic and proposed to replace it. In 1863 and 1864, Congress passed banking acts that established a national currency issued by federally chartered banks and backed by government bonds. The country had a federal banking system once again.

The northern economy also changed under wartime demands. Agriculture expanded, as did investment in farm machinery, notably McCormick reapers, which performed the work of four to six men. During the war, McCormick sold 165,000 of his machines. Northern farmers

Ruined buildings and mourning women were common sights in Richmond as the war came to an end. This photograph gives a vivid sense of the devastation of the South in 1865.

not only grew enough grain to feed civilians and soldiers but gathered a surplus to export as well.

The war also selectively stimulated manufacturing, although it retarded overall economic growth. Industries that produced for the war machine, especially those with advantages of scale, expanded and made large profits. Each year, the Union army required 1.5 million uniforms and 3 million pairs of shoes; the woolen and leather industries grew accordingly. Meatpackers and producers of iron, steel, and pocket watches all profited from wartime opportunities. Cincinnati was one city that flourished from supplying soldiers with everything from pork to soap and candles.

On the Home Front, 1861–1865

In numerous, less tangible ways, the war transformed northern and southern society. Civilians read newspapers and national weekly magazines with a new eagerness. The use of the mails increased dramatically as they corresponded with faraway relatives and friends. The war helped to make Americans less parochial, integrating them into the larger world.

For some Americans, like John D. Rockefeller and Andrew Carnegie, war brought army contracts and profits. In the South, blockade runners made fortunes slipping luxury goods past Union ships. For the majority of Americans, however, war meant deprivation. To be sure, the demand for workers ended unemployment. Large numbers of women and blacks entered the work force, a phenomenon that would be repeated in all future American wars. But while work was easy to get and wages appeared to increase, real income actually declined. Inflation, especially destructive in the South, was largely to blame. By 1864, eggs sold in Richmond for $6 a dozen; butter brought $25 a pound. Strikes and union organizing pointed to working-class discontent.

Low wages particularly harmed women workers. As more women entered the work force, employers cut costs by slashing wages. In 1861, the Union government paid Philadelphia seamstresses 17 cents per shirt. At the height of inflation, three years later, the government reduced the piecework rate to 15 cents per shirt. Private employers paid even less, about eight cents a shirt. Working women in the South fared no better. War may have brought prosperity to a few Americans, North and South, but for most it meant trying to survive on an inadequate income.

Shortages and hardships were severe in the South, especially in cities, where carts brought in vital supplies since trains were reserved for military use. Hunger was rampant. Food riots erupted in Richmond and other cities; crowds of hungry whites broke into stores to steal food. The very cleanliness of southern cities pointed to urban hunger. As one Richmond resident noted, everything was so "cleanly consumed that no garbage or filth can accumulate."

Thousands of southerners who fled as Union armies advanced suddenly found themselves homeless. "The country for miles around is filled with refugees," noted an army officer in 1862. "Every house is crowded and hundreds are living in churches, in barns and tents."

One slave described the upsetting arrival of the Yankees at his plantation in Arkansas: "Them folks stood round there all day. Killed hogs ... killed cows.... Took all kinds of sugar and preserves.... Tore all the feathers out of the mattresses looking for money. Then they put Old Miss and her daughter in the kitchen to cooking." So frightened was this slave's mother that she hid in her bed, only to be roused by the lieutenant, who told her, "We ain't a-going to do you no hurt. ... We are freeing you." But the next day, the Yanks were gone and the Confederates back. "Pa was 'fraid of both" and resolved the problem by hiding out in the cotton patch.

Wartime Race Relations

The journal kept by Emily Harris in South Carolina conveys some of the character of life behind the lines. Emily and her husband, David, lived on a 500-acre farm with their seven young children and ten slaves. When David went to war, Emily had to manage the farm, even though David worried that she would be "much at a loss with the . . . farm and the negroes."

Indeed, Emily's relations with her slaves proved a major problem. As so many southerners discovered, war transformed the master-slave relationship. Because Emily was not the master David had been, her slaves gradually began to take unaccustomed liberties. At Christmas in 1864, several left the farm without her permission; others stayed away longer than she allowed. "Old Will" boldly requested his freedom. Worse yet, she discovered that her slaves helped three Yankees who had escaped from prison camp.

The master-slave relationship was crumbling, and Emily reported in her journal, "It seems people are getting afraid of negroes." In March she wrote, "The Negroes are all expecting to be set free very soon and it causes them to be very troublesom."

Such scenes, which occurred throughout the South, and the thousands of blacks (probably 20 percent of all slaves) who fled toward Union lines after the early months of the war were proof of the changing nature of race relations and the harm slaves could do to the southern cause.

Women and the War

Emily Harris's journal illustrates how the war affected women's lives. So many men on both sides had gone off to fight that women had to find jobs and had to carry on farming operations. During the war years, southern women who had no slaves to help with the farmwork and northern farm wives who labored without the assistance of husbands or sons carried new physical and emotional burdens.

Women also participated in numerous war-related activities. In the North, hundreds of women became military nurses. Under the supervision of Drs. Emily and Elizabeth Blackwell; Dorothea Dix, superintendent of army nurses; and Clara Barton, northern women nursed the wounded and dying for low pay or even for none at all. They also attempted to improve hospital conditions by attacking red tape and bureaucracy. The diary of a volunteer, Harriet Whetten, revealed the activist attitude of many others:

> I have never seen such a dirty disorganized place as the Hospital. The neglect of cleanliness is inexcusable. All sorts of filth, standing water, and the embalming house near the Hospital. . . . No time had to be lost. Miss Gill and I set the contrabands at work making beds & cleaning.

Although men largely staffed southern military hospitals, Confederate women also played an important part in caring for the sick and wounded in their homes and in makeshift hospitals behind the battle lines. Women also worked as volunteers in soldiers' aid societies and in the United States Sanitary Commission. Many others made bandages and clothes, put together packages for soldiers at the front, helped army wives and disabled soldiers find jobs, and joined in war-related fund-raising activities.

Many of the changes women experienced during war years ended when peace returned and the men came home. But for women whose men came home maimed or not at all, the work had not ended.

The Election of 1864

In the North, the election of 1864 brought some of the transformations of wartime into the political arena. The Democrats, capitalizing on war weariness, nominated General George McClellan for president and demanded an armistice with the South. They accused Lincoln of arbitrarily expanding executive power and insinuated that if the Republicans won, a fusion of blacks and whites would result.

Although Lincoln easily gained Republican renomination because of his tight control over party machinery and patronage, his party did not unite behind him. His veto of the radical reconstruction plan for the South, the Wade-Davis bill, led to cries of "usurpation." The Emancipation Proclamation did not sit well with conservatives. But Sherman's capture of Atlanta in September 1864 and the march through Georgia to Savannah helped swing voters to Lincoln. He won 55 percent of the popular vote and swept the electoral college.

Why the North Won

In the months after Lincoln's reelection, the war drew to an agonizing conclusion. Sherman moved north from Atlanta to North Carolina, while Grant pummeled Lee's forces in Virginia. The losses Grant would sustain were staggering: 18,000 in the Battle of the Wilderness, over

8,000 at Spotsylvania, and another 12,000 at Cold Harbor. On April 9, 1865, Grant accepted Lee's surrender at Appomattox, and the war was finally over.

Grant's military strategy succeeded because the Union could survive staggering losses of men and equipment while the Confederacy could not. As Union armies pushed back the borders of the Confederacy, the South lost control of territories essential for their war effort. Finally, naval strategy eventually paid off because the North could build enough ships to make its blockade work. In 1861, fully 90 percent of the blockade runners were slipping through the naval cordon. By the war's end, only half made it.

The South had taken tremendous steps toward meeting war needs. But, as one civilian realized, "The question of bread and meat . . . is beginning to be regarded as a more serious one even than that of War." Women farming alone or with disgruntled slaves and worn-out farm equipment could not produce enough food. The government's impressment of slaves and animals cut production. The half million blacks who fled to Union lines also played their part in pulling the South down in defeat.

Advancing Union forces destroyed many industries. A Confederate officer in northern Virginia observed, "Many of our soldiers are thinly clothed and without shoes and in addition to this, very few of the infantry have tents. With this freezing weather, their sufferings are indescribable." By 1864, the Union armies were so well supplied that soldiers often threw away heavy blankets and coats as they advanced.

The South's woefully inadequate transportation system also contributed to defeat. Primitive roads became all but impassable without repairs. The railroad system, geared to the needs of cotton, not war, was inefficient. When tracks wore out or were destroyed, they were not replaced. Thus food intended for the army rotted awaiting shipment. Food riots in southern cities pointed to the hunger, anger, and growing demoralization of civilians.

Ironically, measures the Confederacy took to win the war undermined its own war effort. Conscription, impressment, and taxes all contributed to resentment and sometimes open resistance. The many southern governors who refused to contribute men, money, and supplies on the scale Davis requested implicitly condoned disloyalty to the cause. The belief in states' rights and the sanctity of private property that gave birth to the Confederacy also helped kill it.

It is tempting to compare Lincoln and Davis as war leaders. There is no doubt that Lincoln's humanity, eloquence, and determination to save the Union set him apart as one of this country's most extraordinary presidents. Yet the men's personal characteristics were probably less important than the differences between the political and social systems of the two regions. Without the support of a party behind him, Davis failed to engender enthusiasm or loyalty. Lincoln, commanding considerable resources of patronage, was able to line up federal, state, and local officials behind his party and administration.

Just as the northern political system provided Lincoln with more flexibility and support, its social system also proved more able to meet the war's extraordinary demands. Northerners were more cooperative, disciplined, and aggressive in meeting the organizational and production challenges of wartime. In the southern states, old attitudes, habits, and values impeded the war effort. Southern governors, wedded to states' rights, refused to cooperate with the Confederate government. North Carolina, the center of the southern textile industry, actually kept back most uniforms for its own regiments. At the war's end, 92,000 uniforms and thousands of blankets, shoes, and tents still lay in its warehouses. Even slaveholders whose property had

been the cause for secession resisted the impressment of their slaves for war work.

One northerner described southerners as they surrendered at Appomattox:

> Before us in proud humiliation stood the embodiment of manhood: men whom neither toils and sufferings, nor the fact of death, nor disaster, nor hopelessness could bend from their resolve; standing before us now, thin, worn, and famished, but erect, and with eyes looking level into ours, waking memories that bound us together as no other bond.

The Costs of War

In the end, the Confederacy collapsed, exhausted and bleeding. The long war was over, but the memories of that event would fester for years to come. About three million American men, a third of all free males between the ages of 15 and 59, had served in the army. Each would remember his own personal history of the war. For George Eagleton, who had worked in army field hospitals, the history was one of "Death and destruction! Blood! Blood! Agony! Death! Gaping flesh wounds, broken bones, amputations, bullet and bomb fragment extractions." Of all wars Americans have fought, none has been more deadly. The death rate during this war was over five times as great as the death rate during World War II. About 360,000 Union soldiers and another 258,000 Confederate soldiers died, about a third of them because their wounds were either improperly treated or not treated at all. Disease claimed more lives than combat.

Many men would be reminded of the war by the missing limbs that marked them as Civil War veterans. About 275,000 on each side were maimed. Another 410,000 (195,000 northerners and 215,000 southerners) would recall their time in wretchedly overcrowded and unsanitary prison camps, such as Andersonville in Georgia, where 31,000 Union soldiers were confined. At the war's end, over 12,000 graves were counted there.

Some Americans found it hard to throw off wartime experiences and return to civilian routines. Even those who adjusted successfully discovered that they looked at life from a different perspective. The experience of fighting, of mixing with all sorts of people from many places, of traveling far from home had lifted former soldiers out of their familiar local world and widened their vision. Fighting the war made the concept of national union real.

Unanswered Questions

What, then, had the war accomplished? On the one hand, death and destruction. The South suffered an estimated 43 percent decline in wealth during the war years, exclusive of the value of slaves. Great cities like Atlanta, Columbia, and Richmond lay in ruins. Fields lay uncultivated, much livestock had disappeared, and two-thirds of the railroads had been destroyed. Thousands were hungry, homeless, and bitter, and over three million slaves, a vast financial investment, were free.

On the other hand, the war had resolved the question of union and ended the debate over the relationship of the states to the federal government. During the war, Republicans seized the opportunity to pass legislation that would foster national union and economic growth: the Pacific Railroad Act of 1862, which set aside huge tracts of public land to finance the transcontinental railroad; the Homestead Act of 1862, which was to provide yeoman farmers cheaper and easier access to the public domain; the Morrill Act of 1862, which established support for agricultural (land-grant) colleges; and the banking acts of 1863 and 1864.

The war had also resolved the issue of slavery, but new questions had to be faced. What would happen to the former slaves? Were blacks to have the same civil and political rights as whites? Would they be given land, the means for economic independence? What would be their relations with their former owners?

What, indeed, would be the status of the conquered South in the nation? Should it be punished for the rebellion? Some people thought so. But Lincoln, as early as December 1863, had announced a generous plan of reconciliation. He was willing to recognize the government of former Confederate states established by a group of citizens equal to 10 percent of those voting in 1860, as long as the group swore to support the Constitution and to accept the abolition of slavery. He began to restore state governments in three former Confederate states on that basis. But not all northerners agreed with his leniency, and the debate continued.

In his 1865 inaugural address, Lincoln urged Americans to harbor "malice towards none . . . and charity for all." "Let us strive," he urged, "to finish the work we are in; to bind up the nation's wounds . . . to do all which may achieve a just and lasting peace." Generosity and goodwill would pave the way for reconciliation. On April 14, he pressed the point home to his cabinet. His wish was to avoid persecution and bloodshed.

That same evening, only five days after the surrender at Appomattox, the president attended a play at Ford's Theater. There, as one horrified eyewitness reported,

> a pistol was heard and a man . . . dressed in a black suit of clothes leaped onto the stage apparently from the President's box. He held in his right hand a dagger whose blade appeared about 10 inches long. . . . Every one leaped to his feet, and the cry of 'the President is assassinated' was heard—Getting where I could see into the President's box, I saw Mrs. Lincoln . . . in apparent anguish.

John Wilkes Booth, a southern sympathizer, had killed the president.

CONCLUSION

AN UNCERTAIN FUTURE

As the war ended, many Americans grieved for the man whose decisions had so marked their lives for five years. "Strong men have wept tonight & the nation will mourn tomorrow," wrote one eyewitness to the assassination. Many more wept for friends and relations who had not survived the war but whose actions had in one way or another contributed to its outcome. Perhaps not all Americans realized how drastically the war had altered their lives, their futures, their nation. It was only as time passed that the war's impact became clear to them. And it was only with time that they recognized how many problems the war had left unsolved. It is to these years of Reconstruction that we turn next.

Recommended Reading

Good general introductions are Peter J. Parrish, *The American Civil War* (1985); and James McPherson, *Battle Cry of Freedom: The Civil War Era* (1988). Careful studies of the Confederacy include Emory M. Thomas, *The Confederate Nation, 1861–1865* (1979); and Paul D. Escott, *After Secession: Jefferson Davis and the Failure of Confederate Nationalism* (1978). For economic matters, consult David Gilchrist and W. David Lewis, eds., *Economic Change in the Civil War Era* (1965). On social history, see Maris Vinovskis, ed., *Toward a Social History of the American Civil War* (1990).

The military aspects of the war can be followed in Richard E. Beringer, Herman Hattaway, Archer Jones, and William N. Still, Jr., *Why the South Lost the Civil War* (1986); and Henry S. Commager, ed., *The Blue and the Gray: The Story of the Civil War as Told by Participants*, 2 vols. (1950).

Eric Foner's essays, collected in *Politics and Ideology in the Age of Civil War* (1980), are valuable for understanding the political context of the Civil War. Also helpful is John L. Thomas, ed., *Abraham Lincoln and the American Political Tradition* (1986). For a biography, see Stephen B. Oates, *With Malice Towards None: The Life of Abraham Lincoln* (1977).

Benjamin Quarles studies southern blacks in *The Negro in the Civil War* (1968 ed.), while Leon F. Litwack illuminates changing race relations in *Been in the Storm So Long: The Aftermath of Slavery* (1979). A good primary source is James M. McPherson, ed., *The Negro's Civil War* (1965). The strength of white racism is portrayed in George M. Frederickson, *The Black Image in the White Mind* (1971); and in C. Vann Woodward, *American Counterpoint: Slavery and Racism in the North-South Dialogue* (1971).

The experience of women is treated in Catherine Clinton and Nina Silber, eds., *Divided Houses: Gender and the Civil War* (1993); John P. Bugardt, ed., *Civil War Nurse* (1980); and in more general works such as Sara M. Evans, *Born for Liberty: A History of Women in America* (1989); and Eleanor Flexner, *Century of Struggle: The Woman's Rights Movement in the United States* (1975). Although Mary Boykin Chesnut's diary was actually written after the war, her vivid account, *Mary Chesnut's Civil War* (1981), is well worth consulting. Southern Unionists are explored in Phillip Shaw Paludan's *Victims: A True Story of the Civil War* (1981).

Novels about the Civil War include Stephen Crane, *The Red Badge of Courage* (any ed.), and MacKinlay Kantor, *Andersonville* (1955).

Time Line

1861	Lincoln calls up state militia and suspends habeas corpus First Battle of Bull Run Union blockades the South
1862	Battles at Shiloh, Bull Run, and Antietam *Monitor* and *Virginia* battle First black regiment authorized by Union Union issues greenbacks South institutes military draft Pacific Railroad Act Homestead Act Morrill Land-Grant College Act
1863	Lincoln issues Emancipation Proclamation
1863	Congress adopts military draft Battles of Gettysburg and Vicksburg Union Banking Act Southern tax laws and impressment act New York draft riots Southern food riots
1864	Sherman's march through Georgia Lincoln reelected Union Banking Act
1865	Lee surrenders at Appomattox Lincoln assassinated Andrew Johnson becomes president Congress passes Thirteenth Amendment, abolishing slavery

chapter 16

....

The Union
Reconstructed

In April 1864, one year before Lincoln's assassination, Robert Allston died of pneumonia. His wife, Adele, and daughter, Elizabeth, took over the affairs of their many rice plantations. With Yankee troops moving through coastal South Carolina in the late winter of 1864–1865, Elizabeth's sorrow over the loss of her father turned to "terror" as Union soldiers arrived seeking liquor, firearms, and hidden valuables. The Allston women endured an insulting search and then fled. In a later raid, Yankee troops encouraged the Allston slaves to take furniture and other household goods from the Big Houses, some of which the blacks returned when the Yankees were gone. But before they left, the Union soldiers, in their role as liberators, gave the keys to the crop barns to the semifree slaves.

When the war was over, Adele Allston took an oath of allegiance to the United States and secured a written order commanding the blacks to relinquish these keys. She and Elizabeth made plans to return in the early summer of 1865 to resume control of the family plantations, thereby reestablishing white authority. Possession of the keys to the barns, Elizabeth wrote, would be the "test case" of whether former masters or their former slaves would control land and labor.

Not without some fear, Adele and Elizabeth Allston rode up in a carriage to their former home, Nightingale Hall, to confront their ex-slaves. To their surprise, a pleasant reunion took place. A trusted black foreman handed over the keys to the barns. This harmonious scene was repeated elsewhere.

But at Guendalos, a plantation owned by a son absent during most of the war fighting with the Confederate army, the Allston women met a very different situation. As their carriage arrived, a defiant group of armed ex-slaves lined both sides of the road, following the carriage as it passed by. Tension grew when the carriage stopped. A former black driver, Uncle Jacob, was unsure whether to yield the keys to the barns full of rice and corn, put there by black labor. An angry young man shouted out: "Ef yu gie up de key, blood'll flow." Uncle Jacob slowly slipped the keys back into his pocket.

The tension increased as the blacks sang freedom songs and brandished hoes, pitchforks, and guns in an effort to discourage anyone from going to town for help.

The Allstons spent the night safely, if restlessly, in their house. Early the next morning, they were awakened by a knock at the unlocked front door. Adele slowly opened the door, and there stood Uncle Jacob. Without a word, he gave her the keys.

The story of the keys reveals most of the essential human ingredients of the Reconstruction era. Despite defeat and surrender, southern whites were determined to resume control of both land and labor. Rebellion aside, the law, property titles, and federal enforcement were generally on the side of the original owners of the land.

In this encounter between former slaves and the Allston women, the role of the northern federal officials is most revealing. The Union soldiers, literally and symbolically, gave the keys of freedom to the blacks but did not stay around long enough to guarantee that freedom. Understanding the limits of northern help, Uncle Jacob handed the keys to land and liberty back to his former owner. The blacks at Guendalos knew that if they wanted to ensure their freedom, they had to do it themselves.

The goals of the groups at the Allston plantations were in conflict. The theme of this chapter is the story of what happened to people's various dreams as they sought to form new social, economic, and political relationships during Reconstruction.

For much of the twentieth century, Reconstruction was seen as a disgraceful period in which vindictive northern Radical Republicans imposed a harsh rule of evil carpetbaggers, scalawags, and illiterate blacks on the helpless, defeated South. *Gone with the Wind* reflects this view. In 1935, the black scholar W. E. B. Du Bois challenged this interpretation, suggesting instead that an economic struggle over land and the exploitation of black workers was the crucial focus of Reconstruction. Other historians have shown the beginnings of biracial cooperation and political participation in some southern states and the eventual violent repression of the freedmen's dreams of land, schooling, and votes. This chapter reflects this later interpretation, enriched by an awareness of the ambiguity of human motives and the devastation and divisions of class and race in pursuit of conflicting goals.

THE BITTERSWEET AFTERMATH OF WAR

"There are sad changes in store for both races," the daughter of a Georgia planter wrote in her diary early in the summer of 1865, adding, "I wonder the Yankees do not shudder to behold their work." In order to understand the bittersweet nature of Reconstruction, we must look at the state of the nation in the spring of 1865, shortly after the assassination of President Lincoln.

The United States in 1865

The "Union" was in a state of constitutional crisis in April 1865. The status of the 11 states of the former Confederate States of America was unclear. Lincoln's official position had been that the southern states had never left the Union, which was "constitutionally indestructible." As a result of their rebellion, they were only "out of their proper relation" with the United States. The president, therefore, as commander in chief, had the authority to decide on the basis for setting relations right and proper again.

Lincoln's congressional opponents argued that by declaring war on the Union, the Confederate states had broken their constitutional ties and reverted to a kind of prestatehood status like territories or "conquered provinces." Congress, therefore, which decided on the admission of new states, should resolve the constitutional issues and assert its authority over the reconstruction process. This conflict between Congress and the president reflected the fact that the president had taken on broad powers necessary for rapid mobilization of resources and domestic security during the war. As soon as the war was over, Congress sought to reassert its authority, as it would do after every subsequent war.

In April 1865, the Republican Party ruled victorious and virtually alone. Although less than a dozen years old, the Republicans had won the war, preserved the Union, and enacted a program for economic growth. The Democratic Party, by contrast, was in shambles. Nevertheless, it had been politically important in 1864 for the Republicans to show that the war was a bipartisan effort. A Jacksonian Democrat and Unionist from Tennessee, the tactless Andrew Johnson, had therefore been nominated as Lincoln's vice president. In April 1865, he headed the government.

The United States in the spring of 1865 was a picture of stark economic contrasts. Northern cities hummed with productive activity while southern cities lay in ruins. Roadways and railroad tracks laced the North, while in the South railroads and roads had been devastated. Southern financial institutions were bankrupt, while northern banks flourished. Northern farms,

under increasing mechanization, were more productive than ever before. Southern farms and plantations, especially those that had lain in the path of Sherman's march, were like a "howling waste."

Despite pockets of relative wealth, the South was largely devastated as soldiers demobilized and returned home in April 1865. Yet, as a later southern writer, Wilbur Cash, explained, "If this war had smashed the Southern world, it had left the essential Southern mind and will . . . entirely unshaken." Many southerners wanted nothing less than to resist Reconstruction and restore their old world.

The dominant social reality in the spring of 1865, however, was that nearly four million former slaves were on their own, facing the challenges of freedom. After an initial reaction of joy and celebration, the freedmen quickly became aware of their continuing dependence on former owners.

Hopes Among Freedmen

Throughout the South in the summer of 1865, there were optimistic expectations in the old slave quarters. As Union soldiers marched through Richmond, prisoners in slave-trade jails chanted: "Slavery chain done broke at last! Gonna praise God till I die!" The slavery chain, however, was not broken all at once but link by link. After Union soldiers swept through an area, Confederate troops would follow, or master and overseer would return, and the slaves learned not to rejoice too quickly or openly. "Every time a bunch of No'thern sojers would come through," recalled one slave, "they would tell us we was free and we'd begin celebratin'. Before we would get through somebody else would tell us to go back to work, and we would go." So former slaves became cautious about what freedom meant.

Gradually, the freedmen began to test their new freedom. The first thing they did was to leave the plantation, if only for a few hours or days. Some former slaves cut their ties entirely, leaving cruel and kindly masters alike.

Many freedmen left the plantation in search of members of their families. For some, freedom meant getting married legally. Legal marriage was important morally, but it also served such practical purposes as establishing the legitimacy of children and gaining access to land titles and other economic opportunities. Marriage also meant special burdens for black women who took on the now familiar double role as housekeeper and breadwinner. For many newly married blacks, however, the initial goal was to create a traditional family life, resulting in the widespread withdrawal of women from plantation field labor.

Another way in which freedmen demonstrated their new status was by choosing surnames; names associated with the concept of independence, such as Washington, were common. Emancipation changed black manners around whites as well. Masks were dropped, and old expressions of humility—tipping a hat, stepping aside, feigning happiness, addressing whites with titles of deference—were discarded. For the blacks, these were necessary symbolic expressions of selfhood; they proved that things were now different. To whites, these behaviors were seen as acts of "insolence," "insubordination," and "puttin' on airs."

However important were choosing names, dropping masks, moving around, getting married, and testing new rights, the primary goal for most freedmen was the acquisition of their own land. During the war, some Union generals had placed liberated slaves in charge of confiscated and abandoned lands. In the Sea Islands off the coast of South Carolina and Georgia, blacks had been working 40-acre plots of land and harvesting their own crops for several years. Some blacks held title to these lands. Northern philanthropists had organized others to grow cotton for the Treasury Department to prove the superiority of free labor over slavery.

Many freedmen expected a new economic order as fair payment for their years of involuntary work on the land. As one freedman put it, "Gib us our own land and we take care ourselves; but widout land, de ole massas can hire us or starve us, as dey please." However cautiously expressed, the freedmen had every expectation, fed by the intensity of their dreams, that "forty acres and a mule" would be provided.

The White South's Fearful Response

White southerners had mixed goals at the war's end. Yeoman farmers and poor whites stood side by side with rich planters in bread lines as together they looked forward to the restoration of their land and livelihood. Suffering from "extreme want and destitution," as a Georgia resident put it, white southerners responded with feelings of outrage, loss, and injustice. "I tell you it is mighty hard," said one man, "for my pa paid his own money for our niggers; and that's not all they've robbed us of. They have taken our horses and cattle and sheep *and everything.*"

A more dominant emotion, however, was fear. The entire structure of southern society was shaken, and the semblance of racial peace and order that slavery had provided was shattered. Many white southerners could hardly imagine a society without blacks in bondage. Having lost control of all that was familiar and revered, whites feared everything from losing their cheap labor supply to having to sit next to blacks on trains.

The mildest of their fears was the inconvenience of doing various jobs and chores they had rarely done before, like housework. The worst fears of southern whites were rape and revenge. The presence of black soldiers touched off fears of violence. Although demobilization occurred rapidly after Appomattox, a few black militia units remained in uniform, parading with guns in southern cities. Acts of violence by black soldiers against whites, however, were rare.

Believing that their world was turned upside

Both white southerners and their former slaves suffered in the immediate aftermath of the Civil War, as illustrated by this engraving from Frank Leslie's Illustrated Newspaper.

places marauding groups of whites were assaulting and terrorizing virtually defenseless freedmen, who clearly needed protection and the right to testify in court against whites.

Because white planters needed the freedmen's labor, the crucial provisions of the black codes were intended to regulate the freedmen's economic status. "Vagrancy" laws provided that any blacks not "lawfully employed," which usually meant by a white employer, could be arrested, jailed, fined, or hired out to a man who would assume responsibility for their debts and future behavior. The codes regulated the work contracts by which black laborers worked in the fields for white landowners, including severe penalties for leaving before the yearly contract was fulfilled and rules for proper behavior, attitude, and manners. In this way, southern leaders sought to reestablish their dominance.

down, the former planter aristocracy set out to restore the old plantation order and appropriate racial relationships. The key to reestablishing white dominance were the "black codes" that state legislatures passed in the first year after the end of the war. Many of the codes granted freedmen the right to marry, sue and be sued, testify in court, and hold property. But these rights were qualified. Complicated passages in the codes explained under exactly what circumstances blacks could testify against whites or own property (mostly they could not) or exercise other rights of free persons. Some rights were denied, including racial intermarriage and the right to bear arms, possess alcoholic beverages, sit on trains except in baggage compartments, be on city streets at night, or congregate in large groups.

Many of the alleged rights guaranteed by the black codes—testimony in court, for example—were passed to induce the federal government to withdraw its remaining troops from the South. This was a crucial issue, for in many

NATIONAL RECONSTRUCTION

The question facing the national government in 1865 was whether it would use its power to support the black codes and the reimposition of racial intimidation in the South or to uphold the newly sought rights of the freedmen. Would the federal government side with the democratic reform impulse in American history, which stressed human rights and liberty, or with the forces emphasizing property, order, and self-interest? Although the primary drama of Reconstruction took place in the conflict between white landowners and black freedmen over land and labor in the South, the struggle over Reconstruction policy among politicians in Washington played a significant role in the local drama, as well as the next century of American history.

The Presidential Plan

After initially calling for punishment of the defeated Confederates for "treason," President

Johnson soon adopted a more lenient policy. On May 29, 1865, he issued two proclamations setting forth his reconstruction program. Like Lincoln, he maintained that the southern states had never left the Union. His first proclamation continued Lincoln's policies by offering "amnesty and pardon, with restoration of all rights of property" to all former Confederates who would take an oath of allegiance to the Constitution and the Union of the United States. However, he made exceptions: ex–Confederate government leaders and rich rebels whose taxable property was valued at over $20,000. Any southerners not covered by the amnesty proclamation could, however, apply for special individual pardons, which Johnson granted to nearly all applicants. By the fall of 1865, only a handful remained unpardoned.

Johnson's second proclamation laid out the steps by which southern states could reestablish state governments. First, the president would appoint a provisional governor, who would call a state convention representing "that portion of the people of said State who are loyal to the United States." This included those who took the oath of allegiance or were otherwise pardoned. The convention should ratify the Thirteenth Amendment, which abolished slavery, void secession, repudiate all Confederate debts, and then elect new state officials and members of Congress.

Under this lenient plan, each of the southern states successfully completed reconstruction and sent newly elected members to the Congress that convened in December 1865. Southern voters defiantly elected dozens of former officers and legislators of the Confederacy, including a few not yet pardoned. Some state conventions hedged on ratifying the Thirteenth Amendment, and some asserted their right to compensation for the loss of slave property. No state provided for black suffrage, and most did nothing to guarantee civil rights, schooling, or economic protection for the freedmen. Less than eight months after Appomattox, Reconstruction seemed to be over.

Congressional Reconstruction

As they looked at the situation late in 1865, northern leaders painfully saw that almost none of their postwar goals were being fulfilled. The South was taking advantage of the president's program to restore the power of the prewar planter aristocracy. The freedmen were receiving neither equal citizenship nor economic independence. And the Republicans were not likely to maintain their political power and stay in office. Would the Democratic Party and the South gain by postwar politics what they had been unable to achieve by civil war?

Congressional Republicans, led by Congressman Thaddeus Stevens of Pennsylvania and Senator Charles Sumner of Massachusetts, decided to assert their own policies for reconstructing the nation. Although branded as "radicals," only for a brief period in 1866 and 1867 did "radical" rule prevail. Rejecting Johnson's notion that the South had already been reconstructed, Congress asserted its constitutional authority to decide on its own membership and refused seats to the newly elected senators and representatives from the old Confederate states. Congress then established the Joint Committee on Reconstruction to investigate conditions in the South. Its report documented disorder and resistance and the appalling treatment and conditions of the freedmen. Even before the report was made final in 1866, Congress passed a civil rights bill to protect the fragile rights of the blacks and extended for two more years the Freedmen's Bureau, an agency providing emergency assistance at the end of the war. President Johnson vetoed both bills, arguing that they were unconstitutional and calling his congressional opponents "traitors."

Johnson's growing anger forced moderates into the radical camp, and Congress passed both bills over his veto. Both, however, were watered down by weakening the power of enforcement.

A white mob burned this freedmen's school during the Memphis riot of May 1866.

Southern civil courts, therefore, regularly disallowed black testimony against whites, acquitted whites charged with violence against blacks, sentenced blacks to compulsory labor, and generally made discriminatory sentences for the same crimes. In this judicial climate, racial violence erupted with discouraging frequency.

In Memphis, for example, a race riot occurred in May 1866 that typified race relations during the Reconstruction period. A street brawl erupted between the police and some recently discharged but armed black soldiers. After some fighting and an exchange of gunfire, the soldiers went back to their fort. That night, white mobs, led by prominent local officials, invaded the black section of the city. With the encouragement of the Memphis police, the mobs engaged in over 40 hours of terror, killing, beating, robbing, and raping virtually helpless residents and burning houses, schools, and churches. When it was over, 48 persons, all but two of them black,

had died in the riot. The local Union army commander took his time intervening to restore order, arguing that his troops had "a large amount of public property to guard [and] hated Negroes too." A congressional inquiry found that in Memphis, blacks had "no protection from the law whatever."

A month later, Congress proposed to the states the ratification of the Fourteenth Amendment, the single most significant act of the Reconstruction era. The first section of the amendment sought to provide permanent constitutional protection of the civil rights of freedmen by defining them as citizens. States were prohibited from depriving "any person of life, liberty, or property, without due process of law," and all persons were guaranteed "the equal protection of the laws." In section 2, Congress paved the way for black male suffrage in the South by declaring that states not enfranchising black males would have their "basis of representation reduced" proportionally. Other sections of the amendment denied leaders of the Confederacy the right to hold national or state political office (except by act of Congress), repudiated the Confederate debt, and denied claims of compensation by former slave owners for their lost property.

President Johnson urged the southern states not to ratify the Fourteenth Amendment, and ten states immediately rejected it. Johnson then went on the campaign trail in the midterm election of 1866 to ask voters to throw out the radical Republicans. Vicious name calling and other low forms of electioneering marked this first political campaign since the war's end. The result of the election was an overwhelming victory for the Republicans and a repudiation of Andrew Johnson and his policies.

Therefore, early in 1867, Reconstruction Acts were passed dividing the southern states into five military districts to maintain order and protect the rights of property and persons and defining a new process for readmitting a state.

Qualified voters, which included blacks and excluded unreconstructed rebels, would elect delegates to state constitutional conventions, which then would write new constitutions guaranteeing black suffrage. After the new voters of the states had ratified the constitutions, elections would be held to choose governors and state legislatures. When a state ratified the Fourteenth Amendment, its representatives to Congress would be accepted, thus completing readmission to the Union.

The President Impeached

At the same time as it passed the Reconstruction Acts, Congress also approved bills to restrict the powers of the president and to establish the dominance of the legislative branch over the executive. The Tenure of Office Act, designed to protect the outspoken secretary of war, Edwin Stanton, from removal by Johnson, limited the president's appointment powers. Other measures restricted his power as commander in chief. Johnson behaved exactly as congressional Republicans had anticipated, vetoing the Reconstruction Acts, issuing orders to limit military commanders in the South, and removing cabinet and other government officials sympathetic to Congress's program. The House Judiciary Committee investigated, charging the president with "usurpations of power," but moderate House Republicans defeated impeachment resolutions to remove Johnson from office.

In August 1867, Johnson finally dismissed Stanton and asked for Senate consent. When the Senate refused, the president ordered Stanton to surrender his office, which he refused, barricading himself inside. This time the House rushed impeachment resolutions to a vote, charging the president with "high crimes and misdemeanors" as detailed in 11 offenses while in office, mostly focusing on alleged violations of the Tenure of Office Act. The three-month trial in the Senate early in 1868 featured impassioned oratory, but in the end, seven moderate Republicans joined Democrats against conviction, and the effort to find the president guilty as charged fell short of the two-thirds majority required by a single vote.

As the moderate or regular Republicans gained strength in 1868 through their support of the presidential election winner, Ulysses S. Grant, radicalism lost much of its power within Republican ranks. Not for another 100 years would a president again face removal from office through impeachment.

Congressional Moderation

The impeachment crisis revealed that most Republicans were more interested in protecting themselves than the freedmen and in punishing Johnson rather than the South. It is revealing to look not only at what Congress did during Reconstruction but also at what it did not do.

With the exception of Jefferson Davis, Congress did not imprison Confederate leaders, and only one person, the commander of the infamous Andersonville prison camp, was put to death. Congress did not insist on a long-term probationary period before southern states could be readmitted to the Union. It did not reorganize southern local governments. It did not mandate a national program of education for the four million ex-slaves. It did not confiscate and redistribute land to the freedmen, nor did it prevent President Johnson from taking land away from freedmen who had gained possessory titles during the war. It did not, except indirectly, provide economic help to black citizens.

What Congress did do, and that only reluctantly, was grant citizenship and suffrage to the freedmen. Black suffrage gained support after the election of 1868, when General Grant, a military hero regarded as invincible, barely won the popular vote in several states. Congressional Republicans, who had twice rejected a suffrage amendment, took another look at the idea as a way of adding grateful black votes to party rolls. After a bitterly contested fight, repeated in several state ratification contests, the Fifteenth

Amendment, forbidding all states to deny the vote to anyone "on account of race, color, or previous condition of servitude," became part of the Constitution in 1870. A black preacher from Pittsburgh observed that "the Republican party had done the Negro good, but they were doing themselves good at the same time."

For political reasons, therefore, Congress gave blacks the vote but not the land, the opposite priority of what the freedmen wanted. Almost alone, Thaddeus Stevens argued that "forty acres . . . and a hut would be more valuable . . . than the . . . right to vote." But Congress never seriously considered his plan to confiscate the land of the "chief rebels" and to give a small portion of it, divided into 40-acre plots, to the freedmen.

Although most Americans, in the North as well as the South, opposed confiscation and black independent landownership, Congress passed an alternative measure. Proposed by George Julian of Indiana, the Southern Homestead Act of 1866 made public lands available to blacks and loyal whites in five southern states. But the land was of poor quality and inaccessible, and claimants had only until January 1, 1867, to claim their land. But that was nearly impossible for most blacks because they were under contract with white employers until that date. Only about 4,000 black families even applied for the Homestead Act lands, and fewer than 20 percent of them saw their claims completed. The record of white claimants was not much better. Congressional moderation, therefore, left the freedmen economically weak as they faced the challenges of freedom.

Women and the Reconstruction Amendments

One casualty of the Fourteenth and Fifteenth amendments was the goodwill of the women who had been petitioning and campaigning for suffrage for two decades. They had hoped that grateful male legislators would recognize their support for the Union effort during the war and the suspension of their own demands in the interests of the more immediate concerns of preserving the Union, nursing the wounded, and emancipating the slaves. They were therefore shocked to see the wording of the Fourteenth Amendment, which for the first time inserted the word *male* in the Constitution in referring to a citizen's right to vote. Stanton and Anthony campaigned actively against the Fourteenth Amendment, and when the Fifteenth Amendment was proposed, they wondered why the word *sex* could not have been added to the "conditions" no longer a basis for denial of the vote.

Disappointment over the suffrage issue was one of several reasons that led to a split in the women's movement and the formation of two competing organizations in 1869. While some women's rights activists felt that the struggle for black rights should have its day and should not be hindered by linkage to women's demands for the vote, others pointed out that some blacks were also women. Anthony and Stanton, determined to continue their fight for a national amendment for woman suffrage and a long list of other rights, founded the National Woman Suffrage Association (NWSA). The rival American Woman Suffrage Association (AWSA) concentrated its hopes on securing the vote on a state-by-state basis. In the end, both blacks and women would have a long path of struggle ahead of them.

LIFE AFTER SLAVERY

Clinton Fisk, a well-meaning white who helped to found a black college in Tennessee, told freedmen in 1866 that they could be "as free and as happy" working again for their "old master . . . as any where else in the world." For many blacks such pronouncements sounded familiar, reminding them of white preachers' exhortations during slavery to work hard and obey their masters. Ironically, though, Fisk was an agent of the Freedmen's Bureau, the crucial agency intended to ease the transition from slavery to freedom for the four million ex-slaves.

The Freedmen's Bureau

Never in American history has one small agency—underfinanced, understaffed, and undersupported—been given a harder task than was the Bureau of Freedmen, Refugees and Abandoned Lands. Its purposes and mixed successes illustrate the tortuous course of Reconstruction.

The activities of the Freedmen's Bureau included issuing emergency rations of food and providing clothing and shelter to the homeless, hungry victims of the war; establishing medical care and hospital facilities; providing funds for transportation for the thousands of freedmen and white refugees dislocated by the war; helping blacks search for and put their families back together; and arranging for legal marriage ceremonies. The bureau also served as a friend in local civil courts to ensure that the freedmen got fair trials. Although not initially empowered to do so, the agency was responsible for the education of the ex-slaves. To bureau schools came many idealistic teachers from various northern Freedmen's Aid societies.

In addition, the largest task of the Freedmen's Bureau was to serve as an employment agency, tending to the economic well-being of the blacks. This included settling them on abandoned lands and getting them started with tools, seed, and draft animals, as well as arranging work contracts with white landowners. In the area of work contracts, the Freedmen's Bureau served more to "reenslave" the freedmen as impoverished fieldworkers than to set them on their way as independent farmers.

Although some agents were idealistic young New Englanders eager to help slaves adjust to freedom, others were Union army officers more concerned with social order than social transformation. On a typical day, these overworked and underpaid agents would visit courts and schools in their district, supervise the signing of work contracts, and handle numerous complaints, most involving contract violations between whites and blacks or property and domestic disputes among blacks. They were helpful in finding work for the freedmen, but more often than not the agents found themselves defending white landowners by telling the blacks to obey orders, to trust their employers, and to sign and live by disadvantageous contracts.

Despite mounting pressures to support white landowners, personal frustrations, and even threats on their lives, the agents accomplished a great deal. In little more than two years, the Freedmen's Bureau issued 20 million rations (nearly one-third to poor whites), reunited families and resettled some 30,000 displaced war refugees, treated some 450,000 cases of illness and injury, built 40 hospitals and hundreds of schools, provided books, tools, and furnishings—and even some land—to the freedmen, and occasionally protected their economic and civil rights. The historian W. E. B. Du Bois wrote an epitaph for the bureau that might stand for the whole of Reconstruction: "In a time of perfect calm, amid willing neighbors and streaming wealth," he wrote, it "would have been a herculean task" for the bureau to fulfill its many purposes. But in the midst of hunger, sorrow, spite, suspicion, hate, and cruelty, "the work of any instrument of social regeneration was . . . foredoomed to failure."

Economic Freedom by Degrees

The economic failures of the Freedmen's Bureau forced the freedmen into a new economic dependency on their former masters, and both were affected by the changing character of southern agriculture in the postwar years. First, land ownership was concentrated into fewer and even larger holdings than before the Civil War. From South Carolina to Louisiana, the wealthiest tenth of the population owned about 60 percent of the real estate in the 1870s. Second, these large planters increasingly concentrated on one crop, usually cotton, and were tied into the international market. This resulted in a steady drop in food production in the postwar period. Third, reliance on one-crop farming meant that a new credit system emerged whereby most farmers, black and white, depended on local merchants for renting seed, farm implements and animals, provisions, housing, and land. These changes affected race relations and class tensions among whites.

This new system, however, took a few years to develop after emancipation. At first, most freedmen signed contracts with white landowners and worked in gangs in the fields as farm laborers very much as during slavery. But what the freedmen wanted, a Georgia planter correctly observed, was "to get away from all overseers, to hire or purchase land, and work for themselves."

Many blacks therefore broke contracts, ran away, engaged in work slowdowns or strikes, burned barns, and otherwise expressed their displeasure with the contract labor system. Blacks' insistence on autonomy and land of their own was the major impetus for the change from the contract system to tenancy and sharecropping. As a South Carolina freedman put it, "If I can't own de land, I'll hire or lease land, but I won't contract." The sharecroppers were given seed, fertilizer, farm implements, and all necessary food and clothing to take care of their families. In return, the landlord (or a local merchant) told them what to grow and how much and took a share—usually half—of the harvest. The half retained by the cropper, however, was usually needed to pay for goods bought on credit (at huge interest rates) at the landlord's store. Thus the sharecroppers were semiautonomous but remained tied to the landlord's will for economic survival.

Sharecroppers and tenant farmers, though more autonomous than contract laborers, remained dependent on the landlord for their survival.

Under the tenant system, farmers had only slightly more independence. In advance of the harvest, a tenant farmer promised to sell his crop to a local merchant in return for renting land, tools, and other necessities. He was also obligated to purchase goods on credit (at higher prices than whites paid) against the harvest from the merchant's store. At "settling up" time, the income from the sale of the crop was matched with debts accumulated at the store. But tenants usually remained in debt at the end of each year and were then compelled to pledge the next year's crop. Thus a system of debt peonage replaced slavery. Only a very few blacks became independent landowners—about 2 to 5 percent by 1880, but closer to 20 percent in some states by 1900.

These changes in southern agriculture affected yeoman and poor white farmers as well as the freedmen, especially as cotton production doubled between the Civil War and 1880. Like the freedmen, whites, too, were forced to concentrate on growing staples, to pledge their crops against high-interest credit from local merchants, and to face perpetual indebtedness.

Larger planters' reliance on cotton meant fewer food crops, which led to greater dependence on local merchants for provisions and a poorer diet. Poor whites thus faced diminishing fortunes throughout the South. Some became farmhands, earning $6 a month (with board) from other farmers. Other fled to low-paying jobs in urban cotton mills.

In part because their lives were so hard, poor whites persisted in their belief in white superiority. As a federal officer reported in 1866, "The poorer classes of white people ... have a most intense hatred of the Negro, and swear he shall never be reckoned as part of the population." Many poor whites, therefore, joined the Ku Klux Klan and other southern white terror groups that emerged between 1866 and 1868. But however hard life was for poor whites, blacks were far more often sentenced to chain gangs for the slightest crimes and were bound to a life of debt, degradation, and dependency. The

high hopes with which the freedmen had greeted emancipation turned slowly to resignation and disillusionment. Felix Haywood, a former Texas slave, recalled:

> We thought we was goin' to be richer than white folks, 'cause we was stronger and knowed how to work, and the whites ... didn't have us to work for them anymore. But it didn't turn out that way. We soon found out that freedom could make folks proud but it didn't make 'em rich.

Black Self-Help Institutions

It was clear to many black leaders that since white institutions could not fulfill the promises of emancipation, black freedmen would have to do it themselves. Fortunately, the tradition of black community self-help survived in the organized churches and schools of the antebellum free Negro communities and in the "invisible" cultural institutions of the slave quarters. Religion, as usual, was vital. Emancipation brought an explosion in the growth of membership in black churches. The Negro Baptist church grew from 150,000 members in 1850 to 500,000 in 1870. The various branches of the African Methodist Episcopal church increased fourfold in the decade after the Civil War, from 100,000 to over 400,000 members.

Black ministers continued their tradition of community leadership and revivalist preaching. An English visitor to the South in 1867 and 1868, after observing a preacher in Savannah arouse nearly 1,000 people to "sway, and cry, and groan," noted the intensity of black "devoutness."

The freedmen's desire for education was as strong as for religion. A school official in Virginia echoed the observation of many when he said that the freedmen were "down right crazy to learn." This enthusiasm was dampened by the demands of fieldwork and scarce resources for black schools. The first teachers of the black children in the South were unmarried northern women, the legendary "Yankee schoolmarms," sent by groups such as the American Missionary

Along with equal civil rights and land of their own, what the freedmen most wanted was education. Despite white opposition and limited facilities for black schools, one of the most positive outcomes of the Reconstruction era was education in freedmen's schools.

Association. But blacks increasingly preferred their own teachers, who could better understand former slaves. To ensure the training of black preachers and teachers, northern philanthropists founded Howard, Atlanta, Fisk, Morehouse, and other black universities in the South between 1865 and 1867.

Black schools, like churches, became community centers. They published newspapers, provided training in trades and farming, and promoted political participation and land ownership. These efforts made black schools objects of local white hostility. In 1869, in Tennessee alone, 37 black schools were burned to the ground.

White opposition to black education and land ownership stimulated the rise of black nationalism and separatism. In the late 1860s, Benjamin "Pap" Singleton, a former Tennessee slave who had escaped to Canada, organized a land company in 1869 and promoted relocation of blacks to separatist communities in Kansas, where they would be able to manage their own affairs apart from white interference. When these schemes failed, Singleton and other nationalists urged emigration to Canada and Liberia. Other black leaders, notably Frederick Douglass, continued to assert that suffrage would eventually lead to full citizenship rights within the United States.

RECONSTRUCTION IN THE STATES

Douglass's confidence in the power of the ballot seemed warranted in the enthusiastic early months under the Reconstruction Acts of 1867. With President Johnson neutralized, national Republican leaders were finally in a position to accomplish their political goals. Local Republicans, taking advantage of the inability or refusal of many southern whites to vote, overwhelmingly elected their delegates to state constitutional conventions in the fall of 1867. With guarded optimism and a sense of the "sacred importance" of their work, black and white Republicans turned to the task of creating new state governments.

Republican Rule

Despite popular belief, the southern state governments under Republican rule were not dominated by illiterate black majorities intent on "Africanizing" the South by passing compulsory racial intermarriage laws, as many whites feared. Nor were these governments unusually corrupt or financially extravagant. Nor did they use massive numbers of federal troops to enforce their will. Rather, they tried to do their work in a climate of economic distress and increasingly violent harassment.

A diverse combination of political groups made up the new governments elected under congressional Reconstruction. Labeled the "black and tan" governments by their opponents to suggest domination by former slaves and mulattoes, they were actually predominantly white, with the one exception of the lower house of the South Carolina legislature. The new leadership included an old Whiggish elite class of bankers, industrialists, and others interested far more in economic growth than in radical social reforms; northern Republican capitalists seeking investment opportunities; retired Union veterans; and missionaries and teachers. Such people were unfairly labeled "carpetbaggers."

Moderate blacks also participated in the Republican state governments. A large percentage of black officeholders were mulattoes, many of them well-educated preachers, teachers, and soldiers from the North. Others, such as John Lynch of Mississippi, were self-educated tradesmen or representatives of the small landed class of southern blacks. This class composition meant that black leaders often supported land policies that largely ignored the economic needs of the black masses.

These black politicians were more interested in pursuing political influence and education than land redistribution or state aid to black peasants. They sought no revenge or reversal of power, only, as an 1865 petition said, "that the same laws which govern white men shall govern black men [and that] we be dealt with as others are—in equity and justice."

The primary accomplishment of Republican rule in the South was in eliminating the undemocratic features of earlier state constitutions. All states provided universal men's suffrage and loosened requirements for holding office. The basis of state representation was made fairer by apportioning more legislative seats to the interior regions of southern states. Social and penal laws were also modernized.

Republican governments undertook the task of financially and physically reconstructing the South, overhauling tax systems, and approving generous railroad and other capital investment bonds. Most important, the Republican governments provided for a state-supported system of public schools, absent before in most of the South. As in the North, these schools were largely segregated, but for the first time, rich and poor, black and white alike had access to education. As a result, black school attendance increased from 5 to over 40 percent and white from 20 to over 60 percent by the 1880s. All of this cost money, and the Republicans did indeed greatly increase tax rates and state debts. All in all, the Republican governments "dragged the South, screaming and crying, into the modern world."

Despite its effectiveness in modernizing southern state governments, the Republican coalition did not last very long. In fact, as the map indicates, Republican rule lasted for different periods of time in different states. In some

The Return to the Union During Reconstruction

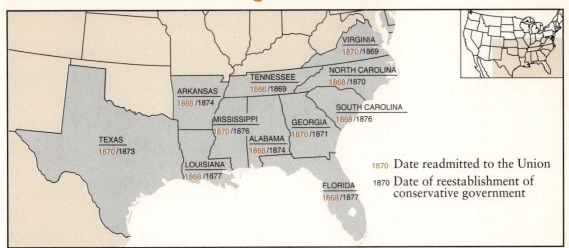

TEXAS
1870/1873

LOUISIANA
1868/1877

ARKANSAS
1868/1874

MISSISSIPPI
1870/1876

ALABAMA
1868/1874

TENNESSEE
1866/1869

GEORGIA
1870/1871

FLORIDA
1868/1877

VIRGINIA
1870/1869

NORTH CAROLINA
1868/1870

SOUTH CAROLINA
1868/1876

1870 Date readmitted to the Union
1870 Date of reestablishment of conservative government

states, Virginia, for example, the Republicans ruled hardly at all. In South Carolina, the unwillingness of black leaders to use their power to help black laborers contributed to their loss of political control to the Democrats. Class tensions and divisions among blacks in Louisiana helped to weaken that Republican regime as well. Republican rule lasted the longest in the black-belt states of the Deep South, where the black population was equal to or greater than the white.

Violence and "Redemption"

Democrats used racial violence, intimidation, and coercion to restore their power. The Ku Klux Klan was only one of several secret organizations that used force and violence against black and white Republicans. The cases of North Carolina and Mississippi are representative in showing how conservative Democrats were able to regain control.

After losing a close election in North Carolina in 1868, conservatives waged a concentrated campaign of terror in several counties in the piedmont area. If the Democrats could win these counties in 1870, they would most likely win statewide. In the year prior to the election, several prominent Republicans were killed, including a white state senator, whose throat was cut, and a leading black Union League organizer, who was hanged in the courthouse square with a sign pinned to his breast: "Bewar, ye guilty, both white and black." Scores of citizens were flogged, tortured, fired from their jobs, or forced to flee in the middle of the night from burning homes and barns. The courts consistently refused to prosecute anyone for these crimes. Local papers, in fact, charged that "disgusting negroes and white Radicals" had committed the crimes. The conservative campaign worked. In the election of 1870, some 12,000 fewer Republicans voted in the two crucial counties than had voted two years earlier, and the Democrats swept back into power.

In the state election in Mississippi in 1875, Democrats used similar tactics. In what was called the Mississippi Plan, local Democratic clubs organized themselves into armed militias, marching defiantly through black areas, breaking up Republican meetings, and provoking riots to justify the killing of hundreds of blacks. Armed men were posted during voter registration to intimidate Republicans. At the election itself, anyone still bold enough to attempt to vote was either helped by gun-toting whites to cast a Democratic ballot or driven away from the polls with cannon and clubs. Counties that had earlier given Republican candidates majorities in the thousands managed in 1875 a total of less than a dozen votes!

Democrats called their victory "redemption." As conservative Democratic administrations resumed control of each state government, Reconstruction came to an end. Redemption resulted from a combination of the persistence of white southern resistance, including violence and other coercive measures, and a loss of will to persist in the North.

Congress and President Grant did not totally ignore the violence in the South. Three Force Acts, passed in 1870 and 1871, gave the president strong powers to use federal supervisors to make sure that citizens were not prevented from voting by force or fraud. The third act, known as the Ku Klux Klan Act, declared illegal secret organizations that used disguise and coercion to deprive others of equal protection of the laws. Congress created a joint committee to investigate Klan violence, which reported in 1872 in 13 huge volumes of horrifying testimony. Grant issued proclamations condemning lawlessness and sent some additional troops to South Carolina. However, as reform Republicans realized that black voters supported Grant, they lost interest in defending those voters. Regular Republicans were also not very supportive, since many felt that they could do without black voters. In 1875, Grant's advisers told him that Republicans might lose important Ohio elections if he continued to protect blacks. Thus he decided that year to reject appeals by Mississippi blacks that troops be stationed in their state to

guarantee free elections. Grant declared instead that he and the nation "had tired of these annual autumnal outbreaks."

The federal government did little to stop the reign of terror against black and white Republicans throughout the South. The Force Acts were wholly inadequate and were themselves weakly enforced. Although the Ku Klux Klan's power was officially ended, the attitudes (and tactics) of Klansmen would continue long into the next century.

Reconstruction, Northern Style

The American people, like their leaders, were tired of battles over the freedmen and were shifting their attention to other matters. Frustrated with the difficulties of trying to transform an unwilling South and seemingly ungrateful blacks, the easiest course was to give blacks their citizenship and the vote and move on to something else. After the interruptions of civil war and its aftermath, most Americans were primarily interested in starting families, finding work, and making money. This meant firing furnaces in the new steel plant in Wheeling, West Virginia, pounding in railroad ties for the Central Pacific in the Nevada desert, struggling to teach in a one-room schoolhouse in Vermont for $23 a month, or battling heat, locusts, and railroad rates on a family homestead in Kansas.

At both the individual and national levels, Reconstruction, northern style, meant the continuation of the enormous economic revolution of the nineteenth century. Although failing to effect a smooth transition from slavery to freedom for ex-slaves, Republican northerners were able to accelerate and solidify their program of economic growth and industrial and territorial expansion.

The years between 1865 and 1875 featured not only the rise (and fall) of Republican governments in the South but also the spectacular rise of working-class activity and organization. Stimulated by the Civil War to improve working conditions in northern factories, such groups as trade unions, labor reform associations, and labor parties flourished, culminating in the founding of the National Labor Union in 1866. Before the depression of 1873, an estimated 300,000 to 500,000 American workers had enrolled in some 1,500 trade unions, the largest such increase in the nineteenth century. This growth would inevitably affect class tensions. In 1876, hundreds of freedmen in the rice region along the Combahee River in South Carolina went on strike to protest a 40-cent-per-day wage cut, clashing with local sheriffs and white Democratic rifle clubs. A year later, also over wage cuts, thousands of railroad workers in Pittsburgh, St. Louis, Omaha, and other northern cities went out in a nationwide wave of strikes, clashing with local police and the National Guard.

As economic relations changed, so did the Republican Party. It changed from the party of moral reform to one of material interest. In the continuing struggle in American politics between "virtue and commerce," self-interest was again winning. No longer willing to support an agency like the Freedmen's Bureau, Republican politicians had no difficulty backing huge grants of money and land to the railroads. As blacks were told to go to work and help themselves, the Union Pacific was being given subsidies of between $16,000 and $48,000 for each mile of track laid across western plains and mountains.

By 1869, the year financier Jay Gould almost succeeded in cornering the gold market, the nation was increasingly defined by materialistic "go-getters" and by sordid grasping for wealth and power. Ulysses Grant himself was an honest man, but his judgment of others was flawed. His administration featured a series of scandals that touched several cabinet officers and relatives and even two vice presidents. Under Grant's appointments, outright graft flourished in a half dozen departments. Most scandals involved large sums of public money. The Whiskey Ring affair, for example, cost the public millions of dollars in lost tax revenues siphoned off to government of-

ficials. Gould's gold scam received the unwitting aid of Grant's Treasury Department and the knowing help of his brother-in-law.

Nor was Congress pure in these various schemes. Crédit Mobilier figured in the largest of several scandals in which construction companies for transcontinental railroads (in this case a dummy company) received generous bonds and work contracts in exchange for giving congressmen gifts of money, stocks, and railroad lands. Henry Adams spoke for many Americans when he said that Grant's administration "outraged every rule of decency."

The election of 1872 marked the decline of public interest in moral issues. A "liberal" faction of the Republican Party, unable to dislodge Grant and disgusted with his administration, formed a third party with a reform platform and nominated Horace Greeley, editor of the New York *Tribune,* for president. Democrats, lacking notable presidential candidates, also nominated Greeley, even though he had spent much of his earlier career assailing Democrats as "rascals." Despite his wretched record, Grant easily won a second term.

The End of Reconstruction

Soon after Grant's second inauguration, a financial panic, caused by overconstruction of railroads and the collapse of some crucial eastern banks, created a terrible depression that lasted throughout the mid-1870s. In times of hardship, economic issues dominated politics, further pulling attention away from the plight of the freedmen. As Democrats took control of the House of Representatives in 1874 and looked toward winning the White House in 1876, politicians talked about such issues as new scandals in the Grant administration, unemployment, various proposals for public works expenditures for relief, the availability of silver and greenback dollars, and high tariffs.

No one, it seemed, talked much about the rights and conditions of southern freedmen. In 1875, a guilt-ridden Congress passed Senator

Charles Sumner's civil rights bill, intended to put teeth into the Fourteenth Amendment. But the act was not enforced and was declared unconstitutional by the Supreme Court eight years later. Congressional Reconstruction, long dormant, had ended. The election of 1876 sealed the conclusion.

As their nominee for president in 1876, the Republicans turned to a former governor of Ohio, Rutherford B. Hayes, partly because of his reputation for honesty, partly because he had been an officer in the Union army (a necessity for post–Civil War candidates), and partly because, as Henry Adams put it, he was "obnoxious to no one." The Democrats chose Governor Samuel J. Tilden of New York, who achieved national recognition as a civil service reformer in breaking up the corrupt Tweed Ring.

Tilden won a majority of the popular vote and appeared to have enough electoral votes for victory. Of 20 disputed electoral votes, all but one came from states in the Deep South, where Democrats had applied various versions of the Mississippi Plan to intimidate voters. To resolve the disputed votes, Congress created a special electoral commission, which awarded Hayes all 20 votes, enough to win, 185 to 184.

Outraged Democrats threatened to stop the Senate from officially counting the electoral votes, thus preventing Hayes's inauguration. The country was in a state of crisis, and some Americans wondered if civil war might break out again.

As the inauguration date approached and newspapers echoed outgoing President Grant's call for "peace at any price," the forces of mutual self-interest concluded the "compromise of 1877." The Democrats agreed to suspend resistance to the counting of the electoral votes, and on March 2, Rutherford B. Hayes was declared president. In exchange for the presidency, Hayes ordered the last remaining troops out of the South (South Carolina, Louisiana, and Florida being the last states under military Reconstruction), appointed a former Confederate general to his cabinet, supported federal aid to bolster economic and railroad development in the South, and announced his intentions to let southerners handle race relations themselves. Hayes let it be known that he would not enforce the Fourteenth and Fifteenth amendments, thus initiating a pattern of executive inaction not broken until the middle of the twentieth century. The immediate crisis was averted, officially ending the era of Reconstruction, but the unfulfilled hopes of freedmen continued to smolder beneath the surface of everyday life.

CONCLUSION

A MIXED LEGACY

In the 12 years between Appomattox and Hayes's inauguration, the diverse dreams of victorious northern Republicans, defeated white southerners, and hopeful black freedmen conflicted. There was little chance that all could be realized, yet each group could point to a modest fulfillment of its goals. The compromise of 1877 cemented the reunion of South and North, thus providing new opportunities for economic development in both regions. The Republican Party achieved its economic goals and preserved its political hold on the White House, though not Congress, with two exceptions, until 1932. The ex–Confederate states were brought back into the Union, and southerners retained their firm control of southern lands and black labor, though not without struggle and some changes. To the extent that the peace of 1877 was preserved "at any price," that price was paid by the freedmen.

In 1880, Frederick Douglass summarized Reconstruction for the freedmen, saying that it was a wonder to him "not that freedmen have made so little progress, but, rather, that they have made so much; not that they have been standing still, but that they have been able to stand at all." Indeed, despite their liabilities, the freedmen had made admirable gains in education and in economic and family survival. Although sharecropping and tenancy were harsh systems, black laborers organized themselves to achieve a measure of autonomy and opportunity in their lives that could never be diminished. Moreover, the three great Reconstruction amendments to the Constitution, despite flagrant violation over the next 100 years, held out the promise that the rights of equal citizenship and political participation would yet be fulfilled.

Recommended Reading

The best overviews of the Reconstruction era are John Hope Franklin, *Reconstruction After the Civil War* (1961); Kenneth Stampp, *The Era of Reconstruction, 1865–1877* (1965); and the brilliant work by Eric Foner, *Reconstruction: America's Unfinished Revolution, 1863–1877* (1988).

The fullest, most moving account of the black experience in the transition from slavery to freedom is Leon Litwack's massive and sensitive work, *Been in the Storm So Long: The Aftermath of Slavery* (1980). The southern white response to emancipation is described in Dan T. Carter, *When the War Was Over: The Failure of Self-Reconstruction in the South, 1865–1867* (1985).

The economy of the South and the freedmen's experience with land and labor are described in Roger Ransom and Richard Sutch, *One Kind of Freedom: The Economic Consequences of Emancipation* (1977); and Eric Foner, *Nothing but Freedom: Emancipation and Its Legacy* (1983). An excellent work showing the white experience with tenancy in the changing economy of the South is Stephen Hahn, *The Roots of Southern Populism* (1983). The Freedmen's Bureau is the subject of Donald Nieman, *To Set the Law in Motion: The Freedmen's Bureau and the Legal Rights of Blacks, 1865–1868* (1979). Continuing racial prejudice in the South and North is the subject of C. Vann Woodward, *The Strange Career of Jim Crow*, 3d rev. ed. (1974). See also W. E. B. Du Bois's *Black Reconstruction* (1935) and *The Souls of Black Folk* (1903).

Northern politics during Reconstruction have been widely discussed. See David Donald, *The Politics of Reconstruction* (1965); and Michael Les Benedict, *A Compromise of Principle: Congressional Republicans and Reconstruction, 1863–1869* (1974). Southern politics is best seen in Michael Perman, *The Road to Redemption: Southern Politics, 1869–1879* (1984). Grant's presidency and the abandonment of the freedmen by northern Republicans can be traced in William McFeeley, *Grant: A Biography* (1981); and William Gillette, *Retreat from Reconstruction, 1869–1879* (1979). The campaign of violence that ended the Republican governments in the South is told with gripping horror in George C. Rable, *But There Was No Peace: The Role of Violence in the Politics of Reconstruction* (1984).

Five novels written at different times and representing different interpretations of the story of Reconstruction are Albion Tourgée, *A Fool's Errand* (1879); Thomas Dixon, *The Clansman* (1905); W. E. B. Du Bois, *The Quest of the Silver Fleece* (1911); Howard Fast, *Freedom Road* (1944); and Ernest Gaines, *The Autobiography of Miss Jane Pittman* (1971).

Time Line

1865	Civil War ends
	Lincoln assassinated; Andrew Johnson becomes president
	Johnson proposes general amnesty and reconstruction plan
	Racial confusion, widespread hunger, and demobilization
	Thirteenth Amendment ratified
	Freedmen's Bureau established
1865–1866	Black codes
	Repossession of land by whites and freedmen's contracts
1866	Freedmen's Bureau renewed and Civil Rights Act passed over Johnson's veto
	Southern Homestead Act
	Ku Klux Klan formed
	Tennessee readmitted to Union
1867	Reconstruction Acts passed over Johnson's veto
	Impeachment controversy
	Freedmen's Bureau ends
1868	Fourteenth Amendment ratified
	Johnson acquitted
	Ulysses S. Grant elected president
1868–1870	Ten states readmitted under congressional plan
1869	Georgia and Virginia reestablish Democratic Party control
1870	Fifteenth Amendment ratified
1870s–1880s	Black followers of Pap Singleton migrate to Kansas
1870–1871	Force Acts
	North Carolina and Georgia reestablish Democratic control
1872	General Amnesty Act
	Grant reelected president
1873	Crédit Mobilier scandal
	Panic causes depression
1874	Alabama and Arkansas reestablish Democratic control
1875	Civil Rights Act
	Mississippi reestablishes Democratic control
1876	Hayes-Tilden election
1876–1877	South Carolina, Louisiana, and Florida reestablish Democratic control
1877	Compromise of 1877; Rutherford B. Hayes assumes presidency and ends Reconstruction
1880s	Tenancy and sharecropping prevail in the South
	Disfranchisement and segregation of southern blacks begins

Appendix

Declaration of Independence in Congress, July 4, 1776

THE UNANIMOUS DECLARATION OF THE THIRTEEN UNITED STATES OF AMERICA

When, in the course of human events, it becomes necessary for one people to dissolve the political bonds which have connected them with another, and to assume, among the powers of the earth, the separate and equal station to which the laws of nature and of nature's God entitle them, a decent respect to the opinions of mankind requires that they should declare the causes which impel them to the separation.

We hold these truths to be self-evident: That all men are created equal, that they are endowed by their Creator with certain unalienable rights; that among these are life, liberty, and the pursuit of happiness; that, to secure these rights, governments are instituted among men, deriving their just powers from the consent of the governed; that whenever any form of government becomes destructive of these ends, it is the right of the people to alter or to abolish it, and to institute new government, laying its foundation on such principles, and organizing its powers in such form, as to them shall seem most likely to effect their safety and happiness. Prudence, indeed, will dictate that governments long established should not be changed for light and transient causes; and accordingly all experience hath shown that mankind are more disposed to suffer, which evils are sufferable, than to right themselves by abolishing the forms to which they are accustomed. But when a long train of abuses and usurpations, pursuing invariably the same object, evinces a design to reduce them under absolute despotism, it is their right, it is their duty, to throw off such government, and to provide new guards for their future security. Such has been the patient sufferance of these colonies; and such is now the necessity which constrains them to alter their former systems of government. The history of the present King of Great Britain is a history of repeated injuries and usurpations, all having in direct object the establishment of an absolute tyranny over these states. To prove this, let facts be submitted to a candid world.

He has refused his assent to laws the most wholesome and necessary for the public good.

He has forbidden his governors to pass laws of immediate and pressing importance, unless suspended in their operation till his assent should be obtained; and, when so suspended, he has utterly neglected to attend to them.

He has refused to pass other laws for the accommodation of large districts of people, unless those people would relinquish the right of representation in the legislature, a right inestimable to them, and formidable to tyrants only.

He has called together legislative bodies at places unusual, uncomfortable, and distant from the depository of their public records, for the sole purpose of fatiguing them into compliance with his measures.

He has dissolved representative houses repeatedly, for opposing, with manly firmness, his invasions on the rights of the people.

He has refused for a long time, after such dissolutions, to cause others to be elected; whereby the legislative powers, incapable of annihilation, have returned to the people at large for their exercise; the state remaining, in the mean time, exposed to all the dangers of invasions from without and convulsions within.

He has endeavored to prevent the population of these states; for that purpose obstructing the laws for naturalization of foreigners; refusing to pass others to encourage their migration hither, and raising the conditions of new appropriations of lands.

He has obstructed the administration of justice, by refusing his assent to laws for establishing judiciary powers.

He has made judges dependent on his will alone, for the tenure of their offices, and the amount and payment of their salaries.

He has erected a multitude of new offices, and sent hither swarms of officers to harass our people and eat out their substance.

He has kept among us, in times of peace, standing armies, without the consent of our legislatures.

He has affected to render the military independent of, and superior to, the civil power.

He has combined with others to subject us to a jurisdiction foreign to our constitution, and unacknowledged by our laws, giving his assent to their acts of pretended legislation:

For quartering large bodies of armed troops among us;

For protecting them, by a mock trial, from punishment for any murders which they should commit on the inhabitants of these states;

For cutting off our trade with all parts of the world;

For imposing taxes on us without our consent;

For depriving us, in many cases, of the benefits of trial by jury;

For transporting us beyond seas, to be tried for pretended offenses;

For abolishing the free system of English laws in a neighboring province, establishing therein an arbitrary government, and enlarging its boundaries, so as to render it at once an example

and fit instrument for introducing the same absolute rule into these colonies;

For taking away our charters, abolishing our most valuable laws, and altering fundamentally the forms of our governments;

For suspending our own legislatures, and declaring themselves invested with power to legislate for us in all cases whatsoever.

He has abdicated government here, by declaring us out of his protection and waging war against us.

He has plundered our seas, ravaged our coasts, burned our towns, and destroyed the lives of our people.

He is at this time transporting large armies of foreign mercenaries to complete the works of death, desolation, and tyranny already begun with circumstances of cruelty and perfidy scarcely paralleled in the most barbarous ages, and totally unworthy the head of a civilized nation.

He has constrained our fellow-citizens, taken captive on the high seas, to bear arms against their country, to become the executioners of their friends and brethren, or to fall themselves by their hands.

He has excited domestic insurrection among us, and has endeavored to bring on the inhabitants of our frontiers the merciless Indian savages, whose known rule of warfare is an undistinguished destruction of all ages, sexes, and conditions.

In every stage of these oppressions we have petitioned for redress in the most humble terms; our repeated petitions have been answered only by repeated injury. A prince, whose character is thus marked by every act which may define a tyrant, is unfit to be the ruler of a free people.

Nor have we been wanting in our attentions to our British brethren. We have warned them, from time to time, of attempts by their legislature to extend an unwarrantable jurisdiction over us. We have reminded them of the circumstances of our emigration and settlement here. We have appealed to their native justice and magnanimity; and we have conjured them, by the ties of our common kindred, to disavow these usurpations, which would inevitably interrupt our connections and correspondence. They, too, have been deaf to the voice of justice and of consanguinity. We must, therefore, acquiesce in the necessity which denounces our separation, and hold them, as we hold the rest of mankind, enemies in war, in peace friends.

We, therefore, the representatives of the United States of America, in General Congress assembled, appealing to the Supreme Judge of the world for the rectitude of our intentions, do, in the name and by the authority of the good people of these colonies, solemnly publish and declare, that these United Colonies are, and of right ought to be, FREE AND INDEPENDENT STATES; that they are absolved from all allegiance to the British crown, and that all political connection between them and the state of Great Britain is, and ought to be, totally dissolved; and that, as free and independent states, they have full power to levy war, conclude peace, contract alliances, establish commerce, and do all other acts and things which independent states may of right do. And for the support of this declaration, with a firm reliance on the protection of Divine Providence, we mutually pledge to each other our lives, our fortunes, and our sacred honor.

Constitution of the United States of America[*]

PREAMBLE

We the people of the United States, in order to form a more perfect union, establish justice, insure domestic tranquillity, provide for the common defense, promote the general welfare, and secure the blessings of liberty to ourselves and our posterity, do ordain and establish this Constitution for the United States of America.

ARTICLE 1

Section 1   All legislative powers herein granted shall be vested in a Congress of the United States, which shall consist of a Senate and a House of Representatives.

Section 2   The House of Representatives shall be composed of members chosen every second year by the people of the several States, and the electors in each State shall have the qualifications requisite for electors of the most numerous branch of the State Legislature.

No person shall be a Representative who shall not have attained to the age of twenty-five years, and been seven years a citizen of the United States, and who shall not, when elected, be an inhabitant of that State in which he shall be chosen.

Representatives and direct taxes shall be apportioned among the several States which may be included within this Union, according to their respective numbers, *which shall be determined by adding to the whole number of free persons, including those bonded in service for a term of years and excluding Indians not taxed, three-fifths of all other persons.* The actual enumeration shall be made within three years after the first meeting of the Congress of the United States, and within every subsequent term of ten years, in such manner as they shall by law direct. The number of Representatives shall not exceed one for every thirty thousand, but each State shall have at least one Representative; *and until such enumeration shall be made, the State of New Hampshire shall be entitled to choose three, Massachusetts eight, Rhode Island and Providence Plantations one, Connecticut five, New York six, New Jersey four, Pennsylvania eight, Delaware one, Maryland six, Virginia ten,*

---

[*]The Constitution became effective March 4, 1789.

NOTE: Any portion of the text that has been amended appears in italics.

North Carolina five, South Carolina five, and Georgia three.

When vacancies happen in the representation from any State, the Executive authority thereof shall issue writs of election to fill such vacancies.

The House of Representatives shall choose their Speaker and other officers; and shall have the sole power of impeachment.

Section 3   The Senate of the United States shall be composed of two Senators from each State, *chosen by the legislature thereof,* for six years; and each Senator shall have one vote.

Immediately after they shall be assembled in consequence of the first election, they shall be divided as equally as may be into three classes. The seats of the Senators of the first class shall be vacated at the expiration of the second year, of the second class at the expiration of the fourth year, and of the third class at the expiration of the sixth year, so that one-third may be chosen every second year; *and if vacancies happen by resignation or otherwise, during the recess of the legislature of any State, the Executive thereof may make temporary appointments until the next meeting of the legislature, which shall then fill such vacancies.*

No person shall be a Senator who shall not have attained to the age of thirty years, and been nine years a citizen of the United States, and who shall not, when elected, be an inhabitant of that State for which he shall be chosen.

The Vice-President of the United States shall be President of the Senate, but shall have no vote, unless they be equally divided.

The Senate shall choose their other officers, and also a President *pro tempore,* in the absence of the Vice-President, or when he shall exercise the office of President of the United States.

The Senate shall have the sole power to try all impeachments. When sitting for that purpose, they shall be on oath or affirmation. When the President of the United States is tried, the Chief Justice shall preside; and no person shall be convicted without the concurrence of two-thirds of the members present.

Judgment in cases of impeachment shall not extend further than to removal from the office, and disqualification to hold and enjoy any office of honor, thrust or profit under the United States: but the party convicted shall nevertheless be liable and subject to indictment, trial, judgment and punishment, according to law.

Section 4   The times, places and manner of holding elections for Senators and Representatives shall be prescribed in each State by the legislature thereof; but the Congress may at any time by law make or alter such regulations, except as to the places of choosing Senators.

The Congress shall assemble at least once in every year, and such meeting *shall be on the first Monday in December, unless they shall by law appoint a different day.*

Section 5   Each house shall be the judge of the elections, returns and qualifications of its own members, and a majority of each shall constitute a quorum to do business; but a smaller number may adjourn from day to day, and may be authorized to compel the attendance of absent members, in such manner, and under such penalties, as each house may provide.

Each house may determine the rules of its proceedings, punish its members for disorderly behavior, and with the concurrence of two-thirds, expel a member.

Each house shall keep a journal of its proceedings, and from time to time publish the same, excepting such parts as may in their judgment require secrecy; and the yeas and nays of the members of either house on any question shall, at the desire of one-fifth of those present, be entered on the journal.

Neither house, during the session of Congress, shall, without the consent of the other, adjourn for more than three days, nor to any other place than that in which the two houses shall be sitting.

Section 6   The Senators and Representatives shall receive a compensation for their services, to be ascertained by law and paid out of the treasury of the United States. They shall in all cases except treason, felony and breach of the peace be privileged from arrest during their attendance at the session of their respective houses, and in going to and returning from the same; and for any speech or debate in either house, they shall not be questioned in any other place.

No Senator or Representative shall, during the time for which he was elected, be appointed to any civil office under the authority of the United States, which shall have been created, or the emoluments whereof shall have been increased, during such time; and no person holding any office under the United States shall be a member of either house during his continuance in office.

Section 7 All bills for raising revenue shall originate in the House of Representatives; but the Senate may propose or concur with amendments as on other bills.

Every bill which shall have passed the House of Representatives and the Senate, shall, before it becomes a law, be presented to the President of the United States; if he approve he shall sign it, but if not he shall return it with objections to that house in which it originated, who shall enter the objections at large on their journal, and proceed to reconsider it. If after such reconsideration two-thirds of that house shall agree to pass the bill, it shall be sent, together with the objections, to the other house, by which it shall likewise be reconsidered, and, if approved by two-thirds of that house, it shall become a law. But in all such cases the votes of both houses shall be determined by yeas and nays, and the names of the persons voting for and against the bill shall be entered on the journal of each house respectively. If any bill shall not be returned by the President within ten days (Sundays excepted) after it shall have been presented to him, the same shall be a law, in like manner as if he had signed it, unless the Congress by their adjournment prevent its return, in which case it shall not be a law.

Every order, resolution, or vote to which the concurrence of the Senate and House of Representatives may be necessary (except on a question of adjournment) shall be presented to the President of the United States; and before the same shall take effect, shall be approved by him, or being disapproved by him, shall be repassed by two-thirds of the Senate and House of Representatives, according to the rules and limitations prescribed in the case of a bill.

Section 8 The Congress shall have power:

To lay and collect taxes, duties, imposts, and excises, to pay the debts and provide for the common defense and general welfare of the United States; but all duties, imposts and excises shall be uniform throughout the United States;

To borrow money on the credit of the United States;

To regulate commerce with foreign nations, and among the several States, and with the Indian tribes;

To establish an uniform rule of naturalization, and uniform laws on the subject of bankruptcies throughout the United States;

To coin money, regulate the value thereof, and of foreign coin, and fix the standard of weights and measures;

To provide for the punishment of counterfeiting the securities and current coin of the United States;

To establish post offices and post roads;

To promote the progress of science and useful arts by securing for limited times to authors and inventors the exclusive right to their respective writings and discoveries;

To constitute tribunals inferior to the Supreme Court;

To define and punish piracies and felonies committed on the high seas and offenses against the law of nations;

To declare war, grant letters of marque and reprisal, and make rules concerning captures on land and water;

To raise and support armies, but no appropriation of money to that use shall be for a longer term than two years;

To provide and maintain a navy;

To make rules for the government and regulation of the land and naval forces;

To provide for calling forth the militia to execute the laws of the Union, suppress insurrections, and repel invasions;

To provide for organizing, arming, and disciplining the militia, and for governing such part of them as may be employed in the service of the United States, reserving to the States respectively the appointment of the officers, and the authority of training the militia according to the discipline prescribed by Congress;

To exercise exclusive legislation in all cases whatsoever, over such district (not exceeding ten miles square) as may, by cession of particular States, and the acceptance of Congress, become the seat of government of the United States, and to exercise like authority over all places purchased by the consent of the legislature of the State, in which the same shall be, for erection of forts, magazines, arsenals, dockyards, and other needful buildings;—and

To make all laws which shall be necessary and proper for carrying into execution the foregoing powers, and all other powers vested by this Constitution in the government of the United States, or in any department or officer thereof.

Section 9   The migration or importation of such persons as any of the States now existing shall think proper to admit shall not be prohibited by the Congress prior to the year 1808; but a tax or duty may be imposed on such importation, not exceeding $10 for each person.

The privilege of the writ of habeas corpus shall not be suspended, unless when in cases of rebellion or invasion the public safety may require it.

No bill of attainder or ex post facto law shall be passed.

No capitation or other direct tax shall be laid, unless in proportion to the census or enumeration herein before directed to be taken.

No tax or duty shall be laid on articles exported from any State.

No preference shall be given by any regulation of commerce or revenue to the ports of one

State over those of another; nor shall vessels bound to, or from, one State be obliged to enter, clear, or pay duties in another.

No money shall be drawn from the treasury, but in consequence of appropriations made by law; and a regular statement and account of the receipts and expenditures of all public money shall be published from time to time.

No title of nobility shall be granted by the United States: and no person holding any office of profit or trust under them, shall, without the consent of the Congress, accept of any present, emolument, office, or title, of any kind whatever, from any king, prince, or foreign state.

Section 10   No State shall enter into any treaty, alliance, or confederation; grant letters of marque and reprisal; coin money; emit bills of credit; make anything but gold and silver coin a tender in payment of debts; pass any bill of attainder, ex post facto law, or law impairing the obligation of contracts, or grant any title of nobility.

No State shall, without the consent of Congress, lay any imposts or duties on imports or exports, except what may be absolutely necessary for executing its inspection laws: and the net produce of all duties and imposts, laid by any State on imports or exports, shall be for the use of the treasury of the United States; and all such laws shall be subject to the revision and control of the Congress.

No State shall, without the consent of Congress, lay any duty of tonnage, keep troops or ships of war in time of peace, enter into any agreement or compact with another State, or with a foreign power, or engage in war, unless actually invaded, or in such imminent danger as will not admit of delay.

ARTICLE II

Section 1   The executive power shall be vested in a President of the United States of America. He shall hold his office during the term of four years, and, together with the Vice-President, chosen for the same term, be elected as follows:

Each State shall appoint, in such manner as the legislature thereof may direct, a number of electors, equal to the whole number of Senators and Representatives to which the State may be entitled in the Congress; but no Senator or Representative, or person holding an office of trust or profit under the United States, shall be appointed an elector.

The electors shall meet in their respective States, and vote by ballot for two persons, of whom one at least shall not be an inhabitant of the same State with themselves. And they shall make a list of all the persons voted for, and of the number of votes for each, which list they shall sign and certify, and transmit sealed to the seat of government of the United States, directed to the President of the Senate. The President of the Senate shall, in the presence of the Senate and House of Representatives, open all the certificates, and the votes shall then be counted. The person having the greatest number of votes shall be the President, if such number be a majority of the whole number of electors appointed; and if there be more than one who have such majority, and have an equal number of votes, then the House of Representatives shall immediately choose by ballot one of them for President; and if no person have a majority, then from the five highest on the list said house shall in like manner choose the President. But in choosing the President the votes shall be taken by States, the representation from each State having one vote; a quorum for this purpose shall consist of a member or members from two-thirds of the States, and a majority of all the States shall be necessary to a choice. In every case, after the choice of the President, the person having the greatest number of votes of the electors shall be the Vice-President. But if there should remain two or more who have equal votes, the Senate shall choose from them by ballot the Vice-President.

The Congress may determine the time of choosing the electors and the day on which they shall give their votes; which day shall be the same throughout the United States.

No person except a natural-born citizen, *or a citizen of the United States at the time of the adoption of this Constitution,* shall be eligible to the office of President; neither shall any person be eligible to that office who shall not have attained to the age of thirty-five years, and been fourteen years a resident within the United States.

In case of the removal of the President from office or of his death, resignation, or inability to discharge the powers and duties of the said office, the same shall devolve on the Vice-President, and the Congress may by law provide for the case of removal, death, resignation, or inability, both of the President and Vice-President, declaring what officer shall then act as President, and such officer shall act accordingly, until the disability be removed, or a President shall be elected.

The President shall, at stated times, receive for his services a compensation, which shall neither be increased nor diminished during the period for which he shall have been elected, and he shall not receive within that period any other emolument from the United States, or any of them.

Before he enter on the execution of his office, he shall take the following oath or affirmation:—"I do solemnly swear (or affirm) that I will faithfully execute the office of the President of the United States, and will to the best of my ability preserve, protect and defend the Constitution of the United States."

Section 2 The President shall be commander in chief of the army and navy of the United States, and of the militia of the several States, when called into the actual service of the United States; he may require the opinion, in writing, of the principal officer in each of the executive departments, upon any subject relating to the duties of their respective offices, and he shall have power to grant reprieves and pardons for offenses against the United States, except in cases of impeachment.

He shall have power, by and with the advice and consent of the Senate, to make treaties, provided two-thirds of the Senators present concur;

and he shall nominate, and by and with the advice and consent of the Senate, shall appoint ambassadors, other public ministers and consuls, judges of the Supreme Court, and all other officers of the United States, whose appointments are not herein otherwise provided for, and which shall be established by law: but Congress may by law vest the appointment of such inferior officers, as they think proper, in the President alone, in the courts of law, or in the heads of departments.

The President shall have power to fill up all vacancies that may happen during the recess of the Senate, by granting commissions which shall expire at the end of their next session.

Section 3 He shall from time to time give to the Congress information of the state of the Union, and recommend to their consideration such measures as he shall judge necessary and expedient; he may, on extraordinary occasions, convene both houses, or either of them, and in case of disagreement between them, with respect to the time of adjournment, he may adjourn them to such time as he shall think proper; he shall receive ambassadors and other public ministers; he shall take care that the laws be faithfully executed, and shall commission all the officers of the United States.

Section 4 The President, Vice-President and all civil officers of the United States shall be removed from office on impeachment for, and on conviction of, treason, bribery, or other high crimes and misdemeanors.

ARTICLE III

Section 1 The judicial power of the United States shall be vested in one Supreme Court, and in such inferior courts as the Congress may from time to time ordain and establish. The judges, both of the Supreme and inferior courts, shall hold their offices during good behavior, and shall, at stated times, receive for their services a compensation which shall not be diminished during their continuance in office.

Section 2 The judicial power shall extend to all cases, in law and equity, arising under this Constitution, the laws of the United States, and treaties made, or which shall be made, under their authority—to all cases affecting ambassadors, other public ministers and consuls;—to all cases of admiralty and maritime jurisdiction;—to controversies to which the United States shall be a party;—to controversies between two or more States;—*between a State and citizens of another State;*—between citizens of different States;—between citizens of the same State claiming lands under grants of different States, and between a State, or the citizens thereof, and foreign states, citizens or subjects.

In all cases affecting ambassadors, other public ministers and consuls, and those in which a State shall be party, the Supreme Court shall have original jurisdiction. In all the other cases before mentioned, the Supreme Court shall have appellate jurisdiction, both as to law and fact, with such exceptions, and under such regulations, as the Congress shall make.

The trial of all crimes, except in cases of impeachment, shall be by jury; and such trial shall be held in the State where said crimes shall have been committed: but when not committed within any State, the trial shall be at such places or places as the Congress may by law have directed.

Section 3 Treason against the United States shall consist only in levying war against them, or in adhering to their enemies, giving them aid and comfort. No person shall be convicted of treason unless on the testimony of two witnesses to the same overt act, or on confession in open court.

The Congress shall have power to declare the punishment of treason, but no attainder of treason shall work corruption of blood, or forfeiture except during the life of the person attainted.

ARTICLE IV

Section 1 Full faith and credit shall be given in each State to the public acts, records, and judicial proceedings of every other State. And the

Congress may by general laws prescribe the manner in which such acts, records, and proceedings shall be proved, and the effect thereof.

Section 2   The citizens of each State shall be entitled to all privileges and immunities of citizens in the several States.

A person charged in any State with treason, felony, or other crime, who shall flee from justice, and be found in another State, shall on demand of the executive authority of the State from which he fled, be delivered up, to be removed to the State having jurisdiction of the crime.

No person held to service or labor in one State, under the laws thereof, escaping into another, shall, in consequence of any law or regulation therein, be discharged from such service or labor, but shall be delivered up on claim of the party to whom such service or labor may be due.

Section 3   New States may be admitted by the Congress into this Union; but no new State shall be formed or erected within the jurisdiction of any other State; nor any State be formed by the junction of two or more States, or parts of States, without the consent of the legislatures of the States concerned as well as of the Congress.

The Congress shall have power to dispose of and make all needful rules and regulations respecting the territory or other property belonging to the United States; and nothing in this Constitution shall be so construed as to prejudice any claims of the United States, or of any particular State.

Section 4   The United States shall guarantee to every State in this Union a republican form of government, and shall protect each of them against invasion; and on application of the legislature, or of the executive (when the legislature cannot be convened), against domestic violence.

ARTICLE V

The Congress, whenever two-thirds of both houses shall deem it necessary, shall propose amendments to this Constitution, or, on the application of the legislatures of two-thirds of the several States, shall call a convention for proposing amendments, which, in either case, shall be valid to all intents and purposes, as part of this Constitution, when ratified by the legislatures of three-fourths of the several States, or by conventions in three-fourths thereof, as the one or the other mode of ratification may be proposed by the Congress; provided *that no amendments which may be made prior to the year one thousand eight hundred and eight shall in any manner affect the first and fourth classes in the ninth section of the first article; and* that no State, without its consent, shall be deprived of its equal suffrage in the Senate.

ARTICLE VI

All debts contracted and engagements entered into, before the adoption of this Constitution, shall be as valid against the United States under this Constitution, as under the Confederation.

This Constitution, and the laws of the United States which shall be made in pursuance thereof; and all treaties made, or which shall be made, under the authority of the United States, shall be the supreme law of the land; and the judges in every State shall be bound thereby, anything in the Constitution or laws of any State to the contrary notwithstanding.

The Senators and Representatives before mentioned, and the members of the several State legislatures, and all executive and judicial officers, both of the United States and of the several States, shall be bound by oath or affirmation to support this Constitution; but no religious test shall ever be required as a qualification to any office or public trust under the United States.

ARTICLE VII

The ratification of the conventions of nine States shall be sufficient for the establishment of this Constitution between the States so ratifying the same.

Done in Convention by the unanimous consent of the States present, the seventeenth day of September in the year of our Lord one thousand seven hundred and eighty-seven and of the Independence of the United States of America the twelfth. In witness whereof we have hereunto subscribed our names.

AMENDMENTS TO THE CONSTITUTION*

Amendment I [1791]

Congress shall make no law respecting an establishment of religion, or prohibiting the free exercise thereof; or abridging the freedom of speech, or of the press; or the right of the people peaceably to assemble, and to petition the government for a redress of grievances.

Amendment II [1791]

A well-regulated militia being necessary to the security of a free State, the right of the people to keep and bear arms shall not be infringed.

Amendment III [1791]

No soldier shall, in time of peace, be quartered in any house without the consent of the owner, nor in time of war, but in a manner to be prescribed by law.

Amendment IV [1791]

The right of the people to be secure in their persons, houses, papers, and effects, against unreasonable searches and seizures, shall not be violated, and no warrants shall issue but upon probable cause, supported by oath or affirmation, and particularly describing the place to be searched, and the persons or things to be seized.

Amendment V [1791]

No person shall be held to answer for a capital or otherwise infamous crime, unless on a presentment or indictment of a grand jury, except in cases arising in the land or naval forces, or in the militia, when in actual service in time of war or public danger; nor shall any person be subject for the same offense to be twice put in jeopardy of life or limb; nor shall be compelled in any criminal case to be a witness against himself, nor be deprived of life, liberty or property, without due process of law; nor shall private property be taken for public use without just compensation.

Amendment VI [1791]

In all criminal prosecutions, the accused shall enjoy the right to a speedy and public trial, by an impartial jury of the State and district wherein the crime shall have been committed, which district shall have been previously ascertained by law, and to be informed of the nature and cause of the accusation; to be confronted with the witnesses against him; to have compulsory process for obtaining witnesses in his favor, and to have the assistance of counsel for his defense.

Amendment VII [1791]

In suits at common law, where the value in controversy shall exceed twenty dollars, the right of trial by jury shall be preserved, and no fact tried by a jury shall be otherwise reexamined in any court of the United States, than according to the rules of the common law.

Amendment VIII [1791]

Excessive bail shall not be required, nor excessive fines imposed, nor cruel and unusual punishments inflicted.

Amendment IX [1791]

The enumeration in the Constitution, of certain rights, shall not be construed to deny or disparage others retained by the people.

*The first ten amendments are known as the Bill of Rights.

Amendment X [1791]

The powers not delegated to the United States by the Constitution, nor prohibited by it to the States, are reserved to the States respectively, or to the people.

Amendment XI [1791]

The judicial power of the United States shall not be construed to extend to any suit in law or equity, commenced or prosecuted against one of the United States by citizens of another State, or by citizens or subjects of any foreign state.

Amendment XII [1804]

The electors shall meet in their respective States, and vote by ballot for President and Vice-President, one of whom, at least, shall not be an inhabitant of the same State with themselves; they shall name in their ballots the person voted for as President, and in distinct ballots the person voted for as Vice-President, and they shall make distinct lists of all persons voted for as President, and of all persons voted for as Vice-President, and of the number of votes for each, which lists they shall sign and certify, and transmit sealed to the seat of government of the United States, directed to the President of the Senate;—the President of the Senate shall, in the presence of the Senate and House of Representatives, open all the certificates and the votes shall then be counted;—the person having the greatest number of votes for President shall be the President, if such number be a majority of the whole number of electors appointed; and if no person have such majority, then from the persons having the highest numbers not exceeding three on the list of those voted for as President, the House of Representatives shall choose immediately, by ballot, the President. But in choosing the President, the votes shall be taken by States, the representation from each State having one vote; a quorum for this purpose shall consist of a member or members from two-thirds of the States, and a majority of all the States shall be necessary to a choice. And if the House of Representatives shall not choose a President whenever the right of choice shall devolve upon them, before *the fourth day of March* next following, then the Vice-President shall act as President, as in the case of the death or other constitutional disability of the President.

The person having the greatest number of votes as Vice-President shall be the Vice-President, if such number be a majority of the whole number of electors appointed; and if no person have a majority, then from the two highest numbers on the list the Senate shall choose the Vice-President; a quorum for the purpose shall consist of two-thirds of the whole number of Senators, and a majority of the whole number shall be necessary to a choice. But no person constitutionally ineligible to the office of President shall be eligible to that of Vice-President of the United States.

Amendment XIII [1865]

Section 1 Neither slavery nor involuntary servitude, except as a punishment for crime whereof the party shall have been duly convicted, shall exist within the United States, or any place subject to their jurisdiction.

Section 2 Congress shall have power to enforce this article by appropriate legislation.

Amendment XIV [1868]

Section 1 All persons born or naturalized in the United States, and subject to the jurisdiction thereof, are citizens of the United States and of the State wherein they reside. No State shall make or enforce any law which shall abridge the privileges or immunities of citizens of the United States; nor shall any State deprive any person of life, liberty, or property, without due process of law; nor deny to any person within its jurisdiction the equal protection of the laws.

Section 2 Representatives shall be apportioned among the several States according to their respective numbers, counting the whole number of persons in each State, excluding Indians not taxed. But when the right to vote at any election for the choice of Electors for President and Vice-President of the United States, Representatives in Congress, the executive and judicial officers of a State, or the members of the legislature thereof, is denied to any of the male inhabitants of such State, being twenty-one years of age and citizens of the United States, or in any way abridged, except for participation in rebellion, or other crime, the basis of representation therein shall be reduced in the proportion which the number of such male citizens shall bear to the whole number of male citizens twenty-one years of age in such State.

Section 3   No person shall be a Senator or Representative in Congress, or Elector of President and Vice-President, or hold any office, civil or military, under the United States, or under any State, who, having previously taken an oath, as a member of Congress, or as an officer of the United States, or as a member of any State legislature, or as an executive or judicial officer of any State, to support the Constitution of the United States, shall have engaged in insurrection or rebellion against the same, or given aid or comfort to the enemies thereof. Congress may, by a vote of two-thirds of each house, remove such disability.

Section 4   The validity of the public debt of the United States, authorized by law, including debts incurred for payment of pensions and bounties for services in suppressing insurrection or rebellion, shall not be questioned. But neither the United States nor any State shall assume or pay any debt or obligation incurred in aid of insurrection or rebellion against the United States, or any claim for the loss of emancipation of any slave; but all such debts, obligations, and claims shall be held illegal and void.

Section 5   The Congress shall have power to enforce, by appropriate legislation, the provisions of this article.

Amendment XV [1870]

Section 1   The right of citizens of the United States to vote shall not be denied or abridged by the United States or by any State on account of race, color, or previous condition of servitude.

Section 2   The Congress shall have power to enforce this article by appropriate legislation.

Amendment XVI [1913]

The Congress shall have power to lay and collect taxes on incomes, from whatever source derived, without apportionment among the several States, and without regard to any census or enumeration.

Amendment XVII [1913]

Section 1   The Senate of the United States shall be composed of two Senators from each State, elected by the people thereof, for six years; and each Senator shall have one vote. The electors in each State shall have the qualifications requisite for electors of [voters for] the most numerous branch of the State legislatures.

Section 2   When vacancies happen in the representation of any State in the Senate, the executive authority of such State shall issue writs of election to fill such vacancies: Provided that the legislature of any State may empower the executive thereof to make temporary appointments until the people fill the vacancies by election as the legislature may direct.

Section 3   The amendment shall not be so construed as to affect the election or term of any Senator chosen before it becomes valid as part of the Constitution.

Amendment XVIII [1919]

Section 1   After one year from the ratification of this article the manufacture, sale, or transportation of intoxicating liquors within, the importation thereof into, or the exportation thereof from the United States and all territory subject to the jurisdiction thereof, for beverage purposes, is hereby prohibited.

Section 2   The Congress and the several States shall have concurrent power to enforce this article by appropriate legislation.

Section 3   This article shall be inoperative unless it shall have been ratified as an amendment to the Constitution by the legislatures of the several States, as provided by the Constitution, within seven years from the date of the submission thereof to the States by the Congress.

Amendment XIX [1920]

Section 1   The right of citizens of the United States to vote shall not be denied or abridged by the United States or by any State on account of sex.

Section 2   The Congress shall have power to enforce this article by appropriate legislation.

Amendment XX [1933]

Section 1   The terms of the President and Vice President shall end at noon on the 20th day of January, and the terms of Senators and Representatives at noon on the 3d day of January, of the years in which such terms would have ended if this article had not been ratified; and the terms of their successors shall then begin.

Section 2   The Congress shall assemble at least once in every year, and such meeting shall begin at noon on the 3d day of January, unless they shall by law appoint a different day.

Section 3   If, at the time fixed for the beginning of the term of the President, the President-elect shall have died, the Vice-President-elect shall become President. If a President shall not have been chosen before the time fixed for the beginning of his term, or if the President-elect shall have failed to qualify, then the President-elect shall act as President until a President shall have qualified, and the Congress may by law provide for the case wherein neither a President-elect nor a Vice-President-elect shall have quali-

fied, declaring who shall then act as President, or the manner in which one who is to act shall be selected, and such persons shall act accordingly until a President or Vice-President shall have qualified.

Section 4   The Congress may by law provide for the case of the death of any of the persons from whom the House of Representatives may choose a President whenever the right of choice shall have devolved upon them, and for the case of the death of any of the persons from whom the Senate may choose a Vice-President whenever the right of choice shall have developed upon them.

Section 5   Sections 1 and 2 shall take effect on the 15th day of October following the ratification of this article.

Section 6   This article shall be inoperative unless it shall have been ratified as an amendment to the Constitution by the legislatures of three-fourths of the several States within seven years from the date of its submission.

Amendment XXI [1933]

Section 1   The eighteenth article of amendment to the Constitution of the United States is hereby repealed.

Section 2   The transportation or importation into any State, Territory, or Possession of the United States for delivery or use therein of intoxicating liquors, in violation of the laws thereof, is hereby prohibited.

Section 3   This article shall be inoperative unless it shall have been ratified as an amendment to the Constitution by conventions in the several States, as provided in the Constitution, within seven years from the date of submission thereof to the States by the Congress.

Amendment XXII [1951]

Section 1   No person shall be elected to the office of President more than twice, and no person who has held the office of President, or acted as

President, for more than two years of a term to which some other person was elected President shall be elected to the office of President more than once. But this article shall not apply to any person holding the office of President when this article was proposed by the Congress, and shall not prevent any person who may be holding the office of President, or acting as President, during the term within which this article becomes operative from holding the office of President or acting as President during the remainder of such term.

Section 2   This article shall be inoperative unless it shall have been ratified as an amendment to the Constitution by the legislatures of three-fourths of the several States within seven years from the date of its submission to the States by the Congress.

Amendment XXIII [1961]

Section 1   The District constituting the seat of Government of the United States shall appoint in such manner as the Congress may direct:

A number of electors of President and Vice-President equal to the whole number of Senators and Representatives in Congress to which the District would be entitled if it were a State, but in no event more than the least populous State; they shall be in addition to those appointed by the States, but they shall be considered for the purposes of the election of President and Vice-President, to be electors appointed by a State; and they shall meet in the District and perform such duties as provided by the twelfth article of amendment.

Section 2   The Congress shall have the power to enforce this article by appropriate legislation.

Amendment XXIV [1964]

Section 1   The right of citizens of the United States to vote in any primary or other election for President or Vice-President, for electors for President or Vice-President, or for Senator or Representative in Congress, shall not be denied or abridged by the United States or any State by reason of failure to pay any poll tax or other tax.

Section 2   The Congress shall have the power to enforce this article by appropriate legislation.

Amendment XXV [1967]

Section 1   In case of the removal of the President from office or of his death or resignation, the Vice-President shall become President.

Section 2   Whenever there is a vacancy in the office of the Vice-President, the President shall nominate a Vice-President who shall take office upon confirmation by a majority vote of both houses of Congress.

Section 3   Whenever the President transmits to the President pro tempore of the Senate and the Speaker of the House of Representatives his written declaration that he is unable to discharge the powers and duties of his office, and until he transmits to them a written declaration to the contrary, such powers and duties shall be discharged by the Vice-President as Acting President.

Section 4   Whenever the Vice-President and a majority of either the principal officers of the executive departments or of such other body as Congress may by law provide, transmit to the President pro tempore of the Senate and the Speaker of the House of Representatives their written declaration that the President is unable to discharge the powers and duties of his office, the Vice-President shall immediately assume the powers and duties of the office as Acting President.

Thereafter, when the President transmits to the President pro tempore of the Senate and the Speaker of the House of Representatives his written declaration that no inability exists, he shall resume the powers and duties of his office unless the Vice-President and a majority of either the principal officers of the executive department[s] or of such other body as Congress may by law provide, transmit within four days to the President pro tempore of the Senate and the Speaker of the House of Representatives their written declaration that the President is unable to discharge the powers and duties of his office. Thereupon Congress shall decide the issue, assembling within forty-eight hours for that purpose if not in session. If the Congress, within twenty-one days after receipt of the latter written declaration, or, if Congress is not in session, within twenty-one days after Congress is required to assemble, determines by two-thirds vote of both Houses that the President is unable to discharge the powers and duties of his office, the Vice-President shall continue to discharge the same as Acting President;

otherwise, the President shall resume the powers and duties of his office.

Amendment XXVI [1971]

Section 1 The right of citizens of the United States, who are eighteen years of age or older, to vote shall not be denied or abridged by the United States or by any State on account of age.

Section 2 The Congress shall have power to enforce this article by appropriate legislation.

Presidential Elections

Year	Candidates	Parties	Percent of Popular Vote*†	Electoral Vote‡	Percent of Voter Participation†
1789	GEORGE WASHINGTON	No party designations		69	
	John Adams			34	
	Other candidates			35	
1792	GEORGE WASHINGTON	No party designations		132	
	John Adams			77	
	George Clinton			50	
	Other candidates			5	
1796	JOHN ADAMS	Federalist		71	
	Thomas Jefferson	Democratic-Republican		68	
	Thomas Pinckney	Federalist		59	
	Aaron Burr	Democratic-Republican		30	
	Other candidates			48	
1800	THOMAS JEFFERSON	Democratic-Republican		73	
	Aaron Burr	Democratic-Republican		73	
	John Adams	Federalist		65	
	Charles C. Pinckney	Federalist		64	
	John Jay	Federalist		1	
1804	THOMAS JEFFERSON	Democratic-Republican		162	
	Charles C. Pinckney	Federalist		14	
1808	JAMES MADISON	Democratic-Republican		122	
	Charles C. Pinckney	Federalist		47	
	George Clinton	Democratic-Republican		6	
1812	JAMES MADISON	Democratic-Republican		128	
	DeWitt Clinton	Federalist		89	
1816	JAMES MONROE	Democratic-Republican		183	
	Rufus King	Federalist		34	

YEAR	CANDIDATES	PARTIES	PERCENT OF POPULAR VOTE*†	ELECTORAL VOTE‡	PERCENT OF VOTER PARTICIPATION†
1820	JAMES MONROE	Democratic-Republican		231	
	John Quincy Adams	Independent Republican		1	
1824	JOHN QUINCY ADAMS	Democratic-Republican	30.5	84	26.9
	Andrew Jackson	Democratic-Republican	43.1	99	
	Henry Clay	Democratic-Republican	13.2	37	
	William H. Crawford	Democratic-Republican	13.1	41	
1828	ANDREW JACKSON	Democratic	56.0	178	57.6
	John Quincy Adams	National Republican	44.0	83	
1832	ANDREW JACKSON	Democratic	54.5	219	55.4
	Henry Clay	National Republican	37.5	49	
	William Wirt	Anti-Masonic	8.0	7	
	John Floyd	Democratic		11	
1836	MARTIN VAN BUREN	Democratic	50.9	170	57.8
	William H. Harrison	Whig		73	
	Hugh L. White	Whig		26	
	Daniel Webster	Whig	49.1	14	
	W. P. Mangum	Whig		11	
1840	WILLIAM H. HARRISON	Whig	53.1	234	80.2
	Martin Van Buren	Democratic	46.9	60	
1844	JAMES K. POLK	Democratic	49.6	170	78.9
	Henry Clay	Whig	48.1	105	
	James G. Birney	Liberty	2.3	0	
1848	ZACHARY TAYLOR	Whig	47.4	163	72.7
	Lewis Cass	Democratic	42.5	127	
	Martin Van Buren	Free-Soil	10.1	0	
1852	FRANKLIN PIERCE	Democratic	50.9	254	69.6
	Winfield Scott	Whig	44.1	42	
	John P. Hale	Free-Soil	5.0	0	
1856	JAMES BUCHANAN	Democratic	45.3	174	78.9
	John C. Frémont	Republican	33.1	114	
	Millard Fillmore	American	21.6	8	
1860	ABRAHAM LINCOLN	Republican	39.8	180	81.2
	Stephen A. Douglas	Democratic	29.5	12	
	John C. Breckinridge	Democratic	18.1	72	
	John Bell	Constitutional Union	12.6	39	
1864	ABRAHAM LINCOLN	Republican	55.0	212	73.8
	George B. McClellan	Democratic	45.0	21	
1868	ULYSSES S. GRANT	Republican	52.7	214	78.1
	Horatio Seymour	Democratic	47.3	80	
1872	ULYSSES S. GRANT	Republican	55.6	286	71.3
	Horace Greeley	Democratic	44.0	0§	

YEAR	CANDIDATES	PARTIES	PERCENT OF POPULAR VOTE*†	ELECTORAL VOTE‡	PERCENT OF VOTER PARTICIPATION†
1876	RUTHERFORD B. HAYES	Republican	48.0	185	81.8
	Samuel J. Tilden	Democratic	51.0	184	
1880	JAMES A. GARFIELD	Republican	48.5	214	79.4
	Winfield S. Hancock	Democratic	48.1	155	
	James B. Weaver	Greenback-Labor	3.4	0	
1884	GROVER CLEVELAND	Democratic	48.5	219	77.5
	James G. Blaine	Republican	48.2	182	
1888	BENJAMIN HARRISON	Republican	47.9	233	79.3
	Grover Cleveland	Democratic	48.6	168	
1892	GROVER CLEVELAND	Democratic	46.0	277	74.7
	Benjamin Harrison	Republican	43.0	145	
	James B. Weaver	Populist	8.5	22	
1896	WILLIAM McKINLEY	Republican	51.1	271	79.3
	William J. Bryan	Democratic	46.7	176	
1900	WILLIAM McKINLEY	Republican	51.7	292	73.2
	William J. Bryan	Democratic; Populist	45.5	155	
1904	THEODORE ROOSEVELT	Republican	56.4	336	65.2
	Alton B. Parker	Democratic	37.6	140	
	Eugene V. Debs	Socialist	3.0	0	
1908	WILLIAM H. TAFT	Republican	51.6	321	65.4
	William J. Bryan	Democratic	43.1	162	
	Eugene V. Debs	Socialist	2.8	0	
1912	WOODROW WILSON	Democratic	41.9	435	58.8
	Theodore Roosevelt	Progressive	27.4	88	
	William H. Taft	Republican	23.2	8	
	Eugene V. Debs	Socialist	6.0	0	
1916	WOODROW WILSON	Democratic	49.4	277	61.6
	Charles E. Hughes	Republican	46.2	254	
	Allan L. Benson	Socialist	3.2	0	
1920	WARREN G. HARDING	Republican	60.4	404	49.2
	James M. Cox	Democratic	34.2	127	
	Eugene V. Debs	Socialist	3.4	0	
1924	CALVIN COOLIDGE	Republican	54.0	382	48.9
	John W. Davis	Democratic	28.8	136	
	Robert M. La Follette	Progressive	16.6	13	
1928	HERBERT C. HOOVER	Republican	58.2	444	56.9
	Alfred E. Smith	Democratic	40.9	87	
1932	FRANKLIN D. ROOSEVELT	Democratic	57.4	472	56.9
	Herbert C. Hoover	Republican	39.7	59	

Year	Candidates	Parties	Percent of Popular Vote*†	Electoral Vote‡	Percent of Voter Participation†
1936	FRANKLIN D. ROOSEVELT	Democratic	60.8	523	61.0
	Alfred M. Landon	Republican	36.5	8	
1940	FRANKLIN D. ROOSEVELT	Democratic	54.8	449	62.5
	Wendell L. Willkie	Republican	44.8	82	
1944	FRANKLIN D. ROOSEVELT	Democratic	53.5	432	55.9
	Thomas E. Dewey	Republican	46.0	99	
1948	HARRY S TRUMAN	Democratic	49.5	303	53.0
	Thomas E. Dewey	Republican	45.1	189	
	J. Strom Thurmond	States' Rights	2.4	39	
	Henry A. Wallace	Progressive	2.4	0	
1952	DWIGHT D. EISENHOWER	Republican	55.1	442	63.3
	Adlai E. Stevenson	Democratic	44.4	89	
1956	DWIGHT D. EISENHOWER	Republican	57.4	457	60.6
	Adlai E. Stevenson	Democratic	42.0	73	
1960	JOHN F. KENNEDY	Democratic	49.7	303	64.0
	Richard M. Nixon	Republican	49.6	219	
	Harry F. Byrd	Independent	0.7	15	
1964	LYNDON B. JOHNSON	Democratic	61.1	486	61.7
	Barry M. Goldwater	Republican	38.5	52	
1968	RICHARD M. NIXON	Republican	43.4	301	60.6
	Hubert H. Humphrey	Democratic	42.7	191	
	George C. Wallace	American Independent	13.5	46	
1972	RICHARD M. NIXON	Republican	60.7	520	55.5
	George S. McGovern	Democratic	37.5	17	
1976	JIMMY CARTER	Democratic	50.0	297	54.3
	Gerald R. Ford	Republican	48.0	240	
1980	RONALD REAGAN	Republican	50.8	489	53.0
	Jimmy Carter	Democratic	41.0	49	
	John B. Anderson	Independent	6.6	0	
1984	RONALD REAGAN	Republican	58.7	525	52.9
	Walter F. Mondale	Democratic	40.6	13	
1988	GEORGE BUSH	Republican	54.0	426	50.1
	Michael Dukakis	Democratic	46.0	111	
1992	WILLIAM J. CLINTON	Democratic	43.0	370	61.3
	George Bush	Republican	38.0	168	
	H. Ross Perot	Independent	19.0	0	

*Candidates receiving less than 2.5 percent of the popular vote have been omitted. Hence the percentage of popular vote may not total 100 percent.

†Prior to 1824, most presidential electors were chosen by state legislatures rather than by popular vote.

‡Before the Twelfth Amendment was passed in 1804, the electoral college voted for two presidential candidates; the runner-up became the vice president.

§Greeley died before the electoral college met. His votes were divided among four other candidates.

Credits

Page abbreviations are as follows: **L** left, **R** right.

Index

with the help of 30 editorial board members from around the world, the DCC publishes *Critical Criminology: An International Journal*, and this progressive collective also produces a quarterly newsletter, *The Critical Criminologist*. A website (www.critcrim.org) is also a valuable source of information for DCC members and others interested in the topics covered in this book and elsewhere.

The DCC is one of only five divisions of the ASC and overlaps with three of the ASC's strongest divisions: the Division on Women and Crime; the Division of International Criminology; and the Division on People of Color and Crime. Also consider that one of the pioneers of critical criminology, William Chambliss, was the president of the ASC and the Society for the Study of Social Problems (SSSP), arguably the second most important organization in sociology. Stephen Pfohl, a postmodern criminologist and deviance theorist, succeeded him as president of the SSSP in the early 1990s. Moreover, Robert Bohm, another widely cited critical criminologist, served as president of the Academy of Criminal Justice Sciences (the national US association for criminal justice scholars and practitioners), and Jeffery Walker held this position in 2006.

There are dozens of other examples of critical criminologists who have held key positions, such as annual meeting or major committee chairs. Critical criminologists also routinely serve on the editorial boards of "mainstream" journals, such as *Criminology*, *Justice Quarterly*, and *Crime and Delinquency*. The key point is this: critical criminologists are a major part of the broader academic criminological community and, as you will discover from reading subsequent chapters of this book, they have made many important theoretical, empirical, and political contributions to the field.

Returning to where this chapter started, many would agree with Jock Young's (1988, p. 293) statement that "If there ever was a need for a new criminology, it is now...." The world is facing a terrifyingly long list of problems, including the proliferation of violent, racist pornography (DeKeseredy and Olsson, in press; Jensen, 2007), new forms of global violence (Currie, 2008b), human-rights violations and genocide (Tepperman, 2010), and the "rise of disaster capitalism" (N. Klein, 2007).

To make matters worse, more US citizens die of homicide every three months than the number of people killed by the September 11 terrorist attacks on the World Trade Center in New York and in the Iraq War as of 2008 (Currie, 2008a). Staying the course has done little, if anything, to make the world safer from violence and related harms. Isn't it time to think critically about crime?[8]

2

CONTEMPORARY CRITICAL CRIMINOLOGICAL SCHOOLS OF THOUGHT

It is important that we recognize that each of the many critical criminologies existing today address some portion of the "intersecting social relations that are fundamental to the study of crime and justice" (Barak, 1995, p. 6). If we keep this in mind, we will all move closer to fulfilling the liberative potential of critical criminology.

(Michalowski, 1996, p. 15)

Often referred to incorrectly by mainstream scholars as "conflict theories" (e.g., Kubrin, Stucky, and Krohn, 2009), critical criminological perspectives on crime, law, and social control are repeatedly accused of focusing "more on a critique of the shortcomings of other criminologists than on offering an alternative explanation of crime" (Akers and Sellers, 2004, p. 237). In addition, as stated in Chapter 1, critical criminologists are frequently criticized for not actually testing theories. There are some major problems with these assertions and since the second claim was responded to earlier (see Chapter 1), the first one will be briefly addressed here. Critical criminologists have devoted (and continue to devote) much time and energy to exposing the weaknesses of mainstream scholars' work (Schwartz, 1991), but so do all criminological theorists. In fact, almost every theory text includes critiques of every theory reviewed by the authors. Criminology, in general, is characterized by much debate, and mainstream criminologists are among the first to point out flaws in their colleagues' writings and research.

Contrary to what many conservative scholars state, critical criminologists are actively involved in developing alternative theories. True, there was a time when most progressives directed much, if not all, of their attention to Marxist analyses of the class-based nature of the origins and functions of law and, for the most part, ignored addressing the causes of inter-personal crimes, such as those committed by poor people in urban ghettos. Martin Schwartz (1991, p. 119) recalls:

> Many of us were sort of idealists 20 years ago. We were outraged that the state only saw crime in the actions of African-American and poor youth. In Albert K. Cohen's terms, some of us were "negativistic" – if James Q. Wilson[1] says yes, then I say no. There was some rooting for the underdog and great concern that any actions against the underdog were giving succor to the "Great Enemy."

There are still critical criminologists who theorize the role of the state and law and how they are biased against those at the bottom of the socioeconomic ladder (e.g., Reiman and Leighton, 2010). Such work is much needed because corporate crime is endemic to capitalist societies, and good theories on this problem help us find effective solutions. As Kurt Lewin (1951), the founder of modern social psychology, correctly pointed out, "There is nothing so practical as a good theory" (p. 169). The same can be said of good theories of street crime, violence against women behind closed doors, hate crime, and a myriad of other harms. Critical criminologists recognize this, and since the late 1980s, a growing mass of them have crafted and tested theories of interpersonal victimization.

One of the main objectives of this chapter, then, is to challenge the myth that contemporary critical criminological perspectives are simply "rhetorical" (Wheeler, 1976), "ideologically charged ideas" (Liska, 1987), and are "untestable" (Akers and

Sellers, 2004). At first glance, some readers might perceive two of the above citations as old and consider that the claims associated with them are no longer in vogue. They are still widely cited in popular textbooks (see, for example, Kubrin *et al.*, 2009) because criminology is still dominated by mainstream thinking and a reluctance to seriously engage with the left.

The second, and equally important, objective of this chapter is to briefly review some major contemporary critical schools of thought. I hasten to mention that this overview is by no means not exhaustive and that the order in which each perspective appears does not reflect a hierarchy of importance. Even more offerings will be created by the time you finish reading this book because critical criminologists have a deep-rooted and ongoing commitment to doing theoretical work that meets the highest contemporary disciplinary standards.

FEMINISM[2]

As noted before, many critical criminologists, especially those who produced theories of crime and its control in the 1970s and early 1980s (e.g., Chambliss and Seidman, 1982; Pearce, 1976; Quinney, 1974), relied on Marxist analyses of capitalist society. Although important and pathbreaking, these perspectives were "gender-blind" (Gelsthorpe and Morris, 1988). Even Taylor, Walton, and Young's (1973) *The New Criminology*, perhaps the most important work of its generation, ignores women and gender. Of course, this criticism can just as easily be leveled against the overwhelming majority of mainstream criminologists, including those considered pioneers in the field. For example, in his book *Causes of Delinquency*, eminent social control theorist Travis Hirschi (1969) states in a footnote that "in the analysis that follows the 'non-negro' becomes 'white' and the girls disappear" (pp. 35–36). Many who followed in Hirschi's footsteps also used all-male samples (Curran and Renzetti, 1994).

It should be noted in passing that over 30 years later, a re-analysis of the Richmond Youth Project data used in his study reveals that perceived racial discrimination is a powerful predictor of delinquency.[3] According to the scholars who revisited this data set, "Hirschi missed a historic opportunity to focus the attention of a generation of criminologists on how the unique experiences of African Americans may shape their criminality" (Unnever, Cullen, Mathers, McClure, and Allison, 2009, p. 378).

It is often said: "That was then and this is now." As Chesney-Lind and Pasko (2004, p. 15) put it, "One might want to believe that such cavalier androcentrism is no longer found in academic approaches to delinquency." Alas, it still exists, even among some relatively new directions in critical criminology. Consider Roger Matthews' (2009) "re-fashioned" left realism that "prioritizes the role of theory" (p. 344). The word "gender" appears only once in the main text of his article and the words "feminism" and "patriarchy" are nowhere to be found (DeKeseredy and Schwartz, in press). From a feminist standpoint, then, contrary to what Matthews claims, his re-fashioned realist criminology is "more of the same" and does not move beyond what US left realist Elliott Currie (2007) refers to as "so what? criminology." Such criminology involves doing a-theoretical, quantitative research on relatively minor issues and presenting the findings in an unintelligible fashion. Jock Young (2004) labels this approach "voodoo criminology."

Much of criminology ignores women and girls in conflict with the law or simply treats sex as a variable to be included in complex statistical analyses, but the last two decades have witnessed an "outpouring of feminist scholarship" (Daly and Chesney-Lind, 1988). Moreover, the American Society of Criminology's (ASC) Division on Women and Crime (DWC), like the ASC's Division on Critical Criminology (DCC), is one of the ASC's strongest divisions and the vast majority of its members publicly identify themselves as feminist scholars. Furthermore, the DWC is now close to 30 years old and its members have made many outstanding empirical, theoretical, and political contributions to the field.

Defining feminism is not an easy task. Still, one thing leading experts in the field all agree with is that "feminism is not merely about adding women onto the agenda" (Currie and MacLean, 1993, p. 6). For the purpose of this book, I offer Kathleen Daly and Meda Chesney-Lind's (1988) definition, which is still one of the most widely used and cited offerings. Throughout this book, "feminism" refers to "a set of theories about women's oppression and a set of strategies for change" (Daly and Chesney-Lind, 1988, p. 502). Nevertheless, it is incorrect to paint all feminists with the same brush because there are at least 12 variants of feminist criminological theory (Maidment, 2006). However, all feminists prioritize gender, which should not be confused with sex even though both terms are often incorrectly used interchangeably. Gender is the "sociocultural and psychological shaping, patterning, and evaluating of female and male behavior" (Schur, 1984, p. 10). Sex, on the other hand, refers to the biologically based categories of "female" and "male," which are stable across history and cultures (Dragiewicz, 2009). For example, violent crimes are committed mainly by men, but many societies have much lower rates of violence than those of the United States, the Russian Federation, or Columbia (Currie, 2008a; Krug, Dahlberg, and Mercy, 2002). So, if "boys will be boys," they "will be so differently" (Kimmel, 2000), depending on where they live, their peer groups, social class position and race, and a host of other factors (DeKeseredy and Schwartz, in press; Messerschmidt, 1993).

Most feminists also agree that the United States, the United Kingdom, Canada, and many other countries are patriarchal societies (DeKeseredy and Schwartz, 1996; Ogle and Batton, 2009). There are conflicting definitions of patriarchy and it is a heavily contested concept (Hunnicutt, 2009), but it is not uncommon to follow scholars such as Dobash and Dobash (1979), who assert that patriarchy consists of two key elements: a structure and an ideology. Structurally, the patriarchy is a hierarchical organization in which males have more power and privilege than women. Certainly, North America is well known for being a continent characterized by gross gender inequity. For example, laws in 30 US states allow a man to receive conditional exemptions if he rapes his wife (Bergen, 2006).[4] Moreover, in Canada, on October 27, 2009, federal Liberal Member of Parliament Caroline Bennett, physician and former Public Health Minister, was heckled and shouted down by male members of the ruling Progressive Conservative Party when she tried to raise the issue of what kind of swine flu vaccination pregnant women should be taking (Delacourt, 2009). On

October 3, 2006, the same government announced that Status of Women Canada (SWC) is no longer eligible for funding for advocacy, government lobbying, or research projects. Further, SWC was required to delete the word "equality" from its list of goals (Carastathis, 2006).

Why do men maintain this power? Why don't most women rebel against their subordinate position? The answer is the other part of patriarchy: the ideology. The ideology of patriarchy provides a political and social rationale for itself. Both men and women come to believe that it is "natural" and "right" that women be in inferior positions. Men feel completely supported in excluding women, and up to a point, women feel their exclusion is correct (DeKeseredy and Schwartz, 1993). To someone (male or female) who believes completely in the ideology of patriarchy, the entire concept of equal rights or women's liberation is a pretty difficult topic, sounding not only wrong but unnatural – literally, it goes against nature (Schwartz and DeKeseredy, 1997).

This sounds fairly simple, and in fact most definitions of patriarchy are fairly simple. There are, though, varieties of patriarchy (Hunnicutt, 2009). For example, many feminist scholars focus on *social patriarchy*, which refers to the type of male domination at the societal level, as discussed above. A subsystem of social patriarchy, often called *familial patriarchy*, refers to male control in domestic or intimate settings (Barrett, 1985; Eisenstein, 1980; Ursel, 1986). These two components cannot be pulled too far apart and one variant cannot be fully understood without reference to the other (DeKeseredy and Schwartz, 2009; Smith, 1990).

It is beyond the scope of this book to examine all the different feminist perspectives on crime, law, and social control. In fact, there are many books on feminist approaches to understanding these issues. Nevertheless, it must be emphasized that feminist criminologists do extensive theoretical work on a myriad of important problems, including female gangs, violence against women, women and girls' pathways to crime, drugs, and moral panics about female youth violence. Further, feminist theorists and researchers alike have had a major impact on criminal justice policy (Lilly, Cullen, and Ball,

2007). For instance, due in large part to the efforts of feminist scholars, police departments and other criminal justice agencies no longer simply ignore women who are physically and sexually abused behind closed doors by their current or former male partners (DeKeseredy, Ellis, and Alvi, 2005).[5] Yet, since feminist theoretical work challenges "male-centered" ways of explaining deviance, crime, and social control, it is constantly challenged and often ridiculed by conservative students, practitioners, and academics.

For example, psychologist Donald Dutton (2006) accuses feminists of "dogma preservation" (p. ix), of "politically conceptualizing" domestic violence (p. xi), and of attempting to "spin" data to be consistent with their "paradigm" (p. 349). Dutton is also among a large group of conservative critics who claim that feminists only offer single-factor explanations of crime that focus exclusively on patriarchy. These are not legitimate criticisms. After all, no social scientific theory, method, or policy proposal is value-free (Harding, 1987). Moreover, as stated before, there is more than one feminist perspective on crime, law, and social control. Although *some* feminists claim that patriarchy is the direct cause of women's victimization, offending, or societal reactions to their behaviors, there is a large feminist literature combining both macro- and micro-level factors, such as unemployment, globalization, deindustrialization, life-events stress, intimate relationship status, familial and societal patriarchy, substance use, and other factors (DeKeseredy and Dragiewicz, 2007). In fact, feminists are among the most critical of single-factor explanations of female victimization or rule-breaking (DeKeseredy *et al.*, 2005).[6]

Feminist criminologists have also been accused of making "no attempt to operationalize patriarchy" (Ogle and Batton, 2009, p. 171), which is an erroneous claim. For instance, the late Michael D. Smith (1990) conducted a representative sample survey of woman abuse in Toronto and measured female respondents' perceptions of their intimate male partners' adherence to the ideology of familial patriarchy. For the purpose of his study, relevant themes of this ideology are an insistence on women's obedience, respect, loyalty, dependency, sexual access, and sexual fidelity (Barrett and McIntosh, 1982; Dobash and Dobash, 1979;

Pateman, 1988). Smith operationalized these themes with two indices. One index measured patriarchal beliefs, and the other measured patriarchal attitudes. DeKeseredy and Schwartz (1998) also administered these indices to men in the Canadian national survey of woman abuse in university/college dating. Cronbach's alpha coefficients (0.79 for beliefs and 0.76 for attitudes) show that these indicators are reliable and consistent with Smith's (1990) item factor analysis of female respondents (0.79 and 0.71, respectively).

Questions about patriarchal control are also used in qualitative studies of woman abuse. For example, DeKeseredy and Schwartz (2009) asked 43 rural Ohio women if their male ex-partners felt that men should be in charge at home. Of these women, 79 percent answered affirmatively. For example, one respondent said that her ex-husband, "wanted to be in control. He was in control for us, or you know I felt it." Similarly, another woman reported that her ex-partner "was the type of person where women were lower than men. And men were able, you know – women had to do what men told them. Which is pretty much my whole relationship with him" (p. 71). In sum, there is growing evidence refuting the claim that "patriarchy is difficult to measure as an independent variable" (Lilly *et al.*, 2007, p. 217).

Another criticism offered by some feminist criminologists is that much of feminist criminology "focuses narrowly" on women's victimization (Miller, 2003), which gives the "false impression that women have only been victims, they have never successfully fought back, and that women cannot be effective social agents on behalf of themselves or others" (Harding, 1987, p. 5). This is a rather dated criticism because we now see a major growth in feminist work on women's criminality and key factors associated with it, including neighborhood disadvantage (Caputo, 2008), the feminization of poverty (Morash, 2006; Steffensmeier and Streifel, 1992), and childhood abuse (Chesney-Lind, 2001). Moreover, heavily influenced by life-course theories, some feminist scholars examine female pathways in and out of criminal behavior (Morash, 2006). One recent example is Judith Grant's (2008) work on marginalized rural Ohio women's pathways to recovery from substance abuse.

In addition, feminist research shows that most women in abusive relationships or in nonviolent intimate unions characterized by other means of patriarchal dominance and control are not weak people unable to take steps on their own behalf and on that of their children (DeKeseredy and Schwartz, 2009). Moreover, most battered women eventually leave abusive men, but separation or divorce alone often does not make them safer (Schwartz, 1989; Sev'er, 2002).[7] Still, there is ample evidence of what Morash (2006, p. 145) refers to as "victims exercising agency."

Feminist theories offer an alternative gendered way of thinking about crime (Vold, Bernard, and Snipes, 2002). So, too, does another school of thought heavily influenced by feminism – masculinities (Gardiner, 2005; Messerschmidt, 2005). The study of masculinities is the gendered study of men (Morgan, 1992), and masculinities theories of crime are examined below.

MASCULINITIES THEORIES[8]

Men commit most crimes, especially violent offences, but this does not mean that all men are criminal and that male crime does not vary across countries, regions, socioeconomic groups, and so on. In fact, certain societies are much more likely than others to teach violence to men (Hottocks, 1994). For example, World Health Organization homicide data show that men's risk of committing murder in Colombia is much higher than it is in Japan or France, which have the lowest rate of homicide deaths in the world (Krug et al., 2002). Further, Oakland, California's population was 375,000 in 2006, but had many more homicides than Sweden, which had a population of nine million at that time (Currie, 2008a). Furthermore, homicide is a relatively infrequent crime and thus "we are not talking about a tendency that is either universal or inevitable" (Newburn and Stanko, 1994, p. 4).

A central argument of masculinities theorists is that there is no simple standard of being a man that guides all male behavior, including crime (Messerschmidt, 1993; Polk, 2003). Although society functions in many ways to promote male violence, there remains in any situation other means of expressing one's masculinity (Connell, 2000). For example, it is well known that professional hockey players can be exceptionally violent; yet, some hockey players will not fight an opponent because they can "do masculinity" in other ways. A prime example is Wayne Gretzky, who holds the record for the most goals scored in the National Hockey League. Gretzky rarely fought. His amazing ability to score goals and help his teams win games and championships were key resources at his disposal to demonstrate he was "manly" (DeKeseredy and Schwartz, 2005a). Those lacking his skills, but under intense pressure from employers, teammates, and spectators to fight opponents who challenge them, commonly feel that they would be derided as of "doubtful moral worth" and "relatively useless to the team" (Smith, 1983, p. 42) if they walked away from violent "honor contests" (Polk, 2003).

Connell (1995) developed the basic vocabulary that many masculinities theorists use. He contends that in most areas there is one *hegemonic* masculinity, which is the dominant form. In the United States, Hollywood movie actors such as Vin Diesel, Sylvester Stallone, or Arnold Schwarzenegger (who became the Governor of California) best exemplify such masculinity. The basic components of hegemonic masculinity are: (1) avoid all things feminine; (2) restrict emotions severely; (3) show toughness and aggression; (4) exhibit self-reliance; (5) strive for achievement and status; (6) exhibit no relational attitudes toward sexuality; and, (7) actively engage in homophobia (Connell and Messerschmidt, 2005; Schwartz and DeKeseredy, 1997; Weitzer and Kubrin, 2009). Masculinities studies show that men are encouraged to live up to these ideals and are sanctioned for not doing so, but that crime is just one of many ways of "doing gender" in a culturally specific way (Sinclair, 2002; West and Zimmerman, 1987). Moreover, masculinities theories remind us that the decision to commit certain crimes is affected by class and race relations that structure the resources available to accomplish what men feel provides their masculine identities (DeKeseredy and Schwartz, 2005a; Messerschmidt, 1997).

For example, many economically and socially marginalized young men, regardless of their ethnic/cultural background, are unable to accomplish masculinity at school through academic achievement, participation in sports, or involvement in extra-curricular activities (Messerschmidt, 1993). This problem results in some boys experiencing status frustration, dropping out of school, and creating a subculture with other boys who share their frustration (Cohen, 1955). This subculture grants members status based on accomplishing gender through violence and other illegitimate means (DeKeseredy and Schwartz, 2005a).

Many inner-city boys of color are not only denied masculine status through the inability to succeed in school, but also through unemployment due to deindustrialization and institutional racism (Hagedorn, 1998; Wilson and Taub, 2008). Numerous Hispanic and Asian young men experience similar problems. Thus, it is not surprising that members of these socially marginalized ethnic groups compose most of the street gangs in North America (M. Klein, 2007). It is not, of course, their skin color that contributes to a higher proportion of these social groups in gangs. Rather, it is what Currie (2008a) refers to as the "historical legacy of discrimination" that disproportionately subjects ethnic minority groups to the "social and economic disadvantages that tend to breed violence" (p. 69).

Corporate masculinity is distinct from masculinities found in schools, on the street, on assembly lines, in the family, and elsewhere. Instead of relying on violence, being a corporate "real man" entails "calculation and rationality as well as struggle for success, reward, and corporate recognition" (Messerschmidt, 1993, p. 136). Male executives compete with each other and measure masculinity according to their success in the business community. Corporate crime, then, is one technique of advancing this "gendered strategy of action."

Uncertain and competitive markets, fluctuating sales, government regulations, and relations with unions all obstruct corporate attempts to increase profits legitimately (Box, 1983; DeKeseredy et al., 2005). Masculinities theorist James Messerschmidt (1993) asserts that these obstacles also threaten white corporate executive masculinity. Thus, corporate crime is a solution to both of these problems. That is, illegal and unethical practices are techniques of re-establishing or maintaining a particular type of masculinity, as well as profit margins.

Masculinities play a role in facilitating men's crime in many more arenas. In fact, there are various forms of masculinities (Connell, 1995; Hatty, 2000), which helps to explain the wide range of responses to the contemporary crises facing men. Among these areas are racist violence and homophobic violence ("gay bashing"). Following Connell (1987), Perry (2003) argues that these harms are linked to white men's desire to assert their superiority and dominance, as well as to the desire to "prove the very essence of their masculinity: heterosexuality" (p. 158). She further asserts that many men do not view such violence as breaking a cultural norm (on violence) as much as affirming "a culturally approved hegemonic masculinity: aggression, domination, and heterosexuality" (p. 158). Of course, men engage in masculinist discourse to justify and allow their own violence in many other areas (DeKeseseredy and Schwartz, 2005a).

Numerous theories attempt to lay out which offender characteristics best predict crime, but the most powerful determinant is whether the offender is male (Schwartz and Hatty, 2003). It is not because of biological composition or factors identified by evolutionary psychologists (e.g., Daly and Wilson, 1988).[9] Masculinities theories remind us that men are not naturally aggressive. As Katz and Chambliss (1991) discovered through an in-depth review of the research on the relationship between biology and crime:

> An individual learns to be aggressive in the same manner that he or she learns to inhibit aggression. One is not a natural state, and the other culturally imposed: both are within our biological potential. Violence, sexism and racism are biological only in the sense that they are within the range of possible human attitudes and behaviors. But nonviolence, equality and justice are also biologically possible.
>
> (p. 270)

On top of motivating criminologists to pay more careful attention to "maleness" and its relationship to crime, masculinities theorists such as Messerschmidt (1993) and Mullins (2006) draw attention to how the intersection of race/ethnicity, class, and gender shape men's involvement in crime (Lilly et al., 2007). Even so, as Connell (2000, p. 82) puts it, "masculinities are not the whole story" about crime. Obviously, there are many other sources of crime. Mullins (2006), among others (e.g., Miller, 2002), correctly point outs, to simply argue that crime "is a way for men to 'do gender' or construct a masculine identity is of no theoretical import for understanding the etiological connections between masculinity and crime, and often obscures more than it illuminates" (Mullins, 2006, p. 19). Still, crime and its reduction cannot be adequately understood without an in-depth understanding of masculinities (Messerschmidt, 2005).

LEFT REALISM[10]

Since its birth in the mid-1980s, left realism has been sharply attacked from the right and the left. For example, according to mainstream criminologist Don Gibbons (1994, p. 170), it "can be best described as a general perspective centred on injunctions to 'take crime seriously' rather than as a well-developed theoretical perspective." Similarly, critical criminologist Stuart Henry (1999) claims that left realists offer a "limited conception of criminal etiology" (p. 139). It is also often said that left realism has "nothing new to say" and that it is no longer a major subdiscipline of critical criminology (DeKeseredy and Schwartz, 2005b). Contrary to what some critics state, left realism is not dormant and has the potential to be just as vibrant now as it was during the Reagan and Thatcher years when it was born. In fact, left realism has been "rediscovered" by Roger Matthews (2009), one of its British founders. The concepts of class, the state, and structure are emphasized in his recent attempt to foster the creation of a "coherent critical realist approach" to explaining crime and punishment (p. 341). On the other side of the Atlantic Ocean, North American left realists Walter DeKeseredy and Martin Schwartz (in press), as well as Elliott Currie (2004), also offer new left realist theories to be briefly summarized later in this section.

Left realists are concerned about the damage done by the crimes of the powerful (e.g., corporate and state crime), but the bulk of their theoretical work focuses on street crime, "hard" police tactics (e.g., stopping and searching people who are publicly drunk), and woman abuse in intimate relationships (DeKeseredy, Schwartz, Fagen, and Hall, 2006; Friedrichs, 2009). The main reason for this is that prior to the 1980s, most critical criminologists focused primarily on corporate and white-collar crime, as well as the influence of class and race/ethnic relations on definitions of crime and the administration of justice. Again, left realists, too, are concerned about these problems, but contend that ignoring crimes committed in urban streets by "the truly disadvantaged" (Wilson, 1987) and behind closed doors by patriarchal, abusive men enables right-wing politicians to manufacture ideological support for draconian criminal justice policies that harm people at the bottom of the socioeconomic ladder and that preclude the creation of society based on class, race/ethnic, and gender equality (Boehringer, Brown, Edgeworth, Hogg, and Ramsey, 1983; Taylor, 1992). Moreover, left realists claim that the left's ongoing neglect in taking working-class victimization seriously contributes to the right's hegemonic control over knowledge about crime and policing (DeKeseredy and Schwartz, 1991a). As US left realist Elliott Currie (1992) observes, ignoring predatory and domestic crimes in socially and economically excluded urban communities only serves to:

> help perpetuate an image of progressives as being both fuzzy-minded and, much worse, unconcerned about the realities of life for those ordinary Americans who are understandably frightened and enraged by the suffering and fear crimes brings to their communities and families.
>
> (p. 91)

Left realists point to the criminogenic consequences of broader social forces such as patriarchy and capitalism, but they also borrow from mainstream theoretical work done by strain theorists Merton (1938) and Cohen (1955). For example, early British left realist theorizing focused heavily on the concepts of relative deprivation and subculture. According to Lea and Young (1984, p. 88), it is

> poverty experienced as unfair (relative deprivation when compared to someone else) that creates discontent; and discontent where there is

no political solution leads to crime. The equation is simple: relative deprivation equals discontent: discontent plus lack of political solution equals crime.

Somewhat similar to what Albert Cohen (1955) argued, Lea and Young also contend that people lacking legitimate means of solving the problem of relative deprivation may come into contact with other frustrated, disenfranchised people and form subcultures, which, in turn, encourage and legitimate criminal behaviors (Young, 1999). Absent from this theory, however, is an attempt to address how criminogenic subcultural development in North America and other industrialized parts of the world is simultaneously shaped by the recent destructive consequences of free-market policies and marginalized men's attempts to live up to the principles of hegemonic masculinity. DeKeseredy and Schwartz's (in press) new left realist theory prioritizes these two variables and offers a more gendered understanding of the linkage between broader social forces and subcultural development.

Briefly, DeKeseredy and Schwartz (in press) assert that the harmful effects of "laissez-faire" economic policies informed by Friedman (1962) and others on the right have caused a relatively "new assault" on workers and have helped make North America "categorically unequal" (Massey, 2007), including corporations moving to developing countries to use cheap labor and take advantage of weak environmental and workplace safety laws (DeKeseredy and Schwartz, 2002; Wacquant, 2008). The main point is that they have excluded a substantial number of North Americans from the labor market, which challenges many men's masculine identity. A major source of many male youth's discontent is their unemployment and "material shortage" relative to the employment and "material abundance" of male members of other social-class groupings (Ellis and DeKeseredy, 1996). Many of these socially and economically excluded youths, regardless of whether they live in urban or rural communities, experience "status frustration" that puts them at great risk of teaming up with others to create a subculture that promotes, expresses, and validates masculinity through violent means (Cohen, 1955; DeKeseredy and Schwartz, 2005b; Hagedorn, 1988; Messerschmidt, 1993).

DeKeseredy and Schwartz (in press) further assert that in communities damaged by deindustrialization, the loss of family-owned farms, the closing of sawmills and coal mines, and so on, there is a greater proportion of all-male peer groups that promote violence against women. Men at the bottom of the socio-economic ladder flocking together with members of all-male sexist subcultures that perpetuate and legitimate woman abuse is not surprising, since they are more likely than their more affluent counterparts to adhere to the ideology of familial patriarchy (DeKeseredy et al., 2003; Smith, 1990). Arguably, such subcultures are likely to flourish in the near future because areas with high levels of poverty and unemployment are fertile breeding grounds for male-to-male and male-to-female violence (Currie, 2008a). This is not to say, however, that middle-class men and boys do not engage in violence. They certainly do, and there is a large empirical and theoretical literature on the strong correlation between patriarchal male peer support and various types of woman abuse in university/college dating, which involves, for the most part, middle- and upper-class young adults (DeKeseredy and Schwartz, 2009). Male peer support is the attachment to male peers and the resources they provide that perpetuate and legitimate woman abuse (DeKeseredy, 1990).

Thus far, this section has only touched on pieces of the complex theoretical background of left realism. For example, left realists also offer a timely, but not widely cited, theoretical model directing attention to the negative outcomes of criminalizing incivilities, such as public drunkenness and panhandling in urban communities (Kinsey, Lea, and Young, 1986). Moreover, left realists have created the "square" of crime that focuses simultaneously on the community, the state, the victim, and the offender (Young, 1992). Jennifer Gibbs (in press) also offers a left realist perspective on terrorism. However, similar to what Friedrichs (2009, p. 214) refers to as "traditional radical criminology," left realism has not addressed crimes committed by white middle-class youth, which is an issue of major concern for US left realist Elliott Currie (2004).

Based on in-depth interviews with young men and women, Currie fills a major gap in left realist theorizing by revealing that many of today's white middle-class youths are on a "road to whatever." "Whatever" is a word that many of his respondents and other teenagers use to describe how they felt before committing dangerous or self-destructive acts. It is, according to Currie, "an emotional place in which they no longer cared about what happened to them and that made trouble not only possible but likely" (Currie, 2004, p. 14). What motivates them to start and continue this journey? The conservative knee-jerk response to this question is leniency, inadequate discipline, the ethos of self-expression, and other symptoms of "liberalism." Currie shows that nothing could be further from the truth. Certainly, since the 1990s, lawmakers in the United States, Canada, and other advanced industrial nations have passed draconian legislation aimed at regulating youth deviance, and zero-tolerance policies are now common approaches to dealing with minor transgressions and incivilities in schools across North America and elsewhere (DeKeseredy, 2007).

Currie offers an empirically informed theory of juvenile troubles that emphasizes the role of modern social Darwinist culture. For example, he asserts that the "road to whatever" starts in youths' families, "which often embody the 'sink or swim' ethos of the larger culture – a neglectful and punitive individualism that sets adolescents up for feelings of failure, worthlessness, and heedlessness that can erode their capacity to care about themselves or others" (Currie, 2004, p. 14). Darwinism also guides techniques helping professionals and teachers to treat troubled middle-class teenagers, and statements made by Currie's interviewees show that "there is no help out there" for many delinquent youths raised in Darwinian households. In fact, teachers and therapists driven by Darwinian thought exacerbated the interviewees' problems.

While, for some people, left realism may be "half-forgotten," it is still very much at the forefront of many scholars' minds (DeKeseredy et al., 2006). Numerous criminologists continue to review (often inaccurately) this school of thought in undergraduate texts and in scholarly books and journals. That Roger Matthews' (2009) re-fashioned realism is published in the widely read and cited journal Theoretical Criminology is a strong indicator that left realism is "making a comeback." More evidence of the rebirth of left realism is the fact that the journal *Crime, Law and Social Change* has published a special issue on left realism, edited by Martin Schwartz and myself. Moreover, Matthews' (2009) call for linking theory, method, and intervention challenges the portrayal of left realism as "representing more of an ideological emphasis than a theory" (Schmalleger and Volk, 2005, p. 300). Such criticisms create an "us versus them" scenario in which conservative or mainstream criminologists are objective scientists pursuing the truth, while left realists and other critical criminologists, at best, only pay lip service to rigorous theoretical, empirical, and policy work (DeKeseredy and Dragiewicz, 2007).

Nevertheless, left realism, like any social scientific school of thought, has limitations. One, in particular, is the ongoing inattention given to female offending (DeKeseredy *et al.*, 2006). Women, too, suffer from relative deprivation, belong to subcultures, and are exposed to the same mass media and cultural influences promoting capitalist and individualist materialist acquisition, all of which should give them the motivation needed to commit street crimes and to obtain desired objects (DeKeseredy and Schwartz, 2005b). Yet, compared to men and boys, most females do not do this. Left realist theory is still weak on this case and could benefit by addressing the work of feminist scholars such as Chesney-Lind and Pasko (2004), Miller (2001), and Walklate (2004).

PEACEMAKING CRIMINOLOGY[11]

The United States is one of the most violent countries in the world. It is also the most punitive nation in the world. The US incarceration rate is over 700 per 100,000 population, and the United States is one of the only advanced industrial countries that still uses the death penalty (Currie, 2008a). US citizens are now imprisoned four times more than in the early 1970s (Foster and Hagen, 2007; Western, Pattillo, and Weiman, 2004), and this "mass incarceration" or "new penalism" is racialized (Chesney-Lind, 2007; DeKeseredy, 2009a). About one out of every three African-American men between the ages of 20 and 29 are under some type of correctional supervision, while Latinos stand a 17 percent chance of being incarcerated (Mauer, 2005).

There is much more evidence showing that the United States has shifted from a "welfare state" to a "penal state" (Wacquant, 2001). Yet, capital punishment, long-term prison sentences, and other harsh sanctions are not making US streets, homes, and intimate relationships safer. In fact, extreme harshness is a conservative social experiment that has clearly failed (Reiman and Leighton, 2010). In response to this ongoing crisis, many criminologists contend that it is now time for politicians, criminal justice officials, and members of the general public to recognize that the United States and other very punitive countries (e.g., Russian Federation) are going about things the wrong way. However, there are many conflicting answers to the question, "What is to be done about crime and its control?"

Some people, including conservative politicians, call for a criminal justice system that is even more punitive than the current one (DeKeseredy, 2009a). One benefit of claiming that the system is not harsh enough is that no matter how harsh it becomes, there is no way of proving that it isn't harsh "enough" (DeKeseredy and Schwartz, 1996). If getting harsher does not seem to have any important effect on crime, there is always room for people to assert that we need to get harsher still. Other people, however, contend that radical individual, structural, and cultural changes constitute the solution to crime problems. Among this group are peacemaking criminologists such as Harold Pepinsky and Richard Quinney (1991). Peacemaking criminologists see crime as only one of many different types of violence – such as war, racism, and sexism – that contribute to human suffering (Thomas and O'Maolchatha, 1989).

In the early 1990s, British criminologist Paul Rock (1992) stated that "one might remark that criminology undergoes a scientific revolution *every* time Jock Young changes his mind" (p. x; emphasis in original). Across the Atlantic Ocean, in the United States, a similar observation was recently made about another prominent critical criminologist. According to Lilly *et al.* (2007, pp. 179–180), "Perhaps nothing exemplifies the way in which the context of the times conditions the development of criminological theory so clearly in the evolution in the thinking of Quinney," especially as he moved into peacemaking criminology. Quinney and other peacemaking criminologists are informed by anarchism, humanism, Christian socialism, liberation theology, Eastern meditative thought, penal abolitionism, feminism, and Marxism.[12] According to Pepinsky (2008, p. 190), "part of the art and science of peacemaking is to work out when and how to draw a balance between offering empathy and resisting abuse and violence." Peacemaking also includes the following basic principles, as outlined by Quinney (1991):

- Crime is suffering, and crime can only be eliminated by ending suffering.
- Crime and suffering can only be ended through the achievement of peace.
- Human transformation will achieve peace and justice.
- Human transformation will occur if we change our social, economic, and political structure.

For peacemaking criminologists, the current criminal justice system is a failure because it is rooted in the very problem it is ostensibly designed to eliminate – violence. A "war on crime," a "war on drugs," and all of the other "wars" we fight are based on the presumption that we can "stamp out," "eradicate," "push back," or otherwise do something violent to crime. Thus, for example, many people presume that crime can be stopped by enacting even harsher sanctions, even for relatively minor incivilities (Kelling and Coles, 1997). When this does not work, we increase penalties further. And then more again. And then still more again (DeKeseredy and Schwartz, 1996). Peacemaking criminologists do not believe that we can end violence through violence; such tactics only lead to violent reactions to our own violence (Pepinksy, 2008).

Peacemaking criminology shares some ideas with other progressive criminological perspectives, including anarchic or abolitionist criminology and restorative justice (de Haan, 2009; Fuller and Wozniak, 2006). However, the restorative justice movement is also embraced by some mainstream criminologists and has been co-opted by the criminal justice system (Friedrichs, 2009). Here, following Ptacek (2010a), restorative justice is defined as an approach that seeks "to decrease the role of the state in responding to crime and increase the involvement of personal, familial, and community networks in repairing the harm caused by crime" (p. ix). On the other hand, abolitionism can in no way be considered conservative, given that it calls for the total elimination of prisons, the death penalty, and solitary confinement, as well as a formal government and its laws (de Hann, 2009; Morris, 1995; Friedrichs, 2009).

What stands peacemaking criminologists apart from others is that they want to "make peace on crime." They call for a nonviolent criminology, one that simultaneously rejects repressive measures (e.g., prisons) and embraces human, progressive, community-based strategies such as mediation, reconciliation, alternative dispute resolution, and other nonpenal means of making our society safer (DeKeseredy and Schwartz, 1996). The success of such strategies and other less punitive community-based initiatives support the argument put forth nearly 30 years ago by Stanley Cohen (1985, p. 131):

> It still makes sense to say that mutual aid, good neighborliness and real community are preferable to the solutions of bureaucracies, professionals and the centralized state.... [I]t should not be impossible to imagine a way of stopping the relentless categorization of deviants.

It is not surprising that conservatives see peacemaking criminology as a "heretical challenge" to their draconian crime control strategies (Friedrichs, 2009). Others, including some who are critical criminologists, simply label peacemaking as utopian (Gibbons, 1994). Again, it has been co-opted by the criminal justice system. For example, judges who feel that probation is not a strong enough sanction might "sentence" a youth to restitution, community service, and charitable donations. Across Canada, the United States, and other countries juvenile court judges do this mainly with the idea that such moves are more a punishment than regular probation (Ptacek, 2010b). The youths themselves figure out quickly that this is a form of punishment, and the probation officers send out that message easily enough. In such an environment, some restitution might be paid and some beer cans picked up on a road outside of town, but no lessons are being learned either by the offenders or by the community (DeKeseredy and Schwartz, 1996).

Restorative practices, such as some of those advanced by peacemaking criminologists, are now found in over 80 countries (Porter, 2005), and the United Nations has adopted the basic principles of restorative justice and encourages countries to implement them (Parker, 2007; Van Ness, 2002). However, many feminists doubt that certain peacemaking responses are effective solutions to male violence against women. Such skepticism is well-founded, because some women abused by male intimates are also harmed during the process of court mediation (Ptacek, 2010b). This is what happened to 34 abused Nova Scotia women:

> Abused women reported intimidation and revictimization in mediation regardless of the form of abuse: physical, sexual, emotional, psychological, or financial. Women reported that their mediator or conciliator minimized emotional, psychological, or financial abuse, or simply did not recognize certain behaviors as abusive. When women brought up the fact that their ex-partner was harassing, stalking, or otherwise continuing to abuse them during the mediation, their mediators did not terminate mediation.
>
> (Rubin, 2000, p. 8)

Although there is much controversy among feminists about peacemaking criminology and violence against women,[13] some left realists claim that a program of reconciliation, re-education, and mutual aid by a caring community would offer the greatest hope of ending many other behaviors that induce a fearful state in wide numbers of women, such as various forms of sexual harassment in public places. Expanding the net of social control could bring in male perpetrators to begin a process of stopping their harassment of women, which, in the long run, would do more to demarginalize women than many other criminology proposals (DeKeseredy and Schwartz, 1991b). Of course, careful attention needs to be paid to the fact that peacemaking solutions are only useful as part of a package that includes structural change in society, or such solutions may render conflict as individual and deny structure (Selva and Bohm, 1987).

In sum, even if peacemaking criminologists' strategies for making the world peaceful stand little, if any, chance of being implemented under the current patriarchal capitalist social order, their work can constantly alert criminologists, politicians, the media, and the general public that there are alternatives to ceaseless and counterproductive wars on crime (DeKeseredy and Schwartz, 1996; Friedrichs, 2009). They can take the first steps toward developing the social changes and interconnections between people that peacemaking criminologists feel are essential to reducing crime. As Martin Schwartz (1991) points out in his evaluation of peacemaking criminology, at the very least this perspective can help us think through our "facile acceptance of violence against others" (p. 123).

POSTMODERN CRIMINOLOGY[14]

With origins mainly in France and Germany, postmodern thought has had a major impact on many academics, especially those based in university English departments and who specialize in literary criticism (Curran and Renzetti, 2001). However, it was not until the late 1980s that postmodernism began to influence a number of critical criminologists (Henry and Milovanovic, 2005).[15] Still, a cautionary note is required here. As Friedrichs (2009, p. 213) observes, "postmodern thought itself is by no means necessarily linked with a progressive agenda; on the contrary, much postmodernist thought is viewed as either consciously apolitical or inherently conservative and reactionary."

What is postmodern criminology? Briefly answering this question is a major challenge because there are numerous postmodern perspectives (Schwartz and Friedrichs, 1994). Further, postmodern theory is so hard to grasp – even for those who have deeply studied the issues involved – that only a superficial overview will be offered here. It is, to say the least, extremely difficult, if not impossible, to adequately explain postmodernism in a short section of a book like this. Thus, following Friedrichs (2009), postmodern criminology can best be described here as "a loose collection of themes and tendencies" (p. 213).

One of postmodernism's central ideas is deep skepticism about knowledge claims. Postmodernists reject claims of objectivity and challenge the modernist notion that we can harness science and logic, discover truth, and then put that truth to work to solve problems like crime (DeKeseredy and Schwartz, 1996). For postmodernists, "truth" is a social construction and a form of domination because it represents a way of looking at things that is imposed by those with more power (Curran and Renzetti, 2001; Wonders, 1999). Reality is not easily knowable, but rather is very complex, hard to read, and contradictory.

Postmodernists do not believe that *any* knowledge is knowable. They think that *any* truth claims are a form of tyranny and reject any claims by anyone who purports to know what is right. If truth is unknowable (Henry and Milovanovic, 2005), then our quest for knowledge must come from an understanding that everything is relative or related to everything else (Schwartz and Friedrichs, 1994). We need to be careful that we are not imposing our values (truth) on other people, which is a key issue for many postmodernists. Whereas progressives in general always try to speak for oppressed social groups, postmodernists warn about trying to speak for these people, rather than allowing them to speak for themselves (Denzin, 1990).

Some theorists argue that postmodern criminology is perhaps best understood in terms of what it opposes (Ferrell, 1998; Lilly *et al.*, 2007). Not surprisingly, postmodernism rejects positivism and the potential of collective social action to change society (Friedrichs, 2009). Postmodernism also, as cultural criminologist Jeff Ferrell (1998) once argued, opposes "the intellectual and legal machinery of modernism" and the "forms of legality, illegality, and crime that criminology conventionally investigates" (p. 63). Postmodernists are also against any broad, general theory of anything, at best suggesting that local people everywhere need to develop their own definitions of their experiences and need to work out their own methods of resistance to oppression (DeKeseredy and Schwartz, 1996).

Another one of postmodernist criminology's central ideas is that written or spoken language always plays a major role in the reality we construct and live (Arrigo, 2003). Hence, postmodernists "deconstruct" the meanings and social processes that we connect to crime and criminal justice (Curran and Renzetti, 2001; Friedrichs, 2009). As postmodern criminologist Bruce Arrigo (2003) puts it:

Deconstruction or "trashing" entails a careful reading and de-coding of a text (written or spoken). The purpose of deconstructing the text is to unveil the implicit assumptions and hidden values (i.e., often inconsistent, contradictory beliefs about social phenomena) embedded within a particular narrative. Deconstruction shows us how certain truth claims are privileged within a given story, while certain others are disguised or dismissed altogether. Because deconstruction focuses on the actual words people use to convey their thoughts, it attempts to uncover the unconscious intent behind the grammar people employ when writing or speaking. Thus, language or entire systems of communication are put under the microscope for closer inspection. In a sense, then, trashing a text entails reading between the lines to ascertain meanings (i.e., ideology) given preferred status in a particular language system.

(p. 48)

What has been described so far is quite abstract. Postmodernists must contend with accusations that they are irrelevant theorists who are more concerned with making petty academic points in obscure terms than they are with effecting serious change in the world (Schwartz and Friedrichs, 1994). Related to this point is that postmodernists have also been accused of being apolitical or being politically neutral (Curran and Renzetti, 2001; Dews, 1987; Melichar, 1990), which is also why much postmodernist work is deemed to be inherently conservative (Friedrichs, 2009). Of course, the problem is that there are so many versions of postmodernism in the social sciences that virtually any broad claims do not encompass everyone working within the tradition (Rosenau, 1992). Therefore, what Curran and Renzetti (2001) stated in their review of postmodern criminology is applicable here: "No doubt, many criminologists who call themselves postmodernists will object to our characterization of it here" (p. 205).

No critical criminology text that focuses on postmodern criminology is complete without a summary of "constitutive criminology," a school of thought developed by Stuart Henry and Dragan Milovanovic (1993, 2003). What is particularly interesting is that they integrate postmodernism into a more traditional criminological framework, with the goal of working on the production of meaning in the area of crime. They argue that such meaning is "co-produced" by those who engage in crime, those who try to control it, and those who study it.

Henry and Milovanovic would agree with much of the left realist and feminist analyses and strongly approve of peacemaking criminology's rejection of the use of state violence to overcome individual violence. However, they would define crime as the power to create pain or harm in any context, so that:

> law is not just a definer of crime, it is also a maker of crime. This is because it conceals some people's harms by reflecting power relations, and it manifests crime through its own exercise of power over others, especially those whose own activities have not been to deny others their own expression, such as is the case of consensual "crime," or crimes without victims.
>
> (Henry and Milovanovic, 1993, p. 12)

Thus, Henry and Milovanovic call for a short-term, "social judo" response to violence, whereby, instead of engaging in violence with the government, those who are oppressed by it must learn to bend or channel others' exercise of power over them into the exercise of power over others. The goal is

> a minimal use of energy toward redirecting the considerable power of those seeking to exercise power over us, such that they are made abundantly aware that the more energy they expend in harming us the more that energy converts into constraining them, limiting their further ability to harm us. This is the challenge of a transformative political agenda.
>
> (Henry and Milovanovic, 1993, p. 12)

This analysis is similar to the arguments of feminist postmodernism generally (DeKeseredy and Schwartz, 1996), which has strongly opposed romantic theorists who have championed their identification with oppressed groups. They argue that gathering strength by such identification is impossible. A better goal would be resisting "group identities that have been formed in hierarchical contexts [that] will only reproduce those hierarchical relationships (or, at best, create new ones)" (Grant, 1993, p. 137).

CULTURAL CRIMINOLOGY

Cultural criminology is one of the newest directions in critical criminology and was born in the mid-1990s (Ferrell, 1994, 1995; Ferrell and Sanders, 1995). This contemporary critical criminological school of thought is also a prime example of intellectual and political cross-fertilization, because its pioneers (e.g., Jeff Ferrell, Mike Presdee, Keith Hayward, and Jock Young) are based in the United States and the United Kingdom. There are, of course, cultural criminologists in other parts of the world, including Canada, where Ryerson University professor Stephen Muzzatti has made several important contributions to the field.[16] Sadly, one of cultural criminology's founders – Mike Presdee – passed away in July 2009.[17] In Box 2.1, Jock Young (2009, pp. 1–2) describes Presdee's contributions to the growth of cultural criminology. Presdee's work will always be remembered, and the ASC's DCC honored him posthumously by awarding him the DCC Lifetime Achievement Award in 2009.

Box 2.1 Mike Presdee: Perceptive Sociologist Who Played a Key Role in the Growth of Cultural Criminology

Mike Presdee, who has died of cancer aged 64, was a sociologist of international acclaim and great personal magnetism. His work focused on the sociology of youth and cultural criminology. He was fascinated by the way in which young people can be criminalized and controlled, and of youth being seen as a problem, rather than young people being the locus of the problems of the system. In later life, he attempted to understand and explain New Labour's neurotic obsession with antisocial behavior.

Cultural criminology was made for Mike and he was one of its chief architects. He was part of a generation of British criminologists entering academia during the post-1960s era of expanded university provision, who no longer looked down the class structure from a position of privilege, gazing with interest, sometimes charity, but always social distance.

Rather, they spoke for those low in the social structure, and were aware not only of the background factors of social action but the foreground rush of consciousness which gives it life and meaning.

Where traditional criminology mistakes textual dullness and robot-like social actors for objectivity, cultural criminology zooms in on the phenomenal experience of crime, victimization and punishment, stressing anger, humiliation, exuberance, excitement, and fear. It reveals the energy of everyday life, whether in the transgressive breaking of rules or in the repressive nature of conformity and boredom.

Mike's *Cultural Criminology and the Carnival of Crime* (2000) epitomized this approach. A firecracker of a book, it focuses on everything from joyriding to hate crimes, from the criminalization of raves to sadomasochism, it explores notions of transgression and resistance. It introduces the work of Mikhail Bakhtin, Gilles Deleuze and Theodor Reik, and is inspired by the earlier work of Jack Katz, Dick Hebdige, and Jeff Ferrell. It is one of the best introductions to cultural criminology and holds students spellbound.

Near the end of the book's acknowledgments, he apologized to his friends for enjoying life too much and to his employers for seeming to enjoy work too little. And that was it: Mike was a bon vivant, an intellectual enthusiast, a committed Marxist, a proud father, an inspired writer, a bit of an agitator – a wonderful man.

Cultural criminology has roots in the writings of US labeling theorists (e.g., Becker, 1973; Lemert, 1951), British youth cultural and subcultural theorists (e.g., Hall, Critcher, Jefferson, Clarke, and Roberts, 1978; Willis, 1977), moral panic theorists (e.g., Cohen, 1980; Young, 1971), and, of course, the "new criminologists" of the 1970s, such as Taylor, Walton, and Young (1973). Social constructionism, postmodern critical theory, and media/content analysis also heavily inform cultural criminology (Hayward, 2007; Hayward and Young,

2004; Muzzatti, 2006). As described by Jeff Ferrell (2003, p. 71), cultural criminology:

> critically investigates the ways in which the dynamics of media and popular culture, the lives and activities of criminals, and the operations of social control and criminal justice come together in everyday life. Cultural criminologists emphasize the role of image, style, and symbolic meaning among criminals and their subcultures, in the mass media's representation of crime and criminal justice, and in public conflicts over crime and crime control.

Like some feminist analyses (e.g., Chesney-Lind and Irwin, 2008), the role of media-generated moral panics is central to cultural criminologists' theoretical work. For example, in the United States and Canada, there is an important battle being waged over the nature of women's violence and aggression (DeKeseredy and Dragiewicz, 2007; Schwartz and DeKeseredy, 1993). Similarly, there is, in typical US style, a "war on girls" (DeKeseredy, in press a). Some well-known and widely used weapons in this war are "condemnatory media images" of teenage girls, such as those involving relational aggression in Hollywood movies like *Mean Girls* (Chesney-Lind and Irwin, 2008; Schissel, 1997). Cultural criminologists, among others, point out that such films, statistically rare cases of brutal female violence reported by the media, and untrue claims of a major surge in female youth violence like that offered in James Garbarino's (2006) controversial trade book, *See Jane Hit*, fuel moral panics about girls deemed to be in conflict with the law or who use various means of rebelling against patriarchal dominance in schools, dance halls, at home, and elsewhere.

The concept of the moral panic was developed by Stanley Cohen (1980) to describe a situation in which a condition, episode, person, or a group of persons come to be defined as a threat to society. The objects of moral panics are usually people. Certainly, the media, together with some social scientists, lawyers, agents of social control, and other "experts," have jumped on the bandwagon to transform girls who violate a myriad of patriarchal gender norms in the United States, Canada, and other parts of the world into folk devils. A folk

devil is "a socially constructed, stereotypical carrier of significant social harm" (Ellis, 1987, p. 199). As vividly pointed out by
scholars who analyze the media with a gendered lens, many
girls are labeled as being made up of "sugar and spice and
everything evil" (Schissel, 1997, p. 51).

As stated above, cultural criminology also draws heavily
from important studies on youth culture and subcultures, and
offers "thick" descriptions of people who live at the edge of
conventional society (e.g., drug users, skydivers, and graffiti
artists) (Ferrell, Hayward, and Young, 2008; Friedrichs, 2009).
However, the use of the concept "culture" is subject to criticism. For instance, it is said that cultural criminologists' definition of culture is more political than analytical (Lilly *et al.*,
2007; O'Brien, 2005). This is, though, a rather old critique and
claims of subjectivity or "blatant violations" of traditional scientific modes of inquiry have been directed at critical criminologists and other progressive scholars for decades (Muzzatti,
2006). Following in the footsteps of critics of 1960s and early
1970s labeling theory, others claim that cultural criminology's
analyses of high-profile crime, social deviants, and moral panics
is similar to a criminology of "nuts, sluts, and perverts" and
"the exotic, the erotic and the neurotic" (Adler and Adler,
2003; Liazos, 1972). Muzzatti (2006, p. 75) responds to such
criticism by stating:

> These critiques incorrectly equate style with a lack of substance. Because
> the mediated reality of crime is fundamentally a political endeavor, cul-
> tural criminology's engagement with these actors, texts and processes
> can be seen as a retaliatory strike in the culture wars. Cultural criminol-
> ogy offers an avenue for intellectual resistance and self-defense against
> conventional constructions of crime and prescriptions for control.

Another frequent criticism of cultural criminology is that it
"overemphasizes" with the subcultures and other "outlaws" and
thus lacks a solid appreciation of the legitimate concerns of those
responsible for responding and preventing their activities, such as
the police, teachers, and the like (Friedrichs, 2009). Nevertheless,
cultural criminology is "here to stay," and it is attracting an
international cadre of dedicated scholars (DeKeseredy and Perry,

2006b). The launch of relatively new journals such as *Crime, Media, Culture*, and special editions of established journals such as *Theoretical Criminology*, as well as the publication of some widely read and cited books (e.g., Ferrell *et al.*, 2008) attest to this emerging orientation (Muzzatti, 2006).

CONVICT CRIMINOLOGY

Prisoners and ex-convicts have long been the subject of criminological inquiry. However, the bulk of the empirical and theoretical work on these groups is done by criminologists who have had little contact with the criminal justice system (Ross and Richards, 2003). There is also another group of criminologists, such as those who specialize in the psychology of criminal conduct (e.g., Andrews and Bonta, 2006), who routinely enter correctional institutions only to subject prisoners to a battery of problematic psychological tests that end up supporting their claim that crime is primarily a property of the individual (Davidson and Chesney-Lind, 2009). Such work fails to address the real experiences of convicts and ex-convicts (Friedrichs, 2009), which is one of the key reasons for the birth of convict criminology.

"Primarily an American contribution" (Lilly *et al.*, 2007, p. 203), convict criminology formally started at the 1997 ASC meeting and includes academic criminologists who have served time in correctional facilities, as well as some progressive scholars who have not been officially designated as criminal or deviant. In the words of Ross and Richards (2003, p. 6):

> This is a "new criminology" (I. Taylor, Walton, and Young, 1973) led by ex-convicts who are now academic faculty. These men and women, who have worn both prison uniforms and academic regalia, served years behind prison walls, and now as academics, are the primary architects of the movement. The convict scholars do what most previous writers could not: merge their past with their present and provide a provocative approach to the academic study of criminology, criminal justice, and corrections. These authors, as a collective, are the future of a realistic paradigm that promises to challenge the conventional research findings of the past.

Not to be confused with penal abolitionism, which calls for abolishing prisons, the death penalty, and solitary confinement (Lilly *et al.*, 2007; Morris, 1995), convict criminology involves the use of ethnographic studies of the prison experience to "tell it like it is" (Ross and Richards, 2003, p. 9). Given their first-hand experiences with penal institutions, convict criminologists are certainly highly qualified experts in their fields and offer unique "inside perspectives" based on rigorous, thoughtful studies of prison life. Further, these critical scholars are among a large group of progressives that point to the destructive nature of prisons and their inability to promote peace, reduce crime, and foster social justice. As Ross and Richards (2003, p. 3) observe, "One cursory look at the gun towers, walls, and razor wire is evidence that prisons were built to warehouse and punish and not to rehabilitate."

Nearly 20 years ago, David Friedrichs (1991) claimed that it is rather premature to consider peacemaking criminologists' contributions a "school of thought." Perhaps the same assertion can be applied to convict criminology. As Alan Mobley (2003, p. 223) puts it, "Criminology is a curious business and it is not clear where, or if, the convict criminologist fits in." Convict criminology is vibrant and the ASC meetings routinely feature dynamic sessions on this new variant of critical criminology. Nevertheless, some critics wonder whether it is doing anything novel except for the fact that a sizeable portion of convict criminologists publicly reveal their status as "ex-cons." Moreover, convict criminologists are somewhat stigmatized for not publishing in mainstream journals, and, of course, the claim of being too subjective is frequently made (Lilly *et al.*, 2007).

What critics are missing, however, is that convict criminologists are opposed to mainstream or "managerial criminology," which is why they publish in alternative venues. The same can be said about many proponents of other new directions in critical criminology. Also, as stated earlier in this book and elsewhere, there is no such thing as value-free research, and every study, theory, or policy is informed by politics. In addition, since convict criminology is a relatively new school of thought, it is destined to generate new ways of thinking critically about crime, law, and social control. Hopefully, what Ross and

Richards (2003) stated at the start of this century will come true: "We predict that over time, this new school of convict criminology will provide the public with a more realistic understanding of crime, criminal justice, and corrections that is based on experience and cutting-edge research" (p. 13).

SUMMARY[18]

Theory construction and testing occur every day. Nevertheless, some of the most popular journals in the field, such as *Criminology*, only pay lip service to new directions in critical criminology, as well as other theories, and are heavily invested in publishing variants of "so what? criminology" characterized by impenetrable statistical analyses (Currie, 2007). Today, especially in the United States, being labeled a theorist or referring to oneself as such results in marginalization and difficulties landing a tenure-track position at a prestigious university or college. On the other hand, those deemed as "good researchers" are more likely to be "in with the in crowd" and stand a much better chance of getting an academic post at a large doctoral institution.

Criminology is fragmented and academic criminology is under siege (DeKeseredy and Schwartz, in press). Moreover, due in large part to the devastating effects of free-market economic policies, universities and colleges are increasingly demanding that faculty obtain more external funds. Doing this is not an easy task for progressive scholars with a vested interest in theory construction. For example, most government agencies that fund criminological work have relatively little money to begin with, and those in charge of them call for research that evaluates the efficiency of mainstream policies, laws, and practices (Savelsberg, King, and Cleveland, 2002; Walters, 2003). Consequently, as Matthews (2009, p. 341) notes, "academic criminology appears to be becoming more marginalized and irrelevant."

There is much public support for the marginalization and gutting of the humanities and social sciences, which is one of the key reasons why conservative politicians get elected. Further, many people view the theoretical work done by scholars in these fields as simply academic products of "impractical mental gymnastics" or "fanciful ideas that have little to do with what truly motivates people" (Akers, 1997, p. 1). However, let us return to Kurt Lewin's (1951) claim about the practicality of theory. Critical criminologists agree with him and assert that one of the key reasons for why much criminological work is not policy relevant is that much of it is a-theoretical (Matthews, 2009). As is the case with illnesses, such as AIDS, prior to finding solutions to crime and injustice, we must first identify the causes, and critical criminologists have long argued for linking theory to practice (Young, 1992).

The main objective of this chapter was to introduce some of the most important current trends in critical criminology. All of them have shown themselves to be important alternatives to traditional criminological theory and more critical perspectives are likely to emerge in the near future. As stated above, although the schools of thought reviewed here were presented in a particular order, all of them are equally important and each one has strengths and limitations. There is no such thing as a perfect theory of crime or social control (Curran and Renzetti, 2001).

In late 1980s and early 1990s, the criminological world saw the development of four new directions in critical criminology: feminism, left realism, peacemaking, and postmodernism. In response to the emergence of these progressive perspectives, Schwartz (1991) stated that critical criminology "is infused with more energy and exciting alternatives than at any point in the past 20 years" and that "there are so many more avenues and ideas to develop" (p. 123). The same can be said today. That more new ways of thinking critically about crime have been developed since Schwartz made his observation offers some support for the hypothesis that "the impact of critical criminology will increase exponentially in the years ahead, perhaps at some point even coming to overshadow mainstream forms of analysis" (Friedrichs, 2009, p. 217). Will such a transition actually occur? This is an empirical question that can only be answered empirically. Yet, given the exciting developments reviewed here and elsewhere, the future looks promising.

3

CONTEMPORARY CRITICAL CRIMINOLOGICAL RESEARCH

It is not the method that designates an approach as critical: critical researchers use a diverse range of methods, and methods are not "inherently positivist, phenomenological or critical" (Harvey, 1990, p. 1). Critical research is shaped "at the level of methodology" (Harvey, 1990, p. 201). Some areas of critical criminology do have an orientation towards a particular method or methods, with a strong tendency towards qualitative approaches such as participant observation or in-depth interviews. However, debates about the relative merits of qualitative or quantitative research commonly express epistemological or methodological differences. At the level of methods, multi-methods approaches (methodological triangulation) commonly employ both qualitative and quantitative methods that have different strengths. For critical criminology, as for other traditions, the appropriate method depends on the research objectives.

(Stubbs, 2008, p. 13)

Critical criminologists examine a myriad of social problems, ranging from violence against women, to predatory street crime, to state or government crime. They also study timely and important issues outside the realm of criminology as it is commonly known. For example, US critical criminologist Raymond

Michalowski and his intimate partner anthropologist Jill Dubisch (2001) conducted an ethnographic study of a "secular pilgrimage" involving a motorcycle journey from southern California to the Vietnam War Memorial in Washington, DC. Consisting of Vietnam veterans, Michalowski and Dubisch joined this "run for the wall" in their hometown of Flagstaff, Arizona and ended up involved in a study that describes, in their words, "a journey that is both a physical passage through the nation and a spiritual and emotional journey toward healing and understanding" (p. ix).

Victoria Pitts-Taylor is another critical criminologist who "wears two hats." In addition to co-developing and testing a feminist routine activities theory of campus sexual assault (see Schwartz and Pitts, 1995), she does in-depth qualitative research on the experience, meanings, and motivations for cosmetic surgeries (Pitts-Taylor, 2007). Joseph Donnermeyer is one more prime example of a prominent critical criminologist who can balance more than one research project at the same time. Widely recognized as a pioneer in rural criminology, Donnermeyer also conducts studies of old order Amish social life in both Canada and the United States.[1] Cultural criminologists, too, are well known for doing empirical work outside the realm of conventional criminology. Consider Jeff Ferrell's (2006) ethnographic project on "dumpster diving" and studies of "edgework,"[2] such as advanced sky diving (Ferrell, Hayward, and Young, 2008; Lyng, 1990, 2005).

Many more examples of non-criminological research done by critical criminologists could easily be provided, such as Canadian scholar Stephen Muzzatti's (2005) analysis of mass media coverage of the outbreak of Severe Acute Respiratory Syndrome (SARS) in the spring of 2003. The key point here is that critical criminology is much more than a theoretical and/or political enterprise. It also entails "cutting edge" research on crimes at the top, crimes at the bottom, societal reactions to these harms, and how crime, law, and social control are influenced by broader social, political, cultural, and economic forces. The main objective of this chapter is to provide some major examples of recent critical criminological empirical contributions. It must be emphasized, though, that the studies reviewed in this chapter should not be considered superior to those not examined. Certainly, critical criminologists have attended to a legion of substantive topics and thus it is impossible to do them all justice in a short chapter or book.

INTERPERSONAL VIOLENCE[3]

It may seem counterintuitive to state that interpersonal violence is a new area of critical criminological inquiry. Still, until relatively recently such crime was not extensively examined by the discipline as a whole (DeKeseredy and Perry, 2006b). Some salient exceptions are studies of woman abuse done by feminists, left realists, and masculinities scholars. Masculinities and left realist research also focuses heavily on predatory street crimes (Friedrichs, 2009). Moreover, some of the methods used in these progressive studies are similar to those employed by mainstream scholars. One example is the victimization survey, a method commonly utilized to uncover "the dark figure of crime" or crimes not reported to the police. The self-report survey helps achieve the same goal; however, the former asks people about crimes committed against them, while the latter asks respondents to report the crimes they committed. What makes the mainstream use of such surveys distinct from how critical criminologists, such as left realists, use them is that conventional survey researchers focus primarily on individual characteristics, "rational calculations and routine activities, situational factors, and the more immediate environment" (Friedrichs, 2009, p. 216). Some of these factors are also addressed by surveys administered by progressive scholars, but there is a very strong emphasis on gleaning data on the influence of macro-level forces, such as the role of the ideology of familial patriarchy.

Even so, some determinants of central concern to critical criminologists have received more attention than others. For example, the ways in which race and class inequalities shape women's victimization in public and private places warrants much more scrutiny. Feminist scholar Jody Miller (2008) recently answered this call and studied gendered violence experienced by African-American girls in poor St. Louis neighborhoods. Miller conducted in-depth, semi-structured interviews with young African-American women and men, as well as surveys with them. Information on the characteristics of the participants' neighborhoods was also gathered. This project makes many important contributions, including being attentive to the victimization experiences of urban minority youth. Historically, criminologists mainly focused on minority youth in conflict with the law, such as street gang members, drug dealers, and so on. Miller (2008, p. 11) points out that:

> This is exacerbated by a general bias within American culture to assign greater importance to the victimization of whites than people of color and to take race into account when evaluating the seriousness of violence against women and the presumed culpability of its victims.

Miller's data also provide further evidence that the abuse of women is fostered by male peer support. Although the bulk of studies on the relationship between male peer support and woman abuse have been done on college campuses dominated by people of European descent, Miller's study supports what Lee Bowker (1983) said more than 30 years ago about all-male patriarchal subcultures of violence:

> This is not a subculture that is confined to a single class, religion, occupational grouping, or race. It is spread throughout all parts of society. Men are socialized by other subculture members to accept common definitions of the situation, norms, values, and beliefs about male dominance and the necessity of keeping their wives in line. These violence-supporting social relations may occur at any time and in any place.
>
> (pp. 135–136)

Race, gender, and inner-city violence are key concerns for Nikki Jones (2010), who also conducted a study of African-American girls. Done in Philadelphia, this ethnographic project demonstrates how these girls manage the threat of daily interpersonal and gendered violence (e.g., sexual violence) in their neighborhoods. Like Miller (2008), Jones used multiple methods, including participant observation, direct observation, and informal interviews with girls who had voluntarily enrolled in a city hospital-based violence reduction project. Jones also participated in long conversations with the grandmothers, mothers, sisters, brothers, cousins, and friends of the young people in her study. Similar to Miller (2008), Jones (2010) does not pathologize her respondents of color. Rather, her work shows, contrary to the popular racist belief, that inner-city African-American girls are "resourceful, normal women" who are trying to negotiate and cope with brutal socioeconomic conditions in their communities.

As stated in Chapter 1, critical criminologists have not given much attention to crime and social control in rural communities, but we are now seeing an emergence of critical research on drug use, woman abuse, racism, and other social problems that plague rural areas in Canada, the United States, Australia, and elsewhere. Collectively, the rural studies cited in Chapter 1 show that rural communities are not less criminogenic than urban areas, a discovery that challenges conventional wisdom. In fact, rural rates may be higher than urban rates in particular types of rural places and for specific kinds of crime (Jobes, Barclay, Weinand, and Donnermeyer, 2004). Note that the official rate of violence for most rural counties in the United States exceeds that for several dozen metropolitan areas, based on the Federal Bureau of Investigation's (FBI) *Uniform Crime Reports* (Donnermeyer, 2007). North of the US border, in Canada, the rate of homicide in rural areas (2.5 per 100,000) is higher than the rate for large urban areas (2.0) and the rate for small urban communities (1.7), and this pattern held constant over a 10-year period (Statistics Canada, 2007a). Evidence also suggests that rural women are at greater risk of being sexually assaulted during and after separation/divorce than their urban counterparts (DeKeseredy and Schwartz, 2009). Indeed, critical criminologists are part of a cadre that alerts us to the fact that "[R]urality does not imply the sociological equivalent of immunity from crime" (Donnermeyer, Jobes, and Barclay, 2006, p. 205).

Structured social inequality is one of the key determinants of rural crime (Donnermeyer and DeKeseredy, 2008). Qualitative studies done in rural Appalachian sections of the United States by DeKeseredy, Schwartz, Fagen, and Hall (2006), Grant (2008), and Websdale (1998) show that woman abuse, alcoholism, and drug addiction are strongly associated with poverty, unemployment, and patriarchal practices and discourses. Similarly, societal reactions to these problems, such as policing, are also influenced by a larger set of economic, political, and social factors (Donnermeyer, DeKeseredy, and Dragiewicz, in press). As Grant (2008, p. 22) observes, "rural areas are often neglected in the creation of national political agenda or plans for reform and change."

Such neglect is also evident at the local level and is often linked to attempts to maintain inequality and oppression. DeKeseredy and Schwartz (2009) found that many rural Ohio men who abuse their ex-partners can rely on their male friends and neighbors, including those who are police officers, to support a violent patriarchal status quo even while they count on these same people to help prevent public crimes such as vandalism. Furthermore, in rural sections of Ohio and other states such as Kentucky, there is widespread acceptance of woman abuse and community norms prohibiting victims from publicly revealing their experiences and from seeking social support (DeKeseredy *et al.*, 2007). Rural women with addiction problems encounter similar processes of informal social control and hence spend long periods of time suffering in silence (Grant, 2008).

Masculinities researchers are another group of progressive scholars who open up new avenues of inquiry, one of which is the relationship between gender, the body, and violent crime. As Messerschmidt (2004, p. 19) notes:

> Feminists and profeminist criminologists historically have neglected how social action, lived experience, and crime are embodied. Not only have feminist and profeminist criminologists concentrated on gender differences in crime – thereby ignoring possible gender similarities in crime – they have also conceptualized the body as a "natural" phenomenon that lies outside their analytical concerns.

Violence is an embodied practice and Messerschmidt's (2000, 2004) life-history research shows that body size helps determine the type of violence boys will use under certain conditions to "do masculinity." For example, Hugh, one of Messerschmidt's (2000) respondents, was a tall and muscular boy who fought older peers on the school playground who confronted him with masculinity challenges, such as trying to force him and his friends off a field because they wanted to play kick ball. Hugh also disliked teachers because he perceived them as a "form of authority" and he used his physical strength to challenge their power by throwing desks. Messerschmidt (2005, p. 205) discovered that "within the social setting of the school, Hugh's body became his primary resource for masculine power and esteem and simultaneously constructed his victims as subordinate."

Zack, another boy interviewed by Messerschmidt, did not have the physical stature to be masculine like the "cool guys" at his school. He was overweight and was continually rejected by girls he asked to date him. Consequently, due to his inability to "measure up" physically to his school's view of the "ideal masculine body," during his sixth-grade year, he started to sexually assault his six-year-old female cousin and did so for three years using nonviolent, manipulative techniques. According to Messerschmidt (2000, pp. 47–48),

> the control, power, and sexual arousal associated with the sexual domination of his youngest cousin provided Zack a contextually based masculine resource when other masculine resources were unavailable – he was now a "cool guy." The sexual violence provided a sense of masculine accomplishment and therefore heightened his masculine self-esteem.

Recent studies reveal that poor inner-city males also face "overwhelming challenges" to their sense of masculinity, which, in turn, results in many of them engaging in street violence under certain situations (Anderson, 2008; Mullins, 2006). Of course, too, as stated in Chapter 2, critical criminologists, such as Perry (2003), show that racist and homophobic violence are also techniques of "doing masculinity." What makes her contribution even more important is that it constitutes a rigorous effort to address "the paucity of hate crime scholarship" within critical criminology (Perry, 2006, p. 155). So does DeKeseredy, Perry, and Schwartz's (2007) representative sample survey of hate-motivated sexual assaults on female undergraduates at two Ontario institutions of higher learning, which is the first Canadian study of its kind. They found that about 11 percent of the 384 women in their sample stated that they experienced one or more of five variants of hate-motivated sexual assault (e.g., sexual relations because of threats or actual use of force) in the past seven months. Ironically, while Canadian universities and colleges contribute to the advancement of learning and broadening of young minds, DeKeseredy *et al.*'s findings support Ehrlich's (1999) claim that these postsecondary institutions are showing dramatic trends towards intolerance, as evidenced by ongoing and even escalating rates of racial, ethnic, and gender harassment. Some US studies have uncovered similar problems on college campuses (e.g., Southern Poverty Law Center, 2003; Van Dyke and Tester, 2008).

Thinking critically about crimes like interpersonal violence entails taking a broader view. Comparative research is a prime example of such an approach and frequently involves examining data on two or more societies. Well known for his work on violence in US society,[4] left realist Elliott Currie (2008a) examined world-wide data on serious acts of interpersonal violence, such as murder. What makes his comparative research novel is that he points to the variability of violence around the world in recent years. For example, based on an analysis of World Health Organization data (see Krug *et al.*, 2002), Colombia and El Salvador "top the list" in murder, with rates of over 60 per 100,000 population in the former and more than 55 per 100,000 in the latter. At the other extreme are countries like Sweden, Ireland, and Greece, with homicide rates at or below the level of 1 per 100,000. Currie's research also shows that except for the United States, richer countries have lower rates of homicide than poorer nations.

Physical and sexual violence, of course, is not only found on the streets, in pubs and taverns, or in domestic/household settings. It is frequently directed at different types of animals (e.g., pets, strays, and livestock) (DeGue and DiLillo, 2008; Merz-Perez and Heide, 2004), at females during the filming of pornographic films or videos (Jensen, 2007), in workplaces (DeKeseredy, 2009b), and elsewhere. Critical criminologists are starting to examine these other harms that are often unnoticed, unreported, or ignored. In addition, although not generally viewed as violent, feminist criminologists have generated much data on offenses that cause just as much, if not more, harm than nonlethal acts of physical violence. Major examples of such behaviors are sexual harassment in private and public domains and coercive control in intimate relationships. Coercive control frequently involves psychologically and emotionally abusive behaviors that are often subtle, hard to detect and prove, and seem to be more forgivable to people unfamiliar with the abuse of women and its consequences. Two prime examples are threatening looks and criticism (Kernsmith, 2008). Many men also use other tactics of coercive control to suppress their intimate female partner's personal freedom, including "microregulating a partner's behavior" (Stark, 2007, p. 229). This, then, is another key reason why many feminist and other critical scholars assert that we should develop and operationalize even broader definitions of interpersonal violence.

CRIMES OF THE POWERFUL[5]

In his book, *Dude, Where's My Country*, film-maker Michael Moore (2003) states, "The fear drug works like this: You are repeatedly told that bad, scary people are going to kill you, so place all your trust in *us*, your corporate leaders, and we will protect you" (p. 138; emphasis in original). The reality is, however, that many corporate and political elites are "trusted criminals," and critical criminologists repeatedly remind us of this problem (Friedrichs, 2007). What Michalowski (1985) pointed out over 20 years ago still holds true today: "corporate crime represents the most widespread and costly form of crime in America" (p. 325). The same can be said about corporate crime in other parts of the world, such as Canada and the United Kingdom. For example, based on their review of the extant literature on corporate violence, some sociologists estimate that the rate of deaths from unsafe work conditions is more than six times greater than the street crime death rate, and the rate of nonlethal assault in the workplace is more than 30 times greater than the rate of predatory street assault (DeKeseredy, Ellis, and Alvi, 2005). Corporate violence is defined here as:

> any behavior undertaken in the name of the corporation by decision makers, or other persons in authority within the corporation, that endangers the health and safety of employees or other persons who are affected by that behavior. Even acts of omission, in which decision makers, etc., refuse to take action to reduce or eliminate known health and safety risks, must be considered corporate violence. It is the impact the action has on the victim, not the intent of the act, which determines whether or not it is violence.
>
> (DeKeseredy and Hinch, 1991, p. 100)

On top of documenting a host of corporate crimes, critical criminologists do extensive research on government or state crimes. One progressive scholar mentioned to David Kauzlarich and Rick Matthews (2006, p. 239) that "such a sustained body of high-quality scholarship from a network of researchers working in concert on a particular problem area was unparalleled in criminology." Nevertheless, defining state crime is subject to heated debates, which are not likely to be resolved soon. Still, most leading experts in the field agree with Rothe and Friedrichs' (2006) call for using international law as a "foundational basis" for understanding state crime, which includes standards such as human rights and social harms (Rothe, 2009).

Major examples of state crimes studied by contemporary critical criminologists include:

- genocidal rape in Rwanda (Mullins, 2009; Mullins and Rothe, 2008)
- child labor and violations of children's rights (Olsson, 2003)
- links between drug traffickers and political elites (Schulte-Bockholt, 2006)
- the Nazi Holocaust (Friedrichs, 2000; Matthews, 2006)
- violations of treaties between the US government and American-Indian tribes (Robyn, 2006)
- US army personnel torturing Iraqi prisoners at Abu Ghraib (N. Klein, 2007; Rothe, Kramer, and Mullins, 2009).

A much longer list of state crimes could be noted here. The same could be said about corporate crimes, which are types of white-collar crime (Friedrichs, 2007). White-collar and corporate crimes are similar in the sense that they occur in the context of occupational roles and are committed by "persons of high or respectable social status" (Helmkamp, Ball, and Townsend, 1996, p. 351). The major difference between the two crimes, however, is in the victims and beneficiaries of the crime. For example, corporate crime benefits both the company and the offender(s), while white-collar crime benefits only the offender. Corporate crime is thus defined here as "the conduct of employees acting on behalf of a corporation, which is proscribed and punishable by law" (Braithwaite, 1984, p. 6).

It is not always easy to distinguish between the two types of crime committed by executives because many corporate crimes also benefit the individuals. For example, executives who save their company money by insisting on maintaining unsafe working conditions for factory workers may be in line for a promotion to a higher salary. In general, though, white-collar crime is committed without the knowledge or permission of the company and is designed to profit only the individual (DeKeseredy et al., 2005). Corporate crime is, on the other hand, designed to benefit the company and only secondarily will profit the individual, if at all (DeKeseredy and Schwartz, 1996).

The most common technique of gathering data on crimes of the powerful, such as state and corporate crime, is the case study method (Matthews and Kauzlarich, 2006; Rothe et al., 2009; Tombs and Whyte, 2007). Case studies are detailed examinations of specific outcomes, events, or processes that occur over varying periods of time. Usually a single case is studied, such as the space shuttle Challenger explosion or the crash of ValuJet Flight 592 (Kramer, 2006; Matthews and Kauzlarich, 2006). Moreover, a variety of data collection methods may be used in conducting case studies, such as listening to and engaging in casual conversations, focused in-depth interviews, reviewing statistics, making tape recordings, taking photographs, making maps, and reading local newspapers, community notices, and records (Alvi, DeKeseredy, and Ellis, 2000).

A major obstacle facing all researchers is eliciting accurate data on the extent and distribution of crimes of the powerful. Some methods are better than others, but none of them can collect accurate data on the experiences of the thousands of North Americans who "continue to work, unaware that they are harboring slowly evolving occupational diseases or that physical ailments will painfully show themselves only after a great deal of accumulated damage is done" (Katz, 1978, p. 6). For this and other reasons, a few critical scholars claim that the victimization survey is an inappropriate means of uncovering reliable data from people harmed by crimes of the powerful that are often hidden or difficult to detect, such as the secretive dumping of toxic waste (Walklate, 1989).

Arguments such as this one are stated so often that they are considered by many to be truisms. Yet no concrete empirical evidence is presented that proves that the victimization survey is an inadequate mode of studying crimes such as corporate violence (DeKeseredy and Goff, 1992). Obviously, people cannot report incidents of unwitting victimization, such as exposure to particular pollutants (MacLean, 1991). This is a problem which no method can avoid, but as Friedrichs (2007, p. 37) puts it, "Surveys can contribute greatly to our under-standing of white collar crime because we still have much to learn about patterns of involvement, rationalizations, and atti-tudes pertaining to white collar crime issues." Left realists cer-tainly agree and those among them who conducted the second sweep of the Islington Crime Survey (ICS II) in the London Borough of Islington uncovered reliable and valid information on three variants of what Pearce (1992) refers to as commercial crime: workplace hazards, unlawful trading practices, and the victimization of housing tenants (Crawford, Jones, Woodhouse, and Young, 1990).

It is beyond the scope of this chapter to provide a detailed description of the data generated by the 1988 ICS II; however, based upon some of the findings reported by Pearce (1992), they provide a much more realistic account of the number of accidents people experience in the workplace than official British statistics did at that time. For example, then, the acci-dent rate per 100,000 workers was found to be approximately

30 times the national average. Another relevant victimization survey was conducted in the United States by the National White Collar Crime Center. Data gathered from a national survey of 1,169 US households showed that more than one out of every three households was victimized in 1999 by fraud through the following offenses:

- Internet transactions
- unauthorized use of their credit cards
- use of 800 or 900 telephone numbers
- unauthorized use of a personal identification number
- a free prize or vacation that turned out not to be free
- a free product sample that turned out not to be free (Rebovich and Layne, 2000).

Arguably, studying crimes of the powerful presents more challenges than collecting data on many "conventional crimes," such as juvenile delinquency. For example, it would be extremely difficult, if not impossible, to get a dictator who ordered the mass execution of citizens who opposed him or her to participate in an in-depth interview for social scientific purposes. Further, there is no crimes-of-the-powerful database equivalent to those maintained for street crimes (e.g., Uniform Crime Reports), and government agencies are uncomfortable funding research that may "hit too close to home" (Friedrichs, 2007). Yet, critical criminologists around the world persist in studying topics such as those briefly covered here and are heavily engaged in developing new ways of gathering data on genocide, price fixing, false advertising, child labor, and a myriad of other crimes of the powerful. For example, Rothe *et al.* (2009a) suggest the creation of a state crime database that takes the following approach:

- delineate the variables available: the scope of the enterprise (e.g., country, years, etc.);
- make a short list of hypotheses and variables that are important to gather data on;
- cull through existing databases (e.g., Human Rights Watch, Amnesty International, Transaction, Polity II, etc.);

- develop a search strategy for missing cases and variables;
- perform relevant statistical tests on hypotheses.

Lynch and Stretesky (2001) provide another example of a novel way of studying crimes of the powerful. They show us the value of examining medical evidence to identify toxic harms, such as hazardous waste. Undoubtedly, such important data cannot be gleaned from police statistics and other criminal justice databases.

In sum, critical criminological research shows that many people assumed to have what Jackson Toby (1957) refers to as a strong "stake in conformity" engage in behaviors that actually do more harm, cost more money, and destroy more lives than predatory street crimes such as mugging, theft, and so on (Reiman and Leighton, 2010). Some types of social control (e.g., policing), too, frequently cause much harm, and it is to recent critical research on this issue that I turn to next.

SOCIAL CONTROL

Critical criminology is well known for pointing to how certain laws and various techniques of social control are tools used by powerful social groups to promote and protect their interests. Particularly during the 1970s and 1980s, scholars such as Richard Quinney (1975), Frank Pearce (1976), William Chambliss (1986), and Colin Goff and Charles Reasons (1978) played an important role in sensitizing us to the class-based nature of the origins and functions of law. Marxist analyses of law and social control are still used today (e.g., Reiman and Leighton, 2010); however, some new theoretical perspectives emerged near the start of this century (e.g., critical race theory), as well as some new empirical directions (Friedrichs, 2001, 2009). On top of constantly showing the failures of the prison system and that those at the bottom of the socioeconomic ladder are more likely to be charged, convicted, and sent to prison, progressive scholars now devote much more attention to how gender and race/ethnicity shape law and social control. Some recent examples are Susan Miller's (1999) multi-method, feminist study of the impact of gender on community policing in a Midwestern

US city. For some readers, such a study may not appear unique, but most policing research still ignores gender and how it is related to police organizations and culture (Corsianos, 2009).

There is also a paucity of research on policing Native American communities, which is of paramount concern to Canadian critical criminologist Barbara Perry (2009b). Her interviews with 278 Native Americans from seven states in the United States reveal that police "under- and over-enforce" the law in Native American communities. In other words, Perry's respondents reported that the police would often turn a blind eye to their victimization, as well as subject them to violence and harassment. There is a large body of knowledge on racist police practices, but most of the extant US literature addresses the plight of African-Americans and Latinos. Thus, like Miller (1999), Perry has opened up a new door on critical inquiry.

The same can be said about the small group of critical criminologists who study crime and social control in rural communities. For example, DeKeseredy and Schwartz's (2009) Ohio study shows that rural male-to-female violence is seldom reported to the police, and when it is, these law-enforcement officials often respond in ways described by one of their respondents:

> Well, out here we deal with the Sheriff's Department outside the city limits. It would be nice if the deputies would stop rolling their eyeballs. You know, it's, uh, I don't think they treat domestic fights with enough seriousness.... I would like for the lawyers and the Sherriff's Department to be a little more sympathetic.
>
> (p. 9)

This response on the part of the legal system is not limited to rural areas. It is well known that many urban police officers ignore the plight of battered women and sexual assault survivors (Iovanni and Miller, 2001). Still, research such as that done by DeKeseredy and Schwartz (2009) and Websdale (1998) reveals that while there is a system of social practices that generally dominates and oppresses rural and urban women alike, it operates differently in rural areas. For example, people in urban communities often complain of feeling anonymous, victims of an uncaring mysterious policing system. In rural communities, violent men are more likely to be protected by an "ol' boys network" (Websdale, 1998). Many women know that the local police not only may be friends of their abusers, but also may refuse to arrest them on the grounds of this friendship (DeKeseredy and Joseph, 2006; Zorza, 2002). Critical scholarship in Australia also shows that the police are not likely to arrest men who abuse female intimates (Hogg and Carrington, 2006).

Within criminology, there is a rich history of observing police work (e.g., Manning, 1997; Skolnick, 1966). Still, until recently, mainstream and critical criminologists alike did not directly observe private policing or "parapolicing." George Rigakos (2002) notes in his book on this topic, "After an extensive literature review I could not locate a single published study of private police that examined the *doing* of security work from the perspective of line officers" (p. 3; emphasis in original). Informed by four bodies of knowledge (risk society, governmentality, Marxist analyses, and pluralist),[6] Rigakos conducted a first-hand ethnographic study of the Intelligarde International parapolice in Toronto,[7] one that addresses the importance of carefully examining the rapidly expanding nature of private policing and how variations of it (e.g., nightclub bouncers) are influenced by broader social forces, such as the capitalist political economy.

If policing is a major focus of critical criminologists, so are courts. New directions in critical research on this topic include Rothe and Mullins' (2006) work on the International Criminal Court (ICC), which also offers an integrated theoretical model of state crime originally developed by Kramer and Michalowski (see Kramer, Michalowski, and Kauzlarich, 2002). Feminists, too, are breaking new ground in court research. For example, Dragiewicz and DeKeseredy (2008) recently conducted a needs assessment and gap analysis for abused women unrepresented in the family law system that helped establish an empirical foundation for policy and programs that serve abused mothers in Ontario, Canada. Despite the frequency of anecdotal reports about problems with family law issues following separation and divorce and a growing awareness of problems for abused women in the family courts around custody, access, and child support, there is still little empirical research in Canada on the experiences of abused women who try to navigate the family law system without legal representation. As an exploratory study, Dragiewicz and DeKeseredy's study answered some important questions and raised many others that need to be addressed in much-needed further research on the topic.

Today, we are also witnessing a growth in feminist research on alternatives to the traditional court system, such as restorative justice in response to violence against women (Ptacek, 2010c). "Race matters" (West, 2001) and new feminist scholarship on restorative justice pays more than just lip service to this concern. For example, included in Ptacek's (2010c) anthology on restorative justice and violence against women are chapters that highlight the importance of carefully examining the implications of restorative justice in Aboriginal communities and in communities of color (e.g., Goel, 2010; Smith, 2010). Nonetheless, regardless of the area of criminal justice inquiry, much more research on the experiences of Asians and other ethnic minority groups is needed. Certainly, most of the critical scholarship produced so far on the relationship between race/ethnicity and legal systems focuses on the plight of blacks (Gabbidon and Greene, 2005), especially work done in the United States.

Critical criminologists, among others (e.g., some journalists), make it clear that there is no "freedom and justice for all" and that the primary targets of criminal justice attention are those at the bottom of the socioeconomic ladder (Lynch *et al.*, 2000; Reiman and Leighton, 2010). This is not to say, however, that the crimes socially and economically disenfranchised people commit are totally harmless. For example, many women are targets of brutal sexual and physical assaults committed by their current or former impoverished male partners (DeKeseredy, Alvi, Schwartz, and Tomaszewski, 2003; Renzetti and Maier, 2002). These and other crime victims (e.g., those harmed by "gay bashing") warrant much empirical, theoretical, and political attention. So does another group of victims that is "rarely in the limelight" (Radelet, 2005). These are, as Susan Sharp (2005) uncovered, the "hidden victims" of the death penalty in the United States. Her in-depth interviews with families of those facing a death sentence are not only innovative, but also reveal much pain and suffering that goes unnoticed.

As one interviewee described to Sharp, her mother was "terribly damaged" after her son's execution:

> It is ... difficult for me to see my mother suffer like she does. She goes to the cemetery often and sits for hours. Sometimes she won't take off her pajamas nor answer her phone. My brother's room is still like it was when he left.... She lives in guilt every day and she is beating herself up for it. She feels totally responsible and she is punishing herself. Her health is failing fast, and she is going to have a heart attack one of these days.
>
> (p. 103)

The death penalty, or the possibility of receiving it, is not the only criminal justice sanction that harms families. For example, in most impoverished urban neighborhoods in the United States, as many as 20 percent of adult males are incarcerated on any given day, and almost every family has a father, son, brother, or uncle who has been in a correctional facility (Clear, 2007). Critical research shows that families impacted by such mass incarceration experience many major problems. In the words of Travis and Waul (2003, pp. 1–2):

> To begin with, families impacted by incarceration are already typically at high risk along several dimensions. A parent's incarceration does not necessarily signal the onset of family and child development needs, but rather in most cases adds to the burdens of a family already struggling to overcome life's obstacles and setbacks. The incarceration of a family member may further exacerbate an environment already characterized by ongoing poverty, stress, and trauma.

Many neighborhoods, too, are also hidden victims of mass incarceration, especially inner-city slums populated primarily by African-Americans. The concentration of ex-convicts in poor communities not only precludes many of them from finding legitimate work because they are "marked" (Pager, 2007), but also harms the labor market prospects of others in the neighborhood, as well as affecting the voting patterns and election outcomes in some communities. Approximately one million Florida citizens are banned from voting for life because of a previous felony conviction, and 50 percent of them are African-American (Clear, 2007). Mass incarceration also increases the number of female-headed, single-parent families on welfare, which contributes to much stigmatization and isolation from conventional society (Browne, 1997; Clear, 2007; Wilson, 1996). Such research highlights the importance of bringing economic disadvantage and social exclusion back into public discussions and policies about crime (Vogel, 2007).

THE MEDIA[8]

Since its inception, critical criminology has attended to how the media contributes to crime, perceptions and meanings of crime, and to social control. Undeniably, in the words of cultural criminologists Ferrell *et al.* (2008), the study of crime and the media is a "well-trodden path" (p. 125). This is not to say, though, that media never change and that critical criminologists and other researchers do not adapt and respond to ongoing transformations, such as the creation of YouTube, Facebook, etc. As communications scholar Joseph Walther and his colleagues observed nearly 10 years ago,

> With the expansion of the Internet and new communications technologies, we are witnessing the diffusion of high-end, high bandwidth multimedia technology for a wide range of people. It is common for many computer-mediated communication (CMC) users to create multi-media World Wide Web sites with graphics and pictures.
>
> (p. 105)

This statement is still relevant and many such sites are beneficial to corporate executives, small business owners, educators, students, and to a myriad of other people eager to enhance their understanding of social, political, cultural, and economic factors that directly or indirectly influence their lives. However, critical scholars identify some highly injurious features of new information technologies, one of which is adult Internet pornography.

Today, we live in a "post-*Playboy* world" (Jensen, 2007), where defining adult pornography is still subject to much debate. Those who produce adult pornography, consume it, and/or oppose prohibiting it typically define harmful, sexually explicit material as erotica. However, there is a big difference between erotica and adult pornography. Erotica refers to "sexually suggestive or arousing material that is free of sexism, racism, and homophobia and is respectful of all human beings and animals portrayed" (Russell, 1993, p. 3). On the other hand, in adult pornography:

> Women are represented as passive and as slavishly dependent upon men. The role of female characters is limited to the provision of sexual services to men. To the extent that women's sexual pleasure is represented at all, it is subordinated to that of men and is never an end itself as is the sexual pleasure of men. What pleases men is the use of their bodies to satisfy male desires. While the sexual objectification of women is common to all pornography, in which women characters are killed, tortured, gang-raped, mutilated, bound, and otherwise abused, as a means of providing sexual stimulation or pleasure to the male characters.
>
> (Longino, 1980, p. 42)

Many women consume adult pornography, but it is created primarily for generating sexual arousal in heterosexual men (Jensen, 2007). From the standpoint of many feminist scholars (e.g., DeKeseredy, 2009b; Dworkin, 1994), pornography, regardless of whether it appears on the Internet, in stores, on television, in literature, or in other media, is also a variant of hate-motivated violence and it, too, has become "normalized" or "mainstreamed" in North America and elsewhere (Jensen and Dines, 1998), despite becoming increasingly more violent and racist (DeKeseredy, 2009b).

It is beyond the scope of this chapter to graphically describe what appears on contemporary pornographic Internet sites, but some brief examples of violence and racism are necessary. For instance, Doghouse Digital is a company that produced the film *Black Bros and White Ho's*, which offers stereotypical images of "the sexually primitive black male stud" (Jensen, 2007, p. 66).

Another example is the interracial film *Blacks on Blondes*, which features a white man in a cage watching black men have sex with his wife (Dines, 2006). An additional common feature of new pornographic films that exist online and elsewhere is painful anal penetration, as well as men slapping women and/or pulling their hair while they penetrate them orally, vaginally, and/or anally (Dines and Jensen, 2008a). Also, many pornographic Internet sites routinely depict black, Asian, Hispanic, and women from other social groups (e.g., those with disabilities) in hurtful ways.

Perhaps "normalized" is an understatement. Pornography is a giant industry and it is estimated that there are over one million pornography sites on the Internet, with as many as 10,000 added every week (Funk, 2006). Note, too, that worldwide pornography revenues from a variety of sources (e.g., Internet, hotel rooms, etc.) recently topped $97 billion. This is more than the revenues of these world-renowned technology companies combined: Microsoft, Google, Amazon, eBay, Yahoo!, Apple, Netflix, and Earthlink (Zerbisias, 2008). Another key point to consider is that rare are men who are not exposed to pornographic images and narratives on the Internet (DeKeseredy and Olsson, in press; Schwartz and DeKeseredy, 1997). Even if people go out of their way to avoid pornography, it frequently "pops up" on people's monitors while they are working or "surfing the web" for information that has nothing to do with sex (Dines and Jensen, 2008b).

To make matters worse, as noted above, contemporary critical criminological research shows that what men and boys watch on adult pornographic Internet sites are not simply "dirty pictures that have little impact on anyone." Rather, the images typically endorse "women as second-class citizens" and "require that women be seen as second-class citizens" (Funk, 2006, p. 165). Another challenge to the assertion that "pornography is just fantasy" are quantitative and qualitative data showing that pornography is strongly associated with various types of violence against women (DeKeseredy, in press a; Jensen, 2007), especially sexual assault. In addition, some studies found that the contribution of pornography to woman abuse in dating, marriage, and during or after separation/

divorce is related to male peer support (DeKeseredy and Schwartz, 2009). For example, many violent, patriarchal men often view pornography in all-male groups and share videos and other media electronically with a "wider circle of friends" via the Internet (DeKeseredy, in press a; Giordano, 1995).

Contemporary critical criminologists uncover misogyny and racism in other media, such as modern rap music (Weitzer and Kubrin, 2009). For Patricia Hill Collins (2000), rap is seen as one of the modern "controlling images" used to oppress black women, and Oliver (2006) asserts that rap's patriarchal or sexist lyrics "provide justifications for engaging in acts of violence against black women" (p. 927). However, Weitzer and Kubrin (2009) contend that such music is a method of controlling all women because it is consumed by a diverse range of youth. For cultural criminologists Ferrell *et al.* (2008), contemporary rap music also "embodies the evolving fusion of crime and consumerism, of transgression and popular art" (p. 139).

Race/ethnicity is an important factor for critical criminologists who study Western media representations of terrorism, which, not surprisingly, gained much attention after September 11, 2001. In-depth analyses of numerous fictional and nonfictional media accounts of events such as 9/11 reveal a "troubling absence of Muslim perspectives," while simultaneously perpetuating and legitimating racist stereotypes of Muslims (Chermak, Bailey, and Brown, 2003, p. 5; Strawson, 2003).

As well as studying how crime is "spun," another group of critical criminologists challenge racist, sexist, and other media-produced stereotypes of crime and criminals by disseminating their own interpretations and arguments through the media, an approach referred to as "newsmaking criminology" (Barak, 1988, 1995b). Since newspapers, television shows, web sites, and magazines reach large audiences, newsmaking criminologists assert that progressive scholars and activists should take every opportunity to offer their research and views to the media, creating a situation where they are "seen and heard, not after the fact, but proactively" (Renzetti, 1999, p. 1236). That articles and letters written by critical criminologists are periodically published by the mainstream press and that some critical scholars have been on television serves as evidence that the media do not totally dismiss or ignore struggles against patriarchal, capitalist, and racist oppression (Caringella-MacDonald and Humphries, 1998; DeKeseredy *et al.*, 2003).

Newsmaking criminology is often vaguely distasteful to academics socialized in an atmosphere of supposedly value-free positivism, even when they intellectually reject their training (Brownstein, 1991). Academics are frequently taught that their job is just to announce the facts, then stand back and allow the politicians and activists to debate and use these "facts" (Schwartz and DeKeseredy, 1997). Unfortunately, the world of understanding is largely a symbolic one where reality is constructed and negotiated (Goodwin, 1983). The struggle to define the "typical case," often called by sociologists *typification*, is an essential one. The group that is most successful in setting up the facts that are recognized in the minds of politicians and the general public as being examples of the problem is going to be the group most likely to have an effect upon the development of the solution (Best, 1990; Schwartz and DeKeseredy, 1993).

SUMMARY

Critical criminologists produce qualitative and quantitative scholarship accounting for both sides of the power equation: how crimes of the powerful are exempt from the purview of the law; and how the powerless become criminalized (DeKeseredy and Perry, 2006b). Similarly, critical criminologists offer rich data on various types of interpersonal violence and media representations of crime, law, and social control. As stated at the beginning of this chapter, these scholars also study topics outside the realm of criminology (e.g., Amish social life). The main objective of this chapter was to offer some recent examples of empirical criminological work done by progressive colleagues. Hopefully, this brief overview of contemporary research will help challenge the myth of critical criminology as simply a critique of mainstream contributions.

Contrary to what many people claim, critical criminologists do not outright reject quantitative methods. In fact, some left-wing scholars frequently use them. Further, many critical criminologists devote considerable time and effort to reading scholarship generated by mainstream scholars for several reasons, one of which is to determine if their empirical contributions have the potential to inform a more progressive understanding of social problems. Rarely, however, is critical research, regardless of whether it is quantitative or qualitative, cited in widely read and cited mainstream journals. Keep in mind the following observation made by David Kauzlarich (2006) in his Foreword to Rothe and Mullins' (2006, p. x) book, *Symbolic Gestures and the Generation of Global Social Control*:

> Hagan and Greer's (2002) article in *Criminology*, among the most prestigious journals in the field, examines the ebb and flow of international criminal justice as it pertains to war crimes and crime against humanity. The authors provide only one brief citation of critical criminological work on these subjects, ignoring the important work that Rothe and Mullins have thoroughly documented and expanded upon in Chapter 1 of this book. How the Hagan and Greer article was published in such a major journal without any attention to, to name a few, the work of Bill Chambliss (1989), Gregg Barak (1991), Ken Tunnell (1993), and Jeffrey Ian Ross (1995, 2000a, 2000b) can only be explained by author, editor, and reviewer unfamiliarity and/or indifference to the work of critical criminologists.

Some readers might add to Kauzlarich's commentary that critical criminology is sharply ridiculed by most mainstream researchers. Regardless of why progressive scholarship receives limited attention in traditional circles, it definitely has much to offer and reflects thoughtful attempts to advance a rigorous empirical understanding of social problems. Moreover, "mutual respect and supportiveness" are key characteristics of the critical criminological community (Friedrichs, 1996), which is a major reason there will be an explosion of new progressive scholarship on a broad range of topics in the coming decades.

4

CONFRONTING CRIME[1]

CRITICAL CRIMINOLOGICAL POLICIES

I am forced to conclude that the fundamental inhumanity of penal
confinement and the corresponding processes of "otherizing"
diminishes all human beings – whether they are female or male.

(Owen, 2005, p. 285)

As stated previously, the United States has shifted from a
"welfare state" to a "penal state" (Wacquant, 2001). So have
other countries, including Canada, a nation deemed by many
people around the world as much more progressive than the
United States. For example, staunch "law and order" advocate
and Progressive Conservative Member of Parliament Stephen
Harper was elected Prime Minister in 2006. Not coincidently,
Canada's incarceration rate increased for the first time in more
than a decade in 2005/2006. An average of 33,123 adults and
1,987 youths were then in custody, which was 3 percent more
than in 2004/2005 (Statistics Canada, 2007b). Imprisonment is
also racialized in Canada. While men of color constitute only
0.02 percent of Canada's population and 0.03 percent of the
province of Ontario's population, they account for more than 5
percent of the federal institution population and 11 percent of
Ontario's institution population (DeKeseredy, 2009a; Griffiths,
2007). Aboriginal people are also overrepresented in Canadian

penal institutions. Aboriginals account for only 2 percent of the adult Canadian population, but they represent 14 percent of federal inmates and 18 percent of their provincial/territorial counterparts (Terrill, 2007).

Chesney-Lind's (2007) commentary on the shift from welfare state to penal state in the United States is therefore also relevant to Canada: "Along with this shift, of course, comes public attitudes about crime issues and criminals that reinforce prison as a viable 'solution' to the many social problems associated with this nation's long struggle with racial justice and income inequality" (p. 212). Note that although the Canadian homicide rate dropped by 10 percent in 2006 compared to 2005 (Li, 2007), one of the Harper government's slogans at that time was "Serious Crime = Serious Time" and it passed the omnibus Tackling Violent Crime Act on February 28, 2008, parts of which "mimic failed US methods" (Travers, 2007), such as the "three-strikes, you're out" sentencing law.[2]

Twenty-six US states and the US federal government now have three-strikes laws. The Canadian federal government's push for similar legislation occurred at roughly the same time Toronto was designated as "Canada's poverty capital" (Monsebraaten and Daly, 2007). There, at that time, close to 30 percent of families (about 93,000 households raising children) lived in poverty, which was a 16 percent increase since 1990 (United Way of Greater Toronto, 2007). It is likely that a sizeable portion of Toronto's poor will soon end up in jail or prison in response to their use of drugs to cope with the daily life-events stress spawned by being socially and economically excluded.

Did the Tackling Violent Crime Act make a difference after it was passed in 2008? Yes, but not in the ways anticipated by proponents of getting "tough on crime." In 2008, there were 611 homicides in Canada, 17 more than in 2007. This constituted a 2 percent increase in the national murder rate. Furthermore, there were 200 homicides committed with a firearm during the same year, 12 more than in 2007. The rate of homicides committed with a firearm also increased by 24 percent since 2002 (Statistics Canada, 2009). These and similar findings support Currie's (2008a) claim that taking a more punitive approach to crime frequently results in higher levels of violence.

Would more progressive or more liberal leaders call for less punitive measures and help cure the "addiction to incarceration" that plagues the United States and other countries, such as the Russian Federation (Pratt, 2009)?[3] This question is partially answered in Chapter 1, but a more detailed response is warranted. Undeniably, there is no evidence of a rapidly growing penal abolition movement in the United States. For example, so-called liberal Bill Clinton did not let the Republicans "out-tough him on crime" when he ran for president in the United States in 1992 (Chesney-Lind, 2007, p. 212). He interrupted his New Hampshire campaign to preside over the execution of mentally disabled Rickey Ray Rector in Arkansas (Sherrill, 2001). North of the US border, in fall 2007, Stephan Dion, then Canadian Liberal Leader of the Official Opposition, also did not want to be "out-toughed on crime" (DeKeseredy, 2009b). The minority government led by Stephen Harper could have easily fallen had Dion called for a parliamentary nonconfidence vote on the Tackling Violent Crime Act. However, he lacked confidence about going into a fall 2007 election and did not want to "trigger one by defeating the populist law-and-order agenda of the Conservatives" (Hebert, 2007, p. A17).

Although very popular among liberal circles, US President Barak Obama doesn't appear to have reducing the incarceration rate and/or eliminating the death penalty on his list of priorities for similar reasons. Perhaps, too, like many people raised in the United States, he grew up in a conservative political economic climate which precludes him from seeing any alternatives to the crime problem beyond the punitive status quo (Chesney-Lind, 2007). It also appears that universities and colleges are not doing much to encourage criminal justice students to think more critically about crime. For example, research done at several US institutions of higher learning reveals that criminal justice students were "more punitive in their attitudes toward crime, criminals, and the criminal justice system" (Courtright, MacKey, and Packard, 2005, p. 140).

So, what is to be done? An obvious, but simplistic, critical criminological answer to this question is radical social, political, and economic change, such as a transition from a capitalist, patriarchal society to one that is socialist and feminist. True, outrageous problems often require outrageous solutions (Gibbons, 1995), but few critical criminologists believe that truly fundamental changes will occur soon in the United States, Canada, and other countries with a similar political economic order. In fact, there is ample evidence that many parts of the world are "moving in precisely the wrong directions" if the goal is to curb violence and other serious crimes (Currie, 2008a, p. 112). As briefly mentioned in Chapter 2, unbridled, "laissez-faire" economic policies are aggressively implemented in North America and elsewhere. As Currie (2008a, pp. 112–113) observes:

> The social arrangements that are characteristic of the most dangerous societies are now, in many places, being enshrined as fundamental virtues: the tolerance of great inequality in the name of economic growth; a willingness to let individuals and families fall into extreme deprivation in the name of encouraging "personal responsibility"; a willingness to leave people's well-being up to the fluctuations of the job market; the shrinking of public supports for the vulnerable in the name of boosting self-reliance and ending dependency.

There is substantial empirical support for Currie's claim. Yet, bigger gaps between the rich and poor, a rabid anti-feminist backlash, government-supported assaults on affirmative action programs, and the like do not weaken critical criminologists' resolve. They continue to propose progressive short-term strategies that chip away at the forces that motivate people to commit crime and that buttress unequal justice. Of course, thousands of alternatives to the status quo could be listed but will not be. Moreover, many readers will notice that conspicuously absent from this chapter are in-depth accounts of how initiatives such as progressive criminal justice reforms, job creation and training, a higher minimum wage, state-sponsored child care, and housing assistance help curb crime. These important strategies are briefly discussed here, but they are not new suggestions and have been covered at length in previous critical criminological books. The main objective of this chapter is not to repeat in detail what has already been proposed, but rather to supplement these suggestions with more contemporary initiatives. The key, though, is to recognize that we must take on these tasks. As Irwin and Austin (1994, p. 167) pointed out nearly 20 years ago:

> Reducing crime means addressing those factors that are more directly related to crime. This means reducing teenage pregnancies, high school dropout rates, unemployment, drug abuse, and lack of meaningful job opportunities. Although many will differ on how to address these factors, the first step is to acknowledge that these forces have far more to do with reducing crime than escalating the use of imprisonment.

CRIMINAL JUSTICE REFORMS

Critical criminologists propose many progressive criminal justice reforms, ranging from democratic accountability of the police (Kinsey, Lea, and Young, 1986), to legalizing the production and sale of "illicit drugs" (Reiman and Leighton, 2010), to stricter legislation aimed at reducing corporate crime. A more recent concern for some scholars who study interpersonal violence is the criminal justice system's response to ice hockey violence (DeKeseredy, in press a), especially the types that occur during National Hockey League games in North America. One widely publicized event that still remains in the minds of many professional hockey fans is former Vancouver Canucks player Todd Bertuzzi's vicious attack on former Colorado Avalanche player Steve Moore on March 8, 2004. From behind, Bertuzzi grabbed Moore's jersey and punched him in the side of his head (an attack that is readily available on the video-sharing website YouTube). Following this assault, several members of both teams, including Bertuzzi, jumped on Moore. Moore suffered major injuries and will never play professional hockey again. Should those who commit acts like Bertuzzi's be labeled violent criminals? Or, are their potentially lethal behaviors "just part of the game"? Many people obviously agree with this statement because Bertuzzi received no criminal record from this incident and went on to play for Team Canada in the 2006 Winter Olympics.

Only a small number of cases such as the assault on Steve Moore have resulted in litigation. Thus, it is fair to conclude that despite the life-threatening nature of some "punch-ups," many people see nothing wrong with "hockey fisticuffs" (Smith, 1983). On the other hand, a growing number of critical criminologists are teaming up with nonprofit organizations (e.g., Canadian Paraplegic Association Ontario) and journalists to demand that the justice system help end hockey violence. As is the case with corporate crime, professional hockey players' crimes on the ice should be responded to as vigorously as predatory street crime. If not, in the words of Toronto sports journalist Dave Perkins (2010, p. S4), "it won't be long now until a hockey player dies on the ice from a stupid and vicious head hit, the kind that show no signs of ceasing any time soon as the game's higher levels."

Some critical criminologists also call for the criminalization of another form of violence that is exempt from prosecution in most countries – the spanking of children. Spanking is the most universal type of physical violence (DeKeseredy, 2009c), but it is illegal in Sweden, Finland, Denmark, Norway, and Austria (Alvarez and Bachman, 2008). There are sound reasons for strictly prohibiting it. For example, spanking is strongly associated with other forms of violence, such as bullying and violence against women in adult intimate relationships (Payne and Gainey, 2006). Further, spanking and other frequent types of physical punishment (e.g., slapping), teach children these four lessons:

- Love is associated with violence, and those who love you also have the right to hurt you.
- Physical punishment is used to train the child, which establishes the moral rightness of hitting other family members.
- When something is really important, it justifies the use of physical force.
- When one is under stress, tense, or angry, hitting is understandable and, to a certain extent, legitimate (Johnson, 1996, p. 5).

Violent and other hurtful acts are also committed by states or governments, and some key examples were given in Chapter 3 (e.g., military personnel torturing prisoners). Thus, Rothe and Mullins (2006) call for legal reforms such as enhancing the jurisdiction of the International Criminal Court (ICC) to address crimes committed by governments and transnational corporations, as well as individuals. Furthermore, two of the major crimes they assert should be covered are state terrorism and "unilateral war mongering" (p. 113). Certainly, much more attention should be devoted to such harms, and Rothe and Mullins, among others (e.g., Friedrichs, 2007), remind us that critical criminological policies should be aimed at both crimes "at the top" and "crimes at the bottom."

FULL AND QUALITY EMPLOYMENT

In North America and other parts of the world once known for being manufacturing strongholds (e.g., Ontario, Canada), work is rapidly disappearing because of factors such as outsourcing of jobs to developing countries and the implementation of new technologies in the workplace. This is also a constant right-wing "race to deunionize" (Massey, 2007), as well as other major economic shifts that simultaneously increase unemployment rates and reduce the number of quality full-time jobs. These are not simply economic issues, because getting and holding a steady job reduces the risk of people committing crime. In fact, a high level of stable employment is one of the main reasons there was a major decline in US crime rates in the 1990s (Currie, 2008a). On the other hand, without meaningful and stable work, people are more prone to committing crimes for reasons outlined by left realists (e.g., relative deprivation) or to survive. For example, thefts and frauds committed by North American women tend to focus on meeting their economic needs or those of their families (Barker, 2009).

The great shortage of both jobs and quality employment not only influences many disenfranchised people to commit street crimes, but can also keep them from escaping being crime victims. For instance, although most battered women do leave their abusers (DeKeseredy and Schwartz, 2009), many unemployed women cannot leave right away because they do not have the money to house and feed themselves and their children (Raphael, 2009).

Some critical criminologists suggest specific ways to deal with these problems. Michalowski (1983), for example, proposed several policies aimed at reducing street crime that place financial burdens on industry rather than on taxpayers. They include:

- tax surcharges on industries attempting to close plants or permanently reduce a community's work force;
- government laws requiring retraining and job placement for all workers displaced by new technology;
- a minimum wage level that is approximately 50 percent higher than the poverty level.

(pp. 14–18)

As we progress through this new millennium, these and somewhat similar initiatives continue to be suggested by an international body of critical criminologists. The problem, and the most discouraging aspect of making such recommendations, is not that political and corporate elites are uncaring or neglectful in their failure to invest in decent, full-time employment. Rather, especially in the United States, they aggressively oppose such policies, even when they are confronted with evidence that these and similar strategies work. Conservative politicians and corporations resist job creation and training initiatives because they do not want to lose the financial gains they have made under the current system (Barak, 1986). In other words, it isn't so much economic obstacles as ideological ones that account for the failure to mount a massive campaign to expand and upgrade the labor force.

HIGHER MINIMUM WAGE

Many countries, such as the United States, have social policies that coerce people into low-paying, "dead end jobs" to help lower embarrassing official unemployment rates (Currie, 2008a). Since many of the "working poor" are not making a decent wage, it is amazing how they survive in the face of being "nickel and dimed" (Ehrenreich, 2001). Hence, rather than continue down the worn path of reminding the working poor that "they are lucky to have a job," the minimum wage should be raised, which increases people's standard of living and reduces crime. For example, when a server in a fast-food restaurant works for a pay check that precludes him or her from eating properly so that the customer can eat more cheaply, this person will experience alienation, social exclusion, and relative deprivation (DeKeseredy, Alvi, Schwartz, and Tomaszewski, 2003), which are major correlates of crimes committed by disenfranchised people (Young, 1999). Moreover, low wages enable those involved in illegal work (e.g., drug dealing) to easily recruit new "employees" (Currie, 1993). For people "systematically deprived of access to avenues of success, how can the 'honest job' of dishwashing compete with the easy money obtained through dishonest behavior"? (Pfohl, 1994, p. 264).

SOCIAL SERVICES AND PROGRAMS

Conservative criminologists such as James Q. Wilson (1985) take much delight in pointing out that state-sponsored social services provided in the 1960s failed to reduce the crime rate in the United States and other capitalist nations. This is because most of the policies of the 1960s were not sensitive to the powerful influences of the political economy, community, and family. For example, in the United States, large numbers of youths were trained in the Job Corps for jobs that did not exist. However, few attempts were made to deal with the structural disintegration of troubled individuals' familial and neighborhood environments (Currie, 1985). It is not surprising that the failure of government-funded social programs was successfully exploited by conservative politicians to gain popular support for a policy of reducing social spending (DeKeseredy and Schwartz, 1996).

At the time of writing this book, conservative politicians are still cutting social programs and services, but claim that this agenda is designed to reduce government debt. As Canadian Prime Minister Stephen Harper stated on January 19, 2010, "As our recovery program comes to an end and we prepare to bring down the deficit once the economy has begun to grow again, it is essential that the government limit public spending" (cited in Whittington and Campion-Smith, 2010, p. A6). The trend in government today, as it was in the past two decades, supported by the media and by more and more voters, is to cut social services because we can't afford them, but at the same time dramatically increase spending on prisons. Much of the reason that many people support these notions is because they assume that the policies will not affect them; they will mainly affect visible minorities, such as African-Americans.

Stephen Harper and politicians with similar beliefs help fuel what Currie (2008a, p. 111) refers to as a "*culture of disregard*, in which people feel little sense of responsibility or solidarity toward others and a 'me-first' ethic of personal gain often dominates public life." The reality is, though, that services such as early-childhood education, effective parenting training, prenatal care, affordable housing, and remedial education are worthwhile and help curb crime (Currie, 1985; DeKeseredy *et al.*, 2003). However, can those who participate in these programs be guaranteed financial security after they complete them (Currie, 1992)? History reveals that the answer to this question is an emphatic "no." For example, what is the point of going back to school or participating in job training if there is no chance of getting a job? To avoid repeating the mistakes of the 1960s, then, social programs and services must be accompanied by the elimination of unemployment and sub-employment.

USING NEW TECHNOLOGIES

Taylor, Walton, and Young's (1973) *The New Criminology* raised questions about the role that progressive scholars should play in the broader arena of political activism (Walton, 1998). Certainly, there are many political actions that do not cost much time, effort, and money. One example is using new computer technologies such as Facebook. For example, as of January 20, 2010, nearly 200,000 Canadians signed a Facebook petition protesting Prime Minister Harper's prorogation of Parliament on December 30, 2009. The Canadian legislature was originally set to reconvene on January 25, 2010, but Harper delayed the return until March 3, 2010. This prorogation eliminates bills tabled at the previous parliamentary session, including some related to important environmental and pension issues (Werbowski, 2010). Prorogation also shut down a public inquiry about the Harper government's knowledge of the torture of detainees handed over to Afghan forces by the Canadian military.

Social networking websites make a difference. Two weeks after the creation of the above petition, the Harper government's lead over the Liberal Party fell to only 1 percent (Hebert, 2010). This is strong evidence that new technologies are effectively used to mobilize large numbers of people to demand government accountability and to challenge attempts to cover up state crime and other state wrongdoings. Further, progressive Facebook initiatives are examples of reinvigorated civic engagement that are also being used to digitally protest white supremacy online (Daniels, 2009). Contrary to what many people claim, social networking sites are now key arenas of political struggle. As University of Bergen scholar Jill Walker Rettberg (2009, p. 1) observes:

> Obviously people find it easier to join a Facebook group to make a political point than to march the streets. Perhaps it's actually more effective, too. Right now, it's entirely possible that you get more press, and thus more national notice for a Facebook group with 2000 members than a demonstration of 500 people. And it's a *lot* easier to get 2000 people to join a Facebook group than to get 500 people to show up at a particular time and place with banners.

Using Facebook to help achieve social justice is a contemporary technique of newsmaking criminology that attracts more and more people each day. So are blogging and other new means of exchanging information. Communication is vital, and if Facebook, Twitter, etc. enable more people to become aware of various injustices, more people will voice their discontent with the prevailing inequitable status quo by electing politicians committed to a more progressive way of dealing with social problems such as crime. At the very least, such newsmaking criminology makes the issues covered in this book and in other sources very visible to the public in the same way that the above Canadian Facebook petition raised considerable public awareness about the problems related to the prorogation of Parliament.

BOYCOTTING HARMFUL COMPANIES[4]

Many companies are criminogenic and corporate crime is far more economically, physically, socially, and environmentally injurious than street crime (Reiman and Leighton, 2010). Further, corporations, such as satellite and cable companies, generate much profit from broadcasting hurtful pornographic images of men and women. Although formal agents of social control are quick to punitively respond to producers and consumers of "child porn," there is no reason to believe that government officials in a capitalist society are going to launch a "war on corporate crime" or adult pornographic television channels or videos in the near future. We seldom hear cries for "three strikes and you're out" in relation to corporate crime. In fact, some evidence suggests that governments around the world are making it easier for corporations to threaten our well-being.

Profit is a corporation's "bottom line." Thus, many people call for boycotting products and services offered by criminogenic companies or those that profit from legal means of causing harm, such as pornographic video stores. Boycotting has a long history and is not a contemporary critical criminological approach. Nevertheless, scholars and activists are using new means of boycotting. For example, since violent and racist pornography are "normalized," "mainstreamed," and easily accessible (Jensen and Dines, 1998), some feminist men's groups, such as the Minnesota Men's Action Network: Alliance to Prevent Sexual and Domestic Violence, participate in variations of the Clean Hotel Initiative.[5] This involves encouraging businesses, government agencies, private companies, and so on to only hold conferences and meetings in hotels that do not offer in-room adult pay-per-view pornography. Further, new groups of men and women join hands to collectively expose and criticize injurious media coverage of woman abuse (e.g., wife beating) and to boycott companies that profit from pornography. Robert Jensen (2007, p. 182) is right to state that "it's not enough for us to change our personal behavior. That's a bare minimum. Such change must be followed by participation in movements to change the unjust structure and the underlying ideology that supports them."

Such efforts make a difference because of their financial impact, but they are also accused of promoting censorship. Therefore, in efforts to formally and informally sensitize people to the harmful nature of pornography, such as boycotts, a few critical criminologists suggest that anti-pornography educators and activists should respond to claims of censorship by stating that there are many types of harmful films that cannot be found in hotels, video stores, and other places, mostly because they do not exist (DeKeseredy, in press a; DeKeseredy and Schwartz, 1998). Rather than constituting outright censorship, citizens of many countries manage to express their disgust and dismay at even the slight hint of harm to animals in motion pictures. Where the plot line requires an animal to be fictionally hurt (e.g., a great white shark eating a swimming dog),[6] Hollywood producers find it essential to report in the credits that their set was inspected and monitored by animal-rights organizations. Even then, however, there are virtually no movies that show animals burned, dismembered, stabbed or shot to death, electrocuted, beaten or kicked, or raped. These images are saved for stories about men and women.

Similarly, it is important to mention to those making claims about censorship that there are no movies available showing, in an approving manner, the mass execution of Jews, gypsies, and the mentally ill by the German Nazis in World War II. There are also no pro-slavery movies showing approvingly how white people need to beat, starve, and torture African slaves to get them to behave "properly." This is because people show a very high intolerance for movies of this nature being publicly available. Why is it that there are very firm reactions against seeing a dog raped, but it is found to be appropriate, or at least a free speech issue, to allow films approvingly showing women being beaten and gang raped by a group of men? Thus, there is a major point to be made to those who accuse opponents of pornography to be "pro-censorship": rather than calling for censorship, anti-porn activists argue that in a better society, it would be considered morally reprehensible to show or attend certain types of films, just as it is now for non-documentary films about animal torture, pro-slavery violence, or Nazi killings (DeKeseredy, in press a; DeKeseredy and Schwartz, 1998).

CREATING A CULTURE OF SUPPORT[7]

Currie (2004) identifies modern social Darwinist culture as a key determinant of many middle-class teenagers' troubles. What is to be done? He suggests progressive ways of developing a "culture of support," such as inclusive schools and offering troubled teenagers welcoming places to go when they leave or are thrown out of their homes. Currie's policy proposals make many people uncomfortable, given the extreme punitiveness of the United States. However, there is considerable support for these strategies. For example, Crespo's (1987) study of skipping school suggests that authorities would be more successful in preventing continued skipping and in reducing drop-out rates if stigmatizing, segregative measures were replaced by reintegrative ones. These could include positive recognition and acceptance of skippers when they do attend classes, pairing regular and conscientious attendees with skippers on school projects, support and reward of the participation of skippers in school activities they do enjoy (e.g., sports and music), and making the curriculum more relevant to the interests and capacities of skippers.

These approaches are examples of what Currie refers to as "inclusive discipline, in which the first priority is to understand why a student is having trouble and in which throwing kids out is the last resort, not the first" (p. 269). If school authorities base their reactions to student's troubles on an understanding of the causes, they may help de-amplify, or at least not amplify, students' use of drugs and involvement in other dangerous activities (DeKeseredy, Ellis, and Alvi, 2005). For example, Jarjoura (1993) found that skipping and dropping out are not in themselves predictors of troublemaking. Rather, the reasons for doing these things are more reliable predictors of delinquency. Hence, students who skip or drop out of school to help their parents or because of the problems at home are as conformist as students who graduate from high school. On the other hand, students who are expelled or who drop out for personal reasons having to do with marriage or pregnancy, or who leave school because of failing grades, are more likely to be delinquent than high-school graduates. Reasons, then, mediate the relationship between skipping or dropping out and delinquency.

SUMMARY

Critical criminologists' paramount concern is eliminating inequality in all realms of society. To do so, they struggle for fundamental social, political, and economic change, and advance short-term progressive policies. The main objective of this chapter was to discuss some contemporary critical criminological initiatives. Most of these proposals stem, in part, from the proposition that the criminal justice system is only one part of society and cannot be responsible all by itself for cleaning up the messes left by broader social forces (Currie, 1985). Throughout this book, it is repeatedly argued that social structural problems cause various types of crime and contribute to problematic and often destructive societal reactions to violations of legal norms.

There are, of course, many more initiatives that could be listed here and have been by others. The goal is for progressives from all walks of life to work closely together to promote the creation and maintenance of peaceful and equitable societies. Unfortunately, in the light of growing joblessness, massive cuts to social services, and other economic factors, "[t]he struggle to keep people focused on pushing for the necessary structural change is going to be more difficult" (Denham and Gillespie, 1999, p. 47). Nevertheless, if critical criminologists and other groups with similar goals do not stay focused and repeatedly promote progressive policies, many families, countries, and communities will continue to suffer from crime, social injustice, and a myriad of other major social problems. Perhaps, then, one of the best ways to conclude this chapter is to quote a section of Currie's (2008a, p. 117) commentary on the future of violence:

> The choice is stark and simple: We can either let that process continue and fortify ourselves against it, with more gated communities and more prisons, or we can decide that it is not tolerable and work to change it. What we cannot do is pretend that we don't know it's happening.

NOTES

1 Critical criminology: definition and brief history

1 Employment insurance (EI) offers temporary income for unemployed Canadians while they seek a job or try to upgrade their skills. EI also assists Canadians who are sick, pregnant, or who look after newborn or adopted children, as well as those who must care for a seriously ill family member at risk of dying (Service Canada, 2009).

2 Milton Friedman was born on July 31, 1912 and died on November 16, 2006. His (1962) book, *Capitalism and Freedom*, had a major impact on advocates of conservative and neo-conservative policies.

3 With the help of progressive organizations such as Legal Momentum, the American Civil Liberties Union, and the American Association of University Women, the plaintiffs appealed the dismissal and it was overturned in September 2007 (Fleury-Steiner and Miller, 2008; Simpson *v*. University of Colorado, Boulder, 2007). After that, the case was settled for approximately US$3 million, and the University of Colorado appointed an independent adviser on Title IX, sexual harassment, and sexual assault (Burnett and Vaughn, 2007).

4 This section includes revised versions of work published previously by DeKeseredy and Schwartz (1991a).

5 Administrative criminologists are often called right realists for their work in helping the state to administer the criminal justice system. James Q. Wilson in the United States and Ron Clarke, who did most of his work in the United Kingdom are two of the best-known administrative criminologists. Because their views tend to coincide more with the views of politicians, administrative criminologists have had a much greater impact on US and Canadian criminal justice policies than any other type of criminologist.

6 Some of the articles that appear in this issue were reprinted in James Incidari's (1980) controversial anthology, *Radical Criminology: The Coming Crises*.

7 This section includes modified sections of work published previously by DeKeseredy and Perry (2006a) and DeKeseredy and Schwartz (1996).

8 This sentence is derived from the title of MacLean and Milovanovic's (1997b) anthology, *Thinking Critically About Crime*.

2 Contemporary critical criminological schools of thought

1 As stated in Chapter 1, James Q. Wilson is an administrative criminologist and author of the widely read and cited conservative text, *Thinking About Crime* (1985).

2 This section includes revised versions of work published previously by DeKeseredy and Schwartz (1996, 2009).

3 Conducted in 1965, the Richmond Youth Project is a self-report survey of 4,075 Richmond, California high-school students.

4 A husband is exempt in these states if his wife is mentally ill or physically impaired, unconscious, asleep, or unable to consent (Bergen, 2006).

5 However, in all cases of wife beating where reasonable and probable grounds exist, charges are still not typical (DeKeseredy and Schwartz, 2009).

6 For example, see Messerschmidt (1993), Miller (1994), and Renzetti (1994).

7 For example, in the United States, between 50 percent and 90 percent of battered women try to leave abusive relationships (Block, 2003; DeKeseredy and Schwartz, 2009; Stark, 2007).

8 Parts of this section include revised sections of work published previously by DeKeseredy and Schwartz (2005a) and Schwartz and DeKeseredy (1997).

9 For example, evolutionary psychologists argue that male violence is the result of competition for sexual access to women. However, men kill not only men, but also women. See DeKeseredy and Schwartz (2005a), Kimmel (2000), and Polk (2003) for more criticisms of the evolutionary theory of male violence.

10 This section includes modified sections of work published previously by DeKeseredy (2007), DeKeseredy *et al.* (2006) and DeKeseredy and Schwartz (in press).

11 This section includes revised sections of work published previously by DeKeseredy and Schwartz (1996).

12 See Pepinsky and Quinney's (1991) edited book for essays giving more detailed descriptions of peacemaking criminology's intellectual, spiritual, philosophical, and political roots.

13 See Ptacek's (2010c) collection of essays on restorative justice and violence against women for more in-depth information on such feminist controversies.

14 This section includes modified sections of work published previously by DeKeseredy and Schwartz (1996).

15 Arguably, of all the European postmodern theorists, Michel Foucault has received the most attention in criminological circles. His (1977) book, *Discipline and Punish*, was especially influential (Schwartz and Friedrichs, 1994).

16 See, for example, his (2006) chapter in DeKeseredy and Perry's (2006c) anthology, *Advancing Critical Criminology*.

17 Presdee's (2000) *Cultural Criminology and the Carnival of Crime* is essential reading for those seeking a richer understanding of cultural criminology. The same can be said of Ferrell *et al.*'s (2008) book, *Cultural Criminology: An Invitation*.

18 This section includes modified sections of work published previously by DeKeseredy and Schwartz (in press).

3 Contemporary critical criminological research

1 See, for example, Donnermeyer, Kreps, and Kreps (1999) and Kreps, Donnermeyer, and Kreps (1997).

2 Edgework is defined as "acts of extreme voluntary risk taking" (Ferrell *et al.*, 2008, p. 72). Rather than being self-destructive, edgework is a means of reacting against the "unidentifiable forces that rob one of individual choice" (Lyng, 1990, p. 870).

3 This section includes slightly modified parts of work published previously by Donnermeyer and DeKeseredy (2008).

4 See, for example, his (1985) seminal book, *Confronting Crime: An American Challenge*.

5 This is the title of Frank Pearce's (1976) pathbreaking Marxist analysis of corporate and organized crime.

6 See Rigakos (2002, p. 5) for sources on these schools of thought.

7 Intelligarde International is a private law-enforcement company founded by Ross MacLeod who first developed the concept of parapolice.

8 This section includes modified sections of work published previously by DeKeseredy and Olsson (in press).

4 Confronting crime: critical criminological policies

1 This chapter includes modified sections of work published previously by DeKeseredy (2009a) and DeKeseredy and Schwartz (1996).

2 The Tackling Violent Crime Act includes the following revisions to the Canadian *Criminal Code*: automatically refusing bail to people charged with gun crimes; making it easier for police to charge people driving under the influence of drugs; raising the legal age of sexual consent to 16 from 14; making it easier to prosecute and indefinitely incarcerate "dangerous offenders" after three convictions for serious crimes; and mandatory minimum prison sentences for drug dealers.

3 The Russian Federation had the second highest incarceration rate in the world and the United States had the highest rate (700 per 100,000 population (Currie, 2008a; International Centre for Prison Studies, 2007)).

4 This section includes modified portions of work published previously by DeKeseredy (in press a) and DeKeseredy and Schwartz (1998).
5 For more information on the Clean Hotel Initiative, go to www.menaspeacemakers.org/programs/mnman/hotels.
6 See, for example, the 1975 Hollywood movie, *Jaws*.
7 This section includes revised sections of work published previously by DeKeseredy (2007) and DeKeseredy *et al.* (2005).

REFERENCES

Adler, P.A., and Adler, P. (Eds). (2003). *Constructions of deviance: Social power, context, and interaction* (4th ed.). Belmont, CA: Wadsworth.

Akers, R.L. (1997). *Criminological theories: Introduction and evaluation* (2nd ed.). Los Angeles, CA: Roxbury.

Akers, R.L., and Sellers, C.S. (2004). *Criminological theories: Introduction, evaluation, and application* (4th ed.). Los Angeles, CA: Roxbury.

Alvarez, A., and Bachman, R. (2008). *Violence: The enduring problem.* Thousand Oaks, CA: Sage.

Alvi, S., DeKeseredy, W.S., and Ellis, D. (2000). *Contemporary social problems in North American society.* Toronto, ON: Addison Wesley Longman.

Anderson, E. (2008). 'Against the wall: Poor, young, black, and male.' In E. Anderson (Ed.), *Against the wall: Poor, young, black, and male* (pp. 1–27). Philadelphia, PA: University of Pennsylvania Press.

Andrews, D.A., and Bonta, J. (2006). *The psychology of criminal conduct* (4th ed.). Cincinnati, OH: LexisNexis.

Arrigo, B.A. (2003). 'Postmodern justice and critical criminology: Positional, relational, and provisional justice.' In M.D. Schwartz and S.E. Hatty (Eds.), *Controversies in critical criminology* (pp. 43–56). Cincinnati, ON: Anderson Publishing.

Austin, J., and Coventry, G. (2001). *Emerging issues on privatized prisons.* Washington, DC: National Institute of Justice.

Barak, G. (1986). 'Is America really ready for the Currie challenge?' *Crime and Social Justice, 25,* 200–203.

Barak, G. (1988). 'Newsmaking criminology: Reflections on the media, intellectuals, and crime.' *Justice Quarterly, 5,* 565–588.

Barak, G. (Ed.). (1991). *Crimes by the capitalist state: An introduction to state criminality.* Albany, NY: SUNY Press.

Barak, G. (1995a). 'Time for an integrated criminology.' *The Critical Criminologist, 7,* 3–6.

Barak, G. (Ed.). (1995b). *Media, process, and the social construction of crime: Studies in newsmaking criminology.* New York, NY: Garland.

Barker, J. (2009). 'A "typical" female offender.' In J. Barker (Ed.), *Women and the criminal justice system: A Canadian perspective* (pp. 63–88). Toronto, ON: Emond Montgomery.

Barrett, M. (1985). *Women's oppression today: Problems in Marxist feminist analysis*. London: Verso.

Barrett, M., and McIntosh, M. (1982). *The anti-social family*. London: Verso.

Basran, G.S., Gill, C., and MacLean, B.D. (1995). *Farmworkers and their children*. Vancouver, BC: Collective Press.

Becker, H.S. (1967). 'Whose side are we on?' *Social Problems, 14*, 239–247.

Becker, H.S. (1973). *Outsiders: Studies in the sociology of deviance*. New York: Free Press.

Bergen, R.K. (2006). 'Marital rape: New research and directions.' *VAWnet*, February, 1–13.

Belknap, J. (2005, November). 'What I saw at the Title IX revolution: University charged as a rape training institution.' Paper presented at the American Society of Criminology meetings, Toronto, Canada.

Best, J. (1990). *Threatened children: Rhetoric and concern about child victims*. Chicago, IL: University of Chicago Press.

Blau, J., and Blau, P. (1982). 'The cost of inequality: Metropolitan structure and violent crime.' *American Sociological Review, 47*, 114–129.

Block, C.R. (2003). 'How can practitioners help an abused woman lower her risk of death.' *NIJ Journal, 250*, 4–7.

Boehringer, G., Brown, D., Edgeworth, B., Hogg, R., and Ramsey, I. (1983). 'Law and order for progressives? An Australian response.' *Crime and Social Justice, 25*, 200–203.

Bourgois, P. (1995). *In search of respect: Selling crack in El Barrio*. New York, NY: Cambridge University Press.

Bowker, L. (1983). *Beating wife beating*. Lexington, MA: Lexington Books.

Box, S. (1983). *Power, crime and mystification*. London: Tavistock.

Braithwaite, J. (1984). *Corporate crime in the pharmaceutical industry*. London: Routledge and Kegan Paul.

Browne, I. (1997). 'The black–white gap in labor force participation among women.' *American Sociological Review, 62*, 236–252.

Brownstein, H. (1991). 'The social construction of public policy.' *Sociological Practice Review, 2*, 132–140.

Bureau of Labor Statistics. (2009). 'Summer youth labor force release.' Washington, DC: US Department of Labor.

Burnett, S., and Vaughn, K. (2007, December 6). 'CU makes $2.85M vow for change: Barnett responds.' *Rocky Mountain News*.

Retrieved May 23, 2008, from www.rockymountainnews.com/news/2007/dec/06/sex-assault-suit-settled.

Caputo, G.A. (2008). *Out in the storm: Drug-addicted women living as shoplifters and sex workers.* Boston, MA: Northeastern University Press.

Carastathis, A. (2006, October 11). 'New cuts and conditions for Status of Women Canada.' *Toronto Star.* Retrieved October 11, 2006, from www.dominionpaper.ca/canadian_news/2006/10/11new_cuts_a.html.

Caringella-MacDonald, S., and Humphries, D. (1998). 'Guest editors' introduction.' *Violence Against Women, 4,* 3–9.

Carrington, K., and Hogg, R. (2008). 'Critical criminologies: An introduction.' In K. Carrington and R. Hogg (Eds), *Critical criminology: Issues, debates, challenges* (pp. 1–12). Portland, OR: Willan.

Chakraborti, N., and Garland, J. (Eds). (2004). *Rural racism.* Portland, OR: Willan.

Chambliss, W. (1975). 'Toward a political economy of crime.' *Theory and Society,* Summer, 167–180.

Chambliss, W. (1986). 'On lawmaking.' In S. Brickey and E. Comack (Eds), *The social basis of law: Critical readings in the sociology of law* (pp. 27–51). Toronto, ON: Garamond.

Chambliss, W., and Seidman, R. (1982). *Law, order, and power* (2nd ed.). Reading, MA: Addison-Wesley.

Chermak, S., Bailey, F.Y., and Brown, M. (2003). 'Introduction.' In S. Chermak, F.Y. Bailey, and M. Brown (Eds), *Media representations of September 11* (pp. 1–14). Westport, CT: Praeger.

Chesney-Lind, M. (2001). 'Girls, violence and delinquency.' In S.O. White (Ed.), *Handbook of youth and justice* (pp. 135–158). New York, NY: Kluwer Academic/Plenum.

Chesney-Lind, M. (2007). 'Epilogue: Criminal justice, gender and diversity – A call for passion and public criminology.' In S.L. Miller (Ed.), *Criminal justice research and practice: Diverse voices in the field* (pp. 210–220). Boston, MA: Northeastern University Press.

Chesney-Lind, M., and Irwin, K. (2008). *Beyond bad girls: Gender, violence and hype.* New York, NY: Routledge.

Chesney-Lind, M., and Pasko, L. (2004). *The female offender: Girls, women, and crime* (2nd ed.). Thousand Oaks, CA: Sage.

Clear, T.R. (2007). *Imprisoning communities: How mass incarceration makes disadvantaged neighborhoods worse.* New York, NY: Oxford University Press.

Cloward, R.A., and Ohlin, L.E. (1960). *Delinquency and opportunity: A theory of delinquent gangs.* New York, NY: Free Press of Glencoe.

Cohen, A. (1955). *Delinquent boys: The culture of the gang*. New York, NY: Free Press.

Cohen, S. (1980). *Folk devils and moral panics*. Oxford: Basil Blackwell.

Cohen, S. (1981). 'Footprints in the sand.' In M. Fitzgerald, G. McLennan, and J. Pawson (Eds), *Crime and society* (pp. 183–206). London: Routledge and Kegan Paul.

Cohen, S. (1985). *Visions of social control*. London: Wiley-Blackwell.

Collins, P.H. (2000). *Black feminist thought* (2nd ed.). New York, NY: Routledge.

Connell, R.W. (1987). *Gender and power*. Stanford, CA: Stanford University Press.

Connell, R.W. (1995). *Masculinities*. Berkeley, CA: University of California Press.

Connell, R.W. (2000). 'Masculinity and violence in world perspective?' In A. Godenzi (Ed.), *Frieden, kultur und geschlecht* (pp. 65–84). Fribourg: University of Fribourg Press.

Connell, R.W., and Messerschmidt, J.W. (2005). 'Hegemonic masculinity: Rethinking the concept.' *Gender and Society, 19*, 829–859.

Corsianos, M. (2009). *Policing and gendered justice: Examining the possibilities*. Toronto, ON: University of Toronto Press.

Courtwright, K.E., Mackey, D.A., and Packard, S.H. (2005). 'Empathy among college students and criminal justice majors.' *Journal of Criminal Justice Education, 16*, 125–144.

Crawford, A., Jones, T., Woodhouse, T., and Young, J. (1990). *Second Islington crime survey*. Middlesex: Centre for Criminology, Middlesex Polytechnic.

Crespo, M. (1987). 'The school skipper.' In E. Rubington and M.S. Weinberg (Eds), *Deviance: The interactionist perspective* (pp. 307–314). New York, NY: Macmillan.

Curran, D.J., and Renzetti, C.M. (1994). *Theories of crime*. Boston, MA: Allyn and Bacon.

Curran, D.J., and Renzetti, C.M. (2001). *Theories of crime* (2nd ed.). Boston, MA: Allyn and Bacon.

Currie, D.H., and MacLean, B.D. (1993). 'Preface.' In D.H. Currie and B.D. MacLean (Eds), *Social inequality, social justice* (pp. 5–6). Vancouver, BC: Collective Press.

Currie, E. (1985). *Confronting crime: An American challenge*. New York, NY: Pantheon.

Currie, E. (1992). 'Retreatism, minimalism, realism: Three styles of reasoning on crime and drugs in the United States.' In J. Lowman and B.D. MacLean (Eds), *Realist criminology: Crime control and policing in the 1990s* (pp. 88–97). Toronto, ON: University of Toronto Press.

Currie, E. (1993). *Reckoning: Drugs, the cities and the American future*. New York, NY: Hill and Wang.

Currie, E. (2004). *The road to whatever: Middle-class culture and the crisis of adolescence*. New York, NY: Metropolitan Books.

Currie, E. (2007). 'Against marginality: Arguments for a public criminology.' *Theoretical Criminology, 11*, 175–190.

Currie, E. (2008a). *The roots of danger: Violent crime in global perspective*. Upper Saddle River, NJ: Prentice Hall.

Currie, E. (2008b). 'Preface.' In K. Carrington and R. Hogg (Eds), *Critical criminology: Issues, debates, challenges* (pp. vii–ix). Portland, OR: Willan.

Daly, K., and Chesney-Lind, M. (1988). 'Feminism and criminology.' *Justice Quarterly, 5*, 497–538.

Daly, M., and Wilson, M. (1988). *Homicide*. Hawthorne, NY: Aldine de Gruyter.

Daniels, J. (2009). *Cyber racism: White supremacy online and the new attack on civil rights*. Lanham, MD: Roman and Littlefield.

Davidson, J.T., and Chesney-Lind, M. (2009). 'Discounting women: Context matters in risk and need assessment.' *Critical Criminology, 17*, 221–246.

De Giorgi, A. (2008). 'Rethinking the political economy of punishment.' *Criminal Justice Matters, 70*, 17–18.

DeGue, S., and DiLillo, D. (2008). 'Is animal cruelty a "red flag" for family violence? Investigating co-occurring violence toward children, partners, and pets.' *Journal of Interpersonal Violence, 24*, 1036–1056.

de Hann, W. (2009). 'Abolitionism and crime control.' In T. Newburn (Ed.), *Key readings in criminology* (pp. 21–274). Portland, OR: Willan.

DeKeseredy, W.S. (1990). 'Male peer support and woman abuse: The current stake of knowledge.' *Sociological Focus, 23*, 129–139.

DeKeseredy, W.S. (2007). 'Review of Elliott Currie's *The Road to Whatever: Middle-class Culture and the Crisis of Adolescence*.' *Critical Criminology, 15*, 199–201.

DeKeseredy, W.S. (2009a). 'Canadian crime control in the new millennium: The influence of neo-conservative policies and practices.' *Police Practice and Research, 10*, 305–316.

DeKeseredy, W.S. (2009b). 'Male violence against women in North America as hate crime.' In B. Perry (Ed.), *Hate crimes volume 3: The victims of hate crime* (pp. 151–172). Santa Barbara, CA: Praeger.

DeKeseredy, W.S. (2009c). 'Patterns of violence in the family.' In M. Baker (Ed.), *Families: Changing trends in Canada* (6th ed.) (pp. 179–205). Whitby, ON: McGraw-Hill Ryerson.

DeKeseredy, W.S. (in press a). *Violence against women in Canada.* Toronto, ON: University of Toronto Press.

DeKeseredy, W.S. (in press b). 'Bourgois, Phillipe: In search of respect.' In F.T. Cullen and P. Wilcox (Eds), *Encyclopedia of criminological theory.* Thousand Oaks, CA: Sage.

DeKeseredy, W.S., Alvi, S., and Schwartz, M.D. (2006). 'Left realism revisited.' In W.S. DeKeseredy and B. Perry (Eds), *Advancing critical criminology: Theory and application* (pp. 19–42). Lanham, MD: Lexington Books.

DeKeseredy, W.S., Alvi, S., Schwartz, M.D., and Tomaszewski, E.A. (2003). *Under siege: Poverty and crime in a public housing community.* Lanham, MD: Lexington Books.

DeKeseredy, W.S., Donnermeyer, J.F., Schwartz, M.D., Tunnell, K.D., and Hall, M. (2007a). 'Thinking critically about rural gender relations: Toward a rural masculinity crisis/male peer support model of separation/divorce sexual assault.' *Critical Criminology, 15,* 295–311.

DeKeseredy, W.S., and Dragiewicz, M. (2007). 'Understanding the complexities of feminist perspectives on woman abuse: A commentary on Donald G. Dutton's *Rethinking Domestic Violence.*' *Violence Against Women, 13,* 874–884.

DeKeseredy, W.S., Ellis, D., and Alvi, S. (2005). *Deviance and crime: Theory, research and policy.* Cincinnati, OH: Anderson Publishing.

DeKeseredy, W.S., and Goff, C. (1992). 'Corporate violence against Canadian women: Assessing left-realist research and policy.' *Journal of Human Justice, 4,* 55–70.

DeKeseredy, W.S., and Hinch, R. (1991). *Woman abuse: Sociological perspectives.* Toronto, ON: Thompson Educational Publishing.

DeKeseredy, W.S., and Joseph, C. (2006). 'Separation/divorce sexual assault in rural Ohio: Preliminary results of an exploratory study.' *Violence Against Women, 12,* 301–311.

DeKeseredy, W.S., and Olsson, P. (in press). 'Adult pornography, male peer support, and violence against women: The contribution of the "dark side" of the internet.' In M. Varga Martin and M.A. Garcia-Ruiz (Eds), *Technology for facilitating humanity and combating social deviations: Interdisciplinary perspectives.* Hershey, PA: IGI Global.

DeKeseredy, W.S., and Perry, B. (2006a). 'Introduction: The never-ending and constantly evolving journey.' In W.S. DeKeseredy and B. Perry (Eds), *Advancing critical criminology: Theory and application* (pp. 1–8). Lanham, MD: Lexington Books.

DeKeseredy, W.S., and Perry, B. (2006b). 'Introduction to part I.' In W.S. DeKeseredy and B. Perry (Eds), *Advancing critical criminology: Theory and application* (pp. 11–17). Lanham, MD: Lexington Books.

DeKeseredy, W.S., and Perry, B. (Eds). (2006c). *Advancing critical criminology: Theory and application*. Lanham, MD: Lexington Books.

DeKeseredy, W.S., Perry, B., and Schwartz, M.D. (2007). 'Hate-motivated sexual assault on the college campus: Results from a Canadian representative sample.' Paper presented at the annual meeting of the American Society of Criminology, Atlanta.

DeKeseredy, W.S., and Schwartz, M.D. (1991a). 'British and U.S. left realism: A critical comparison.' *International Journal of Offender Therapy and Comparative Criminology, 35*, 248–262.

DeKeseredy, W.S., and Schwartz, M.D. (1991b). 'British left realism on the abuse of women: A critical appraisal.' In H. Pepinsky and R. Quinney (Eds), *Criminology as peacemaking* (pp. 154–171). Bloomington, IN: Indiana University Press.

DeKeseredy, W.S., and Schwartz, M.D. (1993). 'Male peer support and woman abuse: An expansion of DeKeseredy's model.' *Sociological Spectrum, 13*, 394–414.

DeKeseredy, W.S., and Schwartz, M.D. (1996). *Contemporary criminology*. Belmont, CA: Wadsworth.

DeKeseredy, W.S., and Schwartz, M.D. (1998). *Woman abuse on campus: Results from the Canadian national survey*. Thousand Oaks, CA: Sage.

DeKeseredy, W.S., and Schwartz, M.D. (2002). 'Theorizing public housing woman abuse as a function of economic exclusion and male peer support.' *Women's Health and Urban Life, 1*, 26–45.

DeKeseredy, W.S., and Schwartz, M.D. (2005a). 'Masculinities and interpersonal violence.' In M.S. Kimmel, J. Hearn, and R.W. Connell (Eds), *Handbook of studies on men and masculinities* (pp. 353–366). Thousand Oaks, CA: Sage.

DeKeseredy, W.S., and Schwartz, M.D. (2005b). 'Left realist theory.' In S. Henry and M. Lanier (Eds), *The essential criminology reader*. Boulder, CA: Westview Press.

DeKeseredy, W.S., and Schwartz, M.D. (2009). *Dangerous exits: Escaping abusive relationships in rural America*. New Brunswick, NJ: Rutgers University Press.

DeKeseredy, W.S., and Schwartz, M.D. (in press). 'Friedman economic policies, social exclusion, and crime: Toward a gendered left realist subcultural theory.' *Crime, Law and Social Change*.

DeKeseredy, W.S., Schwartz, M.D., Fagen, D., and Hall, M. (2006). 'Separation/divorce sexual assault: The contribution of male peer support.' *Feminist Criminology, 1*, 228–250.

Delacourt, S. (2009, October 26). 'Tory heckles drown out Liberal MP's flu questions.' *Toronto Star*, p. A8.

Denham, D., and Gillespie, J. (1999). *Two steps forward … one step back*. Ottawa, ON: Health Canada.

Denzin, N. (1990). 'Presidential address on the sociological imagination revisited.' *The Sociological Quarterly, 31*, 1–22.

Devine, J.A., and Wright, J.D. (1993). *The greatest of evils: Urban poverty and the American underclass*. New York, NY: Aldine de Gruyter.

Dews, P. (1987). *Logic of disintegration: Poststructuralist thought and claims of critical thought*. New York, NY: Verso.

Dines, G. (2006). 'The white man's burden: Gonzo pornography and the construction of black masculinity.' *Yale Journal of Law and Feminism, 18*, 296–297.

Dines, G., and Jensen, R. (2008a). 'Pornography.' In C.M. Renzetti and J.L. Edleson (Eds), *Encyclopedia of interpersonal violence* (pp. 519–520). Thousand Oaks, CA: Sage.

Dines, G., and Jensen, R. (2008b). 'Internet, pornography.' In C.M. Renzetti and J.L. Edleson (Eds), *Encyclopedia of interpersonal violence* (pp. 365–366). Thousand Oaks, CA: Sage.

Dobash, R.E., and Dobash, R. (1979). *Violence against wives: A case against the patriarchy*. New York, NY: Free Press.

Donnermeyer, J.F. (2007). 'Rural crime: Roots and restoration.' *International Journal of Rural Crime, 1*, 2–20.

Donnermeyer, J.F., and DeKeseredy, W.S. (2008). 'Toward a rural critical criminology.' *Southern Rural Sociology, 23*, 4–28.

Donnermeyer, J.F., DeKeseredy, W.S., and Dragiewicz, M. (in press). 'Policing rural Canada and the United States.' In R. Yarwood and R. Mawby (Eds), *Countryside constable*. Aldershot: Ashgate.

Donnermeyer, J.F., Jobes, P., and Barclay, E. (2006). 'Rural crime, poverty, and community.' In W.S. DeKeseredy and B. Perry (Eds), *Advancing critical criminology: Theory and application* (pp. 199–218). Lanham, MD: Lexington Books.

Donnermeyer, J.F., Kreps, G.M., and Kreps, M.W. (1999). *Lessons for living: A practical approach to daily life from the Amish community*. Sugarcreek, OH: Carlisle Press.

Dragiewicz, M. (2009). 'Why sex and gender matter in domestic violence research and advocacy.' In E. Stark and E.S. Buzawa (Eds), *Violence against women in families and relationships, volume 3: Criminal justice and the law* (pp. 201–216). Santa Barbara, CA: Praeger.

Dragiewicz, M., and DeKeseredy, W.S. (2008). *A needs gap assessment report on abused women without legal representation in the family courts*. Oshawa, ON: Report prepared for Luke's Place Support and Resource Centre.

Dutton, D.G. (2006). *Rethinking domestic violence*. Vancouver, BC: University of British Columbia Press.

Dworkin, A. (1994). 'Pornography happens to women.' Retrieved August 15, 2009 from www.nostatusquo.com/ACLU/dworkin/Porn-Happens.html.

Ehrenreich, B. (2001). *Nickel and dimed: On (not) getting by in America*. New York, NY: Metropolitan Books.

Ehrlich, H.J. (1999). 'Campus ethnoviolence.' In F. Pincus and H.J. Ehrlich (Eds), *Ethnic conflict* (pp. 277–290). Boulder, CO: Westview.

Eisenstein, Z. (1980). *Capitalist patriarchy and the case for socialist feminism*. New York, NY: Monthly Review Press.

Elias, R. (1986). *The politics of victimization*. New York, NY: Oxford University Press.

Ellis, D. (1987). *The wrong stuff: An introduction to the sociological study of deviance*. Toronto, ON: Macmillan.

Ellis, D., and DeKeseredy, W.S. (1996). *The wrong stuff: An introduction to the sociological study of deviance* (2nd ed.). Toronto, ON: Allyn and Bacon.

Ferrell, J. (1994). 'Confronting the agenda of authority: Critical criminology, anarchism and urban graffiti.' In G. Barak (Ed.), *Varieties of criminology* (pp. 161–178). New York, NY: Praeger.

Ferrell, J. (1995) 'Culture, crime and cultural criminology.' *Journal of Criminal Justice and Popular Culture, 3*, 25–42.

Ferrell, J. (1998). 'Stumbling toward a critical criminology (and into the anarchy and imagery of postmodernism).' In J.I. Ross (Ed.), *Cutting the edge* (pp. 63–76). Westport, CT: Praeger.

Ferrell, J. (2003). *Cultural criminology*. In M.D. Schwartz and S.E. Hatty (Eds), *Controversies in critical criminology* (pp. 71–84). Cincinnati, OH: Anderson Publishing.

Ferrell, J. (2006). *Empire of scrounge*. New York, NY: New York University Press.

Ferrell, J., Hayward, K., and Young, J. (2008). *Cultural criminology: An invitation*. London: Sage.

Ferrell, J., and Sanders, C. (Eds). (1995). *Cultural criminology*. Boston, MA: Northeastern University Press.

Fleury-Steiner, R.E., and S.L. Miller. (2008). 'Research, dissemination, and activism: Guest editors' introduction.' *Feminist Criminology, 3*, 243–246.

Foster, H., and Hagan, J. (2007). 'Incarceration and intergenerational social exclusion.' *Social Problems, 54*, 399–433.

Foucault, M. (1979). *Discipline and punish: The birth of the prison*. New York, NY: Vintage.

Friedman, M. (1962). *Capitalism and freedom*. Chicago, IL: University of Chicago Press.

Friedrichs, D.O. (1989). 'Critical criminology and critical legal studies.' *Critical Criminologist, 1*, 7.

Friedrichs, D.O. (1991). 'Introduction: Peacemaking criminology in a world filled with conflict.' In B. MacLean and D. Milovanovic (Eds), *New directions in critical criminology* (pp. 101–106). Vancouver, BC: Collective Press.

Friedrichs, D.O. (1996). 'Critical criminology: Strength in diversity for these times.' *Critical Criminology, 7*, 121–128.

Friedrichs, D.O. (2000). 'The crime of the century? The case for the holocaust.' *Crime, Law and Social Change, 34*, 21–41.

Friedrichs, D.O. (2001). *Law in our lives: An introduction*. Los Angeles, CA: Roxbury.

Friedrichs, D.O. (2007). *Trusted criminals: White collar crime in contemporary society* (3rd ed.). Belmont, CA: Wadsworth.

Friedrichs, D.O. (2009). 'Critical criminology.' In J.M. Miller (Ed.), *21st century criminology: A reference handbook, volume 1* (pp. 210–218). Thousand Oaks, CA: Sage.

Fuller, J.R., and Wozniak, J.F. (2006). 'Peacemaking criminology: Past, present, and future.' In F.T. Cullen, J.P. Wright, and K.B. Blevins (Eds), *Taking stock: The status of criminological theory* (pp. 251–273). New Brunswick, NJ: Transaction Publishing.

Funk, R.E. (2006). *Reaching men: Strategies for preventing sexist attitudes, behaviors, and violence*. Indianapolis, IN: Jist Life.

Gabbidon, S.L., and Greene, H.T. (2005). *Race and crime*. Thousand Oaks, CA: Sage.

Galt, V. (2009, August 7). 'Youth bear brunt of job losses: Canada's student unemployment rate hits almost 21 percent in July, the highest on record.' *Globe and Mail*, p. 1.

Garbarino, J. (2006). *See Jane hit: Why girls are growing more violent and what we can do about it*. New York, NY: Penguin Press.

Garcia-Moreno, C., Jansen, A.F.M.H., Ellsberg, M., Heise, L., and Watts, C. (2005). *WHO multi-country study on women's health and domestic violence against women: Initial results on prevalence, health outcomes, and women's responses*. Geneva: World Health Organization.

Gardiner, J.K. (2005). 'Men, masculinities, and feminist theory.' In M.S. Kimmel, J. Hearn, and R.W. Connell (Eds), *Handbook of studies on men and masculinities* (pp. 35–50). Thousand Oaks, CA: Sage.

Gelsthorpe, L., and Morris, A. (1988). 'Feminism and criminology in Britain.' *British Journal of Criminology, 28*, 93–110.

Gibbons, D. (1994). *Talking about crime and criminals: Problems and issues in theory development in criminology*. Englewood Cliffs, NJ: Prentice Hall.

Gibbons, D. (1995). 'Unfit for human consumption: The problem of flawed writing in criminal justice and what to do about it.' *Crime and Delinquency, 41*, 246–266.

Gibbs, J.C. (in press). 'Looking at terrorism through left realist lenses.' *Crime, Law and Social Change*.

Giordano, P.C. (1995). 'The wider circle of friends in adolescence.' *American Journal of Sociology, 101*, 661–97.

Goel, R. (2010). 'Aboriginal women and political pursuit in Canadian sentencing circles: At cross roads or cross purposes?' In J. Ptacek (Ed.), *Restorative justice and violence against women* (pp. 60–78). New York, NY: Oxford University Press.

Goff, C., and Reasons, C. (1978). *Corporate crime in Canada*. Scarborough, ON: Prentice-Hall.

Goodwin, G. (1983). 'Toward a paradigm for humanist sociology.' *Humanity and Society, 7*, 219–237.

Grant, J. (1993). *Fundamental feminism: Contesting the core concepts of feminist theory*. New York, NY: Routledge.

Grant, J. (2008). *Charting women's journeys: From addiction to recovery*. Lanham, MD: Lexington Books.

Griffiths, C.T. (2007). *Canadian criminal justice: A primer* (3rd ed.). Toronto, ON: Thomson.

Hagan, J. (1985). 'The assumption of natural science methods: Criminological positivism.' In R.F. Meir (Ed.), *Theoretical methods in criminology* (pp. 75–92). Beverly Hills, CA: Sage.

Hagedorn, J.M. (1988). *People and folks: Gangs, crime and the underclass in a rustbelt city*. Chicago, IL: Lakeview Press.

Hall, S., Critcher, C., Jefferson, T., Clarke, J., and Roberts, B. (1978). *Policing the crisis: Mugging, the state, and law and order*. London: Macmillan.

Harding, S. (1987). 'Is there a feminist method?' In S. Harding (Ed.), *Feminism and methodology* (pp. 1–14). Bloomington, IN: Indiana University Press.

Harvey, L. (1990). *Critical social research*. London: Unwin Hyman.

Hatty, S.E. (2000). *Masculinities, violence, and culture*. Thousand Oaks, CA: Sage.

Hayward, K. (2007). 'Cultural criminology.' In B. Goldson (Ed.), *The dictionary of youth justice* (pp. 119–120). Cullompton: Willan.

Hayward, K., and Young, J. (2004). 'Cultural criminology: Some notes on the script.' *Theoretical Criminology, 8*, 250–273.

Hebert, C. (2007, October 19). 'Dion now looks down the barrel.' *Toronto Star*, A17.

Hebert, C. (2010, January 15). 'Court of public opinion turns on Tories.' *Toronto Star*. Retreived January 20, 2010, from www.thestar.com/news/canada/article/751087-hebert-court-of-public-opinion-turns-on-tories.

Heilbroner, R. (1980). *Marxism, for and against*. New York, NY: Norton.

Helmkamp, J., Ball, J., and Townsend, K. (Eds). (1996). *Definitional dilemma: Can and should there be a universal definition of white collar crime?* Morgantown, WV: National White Collar Crime Center.

Henry, S. (1999). 'Is Left realism a useful theory for addressing the problems of crime? No.' In J.R. Fuller and E.W. Hickey (Eds), *Controversial issues in criminology* (pp. 137–144). Boston, MA: Allyn and Bacon.

Henry, S., and Milovanovic, D. (1993). 'Back to basics: A postmodern redefinition of crime.' *The Critical Criminologist, 5*(1–2), 12.

Henry, S., and Milovanovic, D. (2003). 'Constitutive criminology.' In M.D. Schwartz and S.E. Hatty (Eds), *Controversies in critical criminology* (pp. 57–70). Cincinnati, OH: Anderson Publishing.

Henry, S., and Milovanovic, D. (2005). 'Postmodernism and constitutive theories of criminal behavior.' In R.A. Wright and J.M. Miller (Eds), *Encyclopedia of criminology, volume 2* (pp. 1245–1249). New York, NY: Routledge.

Hirschi, T. (1969). *Causes of delinquency*. Berkeley, CA: University of California Press.

Hogg, R., and Carrington, K. (2006). *Policing the rural crisis*. Sydney: Federation Press.

Hornqvist, M. (2008). 'Prison expansion without a labour market orientation.' *Criminal Justice Matters, 70*, 19–20.

Hottocks, R. (1994). *Masculinity in crisis*. New York, NY: St. Martin's Press.

Housing Assistance Council. (2002). *Taking stock of rural people, poverty, and housing for the 21st century*. Washington, DC: Author.

Human Rights Watch (2008). *Targeting blacks*. New York, NY: Author.

Hunnicutt, G. (2009). 'Varieties of patriarchy and violence against women: Resurrecting "patriarchy" as a theoretical tool.' *Violence Against Women, 15*, 553–573.

Inciardi, J.A. (Ed.). (1980). *Radical criminology: The coming crises*. Beverly Hills, CA: Sage.

International Center for Prison Studies. (2007). *World prison brief.* Retrieved September 11, 2009, from http://www.kcl.ac.uk/depsta/rel/icps/worldbrief.

Iovanni, L., and Miller, S.L. (2001). 'Criminal justice system responses to domestic violence: Law enforcement and the courts.' In C.M. Renzetti, J.L. Edleson, and R.K. Bergen (Eds), *Sourcebook on violence against women* (pp. 303–328). Thousand Oaks, CA: Sage.

Irwin, J., and Austin, J. (1994). *It's about time: America's imprisonment binge.* Belmont, CA: Sage.

Jacobs, J. (2004). *Dark age ahead.* Toronto, ON: Vintage.

Jarjoura, G.R. (1993). 'Does dropping out of school enhance delinquent involvement? Results from a large scale national probability sample.' *Criminology, 31,* 149–170.

Jensen, R. (2007). *Getting off: Pornography and the end of masculinity.* Cambridge, MA: South End Press.

Jensen, R., and Dines, G. (1998). 'The content of mass-marketed pornography.' In G. Dines, R. Jensen, and A. Russo (Eds), *Pornography: The production and consumption of inequality* (pp. 65–100). New York, NY: Routledge.

Jobes, P.C., Barclay, E., Weinand, H., and Donnermeyer, J.F. (2004). 'A structural analysis of social disorganization and crime in rural communities in Australia.' *The Australian and New Zealand Journal of Criminology, 37,* 114–140.

Johnson, H. (1996). *Dangerous domains: Violence against women in Canada.* Toronto, ON: Nelson.

Johnson, H., Ollus, N., and Nevala, S. (2008). *Violence against women: An international perspective.* New York, NY: Springer.

Jones, N. (2010). *Between good and ghetto: African American girls and inner-city violence.* New Brunswick, NJ: Rutgers University Press.

Katz, J., and Chambliss, W.J. (1991). 'Biology and crime.' In J.F. Sheley (Ed.), *Criminology: A contemporary handbook* (pp. 245–271). Belmont, CA: Wadsworth.

Katz, L. (1978). 'Work: It's more dangerous for public employees.' *The Public Employee, 1,* 6.

Kauzlarich, D. (2006). 'Foreword.' In D. Rothe and C.W. Mullins, *Symbolic gestures and the generation of global social control: The International Criminal Court.* Lanham, MD: Lexington Books.

Kauzlarich, D., and Matthews, R.A. (2006). 'Taking stock of theory and research.' In R.J. Michalowski and R.C. Kramer (Eds), *State–corporate crime: Wrongdoing at the intersection of business and government* (pp. 239–250). New Brunswick, NJ: Rutgers University Press.

Kelling, G., and Coles, C. (1997). *Fixing broken windows*. New York, NY: Free Press.

Kimmel, M.S. (2000). *The gendered society*. New York, NY: Oxford University Press.

Kinsey, R., Lea, J., and Young, J. (1986). *Losing the fight against crime*. Oxford: Blackwell.

Klein, M.W. (2007). *Chasing after street gangs: A forty-year journey*. Upper Saddle River, NJ: Prentice Hall.

Klein, N. (2007). *The shock doctrine: The rise of disaster capitalism*. Toronto, ON: Knopf.

Kramer, R.C. (2006). 'The space shuttle challenger explosion.' In R.J. Michalowski and R.C. Kramer (Eds), *State–corporate crime: Wrongdoing at the intersection of business and government* (pp. 27–44). New Brunswick, NJ: Rutgers University Press.

Kramer, R.C., Michalowski, R., and Kauzlarich, D. (2002). 'The origins and development of the concept and theory of state–corporate crime.' *Crime and Delinquency, 48*, 263–282.

Kreps, G.M., Donnermeyer, J.F., and Kreps, M.W. (1997). *A quiet moment in time*. Sugar Creek, OH: Carlisle Press.

Krug, E., Dahlberg, E.L., and Mercy, J. *et al.* (2002). *World report on violence and health*. Geneva: World Health Organization.

Kubrin, C., Stucky, T.D., and Krohn, M.D. (2009). *Researching theories of crime and deviance*. New York, NY: Oxford University Press.

Lea, J., and Young, J. (1984). *What is to be done about law and order?* New York, NY: Penguin.

Legislative Analyst's Office. (2010). 'Analysis of the California 2008–09 budget bill: Criminal justice.' Retrieved January 27, 2010, from www.lao.ca.gov/analysis_2008/crim_justice/cj_anl08008.aspx.

Lemert, E.M. (1951). *Social pathology*. New York, NY: McGraw-Hill.

Leonard, K. (1974). 'Progressive professors on thin ice here and nationwide.' *New University, 6*(1), 16.

Lewin, K. (1951). *Field theory in social science: Selected theoretical papers*. New York, NY: Harper and Row.

Lewis, O. (1966). *La Vida: A Puerto Rican family in the culture of poverty – San Juan and New York*. New York, NY: Random House.

Li, G. (2007). 'Homicide in Canada, 2006.' *Juristat: Canadian Centre for Justice Statistics, 27*, 1–19.

Liazos, A. (1972). 'The poverty of the sociology of deviance: Nuts, sluts and perverts.' *Social Problems, 20*, 103–120.

Lilly, J.R., Cullen, F.T., and Ball, R.A. (2007). *Criminological theory: Context and consequences* (4th ed.). Thousand Oaks, CA: Sage.

Liska, A.E. (1987). 'A critical examination of macro perspectives on crime control.' *Annual Review of Sociology, 13*, 67–88.

Longino, H. (1980). 'What is pornography?' In L. Lederer (Ed.), *Take back the night: Women on pornography* (pp. 40–54). New York, NY: William Morrow.

Luttwak, E. (1995, November). 'Turbo-charged capitalism and its consequences.' *London Review of Books*, pp. 6–7.

Lynch, M.J., Michalowski, R., and Groves, W.B. (2000). *The new primer in radical criminology: Critical perspectives on crime, power and identity* (3rd ed.). Monsey, NJ: Criminal Justice Press.

Lynch, M.J., and Stretesky, P. (2001). 'Toxic crimes: Examining corporate victimization of the general public employing medical and epidemiological evidence.' *Critical Criminology, 10*, 153–172.

Lyng, S. (1990). 'Edgework.' *American Journal of Sociology, 95*, 851–856.

Lyng, S. (Ed.). (2005). *Edgework*. New York, NY: Routledge.

MacLean, B.D. (1991). 'In partial defense of socialist realism: Some theoretical and methodological concerns of the local crime survey.' *Crime, Law and Social Change, 15*, 213–254.

MacLean, B.D., and Milovanovic, D. (1997a). 'Thinking critically about criminology.' In B.D. MacLean and D. Milovanovic (Eds), *Thinking critically about crime* (pp. 1–16). Vancouver, BC: Collective Press.

MacLean, B.D., and Milovanovic, D. (Eds). (1997b). *Thinking critically about crime*. Vancouver, BC: Collective Press.

Maidment, M.R. (2006). 'Transgressing boundaries: Feminist perspectives in criminology.' In W.S. DeKeseredy and B. Perry (Eds), *Advancing critical criminology: Theory and application* (pp. 43–62). Lanham, MD: Lexington Books.

Manning, P.K. (1997). *Police work: The social organization of policing* (2nd ed.). Prospects Heights, IL: Waveland Press.

Massey, D.S. (2007). *Categorically unequal: The American stratification system*. New York, NY: Russell Sage Foundation.

Matthews, R. (2009). 'Beyond "so what?" criminology: Rediscovering realism.' *Theoretical Criminology, 13*, 341–362.

Matthews, R.A. (2003). 'Marxist criminology.' In M.D. Schwartz and S.E. Hatty (Eds), *Controversies in critical criminology* (pp. 1–14). Cincinnati, OH: Anderson Publishing.

Matthews, R.A. (2006). 'Ordinary business in Nazi Germany.' In R.J. Michalowski and R.C. Kramer (Eds), *State–corporate crime: Wrongdoing at the intersection of business and government* (pp. 116–133). New Brunswick, NJ: Rutgers University Press.

Matthews, R.A., and Kauzlarich, D. (2006). 'The crash of ValuJet flight 592.' In R.J. Michalowski and R.C. Kramer (Eds), *State–corporate* crime: *Wrongdoing at the intersection of business and government* (pp. 82–97). New Brunswick, NJ: Rutgers University Press.

Mauer, M. (2005, October). 'Facts about prisoners and prisons.' *Sentencing Project.*

Melichar, K. (1990). 'Deconstruction: Critical theory or an ideology of despair.' *Humanity and Society, 12,* 366–385.

Merton, R.K. (1938). 'Social structure and anomie.' *American Sociological Review, 3,* 672–682.

Merz-Perez, L., and Heide, K.M. (2004). *Animal cruelty: Pathway to violence against people.* Lanham, MD: AltaMira Press.

Messerschmidt, J.W. (1993). *Masculinities and crime: Critique and reconceptualization.* Lanham, MD: Roman and Littlefield.

Messerschmidt, J.W. (1997). *Crime as structured action: Gender, race, class, and crime in the making.* Thousand Oaks, CA: Sage.

Messerschmidt, J.W. (2000). *Nine lives: Adolescent masculinities, the body, and violence.* Boulder, CO: Westview.

Messerschmidt, J.W. (2004). *Flesh and blood: Adolescent gender diversity and violence.* Lanham, MD: Rowman and Littlefield.

Messerschmidt, J.W. (2005). 'Men, masculinities, and crime.' In M.S. Kimmel, J. Hearn, and R.W. Connell (Eds), *Handbook of studies on men and masculinities* (pp. 196–212). Thousand Oaks, CA: Sage.

Messner, S., and Rosenfeld, R. (2006). *Crime and the American dream.* Belmont, CA: Wadsworth.

Michalowski, R.J. (1983). 'Crime control in the 1980s: A progressive agenda.' *Crime and Social Justice,* Summer, 13–23.

Michalowski, R.J. (1985). *Order, law, and crime: An introduction to criminology.* New York, NY: Random House.

Michalowski, R.J. (1996). 'Critical criminology and the critique of domination: The story of an intellectual movement.' *Critical Criminology, 7,* 9–16.

Michalowski, R., and Dubisch, J. (2001). *Run for the wall: Remembering Vietnam on a motorcycle pilgrimage.* New Brunswick, NJ: Rutgers University Press.

Miliband, R. (1969). *The state in capitalist society: The analysis of the western system of power.* London: Quartet.

Miller, J. (2001). *One of the guys: Girls, gangs, and gender.* New York, NY: Oxford University Press.

Miller, J. (2002). 'The strengths and limits of "doing gender" for understanding street crime.' *Theoretical criminology, 6,* 433–460.

Miller, J. (2003). 'Feminist criminology.' In M.D. Schwartz and S.E. Hatty (Eds), *Controversies in critical criminology* (pp. 15–28). Cincinnati, OH: Anderson Publishing.

Miller, J. (2008). *Getting played: African American girls, urban inequality, and gendered violence.* New York, NY: New York University Press.

Miller, S.L. (1994). 'Expanding the boundaries: Toward a more inclusive and integrated study of intimate violence.' *Violence and Victims, 9*, 183–194.

Miller, S.L. (1999). *Gender and community policing: Walking the walk.* Boston, MA: Northeastern University Press.

Mobley, A. (2003). 'Convict criminology: The two-legged data dilemma.' In J.I. Ross and S.C. Richards (Eds), *Convict criminology* (pp. 209–226). Belmont, CA: Wadsworth.

Monsebraaten, L., and Daly, R. (2007, November 26). 'Canada's poverty capital.' *Toronto Star*, A1, A6–A7.

Moore, M. (2003). *Dude, where's my country?* New York, NY: Warner Books.

Morash, M. (2006). *Understanding gender, crime, and justice.* Thousand Oaks, CA: Sage.

Morgan, D.H.J. (1992). *Discovering men.* London: Routledge.

Morris, R. (1995). *Penal abolition: The practical choice.* Toronto, ON: Canadian Scholars' Press.

Mujica, A., and Ayala, A.I.U. (2008). 'Femicide in Morelos: An issue on public health.' Paper presented at the World Health Organization's 9th World Conference on Injury Prevention and Safety Promotion, Yucatan, Mexico, March 18.

Mullins, C.W. (2006). *Holding your square: Masculinities, streetlife and violence.* Portland, OR: Willan.

Mullins, C.W. (2009). ' "He would kill me with his penis": Genocidal rape in Rwanda as a state crime.' *Critical Criminology, 17*, 15–34.

Mullins, C.W., and Rothe, D. (2008). *Blood, power, and bedlam: Violations of international criminal law in post-colonial Africa.* New York, NY: Peter Lang.

Muzzatti, S.L. (2005). 'Bits of falling sky and global pandemics: Moral panic and Severe Acute Respiratory Syndrome (SARS).' *Illness, Crisis and Loss, 13*, 117–128.

Muzzatti, S.L. (2006). 'Cultural criminology: A decade and counting of criminological chaos.' In W.S. DeKeseredy and B. Perry (Eds), *Advancing critical criminology: Theory and application* (pp. 63–82). Lanham, MD: Lexington Books.

Newburn, T., and Stanko, E.A. (1994). 'Introduction: Men, masculinities and crime.' In T. Newburn and E.A. Stanko (Eds), *Just boys doing business? Men, masculinities and crime* (pp. 1–9). London: Routledge.

O'Brien, M. (2005). 'What is *cultural* about cultural criminology?' *British Journal of Criminology, 45*, 599–612.

Ogle, R.S., and Batton, C. (2009). 'Revisiting patriarchy: Its conceptualization and operationalization in criminology.' *Critical Criminology, 17*, 159–182.

Oliver, W. (2006). 'The streets: An alternative black male socialization institution.' *Journal of Black Studies, 36*, 918–937.

Olsson, P. (2003). *Legal ideals and normative realities: A case study of children's rights and child labor activity in Paraguay.* Lund: Lund University.

Owen, B. (2005). 'Afterword.' In J. Irwin, *The warehouse prison: Disposal of the new dangerous class* (pp. 261–289). Los Angeles, CA: Roxbury.

Pager, D. (2007). *Marked: Race, crime, and finding work in an era of mass incarceration.* Chicago, IL: University of Chicago Press.

Parker, L. (2007). 'United Nations publishes handbook on restorative justice.' *Restorative Justice Online.* Retrieved January 28, 2010, from www.restorativejusice.org/editions/2007/feb07/unhandbook.

Pateman, C. (1988). *The sexual contract.* London: Polity.

Payne, B.K., and Gainey, R.R. (2006). *Family violence and criminal justice: A life course approach* (2nd ed.). Cincinnati, OH: Anderson Publishing.

Pearce, F. (1976). *Crimes of the powerful: Marxism, crime and deviance.* London: Pluto Press.

Pearce, F. (1992). 'The contribution of "left realism" to the study of commercial crime.' In J. Lowman and B.D. MacLean (Eds), *Realist criminology: Crime control and policing in the 1990s* (pp. 313–335). Toronto, ON: University of Toronto Press.

Pepinsky, H. (2008). 'Empathy and restoration.' In D. Sullivan and L. Tift (Eds), *Handbook of restorative justice* (pp. 188–197). London: Routledge.

Pepinsky, H., and Quinney, R. (Eds). (1991). *Criminology as peacemaking.* Bloomington, IN: Indiana University Press.

Perkins, D. (2010, January 22). 'Justice system key to ending hockey violence.' *Toronto Star*, S4.

Perry, B. (2003). 'Accounting for hate crime.' In M.D. Schwartz and S.E. Hatty (Eds), *Controversies in critical criminology* (pp. 147–160). Cincinnati, OH: Anderson Publishing.

Perry, B. (2006). 'Missing pieces: The paucity of hate crime scholarship.' In W.S. DeKeseredy and B. Perry (Eds), *Advancing critical criminology: Theory and application* (pp. 155–178). Lanham, MD: Lexington Books.

Perry, B. (2009a). 'Racist violence against Native Americans.' In B. Perry (Ed.), *Hate crimes volume 3: The victims of hate crime* (pp. 1–18). Santa Barbara, CA: Praeger.

Perry, B. (2009b). *Policing race and place in Indian country: Over- and under-enforcement.* Lanham, MD: Lexington Books.

Pfohl, S. (1994). *Images of deviance and social control: A sociological history.* New York, NY: McGraw-Hill.

Pitts-Taylor, V. (2007). *Surgery junkies: Wellness and pathology in cosmetic culture.* New Brunswick, NJ: Rutgers University Press.

Platt, A.M. (1969). *The childsavers.* Chicago, IL: University of Chicago Press.

Polk, K. (2003). 'Masculinities, femininities and homicide: Competing explanations for male violence.' In M.D. Schwartz and S.E. Hatty (Eds), *Controversies in critical criminology* (pp. 133–146). Cincinnati, OH: Anderson Publishing.

Porter, A. (2005). 'Restorative justice takes the world stage at United Nations crime conference.' *Restorative Practices eForum*, June 14. Retrieved January 27, 2010, from www.realjustice.org/library/uncrimecongress.html.

Pratt, T. (2009). *Addicted to incarceration: Corrections policy and the politics of misinformation in the United States.* Thousand Oaks, CA: Sage.

Presdee, M. (2000). *Cultural criminology and the carnival of crime.* London: Routledge.

Proudfoot, S. (2009, July 23). ' "Honor killings" of females on rise in Canada: Expert.' *The Star Pheonix*, 1.

Ptacek, J. (2010a). 'Editor's Introduction.' In J. Ptacek (Ed.), *Restorative justice and violence against women* (pp. ix–xiii). New York, NY: Oxford University Press.

Ptacek, J. (2010b). 'Resisting co-optation: Three feminist challenges to antiviolence work.' In J. Ptacek (Ed.), *Restorative justice and violence against women* (pp. 5–36). New York, NY: Oxford University Press.

Ptacek, J. (Ed.). (2010c). *Restorative justice and violence against women.* New York, NY: Oxford University Press.

Quinney, R. (1974). *Critique of the legal order.* Boston, MA: Little, Brown.

Quinney, R. (1975). 'Crime control in capitalist society: A critical philosophy of legal order.' In I. Taylor, P. Walton, and J. Young (Eds), *Critical criminology* (pp. 181–202). London: Routledge and Kegan Paul.

Quinney, R. (1991). 'The way of peace: On crime, suffering and service.' In H. Pepinsky and R. Quinney (Eds), *Criminology as peacemaking* (pp. 3–13). Bloomington, IN: Indiana University Press.

Radelet, M.R. (2005). 'Foreword.' In S.F. Sharp, *Hidden victims: The effects of the death penalty on families of the accused* (pp. vii–x). New Brunswick, NJ: Rutgers University Press.

Raphael, J. (2009). 'The trapping effects of poverty and violence.' In E. Stark and E.S. Buzawa (Eds), *Violence against women in families and relationships, volume 1* (pp. 93–110). Santa Barbara, CA: Prager.

Ratner, R.S. (1985). 'Inside the liberal boot: The criminological enterprise in Canada.' In T. Fleming (Ed.), *The new criminologies in Canada: State, crime, and control* (pp. 13–26). Toronto, ON: Oxford University Press.

Rebovich, D., and Layne, J. (2000). *The national survey on white collar crime.* Morgantown, WV: National White Collar Crime Center.

Reiman, J., and Leighton, P. (2010). *The rich get richer and the poor get prison: Ideology, class, and criminal justice* (9th ed.). Boston, MA: Allyn and Bacon.

Renzetti, C.M. (1994). 'On dancing with a bear: Reflections on some of the current debates among domestic violence theorists.' *Violence and Victims, 9,* 195–200.

Renzetti, C.M. (1999). 'Editor's introduction.' *Violence Against Women, 5,* 1235–1237.

Renzetti, C.M., and Maier, S.L. (2002). 'Private crime in public housing: Fear of crime and violent victimization among women public housing residents.' *Women's Health and Urban Life, 1,* 46–65.

Rigakos, G.S. (2002). *The new parapolice: Risk markets and commodified social control.* Toronto, ON: University of Toronto Press.

Robyn, L. (2006). 'Violations of treaty rights.' In R.J. Michalowski and R.C. Kramer (Eds), *State–corporate crime: Wrongdoing at the intersection of business and government* (pp. 186–198). New Brunswick, NJ: Rutgers University Press.

Rock, P. (1992). 'Foreword: The criminology that came in from the cold.' In J. Lowman and B.D. MacLean (Eds), *Realist criminology: Crime control and policing in the 1990s* (pp. ix–xii). Toronto, ON: University of Toronto Press.

Rosenau, P.M. (1992). *Postmodernism and the social sciences: Insights, inroads and intrusions.* Princeton, NJ: Princeton University Press.

Ross, J.I., and Richards, S.C. (2003). 'Introduction: What is the new school of convict criminology?' In J.I. Ross and S.C. Richards (Eds), *Convict criminology* (pp. 1–14). Belmont, CA: Wadsworth.

Rothe, D. (2009). *The crime of all crimes: An introduction to state criminality.* Lanham, MD: Roman and Littlefield.

Rothe, D., and Friedrichs, D.O. (2006). 'The state of the criminology of state crime.' *Social Justice, 3*, 147–161.

Rothe, D., Kramer, R., and Mullins, C.W. (2009). 'Torture, impunity, and open legal spaces: Abu Ghraib and international controls.' *Contemporary Justice Review, 12*(1), 27–43.

Rothe, D., and Mullins, C.W. (2006). *Symbolic gestures and the generation of global social control: The International Criminal Court.* Lanham, MD: Lexington Books.

Rothe, D., Ross, J.I., Mullins, C.W., Friedrichs, D.O., Michalowski, R., Barak, G., Kauzlarich, D., and Kramer, R.C. (2009). 'That was then, this is now, what about tomorrow: Future directions in state crime studies.' *Critical Criminology, 17*, 3–14.

Rubin, P. (2000). *Abused women in family mediation: A Nova Scotia snapshot.* Halifax, NS: Transition House Association of Nova Scotia.

Russell, D.E.H. (1993). *Against pornography: The evidence of harm.* Berkeley, CA: Russell Publications.

Russell, S. (2002). 'The continuing relevance of Marxism to critical criminology.' *Critical Criminology, 11*, 93–112.

Sartre, J.P. (1964). *The words.* London: Penguin.

Savelsberg, J.J., King, R., and Cleveland, L. (2002). 'Politicized scholarship: Science on crime and the state.' *Social Problems, 49*, 327–348.

Schissel, B. (1997). *Blaming children: Youth crime, moral panics and the politics of hate.* Halifax, NS: Fernwood.

Schlosser, E. (1998). 'The prison–industrial complex.' *Atlantic Monthly*, December, p. 54.

Schmalleger, F., and Volk, R. (2005). *Canadian criminology today: Theories and applications* (2nd ed.). Toronto, ON: Pearson Prentice Hall.

Schulte-Bockholt, A. (2006). *The politics of organized crime and the organized crime of politics.* Lanham, MD: Lexington Books.

Schur, E.M. (1984). *Labeling women deviant: Gender, stigma, and social control.* Philadelphia, PA: Temple University Press.

Schwartz, M.D. (1989). 'Asking the right questions: Battered wives are not all passive.' *Sociological Viewpoints, 5*, 46–61.

Schwartz, M.D. (1991). 'The future of critical criminology.' In B.D. MacLean and D. Milovanovic (Eds), *New directions in critical criminology* (pp. 119–124). Vancouver, BC: Collective Press.

Schwartz, M.D., and DeKeseredy, W.S. (1993). 'The return of the "battered husband syndrome" through the typification of women as violent.' *Crime, Law and Social Change, 20*, 249–265.

Schwartz, M.D., and DeKeseredy, W.S. (1997). *Sexual assault on the college campus: The role of male peer support.* Thousand Oaks, CA: Sage.

Schwartz, M.D., and DeKeseredy, W.S. (2008). 'Interpersonal violence against women.' *Journal of Contemporary Criminal Justice, 24,* 178–185.

Schwartz, M.D., and Friedrichs, D.O. (1994). 'Postmodern thought and criminological discontent: New metaphors for understanding violence.' *Criminology, 32,* 221–246.

Schwartz, M.D., and Friedrichs, D.O. (2004). 'Postmodern thought and criminological discontent: New metaphors for understanding violence.' *Criminology, 32,* 221–246.

Schwartz, M.D., and Hatty, S.E. (2003). 'Introduction.' In M.D. Schwartz and S.E. Hatty (Eds), *Controversies in critical criminology* (pp. ix–xvii). Cincinnati, OH: Anderson Publishing.

Schwartz, M.D., and Pitts, V. (1995). 'Exploring a feminist routine activities approach to explaining sexual assault.' *Justice Quarterly, 12,* 9–31.

Schwendinger, H., and Schwendinger, J.R. (1975). 'Defenders of order or guardians of human rights?' In I. Taylor, P. Walton, and J. Young (Eds), *Critical criminology* (pp. 113–146). London: Routledge and Kegan Paul.

Schwendinger, H., Schwendinger, J.R., and Lynch, M.L. (2008). 'Critical criminology in the United States: The Berkeley School and theoretical trajectories.' In K. Carrington and R. Hogg (Eds), *Critical criminology: Issues, debates, challenges* (pp. 41–72). Portland, OR: Willan.

Selman, D., and Leighton, P. (2010). *Punishment for sale: Private prisons and big business.* Lanham, MD: Roman and Littlefield.

Selva, L., and Bohm, R. (1987). 'A critical examination of the informalism experiment in the administration of justice.' *Crime and Social Justice, 29,* 43–57.

Service Canada. (2009). *Employment insurance (EI).* Retrieved September 30, 2009, from www.servicecanada.gc.ca/eng/ei/menu/eihome.shtml.

Sev'er, A. (2002). *Fleeing the house of horrors: Women who have left abusive partners.* Toronto, ON: University of Toronto Press.

Sev'er, A. (2008). 'Discarded daughters: The patriarchal grip, dowry deaths, sex ratio imbalances and foeticide in India.' *Women's Health and Urban Life, 7,* 56–75.

Sharp, S.F. (2005). *Hidden victims: The effects of the death penalty on families of the accused.* New Brunswick, NJ: Rutgers University Press.

Sherrill, R. (2001, January 8). 'Death trip: The American way of execution.' *Nation.* Retrieved January 25, 2010, from www.thenation.com/doc/20010108/sherrill.

Silvestri, M., and Crowther-Dowey, C. (2008). *Gender and crime.* London: Sage.

Simpson *v.* University of Colorado, Boulder, 500 F.3d 1170 (10 Cir. 2007).

Sinclair, R.L. (2002). *Male peer support and male-to-female dating abuse committed by socially displaced male youth: An exploratory study.* Doctoral dissertation. Ottawa, ON: Carleton University.

Skolnick, J. (1966). *Justice without trial.* New York, NY: Wiley and Sons.

Smandych, R. (1985). 'Marxism and the creation of law: Re-examining the origins of Canadian anti-combines legislation, 1890–1910.' In T. Fleming (Ed.), *The new criminologies in Canada: State, crime, and control* (pp. 87–99). Toronto, ON: Oxford University Press.

Smith, A. (2010). 'Beyond restorative justice: Radical organizing against violence.' J. Ptacek (Ed.), *Restorative justice and violence against women* (pp. 255–278). New York, NY: Oxford University Press.

Smith, M.D. (1983). *Violence and sport.* Toronto, ON: Butterworths.

Smith, M.D. (1990). 'Patriarchal ideology and wife beating: A test of a feminist hypothesis.' *Violence and Victims, 5,* 257–273.

Southern Poverty Law Center. (2003). *10 ways to fight hate on campus: A response guide for college activists.* Montgomery, AL: Author.

Sparks, R.F. (1980). 'A critique of Marxist criminology.' In N. Morris and M. Tonry (Eds), *Crime and justice: An annual review, volume 2* (pp. 159–210). Chicago, IL: University of Chicago Press.

Spitzer, S. (1975). 'Toward a Marxian theory of deviance.' *Social Problems, 22,* 638–651.

Stark, E. (2007). *Coercive control: How men entrap women in personal life.* New York, NY: Oxford University Press.

Statistics Canada. (2007a). *A comparison of urban and rural crime rates.* Ottawa, ON: Author.

Statistics Canada. (2007b, November 21). 'Adult and youth correctional services: Key indicators.' *The Daily,* 1–6.

Statistics Canada. (2009). 'Homicide in Canada.' *The Daily.* Retrieved January 6, 2010, from www.statcan.gc.ca/daily-quotidien/091028/dq091208a-eng.htm.

Steffensmeier, D., and Streifel, C. (1992). 'Time series analysis of the female percentage of arrests for property crimes, 1960–1985: A test of alternative explanations.' *Justice Quarterly, 9,* 77–104.

Strawson, J. (2003). 'Holy war in the media: Images of Jihad.' In S. Chermak, F.Y. Bailey, and M. Brown (Eds), *Media representations of September 11* (pp. 17–28). Westport, CT: Praeger.

Stubbs, J. (2008). 'Critical criminological research.' In T. Anthony and C. Cunneen (Eds), *The critical criminology companion* (pp. 6–17). Annandale, NSW: Hawkins Press.

Taylor, I. (1992). 'Left realist criminology and the free market experiment in Britain.' In J. Young and R. Matthews (Eds), *Rethinking criminology: The realist debate* (pp. 95–122). London: Sage.

Taylor, I., Walton, P., and Young, J. (1973). *The new criminology: For a social theory of deviance.* London: Routledge and Kegan Paul.

Tepperman, L. (2010). *Deviance, crime, and control* (2nd ed.). Toronto, ON: Oxford University Press.

Terrill, R.J. (2007). *World criminal justice systems.* Cincinnati, OH: LexisNexis.

Thomas, J., and O'Maolchatha, A. (1989). 'Reassessing the critical metaphor: An opportunistic revisionist view.' *Justice Quarterly, 2,* 143–172.

Toby, J. (1957). 'Social disorganization and stake in conformity: Complementary factors in the predatory behavior of young hoodlums.' *Journal of Criminal Law, Criminology and Police Science, 48,* 12–17.

Tombs, S., and Whyte, D. (2007). *Safety crimes.* Portland, OR: Willan.

Travers, J. (2007, October 23). 'On crime issue, facts don't matter.' *Toronto Star,* A18.

Travis, J., and Waul, M. (2003). 'Prisoners once removed: The children and families of prisoners.' In J. Travis and M. Waul (Eds), *Prisoners once removed: The impact of incarceration and reentry on children, families, and communities* (pp. 1–32). Washington, DC: Urban Institute Press.

Turpin-Petrosino, C. (2009). 'Black victimization: Perceptions and realities.' In B. Perry (Ed.), *Hate crimes volume 3: The victims of hate crime* (pp. 19–44). Santa Barbara, CA: Praeger.

United States Department of Labor. (2009). 'Title IX, education amendments of 1972.' Retrieved September 15, 2009, from www.dol.gov/oasam/regs/statutes/titleIX.htm.

United Way of Greater Toronto. (2007). *Losing ground: The persistent growth of family poverty in Canada's largest city.* Toronto, ON: Author.

Unnever, J.D., Cullen, F.T., Mathers, S.A., McClure, T.E., and Allison, M.C. (2009). 'Racial discrimination and Hirschi's criminological classic: A chapter in the sociology of knowledge.' *Justice Quarterly, 26,* 377–409.

Ursel, E. (1986). 'The state and maintenance of patriarchy: A case study of family and welfare legislation.' In J. Dickinsin and B. Russell (Eds), *Family, economy and state* (pp. 150–191). Toronto, ON: Garamond.

Van Dijk, J. (2008). *The world of crime: Breaking the silence on problems of security, justice, and development across the world*. Los Angeles, CA: Sage.

Van Dyke, N., and Tester, G. (2008). 'The college campus as defended territory: Factors influencing variation in racist hate crime.' Department of Sociology, Washington State University.

Van Ness, D. (2002). 'UN economic and social council endorses basic principles on restorative justice.' *Restorative Justice Online*. Retrieved January 28, 2010, from www.restorativejustice.org/editions/2002/August02/ECOSOC%20Acts.

Vogel, M.E. (2007). 'The irony of imprisonment: The punitive paradox of the carceral turn and the "micro-death" of the material.' In M. Vogel (Ed.), *Crime, inequality and the state* (pp. 1–50). London: Routledge.

Vold, G.B., Bernard, T.J., and Snipes, J.B. (2002). *Theoretical criminology* (5th ed.). New York, NY: Oxford University Press.

Wacquant, L. (2001). 'Deadly symbiosis: When ghetto and prison meet and mesh.' *Punishment and Society, 3*, 95–134.

Wacquant, L. (2008). *Urban outcasts: A comparative sociology of advanced marginality*. Malden, MA: Polity.

Wacquant, L. (2009). *Punishing the poor: The neoliberal government of social insecurity*. Durham, NC: Duke University Press.

Walker Rettberg, J. (2009). 'Joining a Facebook group as political action.' *jill/txt*. Retrieved January 20, 2010, from http://jilltxt.net/?p=2367.

Walklate, S. (1989). *Victimology*. London: Unwin Hyman.

Walklate, S. (2004). *Gender, crime and criminal justice* (2nd ed.). Devon: Willan.

Walters, R. (2003). 'New modes of governance and the commodification of criminological knowledge.' *Social and Legal Studies, 12*, 5–26.

Walther, J.B., Slovacek, C.L., and Tidwell, L.C. (2001). 'Is a picture worth a thousand words: Photographic images in long-term and short-term computer-mediated communication.' *Communication Research, 28*, 105–134.

Walton, P. (1998). 'Big science – dystopia and utopia – establishment and new criminology revisited.' In P. Walton and J. Young (Eds), *The new criminology revisited* (pp. 1–13). London: St. Martin's Press.

Walton, P., and Young, J. (1998). 'Preface.' In P. Walton and J. Young (Eds), *The new criminology revisited* (pp. vii–viii). London: St. Martin's Press.

Warr, M. (2002). *Companions in crime: The social aspects of criminal conduct*. New York, NY: Cambridge University Press.

Watts, C., and Zimmerman, C. (2002, April 6). 'Violence against women: Global scope and magnitude.' *The Lancet*, p. 359.

Websdale, N. (1998). *Rural woman battering and the justice system: An ethnography*. Thousand Oaks, CA: Sage.

Weitzer, R., and Kubrin, C.E. (2009). 'Misogyny in rap music: A content analysis of prevalence and meanings.' *Men and Masculinities, 12,* 3–29.

Werbowski, M. (2010, January 18). 'Prorogation nation in crisis: Is Canada sliding towards dictatorial rule?' *OhmyNews*, Retrieved January 20, 2010, from http://english.ohmynews.com/articleview/article_print.asp?menu=c10400andno=385899andr.

West, C. (2001). *Race matters*. New York, NY: Vintage.

West, C., and Zimmerman, D.H. (1987). 'Doing gender.' *Gender and Society, 1,* 125–151.

Western, B., Pattillo, M., and Weiman, D. (2004). 'Introduction.' In M. Pattillo, D. Weiman, and B. Western (Eds), *Imprisoning America: The social effects of mass incarceration* (pp. 1–18). New York, NY: Russell Sage Foundation.

Wheeler, S. (1976). 'Trends and problems in the sociological study of crime.' *Social Problems, 23,* 525–534.

Whittington, L. (2009a, September 10). 'Easing rules for EI "irresponsible": Liberal proposal to let more jobless quality would be ineffective and too expensive, Finley charges.' *Toronto Star*, A6.

Whittington, L. (2009b, July 7). 'Harper got it all wrong, budget watchdog says.' *Toronto Star*, A1.

Whittington, L., and Campion-Smith, B. (2010, January 20). 'PM makes Day chief cost-cutter.' *Toronto Star*, A6.

Willis, P. (1977). *Learning to labor: How working class kids get working class jobs*. New York, NY: Columbia University Press.

Wilson, J.Q. (1985). *Thinking about crime*. New York, NY: Vintage.

Wilson, W.J. (1987). *The truly disadvantaged: The inner-city, the underclass and public policy*. Chicago, IL: University of Chicago Press.

Wilson, W.J. (1996). *When work disappears: The world of the new urban poor*. New York, NY: Knopf.

Wilson, W.J., and Taub, R.P. (2008). *There goes the neighborhood: Racial, ethnic, and class tensions in four Chicago neighborhoods and their meaning for America*. New York, NY: Knopf.

Wonders, N.A. (1999). 'Postmodern feminist criminology and social justice.' In B.A. Arrigo (Ed.), *Social justice, criminal justice* (pp. 109–128). Belmont, CA: Wadsworth.

Young, J. (1971). *The drugtakers*. London: Paladin.

Young, J. (1988). 'Radical criminology in Britain: The emergence of a competing paradigm.' *British Journal of Criminology, 28*, 159–183.

Young, J. (1992). 'Ten points of realism.' In J. Young and R. Matthews (Eds), *Rethinking criminology: The realist debate* (pp. 24–68). London: Sage.

Young, J. (1998). 'Breaking windows: Situating the new criminology.' In P. Walton and J. Young (Eds), *The new criminology revisited* (pp. 14–46). London: St. Martin's Press.

Young, J. (1999). *The exclusive society*. London: Sage.

Young, J. (2004). 'Voodoo criminology and the numbers game.' In J. Ferrell, K. Hayward, W. Morrison, and M. Presdee (Eds), *Cultural criminology unleashed* (pp. 13–28). London: The Glasshouse Press.

Young, J. (2008). 'Critical criminology in the twenty-first century: Critique, irony and the always unfinished.' In K. Carrington and R. Hogg (Eds), *Critical criminology: Issues, debates, challenges* (pp. 251–274). Portland, OR: Willan.

Young, J. (2009, August 20). 'Mike Presdee: Perceptive sociologist who played a key role in the growth of cultural criminology.' *Guardian*. Retrieved December 3, 2009, from www.guardian.co.uk/education/2009/aug/20/obituary-mike-presdee/print.

Zerbisias, A. (2008, January 26). 'Packaging abuse of women as entertainment for adults: Cruel, degrading scenes "normalized" for generation brought up in dot-com world.' *Toronto Star*, L3.

Zorza, J. (2002). Domestic violence in rural America. In J. Zorza (Ed.), *Violence against women: Law, prevention, protection, enforcement, treatment, and health* (pp. 41-1 to 14-2). Kingston, NJ: Civic Research Institute.

INDEX